W9-BUE-944

THE FRENCH REVOLUTION
AND NAPOLEON

The French Revolution and Napoleon

With New Annotated Bibliography

LEO GERSHOY
NEW YORK UNIVERSITY

Prentice-Hall, Inc., Englewood Cliffs, New Jersey

ST. BONAVENTURE LIBRARY
ST. BONAVENTURE, N.Y.

DC
148
.G4

©1964
by PRENTICE-HALL, Inc.,
Englewood Cliffs, New Jersey

All rights reserved. No part of this book
may be reproduced in any form or by any means,
without permission in writing from the publisher.

Copyright © renewed, 1961 by Leo Gershoy

Printed in the United States of America

ISBN: 0-13-331728-5

Library of Congress Catalog Card Number: 64-12378

10 9 8 7 6 5 4 3

PRENTICE-HALL INTERNATIONAL, INC., *London*
PRENTICE-HALL OF AUSTRALIA, PTY. LTD., *Sydney*
PRENTICE-HALL OF CANADA, LTD., *Toronto*
PRENTICE-HALL OF INDIA PRIVATE LIMITED, *New Delhi*
PRENTICE-HALL OF JAPAN, INC., *Tokyo*

1612827

JUN 2 '80

To

CARL BECKER

With great admiration and affection

PREFACE

Fresh studies on the period of the French Revolution and Napoleon follow one another so rapidly that on first consideration a new book on the subject appears totally unwarranted. On second consideration, however, the very rapidity of production suggests the *raison d'être* of this book. It is the need of presenting the new information in as clear and orderly a fashion as possible for the reader and the student who frequently lack the time or desire to dip into the special studies. The author's whole endeavor has been to satisfy this need.

A number of my colleagues, Professors Crane Brinton of Harvard University, Geoffrey Bruun of New York University, Louis Gottschalk of the University of Chicago, and Wilfred B. Kerr of the University of Buffalo, have aided me greatly by reading different parts of the manuscript and suggesting improvements in emphasis and interpretation. Professor Philip D. Jordan of Long Island University generously gave much time to the reading of the proofs and my friend, Miss Lydia R. Levy, aided me with the proofs and index.

Particular thanks go to my wife and Professor Carl Becker of Cornell University. Without Mrs. Gershoy's industry and her good judgment and fine discrimination in all that pertained to translating my thoughts into words, I should have been embarrassed in presenting this volume to the public. Above all, I am indebted to Professor Carl Becker, who read the entire manuscript, for his patient and meticulous criticism and his many admirable suggestions.

A NOTE ABOUT THE
NEW ANNOTATED BIBLIOGRAPHY

In this comprehensive revision of my original bibliography, many old titles have been dropped, many new ones introduced. Where fresh studies have appeared on the same topic, I have generally substituted them for the older works. Unless otherwise stated, the place of publication of titles in English is New York, and of titles in French, Paris. Many of the new titles reflect important changes in interpretation or shifts in emphasis given by recent research to the long period—from the last years of the Old Regime to the era of Napoleon's domination—covered in this volume.

TABLE OF CONTENTS

TABLE OF CONTENTS

TABLE OF MAPS

THE FRENCH REVOLUTION
AND NAPOLEON

I. THE GOVERNMENT OF FRANCE IN THE OLD RÉGIME

Two full centuries span the magnificent crowning and the grievous decline of the governmental institutions of France in the Old Régime. These two hundred years embrace the history of Bourbon France from the accession of the valiant and indomitable Henry IV in 1589 to the outbreak of the Revolution in 1789 in the fifteenth year of the reign of Louis XVI, a monarch generously benevolent but lacking in resolution and constancy. In the first of those two centuries France rose to a position of uncontested supremacy in Europe, becoming the dominant military power on the Continent, the majestic model of centralized royal absolutism, and the classic pattern of elegance and refinement in manners, learning, and the peaceful arts. When the long and shameful reign of Louis XV (1715–1774) had run its course, France was still a powerful state in Europe, rich in the prestige of her absolutism; but the sun had set forever on the glory that was hers during the brilliant age of Louis XIV (1643–1715).

The prestige that remained to her, the prestige that came from a glamorous court, from a still unrivaled mastery in social intercourse, arts, and letters, and from the very tradition of Bourbon supremacy, had sufficed during most of the eighteenth century to cover the real decline in the fortunes of France. When the young king Louis XVI ascended the throne in 1774 all but the most complacently conservative realized at last that the times were out of joint and that a concerted effort at reform was needed to set them right. A peasantry bitter in its grievances; a bourgeoisie restive under its many restrictions; privileged class and corporate interests at odds with each other but united in their parasitism upon the nation; a government discredited by its ruinous foreign policy, its financial extravagances, and its administrative inefficiency and corruption; and a powerful public opinion that scourged the government for its weakness and its errors of policy and assailed the very theory of absolutist government—such were the factors

3

with which Louis XVI and his ministers had to cope between 1774 and 1789.

France Under the First Bourbons

France still holds in grateful memory the first king of the Bourbon dynasty, the gay, courageous, and enlightened Henry IV (1589–1610), who ended the disorders of the sixteenth century. A Protestant "heretic" by conviction, he became a convert to Catholicism because he judged that Paris and France were well worth a mass. A soldier, he fought valiantly for his country against Spain without and against the Catholic League and Protestant fanaticism within. A contemporary of the French Renaissance, he sought to establish a rule of reason and justice, since "France," he said, "is tired unto death of battles and quarrels." Reason dictated that he make peace with the foreign enemy (Peace of Vervins), that he end the religious wars between Catholics and Huguenots (Edict of Nantes), that he force obedience, whether at the point of the sword or through the largess of a purse, upon rebellious noblemen. With order restored in his realm, the ruler and his chief minister, the duke of Sully, applied their energies to untangle the snarl of royal finances, to increase the resources of the country and promote the general welfare. Supported faithfully by the new and influential middle class of merchants, traders, manufacturers, and financiers, the king and his minister laid the corner stone of the edifice of royal absolutism. To the monarchy the arrangement insured an orderly administrative system conducted on business principles by the most competent class of the state and ever increasing authority within the country. To the bourgeoisie the order and tranquillity that ensued brought material rewards and the promise of political influence and social recognition. To France the wise and firm rule of Henry IV gave prestige such as France had not had in Europe since the thirteenth century.

A grave setback in the fortunes of France followed the assassination of Henry IV by an embittered religious fanatic. The history of the next fourteen years, when Marie de Médicis was queen-regent for her minor son, Louis XIII, was one of strife and disorder which bade fair to undo the achievements of Henry IV. In 1624, however, Louis XIII forced his mother into retirement and became ruler in his own right. For his chief minister he selected an ecclesiastic, Cardinal Richelieu (1585–1642), who for the following eighteen years directed the destinies of the state. Domineering by nature and implacable toward his opponents, resolute of will and experienced in administration, Richelieu methodically devoted his entire ministry to the attainment of that goal he set for himself and his royal master in the very year that he became minister. His program, as he announced it to Louis XIII, was ambitious, and the highest tribute that can be paid him is that he lived to see it fulfilled in almost every detail. "I promise to devote all my efforts and all the authority that you may give me to destroying the Huguenots [as a political menace], humbling the great nobles, restoring all your subjects to their duty, and winning for your majesty the prestige that rightly belongs to you among foreign nations."

When the great cardinal died in 1642, he left the French monarchy secure at home and powerful abroad. Building upon the foundations laid by Henry IV, he had strengthened the royal authority within France, both by elaborating the central administrative machinery and by weakening the local opposition to the royal agents. He died before the Thirty Years' War had ended, but the minister who virtually governed France during the minority of Louis XIV, from 1643 to 1661, the all-powerful Cardinal Mazarin (1602–1661), carried through the foreign policy of Richelieu to a successful conclusion. By the peace of Westphalia (1648) France gained, from the Hapsburgs of the Holy Roman Empire, Alsace (with the exception of Strasbourg); and by the peace of the Pyrenees (1659) France gained, from the Hapsburgs of Spain, Roussillon on the Spanish frontier and Artois and parts of Flanders on the northeast. The pledge of a marriage alliance between Louis XIV and the eldest daughter of the Spanish king was a formal guaranty that the peace of the Pyrenees would be maintained; while the triumphs of the French troops against the forces of the Hapsburgs of Spain and Austria were unmistakable signs that the military hegemony of France over her European rivals was now at hand.

In the face of overwhelming personal unpopularity, in the midst of an unfinished war, Mazarin pursued the policy established by Richelieu, first against the opposition of the great magistrates of the parlement of Paris and of the sovereign courts in the provinces, and later against the great nobles of the realm. For four years, from 1648–1652, the structure of royal absolutism was subjected to a severe strain, but it withstood the shock of attacks directed against it. Many years were to pass before the turbulence of the Fronde [1] was forgotten and the material damages that it caused were repaired, but Mazarin emerged victorious from the bitter struggle. The Fronde was the last attempt before the Revolution to promulgate a charter limiting royal absolutism, and its failure assured the triumph of the doctrine of absolutism in the long personal reign of Louis XIV (1661–1715).

Louis XIV became his own prime minister in 1661 on the death of Mazarin and from that date until his death fifty-four years later he conscientiously plied his "royal profession." Dignified yet gracious, imposing and majestic, even in trivial actions, proud in his self-assurance, he impressed and overawed his subjects by his appearance and delighted them with his industry. His stock of ideas was not great, but he had a great deal of common sense, much patience, and moral courage. Ruling in his own right, punctual and regular in his attendance at the sessions of the royal council, well informed and attentive to details, he was a ruler after the heart of the industrious bourgeoisie.

Like his royal contemporaries, he believed with all his heart in the divine sanction of his absolutism. The meticulous code of etiquette that organized to the last detail the acts of his daily life gave to his court a splendor and brilliance that even today are proverbial. The cult of the royal majesty served not only to satisfy the pride of the Sun King, but also to advance his political calculations. Having stripped the turbulent provincial nobility of their political power, he made it his policy to have them near him at court, where he could check their intrigues and flatter their vanity by bestowing rich sinecures upon them in the church, the army, and the administration.

With the assistance of faithful officials, many of them from the middle class, he organized the most competent bureaucracy, the most adroit diplomatic staff, and the largest, best equipped and organized army in Europe since the days of the Roman Empire. In Colbert, the dour and glacial bourgeois from Reims, he had a financial minister and an administrator of genius. For twenty years Colbert enjoyed the confidence of his master, and in those

---

[1] This rebellion received the name of Fronde from a game played by Parisian urchins which the police frequently broke up.

years he directed the most comprehensive attempt to promote the prosperity of his country. Louis XIV's great wars and his architectural and social extravagances ultimately dissipated the riches that Colbert had stored up and plunged the monarchy into that

Acquisitions 1601-1643
Acquired by Treaty of Westphalia 1648
" " " the Pyrenees 1659
Acquisitions of Louis XIV 1668-1697
" 1697-1766

Boundary of France in 1770

THE EMPIRE

ENGLISH CHANNEL

Calais
ARTOIS
Lille Maubeuge 1678
Arto 1678 Charlemont 1678
  Bouillon 1678
  Montmedy 1659 Longwy 1679
Sedan 1642 Saarlouis 1688
Stenay 1641
Reims Clermont 1632
Paris Strasbourg
  ALSACE
  SUNDGAU

Cherbourg Rouen
Brest
Rennes
Orléans
Troyes
FRANCHE COMTÉ 1678
SWITZERLAND

Loire R.
Nantes
CHAROLAIS
FRANCE
BRESSE 1601 BUGEY
Lyons Geneva
SAVOY

BAY OF BISCAY

Bordeaux
Garonne R.
D. OF ALBRET 1607
C. OF ARMAGNAC 1607
K. OF NAVARRE 1620
C. OF FOIX 1607
Toulouse
Rhone R.
BARCELONETTE 1713
ORANGE 1714
Marseilles

SPAIN
Scale of Miles
0 40 80 120 160
C. OF BIGORRE 1607
CERDAGNE ROUSSILLON 1659
MANHATTAN DRAFTING CO., INC., N.Y.

EXTENSION OF THE FRENCH FRONTIERS 1600-1789

financial disorder from which it never recovered. But his early wars (the War of Devolution, 1667–1668, and the Dutch War, 1672–1678) were successful and gained for France several strategic towns in Flanders and the province of Franche Comté. In view of his own confession, late in his life, that he had loved war and glory too much, it is impossible to defend the later military aggressions of the Grand Monarch; but there is no doubt that his early wars started from "a strategic plan for national security" and ended with an enlarged and strengthened France, secure from Spanish and Austrian pressure.

These victories marked the apogee of Louis XIV's power in France and western Europe. While Paris conferred upon him the title of "Louis le Grand," the splendor of France's civilization complemented the political and military prestige of his reign. This was the golden age of French literature, the age of Molière and La Fontaine, Racine and Boileau, Madame de Sévigné and Bossuet, the age of those classics which everywhere on the Continent were admired and imitated as the only worthy models. In the arts the principles of classicism, the cult of classical antiquity with its emphasis upon order, regularity, and dignity also achieved their triumph. More than any other construction of the age, the château of Versailles embodied the spirit of the absolute monarchy. There in the stately grandeur of its magnificent halls, in the beautiful gardens surrounding the royal residence, the aristocracy of France assembled night and day to do homage to the great ruler, the master whose will had made France rich and powerful, the dictator and the cynosure of Europe in the arts and letters, in manners and tastes, in war and diplomacy.

Yet Versailles, which symbolized the glory of the monarchy of the Old Régime, was also the mark of its decline. Its cost to the French nation must be evaluated not only in terms of the expense of its construction and the lavish wastefulness of court existence, but also in terms of the barrier that it established between the monarchy and its subjects. It isolated Louis XIV, as it was to isolate his successors, from the nation. In the profound words of Emile Bourgeois, "A complete, over-long separation, ultimately constituting a divorce, replaced the close secular association between the French people and their monarch." This "separation," this "divorce," became most evident in the painful thirty years' decline of Louis XIV's and France's fortune from 1685 to 1715.

The king's religious policy and his later wars largely nullified the achievements of the first part of his reign. His persecution of the Huguenots (culminating in the revocation of the Edict of Nantes in 1685) inflicted a rude blow to the material prosperity of France, for thousands of skilled artisans, professional men, and merchants fled the country. By siding with the Jesuits against the Jansenists in their bitter doctrinal dispute he precipitated a political controversy that ultimately weakened the unity of the Catholic Church in France and undermined the prestige of the monarchy. More than anything else, the disastrous wars of the League of

Augsburg (1689–1698) and of the Spanish Succession (1701–1714), which united Europe against Louis XIV, began the discrediting of absolutism. The chorus of praise which his subjects had sung turned to angry, despairing maledictions. The great monarch's final bequest to his successors was the repudiation of that policy of common sense which had guided Henry IV, Richelieu, and Mazarin. He left France poor, with her finances in disorder, her population diminished by war, her most industrious craftsmen in exile, and her peasantry hungry, bent under staggering fiscal obligations and ripe for revolt. The government was absolutist and the privileged classes were secure in their prerogatives, but defeat and suffering stimulated critical speculation that examined the very foundations of a government that could wreak such hardships upon the nation.

The Grand Monarch was succeeded by his great-grandson, Louis XV, who was only five years of age when his predecessor died. The first part of his reign of fifty-nine years falls into the period of the regency from 1715–1723, when the duke of Orléans, his great-uncle, ruled in his name. The confusion and disorder of the regency was followed by almost two decades of orderly rule and material prosperity under the cautious leadership of the aged Cardinal Fleury (1726–1743). From 1743 until his death in 1774 Louis XV attempted to exercise direct control over the government, with consequences only too dire for the stability of the monarchy.

The regency was a period of almost complete reaction against the later policy of Louis XIV, in morals, in religious policy, and in foreign relations. In those years the Scots adventurer and banker, John Law, essayed to wipe out the public debt of France, but his ambitious scheme collapsed, leaving the financial situation worse than before.

Under the prudent administration of Cardinal Fleury a measure of financial stability was restored. Expenses were rigidly curtailed, the taxes lowered, and the budget was balanced for the first time since the days of Colbert. Thanks in great measure to his policy of preserving peace, merchants and traders enjoyed great prosperity, particularly those in the Atlantic ports, which did a flourishing business with the sugar-growing islands of the Antilles. His not unskillful conduct of foreign affairs also increased Bourbon prestige, France's intervention in the War of the Polish Succession

(1733–1738) gaining for her the promise of a later annexation of Lorraine, while the renewal of France's religious and commercial privileges in the Ottoman Empire (1740) gave her a predominance in the Levant trade. Despite the renewal of the acrimonious Jesuit and Jansenist controversy [2] Fleury kept intact the government's prestige. When he died in 1743 and Louis XV became his own master, the prospects for France were bright.

Louis XV's native defects quickly destroyed the popularity that he enjoyed in 1743, when his subjects called him Louis the Well Beloved. He was no dullard; on the contrary, he had a supple mind and quick intelligence. But he displayed an apathy and an indifference to affairs of state that boded ill for France. He was concerned primarily, if not exclusively, with the search for pleasure, and all his life he sought to escape from the boredom that lay like a pall about him. He sought escape in a mad and vicious round of pleasures, in hunting, in gambling, in lust, in moving his court from palace to palace, in indulging his caprices, in gratifying the whims and the follies of his numerous mistresses and favorites. In his gilded captivity at court, surrounded by his parasitical courtiers, he cut himself and his administration off from France, from a nation prosperous in spite of him, a nation transformed by economic and social changes to which the monarchy was largely indifferent.

For more than thirty years Louis XV persevered in a shameful policy that intensified the worst features of the Old Régime. A disastrous foreign policy, culminating in the humiliation of the Seven Years' War (1756–1763), a capricious government controlled by royal mistresses, a reckless prodigality of court expenditures, and the renewal of the religious controversy that turned into an onslaught of the thirteen parlements against the theory and practice of royal absolutism—all these developments opened the gates to the deluge that swept over France. Louis XV escaped the disaster and temporarily checked the pretensions of

[2] The controversy between the Jesuits and the Jansenists, originally over questions of theology involving grace and predestination, became political in consequence of the fact that the Jesuits supported the papal condemnation of the Jansenist doctrines, while the parlement of Paris, out of opposition to ultramontane influence, sided with the Jansenists. The Parisians, largely for the same reason, supported the magistrates of parlement. "Everybody in Paris," wrote a contemporary lawyer, "men, women, little children, uphold this doctrine, blindly, without in the least understanding the disputed points, solely out of hatred for Rome and the Jesuits."

the great titled magistrates by confiscating their offices (1771–1774) and exiling the incumbents to their estates. But he could not stay the progress of the new political and social philosophy that repudiated the practice and the theory of irresponsible and arbitrary royal absolutism.

Louis XV's reign ended in 1774 in a chorus of criticisms of the monarch and his hard-pressed ministers. The king that was once Well Beloved died unmourned, his cortège attended by the insulting gibes and epithets of a relieved nation. To his successor, he left an unenviable heritage of military defeat, financial embarrassment, governmental incompetence, parlementary opposition, and intellectual resistance to the existing political and social régime.

THE INTENDANTS AND THE INTENDANCIES

The only large administrative units of any significance in France in the century and a half preceding the Revolution were the generalities, or intendancies. The historic provinces, which had been independent kingdoms or duchies before their absorption into the French state, still retained their distinctive characteristics of custom and culture, dress and speech, but they no longer possessed any importance in the governmental system. For all practical purposes they had become nominal military districts under the jurisdiction of a governor who was invariably chosen from the highest nobility. The title of governor was impressive but purely honorary, for while it entitled the incumbent to a princely salary and great prerogatives, it endowed him with no real authority. The great majority of these royal governors resided at Versailles and appeared in their provinces only on formal occasions when their presence was absolutely required. Some provinces were officially designated as the *pays d'états*, provinces in which the periodic assembly of representatives of the three orders or estates had been perpetuated. In general these provinces were situated on the frontiers of France and had been conquered or otherwise acquired comparatively recently. The central provinces, which had lost the right to convoke the provincial assembly, were known officially as *pays d'élections*, from the subordinate district, the *élection*, which served as a fiscal unit. Only in the apportionment and collection of taxes did the inhabitants of the *pays d'états* enjoy greater self-government than those living in the central provinces, though it is also true that their burdens under the regular government were less heavy.[3]

The thirty-four intendancies, or generalities, into which France

THE ADMINISTRATIVE DIVISIONS OF FRANCE
IN 1789

▨ "Pays d' Élections"	━━ Dividing line between the "customary law" and the "written law"
▨ "Pays d' États"	B – Bishopric C– County

MANHATTAN DRAFTING CO., INC.,N.Y.

was divided in 1789 were the only administrative units of any significance. In some cases several provinces had been combined to form a single intendancy, as in the case of the intendancy of Tours, which was formed by combining the three provinces of Maine, Touraine, and Anjou; while in other cases one large

[3] Cf. below, p. 24.

province had been divided to form several intendancies, as in Normandy, which was split up into three intendancies. In all cases the intention of the government was to have one large city included within each intendancy, and it was after these cities that the intendancies were named.[4]

The intendants, selected at first from the ranks of the bourgeoisie, ruled the provinces. Richelieu had been the first to discern the possibilities of the tried lawyers known as masters of petitions (*maîtres des requêtes*). At that time they regularly handled administrative details in one of the sections of the royal council and under exceptional circumstances some of them were dispatched into the provinces to serve as intendants of police, justice, and finance. Richelieu made the office of intendant an integral part of the machinery of local government, and Mazarin, pursuing his policy, increased the authority of the intendants and assigned them to fixed posts within territorial units called intendancies, or generalities.[5] When Louis XIV began his personal rule in 1661 the intendants were *par excellence* the regular administrative officials of the royal government. The selection of commoners for the office of intendant was a systematic policy of Louis XIV. "It was important," he wrote in his *Memoirs*, "that the public could judge, by the rank of those whom I employed, that I had no intention of sharing authority with them, and that they, themselves, knowing what they were, would not entertain higher hopes than those I would grant them." His policy of raising them to the nobility only emphasized his point, that his power was absolute and that these actual rulers of the provinces of France owed everything to his royal will.

Rulers they were indeed, for their authority in their intendancy was unbounded. They had the right to administer justice in all royal courts (save the parlements), to preside over inferior courts, remove cases from one court to another jurisdiction, and if need be, to settle them themselves. They verified the accounts of their

---

[4] In 1789 there were twenty generalities in the *pays d'élections*—Caen, Rouen, Amiens, Soissons, Paris, Châlons, Orléans, Alençon, Tours, Poitiers, La Rochelle, Bourges, Moulins, Lyons, Riom, Grenoble, Montauban, Limoges, Auch, and Bordeaux—and fourteen intendancies in the *pays d'états*—Aix, Dijon, Rennes, Toulouse, Montpellier, Perpignan, Lille, Valenciennes, Metz, Nancy, Strasbourg, Besançon, Pau, and Corsica. The term "generality" was derived from the *généraux des finances*, royal officials of the fourteenth century.

[5] Strictly, intendancy was applied only to the *pays d'états*, but in the eighteenth century the two terms were practically synonymous.

subordinate financial administrators and attended, in person or through these subdelegates, to the assessment and the levy of the direct taxes. They had a large control over the movement of the military, calling out recruits for the regular army, supervising the conscription of the militia, and directing the activities of the municipal police. They also had competence over the religious activities of their unit and directed the affairs of schools and higher institutions of learning. Economic activities, such as the varied details of agricultural production, regulation of public markets, and the construction of public works, fell under their jurisdiction. Spurred by the officials of the central administration with whom they were in close communication, they familiarized themselves with all the multiple details of local life, issuing special ordinances and even general regulations as circumstances demanded.

During the seventeenth century, their greatest service was to hold in firm check all the old and new forces that might have resisted the central monarchy, such as the provincial parlements, the provincial estates, the local nobility, and all the officials of the state who owned their offices independently of the monarch. During the eighteenth century, when most of them held office for twenty years and some for even longer periods, their problems were less concerned with impressing obedience to the government upon the inhabitants than with administrative reforms and increasing the public welfare. Under their severe control neither village parishes nor municipal governments enjoyed even the semblance of political independence. Either directly by a royal edict or through the agency of the intendant and his subordinates local officials were elected, local finances and justice administered, local problems settled. The forms of municipal governments existed, but the control of administration belonged to the monarchy. Paris, as the most important city of the realm, boasted a more complex municipal organization, which was partly mediaeval and partly royal, but the monarchical supervision was not less pronounced there than elsewhere. Allowing for a certain exaggeration, De Tocqueville's commentary admirably sums up the situation: "There was no city, town, borough, village, or hamlet in the kingdom; there was neither hospital, church fabric, nor religious house which could have an independent will or the management of its private affairs, or which could administer its own property after its own plans."

The tremendous power held by the intendants and their subordinates led all thinking men of the eighteenth century to denounce "the thirty tyrants of France." In reality, the last generation of intendants before 1789 was exceptionally competent and conscientious. The weakness of the governmental system lay not with individual intendants, nor even with the intendants as a class of administrators. It lay first with the theory of government, in the fact that the newer forms of a centralized royal administration were superimposed upon a semifeudal society in which privileged individuals clung tenaciously to innumerable older offices and prerogatives; and secondly with the chaos of the central administration and the incompetence of Louis XVI.

THE CENTRAL ADMINISTRATION

The development of the central administrative system went back to the remote days of the mediaeval monarchy, and after many checks and reversals caused by historical circumstances the system attained, during the seventeenth century, as high a degree of stability as it was ever to attain before the Revolution. Louis XIV did not inaugurate the systematized organization of the central government, for that work had been well advanced by Richelieu and Mazarin. He completed their work and made the system function more efficiently, with less friction and caprice than it ever had before or did again under his two successors. He was his own master, for he had no principal minister in the sense that Mazarin had been of his predecessor, Louis XIII. He practiced his "royal profession" methodically and imperiously, attending with meticulous care to the innumerable details of administration. Perhaps too methodically and imperiously and with too much care, for the excessively centralized government that he had both the strength of character and the ability to control was a legacy of dubious worth without the strong hand of the master. Even during the latter part of his own reign, when his control began to falter, evidence was not lacking that the centralized administration was becoming a Frankenstein monster, no longer an instrument of efficiency and prosperity, but a force for incalculable mischief.

The chief administrative subordinates of the king were the chancellor, the controller-general of finance, the four secretaries of state,[6] and the members of the royal council. The chancellor was the chief judicial and legislative official of the state, presiding when the king was absent, at all sessions of the councils and, with the aid of his staff, drawing up all the legislative edicts of the realm. In addition, he had jurisdiction over the administration of secondary and higher education, all bookstores and publications, and all royal censors, whom he appointed to office. Of all the high officials he alone was not removable; the others held office at the pleasure of the monarch. From the days of Colbert, who displayed an amazing activity in the exercise of his many duties, to the end of the Old Régime, the controller-general of finance had heavier responsibilities and a wider scope of activities than any other member of the central administration. While each of the four secretaries had certain clearly defined, specialized functions, as well as immediate administrative authority over certain specified territorial districts, the very vagueness and undefined limits of the controller-general's authority permitted an energetic and enterprising incumbent of the office to infringe upon the duties that nominally belonged to his associates. A competent ruler like Louis XIV succeeded in keeping the petty jealousy and the dissensions among his subordinates within bounds. A monarch indifferent to affairs of state, like Louis XV, failed utterly to supply the initiative and the regulatory control that were necessary for the efficient functioning of the system.

From 1661 almost to the close of the Old Régime there were four more or less definite sections of the royal council. The council of dispatches and the council of finance, meeting separately or together, determined the general internal policy of the administration. There the dispatches of the intendants were read and discussed, there the financial edicts were drafted for the king's signature. A third and smaller section, the upper council (sometimes called the council of state), dealt with all questions of state, though more particularly with the foreign policy of the government. To the sessions of the upper council only the king, the chancellor, and the three or four officers who held the title of "minister" were admitted, an arrangement which like many another made for misunderstandings and mystification. The largest of the councils was the privy council, which was a sort of supreme court for conten-

[6] These were the secretary of state of the royal household, secretary of state for foreign affairs, secretary of state for war, and secretary of state for the navy.

tious civil and administrative matters. To its deliberations were admitted the leading executive officers, certain high magistrates designated as councilors of state, and the large group of young lawyers, known as masters of petitions, from whose ranks it was customary to select the intendants.

The scantiest examination of the administrative system suggests explanations of its inefficiency. The intendants derived their authority directly from the councils, and legally the councils and the ministers had only an advisory capacity. They were responsible only to the king, for according to absolutist theory the king's will was law. There was neither a representative assembly nor a written constitution to limit the authority of the administrators; nothing but the royal pleasure, the loose body of precedents and traditions which were characteristically misnamed "the fundamental laws of the kingdom," and the right of the High Court of Paris (the parlement of Paris) to register all new legislation on the records of the state. Under the circumstances coöperation among the high officials at Versailles was difficult at best and well-nigh impossible at worst. Conflict of jurisdiction and rivalries among the administrators, the absence of an executive head in their own midst to formulate long-term policies and projects, overlapping, non-differentiated departments and superfluous officials, traditions of graft and irresponsible, high-handed procedure, taxed the patience and sapped the strength of even the most conscientious and determined servant of the state. If the supervision of a strong king, like Louis XIV, made for greater dispatch and efficiency, the occasional intervention of an arbitrary and indifferent monarch, like Louis XV, only served to accentuate the confusion of an irrational and socially indefensible system.

Two great forces saved it from disaster. The first was the relative stability of the local administration under the capable and loyal hands of the intendants. The second was the almost absolute stability of the lesser subordinates of the administrative bureaucracy. Major changes, dismissals and appointments of ministers, scarcely affected the personnel of the lesser bureaus, commissions, and secretariats. These petty officials were wedded to routine and unalterably attached to precedent. The routine was slow, cumbersome, and wasteful, but the very inertia was an obstacle to the caprices of an arbitrary monarch. Habit, not reason, furnished the motive force of government under the last Bourbons.

The Administration of Justice

According to absolutist theory all justice in France emanated from the monarch, whose officials administered it in his name in the many royal courts of justice that were established throughout the entire country. Neither the remaining church courts nor the many petty manorial courts of justice seriously rivaled, in jurisdiction or in influence, the courts which administered royal justice. Of these there were a great variety, a variety without uniformity, a mosaic directly traceable to the process of historic growth which had created the monarchy.

The chief reason for the existence of many hundred courts of regular royal jurisdiction, and an equal or greater number of extraordinary royal jurisdiction, is to be found in the procedure of selling public offices during the Old Régime. Most of the minor administrative offices, particularly in the administration of justice and finance, were owned by their incumbents. They could not be abolished except through judicial condemnation, and the monarchy was also too poor to buy back the offices that it had established. Consequently they remained the family possessions of men of wealth, who could bequeath them to their heirs or sell them, even when they had ceased to perform the services for which they had been created. "When his Majesty created an office," wrote a royal administrator, "Providence called into being an imbecile to buy it." This state of affairs, particularly in the administration of justice and finance, furnishes an interesting commentary upon the authority of the king. Supposedly absolute, in reality it was checked by irremovable office holders over whom he was powerless.

Below the thirteen parlements of the realm, which were the supreme courts of appeal in civil and criminal cases, there existed a veritable hodgepodge of courts of primary and appellate jurisdiction. In the country districts there were simple police courts; in towns and cities, the courts of the bailiffs and seneschals and courts of the presidencies that were rapidly being merged with other tribunals. Besides these courts of general royal jurisdiction, there were many others that took cognizance of litigation in certain specified cases, mainly finance and taxation. There were also administrative courts, military courts, admiralty courts, commercial courts, and inferior and appellate courts that had jurisdiction over cases involving specified taxes and monopolies, such as the excises, the salt tax, hunting and fishing in the royal domains. The administration of justice in these courts was cumbersome, slow, costly, corrupt, and arbitrary. France had no single code of laws either for civil or for criminal cases. No attempt was made after Colbert's efforts in the seventeenth century to codify the laws. The principles of Roman imperial legislation prevailed largely in the south (*pays de droit écrit*), and the many systems of customary law, based upon the principles of feudal and Frankish law, prevailed in the north of France (*pays de droit coutumier*).

This lack of uniformity was the primary cause of confusion. On such litigious matters as marriage, dowries, legacies, inheritances, adoption, wills, entails, and paternal authority the two systems of common law differed widely, though both systems had been profoundly modified by feudal practice. Since the exact geographical limits of the jurisdiction of each court were not clearly fixed, disputes frequently arose among the different tribunals. The uncertainty concerning interpretation of the law and the competence of individual courts made the administration of justice not only dilatory, but expensive and corrupt as well, for the uncertainty promoted appeals from one court to another. Appeals were expensive for litigants, but profitable for magistrates and attorneys. Though these owned their offices, their salaries were slight, and they counted upon the largess of the litigants to earn a fair return upon what was actually a financial investment. The litigants fully understood the advisability of bestowing fees, called *épices*, upon the men of the courts, and there was only too much truth in La Bruyère's cynical epigram that "the duty of judges is to dispense justice, their profession to postpone it; some of them know their duty, but practice their profession."

The administration of justice was as arbitrary as it was slow and costly for the litigants. As the source of all justice in France, the king had the right of overriding the due processes of law. By issuing a writ, he could remove the offender from the jurisdiction of the regular court and have him tried before any of the many courts or commissions of extraordinary royal justice. He could imprison a litigant before he was judged guilty or pardon him after he was convicted. This arbitrary intercession did frequently expedite matters, but, in the majority of cases, to the advantage of the king's privileged subjects and at the expense of justice itself. The king could also issue writs, called *lettres de cachet*, by virtue of which he could imprison any subject without inquiry or trial, so long as it pleased the royal will. Apologists for the Old Régime have shown that this singular right was paternal in spirit and exercised largely for the honor of a respected family, and that such prisoners were better treated than others. Without denying the cogency of their arguments or the fervor of their pleading, it is well to note that the lettre de cachet was also used to gratify personal caprices or hatreds and that, in any case, it constituted a flagrant violation of what enlightened minds then considered the most elementary personal rights of the individual.

The procedure in criminal cases partook of the worst characteristics of civil procedure and added a few abuses peculiar to itself. The accused was examined privately by the magistrate without the aid of counsel. Witnesses were heard in secret, no public hearings were held, and no jury passed on the facts. Torture of the accused was part of the routine, and capital punishment, barbarously inflicted for comparatively trivial crimes, was frequent. The magistrates, hardened to a profession that was sinister, not infrequently made convictions purely from a sense of professional pride. There were indeed humanitarian spirits among them, men learned in the law, just and generous in their sympathies, men who protested indignantly over the abuses of their colleagues. But these liberal judges were not numerous save among the members of those sovereign courts, the parlements of France.

The parlement of Paris and the twelve provincial parlements were the highest tribunals of the realm, supreme courts of appeal for civil and criminal cases and courts of original jurisdiction for many cases over which the extraordinary royal justice had jurisdiction. Their function was to receive appeals and to pass final decisions on the basis of the fundamental laws of the realm. To them the monarch sent his royal edicts, so that they might be registered and, when registered, guide these magistrates in their decisions. Before registering the edicts the parlements were permitted to make comments, to pass judgment on the legality of the edicts. These observations were called "remonstrances," which the king heeded or not as he saw fit. During the reign of the imperious Louis XIV the parlements passively accepted the royal edicts, for Louis XIV had taken from them the right to issue remonstrances. In the period immediately preceding his reign and again, with redoubled vigor, during the entire eighteenth century, the parlements defended their claims to pass on all royal legislation and to ratify by their approval all edicts concerning finance and taxation; and in so doing they elaborated a theory to justify their opposition.

Among them the parlements had appellate jurisdiction over all of France. Only one of these supreme courts, the parlement of Paris, derived from the ancient *curia regis*, which had assisted and tempered the authority of the early Capetians. The other twelve had been established separately in the course of several centuries. Yet in their struggle with Louis XV and Louis XVI their claim was that they formed one single *corps*, that they were the representative body of the nation or the mandatories of the people, who alone defended "the fundamental laws" of France against the caprice of an arbitrary ruler. In that period there was indeed no other representative body, for since 1614 the Estates General had not been convoked. Yet these aristocratic, wealthy, and arrogant magistrates could only by default be regarded as "the fathers of the nation." The *parlementaires* were not mandatories of the people, for they were officers of the royal administration. They were men of wealth and of noble birth who owned their offices and were bound by honor and their oaths to give obedience to the king. They formed a small exclusive caste, the nobility of the robe,[7] occupying, by reason of their wealth and status, a high place in society; exercising by virtue of the numerous personnel of lesser officials who depended upon them, tremendous authority over the entire administration of justice.

Only a few liberal spirits among the magistrates opposed despotism in order to advance liberty. Most of their opposition was really designed, under the name of liberty, to safeguard privilege and to oppose reform. They prevented the reform of judicial abuses, and they defended the barbaric criminal procedure. They thwarted the efforts of Louis XVI's reforming ministers. They disapproved of the freedom of the press, and they opposed the declaration granting civil status to Protestants. They protested against the lettres de cachet, not out of love of freedom, but to defend their own judicial prerogatives. They resisted the registration of new taxes, not to lighten the burden of the taxpayers, but to maintain the fiscal exemptions of the privileged class to which

---

[7] This *noblesse de la robe* included not only the judicial aristocracy which owned offices, but also the independent financial officers.

they belonged. Override their protests the monarch could and did by means of solemn sessions of the court, called *lits de justice,* at which the king would order the registration of his edict. Whether successful or not in a given protest, the parlement of Paris, supported by the provincial parlements, succeeded in embarrassing the government and, by embarrassing it, helped to discredit it and to pave the way to a juster limitation of absolute rule.

Finance and Taxation in the Old Régime

The principle of taxation by the will of the taxpayers was not raised in the Bourbon monarchy, and the financial administration, like the administration of justice and the government, was arbitrary and absolute. While liberal opposition to this particular absolutism demanded nothing more radical than that all financial edicts be registered with the sovereign courts, personal protests were bitter and constant. The system of taxation was of a piece with the very conception of government. It functioned in confusion and disorder, at high cost to the treasury and with a cost still greater to the economic activities of France. Taxes fell unequally upon his Majesty's subjects: the privileged classes were for the most part exempt from taxation, and the peasantry bore the brunt. The methods of collection were financially wasteful and corrupt, socially offensive, and economically indefensible; in the case of indirect taxes the methods were vexatious and brutal as well.

The weakness of the system was fully apparent at the end of the reign of Louis XIV, when the royal treasury was in sore straits, but no radical reforms were attempted until later in the eighteenth century. Incapable of modifying the system, the monarchy resorted, in ever greater measure, to the various fiscal expedients that had been attempted in earlier days, such as establishment and sale of new public offices, loans from the financiers, taxation of government and private securities, irregular funding of the national debt (on which payments were frequently suspended), debasement of the currency, alienation of the royal domain, anticipatory expenditure of tax receipts, and the creation of new taxes. These measures ruined public confidence in the treasury while, at the same time, lavish and useless expenditure of millions at the court of Versailles went on unabated. Pensions,

gifts to favorites, blank drafts upon the treasury, riotous extravagance, and an orgy of wastefulness doomed the monarchy. The
Old Régime destroyed itself by the disorder of its financial
system.

In 1789 the state levied 560,000,000 livres in taxes, of which
85,000,000 livres, or approximately fourteen per cent, went to
defray the costs of collection.[8] In the absence of accurate statistics,
it is impossible to correlate these figures with the national wealth
or income, but most authorities agree that if the taxes had been
distributed equitably the total would not have been excessive.
The inequality of the per capita average tax is strikingly illustrated
in the figures given shortly before the Revolution by Necker, the
director-general of finance. He estimated that the average varied
from fourteen livres in Strasbourg to sixty-four in Paris.[9] If
properly distributed, it would have been about thirty-two livres
per capita. Efforts to reform the financial administration took various forms. Under Louis XIV, Colbert sought to introduce economies and order, to balance the budget, and to do away with the
inequitable incidence of taxation, but his reforms had no lasting
influence. In the following century the liberal economists known
as the Physiocrats endeavored to simplify the multiplicity and
complexity of taxation by introducing a studied, uniform system
of land taxes; but no important changes were made until the reign
of Louis XVI, and those which were made were temporary and
partial.

The most important direct taxes were the *taille*, the *capitation*,
and the *vingtièmes*, the last two being established in the last years
of the reign of Louis XIV to cover the growing deficit of the
government. Originally (from 1439) a levy for military purposes,
the taille was from the beginning almost exclusively a tax upon
the peasantry. Exempt from it were the nobility, because the duty
of the nobles was to wage war, the clergy (from the time of
Francis I), which periodically paid a lump sum known as the
"free gift," the many thousand royal officers, the bourgeois of

---

[8] The livre was worth 19½ cents and was equivalent to the franc.
[9] This estimate applies to members of the Third Estate. The estimate made by the
famous historian Taine that the average peasant paid fifty-three per cent of his income in direct taxes alone is impossibly high, for the indirect taxes to the government which he evaluated at fourteen per cent to the government (and an additional
fourteen per cent to the church) in reality brought the government more than all
the direct taxes.

the most important cities, and many lesser towns which compounded for the taille by paying a lump sum derived from city tolls (*octrois*) upon farm produce. The taille was not assessed uniformly throughout the country. In the pays d'états it was real, that is, a tax upon landed property, though peasants who rented land from the nobles paid less than the peasants who worked non-noble land. Elsewhere in France, in the pays d'élections, the taille was a personal tax, that is, levied upon the presumed wealth of the peasant rather than upon his land. As a result, the assessment was arbitrary and invariably gave rise to many instances of injustice. Finally, there was no uniformity in the incidence and collection of the taille. In the regions of the personal taille the royal council arbitrarily fixed the amount for each pays d'élections, and the various local officials apportioned it and collected it from the inhabitants. In the districts where the real taille was in force, the provincial estates determined their own quotas, which were then apportioned and collected locally.

The captitation and the vingtième were intended as general taxes payable by all subjects, the former as a poll tax and the latter as an income tax on all revenue whether from the land, commerce, industry, or the liberal professions. But these attempts to equalize the burden of taxation eventually only increased the tax rate for the peasantry. The schedules for the classification of personal income were not adhered to, nor were the personal declarations of income rigorously checked. The privileged classes largely evaded paying the capitation, which virtually became, for the peasantry who bore its brunt, a second or supplementary taille. The vingtième, of which there were two or three at different periods during the eighteenth century, also failed of its intended effect, for fiscal equality was an impossibility in a social régime grounded upon privilege. It has already been noted that the parlements steadfastly opposed the equitable management of the vingtièmes, refusing first to register them and later to modify the unfair assessments then existing. In addition to these direct taxes already mentioned there was the royal *corvée*, which also fell exclusively upon the peasantry. The corvée was practically a direct tax, payable in labor instead of money, for it bound the peasants to contribute a stipulated number of days' service on the royal highways and in the transport of troops.

The local collections were ruinous to all concerned, for the collectors and the richest peasants were held personally responsible for the local quota, a state of affairs which favored partiality, corruption, and violence. To lessen their assessment the peasants concealed their goods in order to give an appearance of poverty, or less frequently, had recourse to the law courts to seek, often in vain, redress for their grievances.

The system of indirect taxes was still more unjust and vicious. These were not collected directly by the state, but by private tax collectors.[10] The management of the principal indirect taxes— which were the salt tax (*gabelle*), the excise tax (*aides*), the customs duties (*traites* and *douanes*), the government tobacco monopoly, and the income from the royal domains—provided wealthy financiers with an excellent opportunity to amass enormous fortunes. The system which enriched them was a true abomination, for it was to the pecuniary interest of these farmers-general not to display leniency. Supported by the authority of the government, the vast staffs of fiscal agents in the administrative courts used inquisitorial methods to collect their quotas, practicing domiciliary visits and terrorizing their victims with their power to make arrests.

The abuses connected with the administration of the salt tax were the most flagrant, and of all the fiscal agents the salt tax collectors (*gabelous*) were the most detested. Each family was required by law to buy annually a specified amount of salt for household use. The amount required was not excessive in itself, but the management of this government monopoly was atrocious, varying from district to district and according to the rank of the individual. The price of this obligatory household salt was exceedingly high in the northern and central provinces, less in others, and almost nothing in some, such as Brittany. On the other hand many cities and individuals were entirely exempt from the obligations of the gabelle. Consequently, many individuals turned smugglers, bringing in salt from the provinces where the rate was cheapest to the ones where it was dearer. The gabelous made house-to-house searches and thousands of arrests, many of their

[10] The lease was let, usually for six years, to an individual whose underwriters were the financiers known as farmers-general, each of whom paid a large security on which he received interest. Frequently a portion of the profit went to the silent partners called *croupiers* who helped raise the surety that was required of each farmer-general. In 1773 it was discovered that Louis XV himself as well as the then reigning favorite Madame du Barry were such silent partners in several tax farms.

ST. BONAVENTURE LIBRARY
ST. BONAVENTURE, N.Y.

victims being sent to the galleys in punishment. If the figures given out by one of Louis XVI's ministers are accurate or even approximately accurate, the situation was appalling. Every year, he states, for infractions of the gabelle, there were "four thousand attachments on houses, thirty-four hundred imprisonments, five hundred condemnations to the whipping-post, banishment or galleys." The exactions of the excisemen and the interference of the customs officials, while not so palpably unjust, alike cried for correction.

Interior customs boundaries and a baffling variety of weights and measures also reduced the efficiency of the administration. For the conduct of internal trade France was divided into three large sections. A belt of twelve central provinces around Paris, known as the region of the Five Great Farms (*Cinq Grosses Fermes*, so called because the five most important customs taxes or farms were involved), constituted a sort of tariff union within which the traffic of goods was free. Roughly encircling this belt was a group of provinces which were "reputed foreign" (*provinces réputées étrangères*), and in which transit fees were levied upon goods passing from one province to another and customs duties (traites or douanes) were levied on goods passing out of this division either into the Five Great Farms or to other parts of the kingdom. A third group of provinces, those acquired since 1664 and situated on the eastern political frontiers, such as Alsace and Lorraine, were actually foreign (*provinces d'étranger effectif*) in their trading relations with the rest of France. The discriminatory tariff on foreign goods that was established by the tariff of 1664 was applied to their goods when they entered France. Lastly, there existed a tariff upon country produce that entered city walls (the octroi) which maintained an unnecessary distinction between Frenchmen who produced in the country and those who consumed that produce in the city.

There was no division of the French government of the Old Régime which contemporaries did not condemn, no function whose execution failed to arouse great criticism. The rule of an arbitrary monarch, vigorous and forceful under Louis XIV, had degenerated under his successor into caprice and indifference tempered by vice and cynicism. The governmental system, both local and central, was handicapped at every turn by its paralyzing internal weaknesses, by the lack of responsible leadership, by the tangible

THE CUSTOMS DIVISIONS
OF FRANCE
IN 1789

"Cinq grosses fermes"
(subject to tariff of 1664)

"Provinces réputées étrangères"
(as regards the tariff of 1664)

"Provinces d'étranger effectif"
(acquired since 1664 or endowed
with special privileges)

B.– Bishopric   C.– County

opposition of many individuals and powerful corporate groups,
and by the intangible resistance of ingrained habits, deep-rooted
traditions, and ancient loyalties. Absolutism in practice, whether in
the administration of the government, justice, or finances, gave
meagre returns for the injuries that willfully or otherwise it inflicted upon the nation. But the social structure of France was
itself hardly conducive to promoting man's pursuit of his inalienable and imprescriptible rights of life, liberty, and happiness—
unless he happened to be of the fortunate few who were well born.

II. SOCIETY IN THE OLD RÉGIME

THE CHURCH AND THE CLERGY

THE clergy made up the first class or "Estate" of France, and the church, that is, the corporation of the clergy, was the most influential corporate body in the kingdom. As such it exercised an extraordinary influence in governmental administration. By reason of its great wealth, its varied and extensive privileges in financial, judicial, and educational matters, and its internal discipline, it held a dominant position in the life of the nation. But its dependence upon the monarchy was very marked, and the clergy of the Old Régime no longer had any real political authority. The king had the right to make appointments to the principal benefices, which were the bishoprics, the abbeys, and the priories. By the Declaration of the Liberties of the Gallican Church he was empowered to regulate the internal affairs of the clergy—which, in practice, gave the monarchy police powers over ecclesiastics and supervisory rights over the domains and revenue of the church. This same Declaration not only reaffirmed the independence of the monarchy from the ecclesiastical power in temporal affairs, but virtually made the French clergy an autonomous body in so far as papal control was concerned. But what the French clergy gained in independence from Rome they lost in further dependence upon the king. While all estimates concerning the number of the clergy are uncertain at best, the following figures appear most credible for the end of the Old Régime. There were from 10,000 to 11,000 members of the upper clergy, including archbishops, bishops, vicar-generals, cathedral and collegiate canons, abbots in commendation, bishops *in partibus;* about 60,000 members of the lower secular clergy, which included parish priests and their assistants; and not more than 60,000 monks and nuns living in abbeys, monasteries, priories, and convents. The total of 130,000 secular and regular ecclesiastics composed less than one per cent of the total population of France.

The civil authority of the church was far-reaching. It kept all public registers and recorded all baptisms, marriages, and deaths in the kingdom. Public welfare and charity were in its hands. Church courts were still numerous, and their jurisdiction, although much diminished, was still effective over cases involving ecclesiastics. Education, from the simple parish school or the *école de charité* to the universities, was controlled by individual ecclesiastics or religious orders. At the periodic assemblies, the representatives of the clergy of the kingdom discussed the censorship of books and the press, drafted regulations against heretics and Protestants, and laid down the educational policy of the church.

The net income of the property which the clergy possessed did not exceed 120 million livres and may have been as low as 80 million, but an additional source of income was the tithes, which brought the church about 123 millions annually. The division of that landed property and the apportionment of the annual income from land and tithes, however, were far from equal. The landed property was controlled, or at least administered, by the noble prelates of the secular clergy and the wealthy, old-established monastic orders. To the fortunate few of the upper clergy went not only the income from these estates but the greater part of the tithes as well, while the parish churches and clergy were impoverished.

In the eighteenth century the tithe no longer corresponded to the tenth part of the produce,[1] being as little as one-sixtieth in some districts of Dauphiné and Provence and one-eighth in the southwest of France. One-thirteenth of the farm and dairy produce would represent an average for the entire country. The lower clergy, the peasantry, and the liberal economists joined in denouncing the institution of the tithes: the economists on the grounds that the tithes were deflected from the original purpose for which they had been intended, and also that that purpose should have been fulfilled by the state; the peasantry, because of the hardships and the abuses incidental to their levy; the lower clergy, because the preponderant share of the tax went to the upper clergy, who needed it least. In some instances the tithes had become the per-

---

[1] The tithes were originally a ten per cent tax upon the crops and the flocks, legally established as far back as the time of Charlemagne, for the local needs of the parish. A common classification distinguished between the great tithes (*grosses dimes*), levied upon wheat and wine, and the lesser tithes (*dimes menues*), levied upon millet, buckwheat, hemp, flax, fruit, and vegetables

sonal possession of wealthy lay proprietors or monastic establishments. Such tithes were known as infeudated tithes and were collected by the local agents of tax farmers.

The clergy, whether regular or secular, were civilly dead and therefore exempt from the obligations which the state laid upon the laity. Ecclesiastical property, moreover, was not subjected to royal taxation. Every five years, and sometimes more frequently, the clergy of France held a general assembly for the purpose of regulating their internal financial affairs and voting a "free gift" to the king.[2] To raise the moneys due to the government and necessary for their corporate expenses, the clergy taxed themselves. The amount thus levied by the "free gift" was indubitably less than the clergy would normally have paid if subject to the ordinary royal taxes. The government customarily refunded part of the sum in the form of payment of interest for money borrowed by the church, and frequently it made special concessions in return for this voluntary offering.

At the end of the Old Régime, almost all the one hundred and thirty-nine dioceses, both large and small, were held by nobles. There were whole dynasties of ecclesiastical dignitaries, such as the Rohans, the Montmorencys, the La Rochefoucaulds; the Talleyrand-Périgords, all of them of ancient and famous noble families. One such sinecure for the younger sons of the great noble families was the position of grand vicar at an episcopal diocese. The post was lucrative and required few qualifications save noble birth and formal theological training at the Sorbonne. Another well-paying sinecure was the charge of canon either in a cathedral or in a collegiate chapter. For the nominal duty of relieving the bishop of his temporal obligations in the diocese the canon drew a wholly extravagant income from the chapter to which he was attached. There were approximately 800 canonicates for nobles at the king's disposal. The noble chapters for women, particularly the notorious ones in Lorraine, of which Remiremont and Epinal were the best known, abused the income of the church in yet more flagrant fashion. In return for temporary celibacy and the celebration of a few masses a needy noblewoman retired, for a brief time, to the seclusion of those secularized convents only to emerge into

---

[2] At the periodical assemblies, the clergy also dealt with education, doctrinal matters, and the discipline of their members. The "free gift" was first voted in the early sixteenth century.

the world the richer for a marriage dowry acquired by such exemplary piety. The ancient and pernicious practice of entrusting the titular administration of a prosperous abbey to a commendatory abbot (*abbé en commende*) provided additional sinecures for needy noblemen. Commendatory abbots were either secular ecclesiastics or else laymen who were hastily tonsured in preparation for their new dignity. The typical abbé en commende lived away from his abbatial residence, entrusting the actual administration of his charge to a prior. The literature of the age paints him as a common figure of the salons and the theaters of Paris, popular for his wit, his easy charm, and his large supply of ready money. For such signal devotion to his religious duties he usually received an income that could have brought material comfort to many curés and relief to many a needy parishioner.

The yearly income of a bishopric varied according to the territorial extent and the location of the diocese. The bishop of Strasbourg had an annual income of 400,000 livres, though the average episcopal income did not exceed 30,000 or 40,000. The average income of archbishops was not much higher, though a half-dozen archbishops received between 100,000 and 200,000 livres annually. We must bear in mind that those figures do not reveal the whole story, for many of those prelates also held abbeys in commendation and practically doubled their episcopal incomes. The archbishop of Rouen, for instance, had 100,000 livres from his diocese and an additional 130,000 from the receipts of the abbeys that he held in commendation.

Only a few of the upper clergy could be accused of immorality, but many of them preferred the amenities of Paris to the drabness of their provincial dioceses. There were never fewer than twoscore who maintained residences in Paris, turned their flocks over to their grand vicars or their suffragan bishops, and shared in the pleasures of the court nobility. A much larger number, however, administered the sacraments, made pastoral visits, provided for the instruction of their parishioners, and defended the faith against the indifference of the masses and the rationalism of non-believers. A smaller group among the bishops busied themselves with practical social problems, and were characterized by a contemporary as "men whom a beneficent philosophy had stimulated to prove that public welfare was the real and the sole religion of the state." They presided over provincial estates, pored over financial accounts, built roads and canals, reclaimed waste lands, introduced improved agricultural methods, and "turned the sanctuary into a political laboratory." With the exception of these bishop-administrators, the upper clergy remained adamant to the propaganda of the liberals who held themselves enlightened.

In mode of life no less than in outlook, in birth and social status, in receptivity to current philosophical generalizations, the parish priests and their assistants were entirely distinct from their ecclesiastical superiors. Relatively few of them were actually appointed by their diocesan bishop; in the majority of cases appointments depended upon monastic establishments or else upon various chapters or simple laymen. In those cases where the appointive power did not belong to the bishop, there were frequently two curés for each parish. One, the *curé primitif*, was a convenient figurehead who allowed the patron of the parish to retain most of the tithes; the other, the real curé, who performed all the functions of the office, received a fixed salary, the so-called "congruous portion," which was only a scant portion of the tithes collected in his parish.[3] If the parish priest received more than the congruous portion, he was fortunate, for he could hold up his head against the innumerable demands of his duties and his parishioners. In city parishes salaries were higher than in country, and the parishioners more likely to be generous with their casual fees. In the country parishes the clergy had to rest contented or discontented with their salaries. Even after an increase from 550 to 750 livres salary for the curés, the lot of the latter was difficult, being exceeded only by the condition of the priests who had no parishes and lived entirely on fees from masses, marriages, baptisms, and burials.

The daily tasks of the parish priest were many and trying. He dwelt in the midst of his flock, ate the rough food of his parishioners, wrapped his gaunt form in tattered, threadbare garments, and trod the oft impassable country roads on his errands of faith and mercy. The peasants held him in high reverence and looked to him for the solution of their homely problems. His church was the center of their communal existence, he himself their guide

[3] In the diocese of Chartres, not far from Paris, the heirs of the original "patron" of the village parishes were a group of opulent convents whose control of appointments gave them the nomination of 875 curés of the 943 in the diocese, thus leaving only 68 for the bishop to name.

and good friend. It was at the village church that the various local activities were determined. There the peasants came with their requests and difficulties; there the curé kept the civil records of the village; there he passed on the qualifications of the village teachers, conferring teaching privileges and supervising the few public schools or the more numerous private schools kept and subsidized by the Catholic Church. In cases of necessity he himself went out to teach the rudiments of primary education. It was on the green, before the church doors, that he summoned his communicants when mass was said, and that he read such official news as he had received from the intendant. Almost every page of the peasants' cahiers attested their veneration for the curé, and every cahier of the curés expressed their resentment over the indifference and the neglect of their superiors.[4]

Relations between the upper and lower clergy were an exchange of arrogance on the one part and open or suppressed hostility on the other. The parish clergy demanded a voice at the periodic assemblies of the clergy; they demanded a more equitable assessment of the corporate taxes called *décimes* and an end to the abuse of the tithes; they asked for a break-up of the monopoly of promotions which the nobles guarded so jealously. They resented the insulting attitude of the upper clergy, who looked down upon them as a race apart—"coarse, dirty, and ignorant." These demands, voiced in their cahiers, reveal the independent spirit of the curés as well as their partial conversion to the doctrines of the *philosophes*. It was through no accidental, impulsive propulsion of emotion that the lower clergy forsook their order and joined the Third Estate in 1789. It was the reasoned consciousness of their grievances against the episcopate and the full realization of their common bond with the lower classes that led them to take the decisive step.

For the regular clergy, who lived according to a rule (*regula*) in a conventual establishment, the eighteenth century was a period of decline. Monastic life held little attraction for men or women in the age of reason, and we may gravely doubt whether as many as 60,000 men and women still belonged to the regular orders in 1789, though before the middle of the century authorities had enumerated as many as 100,000. The monarchy contributed to the rapid decline. Since capital that was invested in a monastic estab-

---

[4] There were some curés less worthy of respect, but the complaints about them in the cahiers were not numerous.

lishment came under the "dead hand" (*mainmorte*) of the church, the monarchy utilized various pretexts to dissolve congregations and take over their property. The notorious irregularity of many monasteries and convents also discouraged aspirants to the monastic life. The great prelates themselves took a stern attitude toward the erring monks and nuns and bent resolutely to the severe task of restoring discipline. In the general assembly of the clergy of 1765 a "Commission for the regular clergy" (*commission des réguliers*), was appointed for that purpose. It wrought marvels of purification from 1766 to 1789, suppressing houses in wholesale fashion, uniting small, half-deserted congregations into single groups and, backed by royal legislation, reducing the number of the regular clergy by many thousands.

However, despite such laudable efforts at reform, abuses still undermined the integrity of the orders. At the same time the subversive ideas of the new philosophy invaded the sanctity of monkish cells. Many troubled friars pondered over their shattered faith in the inherent wickedness of man and the sinfulness of mundane society. A few teaching congregations and charitable orders escaped the general contagion of worldly practices and the new philosophy and persevered in their good work, untainted and impoverished in the hurly-burly of corruption. Such examples, however, were rare. Rich, unproductive monastic houses, guarding their wealth from society, abbeys in commendation, convents secularized and turned into fashionable retreats for the daughters of the nobility, corrupt and errant friars—those gave the regular clergy their deservedly evil reputation and led to their suppression in the early days of the Revolution.

The prestige of the church itself was greatly weakened in the Old Régime by the acrimonious doctrinal dispute between the Jansenists and the Jesuits. Skeptics and scoffers made no secret of their feelings toward "the Jesuit assassins" and the "Jansenist bigots." Nothing pleased them more than the quarrel, which gave them an excellent opportunity to ridicule Catholicism and to spread the doctrines of a rational, "natural" religion. In truth the spectacle of the church, which claimed the custody of revealed truth, engaged in cruel strife to determine what that truth was, was as unedifying for its supporters as it was pleasing to its critics. Voltaire, more than any other writer of his time, took the lead in denouncing the church, castigating it for its brutal punishments of dissenters and branding it as the enemy of progress and enlightenment, as the "infamous thing" which had to be extirpated.

The unyielding front of the church to the new scientific truths and the arguments of natural philosophy sufficed to condemn it among the cultivated leisured classes. The utter absence of solidarity in its own ranks weakened it from within. Its complete dependence upon the monarchy, and the monarchy's defense of its financial parasitism upon the state, together with the flagrant misbehavior of many ecclesiastics, alienated the support of the popular classes. That evil combination of circumstances made reorganization of the ecclesiastical system necessary; and the Revolution made it inevitable.

The Nobility

De Tocqueville first established the paradox that at no period in French history was it so easy for a commoner to rise to the ranks of the nobility as in the eighteenth century, and yet never were nobles and commoners so distinct and separate. The nobility constituted the second Estate of the realm. An English peerage descended only to the eldest son; in France all the children of a nobleman retained the rank. Estimates of the number of the nobility on the eve of the Revolution vary most widely. The most likely figures are 50,000 or more families and between 200,000 and 250,000 individuals.

The rank of nobility was acquired by birth, by military service, by the purchase of patents of nobility, or by the possession of certain public offices. The mediaeval military nobility (*noblesse de l'épée*) was, in the eighteenth century, virtually extinct, and the self-styled nobility of the sword of that period had exceedingly few representatives who could trace their lineage beyond the sixteenth century. In that century of the Commercial Revolution wealthy commoners began to acquire the vast estates of the old nobility of blood. With the great landed domains they acquired the patents of nobility, seigniorial rights, and the titles of dukes, marquises, counts, and viscounts. In the next two centuries the monarchy, ever embarrassed for funds, created and sold public offices that conferred nobility. Through the purchase and inheritance of these positions in the judiciary, in the treasury, and in the central and municipal administration, many thousands of rich bourgeois acquired rank. These constituted the nobility of the robe and the nobility of the town belfry (*noblesse de la robe* and *noblesse de la cloche*). Nobility could be lost as well as acquired. A nobleman derogated if he engaged in activities which were considered prejudicial to the dignity of his class. He could sell the produce of his land, but he was forbidden under pain of derogation to engage in legitimate trade or commerce. For the sons of the nobleman the only careers that were open were in the army, the church, the law, and the administration.

The subdivisions among the nobility then were very numerous, depending upon manner of acquisition, functions, residence, and wealth. Essentially, the real distinctions were based upon differences of wealth and social position. At the top of the ladder were the nobles of the court—the princes of the blood and all the wealthy and distinguished noblemen who had been officially presented to the king. Since the road to preferment lay through the favor of the king, all those who could possibly do so flocked to Versailles, hoping, often against hope, to be presented and earn the right to live at or be admitted to the royal court.

The country nobility included nobles of varying financial circumstances. There were the comparatively few but enormously wealthy and pretentious magistrates, the nobles of the robe, who dwelt in their châteaux or in their sumptuous mansions in the provincial towns. Then there were the more numerous but generally less wealthy noblemen who held posts in the administration or in the local municipalities. Lastly, and most numerous of all, were the *hobereaux*, the "sparrow hawks," those impecunious country nobles who were too poor to flee from their poverty to Versailles and forbidden by their noble status to pursue legitimate activities that might rescue them from their plight.

Those who belonged, or claimed to belong, to the nobility of the sword, affected a deep scorn of those nobles whose office may have been noble, but whose blood, alas, was not. This scorn was returned with generous interest by the office-holding magistrates and public officials. It is perhaps superfluous to note that the hobereaux were intensely envious of the court nobility, and the latter contemptuous of the ruined country gentry. Yet jealousy, envy, and scorn apart, the nobles regarded themselves as infinitely superior to the commoners. Irrespective of social classification, they had seigniorial rights, rights of administering manorial justice, tax exemptions, a monopoly of the most important public offices in the courts, the administration, and in the army, and a veritable vested interest in the church benefices.

These privileges were least valuable to the hobereaux, whose condition was particularly sorry in the western and west-central provinces. They quarreled over the trifling manorial dues which their tenant peasants owed them and they insisted, with a haughtiness bordering on the ridiculous, upon the recognition of their petty social prerogatives. Without patronage their sons could not aspire to any of the governmental or ecclesiastical sinecures. Their mortgaged lands reverted to rich nobles or to wealthy commoners from near-by towns. To escape paying the poll tax they posed as commoners. They sold their rents, their judicial privileges, and their uncultivated lands. Their daughters took the veil, and their sons remained in the tumbling manor house, wasting their time in idleness or debauch, or else drifted away to join the urban unemployed. There were of course more progressive country noblemen who lived on terms of friendly intimacy with their tenants, acting as benevolent counselors to the peasants, but their number was not great.

The court nobility fared better. Montesquieu acidly defined a great noble as a man who saw the king, spoke with his ministers, and had ancestors, debts, and pensions. We have already referred to the splendor of the royal court during the eighteenth century. Never before was social intercourse so gay, so refined, and so graceful. Never were manners so good, conversation so sparkling, and morals so low as they were at the court. Never was the cult of luxury so assiduously served and defended by its devotees. Indeed, in the eyes of many, extravagance in dress and entertainment seemed the triumphant vindication of the prevailing philosophical doctrine of progress. Refined taste and exquisite manners condoned great vices, and elegance of speech gilded base topics of conversation. Court society was "a charming and wicked moment, a world which had brought the art of sensuous enjoyment to its perfection and was going to ruin with a smile." Elaborate retinues, huge establishments, garments of gold and silver cloth, hunting, gambling, theatricals, gala balls, sumptuous spectacles, extravagant repasts exhausted the largest fortunes. The spendthrift monarchy of Louis XV was generous in its assistance, dispensing well-paying sinecures and rich bounties to its favorites, encouraging, even taking the lead, in the mad whirl of profligate extravagance. The more unscrupulous nobles speculated on the Bourse (the stock exchange) or maintained gambling dens in their homes and skimmed closely around the rim of the penal code. Worldly prelates and the rakish court abbés vied with their secular brethren. Not a few court nobles escaped the contagion, but the folly of their fellows was more than ample to damn them in the eyes of contemporaries and posterity.

In real influence the nobility of the robe, which included the magistrates of the parlements and the other sovereign courts, easily outranked the more ornamental and wasteful nobles at court. They were enormously wealthy, inheriting the accumulated riches of their bourgeois ancestors and increasing them from the emoluments of their offices and by careful investments in landed property and trade. In the eighteenth century the nobility of the robe became a veritable caste, as rich commoners no longer bought posts in the judiciary. The magistrates arranged marriage alliances for their daughters, seeking a connection with the court nobility and an entry to Versailles. But despite their wealth and the marriage alliances they remained a group apart, "a sort of judicial clergy, holding aloof from the profane, officiating in the severe solemnity of their luxurious and imposing interiors into which none but a magistrate may penetrate." Negligible at Versailles, their social rôle in the provinces was exceedingly important by reason of their wealth and their influence over thousands of lesser judicial officials who solicited their favor.

Attention has already been called to the political rôle of the magistrates of the parlements, in particular of the parlement of Paris, during the reign of Louis XV. Public opinion favored them for their opposition to the arbitrary rule of the monarchy, but that opposition, as we have noted, was not altogether disinterested. They opposed the monarch in order to gain more power for themselves. Yet there were liberal spirits among them as well as in the ranks of the court nobility. Adrien Duport, Hérault de Séchelles, and Servan, all of them important figures during the Revolution, joined the liberal court nobles, such as Lafayette, the Dillons, and the Lameths, in denouncing abuses. One met these enthusiastic apostates to privileged aristocracy in many fashionable and "enlightened" salons of Paris. The impressionable young count of Ségur, fresh from the battle fields of America where he had followed Lafayette, has given us a vivid picture of these young nobles:

> We were scornful critics of the old customs, of the feudal pride of our fathers and of their severe etiquette, and everything that was old seemed annoying and ridiculous to us. . . . Voltaire attracted our intellect, and Rousseau touched our hearts. We took secret pleasure in seeing them attack the old framework, which appeared antiquated and ridiculous to us. . . . We enjoyed at the same time the advantages of the patriciate and the amenities of a plebeian philosophy.

One must beware of exaggerating their influence, for the liberal elements in the nobility were few. Besides, these nobles did not understand their danger, for they thought that their own privileges were unassailable. They did not grasp the fact that once free criticism of accepted institutions was allowed, they themselves would be among the first victims of that criticism.

The day was past when the ministers and the intendants were sworn enemies of the nobility. Almost without exception they too belonged to the nobility. In the fifteen years preceding the Revolution only one minister out of thirty-six was a commoner, and he was Necker, a foreigner and a Protestant. As for the intendants, all in Louis XVI's reign were nobles, forming powerful dynasties that were closely allied with the judicial nobility. Like the latter, the administrative nobles sought popularity with the people, and to gain it they frequently ignored instructions from Versailles and initiated policies of their own. Yet for all their courting of popular favor, they failed to gain it. The people disliked them because of their excessive powers, because they were the official representatives of the monarchy that public opinion condemned. But the temporary solidarity of administrators and magistrates against the monarchy precipitated the final revolutionary dénouement, in which the nobility along with the monarchy met their doom.

Long before 1789 the nobility was destined for destruction. In the first place the internal strife of this social class destroyed its solidarity. Disunited, the nobility fell before the superior strength of the commoners. Secondly, enlightened public opinion condemned the wasteful, parasitic existence of this privileged body. Peasants denied the legitimacy of the entire manorial system, and the bourgeoisie through their spokesmen among the *philosophes* roundly denounced the social discrimination, the fiscal immunities, and the innumerable privileges of the class that kept capital out of circulation, shackled trade, crippled industry, and lived on the toil of the nation.

THE PEASANTS AND THE LAND QUESTION

France was predominantly an agricultural country, and more than twenty million peasants lived on the soil, by their labor feeding themselves and the city inhabitants. The peasant question was necessarily the foremost economic question of the times, particularly in view of the appalling burdens of the peasants and the backwardness of agricultural production. Agrarian conditions in France were unique and unparalleled anywhere else in Europe, for France was a country of many peasant proprietors and tenant farmers cultivating small plots of land. Neither in England nor among France's eastern neighbors were conditions similar. In the former country free peasant ownership during the eighteenth century was being eliminated almost entirely in favor of the landed aristocracy, which acquired possession of most of the land. In central and eastern Europe the feudal nobility not only owned the land but exercised great political and military authority over the peasantry.

The agricultural map of France in the Old Régime showed great variations not only in the mode and intensity of cultivation, in the type of leaseholds, but also in the distribution of the landed property among the different social classes. The relative percentages of these social classes varied considerably from district to district. Between them the nobility and the clergy owned probably not much more than one-third of the land. The holdings of the nobility were greatest in the western provinces, where the clergy held little property, less in the fertile north-central provinces, and least in southern France. The clergy possessed very little either in western or southern France, but held considerable real estate in the north.[5] Much of this privileged land was unproductive, consisting of woodlands, moors, brakes, and meadows of which the peasantry had the communal usufruct. There were relatively few large estates among the aristocracy, for the nobles and the

[5] A recent estimate evaluated the landed possessions of the clergy at not less than six and not more than ten per cent of the total.

clergy leased their lands in small plots to peasant tenants. The wealthy bourgeoisie also owned considerable landed property, particularly in the vicinity of the towns, their holdings ranging from twelve to forty-five per cent in different regions. The most numerous proprietors were the free, non-servile peasants. There were approximately four million male adult peasant landowners, or between seventy and eighty per cent of the total male adult peasantry. While the total amount held by the peasantry was clearly not less than one-third and probably not more than one-half of all the land, most of these proprietors owned much less land than was necessary to enable them, from its produce, to support themselves and their families. Peasant ownership was weakest in the western provinces, more pronounced in the north-central districts, and at its greatest strength in southern France.

In the strict legal sense those peasants who considered themselves landed proprietors were only perpetual leaseholders of land belonging to the feudal overlord. Theoretically, the owner was the feudal lord who received the dues and services. Actually, however, the peasant who bought or sold, inherited and bequeathed his parcel of land regarded himself as the real proprietor, and for that reason he considered intolerable the innumerable manorial dues that he owed to the lord.[6]

Not many of these free proprietors, who were so numerous, could support themselves and their families from their plots. Those few who could were known as the *laboureurs*, and constituted a sort of rural aristocracy. They were most numerous in the north of France. Other peasant proprietors, even when they owned sufficient land to pay government land taxes, did not own enough for their needs and generally tried to better their condition by leasing land as tenants from rich noble, church or bourgeois landowners, or by working as millers and innkeepers. In addition to peasant proprietors and tenants there were many peasants—one-fourth of the entire peasant population—that owned no land at all. In order to make a living they had to compete with one another for work as farm hands and harvesters during the busy season, as household servants, or as workers in rural industry. If they did not

---

[6] A very small proportion of the free peasant proprietors were in theory not subject to the manorial dues. These peasants who held their land in fee simple were known as the *francs-alleux*.

find work, which was often the case, or if their ill paid and temporary work ran out, they averted starvation, or did not avert it, by becoming poachers, smugglers, vagrants, highwaymen, or beggars in the towns.

Of the two most common types of leaseholds, *fermage* was preferable. The tenant *fermier* leased his land for a short period, from three to nine years, paying a money rental and also rental in kind. Until the second half of the eighteenth century this system benefited many petty peasant workers, but after 1750, the owners began to form chains of farms, which not only eliminated many tenants but also greatly increased the rental price. Those who were unable to renew their leases dropped a notch lower in the social scale. The second general type of leasehold was *métayage* (share cropping). The cropper (*métayer*) was most frequent in the south of France, but was found also in the western and central provinces. Wherever he was, his position was precarious. In return for an advance of seed and stock from the proprietor the tenant turned over to him half his entire crop, in addition to paying the usual government taxes and manorial dues. The land-hungry, needy peasant became a métayer, sorry as the lot was, because this status gave him land and at least a prospect of a livelihood. But ordinarily his parcel was too small, his tools too crude and blunted by years of use, his cattle scrawny and sickly, his seed of inferior quality. Small wonder that a contemporary remarked, "It is as impossible for one of these wretches to be a good farmer as for a galley convict to be a good admiral."

The landless proletarians were most numerous in Brittany, Normandy, the northern provinces, and Picardy. In prosperous years the scant wages of the farm hands may barely have sufficed for their simple needs. In years of poor crops, in years of famine, these hapless workers were driven to brigandage or mendicity, or died miserable deaths from starvation or disease. During the off season they competed with the rest of the rural needy in preparing cloth for the entrepreneurs of the towns. Unfortunately, at least in certain regions, that which they earned was lost to the city workers, the gain in all cases going to the incipient capitalist entrepreneur. Domestic servants were comparatively better off than these farm hands, for they at least were hired by the year and were furnished food and lodgings and, occasionally, clothing.

Serfdom still survived in the least fertile regions of the country, most notably in Lorraine and Franche Comté. It was abolished on the crown lands in 1779 and in the neighboring state of Savoy as well, but all efforts failed to induce the nobility of France to follow the royal example. The number of serfs (*mainmortables*) cannot be estimated with any degree of accuracy, but it was probably less than one million in 1789. Their lot was better than that of the serfs of central and eastern Europe. The most oppressive of their obligations was the bond of personal mainmorte which kept them from bequeathing any of their property to children living away from home. Clearly, the French serfs were neither numerous enough nor sufficiently wretched to unleash a revolutionary movement.

Among the numerous obligations which made the peasant "the beast of burden" of the Old Régime, none were more varied or unwarranted than the manorial dues. These the peasant paid in addition to the manifold taxes, direct and indirect, to the state. Practically every peasant cultivator, whether proprietor or tenant, owed certain traditional rents or services to the lord of the manor. The rights of the lord and the obligations of the peasant varied in severity according to the status of the peasant and the traditional custom of the region, though the lord of the manor could, by his intercession, temper the literal execution of the obligations. The extent of each peasant's obligations was recorded in a declaration (*aveu*), which also recorded the type of tenure that he held. These aveux were renewed whenever the land changed hands, and periodically at intervals of ten, twenty, or thirty years. The manor rolls or the archives in which these declarations were kept were known as *terriers*. Toward the end of the Old Régime the aveux were renewed, at the expense of the peasantry, more frequently than they had been in many generations. Because of the wide discussion that raged toward 1776 concerning the entire seigniorial régime, feudal nobles began to pay more attention to their legal titles, employing "feudists," who were lawyers proficient in feudal law, to examine these titles. The result was, generally, that the seigneurs discovered that they were legally entitled to more than they had customarily received from the peasants. As the cost of living was rising steadily the nobles hastened to take advantage of this opportunity to increase what hitherto had been a fixed income.

Most personal dues had either been abolished or been converted into land or money payments.[7] The serfs, or mainmortables, still owed their lord three days' labor a week upon his manorial estate, but the majority of free peasants had little to complain of in respect to manorial labor (corvée). The most general obligation was the payment of the fixed, unchangeable land rent (*cens*), which marked the land as peasant land and subjected its peasant proprietor to the payment of various sales and mutation fees. The cens was almost always a money rent, and consequently it was neither high nor burdensome, since it had been fixed years earlier when the purchasing power of money was much greater than in the eighteenth century. In addition to the cens the peasant owner generally paid another land rent in the form of a specified share of the crop which was known as the *champart*, sometimes called *terrage*, and amounted on the average to one-eighth of the crop. This heavy burden the peasant endeavored to convert, whenever it was possible, into a money payment.[8] The manorial rights most profitable for the lord, when they could be applied, were the various sales and mutation fees that he exacted whenever the land changed hands. The *lods et ventes* were a sales tax amounting theoretically to about one-eighth of the selling price. By the right known as *retrait* the lord could refuse, at any time within thirty years after the date of a given sale, to give his assent to it; a legal right that made for extortionate practices.

The obligation to do road service for the noble (corvée) had largely disappeared in the eighteenth century, but the group of manorial monopolies known as the *banalités* still existed to plague the lives of the peasantry. There had been a real justification for these banalités in the mediaeval period, when it was convenient, if not altogether necessary, for the peasant to bring his grain to the lord's mill, his flour to the manorial bakery, and his grapes to the manorial winepress, but that historical justification no longer survived in the seventeenth and eighteenth centuries. Nor was there any justification for the commutation of these monopolistic rights into money payments. Many manorial tolls on roads, canals, and

[7] Feudal lawyers (but not the peasants) distinguished between *personal* and *real* rights. The former represented prerogatives that the lord enjoyed by virtue of the services that some remote ancestor had performed for his peasants or the interest on loans and advances; the latter rental claims for the concession of land to the peasant cultivator.

[8] The cens of course was not paid by the fermier or the métayer who leased his land from the privileged classes.

rivers, as well as innumerable dues levied on goods at markets and fairs, artificially increased prices and hindered the sale of agricultural produce. The most vexatious and most cordially hated of all the manorial rights were the exclusive hunting monopolies that the nobility enjoyed over the tilled lands of the peasantry. Although the most fertile regions of France fortunately suffered very slightly from the scourge of the chase, the cahiers of 1789 are full of complaints of the damage to their fields that the hunting parties inflicted. One cahier stated with bitter, epigrammatic poignancy that "the stags, the dogs, the boars, and other animals, but no one else, enjoy the produce of the land." Disputes over manorial rights and obligations were heard in the courts of manorial justice. There were many thousands of manorial courts over which the lord or his bailiff presided. The sentiment that Voltaire put into the mouth of his *Seigneur du Village,* "I am judge, bailiff, and notary here, all in one," gives the spirit of manorial justice. It was corrupt, dilatory, and expensive to the peasant litigant, and an instrument of exploitation on the part of the noble.

The relations between the peasantry and the nobility were ever conditioned by the one constant factor—the perpetuation of the manorial rights and obligations. At best these relations were an exchange of benevolent paternal solicitude on the part of the noble and respectful veneration on the part of the peasant. They were at their worst on the estates of the "absentee proprietors" and on the lands owned by the "sparrow hawks," where interminable disputes and lawsuits over manorial dues embittered the contacts of the two classes.

The attitude of the peasantry toward the clergy, particularly the lower clergy, was more amicable. While the lot of the peasant on a clerical estate did not differ in any radical fashion from that of his fellow on the land of a noble, the deep religious feelings of the peasant and his intimate association with and dependence upon the priest established a bond of sympathy between them. Most frequently the priest came from the ranks of the peasants. It is clear from the cahiers that the parish priests and the peasantry were in substantial agreement on the question of civil and political rights. Almost everywhere the curés and the peasantry complained about the unjust distribution of the tithes and the abuse of the infeudated tithes. Common grievances against the financial abuses only intensified the solidarity of the peasantry and the curés. The basic cause of their close coöperation was their traditional association in the duties and tasks of daily existence, in religious devotions, in elementary instruction, in the alleviation of poverty, and in the relief of illness and suffering.

THE CHANGED STATUS OF THE PEASANTRY

Despite the fertility of the soil and the numerous peasantry the population lived in almost constant fear of famine. Withal, France was the largest grain-producing country in western Europe, production generally exceeding consumption. The grain harvest, however, was not uniform throughout the kingdom. About one-third of the provinces produced slightly more than was needed for their own use, another third just barely produced enough, and the remaining provinces scarcely produced any grain crops.

The backwardness of agricultural exploitation in France may be explained by the fact that agriculture was almost exclusively in the hands of the peasantry, and that much of the land of the kingdom did not come under the plow. Two-fifths of the total area in Brittany, for example, was uncultivated. Great stretches of waste land in river valleys, along the edges of forests and on the slopes of foothills, were waiting to be cleared or drained. Peasant cultivation, except in the most fertile and the richest regions, followed primitive methods. The granges and the stables and the granaries were thoroughly unsatisfactory and inadequate. The stock was scrawny and undernourished. The agricultural implements were primitive and not much superior to those used in the Middle Ages. There was no improved farm machinery to aid the cultivator as there was in England during the same period. In most districts intensive culture and the rotation of crops were unknown. The system of fallow land was still in general use, except in Flanders, Alsace, and parts of Normandy. Artificial meadows were infrequent, even after the reformers pointed out the necessity of introducing them. It was not only lack of equipment, but also the spirit of tradition that made the average farmer persevere in the ancient methods. He plowed only the surface land, he was negligent in his weeding, he sowed too late to get a good harvest. A good quality of seed and a plentiful supply of manure for fertilizer would have worked wonders with the crop. But neither was available.

Lack of resources and primitive methods of agriculture alone do not explain the recurrent food shortages and famines that France suffered in the Old Régime. Internal trade, if it had functioned smoothly, could have brought the surplus from one district to other districts where a shortage existed. But innumerable restrictions hampered internal trade. Customs barriers, transit fees, market and fair dues, and varying weights and measures made transportation expensive. The difficulties of land transportation further increased the costs, for travel on country roads was always difficult and sometimes dangerous, while the new state highways were not kept up. Transportation was not only difficult but extremely slow as well. Moreover the peasant's instinctive fear of a shortage or of creating the impression that he was prosperous led him to conceal his grain, particularly if he learned that it was to be shipped out of his local district. Thus mob panic not infrequently created an artificial famine.

Up to the middle of the eighteenth century the government exercised a continual supervision over the trade in grain. It made no serious efforts to remove the restrictions, but it passed numerous and stringent regulations to avert the threat of famine. Grain merchants were licensed by the administration and subject to police inspection. Official regulations governed the conditions on which they bought and sold their grain. The amount, the hours and the place of sale, the price, all were determined by the government. The regulating hand of the government fell also upon the cultivators. Royal ordinances prescribed the amount and the kind of seed that was to be grown. It was forbidden to keep grain reserves longer than two years. Frequent declarations, verified by official search, had to be made under pain of severe penalties.[9] When the harvest was good and bread cheap, these regulations were mildly enforced; but when the danger of a food shortage existed, the government applied them rigorously. Food was requisitioned, the granaries of the nobility and the clergy were opened and the contents sold at the market, and a maximum sales price was fixed by the intendants. Reserve stocks of grain that were accumulated for Paris and the large cities were thrown on the market when the shortage became acute. After 1750 the government made a conscious effort to stimulate agricultural production, but the very

[9] These restrictions upon grain trade were removed for the grain merchants of Paris, who were allowed special privileges to provision the capital.

progress that was accomplished tended, as we shall note, to render the position of the needy peasant still more precarious.

From the mass of contradictory fragmentary reports of the period, many historians have found justification for the view that while in general the lot of the peasant improved, his consciousness of his grievances also became accentuated and imbued him with the spirit of revolutionary discontent. Any generalization to the contrary is likely to be as misleading as the accepted generalization, so different were living conditions, types of agricultural cultivation, kinds of food eaten, clothing worn, and houses inhabited in the various provinces of France. Yet it has become increasingly evident, from the most recent researches, that the lot of the majority of the peasants grew worse rather than better in the thirty years immediately prior to 1789. The evidence of clothing, food, and habitation makes it clear that a small, relatively prosperous category of peasant proprietors improved their status and added to their plots of land and their material comfort. At the same time, however, certain factors more or less constant in their force, as well as certain factors of an exceptional character, tended continuously to impoverish the greater number of rural inhabitants and to bring them inexorably below the lowest level of decent subsistence.

Three principal causes determined the steady decline in fortune of the French peasantry: (1) a sharp and continuous growth in population; (2) a marked upward movement of prices without a corresponding increase in real wages; (3) the influence of the Physiocrats in stimulating agrarian reforms. The population of France grew steadily in the eighteenth century, attaining a level that caused Arthur Young to remark that France would be much more powerful and infinitely more prosperous if her population were five or six million less.[10] This rise in population not only accentuated the hardships of the petty peasant proprietor, now doomed, from his already meagre lands, to support a larger family; but, in conjunction with other factors, it greatly increased the number of the landless peasantry who were driven into the

---

[10] He estimated that the population of France in 1791 was 26,363,074, of which 20,500,000 were rural and less than 6,000,000 urban. By comparing his figures with Necker's estimate of 24,000,000 in 1784, it becomes evident that there was a perceptible increase in the last years of the Old Régime. While these figures are not based upon accurate statistics, they reveal clearly that France was one of the most densely populated countries in Europe.

ranks of beggars and vagrants. A noncomitant development with the increase in population was the steady rise, after 1763, in food prices, which more than counterbalanced the smaller increase in wages. This increase in prices arose essentially from the development of an incipient commercial and industrial capitalism, which, in France as in every other country, brought great wealth to the moneyed interests and economic distress to the rest of the population.[11]

In the amount of gold and silver coins in circulation France was far richer than any other state in Europe, a circumstance in itself sufficient to explain the steady increase in the cost of living. The increase in minted money from 1763 to 1777 took place at an annual rate of two per cent, or more than thirty per cent in that fifteen-year period. The new class of capitalists used their wealth to buy titles of nobility and government offices, while the monarchy relied upon them for its ever more needed loans. To repay these loans the state resorted to increasing the tax rate upon the peasantry, while it perpetuated the fiscal exemption or privileges of those from whom alone it could borrow money.

In the second half of the century the economic theorists known as the Physiocrats began an intensive propaganda to interest the government as well as the privileged landowners in agrarian conditions. Working through a central and district agricultural committees the intendants gave instruction and encouragement to the cultivators in the introduction of new crops, improved methods of animal husbandry, use of improved farming machinery, and the use of artificial meadows. On two separate occasions government regulation of the internal grain trade was suspended, but only to be renewed in the face of a rioting peasantry that found itself at the mercy of private traders. Nor did the projected reforms succeed among the rural masses, for these remained faithful to traditional methods partly because they were too poor and ignorant to alter them, and partly because the establishment of artificial meadows and the rotation of crops curtailed their traditional pasturage rights on cropped land and on meadows where the hay had been cut. Such success as the efforts of the Physiocrats did have tended to benefit only those who had sufficient wealth

---

[11] The encouragement of free internal grain trade (in 1763 and again in 1774) also contributed to the increase in prices, for the prosperous peasants sold their grain as high as they could.

to profit from reforms. The laboureur greatly increased his holding by purchasing the formerly unproductive land that was now
reclaimed for cultivation. In many instances the noble proprietor
himself succeeded in acquiring legal title to, or simply usurping
the greater part of, the reclaimed land, again to the disadvantage
of the poor cultivators, who from time immemorial had enjoyed
the use of the common waste land. From the woods, the moors,
the brakes, and the meadows that constituted the commons they
had gathered litter for their cattle, nuts and acorns for their stock,
and the wood they needed for cooking and heating. Now, at a
moment of greatest stress this right too was to be denied them.

At the same time there developed the so-called "feudal reaction," a widespread movement on the part of the privileged
landowners to increase their revenue from their landed estates.
More harassed than ever by the lack of money, but encouraged
by the signs of agricultural progress, they raised the farm rents
on the lands that they leased to peasant tenants, and they revived
obsolete manorial dues to which doubtless they were legally entitled, but which had fallen into disuse. The second half of the
century witnessed a notable increase in the revenues that the
privileged classes derived from their manorial rights, an increase
which was legally exacted mainly from a miserable peasantry
already sinking deeper and deeper into economic distress.

Under these circumstances the lot of the average peasant in
normal times was at best precarious. It has been estimated that
more than twenty per cent of the rural peasantry was indigent in
times of plenty. In general the poverty was most acute in the
newly industrialized regions of the north and in the provinces of
the east where the manorial system was most strongly intrenched.
But the constant and continuous factors which depressed the condition of the peasantry do not alone explain the situation. At times
of crisis, when harvests were poor or epidemics raged, the number
of the indigent increased appreciably. The reports of the intendants, the memorials of the parish priests, and the writings of other
contemporaries all attest the appalling misery of the needy peasants on such occasions. Then, more than ever, they joined the ranks
of the beggars and vagrants who overran the roads, pillaging the
hamlets and terrorizing the inhabitants. In the face of such crushing poverty private relief was impotent, ecclesiastical relief piti-
fully inadequate, and governmental alms and charity hopelessly

meagre.[12] Owing to the lack of sanitation and medical attention, conditions in hospitals and prisons and workhouses were indescribably bad. In the three years immediately preceding the Revolution the distress of the populace, both in the country and in the towns, reached heights of intensity fully as great as at any earlier period of French history.

We shall relate in a later chapter the development of that acute depression which grew out of three simultaneous crises—the demoralization (after 1786) of industrial activity, the failure (in 1788 and 1789) of the crops, and the merciless winter of 1788–1789. Yet it is certain that even before the final series of calamities that befell them, the peasants, taken as a group, had become a revolutionary element. They required only a signal to break out in revolt, and it was their active participation that made the revolutionary movement of 1789 a success. They needed no propaganda to formulate their grievances against the established order. They demanded more land in order to live; and relief from their obligations to the king, the church, and the nobles in order to enjoy life. They wanted equality of taxation, abolition of the manorial system with all its abuses, and the local application of the tithes for education and poor relief. In these demands the landless peasantry and those who worked tiny parcels of land were united.

The Bourgeoisie and the Urban Proletariat

Only a small percentage of the population lived in cities, and the cities, even the largest, were thinly populated. Paris with its half-million souls was the largest city in France and on the Continent. Lyons, long the seat of a prosperous silk trade and industry, was the second largest city in France with a population of 135,000. No other city in the realm had as many as 100,000 inhabitants. Yet France was the most densely populated country in Europe, and its population increased rapidly toward the end of the Old Régime, particularly in urban centers. Though the ancient obstacles to trade and industry still remained in force, France underwent a remarkable economic development in the eighteenth century. In 1789 France had nearly half the available specie in

[12] Conditions were not so horrible in the urban centers, though by no stretch of the imagination could the condition of the workmen and petty merchants be called anything but precarious. The greatest problem of the towns was the care of rural beggars and unemployed.

Europe, the population was increasing rapidly, and rents and the prices of commodities and land were rising steadily. Internal trade profited by the improvements in the ways of communication and the means of transportation as well as by the application of the liberal commercial policy of the administration. The foreign trade of France was inferior only to that of England, its volume being quadrupled in the period between the death of Louis XIV and the outbreak of the Revolution. This extraordinary commercial expansion not only brought French merchants in closer contact with other European countries, but gave France a predominant share of the Levant trade and tended to modify the restrictive mercantilist policy which hampered colonial trade between France and her colonies in the West Indies.

At the same time, industrial development made notable progress, being stimulated by the great fluid capital that was amassed in commerce as well as by the application of the new doctrines of economic liberalism. All signs indicated that France was entering upon the first stages of that industrial Revolution which had already begun in England. There was a great extension of rural industry, particularly in the textile industry. In the poorer agricultural regions of western France the peasants devoted themselves only to the bleaching and finishing of the cloth, but in the more fertile provinces of northeastern France the peasants received the raw material from the entrepreneurs in the near-by towns and worked under their direction, carrying on production from the first to the last stages. The intervention of the entrepreneurs in the urban centers of the silk and cloth trade was still more pronounced. Great capital was invested in the cloth industry, large plants with costly equipments were built, vast supplies of raw materials were bought, and the labor was subdivided among many classes of specialized workmen. The cloth industry alone occupied more than one hundred factories which employed many formerly independent master workmen who now found themselves reduced to the ranks of wage earners. Machinery, however, had been introduced only in comparatively few industries: very slightly in the silk and paper mills; more pronouncedly in the metallurgical industry, and most commonly in the cotton mills and in the coal mines. Despite these scattered manifestations of increasing capitalistic industry, the era of machinery and industrial concentration was only in its infancy, and the predominant system was that of petty industry employing only few workmen.

It is necessary to distinguish between the social classes among the city dwellers, for they did not profit alike from the astounding increase in the private wealth of the country. The urban population was divided into two large groups, the bourgeoisie and the workmen. The bourgeois lived on their incomes or else from the revenue of a trade or profession which required little manual labor. All other city dwellers belonged to the *gens du peuple,* that is, a group akin to an urban proletariat. Yet the bourgeoisie itself had gradations of rank. Most influential of all were the lordly, though non-noble, owners of offices in the financial and judicial administration, the rich bankers and financiers, and the small group of capitalists who had accumulated great fortunes in commerce and industry. Among the last named were those engaged in wholesale trade and maritime insurance and the directors of the new manufacturing establishments. Some retired from active business careers and lived on their incomes, and others bought offices that ennobled them, or patents of nobility and landed property in the country. They maintained sumptuous residences and vied with the richest nobles in the splendor of their social life.

This "urban patriciate," which monopolized most of the municipal offices, was only a small portion of the bourgeoisie. The great majority of the bourgeoisie, the "middle" and the petty bourgeois, led a simple life without luxury or ostentation. Some, like the masters of the guilds of the printers and book dealers, the apothecaries, the goldsmiths, the haberdashers, and the hosiers, and members of the legal profession (advocates and notaries), lived in easy circumstances. Others, like the physicians and surgeons, professors of the universities, and lesser merchants and subordinate legal officials (sheriffs, clerks, bailiffs), were less endowed with the world's goods. The social distinctions between the various groups were rigidly maintained, but nearly all had sufficient wealth for greater material comforts and leisure for intellectual pursuits. They bought the works of the great writers of the century, mingled in the society of the salons, and joined clubs and Masonic lodges, where they discussed the new liberal and radical ideas and found an audience that listened to and debated the many grievances which they voiced.

In wealth, in ability, in formal education and culture, they felt themselves the equals of the nobility of birth, yet the doors to many offices were closed to them. The government's policy of selling offices enabled a great many bourgeois to become public functionaries, but tradition and royal edicts excluded them from highest positions in the administration, in the army, in the church and in the judiciary. Their pride and self-respect were wounded by the social discrimination and the deliberate snubs administered by the nobility. They demanded a voice in the government in order to check the wastefulness and the inefficiency of a monarchy which failed to respect its financial obligations to its creditors and burdened them with taxes. Though many of them steadily increased their wealth they chafed at the obsolete governmental and feudal restrictions upon free commercial and industrial development, at the unjustifiable barriers against their initiative and resourcefulness. From the ranks of these enterprising merchants, manufacturers, and financiers came the loudest protests against the obsolete system of trade and craft corporations, which the government, for fiscal reasons, attempted to strengthen. They pleaded the cause of commercial and industrial freedom, of laissez faire, against the innumerable obstacles that the guild systems, regulations, and monopolies raised in their path. From the ranks of the cultured and ambitious lawyers came the most enthusiastic and militant response to the new ideas of the century. In 1788–1789 their rôle in undermining the Old Régime was particularly prominent.

On the other hand, the very prosperity that brought wealth and comforts to the upper and middle bourgeoisie increased the hardships of the petty craftsmen [13] and workmen. In most of the cities the small artisans who worked alone or with the assistance of one or two journeymen and apprentices were in an overwhelming majority. As Professor Sée remarks, "This is true not only of all the trades having as their object the feeding, clothing, and housing of the population, but also of all the trades connected with the textile industry, all of which were later included among the great industries." The workingmen who belonged to the guilds or corporations found it increasingly difficult to rise to the status of

---

[13] We have already called attention to the fact that in certain industries, most markedly in the silk and cloth manufactures, the small master became more and more dependent on the wealthy merchant and dropped into the ranks of the wage earners.

master and were doomed to remain wage earners all their lives. They formed secret organizations of their own, but the force of their unions was misspent in petty rivalries rather than directed toward the common defense of the interests of the laboring class against the masters or the government. The first half of the century witnessed an increased stringency in the internal regulations of the corporations, the government coming to the aid of the masters in outlawing strikes and forbidding artisans to form corporate groups of their own. Those who worked in the factories were, in general, docile to the severe discipline that prevailed there. They could not leave their factory without written permission, nor could they obtain a new position without presenting a written dismissal from their previous master or employer.

For the workers the remarkable economic progress of the century was no blessing. It subjected them more closely than ever to the authority of the individual employer in particular and to that of the government in general. It raised prices much more rapidly than it did wages and tended steadily to impoverish them. Whenever a crisis occurred, many workmen were thrown out of employment and were reduced, like the agricultural proletariat, to vagrancy or mendicity. Still, there was no labor question during the Old Régime. The laboring class complained more and more vigorously, but it sought only relief from unemployment, soaring prices, government regulations, and the grim menace of starvation. It did not consider itself as a distinct group nor did it agitate for a new industrial organization. The claims of labor against the employer as voiced in the nineteenth and twentieth centuries were unknown in the Old Régime.

III. THE AGE OF ENLIGHTENMENT

The Philosophes

THE fundamental point at issue in our discussion of French liberal thought during the eighteenth century lies precisely in the relation of that thought to the French Revolution. To make avowedly propagandist literature responsible for the great upheaval that came at the end of the century is to assign to ideas a force that more properly belongs to outmoded institutions and intolerable conditions. To deny the influence of the intellectual movement which grew in intensity and gained increasing acceptance toward the end of the Old Régime is equally false. The truth then lies somewhere between these two extremes, and it will be the endeavor of this chapter to correlate the action of historical circumstances with that of political and social speculation.

The Age of Reason or the Age of Enlightenment—that is, the period roughly from 1715 to 1789—takes on a convenient simplicity and unity only when one chooses to regard the Revolution as the direct product of the movement for reform which dominated French literature. What was simple and clear was the basic concept underlying the many forms of eighteenth century philosophy. But if we examine its origins, we find that they were multiple; if we study its exponents, we find them at odds with one another; if we analyze its content closely, we find differences of emphasis and approach. As its influence was felt widely beyond the confines of France, so some of the doctrines that constituted it came from beyond France. Yet at the same time it contained many French elements, and its development was in consonance with the markedly French traits of logic and clarity. Moreover, many individuals, differing widely in temperament and in intellectual interests, helped mold the forms of that speculation. Nor was it uniform and static throughout the entire century.

On the contrary, in the dynamic speculations of the age there were no fewer than three distinct approaches toward the solution of problems which most interested contemporaries. During the first thirty or forty years of the century the method most favored was the logical and deductive method of reasoning laid down a century earlier by Descartes. One established a premise that apparently was rationally acceptable to everybody and then proceeded, geometrically, to make logical deductions from the premise. This was the appeal to reason, an attempt to solve fundamental problems by going back to first principles. The results were magnificent, but the reliance upon the Cartesian method of doubt and of the examination of traditions by reason was not enough. When the inadequacy of this methodology was perceived (the inadequacy being the arbitrary assumption that the premise was as axiomatic and as self-evident to all as it was to its formulator), the thinkers tried a new tack. They had recourse to the method of experimental science, of making inductions from experience and observation. They made observations and patient investigation in their own right, but, more important, they popularized the accomplishments of other, greater, scientists. Thanks to their efforts the scientific spirit became the common property of humanity and the mainspring of their own social thought.

Then it became apparent toward 1762 that both logical reason and experimental science led to contradictory conclusions, and that their laws failed to supply a satisfactory explanation of the universe. So to explain one's destiny, one's reasons for acting, the secret of one's happiness, men fell back with Rousseau and lesser thinkers upon the mystic promptings of the heart, upon sentiment and intuition. Rousseau was the prophet of this spiritual revolt against the conventionality of civilization, of the movement that rediscovered the importance and dignity of the spiritual nature of man. Yet no one period was dominated exclusively by any one method of approach, and without a doubt French thought during the second half of the century was neither entirely rational nor philosophical, scientific nor experimental, emotional nor mystical. It displayed all these elements, depending on the place or the person, and at times displayed all of them in the same place and the same person.

The Age of Reason was then neither simple nor uniform, yet the cumulative effort of its great spokesmen produced a revolution in men's minds and expressed in many intellectual formulas a new spirit that was far removed from the dominant ideas inherited from the Middle Ages.

The men who effected this fundamental change called themselves *philosophes*. Up to the middle of the century their precursors were few and disunited. Their principal representatives were the mocking exile, Saint-Evremond (1613–1703), the learned philosopher, Bayle (1647–1706), and the witty skeptic, Fontenelle (1657–1757). Of the early *philosophes* the most influential were Montesquieu and Voltaire. Their views made slight headway with the public, and not a few writers remained untouched by their example. During the decade 1750–1760 a new generation of writers, young, forthright, and imbued with the new spirit, reached maturity. With the publication of the first volume of the colossal *Encyclopedia* in 1751 began the determined offensive of the *philosophes,* a movement which assumed the proportions of an organized campaign against the ideas and the institutions of the Old Régime. By the end of the reign of Louis XV they had won an overwhelming triumph in respect to the ideas mainly interesting to their contemporaries. These writers were not philosophers in the academic sense of the word, nor detached seekers after truth. In an earlier day they would have been called humanists; in modern times, publicists. They were men of letters, writers of novels, plays, poetry, students of science, authors of articles and long works on government, religion, morality, education, social and economic problems. Some were men of genius, others of talent, who employed their gifts with amazing effectiveness in "fighting all that was oppressive, cruel, or barbarous in religion, in government, in manners, and in laws; commanding in the name of nature, soldiers, magistrates, and priests to respect human life; . . . finally taking for their battle cry 'Reason, Tolerance, Humanity.' " In short, they deliberately put their literary ability to the practical purpose of molding public opinion in favor of a fundamental transformation of society. Their work was at once destructive and constructive.

The term *philosophes* at once calls to mind the giants of the period, Montesquieu (1685–1755), Voltaire (1694–1778), Rousseau (1712–1778), Diderot (1713–1784), whose contributions will be examined shortly. There were many other men, famous and influential in their day, but now only names save to the student. There was the studious Abbé de Condillac (1714–1780) and the rich farmer-general Helvétius, both vitally interested in ethics and metaphysics; the brilliant mathematician D'Alembert and the wealthy Baron d'Holbach, whose home was the rendezvous of the Encyclopedists; the Abbé Mably (1709–1785), the author of many works on political philosophy, the Abbé Raynal, author of the vast *Philosophical and Political History of the Establishment and the Trade of Europeans in the Two Indies,* the high-minded Condorcet (1743–1794), the experienced and capable administrator Turgot, the adventurous Beaumarchais, author of the devastating *Mariage de Figaro,* and the brilliant coterie of political scientists known as the Physiocrats, whose ranks included such writers as Quesnay, Gournay, and Dupont de Nemours.

THEIR CREDO

These men were not conscious advocates of violent revolution. When the Revolution did come, one of the *philosophes* who lived to witness its violence wrote sadly and apologetically, "The *philosophes* did not want to do all that has been done, nor to use the means that have been employed, nor to act as rapidly as has been done." They were enemies of ancient abuses that long demanded suppression. They neither invented these abuses nor exposed them for the first time. They drew the inevitable inference from realities bitterly experienced and borne by all save the privileged classes. Reason impelled them to attack the forces of superstition, ignorance, and folly that perpetuated an incompetent administration, a crushing financial system, a barbarous judicial procedure, religious cruelty, and economic waste and confusion. Humanity, the spirit of service to one's fellow men, the hope of employing the forces of society for all mankind, forced them to attack cruelty and injustice in every guise—in the grim scandal of judicial procedure, arbitrary arrests, torture and the ferocious cruelty of the penal code.

Frenchmen of the eighteenth century did not have to be told that men were not happy and unable to develop and realize their natural capacities. They well knew that equality, the basic notion of democracy, was denied. Even during the latter years of Louis XIV's reign powerful voices had denounced the burdens of dynastic wars with their crushing legacies of debts and taxation, stagnation of trade, and widespread suffering. A great churchman, Fénelon, delivered an outspoken attack upon his monarch's despotism and championed the constitutional limitation of royal power.

Other critics, such as Boulainvilliers and Vauban, advocated reforms of financial abuses and more equitable systems of taxation. Others still, Boisguillebert and the Abbé de Saint-Pierre, made clear the need of free internal trade and exchange and coöperation instead of rivalry among nations. During the Sun King's reign there appeared also new religious ideas that formed a break with the Middle Ages. Louis XIV himself provided the opportunity by precipitating the prolonged religious controversy between the Jansenists and the Jesuits,[1] a controversy that, by destroying the unity of the church, also undermined the authority of the monarchy. Two remarkable advocates of tolerance, Fontenelle and Bayle, hastened to take advantage of circumstances which showed the church despairingly unable to determine the truths of that revelation upon which it was founded. They perpetuated and restated ancient arguments against the religion of the Middle Ages. They repeated the humanists' doctrine of the goodness and the dignity of man and kept alive the spirit of Rabelais's revolt against asceticism and Montaigne's tolerant skepticism. They strengthened the old doctrines of revolt with arguments logically derived from Descartes. These "fathers of modern incredulity" clearly voiced the new spirit of religious skepticism and eloquently defended the cause of tolerance. Fontenelle developed a rationalistic method in dealing with religious traditions. Bayle's great *Historical and Critical Dictionary* became an armory from which the *philosophes* drew their weapons against revealed religion.

The breakdown of political and religious absolutism was accelerated during the long reign of Louis XV, which perpetuated the worst features of the preceding reign. Simultaneously the disintegration of the old economic system proceeded rapidly, and the vast social and economic changes of the eighteenth century intensified the grievances of the wealthy, influential, and capable middle class of merchants, industrialists, financiers, and professional men. More than ever it was realized that institutions founded upon political absolutism and religious revelation were indefensible before the test of reason and humanity.

The *philosophes* knew that times were out of joint because they, of all people, were sensitive to obvious injustices and obvious suffering. They proclaimed that existing institutions were unnatural and that reason would discover that just and ideal order which the law of

[1] Cf. Chapter I, pp. 8, 10.

nature demanded, because they all subscribed to certain basic ideas concerning the nature of the universe and the nature of man and his mind. In part and in one form or another, those basic ideas had been stated long before their time—by the stoic philosophers of antiquity, by the Roman jurists of the empire, by mediaeval philosophers, by Descartes, by the humanists and scientists since the period of the Renaissance. But the formulation of the characteristically eighteenth century concept of nature and man's place in the universe owed most to two great Englishmen of the seventeenth century, Isaac Newton and John Locke.

SIGNIFICANCE OF ISAAC NEWTON AND JOHN LOCKE

As early as the fifteenth and sixteenth centuries and the early seventeenth century great scientists such as Leonardo da Vinci, Copernicus, Brahe, Kepler, and Galileo had discovered many important laws of nature. But up to the time of Galileo's death in 1642 ordinary men still feared the unknown force of nature, and the church and the institutions of higher learning were still hostile to natural science. To Newton, who was born in the very year that Galileo died, belongs the credit, more than to any other individual, for a great mental revolution. More than any other scientist he succeeded, through his observation of and experiments with the forces of nature, in raising the study of the natural sciences from an occult proceeding fit for sorcerers to the position of the most important branch of learning. Through his work on light, optics, and gravitation he enlarged upon and systematized the work of his great predecessors. He correlated their special laws and proved conclusively that the forces operating in nature were few and universal, that there was one universal law of nature.

Few people were qualified to read Newton's great work, the *Principia* (1686), but before he died in 1727 people everywhere were eager to learn something about the "Newtonian philosophy." So today people are eager to learn something about Einstein's theory of relativity, and so in the nineteenth century people discussed the Darwinian theory of evolution. There were the inevitable popular lectures on Newton's ideas and the innumerable books that gave or attempted to give simple explanations of those ideas. Every phase of human life became affected by science, its pursuit was called "the sum of human wisdom" and the sure road to happiness. France counted some truly remarkable scientists such as Buffon, Lavoisier, Réaumur, and many of the *philosophes* devoted themselves with unsurpassed earnestness to the study of physics, chemistry, and natural history.

No doubt only learned and at least moderately wealthy people gratified their amateur interest in science and experimented in chemistry and physics or studied the laws of mathematics and mechanics. But, thanks more to the popularizers of "Newtonian philosophy" than to Newton himself, it now seemed evident to all who took the trouble to attend those lectures or to listen to the accounts of those who had attended them that Newton had banished mystery from the universe. Nature had stepped in between man and God, and one tried to discover the intention of God by studying the laws of nature. To study nature was to study His handiwork; and to discover all His secrets, it was the duty of man to put himself into harmony with nature.

At the same time, the English philosopher, John Locke, propounded certain new ideas concerning the power of man's mind. These new ideas were developed in his epochal *Essay Concerning the Human Understanding* (1690), which became the psychological gospel of the eighteenth century. Newton showed a physical universe ordered by natural laws; Locke showed that man could live in accordance with nature, because human nature was not innately evil and man was capable of utilizing knowledge and experience for his own advancement. Locke's *Essay* was a blast to the mediaeval and feudal conception of the nature of man and the power of his mind. Man, this view held, was innately evil, a poor creature prone to error and sin unless he were obedient to and were guided by the church in his thinking and by the state in his acts. What Locke did by his famous analogy between the mind of man at his birth and a bare white sheet of paper was to deny the competence of the church and priests to govern man's thinking. Man's mind at birth was perfectly blank. All his ideas came from experience of the outer world through his senses and from experience of the mind by observation of consciousness. By using his mind man could bring himself, his thoughts and his acts, his institutions and his laws, into harmony with the universal order of nature of which he was a part.

The implication was clear. If scientists, Galileo and Newton for instance, by using their minds, could discover laws of nature unknown even to the church, the traditional custodian of the eternal law of God, was it not possible that revelation was inadequate, and that the mind of man might discover the truth concerning nature without the church and revelation? All men were potentially equal. Not birth, heredity, or rank made man what he was, but differences of environment and education.

This was the legacy of the scientists and the philosophers of the seventeenth century to the *philosophes*—that man could find in experience the actual ideas corresponding to the knowledge that he claimed to possess. "Follow reason and experience," Newton and Locke seemed to say, "and you will discover the secrets of the world that God has created." In the application of this basic concept of reason and nature lay the force of eighteenth century liberal thought, in the extension of the simple and clear idea that reason could discover truth and increase knowledge, that man through the power of his mind could make steady progress toward greater wisdom and perhaps perfection. And it was the *philosophes* who, in divers ways, applied this concept to a searching interrogation of governmental and social institutions.

They questioned the bases of authority that existed upon revelation, formulated new theories, aroused new enthusiasms, and fixed new ideals for all mankind. Indeed for all mankind, for the *philosophes* were the standard bearers of a faith that spread from France through all the civilized world. While destroying the old, they established the bases of a new order. Their common credo may be stated as belief in the sovereignty of the people and in the rights and prospects of man. By liberty they meant civil and individual liberty, liberty of conscience, thought, and expression; by equality and fraternity they meant the abolition of special privileges for the aristocracy and the opening of careers to talent. The state, they maintained, exists only for the benefit and the happiness of all its citizens. Man, being a rational animal, can discover that which is beneficial and direct his life by his knowledge and experience. All men can do so because of the equality of their natural capacities and needs. Hence men need liberty and the duty of the state is to preserve their right to liberty.

In short, the *philosophes* were hopeful that ordinary men and women through the exercise of their reason and will could form a society in which they would be happy and in which they could develop and realize all their natural faculties. To bring social institutions into harmony with what they conceived to be natural law, with the essential nature of men and things was their ultimate goal and endeavor.

Voltaire's Fight for Tolerance

The foremost champion of reason and tolerance during the eighteenth century and perhaps of all time was Voltaire. It is impossible to overestimate the importance of his career, first, in gaining acceptance among a wide public for the seminal ideas of Newton and Locke which hitherto had been known to a comparatively small group of thinkers, and second, in pleading the cause of free thought against political and religious absolutism. His name is permanently associated with the campaign whose motto was "Crush the infamous thing"—*Ecrasez l'infâme*—which was the most earnest, the most deadly in its effectiveness, and yet the most intellectually amusing offensive ever launched by a person of genius against religious authority. Voltaire early discovered his talent for raillery and cutting mockery, but some years elapsed before he chose to direct that talent against revealed religion in general and Christianity in particular.

The occasion was a humiliating experience with a lesser nobleman who, not content with having the young Voltaire roundly beaten by his lackeys, succeeded also in having the ambitious poet and dramatist incarcerated in the Bastille. Up to this time Voltaire was known in the brilliant and sophisticated circles of the capital as a wit and a poet of highest promise, and it was indeed as a dramatist that he was still known for many years. But a change of paramount significance in Voltaire's thinking was to set in. He obtained his release from the Bastille on the promise to leave France and in 1726, when he was thirty-two years of age, he went to England, where he lived for three years.

England was a revelation to him, and he proceeded almost at once to write down, while they were still fresh in his mind, the impressions produced on him by a country that was so different from France. These observations were published in England in 1733 in a volume entitled *Letters on the English*. A year later several editions of this work were published in French in his own country, only to meet with the fate then commonly reserved for works of that nature. A copy was solemnly burned by the public hangman as "scandalous, contrary to religion, to morals, and to respect for authority." These letters were journalism of genius. They make no pretense of describing England and the English in detail; they describe only those things that might be used to make odious the corresponding French institutions. By describing a country where opinion was free and the government constitutional, where religious persecution was unknown and every one was "permitted to go to Heaven in his own way," where the middle class was socially as respectable as the nobility, where civil liberties were guaranteed and men of letters and science were honored, Voltaire pointed the obvious lesson of the absence of all those praiseworthy features from French life.

After the formal suppression of his book—which scarcely prevented people from reading it—Voltaire once more fled Paris. For fifteen years he lived with the learned Madame du Châtelet at her château in Lorraine. After her death in 1749 he accepted the insistent invitation of the philosopher-king, Frederick the Great, to grace the royal court at Berlin. Three years sufficed to prove that the two men could not live together, and Voltaire, fleeing from Berlin, finally found a refuge at Ferney, near the Swiss frontier.

At Ferney, where he was safe from persecution, Voltaire settled down to the fulfillment of the task that he had not been free to accomplish. For twenty-five years he flooded France with "plays, poems, philosophical tales, satires, burlesques, histories, essays, diatribes, deistic sermons and anti-biblical pamphlets, and won for himself the reputation of the intellectual ruler of his age." For twenty-five years he waged war upon intolerance through his writing and through his deeds. Voltaire was not atheistic; he accepted the few and brief fundamental tenets of "natural religion"—belief in a transcendent Deity and obedience to the moral precepts that God had revealed to man through his reason. What he attacked were the particular dogmas, the accretions of theology, the complex mysteries and contradictory ceremonials of Christianity that through the ages had engendered fanaticism, persecution, and bloodshed, suppressed reason, and persecuted free thought. For a quarter of a century, this inspired publicist, this man of prodigious intellectual and literary gifts, preached the cause of tolerance through enlightenment. In his *Philosophical Dictionary*, the definitive edition of which was published in 1764 (notably in the articles "God," "Religion," "Fanaticism," "Liberty of Conscience," and

"Liberty of Thought"), in his vast *Essay on the Manners and Spirit of Nations* (1751–1756), in his *Treatise on Tolerance*, in thousands of letters, he denounced the "infamous thing." He fought intolerance with deeds as well as words. He used his tremendous energy and influence to rehabilitate several obscure victims of religious injustice. Nothing that Voltaire did brought him more honor as a champion of human rights and human justice than his efforts in behalf of the Calas family, the innocent victims of religious hatred. In 1778, when he was eighty-four years old, he returned at last to Paris, where he died in the same year. The tremendous welcome that he received was no doubt a remarkable tribute to an unparalleled career; even more, it was a gauge of the change in the public temper. It was the recognition of the fact that the Patriarch of Ferney had won his long battle for freedom of thought and tolerance.

Voltaire, of course, was not unaided in his endeavor. He was only the foremost and the most famous of the critics of clericalism and fanaticism. Whether deists like Voltaire, Montesquieu, and Condorcet, or atheists like Diderot and many of the Encyclopedists, the *philosophes* were at one in certain fundamental claims. They made the case for intolerance impossible and made certain the principle that the secular state could no longer place itself at the disposal of a religious organization. They announced the supremacy of the state over the secular interests of the community; they advocated the secularization of human life by having the state take jurisdiction over registrations of marriage, birth, and death, education and charity, and they proclaimed the right of the state, in the name of the social good, to supervise, regulate, and control the internal organization of the church.

RATIONAL POLITICS

The application of reason and natural law was soon made to the political organization of society. The rationalist critique was suggested by the weakness of the existing system; and we have already noted the existence of a literature of protest under Louis XIV. Again, it was England that furnished an example to the more outspoken critics of the eighteenth century, an example both in practice and in theory. As the century wore on the influence of this example grew more pronounced and the relationship between prosperity and political freedom in England, between military victories (over France) and constitutional government, impressed itself firmly upon the minds of an ever wider circle of Frenchmen. The first significant and widely read works in France discussing political institutions were Voltaire's *Letters on the English* (published in France as the *Lettres Philosophiques* in 1734) and Montesquieu's *Persian Letters,* which appeared earlier, in 1721. Both works deal with the ensemble of man's relations to society, "moral, intellectual, and social, as well as political." What interested the *philosophes* most was the necessity of security for the individual, protection against arbitrary interference in his private law.

Montesquieu was only too well aware of the perils of the censorship and realized only too fully that his criticism, if it were to be read at all, would have to be at once indirect and sufficiently spicy to win the approval of the wide and gay public in the capital. This accounts for the spectacle of a serious magistrate, a president of the parlement of Bordeaux, penning the mildly licentious *Persian Letters* and using the literary device of having two Persians traveling in Paris describe, in a correspondence with their countrymen in Persia, the principal features of life at the French capital. Withal, he issued the book anonymously. In this charming work Montesquieu made an oblique, though readily comprehended, indictment of the whole system of government under Louis XIV. He ridiculed the corruption of the court, condemned the privileges of the aristocracy, derided the incompetent financial administration, and denounced the vices of fanaticism and intolerance. The sale of the *Persian Letters* was enormous; and Montesquieu gave up his position in the judiciary and devoted the rest of his life to travel and study. Upon him too England and English institutions exerted a profound influence. In 1734 appeared a fresh volume from his pen, *The Greatness and the Decadence of the Romans,* an able and mature work of philosophical reflections upon historical causation and development. Here he first manifested his lifelong interest in history and his insistence upon the significance of climate, geography, and population as determining factors in human history.

His greatest work and the one on which his reputation rests was the vast miscellany entitled *Spirit of the Laws* (*l'Esprit des Lois*), published in 1748. A full discussion of this celebrated work belongs properly to the history of political theory. In it Mon‧ tesquieu displayed the essentially conservative temper of an ex‧ parlementarian. The most significant passages are not those deal‧ ing with the republican form of government, but those dealing with monarchy and despotism. By despotism it is clear that he had in mind the centralized absolute state created by the later Bour‧ bons. He directs against it all his pointed, epigrammatic style and all the shafts of his wit. For the monarchical form of government, the historic monarchy of France before the days of Richelieu and Louis XIV, the historic monarchy of France whose nearest coun‧ terpart was then the constitutional monarchy of England, he re‧ serves his admiration and respect. His discussion of the English constitution, though erroneous, carried great weight with later thinkers and seriously influenced subsequent events both in America and in France during the early years of the Revolution. The separation of the legislative, the executive, and the judicial powers that he thought he discovered in eighteenth century Eng‧ land no longer really existed, for cabinet government and the parliamentary executive were even then in formation, though the judiciary was independent and a powerful check upon the power of the government.

Montesquieu no more than Voltaire dreamed of revolution. He was no democrat, and he did not denounce privilege. He favored the perpetuation of the church, if only as an intermediary power and as a check upon the monarch, but clericalism and fanaticism he too abhorred. Voltaire [2] fought the middle-class cause of con‧ stitutional government, religious toleration, civil freedom, and freedom of thought and expression; Montesquieu, not less "en‧ lightened," preferred to check the arbitrary rule of the monarch by restoring the political power of the nobility. He defended the legitimacy of the sale of magistracies, which Voltaire decried, but both demanded a rational jurisprudence and inveighed against the barbarous use of torture, inhuman penalties, and the benighted practice of considering a prisoner guilty until proven innocent. Yet the most systematic indictment of the secret procedure of the courts

---

[2] Voltaire's political ideas are scattered generously throughout the many volumes of his collected works. He never developed them systematically, for what interested him most was the spirit rather than the form of government. They may most readily be found in his *Letters on the English*, the *Philosophical Dictionary*, his *Corre-spondence*, his *Essay on the Manners and the Spirit of Nations*, and his *Age of Louis XIV*.

and the cruelty of the penal code came not from the *philosophes*, but from an Italian reformer, the Marquis Cesare Beccaria, who in 1764 published his remarkable treatise on *Crimes and Punishments*.

Montesquieu and Voltaire were symptomatic of one exceedingly important attitude toward the political organization of society. Rousseau passionately opposed both their approach and their conclusions; and the Physiocrats developed still a third and somewhat distinct political philosophy. Their advocacy of enlightened despotism stemmed directly from their views on the economic organization of society, which we must now examine.

THE PHYSIOCRATS

The men who applied the general precepts of eighteenth century philosophy to the specific problems of the economic welfare called themselves Economists. Somewhat later the term "Physiocrats" superseded the title which they themselves preferred. Their central doctrine, from which the name Physiocrats was derived, was the belief held by the founder of their school, that the land was the sole source of wealth. They assumed that society, like the material universe, was governed by fixed and easily ascertainable laws; and they were at one in stating that the task of the government was to discover those laws and maintain their free operation. There was a fundamental agreement of interests in society, a natural harmony which could serve all mankind. Moreover, they were confident that they had discovered, through reason and observation, what those laws were. The first was the mutual interdependence of men, which could be secured only by a free exchange of products. Under such conditions particular interest would necessarily serve the social good. The second was the maintenance of man's natural right to property, which he secured by abolishing all governmental regulations and feudal restrictions which prevented him from the fullest enjoyment of his property. Free production and free distribution was their goal, and the only regulation they recognized was that supplied by the natural law of supply and demand and by man's enlightened self-interest.

The leading figures among them were François Quesnay (1694–1774), court physician to Louis XV, and the marquis de Gournay (1712–1759). Quesnay, with the approval of his monarch, expounded his views in his *Tableau économique* (1758). Born on a farm and the son of a prosperous agriculturist, he strongly emphasized the position of agriculture. In his opinion the land was the sole source of wealth, and only that mass of agricultural and mineral products which was not consumed in the process of production should be taxed. He took his stand on his maxim: "Poor peasant, poor kingdom; poor kingdom, poor monarch." The marquis de Gournay, who was an intendant of commerce and a merchant himself, supplemented Quesnay's views. From his experience he concluded that industry and commerce could flourish only through free competition; hence, his maxim, *"Laissez faire et laissez passer."* Both agreed in demanding the abolition of customs duties, protective tariffs, and guild regulations. Both denounced the prevailing Colbertism in its industrial aspect of minute regulation and in its commercial aspect of mercantilism. The government should not interfere and had no right to interfere with the free play of natural economic forces.

Their followers were numerous, and their influence, considerable. Dupont de Nemours was the most brilliant of their theorists, and Trudaine and Turgot the most effective in the practical application of their views. It is not untrue to state that the whole movement of agricultural reform [3] owed much to their efforts. Turgot's successful administration of the generality of Limoges (1761–1774) gave practical point to their theories. The liberalizing of guild regulations in the second half of the century and the phenomenal development of the cloth industry were in part the consequences of their teaching. Across the Channel in Scotland one of their admirers, Adam Smith, who was a professor of philosophy at Glasgow, published his famous *Wealth of Nations* (1776). This was the clearest and the most complete account of the doctrines of economic liberalism. Smith enlarged upon the views of his friends Quesnay and Turgot and showed that labor in all its forms was the true source of wealth and the standard of value—value of use if not value of exchange.

The Physiocrats also advanced economic arguments for international coöperation. The indictment of the international anarchy that was Europe had already been made in 1625 by the great Dutchman, Hugo Grotius, in one of the most famous books ever written, *De jure belli et pacis* (*The Law of War and Peace*). His

---

[3] Cf. Chapter II, pp. 49–50.

learned and eloquent endeavor to find the rights of war and peace in the law of nature found no response in the ways of rulers and states. But in the following two centuries various individuals, the duke of Sully, William Penn, and the Abbé de Saint-Pierre, devised separate plans for abolishing war and establishing a league of European states. The *philosophes,* notably Montesquieu, Voltaire, and Condorcet, all passionately denounced the menace of militarism and the cruel inhumanity and waste of war. The Physiocrats based their arguments for international coöperation on the doctrines subsequently made popular by the liberal economists of the Manchester School of the nineteenth century. The natural harmony of interests, they maintained, existed not only within each nation, but among all nations. States grew rich only by supplying wants. Money intrinsically was worthless and was useful only in facilitating free trade. If there were free exchange among nations, the surplus of one would supply the needs of another, and vice versa, to the benefit of all producers and consumers. Nations therefore should coöperate with one another instead of striving to weaken one another through economic tariffs and military adventures. Nothing was more abhorrent to these "citizens of the world" than the concept of a narrow, arrogant nationalism.

Their political views were not what one might expect of opponents of governmental interference. One might have expected them to advocate checks and balances, division of power, and representative government. Most of them, however, strongly believed in the regeneration of society through the enlightened action of one central authority. "There should be one sovereign authority superior to all the individuals of a society," wrote Quesnay. And his disciple, Dupont de Nemours, added, "The idea of several authorities in the same state suggests nothing less than an absurdity." In general they favored the type of government traditionally misnamed Enlightened Despotism. Their enlightened despot would reorganize society in accordance with the "natural and essential laws of the social order" and thus do swiftly and effectively what enlightenment would accomplish more slowly as it spread to all classes and individuals in the state.

ROUSSEAU AND DEMOCRACY

So much has been written about the life and influence of Jean Jacques Rousseau (1712–1778), and his writings have inspired so many contradictory developments that it is perhaps necessary to state that the best possible guide to this extraordinary individual is his *Confessions* (1782). The *Confessions* tell the story of his life experiences, upon which his entire program of thought and action was largely built. For almost forty years he was a pitiable, self-pitying failure, utterly without significance in the intellectual movement of his times. From earliest boyhood he was virtually alone in the world, undisciplined by his father, untaught, and left to grow up without direction or guidance. When he was sixteen years old, he ran away from his native city of Geneva, where he had been apprenticed to an engraver. For fourteen years he was a homeless wanderer, a tramp who lived by his wits and the generosity of such occasional friends as he made. He drifted from point to point and failed in one occupation after another. In his vagabondage he acquired a smattering knowledge of many things and very definite likes and dislikes about a few things in life. For seven years, from 1741 to 1749, this shy yet eager, embarrassed yet intense, person sought to win friends and recognition in a world utterly removed from his own—in the critical, sophisticated society of the salons of Paris where all the artificial conventions of civilization had reached their fullest flowering. Here too he was a wretched failure, meeting some deserved and many undeserved rebuffs, and sinking deeper and deeper into the feeling that there was no place in the modern Sodom for an honest man like himself. Yet had he died then, in 1749, the world would have been infinitely poorer. In that year this unhappy vagabond entered upon a new phase of his career. He began to pour out his unrestrained, undisciplined genius in a profuse torrent of passionate writings that impressed themselves upon his age as no other books had done.

The work that first brought him renown was his essay submitted in the prize competition of the Academy of Dijon for the best answer to the question, *Has the Progress of Science and the Arts Tended to Corrupt or Purify Morals?* He saw an announcement of the competition quite by chance, but it was not by chance that he wrote the prize essay, the first *Discours*. In this essay he argued that the virtue and the happiness of simple, primitive man had been transformed by the increase of knowledge, by the accumulation of wealth, by the growth of cities and luxury, into corruption and misery. Rousseau's gropings were not yet ended, but they began at last to find expression in words of such passionate sincerity, in a style so persuasive and intense, and in visions so rapturous that he found himself the prophet of a spiritual revolt against his age. This is the cardinal point about Rousseau; he neither represented nor led the age during which he reached maturity. He opposed its dominant credo and voiced a yearning that it had stifled. Both by his mode of life before and after 1749 and in the books that he wrote in rapid succession—*The Origin of Inequality* (1755), *The New Heloïse* (1761), *Emile* (1762), and *The Social Contract* (1762)—he preached a gospel of spiritual revolution. And this gospel of a fresh start won its converts by millions, for it was a reaction against the aridness of reason which had failed to take into account the spiritual nature of man.

To the *philosophes* Rousseau said in substance: "There are many things in heaven and earth undreamed of in your philosophy. The promptings of the heart are more to be trusted than the logic of the mind. This reason which you vaunt, whose achievements you extol, whose promise of infinite perfectibility you accept, is a false guide. It has failed to make society give to me the success and the happiness to which I am entitled. Men everywhere are by nature like myself—simple, honest, kindly, and virtuous; and yet they do evil things which they regret. A society in which the few live in luxury and the many toil in wretchedness, in which a few men of rank profit by the inferiority of the great majority, in which a false education sets at naught the values of virtue and humanity, such a society is corrupt to the core. To alter it is beyond the limits of reason's power; the only society in which man can be happy is one in which he is free to follow the dictates of his spiritual being and to live in virtuous harmony with the purposes of nature."

His contemporaries did not wait for the learned critics of later days to denounce his furious attack upon reason and authority. It required something less than intellectual genius to disclose the appalling jumble of his writings, his contradictions, his inconsistencies, his misconceptions, his ignorance of history and—to use an anachronism—of anthropology. Secular and religious authorities condemned his books and the parlement of Paris ordered his arrest after the publication of *Emile*. Once more he became a vagabond and the last sixteen years of his life (1762–1778) marked the spiritual decay of the most original mind that the eighteenth century had produced. Broken by his persecution and unbalanced by his sorry fate, Rousseau sank into a state of intermittent insanity from which death finally released him. Yet he conquered his age, and when he died almost every one who could read was reading his works.

He constantly advocated a return to nature, like many of his contemporaries who read or wrote about primitive societies, failing to see the essential differences between what was primitive and what was natural. It is easy to understand that in his terrific hatred of the contemporaneous he should go back to a primitive Golden Age, that he should indulge in that spiritual flight from reality which appeals ever more urgently in highly civilized societies to honest men of proud and sensitive fiber. But he himself recognized in his more sober moments that the lost Paradise could not be regained, that Frenchmen of the eighteenth century could not go back to the ways of the untutored Indian and the noble savage. In his most famous book, *The Social Contract*, that amazing and revolutionary tissue of seventeenth century political theory and Calvinist theology, he propounded a new scheme of social salvation. He followed the Locke of the *Two Treatises of Government* (1690) in arguing that all men had certain natural rights and liberties, which were life, liberty, and property; and that men no longer owed obedience to any government that failed to protect them in those rights and liberties. The problem that Rousseau endeavored to solve was the relation of the individual to the authority which governed him. He knew that in society as it existed men had been deprived of their rights and liberties without their consent. In the justly organized society of his vision each individual "would put his person and his power under the supreme direction of the general will," and agree to act only for the common good. In renouncing his natural rights and liberties to the general will each individual recognized that the general will of the community was the real will of all the separate members of the community.

This was Rousseau's famous doctrine of the social contract, which developed and brilliantly formulated the revolutionary theory that the people are sovereign and that governments derive their legitimate authority from the consent of *all* the governed. To us his view is a commonplace, an axiom of political democracy. In Rousseau's time, when the accepted legal principle of the Bourbon monarchy was that the king's will was the law, when the government was absolute and the privileged few were in power, his view was revolutionary in the extreme. "Establish," he seems to say, "social institutions in which there are equal rights available to all, and the goodness inherent in the hearts of men will reassert itself." In *The Social Contract* also he outlined the tenets of a civil religion—belief in a Supreme Being, personal immortality, and future rewards and punishments—a civil religion which directly inspired the revolutionaries of 1793–1794. But his greatest contribution to political speculation remains his doctrine of popular sovereignty, with its attendant corollaries of liberty, equality, and fraternity.

The increasingly radical ideas about government and society that were propagated in the two decades following the publication of *The Social Contract* may or may not have been derived directly from Rousseau. In any case they were not alien to his spirit. The attempts of various writers, the best known of whom is the Abbé Mably (1709–1785), to describe a future society founded upon economic equality may have been a moral protest against current doctrines of economic liberalism. Certainly in the vigorous writings of several publicists immediately before the Revolution may be found all the doctrines of scientific socialism of the nineteenth century—the iron law of wages, the class struggle, the doctrine of surplus value, and the inevitable communist revolution. In their case, the protest was less on moral and Christian grounds and more on a reasoned investigation of social and economic realities.

DISSEMINATION OF THE NEW IDEAS

To Denis Diderot, perhaps the most typical man of his age in his skepticism and his hopefulness, in his inquisitiveness and his energy, in the universality of his interests and his broad humanity, fell the self-imposed task of systematizing the new knowledge. With D'Alembert at first and later with D'Holbach and Helvétius he carried to completion the task of editing the colossal *Encyclopédie* (the *Encyclopedia*) in thirty-five large folio volumes of text and plates (1751–1780). The contributors were numerous and of various opinions. Despite their divergences, or perhaps because of them, they effected a synthesis of the essential ideas of the Age of Enlightenment in politics, religion, morals, metaphysics, and economics. The obstacles in the form of government prohibitions, censorship, desertions, and betrayals were staggering, but the great monument to human knowledge was finally built. Its enormous bulk notwithstanding, the *Encyclopédie* was a most successful vehicle for the propagation of the spirit and the ideals of the *philosophes*. Many sets were printed and eagerly pored over not only in France but everywhere on the Continent. The object of this ambitious survey of all phases of human activity was, in Diderot's own words,

to bring together all the knowledge scattered over the face of the earth; to lay its general system before the men with whom we live, and to transmit it to those that will come after us, so that the labors of past ages may not be labors useless to the ages that will follow; so that our children will know more, and so that they may at the same time be greater in virtue and in happiness; and so that we may not die without deserving well of mankind.

And Condorcet, who was to creep out of his hiding place to die a miserable death during the Revolution, echoed those hopes when he wrote: "Living in this happy age . . . we have seen reason emerge from this struggle, so long, so difficult, and we can at last cry out: Truth has conquered and mankind is saved."

We moderns may gratify our sense of superiority by exposing the false foundations of eighteenth century thought. The new physics of Max Planck and Einstein reveals a material universe infinitely more complex and baffling than the material world known to followers of "Newtonian philosophy." The new psychology of Freud and Watson with its complexes, suppressed desires, and behavior tendencies looks pityingly at the optimistic faith of Locke's disciples who believed in the rule of reason and in enlightened self-interest. The cult of rationalism has broken down and the hope of infinite progress through enlightenment has all but disappeared. Though the conclusions reached by the *philosophes* are no longer tenable, it is far from true to call them abstract reasoners. Most of them had a large measure of practical experience with the problems they attacked. All of them, like their modern counterparts, thought that they were following rigorously scientific methods. All of them distinguished between their theoretical writings—that is, their "systems" of thought—and works that they intended for practical application. *The Social Contract* was not written to guide the conduct of administrators in France or elsewhere. Rousseau meant it to be part of a long *Treatise on Political Institutions,* a theoretical discussion of governmental problems. When he wrote on practical politics in Poland or in Corsica he was cautious enough to satisfy the most fastidious tastes of realists.

It is equally far from the truth to assume that the *philosophes* triumphed easily over the authority of church and state. The rigors of the censorship were maintained to the very eve of the Revolution. Few indeed were the exponents of the new liberal ideas who at one time or another did not taste the bitter joys of prison life. The arrest of a bookseller who had in his possession works forbidden by the censorship was no novelty. The voluntary or imposed exile of a condemned writer occurred too frequently to arouse attention—save in his works. To evade the censor the *philosophes* fell back upon expedients as ingenious as they were amusing. They published works secretly in France under a foreign imprimatur, or had them published in Holland and smuggled into France. They issued their works under the cloak of anonymity or ascribed the authorship to some nonexistent individual of most respectable title. Voltaire's pamphlets were smuggled into France by the thousands, and Voltaire would protest eloquently against the base accusation that he was the author of a scurrilous pamphlet. Could not every one see that even the style was not his! The publication of the *Encyclopédie* was a great victory, but it required the friendly aid of Madame de Pompadour and of the director of the publishing trade. The battle grew easier in the last decade before the Revolution, and Beaumarchais' insolent defiance of the court on the occasion of the showing of his play, *The Marriage of Figaro,* showed that public opinion sided overwhelmingly with the new ideas.

Nevertheless there were hundreds of châteaux and salons where the *philosophes* were unknown, or if known, rejected. The lesser nobility and the bourgeoisie of the provincial towns were not all won over to Voltaire or Rousseau. The old ideas had their grip on millions of adherents of the king and the church. The Age of Enlightenment was also an age of superstition, particularly in Paris, where spiritualists and charlatans like Mesmer and Cagliostro had a tremendous following. Along with the works of the *philosophes* there was a tremendous vogue for books on magic, sorcery, and alchemy.

Still the general influence of the new philosophy of enlightenment was enormous. Through the salons (after the middle of the
century) it penetrated into the French Academy and the *haut
monde* of the noble, ecclesiastical, and financial aristocracy. The
salons of the second half of the century were far removed in spirit
from the charming, gay, and refined gatherings held earlier *chez*
Madame de Tencin or Madame Geoffrin. Not that the charm, the
gayety, or the refinement of spirit *chez* Mademoiselle de
Lespinasse, Madame Helvétius, or Madame Necker was less; but
the discussions were wider in range, the atmosphere more robust,
the conversation freer of feminine artifices and art. At these salons,
and at other less famous centers, gathered the intellectual lumi-
naries of France and all Europe—Hume, Wilkes, Garrick, Adam
Smith, Priestley, and Franklin. Many were the young nobles and
powerful churchmen who welcomed the new gospel. It excused
their faults—and it prepared their ruin.

This new gospel was spread by word of mouth in the cafés and
in the public promenades. Marat, who is reported to have read
aloud *The Social Contract* to an admiring throng on the streets of
Paris in 1788, was only one of many who led public discussions.
The city artisans were, many of them, illiterate; but they had ears
to hear with. To the remote parish priests and the peasantry came
the itinerant country peddler carrying, with other wares, a few
copies of a book that every one was reading in the capital. A trip to
a neighboring town brought one to a book dealer with a larger
stock of books. The number of newspapers, especially of provincial
journals, increased rapidly, but journals and books were expensive.
There were only few public libraries then in existence enabling
their readers to examine "almost all the works forbidden by despotism or the court of Rome." Above all, for the bourgeoisie and
the petty nobility of the provinces, there were the Masonic lodges
and the reading societies and the thinking societies (*sociétés de
lecture; sociétés de pensée*). Many of these societies were simply
old associations transformed by new interests into reading and discussion groups. Some observed class distinctions, others allowed
different social groups to mingle freely. All discussed the topics of
the day, "politics, reform of abuses, equality of taxation." There,
as in the seven hundred Masonic lodges, the members could read
the latest books and the current periodicals. The Freemasons were
not secret conspirators against the government and religion. There

were priests in their ranks, and many nobles as well as bourgeois comfortably situated. In general they displayed a cautious and conservative spirit, but it was natural that they should discuss and even attempt, within their own midst, to carry out their views on tolerance, equality, and fraternity.

The spread of these new opinions may be gauged in still other ways. Changes in the curriculum of the secondary schools and of the religious seminaries, and the new manuals of instruction all attest the extent to which the *philosophes* popularized their ideas. The multitude of new subjects that the provincial academies presented for prize literary competition show the change. Prizes were offered for the best essays on various aspects of social and economic problems, on crime and punishment, public instruction, the influence of the *philosophes,* and the American Revolution. The spread of religious skepticism, shown by the drop in the number of communicants, was attended in many cases by conversion to the ideals of the *philosophes.*

Meantime political unrest deepened in intensity. The long constitutional struggle between the king and the parlements, the failure of the reforming ministers, the violent uprisings of the starving peasantry, the menace of state insolvency were stages in the development of the attitude of protest. The *philosophes* were not the leaders of the general discontent. The causes of the Revolution were imbedded in the economic inconsistencies, in financial mismanagement, in an indefensible system of taxation, in the decaying political and social institutions and a ruling class powerless to alter them. The *philosophes* taught neither democracy nor revolution. But they broke down the traditional attitude of respect for the government and reverence for religion. They made the middle classes conscious both of their grievances and of their power; and they supplied a new basis of authority in their doctrines of civil liberty and constitutional self-government. The middle classes put their faith in civil liberty and wider suffrage to disarm the state, to win freedom for the play of economic forces and their personal energies.

The success of the American Revolution strengthened the faith of those who accepted the principles of the *philosophes.* The Declaration of Independence proclaimed the legitimacy of rebellion against a government contemptuous of the natural rights of man. The Constitution of the United States seemed the triumph of rationalism in politics. The canny Franklin was lionized in the Parisian salons, because he was the very ideal of a *philosophe*—a perfect blend of Voltaire's intelligence and Rousseau's simplicity. Lafayette became the hero of the nation because he had fought side by side with the great Washington in the struggle for liberty. Reforms, liberty, and *philosophie* were definitely established as the new trinity of ideas.

IV. THE REFORM MOVEMENT DURING THE
OLD RÉGIME

Social Conditions

Conditions in France were representative of the Old Régime in Europe. In practically all the countries of Europe certain general characteristics prevailed. Governments were absolute; intolerant state churches forbade the free exercise of dissenting religious beliefs; a privileged aristocracy enjoyed special rights and prerogatives; labor, commerce, and industry suffered under multiple restrictions and regulations; agriculture was still man's chief occupation; and those in authority were suspicious of nonconformity in thought and in deed.

In England the aristocracy lacked the disproportionate power, as well as the variety of privileges and responsibilities, which it had on the Continent. The historical evolution of England had gradually stripped the nobility of their special legal and fiscal privileges and established the civil and political rights of the commoners. The middle class tended to merge with the old landed aristocracy. Rich merchants, financiers, and manufacturers acquired land and settled down as country gentlemen. Some of them won election to the House of Commons; others acquired titles and entered the House of Lords. Conversely, many of the younger sons of the English nobility found careers in business, in the civil service, or in the liberal professions. Deprived of most of their privileges, the English nobility still wielded enormous political power and controlled the appointments to the most lucrative positions.

The nobility in Spain, Portugal, and Italy were as firmly intrenched in their powers as in France; while in central and eastern Europe their influence was even greater. In Prussia the local lords were real rulers, controlling the courts and the administration of the villages within their domains. There were many hundreds of noblemen within the Holy Roman Empire who were as powerful and as wealthy as the nominal rulers of the petty sovereign states that constituted the empire. Still more notorious was the domination of the Polish nobility over the government.

Prosperous and influential as the middle class of France was in comparison with the bourgeoisie east of the Rhine, it yielded in wealth, political influence, social and intellectual distinction to the bourgeoisie of England. There the middle class used its proceeds from commerce, industry, and finance to diminish the political power of the nobility and to share with them in the control of a powerful state. As in France the bourgeoisie comprised not only business men, but the leading lights of the liberal professions—lawyers, physicians and surgeons, scholars, writers, scientists, and artists. In England the guilds had long been deprived of their powers. There were no feudal restrictions, no guild opposition, no considerable government interference in the development of new manufactures and new methods, in the increased use of machinery, and the adoption of large-scale production. The decline of the Dutch commercial supremacy prepared for the great economic expansion of England during the eighteenth century. Abundant natural resources, extensive European and colonial markets, capital derived from commerce, and a great fleet helped develop the Industrial Revolution earlier in England than elsewhere. On the Continent, outside of France, the middle class had most power in Italy and the free cities of the empire. In Prussia a rigid classification separated the nobility from the middle class and the middle class from the peasantry and defined the activities legally permitted to each. Elsewhere in central and eastern Europe the bourgeoisie was either nonexistent or without real influence. No opportunity existed for the free play of individual enterprise in economic activities.

Europe was still predominantly rural. The cities were few and insignificant. It has been estimated that Europe had not more than one hundred cities with a population of 10,000 at the end of the eighteenth century. Attention has already been directed to the unique status of the French peasantry.[1] The peasants of continental Europe outside France were far worse off. Serfdom still prevailed in the Prussian provinces, in Poland, Hungary, Galicia, and Russia. The powers and prerogatives of the local lord were unrestricted, save as in Prussia, where the government intervened solely to prevent the decline of the peasant population. Conditions improved as

[1] For the peasants in France, *cf.* Chapter II, pp. 40 ff.

one traveled westward, especially in the valleys of the Rhine and the Main and along the slopes of the Alps. France was the land of many peasant proprietors and tenants. Central and eastern Europe were the strongholds of serfdom. England was the scene of an agricultural revolution which transformed the countryside and squeezed the free English peasants from the land. The eighteenth century in England witnessed the application of new methods, the cultivation of new crops, improved animal husbandry, and a wide-scale enclosure movement which, in fifty years (1770–1820), fenced in more than six million acres of land. Thousands of tenant farmers, cottagers, and squatters left the country and moved to the new industrial cities in northern England. Most of those who remained worked on as farm hands.

In the evolution of religious conditions in western and central Europe the two most pronounced characteristics were the development of rationalist criticism and the growth of an evangelical movement. As in France, religious fanaticism abated slowly elsewhere on the Continent, but the practice of toleration was still confined to small groups of enlightened individuals. The rationalist attack upon revelation and supernatural authority, upon what we today call fundamentalism, developed both in scope and in intensity under the vigorous leadership of the French *philosophes*. It spread from England and western Europe to the Germanies, Italy, Spain, and Portugal. But as in France, so in other countries of Europe the most effective defense of religious sentiments came from the growth of the evangelical movement. In England the spiritual inspiration that Anglicanism failed to supply was furnished by the revivalist zeal of the Methodists. In France during the eighteenth century the emotions of the human heart found a champion in Rousseau, whose passionate espousal of naturalness in life and expression promoted a reaction against the ascendancy of reason. In Germany the Pietist movement transformed the formal "dead orthodoxy" of Lutheranism into an emphasis upon moral redemption, charity, prayers, the reading of the New Testament, and missionary activities. To both these developments, rationalism and evangelism, must be traced the humanitarianism and the cosmopolitanism that formed part of the credo of cultivated Europeans of the time.

It is outside of the scope of this work to discuss the literary movement *per se*. Nor is it possible to evaluate the influence exercised upon the transformation of art and manners by the accounts of travelers and missionaries or by the artificial revival of interest in classical antiquity. Yet all these changes in modes of thought and in habits of action made perspicacious contemporaries sense that Europe was on the verge of a new era. Fundamental changes were impending in the whole structure of civilized life. In France a popular revolution effected these changes, violently. In the period immediately prior to the Revolution, various rulers in Europe recognized the need of reforms and endeavored, not altogether admirably nor wisely, to carry them out.

The Enlightened Despots

In a very real sense the monarchs and the statesmen who initiated these reforms merited their title of enlightened despots. In certain significant respects they did not. They all subscribed to the liberal ideas of the Age of Enlightenment, and they strove to govern according to reason and for the general welfare of their subjects. At least they professed such intentions. The movement of reform varied according to the personality of the monarch and the circumstances of his reign. In some countries its measure of success was greater than its measure of failure, but everywhere on the Continent its tendencies and program were identical. The enlightened despots attempted to establish religious tolerance and to limit the authority of the state church. Their humanitarian impulses made them seek to abolish serfdom and eliminate the use of torture from the code of criminal procedure. They improved the system of instruction and encouraged intellectual activities in all their manifestations. They instituted administrative reforms of wide scope, and they stimulated all forms of productivity that would at once bring prosperity to their peoples and increased revenue to the government.

The most famous of these reformers were Frederick the Great of Prussia, the Emperor Joseph II, and the Czarina Catherine the Great of Russia. There were reformers of lesser renown elsewhere on the Continent. In Portugal a determined minister, Pombal, struck severe blows at the native aristocracy and broke the power of the Jesuits by expelling them from the country and confiscating their estates for the benefit of the crown. At the same time their schools were taken over by the state and changed into lay establishments. The benevolent Charles III of Spain (1759–1788), ably assisted by his reforming ministers, followed the example of the Portuguese in dealing with the Jesuits, whom he expelled from his realm in 1767. The power of the church was narrowly curtailed. A comprehensive series of economic reforms checked the decadence into which the country had fallen since the glorious days of the sixteenth century. In the Italian states the most distinguished of the reformers was Leopold I of Tuscany (1765–1790), the brother of Joseph II and his successor as emperor in 1790. He suppressed the Holy Inquisition, and he adopted the principles of Beccaria in reforming the penal code and criminal procedure. He also established freedom of commerce and industry. He instituted proportional equality of taxation and substituted a single tax for the many existing levies. The best known of the reformers in the Scandinavian states were Gustavus III of Sweden (1771–1792) and the minister Struensee in Denmark.

The most successful of all the enlightened rulers and the model for the others was the great Frederick II of Prussia (1740–1786). Of Frederick's intensely personal form of enlightenment and of his keen appreciation of things of the spirit there can be no question. But even a superficial examination of his policy reveals that he tempered his benevolence and enlightenment with copious applications of practical considerations. If he sympathized with the ideals of the *philosophes*, he also followed the traditions of his ancestors in Brandenburg and of Louis XIV in France. His religious tolerance, his zeal for the diffusion of learning, and his judicial reforms all derived from his philosophical principle that the monarch was not the absolute master but was only the first servant of the state. But his unending preoccupation with national finance, his efforts to increase prosperity through the encouragement of immigration and the development of commerce and industry, his administrative reforms, and his steady determination to strengthen his military forces, all those activities derived from the historical traditions of Prussia. In many ways they flagrantly violated the theory of enlightened despotism to which Frederick subscribed and which the *philosophes* elaborated. The theory, particularly as expounded by the Physiocrats,[2] sponsored the ultimate fraternity of peoples via fraternity of monarchs. For this hopeful prospect Frederick substituted the more realistic principle of *raison d'état*,

[2] For the political views of the Physiocrats, *cf.* Chapter III, p. 71.

that is, the supreme interest of the Prussian state. Thus, his economic principles favored not free trade and industry, but government intervention through subsidies and tariffs. His foreign policy was the consecration of force and ruse. The security of his dynasty and the territorial aggrandizement of his state were his goal. His mentor may have been Voltaire, but his model was Louis XIV. The seizure of Silesia, his share in the first partition of Poland (1772), and his long years of foreign wars were not instances of "enlightenment." When he died in 1786, the kingdom of Prussia was one of the great powers of Europe. Its population had more than doubled and its revenue had almost doubled. The Prussian army of almost 200,000 men was undoubtedly the strongest in Europe.

Frederick's younger contemporary and intense admirer, Joseph II, was less fortunate. From 1765 to 1780, when he shared his nominal authority as emperor with his mother and coregent, Maria Theresa, Joseph had ample opportunity to philosophize and to indulge in self-pity; for at every turn his mother checked him in his great yearning to make "philosophy the lawgiver of his empire." After her death in 1780 this fanatical disciple of the enlightenment became the sole ruler of the bizarre congeries of nationalities that made up the Holy Roman Empire. For ten years, with his head filled with liberal ideas and his heart increasingly heavy over the failure that met his efforts, he persevered in the path of reform. Unlike Frederick he did not use the brake of traditional practices to check his advance toward a fundamental social, political, and religious reconstruction of his state.

Barely a month after his accession, he issued a proclamation abolishing serfdom in the Slavic provinces of his empire and strengthening the property rights of the peasantry over the land that they occupied. He announced the equality of all his subjects before the law. His administrative reforms did away with ancient local privileges and established, at least on paper, a centralized and unified administration at Vienna. Of all his measures this one was the most signal failure, for the attempt to uproot political habits and institutions sanctioned by traditional practice aroused fierce resistance. It had to be abandoned in Hungary, and it was received with a rebellious uprising in the Netherlands. Joseph's religious reforms were characteristic. By edict, he extended freedom of worship and civil equality to all non-Catholics in the state. In all matters save dogma, he subordinated the church to the authority of the government. He suppressed many hundred conventual establishments, diverting their funds for services that he deemed more beneficial to humanity.

Yet he died in 1790, bitterly aware of the failure of his career. Ecclesiastics, noblemen, and the subject nationalities rallied in opposition to his reform edicts. The break with the past was too sudden. His foreign policy, arrogantly ambitious, was dismally unsuccessful. Nevertheless, he did not fail as completely as his tortured mind imagined. He strengthened the bond between the hereditary Austrian duchies and strove to create a German state out of those distinct regions. He left for his successors a broad program of liberal reform and humanitarian action. To his immediate successor, Leopold, he bequeathed a well trained and well equipped army that played no small rôle in the struggle that broke out two years later between monarchic Europe and revolutionary France.

Another monarch whose policies won the praise of the *philosophes,* even as their ideas elicited her admiration, was Catherine the Great of Russia (1762–1796). One of the publicists in France wrote somewhat ecstatically of "that government which the genius of a great empress is raising even now for the happiness of her subjects amid the frozen wastes of the North." Though Catherine encouraged the spread of liberal ideas in Russia, at least during the earlier years of her reign, she never for a minute contemplated renouncing the autocratic form of government for her country. After 1789 she turned her back upon reform, but in her heyday as an enlightened despot her reforming zeal had operated within a rather narrow circle of endeavors.

At the very beginning of her long reign this German-born princess undertook the immense task of revising the legal code of her adopted country. From all parts of her realm came many hundred delegates of a legislative commission for whose enlightenment she, herself, prepared an elaborate set of instructions. They deliberated earnestly for two years, and the spirit of liberty, tolerance, and humanity hovered over their discussions. But the sober reality of a war with Turkey recalled Catherine to her duty, and the commission was dissolved. The code was never drawn up. The great empress also spoke frequently of ameliorating the lot of the serfs, but she consistently practiced the traditional policy of the Russian government of attaching them more closely to the soil. By the end of her reign, despite certain paper regulations to the contrary, the lord could do what he willed with his serfs, exploit their labor without remunerating them, and sit in full judgment over them. Within the same span of years the nobility increased their privileges and became a special caste granted, by an imperial charter, exclusive economic and social rights for which they gave no services.

On the other hand, Catherine was a sincere patron of the arts and letters. She gave her support to the dissemination of French liberal ideas among the comparatively few Russians whom one could consider educated. She strengthened the existing system of secondary education. The formation of public opinion—which was not always favorable to Catherine's double-edged liberalism—the development of literary expression, and the beginnings of a press and publishing activities were all products of the empress's interest in the ideas of the enlightenment. The slow conversion of the semi-Oriental Russian autocracy into a monarchy imbued with a modicum of Western ideas was undoubtedly furthered by her example. Like Peter the Great she believed in the civilizing mission of the Russian government within the limits of its own boundaries. Though she made no noteworthy changes in the central administration, she introduced sweeping modifications in the organization of local government which were perpetuated for almost a century after her death.

The most important accomplishments of her reign came from her foreign policy. Catherine accepted the guiding ideals of her Russian predecessors, which were the attainment of Russia's "natural boundaries" in Europe. In the south she wrested the Crimean peninsula and the north shore of the Black Sea from the Ottoman Empire. In the west the successive partitions of Poland extended Russia's boundary to central Europe. When Catherine died in 1796, Russia's imperial position was secure. Her educated classes had acquired a training in Western manners and ideas, but "the happiness of her subjects" was no nearer reality than it had been in 1762, when she ascended the throne.

Behind the zeal of the enlightened despots for humanitarian reform lay their deep concern with dynastic security and territorial aggrandizement. Territorial aggrandizement could come, however, only through skillful diplomacy and victorious wars. The prerequisites of a successful foreign policy were therefore sound finance, a numerous population, and strong armies. This is another way of stating that the achievements of the internal policy of the enlightened despots were put to the account of an aggressive for-

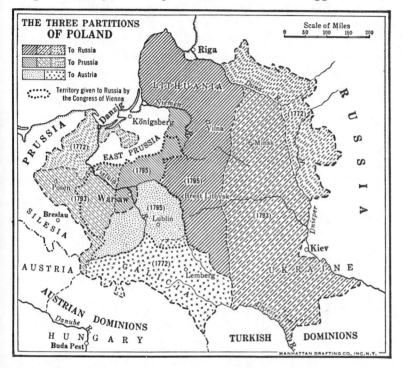

THE THREE PARTITIONS OF POLAND

Scale of Miles
0   50   100   150   200

eign policy. It is an historical commonplace that the age of the enlightened despots furnished the spectacle in Europe of long-drawn-out dynastic strife, replete with selfish calculations, cynical intrigues, and barefaced seizure and partitions of territory. Silesia, Poland, and the Ottoman Empire in Europe are cases in point.

Enlightened despotism as an experiment in government was neither altogether noble nor altogether successful. Perhaps it is nearer the truth to say that it failed to bridge the gap between a government of less liberty and a government of more liberty. It assumed, almost as a logical complement to the "enlightenment" of the ruler, the "unenlightenment" of his subjects. Consequently, the ruler did what *he* deemed best for the interests of his people. But, when it failed to effect reforms, it only accentuated the abuses that remained; when its reforms proved effective, people became anxious for further amelioration. Moreover, even the most "enlightened" despot was only mortal; and the only way in which his reforms could be perpetuated was to have as his immediate successor a ruler equally benevolent and capable. This contingency, unfortunately, was realized neither in Prussia, nor in Spain, nor in Sweden. If we may excuse the comparative failure of the domestic policy of the despots by pleading their benevolent intentions, we may not make a similar plea for their foreign policy. Ultimately this policy destroyed the prosperity produced by their internal reforms, for the years of peace were few and the ravages of many years of war were murderous of men and resources.

Reforms in France: Turgot (1774–1776)

Enlightened despotism did not fail in France, for there its principles were never consistently applied. Had Louis XVI, who succeeded his grandfather in 1774, been capable of playing the part of a great ruler, France might have been spared a great revolution. Consider his opportunity. He was popular with his subjects, mainly one feels, because they were happy at the thought of a young ruler in the place of the aged and hated Louis XV. No constitutional obstacle to enlightened despotism on the pattern of Frederick the Great existed, for the parlements had been abolished in 1771. In the absence of organized opposition he might have appointed an able ministry and given them a free hand to introduce the necessary reforms. He gave himself a good start by appointing excellent officials, of whom Turgot, the controller-general of finances, was the most notable. But his weak and vacillating character and a lamentable incapacity for sustained thinking, led him into error. Courting popularity and believing that his act would effect a reconciliation between the government and its powerful critics, he reëstablished the abolished parlements, despite Turgot's plea to the contrary. Perhaps the outcome would have been the same even if the king had not restored the parlements, for Louis XVI would have remained weak and vacillating in character; but there is no doubt that his first act immeasurably strengthened the opponents of enlightened reforms.

Turgot, the hope of the *philosophes*, since he was himself a philosopher and a practical administrator, set to work with that characteristic energy and thoroughness which had distinguished his career as intendant at Limoges. On the subject of finances his mind was made up. In the first place he would institute a policy of the strictest retrenchment. In a letter to the king he outlined his views, summarizing them in the phrase: "No bankruptcies, no new taxes, and no loans." By rigid economy he did effect gratifying savings for the treasury, though his example did not influence the monarch to cut down royal pensions and gifts and court expenditures.

Despite the abolition of several lesser abuses in the collection of taxes and his success in reducing the national debt, Turgot expected more considerable results from his efforts to increase the income of the government, which was the more important part of his program. The first reform edict, which concerned the grain trade, was issued in September, 1774, almost immediately after he assumed office. This edict abolished all government regulations concerning the purchase and sale of grain and allowed the fullest freedom of interprovincial grain trade. Turgot's edict had no greater success than similar measures had had in 1754 and 1763. Nature, in the form of a crop shortage, and his enemies in the guise of those interested in the old system, offered opposition to his edict. Once again fear of famine brought disorder and, by accentuating the real shortage, hoisted retail prices. Turgot finally quelled the disturbances of the so-called "grain war," but his experiment in agricultural liberalism must be counted a failure.

Undismayed, he pursued his course, and early in 1776 presented for registration before the parlement of Paris several other reform edicts. Of these the two most important abolished the royal corvée and most of the guild corporations. In doing away with the heavy burden of the corvée Turgot also proposed to introduce the principle of tax equality. He planned to have the costs of road service taken care of by means of an increase in the vingtièmes, which already affected nobles as well as commoners. The edict concerning the guilds proposed to destroy their monopolies and to restore the natural law of free competition. By doing away with the guilds, he would liberate industry, advance commercial development, lower prices, and allow the artisan the enjoyment of his natural right to labor. With the exception of several corporations, the guilds were ordered to liquidate their affairs and to suspend activities.

The monarch overrode the objections of the parlement and ordered the registration of the edicts, but this was Turgot's final victory over his many and influential critics. The measures that he had already executed earned him the hostility of the most powerful groups and privileged classes—guilds, parlements, court favorites, and especially the queen—while those that he had no opportunity to carry out aroused the anxiety of his last protector, the king himself. Among the many projects that were attributed to him, there was one which might have established a strong yet flexible contact between the central administration and the local governments. This was the organization of elective local assemblies culminating in a national assembly through which the king could gather the sentiments of the nation. But the combination of Turgot's enemies, led by Marie Antoinette, prevailed upon Louis XVI to dismiss him. Turgot did not survive to witness the realization of his prophetic words, uttered in defending himself and in encouraging his monarch to support him: "Never forget, Sire, that it was weakness which brought the head of Charles I to the block."

For the moment all reforms were shelved in the reaction that followed the dismissal of Turgot and the resignation of his liberal colleague, the secretary of state, Malesherbes. Even the abolished guild corporations were reëstablished, though not without retaining some of the changes introduced by Turgot.

The First Ministry of Necker (1776–1781)

After several months Louis XVI called upon the most famous of the bankers to take charge of finances. The man summoned was the Genevese financier and publicist, Necker. As a foreigner and a Protestant, Necker could not be made minister, but he received the powers of controller-general with the title of director-general of finance. Necker's pomp and vanity were slightly ridiculous, and his competence in political economy contestable, but he could manage the intricate details of high finance. At first he resorted to new loans and administrative reforms. His problem was particularly difficult, for in 1778 France signed a treaty of alliance with the colonists in America who had revolted against the British government. The successful war upon which France thus entered proved costly, very costly, increasing the already ruinous national debt by more than one and one-half billion livres.

The administrative reforms of Necker were sound, though

hardly sufficient as a remedy. He suppressed many unnecessary offices, simplified the accounting system, and began to limit the functions of the farmers-general by entrusting the collection of several of the indirect taxes, such as royal domains and the excise, to the government itself. His loans and public lotteries were successful, though more profitable for investors than beneficial for the state. The rapid floating of loans of more than five hundred million livres without increasing taxes during the years of war greatly added to Necker's already tremendous reputation as a financial wizard. To be sure, few of his contemporaries realized at the time that his later loans were paying the interest charges on the earlier ones, and that his entire policy immeasurably aggravated the financial crisis.

His popularity at that time was so great that he resolved, albeit cautiously, to extend his activities and continue the work of earlier reformers. He began an inquiry into the scandalous conditions prevailing at hospitals and prisons. He abolished serfdom on the royal domains and he succeeded in restricting the use of torture in criminal inquiries. The most important administrative reform was an attempt to limit the authority of the intendants by establishing provincial assemblies. The experiment began favorably with the creation of an assembly in Berry (1778) and a second in Haute-Guyenne (1779), which at once began to assist the central government in problems of taxation, police, poor relief, and public works.

Necker had foes as well as admirers, and the necessity of defending his administration against the criticism of the foes forced him in 1781 to publish the famous *Compte rendu au roi*. In this account he pretended very ostentatiously to make public the details of his financial administration. Necker juggled his figures so as to show a favorable balance for the fiscal year, hoping thereby that such inestimable and indispensable service would compel Louis XVI to grant him the title of royal minister, which would have the double effect of strengthening his position and increasing the confidence of the public. The treasury situation in reality was quite different. War expenditures and certain other "extraordinary" charges for that year established a deficit of almost ninety million livres, to which had to be added an additional sum of one hundred and twenty-nine millions for "anticipations" or claims upon the following year's revenues.

Distorted as it was, the *Compte rendu* nevertheless was highly illuminating. One hundred thousand copies of it were sold the year of its publication, and the readers got their first glimpse into the mysterious transactions of the royal treasury. The great majority of these readers now learned that which a few had suspected; namely, the reality of the enormous sums paid by the court in pensions and gifts to the courtiers. These "drones" of the court, aroused by Necker's presumption, now led the attack upon him, aided by the king's brothers, by members of the parlement, and by the same minister, Maurepas, who had undermined Turgot's position. When Necker's demand for the title of minister was refused, he resigned his position, leaving the treasury in a desperate plight and the moneyed interests in consternation.

THE GATHERING OF THE STORM (1781–1789)

While the financial aristocracy derived handsome profits from lending money at usurious interest to the embarrassed government they were now far from sanguine about recovering their principal. What if the government became insolvent? How much, then, would they receive for the state securities to which they had subscribed so heavily? Financiers became dismayed, but on the other hand thousands of less wealthy but not less liberal disciples of the *philosophes* confidently awaited the inauguration of great political changes. Imbued with the critical revolutionary doctrine, they now hailed the events of the American Revolution as a sweeping confirmation of their views—not only a confirmation, but an example for them to follow—of course, within certain limits and with certain reservations due to conditions in France. The large cities, Paris in particular, buzzed with excitement. People talked politics, or read about politics in the press, and many joined reading and debating clubs where they could hear the illuminating or merely exciting comments by self-appointed political mentors. For five or six years after the resignation of Necker the impending crisis was averted. Necker's immediate successors (from 1781 to 1783) grappled with the additional burdens bequeathed to them by the costs of the war with England, but they found the road too difficult. In November, 1783, the king appointed Calonne, an experienced intendant and a highly intelligent and resourceful person, to the pivotal position of controller-general. Calonne undertook his duties with a full realization of the gravity of the situation. He knew that the budget was in arrears, that future revenues had been discounted, that the treasury was empty, and that the moneyed classes had lost confidence.

His great nostrum for financial ailments was the restoration of public confidence; and he averred the best way to restore confidence was to give the appearance of prosperity. Therefore he threw economy to the winds and expanded the credit of the government by borrowing heavily from the capitalists. His first success in increasing the general purchasing power through these loans encouraged financiers to make additional loans. In the three years from 1783 to 1786 he borrowed the immense sum of 653 million livres.

A small part of the expenditures went to silence the opposition of publicists and the parlements and to win the support of the royal family and the court with gifts and pensions. The greater part went to meet outstanding indebtedness and to further public works. Thus an artificial prosperity set in, a boom period, when increased productions poured out new goods and employed labor, and the income of workers rose appreciably. This revival developed all the more rapidly because crops too were exceptionally good in those few years and commerce and industry no longer suffered from the restrictive conditions imposed by war with England. The national wealth was considerable, for more than half of the specie of Europe lay in French coffers. But much of this increased purchasing power was channeled off into profits for a comparatively small number of producers. Those who did not share in the profits gradually restricted their own expenditures, and the markets for goods began to collapse. The boom had also steadily increased prices while wages rose less rapidly; and though the government expenses multiplied, its income from taxation lagged behind, thus further decreasing its ability to meet its obligations.

Toward 1786 the process of deflation had set in, and the confidence of the capitalists vanished more rapidly than it had been restored. Necker's three volumes on the *Administration of the Finances* (1785) were a rude revelation to hard-headed business men who had imagined that prosperity could be maintained permanently by inflating the purchasing power instead of balancing the government budget. Calonne exhausted all expedients to meet the interest charges on the loans. The parlements once more raised protests against new loans and huge expenditures. Despite the steady increase in taxes, the annual deficit had risen to more than one hundred million livres. The versatile Calonne turned reformer. It was indeed high time, for the deflation was developing into a severe crisis to which the commercial treaty with England in 1786 greatly contributed. By that treaty the French textile industry suffered a sharp setback and thousands of part-time industrial workers of northeastern France were thrown into unemployment.

Besides, Calonne could hardly expect much from the royal approval of his policy. Marie Antoinette, whose influence over her husband had increased steadily since the beginning of the reign, unwittingly brought shame to herself and her consort. Surrounded by friends as gay and charming, and as irresponsible, as herself, Marie Antoinette lived for pleasure, for dancing and theatricals, for clothes and jewelry. An adventuress and her associates convinced the notorious spendthrift Cardinal Rohan that he could gain the queen's lost favor by buying her a famous diamond necklace worth more than a million and a half livres. Rohan was duped from start to finish, from buying the necklace and holding moonlight interviews with a woman who impersonated the queen to passing on a contract for payment which bore her forged signature. Eventually suspicion was aroused, for thieves and necklace disappeared and Marie Antoinette indignantly refused to make payments to the jeweler who had sold the necklace. Outraged, the king had Rohan arrested and brought to trial before the parlement of Paris (1785). The honor of His Majesty was not vindicated, for the magistrates acquitted Rohan. If the wild applause of the populace meant anything, it meant that the Parisians agreed with the cardinal in thinking that the queen's favors were not reserved exclusively for her husband. Moreover, this verdict gave the princes of the blood hope that perhaps the king might be ousted from the throne.

Later in the summer of 1786 Calonne presented a secret memorandum in which he elaborated a comprehensive plan of reform. At first overwhelmed by its radical provisions, Louis XVI later reluctantly gave Calonne his support and agreed to summon an Assembly of Notables before whom the plan would be laid. Calonne knew perfectly well that the parlements would never register his edicts, hence his anxiety to have his reforms approved by the notables. He proposed to abolish the corvée, to suppress internal customs, to permit free grain trade within France, to extend the system of provincial assemblies throughout the kingdom, to decrease the burden of the taille and the gabelle, and to transform the Bank of Discount that Turgot had established into a State Bank. And most important of all, he proposed to replace the vingtièmes with a land tax, payable by all proprietors whether of the clergy, the nobility, or the Third Estate.

The Assembly of Notables met in February, 1787, one hundred and forty-four representatives of the first three orders of France being present. As might have been foreseen, these distinguished princes of the blood, prelates, officials of the parlements, and municipal and provincial administrators had no inclination to sacrifice their privileges. Calonne came before them, read an indictment of the Old Régime of remarkable clarity and vigor, and then presented his proposals. His very clarity and vigor served only the better to show them that by their approval of his projects they would end their social superiority, destroy their fiscal privileges, and ratify a sweeping reform of the entire political, social, and economic structure of France. The huge deficit that Calonne had incurred gave them their opportunity to mask their essentially selfish opposition to tax reform under the cloak of public interest. Calonne's financial administration was, as we have seen, more than vulnerable, particularly so when scurrilous pamphlets proceeded to analyze it. The resistance was too much for the king and Calonne. Louis XVI dismissed his minister, who fled to England. The Assembly of Notables thus continued what the preambles to Turgot's, Necker's, and Calonne's reform edicts had begun: it gave the widest publicity to the discussion of the evils of the financial system.

The Struggle with the Parlements

For slightly more than a year the administration of finance was in the hands of Calonne's successor, Loménie de Brienne, the archbishop of Toulouse and one of the leaders in the Assembly of Notables. A brief experience as financial administrator speedily convinced him not only of the solid merits of Calonne's projects but of the necessity of supplementing them by a stamp tax on legal transactions. But when he presented his plans the notables held firm to their position. On May 25, 1787, the king dismissed them. Brienne's sole recourse now lay with the parlements, for Louis XVI flatly refused to summon the Estates General. The officers of the judiciary displayed a spirit no less hostile than the notables. To the proposals concerning the corvée, the provincial assemblies, and the grain trade, the parlement of Paris had no objection, but the land tax and the stamp tax it emphatically rejected. It then formulated its position in exceedingly outspoken terms: that only the nation speaking through the Estates General had the right to consent to new taxes. In short, the *parlementaires* took the stand of no taxation without representation.

This formula became the rallying cry of all the opponents of the administration, of the magistrates of the sovereign courts in Paris and the provinces, and of the more liberal group of "Patriots" or "Nationals" who struck a temporary alliance with them. To secure the registration of the decrees on the two new taxes the government held a *lit de justice*, but the parlement promptly declared the registration illegal. For this revolutionary act the magistrates were exiled to Troyes. The sincerity of most of the parlementaires in appealing for the convocation of the Estates General was at the moment questionable. In September of the same year, 1787, they struck a bargain with the government. The government agreed to drop the land tax and the stamp tax, and the parlementaires consented to prolong the collection of the two existing vingtièmes and make them applicable to all classes without distinction or exception. The "Patriots" were keenly disappointed. They felt that the judges had used the threat of the Estates General only as a subterfuge to avoid the basic land tax upon the privileged classes.

The compromise broke down when the government held another lit de justice to register a series of loans amounting to four hundred and twenty million livres (November, 1787), promising at the same time to summon the Estates General within five years. Once more the judges declared the government's act illegal and staunchly demanded the *immediate* convocation of the Estates General. To end the hostile agitation that, in the following six months, swept France, the king decided upon radical measures. Through Lamoignon, the keeper of the seals, he effected a complete reorganization of the courts (May, 1788), creating a supreme plenary court for the registration of all edicts and establishing forty-seven grand bailiwicks for the settlement of civil and criminal litigation. That the reorganization might win public approval, he agreed to abolish the use of torture, reduce the costs of justice, and begin the codification of the laws.

This firmness came too late, for all the supporters of liberal reforms, all the advocates of a revolution on the American model, rallied to the support of the parlements against what they called "monarchical despotism." A "bed of justice" compelled the parlement of Paris to register the decree concerning the new courts, but the monarchy could not cope with the resistance of the provincial parlements. Petitions and protests flowed from every corner of the country. The magistrates formed correspondence committees, communicated with each other from town to town, stirred up the army of their subordinates and dependents, and circulated violent pamphlets against the ministry. Irritated by an ill timed reduction of pensions, the court nobles added their force to the opposition, while the general assembly of the clergy voted to reduce its subsidy to the government. Meantime the "Patriots" conducted an active campaign of propaganda for the convocation of the Estates General and the drafting of a constitution.

There were riots in Toulouse and Dijon and rebellious demonstrations in the province of Béarn. In Brittany the movement reached alarming proportions and the military had to be called out to suppress the rioting. In Dauphiné the attempt of government troops to enforce the decree first provoked violent rioting and then inspired a political act of high significance. Under the guidance of two future revolutionary leaders, Barnave and Mounier, the three legal classes of Dauphiné revived the ancient estates of that province, the deputies sitting together and voting by head, with the Third Estate having as many deputies as the two upper classes combined. These deputies of Dauphiné petitioned the king to convoke the Estates General of the nation, and they took an oath to pay no taxes until that assembly was convoked. A popular revolt menaced the stability of the government. The army was honeycombed with malcontents. The subordinate officers were still smarting under the recent regulation of 1781 which restricted the number of higher offices that were open to commoners, and the soldiers were growing restive under the influence of seditious propaganda. The suspension of the law courts was disrupting civil life. The economic crisis steadily grew worse, now accentuated by a partial failure of the crops. Worst of all, bankruptcy threatened, for the bankers had withdrawn all support from the royal treasury.

On July 5, 1788, the government yielded to the clamor. A royal edict announced the speedy convocation of the Estates General, and on August 8 a second edict fixed May 1, 1789, as the definite date for the opening session. The reorganization of the law courts was dropped and the parlements were reinstated. On August 16, Brienne was compelled to suspend treasury payments. Though the notes of the Bank of Discount were made legal tender in Paris, Brienne's suspension of payments was a confession of his inability to cope with the situation. The financiers joined the opposition of the parliamentary nobility and the "Patriots," and Brienne was forced to resign his office. Louis XVI then recalled Necker, again appointing him director-general of finance and now, minister of state. An index to the popular confidence in Necker was an immediate rise in the market value of government securities and the stock of the Discount Bank. From the latter institution and from private individuals Necker obtained sufficient funds to tide the government over until the spring of 1789.

The Elections to the Estates General and the Cahiers

Liberal opinion was only momentarily satisfied by the crown's resolution to summon the Estates General, for two new questions immediately came up for discussion. Those questions were, first, how many deputies would there be to represent the Third Estate, and secondly, what was to be the method of voting in the Estates General. Here the erstwhile united opponents of "royal despotism" parted company. The "conscript fathers"—that is, the magistrates of the parlements, the upper clergy, and almost all of the nobility—had led the attack upon the crown's prerogatives in order to strengthen their own influence in the state. This conservative bloc, which was strongly intrenched in the administration by virtue of owning the most important offices, was indeed responsible for the convocation of the Estates General. But these "aristocrats" (called "aristos" by the masses) desired an Estates General on the model of the one that had been assembled in 1614. Each order would have an equal number of deputies, and deliberations and voting would be by separate orders and not in common. Moreover, the vote of the individual deputies would be counted only to determine the majority within each order. Each order would have one vote in the assembly and a unanimous vote of the orders would determine the decision of the entire assembly.

This method seemed theoretically just, but the "Patriots" objected strenuously to this procedure. They entertained no hopes of getting the consent of the "aristocrats" to the comprehensive reforms that they had in mind. Had not the latter made it clear that their own program was merely the replacement of the royal despotism by an aristocratic oligarchy! An Estates General modeled on that of 1614 would mean a deadlock and an end of the liberal crusade for reform. The "Patriots" took their stand for a true national assembly. Their program called for (1) double representation for the Third Estate, that is, for as many representatives for the commoners as for the two privileged orders combined, and (2) for the vote by poll instead of by order, that is, to have each individual vote counted instead of having the vote of each order count for one.

The "Patriots" were well organized and had capable leaders who formed a steering committee, the Society of Thirty. Among them were such notables as Lafayette, Condorcet, Mirabeau, and Adrien Duport. They conducted an active propaganda campaign throughout the entire country. In part their campaign was verbal, carried by word of mouth in the many clubs, reading circles, Masonic lodges, and in modest cafés and elegant salons. In part it was literary, for they spread innumerable pamphlets and drew up petitions that circulated rapidly from hand to hand. From July, 1788, when the king had invited officials and other "instructed" persons to delve into the past history of France for information concerning the convocation of the Estates General, there was virtual liberty of the press in France. Pamphlets by the hundreds were struck off the presses, most of them expressing the views of the reformers. No abuses were left untouched; all possibilities of reform were exhausted. Not all of the pamphlets were well informed, for in many instances the author's sole qualifications were his ambition and his enterprising spirit. Not a few, however, were well written, in particular those that emphasized the fact that the Third Estate constituted the overwhelming majority, more than ninety-eight per cent, of the entire population, a fact which entitled the unprivileged commoners to double representation and the vote by poll. Easily the most widely read of all these pamphlets was the famous one written by the Abbé Sieyès, *What Is the Third Estate?* which began in the following vein: "What is the Third Estate? Everything. What has it been in the political order up to the present? Nothing. What does it ask? To become something."

The government delayed making its decision on the two questions, for Necker was sorely perplexed and desperately anxious to maintain harmony. His interest lay in balancing the budget; the discussion of greater social and economic problems would serve only to increase his difficulties. But the demonstrations in the provinces and the flood of political pamphlets convinced him at length that he would have to yield to the popular clamor or risk the loss of his already waning prestige. On December 27, 1788, the government answered the first of the two questions by allowing the Third Estate to have as many deputies as the other two orders combined. At the same time Necker presented the government's plan of reform, a meagre and unsatisfactory program that left much to be desired. It gave control of taxation to the Estates General and limited royal and ministerial expenditures. It promised liberty of the press and the legal regulation of lettres de cachet. It expressed confidence that the clergy and the nobility would voluntarily give up their tax exemptions, but Necker staunchly defended the maintenance of the feudal rights and prerogatives. This concession, "Necker's New Year's Gift to France," still left the second question concerning the method of voting unanswered. Yet for all its shortcomings it was enthusiastically received by the commoners and bitterly opposed by the privileged classes. So extreme were the two types of opinion that street fighting broke out in several districts on the news of the government's decision. On January 24, 1789, the royal letter of convocation prescribed the mode of election to the Estates General and loosely defined the work set for the coming assembly.

The opening of the electoral campaign coincided with the peak of the economic distress. The commercial treaty of 1786 with England which had opened the French market to cheaper English goods, textiles in particular, had dealt that French industry a heavy blow. In the industrial regions of the north and the northeast the effects were most keenly felt. It has been estimated that 200,000 workers were unemployed in 1788. The suffering of the needy became unbearable when torrential rains in some regions and fierce midsummer hailstorms in others ruined the grain harvest and bread reached famine prices, the highest on record for the entire century. To cap the climax the winter of 1789 was of heart-rending severity. The municipal government of Paris kept huge fires burning throughout the city so that the poor might not freeze to death. The Seine was frozen during most of the winter, a calamity which seriously impeded the transit of prime commodities to the capital. In all France starving peasants and workers formed bands and pillaged granaries and markets, demanding an end to crushing taxes and seigniorial dues and clamoring for bread. The scarcity was real, for much of the surplus harvest of earlier years had been exported, though it is true that speculators and hoarders had not been idle. To relieve the situation Necker restored government regulation of the grain trade, but the remedy afforded no appreciable relief. In Paris alone, a fifth of the entire population went hungry. At the end of April, 1789, just before the scheduled opening session of the Estates General a mob of unemployed artisans, peasants, and rural vagrants sacked a large paper-hanging factory in the workingmen's section, the Faubourg Saint-Antoine. Order was restored after a bloody struggle with the police authorities. A general uprising seemed inevitable, an uprising of despair. Professor Lefebvre puts the subsequent events very succinctly: "Had bread been cheaper the violent intervention of the masses, which was essential for the overthrow of the Old Régime, would perhaps not have taken place, and the bourgeoisie would have triumphed less easily."

The elections took place in that troubled atmosphere. The method prescribed was liberal, but extremely complicated; and in many instances confusion and turbulence prevailed at the elections. The nobles chose their 270 deputies directly at the electoral assemblies of the bailiwicks which, in general, were the units of election, electing a majority that was opposed to reform and a liberal minority of almost ninety nobles. The vote of the clergy was in some instances direct, in others indirect. Since the royal regulations permitted the lower clergy to vote, the numerical superiority of the latter enabled them to elect a majority of over 200 parish priests. This circumstance was to prove a decisive factor in the coming months. Even among the minority of ninety-four great prelates there were several liberal ecclesiastics, the most notable of whom were Talleyrand and Champion de Cicé.

The voting of the Third Estate was less turbulent but more

complicated. Every Frenchman of twenty-five years of age and over who was inscribed on the tax rolls had the right to vote, though not directly, for the deputies of his order. In the towns and cities guild members met in one primary assembly, members of the corporations of the liberal arts formed a second primary assembly, and all other voters formed a third. Representatives from each of these primary assemblies formed a secondary assembly for the town. These representatives in turn chose delegates to the bailiwick assembly, and the last named elected the deputies to the Estates General. In general the peasants met in their parish assemblies and named delegates to the bailiwick assembly, where they joined with the delegates from towns in making the final choice. Just as in the towns the electors representing the upper and middle bourgeoisie outnumbered the craftsmen and petty traders, so in the bailiwick assemblies the peasant delegates outnumbered those from the towns and cities. Paris and several of the larger cities voted under special arrangements, whereby the deputies of the commoners were elected directly.

All told, the Third Estate elected 578 deputies, more than half of whom were members of the legal profession, provincial lawyers predominating. The other liberal professions too were well represented, as were publicists and men of the pen. It can hardly be gainsaid that the pick of the upper and middle bourgeoisie were named to go to Versailles to speak in the name of the collective Third Estate, to represent millions of nameless proletarians and many petty landowners who were untouched by their spokesmen's revolutionary idealism.

At the same time that they voted for their delegates or their deputies the voters of each order, in each parish, in each town, in each bailiwick, drew up cahiers. This was done in conformity with the traditions of the Estates General and at the express wish of the government, which hoped thus to learn the real grievances and desires of the entire population. Many of the local cahiers are still unpublished, though the work of publication is now proceeding rapidly. Those that the deputies of the Third Estate took with them to Versailles were compilations supposed to be based upon the many local ones. Nevertheless, in spite of the fact that certain model cahiers were in circulation, despite the fact that provincial notaries or other literate townsfolk drew up many village cahiers, despite the final editing of the local cahiers in the bailiwick assemblies, these "notebooks of grievances" remain the most faithful and sincere expression of the French people on the eve of the Revolution.

The agreement of general ideas is all the more striking because of the diversity in their details. It was the general belief that the Estates General would undertake a wide, comprehensive program of constitutional reform. The royal letter of convocation of January 24, 1789, seemed to indicate that the king expected the Estates General to settle the principles of government and to partake of the functions of a constitutional committee. On the main points of that constitutional reform the three estates were agreed; namely, (1) a hereditary monarchy, not absolute but limited in power, with the royal ministers directly responsible for their actions either to civil tribunals or to the representative assembly; (2) a representative assembly, meeting periodically and exercising supervision over taxation, legislation, and administration; (3) proportional equality of taxation for the three estates; (4) the establishment of the fundamental civil rights of the citizen—in freedom from arbitrary arrest and imprisonment, trial by jury, freedom of speech and the press, religious freedom (though the clergy were not unanimous on the last two points); (5) the decentralization of government by the establishment of a system of local government and administration. Many of the deputies, even of the privileged orders, had also received instructions not to vote further subsidies to the government until the constitution had been adopted. Thus on all important matters pertaining to the constitution, save the most important issue of all, the deputies were in general agreement.

It seems almost incredible that the government should not have decided in advance a matter of such cardinal importance as whether the Estates General should remain a body composed of representatives of three orders or become a true national assembly; yet such was the case. Consequently the deputies wrangled continuously over the method of voting that should be prescribed for the Estates General. The nobles took the stand that France already had a constitution, submerged in the past history and laws of France, which only had to be "restored," and they insisted therefore that the three orders should sit and vote separately according to tradition. The deputies of the Third Estate denied that France had a constitution, asserting that they had come to "create" one for France. Therefore they insisted that all the deputies should sit and vote together in a common assembly. The nobles asserted that their claims were based upon law and history, while the commoners maintained that *their* arguments were founded upon natural law and reason.

The cahiers of the nobility generally agreed with those of the Third Estate in defending the fundamental civil rights of the citizen, to the grant of which the clergy were generally opposed. The long-standing grievances of the lower clergy against ecclesiastical superiors were generously aired. Nobles and Third Estate also stood together in their willingness to sequestrate the ecclesiastical estates for the payment of the national debt. To the admission of commoners to all civil, religious, and military offices the nobility and the clergy were adamant in opposition.

The most striking divergence of views was shown on the question of social and economic reform. Not only did the cahiers of the Third Estate differ from those of the other orders, but they differed widely among themselves. The demands of the peasantry varied according to the economic status of the formulators, whether they were landless peasants, petty tenants, or prosperous proprietors. Urban workers voiced few specific grievances that were peculiar to them alone. The most lucid and comprehensive statements of grievances and programs of reforms are found in the cahiers of the prosperous commercial and industrial bourgeoisie. The class that assumed control of the Revolution achieved its results through no accidental fortune. It had a program and an organization to promote it; and it used its resources of wealth and intelligence both cautiously and wisely.

It is a gross error then to assume from what followed that the cahiers of the commoners were a clarion call to violence. Indeed their most striking characteristic was moderation and restraint. They abounded with expressions of fidelity to Louis XVI and the monarchy, of respect for the established religion, of faith in the unity and integrity of family life, and in the safeguarding of property rights. They advocated not "red revolution," but a radical reform of enormous magnitude.

As the scattered groups of deputies wended their slow way along the long and dusty roads to Versailles, their hopes ran high. They advanced confidently, rich in the faith that by their actions they would usher in a new era for France and all humanity.

V. THE DESTRUCTION OF THE OLD RÉGIME

The Establishment of the National Assembly

EVERYWHERE except in Paris the elections were over in April; and by May 1, 1789, almost all deputies were at Versailles. There were approximately seventeen hundred of them, including the alternates for all the orders. In a variety of petty ways the deputies of the Third Estate were made to feel their inferiority. Their somber and outlandish costumes of black cloth contrasted dismally with the splendid attire worn by the clergy and the nobles. At the formal and highly stilted reception for all the deputies (May 2), the king kept the commoners waiting for hours and then, while the high officials of the court stared at them with condescending curiosity, received them coldly. The formal mass in state which opened the Estates General on May 4 furnished another occasion for humiliation, but the commoners took what comfort they could from the enthusiastic cheers of the townspeople of Versailles. After a long, almost interminable, day they retired to await the real opening of the Estates General on the morrow. Their hopes were still fervent, though their spirits had been depressed by the chill of the royal reception.

Their disappointment in the king was not abated by what occurred on May 5, but changed from irritation to suspicion. To begin, the royal family delayed proceedings for hours; then the king appeared supposedly to announce the royal program. He read a short speech which was received well enough, though it could scarcely have had less content. The keeper of the royal seals followed with a longer address, which intimated that the crown did not object to the vote by head on financial matters, but opposed such a procedure for the discussion of political reform. Necker, on whom the commoners pinned their hopes, spoke last and at great length, leaving a spokesman to conclude his address. The king seemed impressed, probably less by the speech than by the applause of the commoners, which implied strongly that it might be unwise to dismiss powerful ministers, as the court faction desired. Necker spoke almost entirely about financial administration and the deficit, explaining that a few reforms and a program of economy would restore financial stability. He avoided the question of constitutional reforms and made hedging allusions to the question of the vote, intimating, however, that on certain matters it would be desirable to vote by order. When Necker's mouthpiece had finished, the master of ceremonies requested all the deputies to show their credentials.

The commoners, as their many commentaries reveal, were aghast at the proceedings. They had come to the capital to serve as true legislators of the nation; now the king and his principal minister served warning that the old order would be maintained, that no opportunity would be given them to "create" a constitution for France, to regenerate the administration and society. Spontaneously, they resolved to resist the policy of the court. They showed their independence by refusing to present their credentials, and the verification was accordingly postponed until the following day. Each order was assigned to separate rooms in the Salle des Menus Plaisirs.

The events of that day disclosed attitudes and tempers that boded ill for the future. Necker revealed his basic unimaginative mediocrity by failing to grasp the significance of the occasion. He had it in his power to guide the movement for reform under the aegis of the king. But his eye was dimmed to the future; it had grown weary contemplating the figures of receipts and expenditures. He had the soul of a bank clerk; the flame of the statesman did not burn in him. Had Louis XVI been as firm in character as he was benevolent in intention, he might have risen to the heights demanded of a leader. He was not craven, but he was readily influenced by those about him, too open to suggestions; and the suggestions emanating from his court counselors advised him to maintain the *status quo*, to keep the commoners in their place. The commoners were nettled, and in their impatience with the leaders on whom they had counted, but who had failed them, they sought new leaders in their own ranks. Unlike the privileged orders, they refused to verify their credentials separately.

One leader they found in Mirabeau, that *déclassé* noble of imposing ugliness whom frequent imprisonment, crushing debts, and innumerable scandalous adventures had not suppressed. His own order had rejected him, but such was his wide reputation for liberalism that the Third Estate of Aix-en-Provence had elected him to the Estates General. Thanks to his many amanuenses and his own vigorous and capable gifts he had amassed an extraordinarily rich store of information and experience on problems of state. Experienced, of supple intellect, sure in his political faith of a constitutional monarchy, daring in his acts, and brilliant in oratory, Mirabeau rose rapidly to the leadership of the commoners. When the deputies of the Third Estate, or the Commons as they preferred to call themselves, resolved not to organize a separate body, nor to recognize the verification of the credentials of the deputies save in a common assembly, they adopted a policy that required political finesse and courage. These qualities they found in Mirabeau. With the sure sense of a political realist he directed the united commoners against the weaker of the privileged orders. "Send delegates to the clergy, gentlemen," he cried. "Do not send any to the nobles, for the nobles give orders and the clergy will negotiate."

After five weeks of unseemly bickering over the crucial matter of the organization of the Estates General the commoners ended their inactivity. Upon the initiative of Abbé Sieyès, who had only recently taken his seat with them, and in defiance of the king's express command for the separate verification of credentials, they began to verify not as deputies of the Third Estate, but as representatives of the nation (June 12). During the next few days some of the parish priests came over, and on June 17 the commoners and their adherents among the ecclesiastics, declared themselves the *National Assembly* of France and proceeded to act as the representative body of the nation.

Their declaration was the first act of the Revolution; indeed, their declaration contained the whole theory and achievement of the Revolution. In a few deliberate and coldly logical phrases they set aside the entire theory and practice of a government and society based upon *privileged* orders and asserted the *democratic* theory of numbers and of popular sovereignty. "The denomination of National Assembly is the only one which is suitable for the Assembly in the present condition of things; because the members who compose it are the only representatives lawfully and publicly known and verified; because they are sent directly by almost the totality of the nation; because, lastly, the representation being one and indivisible, none of the deputies in whatever class or order he may be chosen, has the right to exercise his functions apart from

the present Assembly." The commoners represented "at least
ninety-six per cent of the nation"; therefore they constituted the
National Assembly. The Assembly took pains to reassure the creditors of the state that the debt would be paid, ordered the provisional collection of the existing taxes, declared that new taxes
were not valid without its consent, and denied the king the right
to veto its future resolutions. Two days later, June 19, Mirabeau's
expectations were realized, for by a small majority the clergy voted
to join the Commons in the National Assembly and in that way
gave indorsement to the illegal and revolutionary act of June 17.

At once the court party, led by the queen and the count of
Artois, the younger of the two brothers of Louis XVI, urged the
harried monarch to take repressive measures; while Necker,
equally insistent, outlined a program of reforms. Louis XVI half
acquiesced in Necker's view, but at the same time he had decided
to annul the measures of the Commons. Despite Necker's objections he made plans to hold a "royal session" of the Estates General on June 22, on which occasion he intended to announce the
policy of the court on the manner of voting and the question of
reforms and thus settle the constitutional dispute which had made
impossible the solution of the nation's problems.

The "Royal Session" of June 23

On the morning of June 20 the deputies of the Commons found
the doors of their Assembly room closed to them, supposedly to
allow necessary repairs within the hall for the holding of a special
royal session two days later. It was a two minutes' walk to the
near-by indoor tennis court, a bare little building with only a floor
space and galleries for spectators. There the determined deputies
betook themselves, resolved not to yield. Discussion began at once;
several deputies were in favor of going to Paris, but from this decision Mounier dissuaded them. He boldly proposed that they
should all take an oath "never to separate and to reassemble wherever circumstances demanded until the constitution of the realm
was established and affirmed upon a solid basis." In the midst of
great enthusiasm, Bailly, the astronomer and savant, who was the
presiding officer of the Assembly, read the oath, and the deputies
swore it after him. The "Tennis Court Oath" was a dramatic and
stirring declaration, not, to be sure the beginning of the Revolu-

tion, for that had already begun, but an emphatic and courageous reaffirmation of the resolution passed three days earlier.

The immediate future of France lay with Louis XVI. He could have summoned the troops against the rebellious deputies, but such a course would have been catastrophic to France. He determined to intimidate the commoners with *threats* of force. He rejected Necker's conciliatory plan and postponed the royal session to June 23. Meantime a majority of the clergy and a bare sprinkling of noblemen joined the deputies of the Third Estate in the hall of the National Assembly. The Assembly was now composed of the majority of orders as well as of deputies.

Louis XVI was ready with his program on June 23. Before the royal session opened the commoners received a taste of what was to come. In spite of a heavy rain they were kept waiting for an hour before they were admitted, by a rear entrance, to the Salle des Menus Plaisirs. Spectators were excluded and a detachment of troops surrounded the hall. Necker's seat was empty, which gave rise to the rumor that he had resigned, though in fact his resignation in protest over the king's policy did not come until after the session.

The speech delivered by the king gave point to the obvious preparations that had been made to intimidate the deputies of the Third Estate. He spoke coldly, with majestic haughtiness ignoring the resolutions of June 17 and June 20. It was his royal wish to have "the ancient distinction of the three orders of the state maintained in its entirety." Subject to his approval, certain stipulated matters might be discussed in common, but constitutional questions were to be discussed separately. Having stated his policy on the disputed points, the monarch outlined the royal program of reform and indicated how far he was ready to go. All property rights without exception (signifying ecclesiastical and feudal property) were to be respected; and no change was to be made in the organization of the army. On the other hand the king promised wide and important financial powers to the Estates General, agreed to the abolition of the most obnoxious feudal and fiscal abuses, and promised equality of taxation to his subjects. He signified his readiness to grant the basic rights of personal liberty to all citizens and ordered the establishment of provincial estates throughout the realm.

Submitted to the Estates General on May 5, the king's program would undoubtedly have served as a basis for discussion. On June 23 it was outmoded since the Commons not only had gone beyond the royal program, but had taken a solemn oath to do that which the king forbade; namely, to draw up a new constitution. Consequently, his final words, an unveiled threat to dismiss the Estates General and carry out his plans alone, if the commoners would not coöperate with him, and his command for the immediate separation of the three orders thrust the decision squarely upon the deputies of the Third Estate. The nobles and most of the clergy followed Louis XVI as he left the hall, but the commoners defied him and his threats. When the master of ceremonies repeated the royal command to Bailly, the thundering voice of Mirabeau filled the hall: "Go and tell those who sent you that we are here by the will of the people, and that we will go only if we are driven at the point of the bayonet."[1] Sieyès in his cold, imperturbable fashion proposed that the Assembly pass a resolution that it adhered to all its previous declarations. The resolution was passed. On Mirabeau's plea the Assembly voted that whoever attacked the inviolability of a deputy (arrested him for what he said in the Assembly) was guilty of a treasonable act punishable by death. Now the decision lay with Louis XVI, rather than with the commoners. He could choose between crushing the rebels or yielding. For the present he chose to yield and gave an order for the withdrawal of the royal bodyguard that had invested the hall.

The Appeal to the Troops

For a few days the king acted as though he had sincerely accepted the *fait accompli*. He prevailed upon the court faction to make its peace with Necker, who withdrew his resignation and remained in office. Within the following three days the deputies of the privileged orders again began to join the commoners, and by the 26th of June a majority of the clerics and a large minority of the nobles had taken their seats in the National Assembly. On the 27th, Louis XVI recognized realities by ordering the rest of the

[1] Mirabeau's exact words are in dispute. Although there is no question of his intervention on this occasion, it is not unlikely that its importance has been exaggerated. For the accounts given by Mirabeau himself, the contemporary press, and the memoirs of the other deputies, consult Fling, *Source Book of the French Revolution*, pp. 123–148; and A. Brette, "La Séance royale du 23 juin," in *La Révolution française*, vol. XXII.

clergy and nobles to join the deputies of the Third Estate in the National Assembly. The struggle was over. The Estates General was no more; the union of the three classes in a genuine representative assembly of the nation was complete. In these new circumstances the Assembly settled down to its task of regenerating the government and society of France. On July 8, it appointed a committee on constitutional procedure, and on the morrow it assumed the name by which it was subsequently known, the National Constituent Assembly. With the loyal support of the king it would give France the new constitution that the nation desired.

Louis XVI's surrender to the rebellious commoners was more apparent than real. Yielding again to the conservative court faction, he determined to use force against the Assembly and restore the ancient order. He secretly called upon the soldiery, summoning to his aid seventeen regiments, totaling twenty thousand men, most of whom were Swiss and German mercenaries, ostensibly to protect life and property against the threatening crowds that gathered in Paris. The menace of the Parisian mob was only a pretext, for, turbulent as the populace was, it contemplated no outbreak against the government. The foreign mercenary troops were called because the regular troops of the government could not be relied upon to support repression. The French Guard, the most disciplined body of soldiers in France, was in mutiny, refusing to use arms against the demonstrators and shouting, "We are the soldiers of the nation! Long live the Third Estate!" The royal plan was ingenious. If the deputies permitted the troops to surround Versailles and Paris, the dissolution of the Assembly would be comparatively simple; if on the other hand they should protest, the king could denounce their action as an incitation to mob violence in Paris and direct the troops all the more legitimately against them. By the beginning of July the preparations for the royal coup d'état against the Assembly were well under way.

The troops, summoned from the frontiers and the provincial cities of the interior, began to arrive early in July. They were stationed before the royal palace at Versailles and along the road between Versailles and Paris. A smaller detachment was encamped in the Champ-de-Mars at Paris. The news of their coming threw the populace of Paris into consternation. All sorts of disquieting rumors circulated, predicting the arrest of prominent deputies and the dissolution of the Assembly. The peace was disturbed not only

PLAN OF PARIS
IN 1789

Scale of Miles
0   1/8   1/4   1/2

KEY TO NUMBERS

1 The Madeleine	7 The Feuillants	13 Châtelet	19 Place du Dauphin	25 The Carmelites
2 The Capuchins	8 St Roch	14 Hôtel de Ville	20 St.Germain des Prés	26 Odéon
3 St. Lazare	9 Palais Royal	15 Place de Grève	21 Conciergerie	27 The Sorbonne
4 Filles St.Thomas	10 The Tuileries	16 La Force	22 Notre-Dame	28 Ste. Geneviève
5 Bibliothèque	11 Halles	17 La Charité	23 Hôtel Dieu	29 Val de Grâce
6 The Jacobins	12 Soubise	18 Collège Mazarin	24 Archevêché	30 The Cordeliers

by redoubtable rumors but by bands of beggars and criminals who flocked into Paris from the country and other cities, driven there by hunger and the hope of plunder. Paris, at its quietest, was a turbulent city, prone to mob violence and sporadic outbreaks against the constituted authorities. Now its narrow crooked streets surged with excited and suspicious crowds of men and women. There were desperate figures among them, men who were contemptuous of the police and ready for any action that would bring them food and shelter; and there were patriotic enthusiasts, eager reformers, and fiery demagogues whose spirits had been inflamed by revolutionary journalism and the gripping events of the past few months. To such men came the news that the king had summoned his troops against the Assembly and Paris.

In the disorder the municipal authorities were powerless, so long as the French Guard fraternized with the newcomers to Paris and the unemployed masses of the city. On July 8, the Assembly adopted a motion made by Mirabeau and sent a delegation to the king, protesting against the concentration of troops and demanding the formation of a bourgeois guard to preserve order. Among the members of the delegation was a young lawyer from Arras, a certain Maximilien Robespierre, whose name was to loom large across the pages of the Revolution. The king's reply was a disingenuous proposal that the Assembly hold its meeting at some other city (farther from Paris), if the deputies feared the presence of troops which he had summoned to maintain order. But the Assembly refused to move and renewed its protests. On July 11, Louis showed his hand. He dismissed Necker and other liberal ministers, whose presence at the royal council thwarted the plans of the court faction, and ordered Necker to leave the country without further delay. He then formed a new ministry, composed of pronounced conservatives, Foulon, Breteuil, and Marshal de Broglie. His act was a formal challenge to the revolutionists, for there could no longer be any question of his ultimate intentions.

The destiny of the Revolution lay in the hands of the Parisians; and in Paris the center of revolutionary agitation was the Palais Royal. The police could not patrol it because it belonged to the duke of Orléans. Around the inner gardens, which were more than two hundred yards in length and a hundred in width, ran a vast framework of edifices housing sumptuous cafés, luxurious shops, bookstores and innumerable gambling dens. The space before the street level of the buildings, which was sheltered against sun and rain, furnished a covered gallery-promenade for the throngs of curiosity seekers, patriotic agitators, unemployed, and lawless vagrants from the rural districts who swarmed all over the enclosed gardens. There the Parisian crowds had brought the "soldier patriots" (the French Guard) when they liberated the soldiers of this mutinous regiment. There the French Guard and thousands of petty bourgeois sat around the café tables or trod the paths that ran through the gardens, discussing revolutionary politics and commenting noisily on the latest news from Versailles. There too, on the 12th of July, came the first report of the dismissal of Necker, confirming the disquieting rumors of the past week.

The excitement in the Palais Royal became feverish when one of the fiery revolutionary journalists of Paris, Camille Desmoulins, leaped upon a table and passionately denounced the impending massacre of patriots. "There is not a moment to lose," he exclaimed; "we have only one course of action—to rush to arms . . ." The crowd rushed out, paraded the streets, Camille at the head, wearing green cockades (the color of Necker's liveries) and carrying the busts of Necker and the duke of Orléans in triumph before them. Later in the day the marchers clashed with a regiment of foreign cavalry, the Royal-German, at the Tuileries Gardens. The demonstrators sustained only insignificant physical injuries but suffered an emotional shock sufficient to provoke them to search for weapons and ammunition. From shop to shop the swelling crowd scurried in quest of arms, its ranks increased by many lawless recruits and by the French Guard, who hastily quit their barracks to join the rioters. Besenval, the commander of the royal troops, was extremely loath to use force against the demonstrators, and kept his men well within the limits of the Champ-de-Mars. The mob was unchecked all through the night of July 12, breaking into shops and pilfering, arms by preference but anything else that was available.

At this juncture the electors of Paris intervened to protect life and property against the lawless rioters, as well as to prevent the massacre of patriots which they imagined the mercenary royal troops were contemplating. After the election of the deputies of the Third Estate had ended, the electors returned to their homes; but they reorganized later in the sixty electoral districts of the city and petitioned the Assembly to form a civic guard to maintain order. On the 13th the electors assumed control of the situation and improvised a provisional municipal government. They named Flesselles, the provost of the merchants, chairman, and ordered the formation of a "civic militia," or bourgeois guard, to maintain order in the city. Within a few hours the volunteer force, which included nobles, financiers, merchants, and even priests, was organized. It patrolled the city, with the help of the French Guard preserving comparative order during the day and far into the night of July 13.

THE FALL OF THE BASTILLE

In the early morning of July 14, while the tocsin at the Hôtel de Ville summoned the volunteers to their task, the mob was roaming restlessly about the city, desperately intent upon getting arms. The news came that there were plenty at the Hôtel des Invalides and at the Bastille. Part of the mob stormed the Invalides and carried out great quantities of muskets and shot, while another group made its way to the eastern part of the city and surrounded the Bastille. The citizen guard of volunteers had also gathered before its walls during the forenoon, equally anxious to procure arms.

Originally a fortress outside the city walls, the gray rock of the Bastille with its walls ten feet thick and its towers more than ninety feet high then lay in the heart of the workingmen's section and was used as a state prison. Many horrifying stories were told about it, tales of vaults and dungeons deep in the earth, of prisoners doomed for years to maddening darkness, of cruel tortures and agonizing deaths. The stories were largely false, but the Parisians believed them; and in the eyes of all liberty-loving people in Europe the Bastille was the hateful symbol of despotism and oppression.

The governor of the Bastille, De Launay, was not unprepared for the mob. His garrison was ready, and the cannon were in place. Two drawbridges and the outer and inner courts separated the fortress from the milling crowd without. It seemed safe against attack. For hours the attack did not come, though the crowd in the streets before the Bastille grew thicker and more menacing. When it came, the attack was a terrible accident. De Launay had just rejected a petition demanding arms for the volunteer civic militia; but he had also given assurances that the cannon would not be used against the crowd unless he were attacked. To allow the deputation to leave, the drawbridge over the moat had been lowered, and a feverish throng poured over it until they stood under the very walls of the fortress. The drawbridge was then raised behind them, and from within the Bastille shots were fired upon the unarmed people.

Then the siege began. Despite the fury of the assailants, who dragged cannon through the streets of Paris, despite the valor of the experienced French Guard who directed operations, the Bastille might have held out for many hours. But the garrison grew mutinous and De Launay lowered the drawbridge of the fortress admitting the mob. The officers of the French Guard had granted De Launay and his men an honorable capitulation, but the promise could not be kept, for the besiegers were not to be restrained. Maddened by the losses in their own ranks and infuriated by what they regarded the governor's treachery in luring them into the inner court, they fell upon De Launay and the Swiss garrison and killed them. The sickening slaughter and the mutilation of the bodies were the deeds of an unleashed mob that was beyond the control of justice and mercy; but they were the deeds of a people whom an oppressive government had rendered callous to cruel violence and brutality. The verdict of posterity strongly condemns their actions, but many of their contemporaries everywhere in France and Europe rejoiced that they had stormed the stronghold of repression.

The royal plot against the Assembly had completely miscarried. Though the anxious Parisians still expected a movement of the troops, Louis XVI conceded the victory of the people. On the 15th he came before the Assembly to report that he had ordered the royal troops to leave Versailles, and on the following day he recalled Necker to the ministry. His advisers urged him to flee from France, but he had more courage than they. He recognized the new municipal government of Paris, and he went in person to give his sanction to its proceedings. With him went a deputation from the National Assembly and a detachment of the citizen militia of Paris, now renamed the National Guard. He recognized Bailly as the mayor of Paris and Lafayette as commander of the National Guard. In testimony of his good faith he put on his hat the red, white, and blue cockade which Bailly gave him. By this gesture he accepted the events that had occurred, for if the white of the tricolor was the color of the Bourbons, the blue and the red were the colors of Paris.

Louis XVI might accept the Revolution, but the count of Artois, some of the court nobles, and other partisans of the Old Régime fled their country, disgusted and indignant over what they deemed the monarch's cowardice. Theirs was the first emigration, the precursor of others. July 14, 1789, ended the royal offensive against the Revolution. The English ambassador wrote to London that France was now a free country and its king a constitutional monarch. Louis XVI retained his throne, but henceforth he was secretly on the defensive, his authority and his security troubled by each new wave of popular emotion. The people led, and he followed; they led at first through the organ of the Assembly and later through more brutal and direct intervention.

The "Great Fear"

The fall of the Bastille was not the spark that ignited the provinces of France, for the provinces were already aflame before the news reached the peasantry. The anxious quiet that had followed the spring disturbances of 1789 was shattered, *first*, not by the dramatic events of July 14, but by actual famine and the fear that all was not going well at Versailles and Paris. In the absence of definite news the peasants took their fears for realities, fear of the "aristocrats" at Versailles and fear of the "brigands" whom the nobles were suspected of sending into the rural districts to butcher the peasantry. Early in July, as soon as the spring harvest began to ripen, starving farm hands began to pillage the fields. Those whose crops were menaced feared that the worst had come, that the "aristos" had struck. Maddened by their fears, they struck back at their hereditary oppressors, the feudal lords and the stewards of the seigneur. Even before the news of the fall of the Bastille could reach them, the peasants of Franche-Comté in the east of France were in full rebellion against their feudal lords. On July 27, 1789, Arthur Young wrote, "For what the country knows to the contrary, their deputies are in the Bastille, instead of the Bastille being razed; so the mobs plunder, burn and destroy in complete ignorance."

When the news of the Bastille finally did come, the peasants redoubled their attacks, and by the end of July and the beginning of August anarchy reigned in the provinces of western and eastern France. The fear that possessed the peasants—the "Great Fear," as their terror has been called—may not have been entirely spontaneous, but one need not accept the puerile explanation made by royalist historians that this amazing psychological phenomenon was inspired by "conspirators," by the duke of Orléans, or Mirabeau, or other Freemasons. It was a many-sided phenomenon that fed on its own strength until it ultimately consumed itself. Different peasant groups feared different things: some, that royalists were planning to starve them by raising the price of grain; others, that the city dwellers were marching upon the fields to cut down the harvest, or that brigands were coming to slay them; others still, that the country nobles were plotting with the court aristocracy, or perhaps with émigré nobles, to massacre them. The news that the Bastille had fallen only accentuated the panic and the anarchy by making the fears more credible and encouraging the violence of the peasants.

The rural police were powerless to curb the anarchy, and the king could not count upon the troops of the regular army. Not until the "Great Fear" had run its course could the newly formed National Guard gain control of the situation. The first mad wave of fear gradually spent itself, when the peasants realized that there were no brigands, and that those whom they suspected of coming to attack them were their fellow peasants, similarly armed against a nonexistent foe. The fear subsided, but the violence persisted. Vagrants and desperate criminals, unemployed workers from neighboring towns, and landless farm hands sacked granaries, cut down the harvest in fields, and terrorized the countryside. Whether landed or landless, the peasants turned instinctively upon their hated oppressors.

In many cases the lords of the manor gladly surrendered the manor rolls containing the record of the peasants' feudal dues; but where the châtelain lacked the grace or sense to give them up voluntarily, the peasants used violence. If a particularly hated steward was massacred, or even if the manor house itself went up in flames, what mattered it to the peasants so long as the flames consumed the records? To a certain extent Jaurès's opinion that the peasant movement was "the violent abolition of the entire feudal system" is justified, for the peasant felt that he had been relieved of a crushing burden. His harvest was now his own (if it was not plundered), and no one dared ask him to pay his feudal dues. The proprietors of feudal land were not the sole victims of the "Great Fear," for the artisans in the towns also rose against their old oppressors, harsh judges, corrupt civil officials, money lenders, and grasping merchants. The Revolution was becoming a war of the classes.

In the meantime the provincial municipalities were responding to the stimulus of events in Paris. The townsmen had carefully followed the course of events in Paris, receiving detailed, if not always impartial, reports from their representatives in the Assembly. In certain cities, like Lyons, the bourgeoisie had not waited for the news of July 14 to form a new municipal government. Somewhat later elsewhere, but substantially in the same manner in all cities, large or small, at Bordeaux and Marseilles, at Nîmes, Valence, and Tours, the citizens ousted the old oligarchic

munipical administrations and elected new revolutionary councils
or else combined the old government with a new council. In general their first action was to follow the example of the new government in Paris and organize local divisions of the National
Guard. Indeed, these new municipalities and the local National
Guard, which soon formed regional federations for mutual protection, were the most important consequences of the capture of the
Bastille by the propertyless mob of Paris.

Before long the guardsmen were directed against the peasant
rioters. The anarchy in the country frightened the stout burghers
in the towns. It was one thing to destroy the local bastille, which
symbolized the despotic tyranny of the upper classes, but an entirely different matter to attack property itself. The bourgeois, who
possessed considerable landed property in the country, and prosperous peasant proprietors now feared that their own possessions might be seized by the pillagers. The municipalities had
troops at their disposal, and they prepared to use them—to maintain order and enforce the rights of property. First they made sure
of the loyalty of the National Guard. The soldiers took an oath of
fidelity to the nation (rather than to the king) and the officers
swore never to use their men against citizens *"except at the requisition of the civil and municipal authorities."* Thus the citizen soldiers were turned against the riotous peasantry. The undisciplined
violence of the latter was no match for the disciplined violence of
the former. The victims of the struggles between rioters and the
forces of law and order fell by hundreds. The war of the classes
had become a grim reality, at least in the country districts.

THE AUGUST FOURTH DECREES

The Constituent Assembly was busily discussing the draft of a
Declaration of Rights when the terrifying news from the provinces
interrupted its constitutional debates. Assuredly, the deputies could
not condone the terrorism that the unemployed in the cities practiced toward the bourgeois merchants. On the other hand, the reforming deputies could not defend the claims of the feudal nobility against the peasants and remain true to their principles of
civil equality. Yet feudal property was also private property, and
not a few commoners derived feudal rents from their landed estates. A committee, drawn up to consider the question, made a re-

port recommending measures of repression, without relief or even discussion of the peasants' claims. Fortunately, there were liberal nobles in the Assembly who had a keener sense of realities than the best legal minds among the bourgeois deputies. They realized that, if the Assembly adopted the report of the committee, prolonged class war would follow between the landholding classes on the one hand and the propertyless peasantry on the other—a war in which the feudal nobles would pay the costs. Better, they reasoned, to renounce with good grace what was irretrievably lost and salvage whatever was possible.

Accordingly, in the discussion at the Breton Club,[2] which had already furnished the deputies of the Commons a central meeting place outside of the assembly hall, on the evening before the report of the committee, the duke of Aiguillon, one of the greatest landowners of France, declared that on the following day, August 4, he would propose in the Assembly that all feudal rents and rights should be surrendered at once. His proposal was less generous than it sounded, for he renounced only the personal rights outright and demanded a monetary compensation for the rights pertaining to the land. There is no question that the nobility were legally entitled to an indemnity. Yet Aiguillon's proposal was both more generous and wiser than the report of the committee.

On the 4th, after the deputies had listened in consternation to the horrible facts reported by the investigating committee, Aiguillon made ready to take the floor, but the viscount de Noailles, the impoverished cadet of an illustrious family, rose first and made the proposal that Aiguillon would have made. Though Noailles had nothing of his own to give up, Aiguillon heartily seconded the motion in a touching description of the peasants' condition. "The people are trying to shake off a yoke which has been over their heads for centuries," he said, "and we must confess that this insurrection, illegal as it is (for all violent aggression is), can find its legitimate excuse in the grievances of which it is the victim." The motion carried, after a brief discussion, and a frenzy of sacrifice overwhelmed the Assembly.

In an indescribable and sustained movement of interested and disinterested self-sacrifice, deputy after deputy arose to renounce his special rights and privileges on the altar of his country; the

<hr />

[2] The Breton Club was, as its name signifies, an association composed originally of deputies from Brittany; but many deputies from other provinces soon joined it.

nobles, their hunting, fishing, and pigeon rights, and their detested judicial rights over their tenants as well; the clergy, their tithes; the wealthy bourgeois, their individual exemptions; the cities and provinces, their antique customs and privileges. During that long night of August 4 France of the Old Régime came to an end, and a new France was born with the dawn. Henceforth all Frenchmen would be citizens, subject to one law, paying the same taxes, and eligible to all offices. In their joy the deputies decided to proclaim Louis XVI "the Restorer of French liberty."

A cynical explanation of the night of August 4 denies all motives of generosity to the deputies. Contemporaries, as well as later historians, have endeavored to prove that the deputies surrendered what was already lost and, surrendering, sought to be well paid for their gesture.[3] Yet, calculated as the renunciations undoubtedly were, the enthusiastic spirit displayed was genuine. The deputies of the privileged orders found in Aiguillon's proposal a formula to calm the peasantry, end the disorders, and save their own rights at the cost of their privileges. The infectious enthusiasm for self-sacrifice that swept the Assembly made them renounce more than they had intended, but the difference was one of degree rather than of kind.

A week later, the definite decree concerning the abolition of these abuses and privileges was passed and presented to Louis XVI for his sanction. The modification of the original version was conservative; "reactionary," in Mathiez's opinion. The hunting and fishing rights of the nobility disappeared. Serfdom and all dues which represented it were abolished without indemnity, but all *real* or land dues were to be redeemed in a manner that would be prescribed later. Ecclesiastical tithes were abolished outright without indemnity, but it was deemed necessary, by prescribing a mode of money payments for subinfeudated tithes[4] and certain feudal rights, to safeguard the financial interests of the lay owners of those tithes as well as of the poorer nobles. Until the subinfeudated tithes and the feudal rights had been redeemed, ruled the final decree, they were to be paid. Other church dues were also abolished on the understanding that the state would consider other ways of

[3] The *Mémoires* of Barère show that the more foresighted nobles realized the value of making the gesture of voluntary renunciation before their hand was forced by the commoners. Cf. *Mémoires de Barère*, I, 269.

[4] Subinfeudated tithes were those which had been farmed out to the highest bidders. They represented a private financial investment.

maintaining the clergy and providing for the expenses of worship. The payment of annates to the papacy was forbidden. All positions in the church, the administration, and the army were thrown open to the citizens. The administration of justice was to be free, and the sale of offices prohibited. A new system of justice was promised. The interests of workingmen in the towns were neglected, for the guilds were perpetuated. On the whole the August decrees outlined a comprehensive program of social, economic, and religious reforms. To realize this program was the task of the deputies. In theory they had destroyed the régime of privilege and instituted a régime of social and civic equality; but in theory only, for the beneficiaries of the régime which was ended obstructed the work of reconstruction, while those who received no benefits or insufficient benefits under the new program clamored for still more sweeping reforms.

VI. THE ORGANIZATION OF REVOLUTIONARY FORCES

THE SECOND APPEAL TO THE TROOPS

WHILE the provinces remained turbulent, comparative quiet descended upon Paris and Versailles. The National Constituent Assembly resumed its interrupted debates on the Declaration of Rights,[1] which was voted on August 27, despite the sharp discussion as to whether it should precede or follow the constitution. It was the death certificate of the Old Régime, but it contained the promise of a new life for France. Based upon the commonplaces of eighteenth century philosophy and universal in its application, it represented a thorough indictment of the old order and a statement of the general principles upon which the new was to be built.

The division of the deputies into loose groups, or political parties, became more distinct in the course of the debates on the constitution. This was a new feature in French political life—the divergence of political parties, conservatives on the Right (that is, on the right of the presiding officer's table), moderates in the Center, and progressives and radicals on the Left. The sharpest discussion concerned the future relations of the executive and legislative divisions of the constitutional government which the deputies of the Constituent Assembly would establish by their labors. The first constitutional committee proposed that a bicameral legislature be established, that the right of absolute veto over the deliberations of the two chambers be given to the king, as well as the right to dissolve the legislature. On this question the Left split up temporarily into two large groups: the Anglophiles, whose leading spokesman in the Assembly was Jean-Joseph Mounier, of the committee, and the Patriots, whose leaders were Lafayette and Barnave. The first group supported the committee's proposal, for their ideal of government was the English parliamentary system. They hesitated to give too much power to untried representatives,

[1] The full title of the measure is the Declaration of the Rights of Man and of the Citizen. For the discussion of the Declaration, cf. pp. 142–148.

fearing for the political stability of the state and fearing also that the pressure of the discontented people might force those inexperienced deputies to take discriminatory measures against private property. The other group, the Patriots, opposed the recommendations of the committee on the ground that it gave excessive and dangerous powers to the monarch and the aristocracy of birth. Above all they feared the absolute veto, and their fears seemed substantiated when it became known that the king had criticized the August decrees and was withholding his sanction of them. Popular agitators exaggerated his action and led the impressionable and suspicious populace of Paris to feel that the absolute veto was a veritable bogy.

When the constitutional proposals came to a vote, the motion for the upper house was rejected on September 10 by an enormous majority of some 800 votes; and the deputies voted to establish a unicameral legislature. On the following day the Assembly voted the king a suspensive and not an absolute veto [2] which gave him the right to suspend the execution of the laws, though not to refuse them outright. The motives of the different groups furnish an explanation of the voting. The parish priests and the lesser provincial nobles voted against the upper house and the absolute veto because they shared the misgivings of the Patriots. They were not minded to perpetuate the power of the great prelates and the court nobility. The extreme Right opposed the first conservative recommendation of the committee because it seemed likely to succeed. By voting it down, and supporting the proposal which they judged thoroughly unworkable, the more extreme conservatives hoped to bring on new disorders which in turn might lead to a reaction and give them an opportunity to regain their lost prerogatives. Mirabeau, who had at first supported the committee's proposals, reversed his position and voted for the suspensive veto, hoping that his support would gain him a position in the ministry. In reality, there was no difference between a suspensive and an absolute veto, for the suspensive veto delayed a law so long as to be practically equivalent to an absolute veto; but the point was certainly not appreciated outside of the Assembly, and perhaps not by the deputies themselves. At any rate the masses were convinced

[2] After a short debate the deputies voted on September 21 that the veto might continue during the sessions of two legislatures, but it was to "cease at the second legislature following the one which shall have proposed the law."

that an absolute veto meant the restoration of the ancient order of things.

After the debates had ended, Louis XVI signified his willingness to sanction the August decrees, but he utilized pretext after pretext to avoid accepting the Declaration, the unicameral legislature, and the suspensive veto.[3] He fully understood his position, being aware that in deferring the ratification of these measures he could count upon the support of a great many deputies who firmly believed that the National Assembly could not "give the force of law to its decrees without the royal sanction." The Patriots maintained that the monarch had no right to refuse his sanction to the constitutional decrees. Mirabeau declared that the royal veto could not "be exercised when the creation of a constitution is at stake"; and Sieyès denied that the royal sanction was even required, holding that the monarchy existed by virtue of the constitution. This was the view held by the new constitutional committee which was appointed after the resignation of Mounier and his colleagues in the first committtee (September 18). The more moderate deputies and the court faction appealed to Louis XVI to call out his troops, while the more determined deputies of the Left realized that it was to their advantage to have the king and the Assembly in Paris. Again, as in July, Louis XVI followed false counsel. On September 14 he ordered the Flanders Regiment to march to Versailles, and once more foreign uniforms were seen on the streets of Versailles and Paris.

In this crisis the Patriots turned again to Paris for aid; and the Paris to which they appealed was again in ferment. The first emigration and the unsettled political conditions had reacted unfavorably upon business. Thousands of unemployed artisans, idle valets and lackeys, grumbling retail merchants, and petty tradesmen whose livelihood had been ruined by the depression crowded the streets. Bread was scarce, speculators active and food prices rising. Hungry mobs of men and women began anew to sack the bakeries. The radical press and stentorian agitators harangued the populace, thrusting the blame for hard times upon the court nobles and other "aristos," and interpreting Louis XVI's refusal to sanction the con-

---

[3] In a formal letter to the Assembly he wrote: "I approve the general spirit of your decrees [the feudal] and the greater number of articles in their entirety. . . . I have no doubt whatever that I can, with perfect justice, invest with my sanction all the laws that you will pass on the different subjects contained in your decrees."

stitutional decrees as evidence of evil intent against the revolutionary cause. The inevitable consequence of this temper was apparent to Mirabeau, who prophesied that both the king and the queen would meet violent deaths if they persisted in their unfortunate tactics. Louis XVI could not bring himself to accept realities. He took advantage of the agitation in Paris to summon the troops, ostensibly to protect the Assembly against the Paris multitude. The move was most unfortunate, for it seemed to confirm the worst suspicions of the Patriots and the Parisians; and it furnished excellent pretexts to various intriguers who sought to profit from the disorders in the city by urging the crowds to violent action. Some of these worked in the interests of the duke of Orléans, who hoped to be named regent in place of Louis XVI; and it is probable that Mirabeau was involved in this scheme. Others tried to organize a counter-revolutionary movement. Still others saw an opportunity for radical measures. In this turmoil the municipal authorities were helpless. The cure for the disorder lay with the king, but his determination to use the soldiery served not to quiet but to aggravate the disorder.

THE "OCTOBER DAYS"

Presently the Flanders Regiment which the king had summoned entered Versailles. On October 1, at a banquet tendered to its officers by the royal bodyguard, an impromptu demonstration of loyalty to the royal family terminated the evening. Stimulated by the good cheer, the guests drank toasts to the royal couple and trampled the national cockade underfoot, while deliberately omitting toasts to the nation.

Paris received the news of that "act of imprudence" on the 3rd of October. The newspapers raised a terrific din of denunciation. The districts, led by two popular agitators, Jean-Paul Marat and Jacques Danton, urged all good men to march on Versailles and bring the king back to Paris. Danton's district appealed to the municipality to send Lafayette to Versailles and demand the recall of the military. On the 4th, the surging crowd in the Palais Royal threatened violent action against the nation's enemies. Thus prepared and organized, the October rebellion needed only a spark to set it off.

Early the next morning after a disturbance at a baker's shop a crowd of women set out for the Hôtel de Ville of Paris to demand bread from the authorities. En route they were joined by the market women, strong-voiced and something less than gentle in their ways. They failed to obtain bread at the Hôtel de Ville, but it afforded them some satisfaction to ransack the building. Presently Maillard, one of the heroes of the capture of the Bastille, gained their confidence, checked their ardor for destruction, and led them off to Versailles. Recruits swelled their ranks all the way to Versailles, but Maillard kept the fiercer of the viragoes in check. A few hours after their departure Lafayette reluctantly sought and obtained permission from the municipality to follow them with the National Guard of Paris. He confessed that he was afraid that the tide would turn in Orléans's favor unless he directed it himself. His conduct during this crisis was characterized by a caution that bordered either on timidity or on conspiracy. There is no doubt that had he not, also, wished the king brought to Paris, he could have taken more energetic steps to inform Versailles of the coming of the mob, or else to prevent the mob's departure from Paris.

On learning of these occurrences Mirabeau attempted to have the session of the Assembly suspended. But the deputies had, that very forenoon, received a temporizing reply from the king on the constitutional measures and they were heatedly discussing the next step to take. When the women arrived, they had already decided to send Mounier at the head of a delegation to the palace and demand an immediate acceptance of the decrees; but on hearing Maillard's complaint about the scarcity of food and the activity of speculators in Paris they decided to present the women's protests with their own demands and appointed a delegation which left late in the afternoon. Meantime the deputies continued their session. Despite constant interruptions from the steadily increasing number of women whom the rain had forced indoors, they remained patient and good-humored under the strain.

Soon the greater part of the mob assembled before the palace, which was defended by the royal bodyguard. Louis XVI, himself, had been hunting, but on his return he received a number of the women and promised them, in writing, that Paris would be provisioned against famine. Confronted by Mounier's delegation, he was most irresolute. At first he contemplated flight rather than surrender to mob pressure; but on second thought he abandoned the idea of flight as savoring of fear and, toward eight o'clock that evening, announced to the delegation from the Assembly that he gave his sanction to the decrees. Toward midnight Lafayette with thousands of troops, composed of National Guardsmen of Paris and volunteers, arrived at the palace. After Lafayette's arrival, which served to end the strain between the royal bodyguard and the National Guard of Versailles, quiet descended upon the palace.

Lafayette had taken precautions to guard the palace, but not in sufficient measure. Whether this negligence was due to a false sense of security or to a desire to force the king's hand is uncertain. In the morning some of the more venturesome of the crowd found an unguarded entrance and began to look about. One of the royal guardsmen fired at the intruders. These rose in wrath, forced their way into the inner rooms and dispatched two of the defenders, giving Marie Antoinette barely time to escape into the king's apartments. Several members of the mob were also killed in the fighting. In order to end the mêlée the entire royal family, the king, the queen, and the dauphin, agreed to show themselves to the crowd. Accompanied by Lafayette, they stood out on the balcony of the court. There were loud shouts for Louis XVI, and a few mild cheers for Marie Antoinette, but louder than any other cry was the one: "On to Paris!" At length the king agreed to go, to the great joy of the crowd. That same evening (October 6), after a long noisy journey, the royal family, which had been accompanied by the troops and the delegations from the Assembly, reached the Hôtel de Ville at Paris. At ten o'clock Louis XVI and his family arrived at the Louvre in the Tuileries, his destination and his future home. Ten days later, the Assembly followed him to Paris.

"The baker," "the baker's wife," and the "baker's boy"—as the Parisians, half derisively, half gratefully called the royal family— were now in Paris, safe (the Parisians believed) from their evil advisers; but for all that, bread did not immediately become plentiful in the city. A full month elapsed before Paris saw the last of the long lines of women standing in wait at the bakers' shops. Workers were idle as before and disorders were still common. Therefore the first act of the municipal administration was to restore the semblance of order.

Lafayette, "the hero of two worlds," as his opponents ironically called him, undertook the task of curbing the danger of anarchy. This gave him an opportunity to make capital of the insurrection (which openly, at least, he had opposed) and to advertise his indispensability to the king. The day following the arrival of Louis XVI in Paris, he secretly organized a demonstration in favor of the royal family. He also put pressure on the press to disavow the violence of the preceding days and had Marat condemned by a high criminal court. Though an official inquiry into the insurrection failed to inculpate either Mirabeau or Orléans, Lafayette managed to convince the latter that a brief absence from Paris would be salutary. The duke left for London, ostensibly on a diplomatic mission. As for Mirabeau, his influence was temporarily effaced. The inexcusable hanging of a hapless baker gave the Assembly an opportunity to make provision for martial law against unruly gatherings, and thus order was temporarily restored.

A second emigration followed on the heels of the mob's victory over the king. Mounier, fearing further violence, resigned the presidency of the Assembly and betook himself to Dauphiné, but failing to stir up opposition against the Assembly he emigrated. Lally-Tollendal, prominent among the Moderates, also endeavored to arouse sentiment against the Assembly, but he too had little success. Soon a small group of disillusioned liberals, men who had been instrumental in summoning the Estates General and in denouncing royal despotism, fled their country. The National Assembly had won a great victory, though largely because the masses had come to its aid. Blood had been shed, and the émigrés carried their woes and complaints beyond the frontiers to a Europe that gave heed to their recriminations. For those disciples of Montesquieu and of a limited, constitutional monarchy the Revolution was advancing too rapidly. Those who remained, the Monarchists, or Impartials as they were now called, constituted only a small group in the Assembly, whose influence dwindled steadily until it became negligible. Now that his foremost rivals—Orléans, Mirabeau, and Mounier—were out of the way, Lafayette had his opportunity to guide the Revolution on its course. In a memorandum addressed to Louis XVI he outlined his plans and appealed for the monarch's full confidence.

THE ORGANIZATION OF THE ASSEMBLY

With tranquillity somewhat restored, the Assembly settled down in earnest to the stupendous task before it, the reconstruction of France. In this work a beginning had already been made. The

August decrees, it was hoped, would destroy feudalism; and the Declaration of Rights and the September decrees had laid the foundations of a constitution. Much remained to be done. Before turning to the accomplishments of the National Constituent Assembly let us first examine in some detail the composition of the Assembly and the organization of the revolutionary forces outside of it which enabled the deputies to bring their efforts to a successful conclusion in September, 1791.

The deputies held their meetings from November, 1789, in a long, narrow building that abutted on the terrace of the Feuillants in the gardens of the Tuileries. Their seats were arranged in tiers in the form of an amphitheater, while near one end of the long riding school (the *Manège*) in which they met was the raised box of the president. The platform of the orators' tribune was opposite it, and the galleries ran all around the hall. Their sessions were open to the public, which permitted excitable or ill-intentioned spectators to interfere frequently in the debates. Yet at all times the deputies expressed themselves freely, and perhaps too freely if the comments of foreign observers at the meetings can be taken at their face value. Ordinarily the galleries contained partisan but well behaved people, whether of the bourgeoisie or of the aristocracy, but after the king's flight in 1791 a rougher element took possession of the galleries and intimidated the deputies with its noise and its threats. Every fortnight a new president was chosen. To facilitate business most of the proposals were prepared in committees, of which there were thirty-one in the Assembly, and presented to the Assembly by the *rapporteur*. Discussions took heated turns, and the uproar frequently kept the deputies from being heard, but the Assembly methodically continued its work.

The difficulties were staggering. While Lafayette's firmness immediately after the October "revolution" prevented the recurrence of violence in Paris, it could not effectively check the more insistent pressure of public and private opinion. Revolutionary sentiment and sentiment opposed to the Revolution were noisily expressed in the Assembly and without. Petitions and demonstrations, threats and incitations to violence, fiery editorials in the newspapers constantly reminded the deputies of the grave responsibilities that rested upon their shoulders. Neither Louis XVI nor his ministers made any efforts to help. They "shammed dead," as one of the deputies observed.

The Assembly had to destroy at the same time that it created. In theory the institutions of the past had been wiped away by the various decrees of the summer; in reality they clung tenaciously to life. It took time to ring out the old and ring in the new. On the one hand the parlements, various subordinate officials, and individual members of the nobility and the clergy strove fiercely to maintain the old order of things. On the other hand the masses took it for granted that the régime of the future had already been established and refused to obey the old royal officials. Many peasants refused to pay taxes and feudal dues. The new communes and the local detachments of the National Guard prevented a complete relapse into anarchy, but they could not prevent the appalling confusion, especially in the rural districts where the peasantry sought to take matters into their own hands. Fortunately for the Assembly, the harvests of 1789 and 1790 were good and the peasants continued in the main to support the deputies. For some time these were free to carry on their work unimpeded, but their accomplishments were compromised in advance because the Assembly was divided against itself.

Parties, in our sense, did not exist. There were no party organizations with officers, official programs, and party funds. The deputies prided themselves on their independence and their individuality. They followed "the promptings of their heart," made alliances that were only shifting and temporary and dictated by the issue at stake. In general, by November, 1789, the Assembly was divided into three large groups or parties whose members voted together and belonged to the same revolutionary clubs. We have noticed that in the very beginning there had been only two groups—those who opposed the Revolution and the Patriots who supported it. But the events of the summer of 1789 broke up the solidarity of the latter and divided them into several groups. On the right of the president's box were the conservatives, the party of the upper clergy and the great nobles who, out of sincere opposition to reforms, systematically obstructed the Assembly's work. The more extreme leaders of that aristocratic faction were D'Esprémesnil and Mirabeau-Tonneau,[4] the younger brother of the great revolutionary orator, whose favorite tactics were to filibuster and rouse a tumult in the Assembly. A more determined foe than

---

[4] *Tonneau*, or barrel, was an uncomplimentary reference to his form or perhaps a flattering characterization of his drinking prowess.

the younger Mirabeau was the ambitious and courageous Abbé Maury, a popular preacher and a capable orator, though facile and shallow in his judgments. Cazalès, a chivalrous officer of dragoons under the Old Régime and the greatest orator of the Right, also distinguished himself at first by his clear and vigorous speeches, but as time went on he drew nearer the Left in his sympathies.

Next to these conservatives were the Monarchists or the Impartials, about forty in number and now led by the count of Clermont-Tonnerre and Malouet, a former royal intendant under the Old Régime. They sat in the center, but their views were more conservative. They pleaded a hopeless cause, as circumstances had made their dream of a liberal, constitutional monarchy on the English model impossible of attainment.

The great majority of deputies sat with the Left. With the Left-Center were all the moderates of the Assembly, the Constitutionalists, as they were called on account of the fact that they were largely responsible for the new constitution. Among them, the lawyers Target, Tronchet, and Merlin de Douai became the most conspicuous figures in the debates on the constitution. They also had the services of Sieyès—the "prophet Mohammed"—who was distant and aloof in manner and without talent as an orator, but very influential despite those characteristics, especially in committee work. Among them also were several liberal clerics, such as Talleyrand de Périgord, bishop of Autun and a scheming, unscrupulous aristocrat of great ability, and the Abbé Grégoire, a humanitarian ecclesiastic whose Christian piety often forsook him in the heat of discussion. The affable and ambitious young lawyer, Barère de Vieuzac, a good speaker and an indefatigable worker, was with them; and a number of court nobles of liberal convictions, such as the duke of La Rochefoucauld-Liancourt and the aspiring but irresolute Lafayette.

On the farther left, a little group of young men sat together. They were bound by mutual attraction and by political views, and all wanted to "plow deep" while they had a chance. They were known as the Triumvirate, since they were three in number. One was the young lawyer Barnave, surpassed only by Mirabeau as an orator in the Assembly, a clear-headed person of great sincerity; another was Adrien Duport, a famous jurist of great capacity and brilliance; and the third was the energetic and amiable young noble Charles de Lameth, a veteran, like Lafayette, of the American War of Independence. There was a slogan that "what Duport thinks, Lameth does, and Barnave says." Alexander de Lameth, the brother of Charles, a good tactician and an authority on military affairs, was also closely associated with the Triumvirate. Finally, there was the Extreme Left, linked with these three men in the early days of the Constituent Assembly but destined to break sharply with them later. Two future members of the Girondin group voted with these radical deputies, Pétion, a solemn and somewhat conceited lawyer from Chartres, and Buzot, a temperamental and eloquent Norman. There too belonged the young lawyer of Arras, Maximilien Robespierre. He was somewhat timid at first and unwilling to alienate the more famous leaders, but his confidence and his resourcefulness in debate developed rapidly. Before the Assembly had ended its session, the neat, spectacled Robespierre commanded attention, if not always respect, whenever he took the floor. He had much to learn in the art of public speaking and dealing with men, but his unflinching advocacy of what he considered the popular cause and his undoubted sincerity received recognition, more fully it is true in the Jacobin Club than in the Assembly.

Above all others loomed Mirabeau. His reputation was formed long before 1789, but it was not of a nature to inspire the trust of his fellow deputies, who admired him but could not respect him. He set out to win their confidence, in spite of his turbulent past, in spite of his notorious immorality and venality. We shall find him in every debate—on the constitution, the clergy, finances, foreign policy, social reform. What he had no time or inclination to prepare himself, he inspired his collaborators and lieutenants to prepare for him. He was never ill informed; his words always rang with authority. As a debater he was unsurpassed in the entire Revolution. More than once he turned a hostile demonstration into a personal ovation. Whether he read a speech that some one had prepared for him or improvised one of his brilliant flights, he commanded silence and attention. At first he was perhaps the only deputy who ventured to speak without a prepared manuscript; only later did others attempt to make impromptu speeches and commence real debates. Up to the time of his death the whole course of the Constituent Assembly could be traced through his speeches. He opposed royal despotism, but he advocated a strong monarchy. He described himself in his first note to the king as "the defender of a monarchy limited by law and the apostle of liberty guaranteed by a monarchy."

Revolutionary Forces Outside the Assembly

Such was the Assembly, composed of the most distinguished men of France, but men inexperienced in public deliberation. Outside the Assembly were the various revolutionary forces that made its success inevitable. Of these the new municipal administrations and the National Guard that came into being after the fall of the Bastille were perhaps the most powerful. With a few unimportant exceptions they recruited their strength from the bourgeoisie. Lawyers, physicians, men of letters, well-to-do merchants, rich industrialists—the very cream of the liberal forces that had initiated the Revolution—sat in the town halls and filled the ranks of the militia.

In addition to these, the revolutionary clubs and newspapers molded popular opinion in favor of the new administration, though occasionally they presented demands that the Assembly found too radical. Among the clubs the Jacobins with their numerous branches in the provinces dominated all rivals. Officially they were known as the Society of Friends of the Constitution, but they had their more famous name thrust upon them from the fact that their meetings were held in the former convent of the Jacobins, which was only a stone's throw from the Manège where the Assembly met.[5] At first only prominent deputies of the Left were members, but early in 1790 the doors of the club were opened to non-deputies as well, until the membership rose to more than a thousand. Later still, when the public was admitted to its galleries, it was not uncommon to see as many as two thousand spectators at the meetings. Soon there arose clubs in the provincial towns; and, commencing in 1790, these grew in number to more than four hundred in 1791.

The "Mother Society" at Paris held the affiliated clubs well in hand. The Jacobins of Paris corresponded with the Jacobins in the provinces; struck off pamphlets for their benefit by thousands and distributed them, made recommendations, and received petitions.

---

[5] While the Assembly was still at Versailles, the deputies from Brittany had formed the Breton Club, with which many of the Patriots, deputies from other provinces, were soon associated. After the "October days," the club held its sessions in Paris.

Delegations flocked to the doors to extend felicitations or present demands, which the society passed or refused to pass on to the Assembly. In this way the club became the nucleus of the militant and enlightened bourgeoisie. In 1789 and 1790 and in the first months of 1791 the Jacobins followed a moderate, conciliatory policy. They were still debating clubs with parliamentary organization and parliamentary ambitions. Their essential purpose was to keep a vigilant eye on the Assembly and to prepare the country for the sweeping reforms that were being made. Their usurpation of legal authority came later, and with it the tendency of committees within each club to assume control of activities. In 1791 the Jacobins of Paris were unquestionably the strongest and best organized force outside of the Assembly, but much of their influence was due to the fact that the deputies who belonged to the club agreed beforehand on their action when a project was brought forward in the Assembly.

For the petty bourgeoisie, the workers and peasants, there existed other societies where initiation fees and dues were cheaper. Among those the most active was the Society of Friends of the Rights of Man and of the Citizen, or more popularly, the Cordelier Club, so called because, like the Jacobins, the members met in an abandoned convent, the convent of the Cordeliers. The Cordelier Club was opened in the spring of 1790. Marat, Danton, Camille Desmoulins, Hébert, Momoro, Fabre d'Eglantine, all of whom came to prominence in 1793, were the leading spokesmen at its crowded meetings. Here one found more spontaneity and less deliberation; no prudent lawyers but impulsive, violent agitators. Of the less influential revolutionary groups, there was the Abbé Fauchet's *Cercle social*, a Masonic-socialistic organization, which had the services of the newspaper *La Bouche de fer*, and Brissot's circle, *Les Amis des noirs*, which advocated freedom and suffrage for the negroes in the French colonies.

But there were also clubs whose members shared less friendly sentiments toward the progress of the revolutionary cause. The *Société de 1789* recruited its members from the more moderate Jacobins, who followed the inspiration of Lafayette, and whose views were expressed in Condorcet's *Journal de la Société de 1789*. The most reactionary club was the group which met under the joint leadership of Mirabeau-Tonneau and Abbé Maury, while midway in political sentiments between the two clubs mentioned was the *Amis de la constitution monarchique*, whose sponsors were the Monarchists of the Assembly. Emigration and the increasingly radical orientation of the revolutionary movement weakened these conservative clubs in measure as the influence of their sponsors in the National Constituent Assembly dwindled before that of the Left.

Lastly, there were the newspapers and their enterprising editors, a force of incalculable significance in stirring up political passions. Since the beginning of the Revolution restrictions upon the liberty of the press had virtually disappeared. Deputies, like Barère and Mirabeau, founded dailies and reported the debates in the Assembly. An experienced journalist, Panckoucke, in whose salon many deputies were wont to assemble and discuss their work, edited the well informed *Moniteur*, which was sympathetic toward the Constitutionalists. Hosts of ambitious men founded journals, each with its clientele of steady readers. Among the more influential revolutionary newspapers we can cite the *Courrier de Versailles* of Gorsas, the *Patriote français* of Brissot, the *Révolutions de Paris* of Prudhomme and Loustalot, the *Révolutions de France et de Brabant* of the witty, sparkling Camille Desmoulins and last, but not least in popularity and influence, the *Ami du peuple* of Jean-Paul Marat, a suspicious and embittered physician who was becoming the hero of the Parisian populace. In 1790 the denunciatory *Père Duchêne* of Hébert, with its strong language and honest vulgarity, gained tremendous vogue among the working masses and the soldiers. These journals cost little; they were badly printed as a rule and carried little real news, but everybody read them, even the aristocrats who had many newspapers of their own. Among the newspapers that were hostile to the Revolution one may mention the *Petit Gauthier* and Rivarol's *Actes des Apôtres*, which faithfully echoed the views of the Abbé Maury and Mirabeau-Tonneau.

These were the more tangible means by which the revolutionary gospel was spread. But the spirit of the revolutionists was best expressed in the series of spontaneous fêtes of federation which reached their finest form in the *Fête de la Fédération* in Paris on July 14, 1790. Gatherings of this nature were first held during the crisis of the "Great Fear," when a terrible danger seemed to be hovering over the land. From that small beginning when neighboring villages and cities promised each other aid against their common enemy, the movement broadened and deepened.[6] After the federation of the towns of one province, as in Dauphiné and Franche-Comté, came interprovincial federations in January, 1790, and the inspiring fête of the eastern provinces a month later. The National Guard sent their delegates, and representatives came from the civil authorities of the communes. The participants all took a solemn oath to support the new order, to suppress disturbances, to renounce all ancient privileges and distinctions, and to be henceforth "one, immense family of brothers, united under the standard of liberty." At all those fêtes mass was held and the banners of the National Guard were blessed. A great impetus to the federation movement came from the king's public acceptance of the Revolution. On February 4, 1790, Louis XVI appeared before the deputies in the Assembly and promised his complete and unreserved support to the revolutionary program. They were greatly moved, not knowing that he had mental reservations, and in their enthusiasm they rose in their seats and took the oath to be faithful to the nation, the law, and the king.

As the first anniversary of the fall of the Bastille approached, the Assembly decided to join in the movement and to crown it by organizing a national festival. This great national *Fête de la Fédération* was held at the Champ-de-Mars in Paris on July 14, 1790. A vast crowd of Parisians, estimated at 200,000, gathered in the colossal amphitheater which volunteers had built for the occasion and waited patiently in the rain for the coming of the lengthy procession of celebrants. The *fédérés* from the newly established departments, the deputies of the Assembly, the king and the queen, and Lafayette, who was the master of ceremonies, marched in the procession. The banners were blessed, Talleyrand held mass on the altar of *la patrie* (which had been built in the center of the parade grounds), and Lafayette, after receiving the form of the oath from the king, administered it to the *fédérés*. Then the trumpets blew, rifles flashed in the air, guns were fired, and the enormous crowd repeated the oath after Lafayette: "I swear to be faithful forever to the nation, the law and the king, [and] to maintain the constitution decreed by the National Assembly and accepted by the king. . . ." Louis XVI stood in the gallery and with great dig-

---

[6] These manifestations of revolutionary solidarity, of patriotic fraternity, were called *fédérations* because the *fédérés* were the contingents of the National Guard of the different departments.

VII. THE ACHIEVEMENTS OF THE
CONSTITUENT ASSEMBLY

The Constitutional Reforms: The Declaration of Rights

The new constitution which the deputies of the National Constituent Assembly swore that they would create was not drawn up without heated discussion over its numerous articles. The earliest text was voted in the course of a month and a half from August to October, 1789, but many supplementary provisions were subsequently added. Consequently in September, 1790, the Assembly decided to fuse the earliest draft and the later laws into a single organic text. The work was completed, with certain important revisions, in 1791 and accepted by Louis XVI on September 14, 1791. Hence the name, Constitution of 1791, which was given to a body of legislation many of whose provisions were in force as early as 1789.

The voting of the Declaration of the Rights of Man and of the Citizen on August 27, 1789, has already been noted. Whether or not the French Declaration was a literal adaptation from the English models and the Bills of Rights in the constitutions of the various American states (in all probability it was not) is relatively unimportant. The philosophical ideas underlying these declarations were an international commodity of which neither American nor French theorists had a monopoly. There is greater significance in the following observations concerning the French Declaration: (1) Several of its theoretical provisions were ignored or revised in the constitutional legislation of the Assembly. (2) It did not explicitly formulate all the fundamental opinions of the deputies, for it made no reference to economic theories. (3) A number of the provisions were more concerned with practical realities than with absolute theoretical rights. (4) The latent promise of its basic articles enlisted innumerable recruits and adherents to the revolutionary cause from all ranks of the commoners.

A careful study of this famous Declaration will throw light both upon the standpoint of its formulators and many aspects of the Revolution. The complete Declaration which was prefaced to the Constitution of 1791 follows:

DECLARATION OF THE RIGHTS OF MAN AND OF THE CITIZEN [1]

The representatives of the French people, organized in the National Assembly, considering that ignorance, forgetfulness or contempt of the rights of man are the sole causes of the public miseries and of the corruption of governments, have resolved to set forth in a solemn declaration the natural, inalienable, and sacred rights of man, in order that this declaration, being ever present to all the members of the social body, may unceasingly remind them of their rights and their duties; in order that the acts of the legislative power and those of the executive power may be each moment compared with the aim of every political institution and thereby may be more respected; and in order that the demands of the citizens, grounded henceforth upon simple and incontestable principles, may always take the direction of maintaining the constitution and the welfare of all.

In consequence, the National Assembly recognizes and declares, in the presence and under the auspices of the Supreme Being, the following rights of man and of the citizen.

1. Men are born and remain free and equal in rights. Social distinctions can be based only upon public utility.

2. The aim of every political association is the preservation of the natural and imprescriptible rights of man. These rights are liberty, property, security, and resistance to oppression.

3. The source of all sovereignty is essentially in the nation; no body, no individual can exercise authority that does not proceed from it in plain terms.

4. Liberty consists in the power to do anything that does not injure others; accordingly, the exercise of the natural rights of each man has for its only limits those that secure to the other members of society the enjoyment of these same rights. These limits can be determined only by law.

5. The law has the right to forbid only such actions as are

---

[1] F. M. Anderson, *The Constitutions and Other Select Documents Illustrative of the History of France (1789–1901)*, pp. 58–60. Used by permission of The H. W. Wilson Company, publishers.

injurious to society. Nothing can be forbidden that is not inter-
dicted by the law, and no one can be constrained to do that which
it does not order.

6. Law is the expression of the general will. All citizens have
the right to take part personally or by their representatives in its
formation. It must be the same for all, whether it protects or pun-
ishes. All citizens being equal in its eyes, are equally eligible to all
public dignities, places, and employments, according to their capacities, and without other distinction than that of their virtues and
their talents.

7. No man can be accused, arrested, or detained except in the
cases determined by the law and according to the forms that it has
prescribed. Those who procure, expedite, execute, or cause to be
executed arbitrary orders ought to be punished; but every citizen
summoned or seized in virtue of the law ought to render instant
obedience; he makes himself guilty by resistance.

8. The law ought to establish only penalties that are strictly
and obviously necessary and no one can be punished except in virtue of a law established and promulgated prior to the offence and
legally applied.

9. Every man being presumed innocent until he has been pronounced guilty, if it is thought indispensable to arrest him, all
severity that may not be necessary to secure his person ought to be
strictly suppressed by law.

10. No one ought to be disturbed on account of his opinions,
even religious, provided their manifestation does not derange the
public order established by law.

11. The free communication of ideas and opinions is one of the
most precious of the rights of man; every citizen then can freely
speak, write, and print, subject to responsibility for the abuse of
this freedom in the cases determined by law.

12. The guarantee of the rights of man and of the citizen re-
quires a public force; this force then is instituted for the advantage
of all and not for the personal benefit of those to whom it is entrusted.

13. For the maintenance of the public force and for the expenses
of administration a general tax is indispensable; it ought to be
equally apportioned among all the citizens according to their
means.

14. All the citizens have the right to ascertain, by themselves or

by their representatives, the necessity of the public tax, to consent to it freely, to follow the employment of it, and to determine the quota, the assessment, the collection, and the duration of it.

15. Society has the right to call for an account from every public agent of its administration.

16. Any society in which the guarantee of the rights is not secured or the separation of powers not determined has no constitution at all.

17. Property being a sacred and inviolable right, no one can be deprived of it unless a legally established public necessity evidently demands it, under the condition of a just and prior indemnity.

The general theoretical principles of French, English, and American liberal thought of the eighteenth century were clearly and vigorously stated in the preamble and the first three articles. These principles which were universal in their appeal, recognizing neither national boundary lines nor distinctions of race, color, or creed, and emphasizing the sovereign nation's right to resist the oppression of irresponsible governments, carried a singular appeal to contemporaries. Applied to a semi-mediaeval society, where caste distinctions were still enforced, they created a conflict between the handful of privileged individuals and the commoners. In this conflict the latter, more than ninety-eight per cent of the nation, saw their opportunity to win the status to which they were entitled by birth and by their native capacities. In the new state of things they found opportunities and careers open to them; wealth or prestige, fame and fortune, for him who would profit by the leveling of barriers. Hence the enthusiastic response of the masses and their quasi-religious defense of the Revolution. If not they themselves, assuredly their children would share in the fulfillment of the promise of a better world. Later, however, many of them became disillusioned, when the Revolution demanded sacrifices and tightening of the belt, when its leaders showed that their interests were not those of the peasantry and the artisans, when they realized that the great opportunities benefited only the superior individuals and maintained the wretchedness of the many.

The deputies of the bourgeoisie who framed the Declaration believed so implicitly that the interests of their class coincided with the interests of the entire nation that they impressed their class fears and convictions upon a document which was intended to be a charter of universal human rights.[2] The fourth, fifth, and seventh articles reveal their preoccupation with guaranteeing individual liberty against despotism. Had they not suffered most from its lack in the Old Régime! Articles twelve, fourteen, fifteen, and sixteen clearly reveal their lurking fear of the monarch. Public agents were to be responsible to the administration, the military power must obey the law, taxes required the consent of those taxed, and the three powers, executive, legislative, and judicial, were to be separated. Article eleven emphasized the need of liberty of speech and the press, a need apparent to authors and readers of revolutionary writings. Since the deputies were afraid or unwilling to alienate the clergy they granted toleration to non-Catholics but not full liberty of conscience (article ten).[3] The sanctity of private property was taken for granted, but it was not defined, for the question of feudal property was not yet settled. Neither the rights of association and petition nor of association were recognized, for class or corporate organization was precisely the form of inequality which the revolutionary idea was trying to abolish in order that the individual might be free. The propertyless worker and peasant did become free, but they remained defenseless against their more prosperous fellow citizens. For these sins of omission and commission the radical press scolded the deputies; but in practice it is true that the Constituent Assembly allowed the masses to organize in clubs and to draw up petition after petition. If, in the Declaration and the Constitution of 1791, the bourgeois deputies reserved all power for themselves, they did so because they recognized their own capacities and mistrusted those of the masses. It is a gross anachronism to speak of class consciousness or class warfare in the period between 1789 and 1791, although one may readily grant that the constitu-

[2] The negroes in the sugar colonies of the French West Indies had good reason to hope that the Declaration foreshadowed their liberation from slavery. But their champions in the Assembly fought a losing battle against the shipowners and the sugar refiners. Slavery and the slave trade were maintained. On September 24, 1791, the colonial assemblies were empowered to regulate the political status of free negroes and mulattoes. This solution provoked a terrible slave insurrection in Santo Domingo.

[3] The Protestants, who had won their civil rights in 1787, were granted full toleration and political rights in December, 1789. The Jews of southern France gained their political rights in January, 1790, but those of eastern France not before September, 1791.

tional legislation of the Assembly, generous as it was, discriminated against the lower born. Instances of this discrimination will be shown in the discussion of the new constitution.

THE CONSTITUTION OF 1791

After proclaiming in the Declaration, "Men are born and remain free and equal in rights," the Assembly flagrantly contradicted itself by refusing to grant suffrage rights to all Frenchmen. The constitution divided the population into two classes, active and passive citizens. Only members of the former class were given the right to vote and to serve in the National Guard. The distinction was based upon differences in wealth. To be an active citizen one had to be twenty-five years of age or over and pay an annual direct tax equal in value to three times the local rate of a laborer's daily wage. This provision, which was voted in December, 1789, reflected both the theories of the political philosophers of the century and the fears of the bourgeois deputies. They were afraid that the three million Frenchmen whom they debarred from the polls might be misled either by their own ignorance or by the cunning propaganda of the erstwhile aristocrats. Four and one-quarter million male Frenchmen were thus classified as active citizens. In the ranks of the three million passive citizens there were, in addition to the landless peasants and the artisans who could not pay the required minimum tax, debtors, bankrupts, and wage servants.[4]

The classification of citizens according to their wealth did not end with the distinction between active and passive citizens. That was merely a beginning. The active citizens met in the primary assembly to choose the electors, who met in the chief town of the department and elected the deputies to the assembly, the judges, the bishops, the parish priests, and the members of the local administrations. But to be eligible as elector, the active citizen had to pay a tax equivalent to the local value of ten days' labor; and to be eligible as deputy, he had to be a landed proprietor who paid an annual tax equivalent in value to a silver mark (*marc d'argent*), which was worth slightly more than fifty francs. Out of a total population of approximately twenty-six million, there were not

---

[4] As one of the deputies, Duquesnoy, expressed it, "Only property owners are true citizens"; and in the original provision only property owners had been given the vote. But this provision was modified in the final draft.

more than fifty thousand citizens eligible to serve as electors, and fewer still who qualified to serve as deputies. In short, political rights were made a monopoly of the well-to-do, for the new constitution did away with privileges based upon birth, but respected and strengthened those arising out of financial prosperity. Protests poured in upon the Assembly against this discriminatory scheme. It was not revised until the very close of the Constituent Assembly (August 27, 1791) and then too late, after the primary elections under the Constitution of 1791 had been held.[5]

Although the third article of the Declaration declared that sovereign rights resided exclusively in the nation, the sixteenth article stressed the fact that the separation of powers was essential to a well ordered state. Hence the nation delegated the legislative power to its elected representatives, the executive power to a hereditary monarch, and the judicial power to elected judges. The power to make the laws was given to a single assembly, the Legislative Assembly, whose members were to be elected for two years and whose sessions could not be dissolved by the king. The powers given to the Legislative Assembly made it the strongest political authority in the state. The deputies enjoyed full parliamentary immunity for the free expression of their views. The Assembly alone could initiate and vote the laws of France. While the king was given the right of a suspensive veto over legislation, that veto became invalid if three successive assemblies persisted in voting the same law. Moreover, the veto did not apply to constitutional and fiscal laws, proclamations to the nation, and accusations against individual ministers. Still it is true that the suspensive veto operated practically as an absolute veto because it delayed legislation for several years. The Assembly fixed the tax assessments and controlled public expenditures. Declarations of war and ratifications of peace treaties could not be made by the king without its previous consent. It supervised the ministry and directed the diplomacy of the state.

[5] The revision of the electoral law came after the king's flight to Varennes in June, 1791. It abolished the eligibility requirement of the silver mark for the deputy, but on the other hand, increased the tax and property qualifications of the electors. The latter were required to be either the proprietors or the usufructuaries of a piece of property assessed on the tax rolls at a rate equivalent to one hundred and fifty to two hundred days' wages. Under certain conditions they were eligible if they paid in direct taxes a sum equivalent to the local value of labor ranging from one hundred to four hundred days. This revision came too late for the elections of 1791, and the elections of 1792 were held under direct manhood suffrage.

The executive power was entrusted to a hereditary monarch, but precautions were taken to restrict him in his rôle of constitutional ruler. Before the draft of the constitution, Louis XVI had been "Louis, by the grace of God, King of France and Navarre." Now he became "Louis by the grace of God and the Constitution of the state, King of the French." He had been the liege lord and the proprietor of the state; now he was the first servant, who was required to swear an oath to be faithful to the nation and the law, to defend the constitution, and to execute the laws. Previously, he could draw without limit upon all the resources of the state. Now he received a civil list, a generous one, of twenty-five million francs annually for his expenses.

In theory, the power that the constitution gave him was of considerable importance; in practice, the exercise of his power was hedged in by many restrictions. He was granted the right to appoint ambassadors, ministers, and a certain proportion of the higher officers of the military forces. He was supreme commander of the army and navy. By his veto power he could effectively delay legislation for a period of several years, but the veto power could not be applied to the most important legislation. He appointed ambassadors, but found the direction of foreign policy largely in the hands of the deputies of the Assembly. He could not select his ministers from the ranks of the deputies, for it was feared that the promise of a ministerial position might either weaken their loyalty to national interests or else strengthen the king's influence over the debates of the Assembly. The Assembly kept a vigilant eye over the six ministers of the king. It decreed that no royal act was valid unless it were countersigned by one of the ministers, who thus assumed responsibility for it. It required these to give an account of their use of funds to the Assembly, and it subjected them to the possibility of impeachment by a special tribunal. The king's administrative power was tremendously weakened by the fact that he exercised it through local bodies in no way responsible to him. Lest the monarch be tempted to use force against the deputies and dissolve the Assembly, the constitution forbade him to station troops within a thirty-mile radius of the place where the sessions were held. Not without some justification could Louis XVI write in 1791: "The King has been declared the supreme head of the administration of the kingdom, yet he can change nothing without the decision of the Assembly." The Assembly was the real master of the state; and this Assembly was to be composed of deputies indirectly elected on the basis of property qualifications. It is no exaggeration to state that the new constitution organized a middle-class government within the framework of a constitutional monarchy.

THE ADMINISTRATIVE REFORMS

The administrative organization was also completely remodeled.[6] The cahiers had given indication of the direction that the reform would follow, and the indication was corroborated in the summer of 1789 when the establishment of the new municipalities, or communes, showed that the country strongly demanded the decentralization of the government. The old overlapping and confusing divisions of generalities, provinces, bailiwicks, and *pays d'élections* were abolished completely. A new, uniform and simple administrative system was established. France was divided into eighty-three departments, each department into districts, each district into cantons, and each canton into communes. It may have been that the deputies created the new departments in the hope of destroying the old particulàrist spirit of the historic provinces. More likely, the deputies were concerned with establishing a new territorial unit that would make local administration simple and efficient. The departments were small enough for the citizens to reach the chief town (*chef lieu*) and its market in a single day's journey, and numerous enough to be without danger to this central administration. Having adopted these principles, the deputies arranged the delimitation of the new units in the Assembly. In their discussions they were not invariably amicable, but they were realistic and never lost track of the purpose in mind.

With the disappearance of the intendant and the subdelegate, the administrative authority was vested in the hands of the officials elected by the local inhabitants. The new administrative units began to function in the spring of 1790. Except in the case of municipal elections the elections were indirect. Even in the case of municipal elections, where the voting was direct and the voters the active citizens, the poor citizens were excluded from the polls. The

---

[6] The two decrees of December 14 and December 22, 1789, which defined the extent and functions of the new administrative units, were not properly speaking included in the Constitution of 1791, but they were essential parts of it.

central administration had no direct agent of its own in the local administrations. The king could suspend the local authorities, but the latter had the right of appeal to the Assembly against his intervention. Each department, district, and commune had its elected

FRANCE IN 1791
SHOWING THE DEPARTMENTS
Scale of Miles

council, which was a deliberating body, and a permanent executive bureau as well. This executive bureau was called a directory in the department and the district and a municipal corps in the commune. Over the latter body the mayor presided. The elected officials inherited all the former powers of the royal intendant. They apportioned and levied the direct taxes, executed the laws, maintained order, and administered schools and poor relief. Other elected officials, the procurators (*procureurs*), represented the state in the different administrative units and served as a link between them and the ministers of the central administration. The canton had no independent political existence and served as the primary assembly for the election of national officials. The decentralization of the administrative organization was most pronounced in the municipalities. Each commune elected its own mayor, its municipal officers, and the local procurator. The term of municipal office was shorter than that of the department or district, fifty per cent of the officers were renewed annually, and the elections were direct. Consequently the political career of the revolutionary municipality was an active one. It was more in touch with political realities than the other administrative units and more democratic in its tendencies. Unlike the larger units, it could summon the National Guard to maintain order and enforce the laws. Except in isolated cases the commune was unchecked in its local administration of national laws.[7]

The reorganization of judicial administration was effected in the same spirit as that of the administrative service of the government. A new hierarchy of elected judges replaced the former magistrates of the Old Régime who had bought their charges. Justice was to be free and within the reach of all citizens. Judicial procedure was greatly simplified. For civil cases each canton had its justice of the peace and each district its own tribunal composed of five judges. Petty cases and misdemeanors were tried locally; more serious infractions of the law came before the district court. In criminal affairs, matters of simple police were entrusted to the communes, more serious cases to justices of the peace in the cantons, and felonies to a special tribunal in each department. There were two elected juries in criminal affairs, one to pass on the case, the other to determine the innocence or the guilt of the accused. There were no juries for civil cases. Provisions were made to insure the accused a fair and open trial, and the penalties were made proportionate to the crime. Most of the old degrading penalties, such as torture, the pillory, and branding, were abolished, but chains and the death penalty were maintained. A procurator represented the king at the various courts, but he could be heard only in special and limited cases and had no power over the procedure. Justice, like the adminis-

---

[7] Paris was given a special law because of its great population and importance, but the organization of the municipality of Paris followed the main lines of the general system.

tration of the law, became a sovereign right of the people, even though it still was administered in the name of the king. No appeal courts were established, but by an ingenious arrangement each district tribunal was permitted to review cases of other district tribunals. A supreme court of appeals, the court of cassation, was established to pass on the forms of procedure; but it had no competence over the matter, and it could not interpret the law. Finally, a High Court, also composed of elected magistrates, was established at Paris with competence over cases involving the ministers and high officials and over cases involving treason and crimes against the safety of the state.

The military organization was also reformed, but not so profoundly as the other branches of the government. The presence of an ever-armed Europe, which did not welcome the achievements of the Assembly with excessive enthusiasm, forced the deputies to proceed slowly in this respect. The sale of offices was abolished, the pay of the soldiers was raised, and an incomplete system of promotion based on seniority was introduced. Commissions were open to all, but the appointment of the highest officers of the regular army was left to the king. These reforms were beneficial, but did little to reëstablish discipline. The new organization of the National Guard, which was at once a militia and a reserve, took its place beside that of the line troops of the regular army. As a general rule only active citizens could serve in the National Guard. But they numbered from two to three million compared to the one hundred and forty thousand of the line troops. They elected their own officers and wore the prescribed uniform of the nation, blue coat and white waistcoat and breeches. Their flags carried the inscription *Le peuple français. La liberté ou la mort.*

This sweeping reform of the administration had its defects as well as its good qualities. It gave excessive powers to the voters and too little to the king and the central administration. Since all power came from below, the government had slight control over its nominal agents. The reaction against too much centralization, such as France had in the Old Régime and such as it has today, weakened the unity of the nation instead of strengthening it, as the deputies hoped. On the one hand there were too many elections and too many elected officials; on the other, the political experience of the country was slight and the problems overwhelming. If the local officials were chosen from citizens who were hostile to the course of the Revolution, as was the case in 1792 and 1793, or fell under the influence of counter-revolutionary forces, as was true in isolated cases from the very beginning, they could direct the local administration against the Assembly. A political crisis was therefore a potential threat to the stability of the government and to the very existence of the nation.[8]

THE FINANCIAL CRISIS

The financial crisis which had precipitated the Revolution grew steadily worse in the summer months of 1789. The secret opposition of Louis XVI, the intrigues of the aristocrats, the plotting of political schemers, the unappeased hostility of the rural masses, and the accentuation of the economic depression reacted sharply upon the financial situation. The Assembly abolished the taxes of the Old Régime, except the stamp duty and the registration of acts, which the peasants were not paying in any case, and proceeded to reform the system of taxation as the cahiers demanded. Three new direct taxes were substituted for the various direct taxes of the past. Of these the most important was the land tax, since real estate was the principal source of wealth. There was also a personal property tax, calculated according to the rent paid, and a tax upon revenue from commerce and industry. The new direct taxes, like the old indirect taxes, were not paid or were paid only after many protests and much delay. The Assembly was powerless and the new municipalities were unwilling to exercise pressure upon the

[8] Mathiez, in tracing the rôles of the many committees of the Assembly, comes to the conclusion that the decentralization was more apparent than real. He maintains that neither in theory nor in practice did the deputies of the Constituent Assembly intend the separation of powers to become effective until after the Assembly had ended its work. The deputies believed and acted upon the principle that they were extraordinary deputies, representing the nation in all its sovereignty, and endowed with dictatorial rights. "The truth is, that despite the Constitution, the departmental authorities assume no initiative, refer to Paris as before for the slightest difficulties. The only difference is that the committees of the Assembly have replaced the divisions of the Royal Council. The truth is, that the Assembly does not stop with passing laws but governs, or better still, administers to the smallest detail. . . . The committees of the Constituent Assembly functioned as did later the committees of the Convention." If his views are correct—and they seem plausible—we must revise our conventional interpretation of the constitutional legislation from 1789 to 1791 and recognize the fact that the Assembly enjoyed far more real authority over the local administration than historians believed. But, as he says, this authority existed *despite* the constitution and not because of it. *Cf.* Mathiez' critical book review in *Annales historiques de la Révolution française*, janvier-février, 1929, p. 96.

masses. The treasury was empty and the financial burden of the state higher than ever, as the liquidation of the Old Régime and the establishment of the new administrative system enormously increased the public indebtedness. The interest on the debt and the expenses of the administration amounted to six hundred million francs annually.

To retain the support of the investors in state bonds the Assembly declared against a formal proceeding in bankruptcy, i.e., a repudiation of the internal debt, and it tried various expedients to meet the country's current obligations. Necker, the financial miracle-maker, fell back upon his traditional tactics, which were new advances from the Caisse d'Escompte and new public loans. The loans were voted by a desperate Assembly in August and December, 1789, and again in the spring of 1790, but they were not covered by the public. An attempted direct income tax failed, principally because the administrative organization and the personnel required for the collection were nonexistent. In the fall of 1789 private individuals, municipalities, and corporate groups made voluntary patriotic contributions to the Assembly, but the relief from this source was slight. The Caisse d'Escompte advanced all its available funds to the state, but in November, 1789, the directors of that institution avowed their inability to continue their loans. Eighty-nine million of its one hundred and fourteen million of notes in circulation were already at the disposal of the treasury. Inasmuch as the solvency of the Caisse d'Escompte depended upon that of the state, only part of its note issue being covered by its own reserves and the rest by what the state owed it, Necker proposed that the Caisse d'Escompte be transformed into a national bank. In that way he could increase its capital and have it issue new notes. The Assembly rejected his proposal on the ground that the new issue would not be taken up by the public without additional security, and that their value would be better maintained if they were issued directly by the state. Moreover, if a direct issue were to be made by the state, the interest that the Caisse d'Escompte charged would be saved. But what fresh security could the state offer? "Our patrimony," answered one of the deputies, and the patrimony was the possessions of the church, which on November 2, 1789, the Assembly "placed at the disposal of the nation."

The wealth of the church was estimated from two to four billion francs, an amount sufficient to pay the state debt. The question was whether the state had the right to seize the possessions of the church. Precedents favored alienation. Under Louis XV the Commission of the Regular Clergy had suppressed nine monastic orders and used the property that they possessed for purposes of the common good. Calonne had suggested expropriation before the Revolution, the cahiers had proposed a redistribution of ecclesiastical land, and the Physiocrats had used various arguments against the great wealth of the church, prescribing confiscation as the social remedy.

The debates in the Assembly on the right of the state to take over the goods of the church became heated as soon as Talleyrand had made the specific proposal in October, 1789. The most convincing argument was the legal argument against the church as a corporation, i.e., as a corporate political body within the state, possessing the right to tax the people. Even if the church had the rights of possession, ran the argument, the state still had superior rights, for the church was a corporation, and all corporations held their status by virtue of the law. The church did not *own* property, continued the argument, but *possessed* it for certain purposes only. If the church does not fulfill its duties, the state can take back the property on condition of performing the same services itself. Chapelier, one of the active Breton deputies, put the argument tersely: "It was impolitic for great corporations to possess property." Talleyrand even cited canon law and the decisions of church synods to prove that the lands had been given neither to the clergy nor to the corporation of the church, but for the perpetuation of religious services. By assuming the threefold obligations of the clergy, i.e., education, poor-relief, and worship, the state had the right to take over the lands. Another argument emphasized the luxury and corruption of the high prelates and advocated confiscation as a method of restoring the church to its apostolic simplicity. It was claimed that the great revenues of the clergy were deflected from their rightful purposes. A third argument invoked natural law to prove that society derived no benefit from the church lands which were administered by the clergy, i.e., persons who were not recognized by civil society. This was the argument of efficiency.

The defenders of the existing status, Camus, Champion de Cicé, and the Abbé Maury, brought out the fact that it was legally unjust to deprive a corporation of its property, since property was a social creation, whether owned by an individual or by a corporation.

They even fell back on the Declaration of Rights, which defined property as one of the natural rights. The answer to this was that corporations did not enjoy natural rights. They also maintained that the property had been given neither to the Catholic Church nor to the clergy, but to individual ecclesiastical organizations. They endeavored to show that secularization of the estates of the church would benefit speculators and profiteers and leave the clergy without any visible means of support. But on November 2, the Assembly voted to place the ecclesiastical lands at the disposal of the state, which assumed the obligation of paying the clergy, meeting the expenses of worship, and relieving the poor. Progressives were well satisfied with the Assembly's vote, hailing it as a notable victory over an organization whose privileged status had strengthened reaction and blocked reform. Those who favored a radical reform in the church and the redistribution of its estates were also satisfied. But thousands upon thousands of simple believers were sorely perplexed, even violently shocked by this dramatic turn of events which altered immemorial customs. To them the Revolution seemed to threaten religion.

THE ASSIGNATS

For a time the Assembly hesitated to use the enormous resources which its vote had given the state. When the last of Necker's expedients failed, it decided on December 14 to place four hundred million francs' worth of ecclesiastical lands on sale. To cover the sale a bond issue in the form of assignats equivalent in amount to the value of the land on sale was floated. A new bank under the control of the Assembly, the Caisse de l'Extraordinaire, was established to issue the assignats and to receive the proceeds of all exceptional taxations. The first use of the assignats would be to repay the one hundred and seventy million francs which the Caisse d'Escompte had advanced to the state. These assignats, created on December 19 and paying five per cent interest, were to be exchanged for all interest-bearing state notes and received in payment for the ecclesiastical lands. As soon as the land was sold, they were to be returned to the new bank and burnt. They were not currency; they were treasury bonds redeemable in land instead of in cash.

If the Caisse d'Escompte had succeeded in floating the one hundred and seventy million of assignats which had been assigned to it, the entire operation would have remained a financial transaction. But investors hesitated in the early months of 1790 to accept them. "The public felt no confidence in bonds that were merely problematical promises to sell property the acquisition of which was not free of all mortgages and might give rise to inextricable complications." The notes of the Caisse d'Escompte depreciated six per cent by the spring of 1790.

The Assembly realized that two additional steps would have to be taken if its effort to meet the pressing state debts by means of assignats were to be successful: (1) to declare the church lands national property, and (2) to give the assignats the force of legal tender. By April it had taken the first step. It deprived the clergy of their administration of ecclesiastical property, and undertook to clear off all mortgages and other liens upon the property by assuming the debt of the clergy and the expenses of public worship. Once the state had guaranteed the assignats, the Assembly could advantageously substitute them for paper money. The assignats of the first issue which had not been taken up by investors were called in, and a new issue was floated, virtually with the force of legal tender (April 17, 1790).

Although the decree of April 17, 1790, placed the limit of the amount of assignats that could be issued at the figure of 400,-000,000 livres, the success scored by the new emission encouraged the National Assembly to go beyond the limit it set. Assignats, issued now by the state bank (Caisse de l'Extraordinaire), took the place of bank notes. Since their success had wiped out the most pressing state debt, why could not the state wipe out its entire debt by issuing additional assignats likewise secured by the national land! A strong minority group of deputies tried to oppose the projected policy, advancing irrefutable financial arguments against increasing the number of assignats in circulation. In time they saw the accuracy of their forecast revealed. They foresaw the partial avowal of bankruptcy that would ensue, the depreciation of national paper money, inflation, speculation, higher prices, decrease of consumption and production, and a serious economic crisis; but the majority in the Assembly was adamant to the appeal. For a month the deputies debated the question until on September 29 the Assembly voted the payment of the debt of the state and clergy in non-interest-bearing assignats. At the same time it raised the limit of issue of assignats from 400,000,000 to 1,200,000,000 livres. Subsequent decrees raised the issue of assignats up to the alarming total of 1,800,000,000 livres. For this circumstances were partly to blame. The deputies foresaw the difficulties, but they saw no other solution of the financial problems. In May and June, 1790, the National Assembly took over the royal domain and appropriated 25,000,000 livres for the king's annual expenses; in July, 1790, it took over the maintenance of the church. By those two measures the deputies added more than a billion livres to the debt of the state. And, more important still, they pinned the highest hopes on the political consequences of their measures.

One alternative proposal had been made, that non-circulating bonds, bearing five per cent interest, be issued to cover the sale of the additional land that was offered. It was rejected. Without an additional issue of assignats, rightly argued Mirabeau, Chapelier, and Montesquiou, who were the spokesmen of the majority, the public land would not and could not be sold. The sale of the land was the important matter. The sale of land had to be facilitated if the twofold goal of the Assembly were to be realized; viz., (1) the cancellation of the *entire* state debt (and not merely the most pressing obligations), and (2) the creation of a widespread group of land purchasers, who, willy-nilly, would become defenders of the Revolution and the constitution. Montesquiou voiced the prevalent optimism when he said: "The assignats will be the connecting link between the private interests of the individual and the general interests of the state; the very adversaries [of the assignats] will become proprietors and citizens through the Revolution and for the Revolution." And another deputy vividly correlated the sale of the national land with the constitutional labors of the Assembly: "It is a question of strengthening the Constitution, of curbing the hopes of its enemies, of binding them to the new order of things by self-interest."

To a very great extent the political hopes of the deputies were realized. "Self-interest" even more than patriotism induced a large body of Frenchmen to open their pocketbooks and buy national property. As proprietors of land which the Revolution had placed on the market, the purchasers were chained to the revolutionary chariot and were obligated by enlightened calculation to defend the new order against a counter-revolution which would nullify their purchases. In this respect the decision to place the confiscated land on sale and to issue assignats was a political success. However, it must also be noted that the plan of sale and the success of the sales themselves were reflected in and modified by the vicissitudes of the factional political struggles and the political divisions of the country. Such occurrences as the flight of the king, the emigrations of the nobles, the war (from 1792 on), had direct bearing upon the financial question.[9]

The economic and financial consequences of the assignat policy were less happy. The state debt was not canceled. For a passing moment—a very brief one, however—the assignats supplied an artificial stimulus to production, since the big business men quickly disposed of their assignats, investing them in land and in merchandise. Eventually that operation resulted in higher prices. The first issues were in high denominations, 1000 livres, 300 livres and 200 livres, but later issues in 1791 touched as low as 50 livres and 5 livres. By a decree of the Assembly on May 17, 1790, the exchange of metallic currency for paper money was made legal. The paper money depreciated at once, and the rift between specie and paper money rapidly grew wider. The Assembly hesitated a long time before it came to its decision to issue the smaller denominations, for the deputies realized that the hardships of depreciation would in that fashion be transferred to the working population. But the disappearance of specie made the decision inevitable. Coin gradually became more and more scarce in France, because the mercenary troops were paid in specie, as were debts to foreign bankers and payments on foreign imports. Emigrés also carried specie out of the country, and hoarding completed the disappearance of metal currency. The practice of banks, business houses, and regional and local administrations (as in Germany from 1921 to 1924) of issuing private paper money, as well as the depreciation and the final repudiation of private paper money ruined private fortunes, encouraged wild speculation in land as well as in assignats, discouraged thrift and sober living, and created a panic psychology. There were other contributory causes to the fall of the assignats. The country was flooded with counterfeit money that was manufactured by criminals in France and by émigrés out of France. Instead of burning the assignats as they were received by the

[9] The experiences of different countries of Europe after 1918 enable the student of today to appreciate more fully the influence of political developments upon financial policy.

treasury, as had been prescribed by the decrees, the Assembly not only delayed the return of the assignats by giving the purchasers of land a long period of time for payment, but actually reissued them in smaller denominations. A certain amount was canceled by the treasury, but 980,000,000 livres in assignats were still in circulation in May, 1791, and 1,700,000,000 a year later.

The official tables of the depreciation of paper money tell the tragic story of its declining value. By the end of 1791 the assignats had fallen between twenty and twenty-five per cent; in the following spring (1792) the assignat in Paris had lost almost forty per cent of its nominal value. Abroad, at London, Amsterdam, Geneva, and Hamburg, the depreciation was still more marked, the assignat being quoted at a loss of fifty to sixty per cent. There were two periods, in the summer of 1792 and again during the Terror (1793–1794), when the assignat recovered part of its face value, but on the whole the decline was constant until 1796, when this paper money was entirely repudiated.

Agrarian and Economic Measures

The agrarian policy and the economic reforms of the Assembly disappointed the masses as sorely as its fiscal policy. The agrarian policy was expressed in the deputies' treatment of the question of the feudal dues and in the procedure adopted to regulate the sale of ecclesiastical land. While the August decrees abolished the tithe outright, they did not do away *in toto* with the feudal rights. The first clause, which stated that "the National Assembly hereby completely abolishes the feudal system," was sufficient for the peasants, most of whom could not read and paid no attention to the qualifying clauses if they could read. The qualifying clauses distinguished between feudal rights which were to be abolished without indemnification and those which were to be redeemed by monetary payment. Pending their ultimate redemption the latter were to be collected by their owners. When the noble and his feudal lawyer made their appearance to explain the decree and collect the dues, the peasants refused to pay, maintaining that they were being cheated. They sent protests to the Assembly and supplemented their words with deeds of violence against nobles and their châteaux. Indeed, the disturbances of the fall and winter of

1789 and of the spring of 1790 were more extensive and more profound than the peasant insurrections prior to August, 1789.

In the spring of 1790, the Assembly's committee on feudal dues made its recommendations, which were voted by the deputies. The committee was composed entirely of jurists, "a soviet of lawyers," says one historian. Two categories of feudal dues were established according to their supposed origin. Those dues which were assumed to have arisen from the exactions of nobles and the usurpation of the state were classified as *personal* rights. They included servitude, hunting and fishing rights, right of warrens and dovecotes, of justice, banalités, and personal corvées. These were to be abolished outright without compensation. Those which were assumed to have arisen from the concession of land in perpetuity by the lord to the peasant were classified as *real* rights. They included all land rents (cens and champart), all real corvées, lods et ventes, and all dues which had been commuted into money payments. These, which were the most lucrative of the noble's rights, were to be repurchased from the proprietor.

The procedure adopted for the redemption of the real rights placed the burden of proof squarely upon the peasant. In the absence of a legal title, proof that a noble had been in possession of his land for the preceding thirty years was sufficient to validate his rights. While the capitalization of the dues was not unduly high, nor the time limit for redemption too brief, there were several exacting provisions. All arrears in payment had to be made good. Annual dues and dues of mutation had to be redeemed together. The principle of solidarity of redemption was established, so that no one peasant might redeem his dues unless all other tenants of the same fief also redeemed theirs or unless he paid for them all.

Neither the actual course of history during the Middle Ages nor the principles of feudal law justified the policy established by the Assembly. The peasant's instinct, which told him that the whole feudal system hung together, was more correct than the complex distinctions of the jurists. Protests rained in upon the deputies. "Never," says Professor Sagnac, who has made a careful study of the feudal legislation, "have laws let loose a more lively indignation." Under the circumstances redemption was well-nigh impossible. Through all of 1790 and 1791 the peasants vented their opposition in rioting, looting, and attacking the National Guard which were sent to enforce the legislation and quell the disorder.[10]

The peasants expected more from the sale of the ecclesiastical estates than they had derived from the legislation on the feudal system, but again they were doomed to disappointment. The richer peasants and even those peasants who owned small plots took advantage of the terms of sale to increase their holdings, but in general the landless peasant did not realize his dream of acquiring a patch of land for himself and his family. The terms of the sale were not difficult to meet, at least for those who had some financial resources; and former nobles, ecclesiastics, bourgeois, and the richer peasants, including many who bought for speculation, took advantage of them. This ready response was not necessarily motivated by patriotic sentiments, for many a shrewd purchaser saw the economic wisdom of exchanging depreciating assignats for something as tangible and solid as real estate. In a later chapter we shall consider the extent of bourgeois and peasant purchases, but here it is sufficient to note that in failing to satisfy the legitimate land hunger of the rural masses, the National Constituent Assembly chilled the revolutionary enthusiasm of innumerable lowly individuals who had hailed the events of 1789. To all the petitions of the landless peasantry for the division of large estates, the free use of the commons, the abolition of métayage, and the governmental regulation of the grain trade, the deputies turned a deaf ear. They were prisoners of their economic views and of the inexorable necessity of raising great sums of money to satisfy the claims of the creditors of the state.

The economic liberalism of the deputies explains their measures concerning trade and industry, which were of a piece with their legislation concerning the feudal dues and the sale of national land. They abolished the grievous internal customs which had stifled trade within the kingdom. They also abolished the guilds which still hampered trade and industry by denying the workingman the right to use his tools and his initiative for his own benefit, and they laid down the new principle that "every person shall be

[10] In a recent study, a French historian takes the attitude that the legislation of 1790 was not unreasonable, and that its provisions would gradually have been met, at least in the department of the Gironde. The feudal dues were completely abolished without any compensation whatsoever in the course of 1792 and 1793.

free to engage in such business or to practice such profession, art, or craft as he shall find profitable." Partly in consequence of their measures and partly in response to other circumstances, they brought about an artificial prosperity which favored the display of individual initiative and the employment of capital funds. Internal and foreign trade was flourishing, and factories were busy. For a few months in the spring of 1791 there was heightened production and consumption. Business men, anxious to get rid of their assignats, made heavy investments and repeated purchases of commodities, all of which stimulated manufactures. But the boom did not last long. The decline of the assignats and the concomitant rise in prices on the one hand, and the growing unemployment, caused in part by the decline of the luxury trades, tended to produce an economic crisis. The Parisian workingmen went on strike for higher wages. Their cause was ably seconded by the petitions of the newly formed popular societies of the capital. This blending of the demands for economic relief and political equality frightened the middle-class deputies, whose response to the demands was the famous Chapelier law of June 14, 1791.

Fearful lest the movement lead to the restoration of the abolished guilds in a new form, the deputies forbade any kind of association among people engaged in the same trade for the defense of their "alleged common interests." As Jaurès has amply shown, theoretically this law ignored class distinction. Employers as well as employees were forbidden to form trade associations, while the terms of the labor contract were to be arranged between the individual employer and the individual employee. From their own point of view the deputies were consistent in preventing corporative associations of workingmen, for they believed that such associations, indeed any corporate groups at all, represented an attack upon the liberty of the individual. But in denying the workers the right to form unions for collective bargaining, in refusing them the right to go out on strike, and in prescribing heavy penalties for violations of these provisions, the Assembly manifestly showed its fear of the workers' strength. Such protests as were made against the Chapelier law came largely from the democrats of the popular societies, who found in it an excuse to redouble their campaign against the property qualifications of the electoral system. Once the disfranchised workers gained political rights, they reasoned, such discriminatory legislation would become impossible. The conservative deputies retaliated by denouncing the democratic agitators as anarchists who wished to destroy all property rights. Thus a breach was opened between the Constituent Assembly and certain sections of the people, and the way was prepared for a continuance of the unrest.

THE CIVIL CONSTITUTION OF THE CLERGY

The first reforms of the Constituent Assembly made the remolding of religious society imperative in order to harmonize it with the new civil society. To the deputies, who had been educated by the clergy, a separation of church and state was unthinkable. Moreover, the execution of its financial reforms gave the Assembly no alternative to regulating the affairs of the church. The legislation concerning the tithes and the ecclesiastical lands forced the state to assume the financial obligations of the Gallican Church. Those obligations were many and burdensome—the clerical debt, the expenses of the cult, relief of the poor, and support of education and hospitals. To cut down those obligations seemed absolutely necessary to the deputies who were struggling with the problems of putting France on a stable financial basis.

Other motives, however, besides financial considerations lay behind the early religious policy of the Constituent Assembly which culminated in the celebrated Civil Constitution of the Clergy (July 12, 1790). These motives were derived from the political traditions of the Old Régime and from the teachings of the *philosophes* which, paradoxically, had been accepted by many of the lower clergy. The political traditions emphasized the subordination of the church to the state and the independence of the Gallican Church from the authority of the papacy. The cahiers of the clergy agreed that a reform of the Gallican Church was in order. On the other hand the *philosophes* in general agreed that the state could not exist without religion. Rousseau voiced one of the strongest convictions of the political philosophers when he wrote, "Those who would treat morality and politics apart will never understand anything, either about the one or about the other." It is true that the *philosophes* would have preferred a civil religion to Catholicism. But the new revolutionary idealism was developing into a civil or patriotic religion, and parish priests encouraged their parishioners to fuse the new revolutionary religion with Catholicism by quoting Holy Writ to justify the articles of the Declaration of Rights. Of the deputies in the Assembly, many were partisans of the natural rights philosophy of their age, but an overwhelming majority was also profoundly Catholic. Their religious reforms were in no sense an attack upon Catholicism or Christianity; their measures were an effort to associate the clergy with the Revolution. They were fully aware that no one could interpret their decrees to the unlettered masses so well as the local priest.

At first the lower clergy applauded the religious enactments. But the refusal of the deputies, in the spring of 1790, to declare Catholicism the state religion made them lend a willing ear to the complaints of the upper clergy. At that moment Catholicism was the only religion supported by state funds. The Catholic Church kept all civil records and controlled education and poor relief. Why then did the revolutionaries lay themselves open to an accusation of hostility to religion, particularly when so many of them were loyal Catholics? The answer is that they could not help themselves. In the first place, to declare Catholicism the state religion would be to undo their own work, for the Declaration of Rights had already granted religious toleration, and a decree of December 24, 1789, admitted Protestants to all civil and military offices. In the second place, the deputies could not violate those philosophical convictions which lay at the basis of the Declaration of Rights.

The first great reform measure concerned the regular clergy. Demands for a reduction of the number of monastic establishments had been made before 1789; after the Declaration of Rights was voted, the existence of the regular clergy was doomed. Many of the monks themselves had petitioned the National Assembly to abolish the monastic orders. After a provisional suspension (October, 1789), the deputies definitely suppressed all monastic vows and abolished those establishments which required them on February 13, 1790. They gave the members of the religious orders the choice of accepting a pension and reëntering civil life or retiring to one of the designated monastic houses which the law set aside for them. As all future monastic vows were forbidden and no new houses could be founded, the monastic system was doomed to extinction. But no compulsion was put upon the regular clergy. Most of the nuns remained in the educational or charitable institutions until the end of 1792, while the majority of monks did not leave until 1791, to become teachers, librarians, administrators, or priests. There was no pronounced opposition to the decree of February 13, 1790.

The turn of the secular clergy followed. The first ecclesiastical committee of the Assembly, appointed August 12, 1789, was strengthened in February, 1790, by the addition of fifteen new members, and on April 21 it submitted a plan for the reform of the constitution and practices of the clergy. The majority of the committee were "Gallican" (defenders of the national liberties of the Catholic Church in France against the papacy); none of them were outstanding Jansenists or representatives of the *philosophes*. The members were convinced that long precedent had given the state the right to reform the clergy, and that the reform should be effected without the intervention of the pope. The plan was peacefully discussed, article by article, in the Assembly and became law on July 12, 1790. The name applied by the committee to its body of measures, the Civil Constitution of the Clergy, marked its determination not to interfere with the dogma of the Catholic Church, but merely to record the *civic* nature of religious functions.

Since a decree of the National Assembly had divided France into eighty-three departments, each department being further subdivided into districts and cantons, the desire of the committee to end the old chaotic ecclesiastical divisions of France was greatly facilitated. The number of bishoprics and archbishoprics was reduced from one hundred and thirty-nine to eighty-three, each department being made an episcopal diocese, presided over by a bishop. Instead of the old archbishoprics, there were to be ten metropolitan districts in each of which the bishop of the leading city was to serve as metropolitan. Similarly, the parishes would be redivided on new and simpler lines, the very large ones reduced and the small ones increased in size. All cathedral chapters were to be suppressed and all benefices without duties abolished. A permanent episcopal council, composed of the vicars of the seminaries, was to ratify the decisions of the bishop. Inasmuch as the priests were public officials salaried by the state, they like all other functionaries were to be elected. The same departmental electors that chose civil officials were to elect the bishops, and the district electors were to elect the parish priests.[11] There was to be a revision of salaries, both for the bishops and the lower clergy, so that the excessively high remuneration of the former and the pathetically meagre salaries of the latter would be remedied. The bishops were to be instituted by a senior bishop or a metropolitan, and they were forbidden to appeal to the pope for confirmation of the election. However, they might address a letter to him as "the visible head of the Universal Church in testimony of the unity of faith and communion" which united them. Thus the primacy of the papacy was recognized, but its jurisdiction denied. And thus the Catholic Church in France would become a national church, free from the absolute rule of the pope and at one with the civil state in its sentiments of liberty and progress.

The deputies were far from anticipating the hostile reaction that greeted the Civil Constitution of the Clergy. They were not aware of having exceeded their rights. They had abolished the Concordat of 1516, suppressed the plurality of benefices (August 4-11, 1789), and done away with annates; and the papacy had made no protest. Were they not, moreover, in making the church subordinate to the state and transforming the functions of religion into civic duties, applying the eighteenth century philosophy of enlightenment? In *The Social Contract,* Rousseau resolved the natural functions of religion into the ordinary moralities— civic duties—which would be supported and controlled by the state. "The function of the state," wrote the atheist D'Holbach, "is to make good men; the function of religion is to make good citizens." Mirabeau proclaimed that "the service of the altar is the public function."

The French clergy, however, with their traditions of Gallican liberties behind them, took another view of the matter. They were not content to win independence from Rome merely to lose it to the state. The several bishops who were deputies abstained from voting on the Civil Constitution. One of them, Boisgelin, the archbishop of Aix, stated categorically that the measure could not be binding unless it received canonical consecration. The Assembly refused to allow the bishops to form a national council which would take the necessary canonical measures to consecrate the

[11] This meant that even Protestants, Jews, and freethinkers might cast their votes in church elections.

decree, for fear that the counter-revolutionary ecclesiastics would use that council against the revolutionary movement; and by its refusal throw the responsibility of canonical consecration upon the pope. To this Civil Constitution the king could not apply his veto power, for the decree was constitutional in character. His only alternatives were to accept or reject it. Rather than risk his newly regained popularity and the opportunity to strengthen his powers, Louis XVI decided, first, to ratify and publish the Civil Constitution (July 22), and then to appeal to Pope Pius VI for his consecration.

Negotiations dragged for several months. After declaring that he was going to examine the decree, the pope later gave clear signs that he would reject it in its then existing form. But the decree, even if revised, would not have been acceptable to him, for it weakened his disciplinary control over the French clergy. Besides, the deputies had no intention of revising the Civil Constitution. On this side, the pope had a political ax to grind. His subjects in the enclave of Avignon and the Comtat-Venaissin were in full revolt and demanded annexation to France, invoking in support of their aims that doctrine of popular sovereignty which the pope had secretly condemned. The émigrés and Bernis, the French ambassador at Rome, urged him to reject the decree.

Ecclesiastical Opposition to the Assembly

In the meantime the application of the Civil Constitution was being essayed in France, but with slight success. The cathedral canons continued to officiate. The suppressed bishops kept their jurisdictions. Several bishops and priests died, and the voters elected their successors. Sharp protests were raised. Sporadic violence in some parts of the country and indifferent neglect elsewhere complicated the situation. To end the confusion, to force the clergy to commit themselves for or against the reforms, the Assembly determined to use compulsion. On November 27, 1790, it decided that all the ecclesiastics retained in their functions would be required to take an oath to the as yet unfinished constitution, which meant specifically a pledge to support the Civil Constitution of the Clergy. All those who refused to take the oath would be reputed to have renounced their office and would be replaced by other clerics. If the priests who refused to take the oath con-

tinued to exercise their former functions, they would be prosecuted under the law. Otherwise they would be pensioned.

Pope Pius VI continued to play for time, but on December 26,
Louis XVI gave his sanction to the decree on the clerical oath. He
sanctioned the decree on the advice of Boisgelin, who himself intended to refuse to take the oath. Boisgelin advised the king to
give the impression that his acceptance was forced. In that case
his conscience would still be clear, for a forced action did not bind
it. The general opinion prevailed among the deputies that the great
majority of the clergy would take the oath. But that opinion was
wholly erroneous. Only seven bishops took the oath, among them
Talleyrand, Grégoire, Loménie de Brienne, and Gobel, the future
bishop of Paris. The percentage of lower clergy that took the oath
is more difficult to establish, for some took it "with reservations"
and others retracted their oath later, when the pope formally condemned the Civil Constitution. According to the most careful estimates, slightly more than fifty per cent of the parish priests and
vicars refused to take the oath.

The pope's solemn denunciation of the religious enactments in
March and April, 1791, made the situation irremediable. Pius VI
condemned not only the Civil Constitution, but also the abolition
of the tithes, the suppression of the annates, and all the principles
of the Revolution. By this papal action France was cut in two.
Over vast stretches of territory force alone could impose the new
law. Slowly, the scales fell from the eyes of the deputies. They
had tried to create a national church and had succeeded only in
creating two churches, one for the adherents of the revolutionary
order, the other for the supporters of the ancient scheme of things.
The opponents of the Revolution quickly seized the opportunity
that presented itself—"to fish in muddy waters," says Madelin. In
his forty-third note to the king Mirabeau urged him to push the
deputies to measures still more extreme. Here, he thought, was
the great chance to discredit the Assembly and put Louis XVI at
the head of the revolutionary movement.

The advice was not wholly necessary. At first the Assembly
was reluctant to apply the decree about the clerical oath. It allowed many of the refractory clergy to perform their religious
functions, in some cases, for almost two years after the acceptance
of the decree, and it accorded the dismissed clergy a pension of
500 livres. That conciliatory policy was further strengthened by

the slowness with which the new church was organized. Only Talleyrand and Gobel agreed to institute the new bishops into office. Those in turn consecrated others until by April, 1791, sixty new bishops were instituted.

The resistance of the lower clergy and the indignation of the faithful made the conciliatory policy impossible. The dismissed parish priests continued to perform the religious services, while their flocks resented the intrusion of the new clergy. Millions of pious souls still took communion with their "good priests" and followed them into chapels, hospitals, barns, vacant churches. If they addressed themselves to the juring priest for a baptism, or a marriage ceremony, or a burial—for only the new constitutional clergy kept the civil records—they repeated these services secretly with the refractory priest whom they knew and loved. The latter was a martyr for his devout parishioners. He no longer received a salary, his dwelling was taken from him, and the authorities denied him the use of his church, but in spite of these privations he said mass, preached sermons, and administered the sacraments to his flock.

Not infrequently the revolutionary clubs and the National Guard had to be called to install the new parish priests. In some instances the latter also took it upon themselves to break up the services of the nonjuring clergy. Private chapels were raided and sacked; fighting took place in the very sanctuaries. As Easter approached (in 1791) the hostility grew more acute. All available steps were taken to prevent opposition to the religious organization.

The last effort of the Assembly to extend toleration to the dissidents also failed. It decreed on May 7, 1791, following the example already established by Talleyrand for the department of Paris, that the nonjuring clergy could hold services publicly, in full liberty, in any of the suppressed churches. But the disillusioned deputies speedily learned that they could not legislate tolerance into social custom. The decree of toleration was disavowed in practice. The constitutional clergy refused to accept the new ruling. They had risked all, physical danger, the fulminations of the pope, and the freedom of their conscience, in rallying behind the revolutionary law, and they had no intention of submitting quietly to a measure which would make their official services useless. Without the firm support of the administration they could not exist, for their churches would be deserted in favor of the tolerated refractory priests. Secondly, the public authorities refused to apply the decree of toleration on the justifiable ground that the church services of the refractory clergy provoked counter-revolutionary disturbances. To maintain the course of the Revolution, they alleged, both the civil and the religious laws of the state had to be observed, and all those who opposed the law proscribed and prosecuted.

To a large extent the reasoning of the public authorities and the clubs was justified by circumstances, for violence was not entirely on the side of the revolutionary adherents. The constitutional priests had as little safety, or less, in strongholds of the nonjuring clergy as the latter had in those regions where sentiment was hostile to them. Originally and fundamentally a religious protest, the opposition of the faithful Catholics to the impious law gradually became a counter-revolutionary war against the Revolution, a war fomented and led by staunch royalists and "aristocrats" of all shades. "The confessionals [of the refractory clergy]," wrote the departmental authorities of Morbihan, in Brittany, on June 9, 1791, "are schools where rebellion is taught and commanded." The religious laws did more than any other single act of the Constituent Assembly to develop the counter-revolution. They forced the refractory clergy and their millions of followers into the opposition.

The Counter-Revolutionary Movement

The "October days" had virtually made Louis XVI a prisoner at the Tuileries. The Assembly no longer feared that he would have recourse to troops, but the Left suspected that in all other ways he would employ his personal influence against the Revolution. The aim of the more resolute deputies, therefore, was to defeat that possibility by weakening his executive power. On the other hand Lafayette, whom the events of October had made the dominant political figure in France, endeavored to strengthen the royal prerogative. He knew that the masses regarded him with awe and respect, and he dreamed of becoming the Washington of France and the real power behind the throne. Neither the king nor the queen liked him, but in order to win time for their own plan they pretended to place themselves under Lafayette's tutelage. Louis XVI gave him command of the regular troops in the immediate vicinity of Paris and expressed confidence in his "mayor of the palace." At the same time the monarch addressed a secret communication to his Bourbon relative, Charles IV of Spain, protesting firmly against all the arbitrary actions of the Assembly. "I owe it to myself," he wrote, "to my children, to my family, to my entire house, to combat the degradation of the royal prerogative which long centuries have confirmed in my dynasty."

Lafayette was no tyro at the game of practical politics. He subsidized a political press and made a bid for the support of the revolutionary leaders. The road to Mirabeau's support lay through his ambition and his purse. His ambition was fixed upon a ministerial position and his purse was open for the payment of his enormous debts. The Assembly, which recognized his ability but suspected him because of his shady past, defeated his ambition by its unfortunate decree of November 7, 1789. This measure denied the king the right to select any of his ministers from among the deputies of the Assembly, but it is apparent that the decree aimed primarily at Mirabeau. Thereupon Mirabeau showed himself receptive to various secret intermediaries of Louis XVI, who brought him into closer contact with court circles. Lafayette and Mirabeau were jealous of each other, yet they were in substantial agreement in their policy of strengthening the king's executive powers.

For his part, Louis XVI detested Lafayette and despised Mirabeau. Yet he tried his utmost to bring the two rivals together in order that they might serve his interests. In all likelihood, despite his appeal to Charles IV of Spain, the king had not yet abandoned confidence in legal means of strengthening his executive powers. On February 4, 1790, shortly after the flurry of a madcap royalist intrigue fomented by his brother, the count of Provence, he appeared very unexpectedly before the Assembly. In his speech, which had been prepared by Necker and Lafayette, he disavowed all plots against the revolutionary cause, loyally accepted, both for himself and for his consort, the new régime, and summoned all citizens to follow his example. Sincere as he undoubtedly was, for the moment at least, the king had no control over the course of events. The enemies of the Revolution, the so-called "aristocrats," made capital of the popular impatience with and grievances against the National Assembly. The court party circulated pamphlets in which they stressed the shortcomings of the revolutionaries and endeavored to win over the various groups of malcontents to a reactionary policy. Their spokesmen in the Assembly and their counter-revolutionary press heaped ridicule upon the patriots. Dismissed functionaries, impatient peasants fuming over the legal perpetuation of the feudal land dues, the aggrieved clergy, all were grist for the counter-revolutionary mill.

The first measures of ecclesiastical reform in the fall of 1789 and the spring of 1790 gave the "aristocrats" an opportunity to cloak their counter-revolutionary activities under the veil of religion. As Easter approached in 1790, the secret agents of the émigré count of Artois redoubled their activity. "Easter week," wrote one of Artois's agents, "is the time when the bishops and priests can profitably lead back their errant subjects to the true religion and to the king. I hope that they will appreciate their interests and those of the state sufficiently clearly not to neglect this opportunity; if they work together, success seems certain." In the Assembly several hundred deputies filed a protest against the religious decrees. That protest had no echo in most of France, but in the south of France and in Alsace, it served to unleash the ill restrained jealousy and hatred between the Protestants and the Catholics, for there the various measures of the Assembly were falsely represented as the work of Protestants and infidels. In Alsace, the religious animosities covered a variety of grievances against the revolutionary government. The menace of civil war in Alsace, moreover, was particularly dangerous, for the lay and ecclesiastical princes were appealing to the head of the Holy Roman Empire against revolutionary France. In the south of France (the Midi), religious intolerance went hand in hand with economic rivalries in the cloth and silk trades. Disturbances began in April, 1790, and lasted for several months with great loss of property and life. In a skirmish at Nîmes on June 13, three hundred people were killed, most of whom were Catholics and royalists. In Avignon, which had revolted against the political authority of the pope, there were violent conflicts between the partisans of the old rule and the leaders of the new who wanted to have Avignon incorporated into France.

Louis XVI still sought legal and constitutional ways of regaining his lost prerogatives. He had no part in stirring up the civil war in the Midi and saw in its failure only an added reason to follow Lafayette's instructions. Lafayette, in common with most of the moderate leaders, was frightened by the interminable disorders and was more determined than ever to strengthen the monarch's executive powers. In his comment on a memorandum that Lafayette submitted to him the king wrote (April 16): "I promise Monsieur de Lafayette fullest confidence in all measures concerning the establishment of the Constitution, my legitimate authority . . . and the restoration of public tranquillity." At the same time Louis XVI came to full terms with Mirabeau. On May 10 he promised the deputy 200,000 livres for the payment of his pressing debts, 6000 more a month for his expenses, and notes for a million livres payable at the close of the Assembly. Mirabeau's duties were to strengthen the royal authority and advise the king in his conduct. Having already taken money for his services to various individuals, most recently to the duke of Orléans and the count of Provence, Mirabeau found himself in no novel rôle when he became the secret agent of the crown.[1] His new relations

[1] The nature of Mirabeau's relations with the court is best revealed in the three volumes of *Correspondance entre Mirabeau et le comte de la Marck* (Paris, 1891).

with the court did not constitute treason to the cause of the Revolution. He had never made a secret of his royalist convictions, and he firmly believed that France could have tranquillity only under a monarchy, but a monarchy whose king sincerely accepted the achievements of the Revolution. Therefore, in essaying to prevent both a counter-revolution and a more radical orientation of the revolutionary movement, Mirabeau was paid, as Lord Acton says, "to be of his own opinion."

An early opportunity presented itself for the fulfillment of Mirabeau's program in the dispute between England and Spain over control of Nootka Sound and Vancouver Island in the Pacific Ocean. The Assembly spent several weeks in May, 1790, debating the question as to whether France was bound by the terms of the Family Compact of 1761 to come to the assistance of Charles IV, the Bourbon ruler of Spain. But the deputies also considered the grave question of the diplomatic powers of Louis XVI; namely, his right to declare war and ratify peace. In these debates the best speakers of the Right and the Left took part; for the former, Maury and Cazalès, as well as Malouet of the Center; for the latter, Duport, Alexandre Lameth, and Barnave. Mirabeau employed all his oratorical skill to aid the cause of Louis XVI, but it proved unavailing. The deputies voted to limit Louis XVI's power over the military forces of the nation and reduced his diplomatic prerogative to conducting negotiations, which were subject to the ratification of the Assembly.

Perhaps if Mirabeau had prevailed in the debates and succeeded in strengthening the executive power of the king, Louis XVI would have been more willing to accept the Revolution. The deputies' vote prevented the outbreak of war between France and England, but it temporarily discredited Mirabeau, especially with the Jacobins of Paris. He made a desperate effort to convince Lafayette that the use of force against the radical deputies was in order, but again he failed. Lafayette guarded his popularity too jealously to risk it in a futile gesture. The Fête de la Fédération was approaching, and he intended to capitalize it for himself. The Fête de la Fédération on July 14, 1790, was, as we have noted, an impressive ceremony which seemed to mark the harmonious unity of all Frenchmen. Lafayette might well have considered it a personal triumph, for he received wild acclaim from the spectators and shone in all his glory. For a brief interlude after

July, 1790, there was a lull in the counter-revolutionary movement, but once the enthusiasm of the Fête had died down, the struggle was resumed with even greater vigor. Military dissensions grew sharper, and the religious conflict was aggravated.

POLITICAL AND ECONOMIC RADICALISM

"That fête poisoned the spirit of the troops," sorrowfully wrote General Bouillé, meditating over the tumultuous reception received by the regulars and the National Guard (*fédérés*) in Paris on July 14, 1790. It did indeed spread revolutionary sentiment among the troops, but the troops were prepared to receive it. In the six months from January to July, 1790, one could have traced the progressive breakdown of all discipline in the regular army. The more determined aristocrats among the old officers had emigrated; those who remained either maintained a sullen resistance to the democratic current in the troops or else tried to take advantage of the relaxed discipline by heading this opposition. At heart all of them realized their impotence to stop their men from undermining their authority. The regular troops, like the members of National Guard, had taken the oath of allegiance to the nation and were at the disposal of the local government. Like the National Guard the regulars joined the clubs and Masonic lodges. The minister of war realized that the situation was dangerous, but beyond penning eloquent notes to the Assembly, did little to remedy it. The Assembly passed the responsibility of action to the king, recommending the formation of a new army. But an armed Europe gave Louis XVI sufficient cause for hesitation before so vast an undertaking.

Soon mutinies occurred in the principal garrisons of the kingdom, at Toulon, Brest, Strasbourg, and elsewhere. In all the mutinies, Lafayette and the Assembly had tried to steer a middle course, to maintain discipline in the ranks without alienating either the support of the officers or the loyalty of the troops. But Lafayette was a militarist by profession. To support discipline he was not loath to use force. In August, 1790, the garrison troops of Nancy in Lorraine rebelled against their commandant, an action which had the gravest consequences.

The situation at Nancy did not differ from that in any of the other garrison towns. The officers were showered with threats and insults by the zealous patriots, denounced for their aristocratic birth, and hindered in the execution of their commands. The troops were wooed by the revolutionary clubs, and their heads were filled with the intoxicating fumes of the new gospel of equality. They protested against the quality of their rations, demanded that the expense accounts be verified, and not infrequently refused to obey the orders of their superior officers. The officers met those manifestations with the only means at their command, which was military punishment. The Nancy affair got out of hand when the Assembly, under Lafayette's instigation, voted to repress the mutinous troops. In spite of Barnave's opposition, it ordered General Bouillé, Lafayette's cousin and the commander of the Army of the East, stationed at Metz, to march on the rebels at Nancy and suppress the insurrection. He gathered a small army of regular troops and National Guardsmen and cut his way into the city. Some thirty of the rebels were hanged, more than forty condemned to the galleys, and the revolutionary clubs closed. Bouillé's soldiers maintained law and order at the point of the bayonet. At first, the entire country approved of Bouillé's step. The king wrote him a congratulatory letter in which he intimated very plainly that Bouillé's popularity might soon stand the monarchy in good stead. The Assembly and the Jacobins felicitated his National Guard for its vigorous repression of anarchy. The National Guard of the capital held memorial services for the loyal troops that had fallen in the strife. But before three months had passed, the Assembly retracted its praise for Bouillé, and reopened the doors of the Jacobin Club of Nancy. More than ever, during September and October, discipline was relaxed and dissension rife. Lafayette's popularity was waning fast, while Mirabeau was under a cloud; and, despairing of their aid, Louis XVI made ready to appeal to the great powers for intervention.

Precisely at this moment the religious war began in earnest. The schism among the clergy, caused by the enforcement of the Civil Constitution, gave a great impetus to the counter-revolutionary movement. Twenty thousand National Guardsmen, inspired by their attachment to the monarchy and their religion, answered the call of their leaders and marched to the camp of Jalès in the Midi. The cross was their banner. Their leaders, who were counter-revolutionary agents of the émigrés, priests, and nobles, issued a .nifesto that "they would not lay down their arms until they had reëstablished the king in his glory, the clergy in their estates, the nobility in their prerogatives, and the parlements in their old functions." For six months, the camp remained organized, until the Assembly dissolved it by force. The departments in the Midi were not the only ones to resist the application of the religious laws. The pope's anathema against the entire Revolution stiffened the resistance of the northern departments, of the west (Brittany and the Vendée), and particularly of the east, where the contact with the émigrés and the Germanic states was closest.

To make the situation still more critical, Louis XVI cast his lot with the refractory clergy. As we have noted, he had never sincerely accepted the reforms of the Revolution, and least of all, the ecclesiastical legislation. A year had passed since the October uprising, and all constitutional attempts to increase his powers had failed. In the meantime the new administration had painfully come into being: the municipalities were functioning, the courts were organized, the monastic establishments and the religious chapters were being shut down, and plans for the sale of national land well under way. His self-appointed mentor, Lafayette, was daily losing ground against the sweeping democratic forces of the newspapers and the popular clubs. Soon the sections of Paris (the sixty electoral districts had been replaced by forty-eight sections) forced Louis XVI to dismiss almost his entire ministry and accept a new one of less pronounced royalist views. At that juncture the king was forced to sign the decree on the clerical oath (December 26, 1790), secretly protesting as he did so that he would rather be king in Metz than king of France under such tyranny.[2] The bitter hostility between the juring and the refractory clergy and their respective followers contributed indirectly to the growth of an anticlerical faction. But the more immediate consequence was to accelerate the growth of a democratic and republican movement.

This movement developed outside the Assembly and against the desires of most of the deputies.[3] In its political aspects it was a demand for universal suffrage and for an end to the distinction between active and passive citizens. The centers of political agitation were the club of the Cordeliers (opened in April, 1790) and

[2] Metz was the headquarters of Bouillé's army.

[3] In the Assembly hall Robespierre pressed his demand for the inclusion of the passive citizens in the National Guard, for he saw that the poorer citizens would greatly strengthen their political influence if they obtained the legal right to bear arms.

the fraternal societies in the forty-eight sections of Paris. The petty bourgeoisie led the movement at the Cordeliers, but the passive citizens who made up most of its membership supplied the energy. Petty traders and dealers, artisans, hawkers and criers, journeymen and apprentices, in short the greatest proportion of the Parisian citizenry, attended the meetings of the popular societies. Under the leadership of the Abbé Fauchet and a Freemason journalist, Nicholas de Bonneville, a group of mystic Christian-Socialists met weekly to listen to an exegesis on Rousseau's *Social Contract*. Bonneville preached direct government in his newspaper, the *Bouche de fer*, and Marat, in his *Ami du peuple*, seconded the appeal. The radical press launched a republican campaign against the monarchy to which Brissot, the future leader of the Girondins, Danton, Robespierre, and Camille Desmoulins gave guarded support. Sharp reproaches were directed against Lafayette, the deputies of the Right, and the refractory clergy. Somewhat more indirectly, this republican agitation was also preparing the masses to accept the belief that war against kings and aristocrats was the sole means of perpetuating the reforms of the Revolution.

Along with the movement for more radical political reform there developed a movement of social and economic protest against the policy of the Assembly. The peasants had unceasingly manifested their discontent since 1789, but early in 1791 the workingmen of Paris recorded their protest against unemployment, rising prices, and the inflation of paper money. There were strikes in the printing establishments and in the building trades. Both groups of malcontents, peasants and artisans, looked to the state for the satisfaction of their grievances. If those who clamored for more sweeping political reform were successful, radical social and economic reform was certain to follow.

This prospect greatly troubled the more moderate bourgeois deputies. Their anxiety over the radical movement was shown in their support of Mirabeau's campaign for social conservatism. Suspected by only a mere handful of deputies Mirabeau engaged upon a campaign of propaganda and bribery that made an art of political corruption. Fully utilizing the court money at his disposal, he bought newspapers, bribed deputies, silenced some republican leaders, and had conservative pamphlets distributed in great profusion. He regained his popularity with the electorate of Paris and his influence with many of his colleagues in the Assembly. Even Marie

Antoinette regarded him more favorably. But he died on April 2, 1791, his plan unconsummated. His funeral was the occasion for a great ovation to his memory, and his remains were deposited in the Panthéon. All Paris grieved over his untimely death. Perhaps, as many historians have thought, he alone was capable of saving the monarchy, but one may challenge the validity of this view. It is far more likely that Mirabeau's death saved him from the discomfiture and chagrin of seeing the pressure of events defeat his plans. His desperate expedient of provoking extreme, radical utterances in order that these might discredit the Assembly was not likely to succeed. Contrary to his advice Louis XVI had already made up his mind to flee toward the eastern frontier. Mirabeau's scheme contained no fundamental remedy to allay the discontent of the radical extremists or to placate the grievances of the disgruntled conservatives. His death helped make his reputation for statesmanship; but more immediately it gave various other deputies an opportunity to lead the debates.

For the next few months the apprehensive Assembly tried to throw back the wave of radical proposals. The deputies extended toleration to the refractory clergy and passed or attempted to pass measures against the democrats, such as the continued exclusion of passive citizens from the National Guard, prohibition of collective petitions, and the expulsion of the Cordeliers from their meeting place. In measure as Robespierre gained recognition as the defender of the poor, so Barnave stood out as the champion of the propertied class which had carried through the Revolution. In May, 1791, Barnave suffered a reverse by losing a long debate with Robespierre over the question of granting the vote to the colored population of Santo Domingo. The decision to grant the franchise to the mulattoes which ultimately brought on chaos in the French part of the island was a triumph of theory over fact, of idealism over expediency. Its immediate consequences were to strengthen the resolution of the moderates like Barnave to keep the revolutionary movement within bounds.

Shortly after this debate, while the reporter of the constitutional committee was discussing the organization of the next legislature, Robespierre made a motion which filled his opponents with joy. He proposed, and the Assembly decreed, that the members of the present Assembly should not be eligible to the next. Robespierre and the democratic deputies believed that they were saving the coming legislature from the continued presence of the obstructive deputies of the Right; the moderates and conservatives were delighted to save the coming legislature from the continued presence of the deputies who proposed to give a more radical turn to the Revolution. Wise and disinterested, Robespierre's motion assuredly was not. While it brought him added renown, the democrats claimed a triumph over the deputies of the Right. The greatest blow to the latter was the dramatic flight of Louis XVI. On June 20, the king and the royal family fled from Paris toward the eastern frontier. Were the sovereigns of Europe ready to intercede in his behalf?

REVOLUTIONARY PROPAGANDA AND INTERNATIONAL PROBLEMS

At first the liberals of Europe had given an enthusiastic welcome to the French Revolution. Liberal Europe was greatly interested in French affairs, for French philosophical ideas and the analogous doctrines of the German *Aufklärung* had spread over a large part of the Continent. French was still the universal language in Europe, and French civilization still maintained its hegemony on the Continent. From the reports of tourists and more or less permanent residents in France as well as from the information given out by Frenchmen living abroad, the different countries of Europe knew that the judicial aristocracy of France had led the struggle against irresponsible despotism. The fall of the Bastille was at first unwittingly represented in Europe as the work of that aristocracy. Hence an additional reason for the universal approbation that greeted that memorable event. But the disorders in the country districts and the attacks upon the châteaux rapidly disillusioned most European sympathizers.

Gradually the sovereigns of Europe began to realize the danger of the revolutionary movement. This danger lay in the extension of its universal principles, in particular of the Declaration of Rights, beyond the French frontiers and in the possibility that certain national groups might attempt to apply those same principles. In fact those revolutionary principles were extended beyond France through the conscious and unconscious propaganda of enthusiastic Frenchmen and equally enthusiastic nationalists of other European countries. The numerous Frenchmen resident in various cities of Europe, tourists, business men, political refugees, liberal supporters of the French movement who flocked to France from all corners of Europe, all served as agents for the spread of the revolutionary gospel. The "pilgrims of liberty," as the first foreign visitors who came to Paris were called, joined in the political debates of the Assembly. The political refugees from Holland, Switzerland, and Belgium formed clubs for the purpose of bringing on a revolutionary movement in their native lands. The Freemasons of France helped spread revolutionary propaganda into Savoy and the Rhineland.

The revolutionary propaganda was a failure in eastern and southern Europe. Russia and Hungary were protected against the revolutionary infection by their distance from France. In these countries isolated individuals declared themselves partisans of the French, but they had no influence over the masses. In Italy, support of French reforms was slight and superficial, while it was almost nonexistent in Spain and Portugal.

The propaganda was much more effective in England and the Germanies, where the intellectual movement before the Revolution had prepared the liberals. From the point of view of the French, England and the Germanies were of strategic importance. As neighbors of France they could crush the extension of the Revolution by their hostility, while by their support or neutrality they could allow it to develop. Many illustrious Germans hailed the first conquests of the Revolution. It found a supporter in Herder, the chief exponent of German nationalism. The poet Klopstock, the philosophers, Kant, Fichte, and Humboldt, as well as other publicists and professors, approved of the early events. The bourgeoisie of several cities also responded favorably to the news from France, while the peasantry along the Rhineland followed the example of their French neighbors by refusing to pay feudal dues and partaking in violent riots against their landlords.

The bishopric of Liége also responded to the contagious influence of French disturbances. There was a demand for the curtailment of the privileges of the bishop, who fled to Treves at the first visible signs of reform. The peasantry and the artisans joined the revolutionary movement, while the more moderate elements appealed to Prussia, which sent in troops to maintain order. A second revolution took place in the Austrian Netherlands in 1789, the first one having been suppressed in 1788. Here too the inspiration came from France, and the leaders were returned refugees who had been living in France. The returning refugees gained popular support, roused the country, and expelled the Austrian troops from Brussels in December, 1789. The German-speaking cantons of Switzerland were also affected, largely because of their nearness to Alsace, while next door to the Swiss cantons the revolutionary propaganda was effectively spread in Savoy.

There were no violent disturbances in England because the response to the Revolution came from the intellectuals rather than from the masses. Fox, Sheridan, and Bentham were among its first defenders. Pitt also viewed the early events with satisfaction and thought that the overthrow of the Old Régime would be followed by the establishment of an orderly constitutional monarchy. With the French government occupied with the Revolution, he hoped for a period of peace in Europe and an opportunity to reduce taxes at home and introduce the reforms that had long been proposed. The most active apologists of the French Revolution in England were the dissenters and nonconformists, who hoped to ultilize the attack upon arbitrary government and privilege in France to gain fuller religious rights in their own country as well as to further the cause of parliamentary reform. They formed new societies or revived old ones and entered into correspondence with the French revolutionary clubs, particularly with the Jacobins of Paris. The most famous of these societies was the Revolution Society of 1688, which sent a congratulatory address to the National Constituent Assembly in 1789 and celebrated the first anniversary of the fall of the Bastille in 1790.

The fatal weakness of the revolutionary propaganda was that it aroused an intellectual reaction in the countries that it penetrated. The summer and autumn disturbances in France during 1789 frightened the faint-hearted supporters in England and the Germanies. The French émigrés aggravated the fears of the timorous. They established themselves wherever a relative or a protector agreed to receive them—at Turin, at Rome, at Koblenz, Worms, and elsewhere on the Continent. They were most numerous on the Rhineland, where the prince of Condé had collected a small army at Worms in the domains of the elector of Treves. Though they were not popular because their mode of life was, or seemed, scandalous to their more sedate hosts, they made a deep impression with their exaggerated accounts of atrocities and their insistence that all the evils in France resulted from the work of a handful of scoundrels. The failure of the revolt in the Austrian Netherlands also turned sentiment against the French. The revolutionists fell out after their expulsion of the Austrian troops in December, 1789, and became involved in strife between the landed interests and the clerical group on the one hand and the democratic element on the other. An effort to form a federal republic was defeated, and the irreconcilable social and religious differences among the inhabitants brought on a violent struggle which ended with the victory of the privileged classes, the flight of the democrats, and the discrediting of the entire movement because of its attendant violence and bloodshed.

The liberals of Germany still professed their allegiance to the principles of the Revolution, but with many reservations and restrictions. They became more discriminating and less frequent in their praise. Moreover, the loose political confederation and the old local traditions and regional activities in the German-speaking countries greatly weakened the force of the French appeal. Revolutionary propaganda made only slight headway east of the Rhine. The hostile reaction developed most sharply in the countries subject to the influence of the Catholic Church. Bavaria, Sardinia, the states of Italy, Spain, and Portugal took careful precautions against secret societies, revolutionary propagandists, and the communication of revolutionary ideas and ideals. In March, 1791, a cordon of troops was stretched along the Pyrenees to ward off "the French pestilence."

England did not escape the reaction. Anglican churchmen and landed proprietors led the van in denouncing what they regarded, justly or otherwise, as atrocities across the Channel. The most eloquent and the most influential of the critics was Edmund Burke, whose famous *Reflections on the Revolution in France* created a sensation upon its publication in November, 1790. Its effect upon public opinion both in England and on the Continent was marked, though one of the unforeseen consequences of its publication was the barrage of angry rejoinders that it drew from capable pens. The *Reflections* is important also because it was the first methodical indictment of the basic natural rights philosophy of the French Revolution, as well as an impassioned statement of the conservative position. For the natural rights of man of the eighteenth century thinkers Burke substituted the historic rights of nations. He believed—and his views were followed by many nineteenth century political thinkers—that legislation was incapable of inculcating civic morality and respect for political liberty; that such necessary political virtues could arise only from the interplay of established interests. But his criticism of the deeds of the Constituent Assembly and the French people was unfair, because it was grounded upon insufficient information and inadequate understanding of conditions in France both before and after 1789. Among the many replies provoked by his book, the most outstanding were the polished *Vindiciae Gallicae* of the Scot, Sir James Mackintosh, and the blunt, stirring *Rights of Man* of Thomas Paine. The first part of the latter work appeared in 1791 in a cheap edition, and its large sale had much to do with the new interest of the English lower middle classes in the French Revolution.

The political effects of Burke's rhetorical denunciation of the French experiment and his eloquent defense of British institutions and tradition were the strengthening of the Tory majority in Parliament and the weakening of the efforts for parliamentary reform and the abolition of the Test Act. The Whigs split into two factions, the more numerous led by Burke, the other by his old friend and political disciple, Charles James Fox. The governing classes were beginning to show such horror of reform that every effort to carry through the schemes which William Pitt himself had advanced somewhat earlier was regarded askance. The masses followed Burke and William Pitt, whose appeal to history aroused their British patriotism. The parliamentary following of Fox was so slight that it has been called the "weakest and most discredited opposition" that England had ever known. For a full generation England labored under the dread of political and social change, and no improvement was to be recorded until after the Napoleonic period. "Philosophical radicals" like Jeremy Bentham, Joseph Priestley, or William Cobbett (only after 1806) might express their sympathy with some of the revolutionary ideas, but, for all the influence that these ideas exercised upon British institutions from 1789 to 1815, the Revolution might never have taken place. Burke himself advocated an armed crusade, after first proposing that the English government should establish a pacific blockade against the French revolutionary propaganda. The pope's formal anathema against the Revolution in the spring of 1791 gave added force to Burke's proposal against the "French barbarians."

The Assembly was anxious to avert war with the great powers, and on May 22, 1790, the deputies voted the pacifistic decree by which France renounced all wars of conquest and promised to refrain from using her troops against the liberty of other peoples. Mirabeau protested bitterly that that decree forced "France to disarm before a Europe still in arms," but it kept the peace. Soon, however, there arose between revolutionary France and the European sovereigns problems involving questions of territory and basic conceptions of international law.

As early as September, 1789, the German princes in Alsace sent protests to the head of the Holy Roman Empire against the feudal decrees, the abolition of foreign ecclesiastical jurisdiction within France, and the abolition of the tithes. Later they protested against the confiscation of the ecclesiastical estates. Legally their various rights had been secured to them by international treaties (Münster and Ryswick) and by separate agreements with the French kingdom; but on the other hand it would have been difficult for the National Constituent Assembly to treat princely rights in Alsace (which was part of political France) differently from, or more leniently than, the rights of other privileged individuals within France. While the Assembly denied the legal claims of the German princes, among whom were the electors of Treves, Mainz, and Cologne, the bishop of Basel, the duke of Württemberg, and the margrave of Baden, it offered them a money indemnity which the princes refused. The Assembly finally took the position, in November, 1790, that Alsace was French, not by virtue of the treaty of Westphalia (1648), but because the Alsatians felt that they were French and desired union with the French. The dispute hinged on even more vital considerations for the German princes than their rights under international law, for the immediate question as to the effect of the revolutionary reforms in Alsace upon their own neighboring states was involved. The princes demanded that the empire reassert its full rights over Alsace, claiming that France had forfeited its sovereignty of that province by ignoring the reservations made in the treaties concerning Alsace. In December, 1790, Emperor Leopold II supported their claims in a sharp note to the French government which went unheeded.

The papacy too had cause for complaint against the Assembly. Ever since the fourteenth century Avignon and the Comtat-Venaissin had been under the temporal rule of the popes, forming a little papal state within France; but in June, 1790, the more radical inhabitants of Avignon rebelled, expelled the papal legate, and demanded annexation to France. Would revolutionary France accept the invitation, particularly after its decree of the preceding month solemnly renouncing wars of conquest? The deputies of the Left, with Robespierre as spokesman, insisted that that decree allowed the *nation*, rather than the political ruler, to decide its destiny. Hence the annexation of Avignon would not be conquest, but the satisfaction of the expressed desires of its inhabitants. Slowly the Assembly allowed itself to be convinced. In April, 1791, its diplomatic committee reported that Avignon belonged *by right* to France and advised its incorporation with France, with an indemnity to the pope. The proposal was rejected, and Avignon was left for months to the warring factions within its territory. By September of the same year, however, Avignon was formally annexed to France. Thus a new principle of international law, was adopted, the application of the democratic doctrine of popular sovereignty in the field of international relations. To the great powers, France's action ruptured all existing diplomatic bonds between the Revolution and Europe. It seemed as though France gave herself the right to annex, peacefully, any state that desired a revolution against its sovereign. In the words of Gaxotte, a historian hostile to the Revolution, "Instead of being an incident of internal French politics the Revolution was going to become a cosmopolitan venture, a universal religion threatening not only the form but the very existence of all states."

PROJECTS OF INTERVENTION AND THE FLIGHT OF THE KING

If the monarchs of Europe did not then unite in a crusade against France, it was because they thought France too weak to carry out her pretensions. Her military forces were of no moment; her finances were in disorder, and her government had broken her alliances with Spain and Austria. The renunciation of all wars of conquest, the refusal to aid the Belgian revolutionists, the evident desire to defer decisive action on Alsace and Avignon, all pointed to France's helplessness. The Austrian alliance was broken in fact if not in name, and the Family Compact with Spain had been severed by the Assembly in May, 1790, when the deputies failed to come to the aid of Spain against England in the Nootka Sound controversy. France "was destroying herself," wrote Mercy-Argenteau, the Austrian ambassador.

Both Louis XVI and the émigrés appealed to the powers to intervene, the former secretly and the latter openly. To arouse Europe against the Revolution became the sacred duty of these embittered crusaders who had voluntarily exiled themselves from their native land. From Turin, which he made his headquarters, the count of Artois sent emissaries to Rome and Madrid to win support for his intrigues in southern France. Calonne, now the leading spirit among the émigrés in the Rhineland, hoped to use Condé's supporters at Koblenz as the spearhead of a Prussian army of intervention. Needless to say, the émigrés were of dubious value to Louis XVI; the royal princes were less concerned with him than with a counter-revolution which would benefit them. Breteuil, the secret agent of Louis XVI, warned the Emperor Leopold II against the count of Artois, and Louis XVI and Marie Antoinette disavowed the latter's schemes.

The émigrés stopped at nothing short of the entry of foreign troops into France and a full restoration of the Old Régime. Louis XVI, on the contrary, wanted the intervention to end with a military demonstration at the frontier. His object was to intimidate the revolutionists with the spectacle of the powers of Europe united against them. He had no desire to become the prisoner of Artois or any other émigré leader. Even before the passage of the decree of the Civil Constitution of the Clergy he had already appealed for assistance at the courts of Madrid and Vienna. The ecclesiastical legislation strengthened his early decision; it did not determine his action. In October, 1790, Louis XVI commissioned Breteuil to take full measures leading to the kind of intervention that he had in mind. Bouillé, the loyal general who had quelled the Nancy insurrection, received word to hold his troops in Lorraine in readiness for action, while Count Fersen, the secret lover of Marie Antoinette, began to draw up careful plans for the flight of the royal family. The traditions of the seventeenth and eighteenth centuries supported intervention. Louis XVI considered himself the incarnation of the state and felt free to use whatever means he deemed best to protect the state against its enemies. The émigré nobles, in the spirit of vassals rallying to the support of their overlord, gave their loyalty to the *prince*, not to the nation. Hence they did not think of themselves as betraying or deserting their country, but as defending the rightful ruler against his rebellious subjects.

As late as the summer of 1791 the sovereigns of Europe were not prepared to listen to appeals for intervention. The dynastic rivalries of the great European powers which had in part precipitated the interminable wars of the eighteenth century were still acute during the early years of the French Revolution. Not until Austria and Prussia began to compose their differences (at the Congress of Reichenbach in July, 1790), not until Austria concluded peace with the Ottoman Empire while Russia was concluding peace both with the Ottoman Empire and with Sweden, was there any possibility of a European intervention in French affairs. Even then the governments of Austria and Prussia paid as much attention to the situation in Poland, where Catherine the Great of Russia was planning a second partition, as they did to the French Revolution.

The monarch most eager to intervene in behalf of Louis XVI and the émigrés was the Hohenzollern prince Frederick William II, the sorry successor of Frederick the Great on the throne of Prussia (1786–1797). But his conditions were that Austria join Prussia and that he receive territorial compensation on the Rhine for the expenses of intervention, while Austria was to seek compensation in Alsace and Lorraine. The emperor Leopold II (the brother of Marie Antoinette) still hesitated, despite the fact that the settlement of his domestic and foreign affairs now permitted him to intervene in France. Perhaps his earlier experience as an enlightened despot in Tuscany made him less hostile than other rulers to the course of events in France. As late as the spring of 1791, he still turned a deaf ear to Frederick William II, to Artois, and to Breteuil, the accredited representative of Louis XVI, and to the repeated appeals of Marie Antoinette. Catherine urged him on, but he knew that she "was racking her brains" to divert Austria from Poland. Then, more or less abruptly, he agreed to consider the Prussian proposal of intervention. He had received a letter from Marie Antoinette in which his sister announced the imminent flight of the royal family to the eastern frontier of France. At a secret conference held at Mantua, May 20, 1791, Austria, Prussia, several secondary German states, and Spain reached a general agreement to come to the aid of the Bourbons in France.

Secret preparations for the escape from Paris had been going on since December, 1790. Various incidents connected with these preparations led not a few revolutionists to suspect that mischievous plans were afoot, but nothing definite was known. The Assembly took its precautions against the rumored flight. Louis XVI gave credence to the rumors by preparing to spend the Easter season (1791) at Saint-Cloud, outside of Paris, but the National Guard and a large crowd of Parisians stopped his carriages in the courtyard of the palace, and the royal family was obliged to reënter the Tuileries. This incident is still shrouded in some mystery. Louis may have been sincere in his desire to escape the services of the constitutional clergy and take communion with a nonjuring priest at Saint-Cloud, but Lafayette alleges in his memoirs that the entire affair had been arranged in advance so as to enable the king to prove to Europe that he was a prisoner in his own palace. The crowd, at any rate, was convinced that, once the royal family reached Saint-Cloud, it would continue directly to the frontier.

After this affront Louis XVI and Marie Antoinette were more determined than ever to escape from Paris. In order to gain time for the fruition of his plan the king tried to quiet public suspicion by agreeing to the proposals of the Assembly. He consented to hear mass said by a constitutional priest. Requested to address a circular letter to the French embassies on the Continent, he obeyed, stating in the letter that he was perfectly free and had accepted the revolutionary program without any reservations. But he also took the secret precaution of instructing Breteuil to disavow all his public utterances. Count Fersen completed the preparations for flight by June 20, and that night the royal family made its escape from the palace. The objective was Montmédy, a small town near the Luxemburg frontier. General Bouillé, whose troops could be counted on, was to send cavalry detachments from Metz along the road toward Paris in order to convey the refugees to the frontier. Suspicion was to be averted by explaining to the local inhabitants that a consignment of great value was en route from Paris which required the protection of Bouillé's regiments.

The count of Provence left by another route and reached the Austrian Netherlands without any trouble. But the royal family was less fortunate. Valuable time was lost in starting and there were further delays on the road. The fugitives made such slow progress, and the presence of the royal troops aroused such suspicion that Bouillé's officers decided not to wait any longer and led their men away from the main road. Though the king was recognized at several points of the journey, the only person who dared give the alarm was Drouet, the postmaster at Sainte-Menehould. When the heavy traveling carriage reached Varennes, it was delayed again to wait for the relay of post horses. Meanwhile Drouet had galloped through the Lorraine woods from Sainte-Menehould to Varennes and given the alarm. The road was barricaded, and the authorities arrested the entire party. Louis XVI acknowledged his identity and was detained to await orders from Paris. Early the next morning (June 22) couriers arrived from Paris, bearing the Assembly's orders to seize the monarch. The return trip to Paris was tragic. Hooting, menacing crowds blocked the road and threatened the royal family with violence. Midway, Barnave, Pétion, and Latour-Maubourg, the three deputies whom the Assembly had sent out to escort the king to Paris, met the royal carriage. On the 24th of June the convoy passed through the silent streets of Paris. The silence was ominous, and the soldiers guarded the streets of the capital. With marked relief the royal couple heard the grilled gate of the Tuileries swing shut behind them.

The Consequences of the King's Flight

When Louis XVI fled from Paris he left behind him a declaration to the nation. In this document he gave utterance to his indignation against the insults to which he and the queen had been subjected. He criticized the constitution sharply and in detail, averring that it stripped him of most of his powers. He attacked the revolutionary clubs, particularly the Jacobins, for their coercion of public opinion and administrative officials. He appealed to all loyal Frenchmen to rally behind him and the ancient traditions of the French monarchy.

As soon as it was informed of his flight, the Assembly, led by the Left deputies, especially Barnave, promptly ordered the seizure of the king and the arrest of his abductors, adopting the necessary political fiction that Louis XVI had not fled but had been carried off by the enemies of France. To have done otherwise would have required absolute proof that Louis XVI was a declared enemy, but the proof did not exist. As for his statement to the nation, it was possible to question its authenticity or to maintain that it had been "wrung from a deceived king." The Assembly voted that decrees should be promulgated without the monarch's sanction and passed another decree closing the frontiers and forbidding the exportation of all specie, arms, and ammunition. Nonjuring priests and notoriously hostile nobles were placed under surveillance and, in some cases, interned. The Assembly mobilized the National Guard for action, and the frontier garrisons made ready for a siege. Petitions from the provinces flowed into the capital with every courier, most of them clamoring for the punishment of the faithless monarch, and some of them, like that of the Jacobins of Montpellier, demanding a republic. The republican movement gained new adherents in Paris. In the columns of the radical press, in the club of the Cordeliers, in the theaters there were outspoken calls for a republic.

The conservative deputies of the Assembly were adamant to the republican and democratic propaganda. In truth, very few Frenchmen thought monarchy condemned because one king had failed them in 1791. To depose Louis XVI meant either a regency or a republic. A regency would have elevated the duke of Orléans or one of the king's brothers, neither of whom was a suitable candidate; a republic meant the certain disapprobation of the great majority of Frenchmen and probably war with the monarchs of Europe.

The news of Louis XVI's arrest, which reached Paris late in the evening of June 22, and his return to the capital two days later greatly heartened the moderates in the Assembly, who now realized that they had rendered the king's position intolerable. Fearing lest the extremists throughout the country vote in favor of a republic, these deputies had already suspended the elections then being held for a new assembly. They rejoiced over the capture of the king because his presence gave France a hostage against the foreign invasion. On the 25th the Assembly tacitly confirmed its earlier decree which suspended the king and practically made him a state prisoner. Several committees, of whose members Barnave was the most prominent, weighed all possible measures concerning the future government of the country and decided that the least evil decision was to advise the reinstatement of Louis on condition that he give his promise to obey the constitution. In the middle of July the deputies debated the question of responsibility for the flight. Again it was Robespierre who rightly or wrongly pleaded the cause of the radical deputies, but Barnave's inspired oratory swung the Assembly to the support of the committee's proposals. In their final vote, on July 15 and 16, the deputies absolved Louis XVI of all guilt in connection with the flight and agreed to restore him to office on condition that he accept the revised constitution. Until that time his suspension would continue. Barnave, in whom the recent events had instilled a deep fear of mass violence, took especial pains to identify the republic with anarchy. "You have made all men equal before the law, you consecrated civil and political equality . . . one step more in the direction of liberty would be the destruction of the monarchy, one more in the direction of equality the *destruction of property*."

The decision to restore Louis XVI and revise the existing constitution carried great weight with the middle class. But it aroused the radicals to greater exertions. The Cordeliers and the fraternal societies of Paris pressed petition after petition upon the Assembly. One petition, which Robespierre persuaded the Jacobins to repudiate, had proposed only the dethronement of the king and his "replacement by constitutional means," which meant a regency, most likely in favor of the duke of Orléans. The new petition which the Cordeliers placed on the altar of the *patrie* at the Champ-de-Mars on July 16 was more explicit. It called for the trial of the perjured monarch and for a new executive government, which could mean only one thing, a republic.

Two men were discovered hiding under the platform of the altar at the Champ-de-Mars on the morning of July 17 when the crowd gathered to sign the petition. Who they were, what they intended, why they were there, no one knew. The mob jumped to the conclusion that they were counter-revolutionary spies, seized them, and lynched them. At the news of this atrocity Bailly, Lafayette, and Duport agreed that a supreme effort had to be made to maintain law and order. That very afternoon the Assembly ordered the municipality of Paris to declare martial law and forbid all threatening gatherings. Preceded by the red flag, which was the signal of martial law, Lafayette marched the National Guard ino the Champ-de-Mars, where an enormous crowd had gathered. The mob of patriots and curiosity seekers greeted the soldiers with a shower of stones. Exasperated, the Guardsmen fired, first in the air; but when some one in the crowd fired at Lafayette, they shot into the crowd itself. The mob scattered in all directions with the troops in pursuit. The casualties were not heavy, fewer than twenty men being fatally injured.[4]

A repressive movement against the republican leaders developed after this so-called "massacre of the Champ-de-Mars." The Assembly opened an investigation into the disorders, arrested the leaders of the popular societies and brought them up for trial. Danton, the leader of the activities of the Cordeliers, fled to England. The more conservative Jacobins resigned from their club and founded a new revolutionary club in the convent of the Feuillants, near the Assembly hall. Sieyès, Barnave, Lafayette, and the Lameths went over to the Feuillants, as the new club was called, while Robespierre, Pétion, and Grégoire were the most prominent of the deputies who remained with the Jacobins. For several months there were two clubs which called themselves "Friends of the Constitution," one sitting at the Jacobins and the other at the Feuillants. Most of the clubs in the departments remained loyal to the Jacobins, and ultimately most of the seceders in Paris returned to the fold. Meanwhile Barnave, Duport, and Alexandre Lameth, anxious for the position of the middle class, conducted a conservative campaign on two fronts. They tried to get the support of the Right in the conservative revision of the constitution and they carried on secret negotiations for a peaceful termination of the dispute with the emperor over the question of the German princes in Alsace. In this interim many persons defied the Assembly's decree which closed the frontiers and secretly left the country. The army was further weakened by the increased emigration and the resignation of most of the officers, many of whom joined the forces of the émigrés along the Rhine.

The fears of a foreign war were well grounded. After Varennes, the court had quietly resumed its secret correspondence with Leopold II. The new leaders of the Assembly, supported by the Feuillants, advised peace, but Marie Antoinette disavowed their letters

---

[4] Scholars are divided on the question of responsibility of this fusillade. G. Michon, in his *Essai sur l'histoire du parti feuillant: Adrien Duport* (Paris, 1924) maintains that it represented a deliberate effort on the part of the conservative leaders to crush the republican movement. Others insist that it was the result of a misunderstanding. Robespierre himself later characterized it as an unfortunate accident. All students agree, however, that the "massacre" cut an unbridgeable gap between the Barnave-Lameth group and the democrats.

and policy. On August 16 she wrote to Mercy-Argenteau, "In any case, the foreign powers alone can save us"; and on the 26th, "No matter at what price, the powers must come to our aid; but the Emperor must place himself at the head and supervise everything." The states of Europe did not conceal their solicitude over the "liberty and honor of the most Christian king." From Mantua the emperor issued a circular letter, July 5, to the principal sovereigns of Europe inviting them "to unite among themselves" and with him "for counsel, coöperation and measures" against the Revolution. On July 25 he signed the preliminaries of a defensive-offensive alliance with Prussia.

To the circular letter the powers gave a cold response, while the moderate leaders of the Assembly pleaded with Leopold II to preserve the peace. In view of Louis XVI's evident desire to avert war and of the fact that a concert of European powers was out of the question as long as England refused to intervene, the emperor determined to back down. To cover his retreat he consented, at the solicitation of Artois, to sign a joint declaration with the king of Prussia, which seemed to confirm his earlier threats but in reality nullified them. This famous Declaration of Pillnitz of August 27, 1791, declared that the restoration of the monarchy in France was a matter of common interest and expressed the hope that the other powers would not refuse to coöperate for that purpose. In a confidential letter to his chancellor Leopold explained that a qualifying clause of the declaration, "then and in that case Austria and Prussia would be ready to act with sufficient troops," nullified his promise of assistance to the émigrés. The conservative revision of the constitution, then in progress, convinced him that for the present Louis XVI's position was secure. By this declaration he hoped only to intimidate the radicals; but the émigrés turned it to their own ends. In a commentary to the Declaration they represented the invasion of France as imminent, announced severe reprisals against the revolutionary leaders, characterized Louis XVI's acceptance of the revised constitution, if it took place, as an act of base cowardice.

The debates on the constitution were unusually acrimonious, for now the radical deputies were convinced that the Barnave-Lameth group of moderates was working in the interests of the suspended monarch. Among the revisions effected were the abolition of the qualification of the *marc d'argent* for candidates and a high increase in the qualifications of the secondary electors, changes which gave added political power to the prosperous citizens. The Civil Constitution of the Clergy should in the future be regarded as an ordinary law and not as part of the constitution, which meant that the legislature could modify it if modification were deemed desirable. The radicals also accused their opponents of desiring to strengthen the king's appointive powers in the judiciary, advocating a bicameral legislature, and allowing ministers to sit in the legislature, but for these accusations there was no real proof.

On September 14 Louis XVI came before the Assembly and read his acceptance of the revised constitution, which he had been considering for a fortnight. With his acceptance his suspension was lifted. He asked the Assembly to grant a general amnesty, which it voted. Paris was alive with enthusiasm and hope. The bourgeoisie hailed the end of the revolutionary era and organized splendid fêtes to celebrate the completion of the Constitution of 1791. Louis XVI was carried in triumph through the gardens of the Tuileries, and Marie Antoinette was acclaimed at the Opera. Émigrés began to return to France, confident of their future security. Despite the general expectations of a stable, constitutional régime, a violent social revolution menaced the country. The city proletariat and the peasantry were still restive, eager to share the control of affairs with the middle class. The partisans of a republic had not forgotten the Champ-de-Mars fusillade. The last session of the National Constitutent Assembly was held on September 30, and on October 1 a new assembly, called the Legislative Assembly, began to guide the course of the Revolution.

The disorders of the later Revolution should not be used as a brief against the deputies of the National Constituent Assembly. They accomplished the work to which the commoners had consecrated themselves by the "Tennis Court Oath." In their two years of office, from 1789 to 1791, they completed, as best they knew how, the prodigious task of laying the bases of a new social and political organization. They destroyed much, almost all, that was characteristic of the old France of corporate and class interests, and that destruction was the necessary preparation for the new democratic France that they labored to create. Their conception of liberty and equality was that of enlightened men of their age, not of ours, nor yet of their propertyless contemporaries. To measure their success one must judge them not by the radical movements of social and economic protest which condemned their achievements in 1793–1794, but by the decaying institutions and outmoded ideals of the Old Régime to which they gave the final, decisive blow.

IX. THE OUTBREAK OF THE WAR AND THE DOWNFALL OF THE MONARCHY

THE PROBLEMS OF THE LEGISLATIVE ASSEMBLY

PARIS celebrated the end of the Revolution, but the Revolution had not ended with the king's acceptance of the constitution. The deputies of the new Assembly were burdened at the start with the unsolved problems of their predecessors. First of these was the problem of Avignon. Three weeks before the Constituent Assembly held its final session the deputies voted the annexation of Avignon and the Comtat-Venaissin to France. For a long time they had hesitated to take that final step, although they had already justified it in theory. The pope's condemnation of the Revolution in the spring of 1791 removed most of their scruples, while the disturbances caused by the refractory clergy and the violent clashes between patriots and aristocrats in those papal enclaves afforded additional reasons for annexation. The Assembly made the gesture of offering the pope an indemnity for the loss of his territory but did not ask his consent to the proceedings. Farsighted observers regarded such conduct as a deliberate challenge to monarchical Europe.

Another pressing problem was that of the German princes and the émigrés. In the summer of 1791 the diet of the empire had placed itself on record as supporting the claims of the princes in Alsace. Would the emperor, particularly after the annexation of Avignon and the Comtat-Venaissin, refuse to ratify the decision of the imperial diet? Would he allow the revolutionary assembly, in Paris, to settle the rights of the princes even as it had settled those of the pope? To be sure, after Louis XVI had accepted the constitution, the emperor received the French ambassador. At the moment he did not desire intervention and war with France, but he could not repair the mischief of the ill advised Declaration of Pillnitz nor the provocative commentary which the émigré leaders had added to it. Averse to intervention by arms but convinced that the Declaration of Pillnitz had kept the Jacobins in check, he continued his policy of opposition through his chancellor, Kaunitz. Instead of being cowed, the Jacobins of Paris bristled with patriotic indignation at his menaces. They firmly believed that Leopold was biding his time and would declare war on France in the spring of 1792. Besides, they were incensed that he, the head of the empire, allowed the belligerent émigrés to make the border German states the base of their operations against France. To them and to all patriotic Frenchmen it seemed intolerable that he suffered the plotting of the count of Provence, who styled himself regent of France and made his court at Koblenz, that he allowed the prince of Condé to gather a small army of noblemen at Worms.

The internal situation, no less than the international situation, was threatening in October, 1791. Dissension in the armies still continued, and the emigration of many thousand officers made the men more than ever suspicious of the loyalty of their superior officers. Religious bigotry provoked continual disorders in Alsace, in the Midi, and in the Vendée, where the nonjuring priests and their devoted parishioners clashed with the constitutional clergy and the local patriots. The aristocrats and the patriots took part in bloody mêlées in Avignon. The purchasers of national land and the peasants were terrified by the menace of intervention, disturbed by visions of their former feudal lords returning in the victorious train of the foreign troops. A sharp recurrence of the food shortage and a steady decline of the assignats provoked economic distress and disorder which became more pronounced in the course of the following months. With the best intentions in the world of enforcing the constitution the new deputies would have found it difficult to solve their many problems. But various groups and different individuals were calculating the possibilities of methods other than constitutional to end disputes. They were anxious to take advantage of the troubled circumstances to pursue their own policies.

THE GIRONDINS AND THEIR POLICY

In theory, at least, the vast majority of the deputies of the Legislative Assembly called themselves royalists and constitutionalists and were supporters of the monarchical constitution. They were new to parliamentary life and inexperienced, for the Constituent Assembly had decided that none of its members could be reëlected to the Legislative Assembly. Very few of them were landowners or men of means. The greatest number came from the ranks of the petty bourgeoisie, lawyers, professional men, and publicists. Some two hundred and sixty-four enrolled themselves at the Feuillant Club [1] and made up the Right of the new Assembly. On the benches of the Left sat a smaller but more compact and more determined group of about one hundred and thirty deputies, who belonged to the Jacobins or the Cordeliers. Between them in the seats of the Center were the remaining three hundred and forty-five deputies, who voted either with the Right or with the Left as the occasion warranted.

The Feuillant deputies were divided among themselves and had no outstanding leader in the Assembly. Outside of the Assembly they followed the leadership either of the Triumvirate (Barnave, Lameth, and Duport) or of Lafayette. The accord between Lafayette and the Barnave-Lameth group was now at an end, broken mainly on the question of foreign policy. Lafayette's influence had dwindled greatly. He was no longer the "mayor of the palace," the would-be dictator of France. Shortly after the opening of the new assembly he became a candidate for the mayoralty of Paris, but he was overwhelmingly defeated by Pétion, the candidate of the Jacobins. The Triumvirate was also considerably less influential, and its guidance tended to weaken the position of the Feuillant deputies. Neither the Right nor the vacillating deputies of the Center, for all their numerical majority, gained control of the Legislative Assembly. The radical deputies of the Left speedily became the masters and imposed their views upon their colleagues.

Like the Feuillant deputies, the one hundred and thirty radical members professed their adherence to the recently accepted constitution. Like the Feuillants, too, they were divided, some following the leadership of Robespierre, who was in the ascendancy among the Jacobins, the others accepting the guidance of Brissot in the Assembly. Some were more sympathetic to the idea of interpreting the constitution in a republican sense than others, but all were agreed that one move by Louis XVI against the Revolution should earn him his deposition. Nearly all of them were young and ambi-

[1] For the origin of the Feuillant Club after the "Massacre of the Champ-de-Mars," see above, p. 194.

tious for power and glory. They had watched the first Assembly
at work, some from the galleries of the hall, and were convinced
that it would have fared much better if they had been members.
Now that they had their chance to share in the making of the
Revolution, they were eager to have the movement continue. They
were assiduous in their attendance at debates, facile and persuasive
speakers, energetic, daring, and reckless.

By their contemporaries they were generally called Brissotins,
because their foremost leader was the Parisian journalist Brissot.
Later generations knew them as the Girondins, because their ablest
orators, Vergniaud, Gensonné, Guadet, Ducos, and others, came
from the department of the Gironde. This radical wing professed
a loud concern for "the people." In reality they were too fastidious
in their tastes and their habits to mingle with and grasp the attitude
of mind of the uncultivated masses. They preferred the charm of
salon life, where they associated on easy terms with the solid, respectable business men, merchants, industrialists, and financiers, and
their wives. Unconsciously perhaps, they allowed the more immediate interests of this class to guide their revolutionary idealism.
Their own ambition and the interests of their salon hosts encouraged the prospect of curbing the counter-revolutionaries and ending disorders, by the possibility of a foreign war which would give
the Girondins power and their friends profits. Their leading figure
was Brissot, an opportunist and an intriguer, who was not devoid
of talent, but unworthy of his reputation. Vergniaud, their greatest
orator, lacked the energy and the fire of Brissot, but his speeches
in the Assembly were masterly in structure and decisive in their
effect. Condorcet, one of the last of the *philosophes,* became their
oracle and their mentor.

Their first move was against the émigrés of the Rhineland,
whose threats infuriated the members of the clubs and gave
the Girondins their opportunity to pounce upon these enemies of
the Revolution. For more than a week their leaders proposed
measures of extreme severity against the émigré princes, nobles, officials, and army officers. On October 31, 1791, the Assembly gave
the count of Provence two months to return to France under pain
of sacrificing his rights to the throne. A decree of November 9
gave the émigrés until January 1, 1792, to do likewise under penalty of being suspected of counter-revolutionary conspiracy. If, by

January 1, 1792 they were still in arms they were to be regarded as guilty of conspiracy, their estates would be sequestrated by the government, and they would be punished by death if captured.

A few weeks later, on November 29, after bitter and tempestuous debates, the Assembly paid its respects to the nonjuring clergy. Vanished was the tolerant attitude of the Constituent Assembly, for toleration had been tried and found wanting. The nonjuring priests were required to take an oath of loyalty within a week's time, a purely civic oath to the new constitution in general and not specifically to the Civil Constitution of the Clergy. If they refused, they would be classed as suspects, placed under the close supervision of the administration, and deprived of their state pensions.

Again the Lameths advised Louis XVI to use his veto power, and early in December he vetoed that measure even as he had vetoed the decree concerning the émigrés (though he gave his sanction to the decree concerning his brother). The Girondins were not personally attached to the constitutional clergy. Most of them were freethinkers, but there was no doubt in their minds that the refractory priests were the "accomplices of the émigrés." And Louis XVI, who had vetoed both decrees, was regarded by all patriots as the defender of the treacherous priests at home as well as the ally of the conspiring émigrés abroad. Assuredly he was within his rights in vetoing the measures, but his veto only threw suspicion upon him, his secret advisers, and all the moderate deputies, while it gave the Left a pretext to introduce still stronger measures.

The very day the Assembly voted the decree on the nonjuring priests, it urged the king to dispatch a note to the elector of Treves bidding him end the activities of the French émigrés in his territory. Presumably, the elector would then appeal to the imperial diet and the emperor, and the latter would support him, in which case war would follow. Leopold II had done little to press the cause of his royal relatives in France, and Count Fersen had just written to the queen: "The Emperor is deceiving you; he will do nothing in your behalf." But the Girondins were ignorant of the emperor's real intentions and were convinced that the powers were getting ready to intervene. They had their own reasons for desiring war with Austria. Unexpectedly, Louis XVI yielded to the demands of the war party. On December 14 he announced to the deputies that he had dispatched an ultimatum to the elector of

Treves giving him a month's time to disperse the émigrés. If the elector failed to comply, he would be treated as an enemy. Louis XVI then appointed the count of Narbonne minister of war, a move which met with the favor of the Girondins, for Narbonne was known as an advocate of war.

THE RUPTURE WITH AUSTRIA

France was drifting toward war, for which each of the groups that advocated hostilities had its own reasons and its own views. The Girondins wanted war because they were ambitious for power and popularity. They wanted war to unmask the king, whose treason to the Revolution they suspected. Open war would end the equivocal situation and force Louis XVI to form a Girondin ministry to prosecute the war "against tyrants." Convinced of this prospect, Brissot painted a glorious picture of swift military victory and the triumph of the armed Revolution in all countries. Were not the oppressed peoples of the Netherlands and the Rhineland burning to join the "crusade for universal liberty"? So he thought, so thought the refugees in Paris, so thought the Girondins. But Narbonne, Lafayette, and the military clique that had the support of the Feuillant deputies, wanted war, not to weaken but to strengthen the powers of Louis XVI. They themselves would command the troops and conduct operations. Against the German princes a short campaign would suffice. Should Austria give aid to the princes, the results would still be the same, for they counted on the traditional rivalry between Austria and Prussia to turn Prussia against Austria, while England maintained her neutrality. After the conclusion of this war the victorious generals would crush the Jacobins and become the indispensable champions of the king.

Louis XVI had still other views on the matter. Realizing that his only hope lay in the intervention of the powers he resolved to force their hand. He addressed new appeals to Austria, Prussia, Russia, Spain, and Sweden, requesting a congress of powers, "supported by the armed force, as the best means of checking the factions here [at Paris]." A brief war would give him his opportunity. Accordingly on the same day that he addressed an ultimatum to the elector of Treves, he wrote to his confidential agent abroad, requesting Breteuil to inform the emperor that he did not want the elector to meet his demands. "The revolutionary party would be-

come too arrogant. . . . My conduct must be such that when misfortune comes, the nation sees no other alternative but to throw
itself into my arms." He reasoned that the French armies would
be crushed in a single campaign, and that his people would turn
to him as a mediator to save them from the vengeance of the powers. So France drifted toward war, and the war-mongers were glad.
The Feuillant deputies and their leaders outside the Assembly opposed the war, but they favored the adoption of a high tone
toward Austria.

For three months, almost single-handed, Robespierre opposed
the war preparations. He profited from his prestige as the unchal-
lenged leader of the democrats, as the incorruptible, if somewhat
circumspect, protector of the masses, to point out the dangers of
war. At first Danton and a few journals supported Robespierre,
but in the end only Marat, Camille Desmoulins, and a few other
radicals aided the "Incorruptible." He foresaw the king's treason
and the defeat of the troops. Victory for the French would only
strengthen the executive power, would perhaps bring France a
military dictator, a Caesar. He called attention to the unprepared
condition of the French military forces and demanded that, if war
was to be declared, measures should be taken at least to strengthen
the army. On the other hand Brissot and the Girondins counted
heavily upon their revolutionary propaganda and condemned
Robespierre's proposal for strengthening the army and supporting
the ministry as playing into the hands of the Feuillants and the
military leaders. They were loud in their wrath against him, and
again there was dissension among the Jacobins. The Lameths and
Duport were still confident that war could be avoided. They pinned
their hopes on the emperor, whom they had counseled to avoid
war. Barnave was beginning to vacillate and was more than half
sympathetic to Lafayette's plans. The nation was unanimously behind the Girondins. The patriots wanted war, because they believed
that war would deliver their country from the evils which beset it.

On the receipt of the French monarch's ultimatum of December
14, the elector of Treves expelled the émigrés, for only on condition that he do so did the emperor promise him aid and protection.
The émigrés scattered in all directions, only Provence and
Artois being permitted to remain. Leopold II then dispatched an
official note to Paris stating that the French grievances had been
satisfied and the incident closed. But he ratified the "conclusion"

of the diet which extended the protection of the empire to the German princes and notified France that his troops had received orders to defend Treves against possible attack. Still convinced that a strong attitude on his part, rather than war, would curb the Jacobins, he renewed his stiff tone expressing the hope that they would not force him to intervene. He took his precautions, however, and tightened his alliance with Prussia by the defensive treaty of February 7, 1792, which provided that either power send twenty thousand men if the other were attacked. Prussia now hastened her preparations, despite the purely defensive character of the treaty with Austria, and the two powers conferred on the plan of campaign. Frederick William was anxious for war, for in the defensive treaty Austria virtually agreed to abandon the new Polish government to its fate. His troops knew the road to Poland.

It is likely that Leopold still believed that a firm tone would suffice, but he died suddenly on March 1; and his less prudent son and successor, Francis II, was eager to intervene. Moreover, he had now a better pretext than his father. Leopold's note concerning Treves and his warning to the Jacobins had spurred the Girondins to action. On January 25, after Brissot and Vergniaud lashed the deputies with their oratory, the Assembly "invited" the king to ask Leopold whether he renounced "all treaties and conventions directed against the sovereignty, independence, and security of the nation." The Assembly's decree gave the emperor until March 1 to announce whether he intended to adhere to the French-Austrian alliance of 1756 and renounce the Austro-Prussian treaty which he had tentatively arranged in the preceding summer at the time that he issued the Declaration of Pillnitz. Narbonne had just returned from a military inspection of the eastern garrisons and assured the Assembly that all was in readiness for war. On March 1 the emperor's reply was read in the Assembly and created great indignation. Leopold, provoked by the bellicosity of the Legislative Assembly, included in his reply several gratuitous observations about the "pernicious sect" of Jacobins and appealed to "healthy" public opinion against them. Jealous of this affront to France's dignity, Narbonne (with Lafayette behind him) tried to impose his war policy on the king, but he was summarily dismissed from office on March 9. The Girondin war party, led by Brissot, took up the challenge, for if this opportunity were missed, it would prove difficult to precipitate war. The Girondins appealed to their great orators.

Vergniaud delivered one of his most impassioned speeches exhorting the Assembly to punish conspirators and traitors. The Feuillant deputies and Delessart, the pacific minister of foreign affairs, were his visible targets, but behind Delessart was the queen, whom Vergniaud attacked by implication. The Assembly was carried away by the oratory. Delessart was indicted for treason and sent before the High Court for trial. The remaining Feuillant ministers resigned, and Louis XVI appointed a new ministry composed of men who were committed to the war policy.

The leading spirit in the new ministry was Dumouriez, the minister of foreign affairs, a veteran soldier of the Seven Years' War and a cynical adventurer ripened in the secret diplomacy of the French court. He was strongly pro-war and played for the support of the Jacobins, but he also carried on secret negotiations with the king. His ultimate hope was to wage a short victorious war which would make him the power behind the throne. He surrounded himself with Girondin associates or sympathizers—Clavière, a Swiss banker, as minister of finances, Roland, a former inspector of manufactures who, with Madame Roland, was a member of the inner circle of Girondins, as minister of the interior. Somewhat later, through the insistence of Madame Roland, another staunch Girondin supporter, Servan, was made minister of war.

War was now a certainty, for the Girondins were in the ministry and Dumouriez conducted his diplomatic negotiations with Austria in a thoroughly intransigent spirit. The accession of Francis II facilitated the rupture. After an exchange of provocative notes, an ultimatum was sent to Austria to which there was no reply. On April 20 Louis XVI proposed and the Assembly enthusiastically decreed war on the "King of Hungary and Bohemia," in other words, on Austria alone and not on the empire as a whole. To reassure apprehensive neighbors, the Assembly repeated the renunciation of a war of conquest which was incorporated in the constitution. The war against Austria was defined as "the just defense of a free people against the unjust aggression of a king." Dumouriez hoped to isolate Austria by detaching Prussia, but Prussia rejected his overtures and, in accordance with the terms of the alliance, came to the support of Francis II.

Immediate responsibility for the war was divided. On each side there were studied provocations, hidden calculations, and cynical

gambling with human destinies. Each side appealed to lofty principles, but principles were subordinated to meaner interests or, in
the minds of the war advocates, somehow fused with them. Prussia
and Austria were fully as concerned over Poland as they were
over Marie Antoinette, Louis XVI, the German princes of Alsace,
and the émigrés; and they postponed action against France until
the question of Poland was somewhat arranged. The Girondins
cloaked their reckless ambition by a self-deceiving but aggressive
policy of propaganda. War between revolutionary France and
monarchical Europe might have been unavoidable ultimately, but
it came in 1792 because politicians and statesmen, kings, generals,
and peoples, all for different reasons and with different expectations, desired it. Calculations and expectations, however, were not
realized. The war which began in 1792 lasted almost without a
break until 1815 and gave a new direction to the entire course of
European history. In France it gave new intensity to the revolutionary movement. The Girondin leaders were swept from power
and the Jacobins of Paris gained control. The king's hopes of becoming a mediator were thwarted and in the violence and disorder
engendered by the war the French monarchy was overthrown, a
dictatorship was established, and new policies came to the fore.
From this time on the internal changes of the revolutionary movement were brought about less and less by the logic of circumstances
in France and more and more by the pressure of military events.

MILITARY REVERSES

France was ill prepared for the war. The army which Narbonne
had judged ready for action was thoroughly disorganized. Emigration had weakened the strength of the regular army and destroyed its morale. More than half of the 9000 officers had emigrated, and more than 30,000 men had deserted. The 100,000
volunteers whom the Constituent Assembly had summoned to the
colors after the flight of the king were slow to respond, only half
of that number having enlisted by the spring of 1792. The recruits
were eager for action, but they were inexperienced and unreliable.
Between them and the regular troops there was jealousy and ill
feeling, for the raw volunteers were given higher pay and the
privilege of electing their officers and returning home after each

campaign. Both regulars and volunteers suffered from a shortage of equipment and supplies. Discipline was lax and confidence in the command was lacking.

Dumouriez's plan was to invade and conquer Belgium by a sharp unexpected offensive, but the French troops hardly crossed the frontier when panic seized them and they fled in disorder. In their flight they massacred one of their commanders, General Dillon. General Rochambeau resigned his command, subordinate officers deserted, and several regiments went over to the enemy *en bloc*. This was the first reverse, on April 30. A second was the failure of Dumouriez's diplomacy, for Prussia rejected his overtures for a Franco-Prussian alliance against Austria and ordered her troops to march on the Rhine.

Neither Prussia nor Austria was ready to take advantage of France's unpreparedness and military disorganization, since Polish affairs preoccupied the monarchs of both states. During the preceding winter Catherine of Russia had carefully encouraged the opposition of Polish nobles to their new constitution. The very month that war broke out in western Europe, Russia intervened in Poland. In a few months, by the end of July, the Polish constitution of May 3 was only a memory and Russian troops had firm control of the country. But Prussia and Austria had to be reckoned with, and Catherine could not disregard their demand for territorial indemnity. A vague agreement was reached by the prospective spoliators, not entirely satisfactory either to Francis or to Frederick William, who continued negotiations all summer, but sufficiently reassuring to allow them to begin operations against France. Three months were lost in these negotiations. By the time this settlement was reached and the two rulers met to discuss campaign plans and indemnities in France, a crisis had been reached in that country.

The news of the defeat and flight of the French troops threw Paris into consternation, for the frontier was exposed to the enemy; and the full extent of the lack of harmony which held Prussia and Austria back was not realized. Robespierre and Marat, who had prophesied defeat, attacked the generals and called for their dismissal. The generals threw the burden of blame on the troops, alleging their lack of discipline. The Girondin leaders defended the generals and fought back against Marat and Robespierre. Without victory they could not retain political power, but the military leaders were lost to them, for the failure of the offensive and its repercussion on the internal situation completely changed the attitude of the latter. Lafayette made overtures to the former Austrian ambassador for an advance against the Paris Jacobins. The other generals determined to end hostilities in the belief that an offensive war was now out of the question and sent a memoir to that effect to the Girondin ministers. This move ended the Girondin efforts to win over the generals. It confirmed their suspicion, and that of the masses, that a vast conspiracy existed against the success of the troops. Their suspicions were only too well founded, for the court was indeed revealing the French military plans to the Austrians. At the same time religious strife in the west and the Midi became sharper. Dumouriez inclined to Lafayette's views, but his Girondin associates in the ministry and the Girondin deputies acted more rapidly.

The Assembly struck fast. On May 27 it passed a new measure against the nonjuring priests, making them liable to deportation from France. A second decree suppressed the constitutional guard of the king, which was lukewarm or hostile to the Revolution. A third measure provided for an army of 20,000 federated National Guardsmen to be encamped within Paris for its defense against open and secret enemies. These decrees were submitted to Louis XVI for his ratification. Most assuredly he did not approve of the measures. The decree concerning the nonjuring priests was no doubt more severe than the occasion demanded. There was strong suspicion, as Duport pointed out to the king, that the Jacobins might be tempted to use the 20,000 fédérés to attack the royal power rather than defend the capital against the foreign foe. Reluctantly Louis XVI ratified the measure which called for the dissolution of his royal guard, but he withheld his sanction from the other two measures. Roland, the minister of the interior, pointed out to him in a public letter that his veto would confirm popular suspicion about his treasonable connections with the enemy. Roland's summary language gave the king his pretext to rid himself of his Girondin ministers and appeal to his military leaders. Roland, Clavière, and Servan were dismissed on June 13, and Dumouriez undertook to reorganize the ministry. He found his position untenable, however, first, because of the king's refusal to follow his instructions and secondly, because of the manifest hostility of the Girondins in the Assembly. He resigned his ministry and assumed military command of the Army of the North.

The overthrow of the war ministry stirred up popular feeling in Paris. Rumors flew thick and fast that the war would be suspended and that the émigrés would be invited to return. Louis XVI felt sufficiently strong to veto the other two decrees and to form a new ministry chosen from the members of the Feuillant Club and supporters of Lafayette. Lafayette judged that his moment had come and addressed a provocative dispatch to the Assembly, threatening the popular clubs and the Girondin leaders. The reply of the Paris patriots to the military threat was the "day of June 20."

Plans for an Insurrection

The mass protest and demonstration which was fixed for the day of the anniversary of the Tennis Court Oath was sponsored by the Girondin deputies in the salon of Madame Roland and executed under the leadership of professional agitators. But it was enthusiastically supported by the working classes of the two sections which comprised the Faubourgs Saint-Antoine and Saint-Marceau. The purpose was to intimidate the king into signing the decrees and recalling the dismissed ministers. The municipal authorities of the city in the persons of the Mayor, Pétion, and the procureur, Manuel, observed a benevolent aloofness toward the agitators, who marched through the streets of Paris, filed through the halls of the Assembly where they presented their petition, and finally penetrated into the royal apartments at the Tuileries. Louis XVI courageously held his position in the face of the petitioners, who forced him into an embrasure of the palace and kept him and the royal family virtual prisoners for several hours before the soft-spoken Pétion arrived to rescue him from the mob. But he refused to withdraw his veto or to recall the ministers.

There were two different reactions to the action of the mob. The moderate element of France became indignant over the humiliation of the monarch, and the departmental authorities of Paris suspended Pétion and Manuel. Petitions against the Jacobins arrived with every courier from the departments, and royalist demonstrations were held in various parts of the kingdom. A well intentioned but futile move on the part of Lafayette saved the day for the radical leaders. Unsuccessful in having the leaders of the manifestation indicted, he quit his army and hastened to Paris, where he tried frantically to swing the National Guard against the Jacobins and their followers. But the king, and more particularly the queen, scorned his aid—and probably betrayed his plan—and he returned, disappointed, to his troops. The second reaction was one of approval. The Jacobin clubs, the fraternal societies, and various municipalities of the south and the east addressed congratulations to the Assembly and petitioned it for the suspension or the abdication of the king. The simultaneous reverses of the French troops at the front intensified the antimonarchical movement. The danger of invasion was imminent and fear stimulated political passions.

In the new circumstances the Girondins and other Jacobins resumed their tactics. They demanded the indictment of Lafayette and the dismissal of the Feuillant ministry. A new decree of the Assembly circumvented the royal veto of the measure to form a camp within Paris by summoning 20,000 fédérés to Paris, ostensibly to celebrate the anniversary of the Fête de la Fédération on July 14. Many of the federated National Guardsmen were already on the way to Paris. From Marseilles there soon marched some five hundred volunteers, singing a new stirring song which Rouget de Lisle had composed at Strasbourg for the Army of the Rhine, a song which long survived them, to be known as the "Marseillaise." Vergniaud delivered a speech on July 3 that was full of menace against the king and raised the question of his dethronement. Thousands of copies of his words were struck off the press and dispatched throughout the country. The idea of dethroning Louis XVI took shape. The Feuillant ministry fell, July 10, and the Girondin leaders were sanguine that they would be summoned to form a new one. Louis XVI did not disillusion them. Meanwhile the Prussians, reputedly the best troops in Europe, methodically pursued their preparations for invasion.

On the 11th of July, the Assembly declared that the *patrie* was "in danger." That declaration was a solemn appeal to the patriotic emotions of the country. Every administrative body in the country was bidden to be on the alert, all the National Guardsmen were called to arms, 50,000 volunteers were summoned to the colors. The Assembly had appealed to the entire nation. Could good patriots doubt any longer that the king had failed in his trust? Companies of volunteers came marching from all parts of the country. Paris alone raised 15,000 men for the national defense. As the hectic weeks of July and August sped on, the realization came over the country that the war could not be prosecuted successfully without a fundamental change in the constitution.

Nevertheless, the difficulties of the procedure were great. The king's relations with the enemy were not known, as they are now, and the Constitutionalists of the Assembly as well as most of the departmental administrators shrank from the thought of deposing Louis XVI. Could a loyal monarchist suspect his king of treason? The Girondins, who had clamored loudest for the suspension or the dethronement of Louis XVI now hesitated, aghast at the storm they aroused. By temperament and training they were averse to direct, violent action with its injury to business stability. Their ambition also held them in check, for they hoped to regain power in the ministry and become the guides and guardians of the king. Like Mirabeau in 1790, like the Triumvirate in 1791, they took fright at the attitude of the masses and essayed, in divers and devious ways, to save the monarch. The masses whom they had summoned to war and insurrection swept past them. The fédérés were coming in from the departments, several contingents bringing petitions for the deposition of the king; but July 14 came and went and nothing happened save that Louis XVI renewed his oath to the constitution. But the Jacobins and the Cordeliers of Paris, largely under the leadership of Robespierre, moved steadily toward their goal. The workingmen of the capital were solidly behind them, as were many of the newly arrived fédérés. Deliberately, they planned an insurrection and the overthrow of the monarchy.

THE DOWNFALL OF THE MONARCHY

Louis XVI did little to better his position. He rejected the advice of the Feuillants to denounce the insurrectionary leaders, and he refused the proffered aid of Lafayette to escape from Paris to Rouen or Compiègne. Marie Antoinette could never overcome her aversion for Lafayette, and the royal couple determined to brave all affronts until the allies arrived or until the latter dispatched the manifesto against the revolutionary leaders which Louis XVI had requested. Meanwhile, his sole resource lay with the Girondins, for they, with the ministry open to them once more, disavowed the insurrectionary movement and bent their efforts toward keeping him in power. "If there are any men," threatened

Brissot on July 25, "who aspire to establish the republic on the ruin of the Constitution, the law should strike them down as it does the supporters of a bicameral legislature and the counter-revolutionists of Koblenz."

The republican movement had made too great progress to be checked by the Girondins' threats. The volunteers who rose to arms against the foreign foe were equally determined to strike against the aristocrats and the monarchy. Girondin propaganda and patriotic enthusiasm made them desire political reform. The depreciation of the assignats, the disappearance of specie, the rise in prices together with a sudden shortage of food products had brought about an economic crisis which was aggravated by war requisitions. Again, as in 1789, granaries were sacked, food riots broke out, and governmental regulation was demanded. The patriots who marched against the monarchy clamored for restrictions of the abuse of property rights. They had lost their Girondin leaders but they carried on despite these. The forty-eight sections or wards of the city, under the leadership of new and daring popular agitators, Santerre, Panis, Sergent, Manuel, and Chaumette, held daily meetings and discussed plans of operation against the royal palace. They formed a central committee, and at the instigation of their delegates, the Assembly granted the status of active citizen to any one who bore arms. Meanwhile many of the federated guardsmen refused to leave Paris and proceed to Soissons, where they were to have formed a camp of reserve troops. Twice these troops presented petitions for the suspension of the king, but the Assembly tabled their demands—a dangerous policy, as not only Paris, but most of France, was united in its mistrust of Louis XVI. Toward the end of July a battalion of federated guardsmen from Brest arrived in Paris, followed a few days later by the equally republican minded contingent from Marseilles. The insurrectionary movement was accelerated, but what gave it an irresistible driving force was the manifesto of the duke of Brunswick which was published in the *Moniteur* on August 3.

That manifesto was a response to the last despairing appeal of the king and queen, who had entreated the allied monarchs for a pronouncement against the Jacobins. Louis XVI also begged the two powers to repudiate the émigrés and make it clear that allied intervention would not be followed by the restoration of the Old

Régime. Unfortunately, one of the émigrés was allowed to write the text of the manifesto, to which the duke of Brunswick in his capacity as commander-in-chief of the allied forces merely signed his name. This text retained the letter of Louis's instructions but altered the spirit, for the manifesto was full of menace not solely against the Jacobins but against all patriotic Frenchmen as well. The powers disclaimed interference in the internal affairs of France, but they summoned the French to restore Louis XVI to his full powers, to obey the orders of the invaders, and to refrain from any resistance and opposition either to Louis XVI or to the allies. They requested the king to name a frontier town which the allies might consider the capital of a regenerated France, and declared that National Guardsmen in arms would be treated as rebels, that administrative officials and private citizens opposing the invading armies would be punished in accordance with the rules of war. Should Paris and its inhabitants offer the least insult or injury to the royal family or invade the Tuileries, the allied monarchs would "wreak . . . memorable vengeance by giving up the city of Paris to military execution and total ruin."

Louis XVI promptly repudiated the manifesto, but his words carried no weight. The insolent threats seemed to prove his treason more fully than any of the arguments of his critics at home. At once the insurrectionists hastened to complete the plans of attack. On August 3 the sections presented a new petition for the deposition of Louis XVI. The Assembly hesitated and deferred its reply. On August 4, the section of the Quinze-Vingts (the workingmen's section of the Faubourg Saint-Antoine) delivered an ultimatum. If the Assembly did not depose the king before midnight of August 9, the march on the Tuileries would begin.[2]

Louis XVI displayed culpable negligence and incapacity in defending himself against the forthcoming attack. He left his defense to others—to the Girondins of the Assembly, with whom he carried on secret negotiations, and to the director of his secret service, Bertrand de Molleville (intendant of the Civil List), who was given a million livres to buy off the leaders of the insurrection. Many of the leaders doubtless accepted the money, but continued their preparations. The Assembly pinned its faith on the units of

[2] The old contention that Danton played a dominant rôle in the insurrection of August 10 has been effectively disproved by Mathiez in his *Le dix août* (Paris, 1931).

the National Guard from the conservative and more moderate sections of the capital and hoped that the affair would blow over without serious consequences. Pétion assured the deputies that all the necessary steps had been taken for the king's safety, but his assurances meant nothing. He allowed the National Guard from the revolutionary sections to obtain arms and ammunition from the city arsenals. Mandat, the commander of the Paris National Guard, was a fervent royalist. He too counted upon the conservative sections, together with the Swiss Guard whose loyalty was above suspicion, and he drew up a plan of defense of the Tuileries. He never had an opportunity to carry it out.

At midnight of August 9 the ringing of the tocsin and the roll of the drums gave the signal for the advance of the insurrectionists. Their ranks were filled with armed fédérés, National Guardsmen and passive citizens, whose concentration had ably been effected by Santerre and the radicals of the Quinze-Vingts section in the Faubourg Saint-Antoine. The Swiss Guard, a small detachment of loyal National Guard, and a few noblemen defended the Tuileries. Twenty-eight of the sections sent delegates to the Hôtel de Ville where the Commune held its sittings. At first, the representatives of the sections sat in a room adjoining that of the Commune, but in the course of the night they ousted the Commune and took its place, thus giving a semblance of ready-made legality to the proceedings of the insurrectionists. The initial act of the new Commune was to summon Mandat to the Hôtel de Ville, order his arrest, and appoint the brewer Santerre, the hero of the Faubourg Saint-Antoine, in his place as commander-in-chief of the National Guard. Mandat did not live the night out; he was shot down by the mob as he was leaving the Hôtel de Ville. His death demoralized the soldiers who were defending the palace. In Louis XVI, who attempted to address them, they had no confidence. The king and the royal family lost heart. They quit the Tuileries early in the morning of August 10, never to return, and took refuge with the deputies of the Assembly. The deputies greeted them courteously, despite the hostile crowd that thronged the terrace around the Riding School, and assigned them a small box behind the president's seat.

There, from his seat, Louis XVI could hear the sounds of firing, at first scattered, but soon heavy and forbidding as the cannon went into action. The National Guardsmen fraternized with the besiegers or took to their heels. The Swiss held out, but found the battle unequal, and their ammunition was soon exhausted. Toward noon an order from the king reached them, commanding them to lay down their arms. He had been finally convinced of the futility of defense and hoped to win grace for the loyal Swiss. A fierce crowd then took possession of the palace and gardens and, infuriated by the battle and the loss of four hundred men, took brutal vengeance on the living and the bodies of the dead. Nine hundred of the defenders were dead—the Swiss, the royalists, and the palace menials. The palace was wrecked, many valuables were destroyed and the bodies of the fallen were mutilated in horrible fashion. After the first spasm of fury, wiser counsel prevailed, and the mob leaders made determined efforts to prevent looting and pillaging. Outside, in the city, the exultant populace roamed the streets, destroying all the busts and statues of Louis XVI they could find.

The Revolutionary Commune of August 10

The Assembly anxiously followed events, powerless to direct or arrest them. A new power, the revolutionary Commune of August 10, had set itself up beside the deputies, overshadowing them, coercing them, and discrediting them. The leaders of the Commune would have dissolved the Legislative Assembly, but the workers and petty bourgeois who formed a majority in the new municipal government feared to take the responsibility of governing France, particularly since the departments were favorable to the Girondins. The Assembly was maintained, but the legal existence of the revolutionary Commune was recognized. At the same time the Commune gave the Assembly full warning that its "reinvestiture" was merely temporary, until a National Convention elected by universal suffrage was convoked to pass judgment on the events that had occurred. More plainly, the constitution was to be revised and the king brought to trial. The deputies agreed to the terms of the Commune. They refused to dethrone Louis XVI but suspended him until the convocation of the National Convention. They agreed to summon a Convention elected by universal male suffrage but decreed that the elections should be indirect; and they also passed a bill appointing a governor for the little Dauphin and placing the royal family under guard in the Luxembourg Palace. Such magnanimity irked the victors, who had the measure revoked. The royal family was turned over to the revolutionary Commune and imprisoned in the tower of the Temple, a group of buildings once in the possession of the Knights Templars.

The throne was now vacant, but since the constitution was still in force, a new executive was needed. A third body was entrusted with the executive power—the provisory executive council of six ministers: Roland, Clavière, and Servan took up the old posts that they had held before their dismissal on June 13; Monge, a mathematician, was given the ministry of the navy; Lebrun, a journalist friend of Brissot, that of foreign affairs; Danton, that of justice. The latter was the virtual head of the ministry, and the selection of this supposed organizer of the insurrection revealed the weakness of the Assembly and the intention of the deputies to bid for the favor of the Commune. These three authorities, the Legislative Assembly, the Commune, and the Ministry, shared the central power and weakened it. For six weeks there was strife among them; and in the National Convention which met at the end of the six weeks the strife was continued and intensified.

The three authorities had only their fears in common. They feared the generals, to whom Lafayette had given an example by attempting to restore the king. His soldiers refused to follow him in that venture, and he fled across the frontier, where he fell into the hands of the Austrians and was clapped into prison. The danger from the military leaders was not pronounced, but the Assembly was cautious and sent twelve deputies, three to each army, to supervise the military conduct of the generals, and if necessary replace or arrest them. The Commune and the council of ministers also sent out delegates into the departments. Public officials were obliged to take the new civic oath: to be faithful to the nation and to maintain liberty and equality, or die at their posts. The Assembly decreed the arrest of the near relatives of the émigrés and other suspects. Local patriots established surveillance committees to watch over suspects in their districts. In many instances the emergency decrees were disregarded, for their execution depended upon local authorities. There were many clashes between the local patriots and the departmental authorities, for the latter were not unanimously favorable to the events of August 10. To end this conflict the new, self-constituted local authorities "purified" the existing departmental boards by appointing their own nominees in the place of lukewarm officials.

Most stringent of all were the measures against the nonjuring priests. One decree, that of August 18, sequestrated all religious houses without exception and put them on sale for the benefit of the nation. The decree which Louis XVI had earlier rejected was legalized after the August 10 insurrection, but while it filled the prisons with many refractory priests, the extreme patriots found that it was too mild. Even priests with no public function, who had formerly been exempted, were now required to take the civic oath on pain of deportation. A sweeping decree, August 26, prescribed that all nonjuring priests (sexagenarians and those with no public functions were excepted) should leave the country in fifteen days or be deported to the tropical colony of Guiana. In that way the Assembly endeavored to destroy their influence over their parishioners, for the time for the election of new deputies was approaching. Thousands prepared to leave the country and seek refuge in various European states, but many others remained, and for them the decree was a dead letter.

In all those acts the Assembly had followed the lead of the Commune. But the Commune was not satisfied. The leaders wanted the trial and punishment of all those who had defended the king. Weeks before the odious massacres of September the populace cried for vengeance against the "conspirators of August 10," meaning of course the authorities who had resisted the insurrection and not the insurrectionists, who were actually the "conspirators," and threatened to massacre the prisoners. Step by step the Commune wrung concessions from the unwilling deputies until on August 17 the Assembly decreed the formation of an extraordinary tribunal to try all "conspirators." All cases connected with the events of August 10, whether within the jurisdiction of Paris or elsewhere in the country, were to be tried before that revolutionary tribunal. No appeal was to be permitted from the decisions of this court. The members of the Commune had hoped to have the judges and the jurors elected by direct vote, but because of opposition a compromise was reached which allowed their nomination by an electoral assembly. The guillotine (named for Dr. Guillotin, who had first proposed that instrument for public execution) was set up in the Place du Carrousel.

The Commune was not unopposed in its acts. Several of the sections, particularly those of the mercantile bourgeoisie of central and western Paris, protested and withdrew their representatives. Echoes of opposition came in from the near-by departments. Petty incidents were multiplied, exhausting alike the patience of the Assembly and the Commune. There were bitter controversies over the powers of the newly elected departmental administration. There were charges and countercharges concerning the press. The final dispute was precipitated by the Commune's action in arresting the managing editors of Brissot's journal, *Le Patriote français*. The Girondin leaders called on their colleagues to resist the unwarranted interference of the Commune. On the 30th the Legislative Assembly ordered the dissolution of the Commune and the election of a new one within twenty-four hours. The Commune obstinately refused to obey, and two days passed without any effort on the part of the Assembly to carry out its measure. Then came alarming news from the front, and a truce was patched up which retained the Commune in office but doubled the number of its members and gave the sections the right to recall their representatives if they so desired.

All the while patriotic feeling grew more and more intense. On the 19th of August, the Prussians had entered France, and four days later they captured Longwy, one of the frontier fortresses. Paris learned the news a day later. On the 26th, a great funeral demonstration for the revolutionary victims of August 10 turned men's thoughts more strongly to vengeance, that vengeance which the newly formed tribunal was administering too slowly to suit the hot-heads. Rumors circulated about royalist demonstrations in the Vendée and a monarchist plot in Dauphiné. The Commune made desperate efforts to organize the national defense; it rushed the work of digging trenches in the path of the advancing Prussians; it disarmed suspects, stimulated recruiting, and voted a fresh levy of 30,000 men, whom the municipality was to arm and equip for the front.

DANTON AND THE SEPTEMBER MASSACRES

In this crisis Danton was the very personification of national patriotism. He it was who thundered against the proposal of Roland and Servan to abandon Paris and remove the seat of government to Tours or Blois. His ministerial post gave him a chance to employ his talents and his energy and carry the weaker ministers with him. He appointed his friends and associates to subordinate posts, gave various concessions to war contractors, disposed of secret funds, which he never satisfactorily explained, and moved at his ease in the chaos. The situation delighted his strong and ardent nature; he could take the sternest measures and live up to his terrible appearance, or he could display his tolerance, his wide sympathy, or his magnanimity, all of which were equally characteristic of his being.

Certainly, his courage stiffened the morale of the ministry and spurred the people to great efforts; but he had every reason to wish the government to remain in Paris. He was popular in Paris; for three years, he had been in the thick of every democratic movement in the capital; he had taken part in every intrigue and had the confidence of the humble workers and artisans. But that was only one side of the medal. The reverse side shows him implicated in various shady transactions, surrounded by tricky, unscrupulous adventurers, subsidized successively by England, by the duke of Orléans, and by the royalists of Brittany. In 1789, he had been a struggling lawyer, heavily in debt. In 1792 he owned property in his natal town of Arcis-sur-Aube and was prosperous and thriving. In Paris he prided himself on having brought about the insurrection of August 10; in secret he predicted the eventual restoration of the monarchy. From the tribune he was for war to the end; in secret he negotiated with England and discussed peace with Prussia. At the very moment that he denounced Roland's trembling suggestion to move the government to the interior, he was in secret communication with the marquis de la Rouarie, who was organizing a royalist rebellion in Brittany. Whoever won, royalists or revolutionists, he was safe—with a claim on the gratitude of the victors. Danton was not the only revolutionist of prominence who blew hot and blew cold, though perhaps his relations with out-and-out counter-revolutionists were the most flagrant illustration of opportunistic trimming. Even Robespierre, whom one may not accuse of venality or double-dealing, was forced in 1793 to play the game of going fast enough to satisfy the extremists without going too fast to lose the support of the moderates.

On August 28, after he had rejected Roland's motion, Danton

proposed vigorous measures. The Assembly and council of ministers should send commissioners to the departments in order to aid
recruiting, to requisition supplies, and to dismiss lukewarm officials. The Commune should be given the right to conduct house-
to-house searches for the purpose of finding and confiscating arms
for the troops and arresting all suspected persons. The domiciliary
visits began the following day and continued through the 30th
and 31st. Tradition has it that 3000 suspects were arrested and
imprisoned, but it is unlikely that even as many as one hundred
suspects were rounded up. The prisons were already full, largely
with nonjuring priests who had been arrested after August 10.
But the tension was unendurable. The city was in a state of indescribable ferment. The extraordinary tribunal functioned slowly,
too slowly for ardent patriots, who grumbled and threatened direct
action. Rumors of prison deliveries filled the air. Night and day,
search parties passed before the eyes of the fearful citizens. The
nerves of the patriots still tingled from the last of the funeral
celebrations for the victims of August 10.

On September 2 the terrifying news came that Verdun was
besieged and that it could hold out only a few days more. If
Verdun fell, the Prussians had a clear road to Paris, and the
Parisians feared that Verdun would not long withstand the Prussian siege guns. Immediately, the Commune called on all good
citizens to meet at the Champ-de-Mars, to form battalions and
march to the front. The tocsin rang from the church towers; the
alarm cannon was fired; the barriers were closed. The Commune
and the Assembly coöperated in this call for volunteers. Vergniaud
harangued the Assembly, and then Danton gave a crisp burning
speech which ended with the memorable words: "To triumph over
the enemy . . . we must be bold, still more bold, ever bold, and
France is saved."

The volunteers made ready to leave for the front, but their
hearts were heavy with forebodings. Could they leave their wives
and children behind, with the prisons full of enemies, in their eyes
dangerous enemies, even though many of them were priests? Was
it not the part of prudence to forestall any possible move on the
part of the prisoners before they left the city? Their fears were
aggravated by the tense excitement that prevailed in the capital,
by the incendiary posters of Marat, who called for "heads," by
the nerve-racking funeral demonstrations, by the seeming reluc-

tance of the special tribunal to punish the aristocrats. The city authorities awaited some frightful mass action against the suspects in prison, for warning of a massacre of prisoners had been given immediately after August 10. On the 2nd of September the massacres began, instigated by the violent resolutions of several of the sections and abetted by the new Watch Committee of the Commune. The first victims were a group of arrested priests, who were attacked and murdered by their guards as they were being conducted to the prison of the Abbaye. Marat, who has so often been made responsible for the butcheries, was not more guilty than the other assassins. In any case the idea of massacre was not his, and the butchery would have begun without him.

For four days the massacres continued in Paris—at the prisons of the Abbaye and La Force, at the Salpétrière, at the Châtelet, at Bicêtre, and at the convent of the Carmelites. In four days, more than eleven hundred dead lay in gruesome heaps before the prisons. The executioners and the volunteer murderers killed indiscriminately with and without the formality of a hurried trial. They killed political suspects by preference, but they fell upon civil law prisoners as well. The Watch Committee of the Commune gave its approval and sent a circular, on September 3, to other municipalities urging them to follow the example of Paris: "The Paris Commune hastens to inform its brothers in the departments that a number of ferocious prisoners kept in its prisons have been put to death by the people . . . and the entire nation, after the long series of treasons which have led it to the edge of the abyss, will undoubtedly hasten to adopt this necessary method of public security." [3]

The advice was scarcely needed, horrible as it was. Before September 2 there had been sporadic, isolated murders at different points. At Reims, Meaux, and Caen there were similar orgies of butchery after the massacres at Paris. Everywhere in France the state of mind was the same as it was at the capital. Fear and mob hysteria, not isolated individuals, provoked the massacres. The beginning of the September massacres must be placed with the passage of the decree that the *patrie* was "in danger" (July, 1792). From comparatively slight measures such as the surveillance, the disarming, and the arrest of suspects, the panic swelled until it burst the limits of reason and justice and exploded in the butchery

---

[3] The Commune repudiated this circular somewhat later.

of September. For that butchery the exceptional circumstances which prevailed were largely responsible—the insurrection of August 10 and its nerve-racking consequences, the clanging of the tocsin, the boom of the alarm cannon, the suspicion generated by the struggle between the Assembly and the Commune, the funeral demonstrations, the maddening posters, the departure of the volunteers for the front, and the weakness of the government which relied on the Parisians whom it could not restrain. Had similar circumstances prevailed in the spring of 1793 when the patrie was again in danger, there is no doubt whatsoever that similar exhibitions of mob violence would have occurred. The circumstances explain but cannot excuse the participants; the massacres were a hideous outrage on justice. They proved that an unleashed mob could be as cruel and savage as the worst of despots. The Champ-de-Mars affair, about which the radicals had raised such indignant protest, was, compared to this, the merest trifle. The Parisian mob was far more merciless than the aristocrats and Feuillants at their worst.

The Legislative Assembly was too terrified to interfere, and the Commune took no serious steps to stop the slaughter. Indeed, the Commune voted to compensate the murderers for the working days which they had lost. Santerre, the commandant of the National Guard, refrained from calling his men, for he realized that they would have refused to obey his commands. Danton too was powerless to prevent the murder of the prisoners. The massacres had this political significance for him, that they weakened the prestige of the Girondins. But he protected Roland and a number of Girondin deputies when Robespierre and the Watch Committee proposed their arrest. Roland excused the massacres: "Yesterday was a day on whose happenings a veil must be drawn. I know that the people, terrible as they are in their vengeance, temper it with a kind of justice." The press was equally complacent and circumspect. Only later when a reaction set in against the massacres did the Girondin journalists condemn them and demand the punishment of their perpetrators.

Consequences of the Insurrection and the Massacres

The full consequences of the insurrection of August 10 and the September massacres were varied and profound. These events totally discredited the existing government. Henceforth no patriot desired or dared openly to defend the king and queen. The elections to the National Convention, which began at the end of August and in the first week of September, coincided with the peak of the antiroyalist wave. In the entire country only 700,000 out of 7,000,000 qualified voters, a minority of ten per cent, cast their ballots. At Paris and in ten departments the voting was verbal, and citizens who may have been inclined to defend the institution of monarchy allowed discretion to temper their valor. In the country at large the poor citizens kept away from the polls, being unable to sacrifice their daily wage. The Commune used terroristic methods to exclude royalist sympathizers from the polls. The Paris electoral assembly instructed the nominees to vote for the abolition of the monarchy. At the capital the Girondin candidates were snowed under by an avalanche of Jacobin votes. Only sympathizers of the Commune were returned, and these included Marat, Danton, and Robespierre, who formed the nucleus of the Montagnard group in the Convention. Elsewhere the Girondins were more successful, for reasons we shall state later. But the monarchy was doomed.

The religious consequences accentuated the deepening animosity of loyal revolutionists toward the clergy, both nonjuring and juring. The various measures taken against the refractory priests have already been stated. Because of the banishment of many thousands of the nonjuring priests and the unwillingness of the deputies to allow the juring priests to benefit thereby, the Assembly voted on September 20 to entrust the register of births, marriages, and deaths to the civil authorities of each municipality. In the same decree of September 20 the Assembly authorized divorce, which was, of course, forbidden by the church. These measures were the most important as well as the most radical of the innovations introduced into the relations of church and state. Still further to weaken the influence of the clergy the Assembly took steps to strip the church of its outward prestige. It ordered the sale of the sumptuous episcopal palaces and bade the bishops find lodgings in bare furnished rooms. Orders were given for the seizure of bronze objects and monuments in churches so that they might be melted down for the manufacture of cannon. Many of the precious gold and silver vessels in the churches were also seized in order that they might be coined into money. The wearing of ecclesiastical costumes was forbidden except during the exercise of religious functions. Church processions and other ecclesiastical ceremonies in the open might no longer be held. Lastly, to achieve the full ideal of the *philosophes* and transform religion into a civic function, the Assembly extended the state's control over the internal administration of the churches. During the Convention this policy was to reach its logical conclusion in a stringent surveillance of every move that the religious authorities made.

The social consequences of the events which had taken place in August and September were equally profound. There was a direct relationship between these social consequences and the election of many Girondin sympathizers to the Convention. The real nature of the insurrection of August 10 was not known in most departments. Inasmuch as the Girondins had regained control of the ministry, the citizens of many departments considered them the responsible leaders of that movement. In order to retain their new prestige, as well as for less calculated reasons, the Girondin deputies made a radical innovation toward the solution of the vexing problem of feudal dues. Their decrees of August 25 provided for the abolition of all feudal rights, unless the proprietor could produce the original title. This he could not do under ordinary circumstances. Whether he could or could not substantiate his claims, the burden of proof was now shifted from the peasant to the former noble overlord. Legal actions against the peasantry arising from disputes over feudal rights were dropped. The decree provided also that the confiscated estates of émigrés and the common lands should be offered for sale in small parcels on easy terms of payment. The intent of these measures was to show that the downfall of feudalism was the result of the downfall of monarchy, that the Girondins were the benefactors of the peasantry. There is no doubt that this decree helped the cause of Girondin candidates at the polls. But there was an even more significant factor explaining the success of the Girondins at the polls. The secondary electors, representing the views of the revolutionary and patriotic middle class, rejected the more radical candidates because the latter were held responsible for certain recent measures which, rightly or wrongly, seemed to threaten property rights.

We have already shown that France was in the grip of an economic crisis in 1792, which war needs had made more acute, particularly with respect to the shortage of food. In many cities the shortage had forced the local authorities to regulate food prices. The Assembly followed the movement closely and finally authorized the district administration to requisition grain supplies, though it refused to authorize price fixing. For isolated Jacobins in Paris and for many more outside of Paris, this decree was not enough. They advocated a rather vague régime of state socialism stressing the right of the state, in the existing crisis, to regulate or even take over private property. While the Jacobin Club at Paris refrained from supporting these extreme claims, the majority of the members gave a guarded indorsement to the demands on the wholly legitimate ground that they were necessary war expedients. Such was the view taken by the Jacobins who were elected by the Parisians to serve as deputies in the coming National Convention. Their attitude sufficed to give strength to the Girondin argument that the Jacobins were "anarchists" and sponsors of an "agrarian law." And the Girondin argument in turn carried enough weight to insure them, outside of Paris, a pronounced victory in the elections to the National Convention.

The Invasion of France

Meanwhile the military situation was growing worse. Verdun surrendered on September 2, and it seemed as if only a miracle could hold Brunswick back from Paris, which he himself now expected to reach by the middle of October. While the troops under his command were not numerous, totaling no more than 77,000 men, the Prussians' reputation as the best soldiers in Europe made the French cause seem desperate. But the defects of the Prussian tactics and strategy, which were substantially those of the days of Frederick the Great, were revealed at an early date. On the other hand, the Austrians, whose reputation was inferior, were actually superior to the Prussians, for they had gained much from their war experience against the Turks. The duke of Brunswick, the generalissimo of the allied troops, had at first not planned to reach Paris before the spring of 1793. He adhered to the military tradition of the century with its slow advances to keep down the loss of men, with its seizure of fortresses for diplomatic bargaining, with its avoidance of decisive battles unless the terrain were ideal. Moreover, he was old, jealous of compromising his glory, and unsuited by temperament for daring ventures. The émigrés assured

Frederick William that all France was waiting to welcome him, and General Bouillé sent word that the fortresses would not hold out against the Prussians. Though Brunswick disagreed with his counselors, he kept silent, deferred to the wishes of his monarch, and advanced, albeit leisurely.

He reckoned without the torrential rains and also without Dumouriez. The rains which began to fall late in August turned the roads into morasses, made marching difficult and the provisioning of his troops more difficult still. In the meantime, Kellermann and Dumouriez, who replaced Generals Lückner and Lafayette, were whipping the raw French recruits into shape. Since the first skirmishes of April the French troops had gained experience. Dumouriez, in particular, had done marvels with them, infusing them with his own reckless and daring spirit. His heart was set upon a conquest of the Austrian Netherlands, but Servan, the minister of war, gave him stringent orders to effect a junction with Kellermann and block the road to Paris. Not daring to risk battle on a level terrain, Dumouriez took up a defensive position in the passes of the Argonne. Meantime Brunswick advanced slowly, pushing the French back of the passes of the Argonne to Valmy hill and the plateau beyond.

There, on September 20, under instructions from Frederick William, he prepared to attack. To his astonishment, and perhaps theirs, the French troops held firm under the Prussian fire. Indeed, the French artillery so clearly showed its superiority that Brunswick, who at first was reluctant to attack, later did not dare move forward with the bulk of his men. The skirmish at Valmy was incomplete and indecisive, for rain put an end to the fighting, but Brunswick fell back and France was saved from the invaders. The astounded Prussians awoke to the fact that the capture of Paris was not going to be a military parade, while the jubilant French troops suddenly became conscious of their strength. The great German poet Goethe, who was present at the artillery duel, indulged in poetic exaggeration when he exclaimed that a new era in the history of the world began from that date, but it is indisputable that the moral significance of Valmy was tremendous. While Dumouriez and the ministry negotiated with the retreating Prussians, the National Convention which assembled on the very day that the Prussians were checked at Valmy, was holding the first of its dramatic and epoch-making sessions.

X. THE CONVENTION: JACOBINS AND GIRONDINS (1792–1793)

Composition of the National Convention

On September 21, 1792, the newly elected deputies of the National Convention held their first regular session.[1] Toward the end of their meeting, almost apologetically and with little enthusiasm, they passed an unanimous decree abolishing the monarchy. *De facto*, of course, the monarchy had come to an inglorious end on August 10. Now *de jure*, although only the deputies from Paris had been instructed to vote for the abolition, all the deputies recognized the accomplished fact. On the following day, September 22, they passed a supplementary decree stipulating that henceforth all public documents were to be dated from "Year I of the French Republic." In that indirect fashion the era of the venerable French monarchy came to an end. The state which had symbolized royal absolutism in Europe was now a republic. On September 25 the Convention decreed that the republic was "one and indivisible" and placed life and property under the safeguard of the new government. It is possible to see in these resolutions a sign of the mutual fears and suspicions which divided the deputies into bitterly antagonistic groups. These measures, particularly the decree of September 25, showed clearly that many deputies feared that the republic might split up into a weak confederation of states. These measures may also have been intended to calm the fears of other deputies who were afraid that certain of their colleagues were aspiring to a dictatorship. The safeguarding of property rights was no doubt welcome to those who feared a redistribution of property, or "an agrarian law," as it was then phrased. But after the passage of these measures the happy accord between the deputies ended, and two factions, progressively more irreconcilable and mistrustful, struggled desperately first to achieve supremacy and then to eliminate each other. Yet they had more than ever

---

[1] On the preceding day there had been a formal meeting for the purpose of organization. It was attended by about half of the 749 duly elected deputies. Those present named Pétion their first presiding officer.

to fear the hostility of Europe and the opposition of the internal foes of the Revolution.

What were these rival groups, and why did their rivalry lead to exhibitions of collective emotions perhaps unparalleled in political annals? To the right of the president's box sat some 165 deputies, known in history as the Girondins, and to their contemporaries as "Brissotins." To the left of the seat of the presiding officer, on the high benches from which they derived their name, sat the deputies of the Mountain, or the Montagnards as they were called.[2] Between them, occupying the seats of the center, were the great majority of the deputies, the men of the Plain, or more derisively, of the Marsh. If, at first, these men of moderate views, who were led by Sieyès, and Barère and Grégoire, inclined toward the Girondins, they gradually overcame their mistrust of the Mountain and its violent popular leaders and gave them their support.

Not a few of the outstanding deputies had served in the preceding assemblies. Some were newcomers to the business of politics. Among the Girondins there were Brissot, Guadet, and Condorcet, who had sat in the Legislative Assembly. With them were Pétion, Buzot, and the impetuous Lanjuinais, the Breton lawyer, all of whom had seen service in the Constituent Assembly. Among their new adherents there were the handsome and fiery young Barbaroux from Marseilles, and Carra and Gorsas, two stormy petrels from the ranks of Paris journalists. Three of the ministers, Lebrun, Clavière, and the earnest, hard-working Roland, also shared their views. To this list we may add Madame Roland, for it was at her home that the Girondins most frequently gathered to discuss their policies and listen to the advice of that inspiring bluestocking, their hostess.

Among the Montagnards there were several representatives who had already achieved greater or lesser prominence. Marat and Danton were there, and also Panis, Sergent, and Manuel, all former members of the Commune of August 10. Robespierre and his younger brother Augustin sat with them. There were also the effervescent Camille Desmoulins, the haughty, youthful Saint-Just, the former actor and future terrorist, Collot d'Herbois, the unfrocked monk, Fouché, the blunt, outspoken Billaud-Varenne,

---

[2] Since they belonged to the Jacobin Club, from which their rivals were soon excluded, one may also refer to them as the Jacobins.

the paralytic cripple Couthon, and the duke of Orléans (now called "Égalité"), all of whom had been elected because of their support of popular measures. Tallien and Fréron, who later led the attack upon Robespierre, sat by his side; and Merlin de Douai, a famed jurist of the Old Régime, and Anacharsis Clootz, who was to dub himself "the orator of all mankind," sat in the ranks of the Montagnard-Jacobins.

These groups did not constitute political parties in our modern sense. They had no real party organization, no well defined program of action, no funds. Their individual adherents felt free to vote as they pleased, with or against their group. Their individualism was too pronounced to suffer the restraints of party discipline. Political tradition and theory frowned upon the very conception of a party. These individuals of pronounced personal characteristics and opinions formed loose groups or factions partly because the very nature of political assemblies tends to intensify the natural tendency of men to disagree on all points, important or trivial. They aligned themselves with these three large groups —Montagnards, Girondins, and the Plain—because each of these groups offered its supporters opportunities for the kind of action they desired, action concerning individuals or action concerning policies.

There were pronounced disagreements and differences between the Jacobins and the Girondins, inherited, long-standing rivalries and jealousies, both on the score of individuals and on that of policies. Robespierre and Brissot had fallen out at the beginning of 1792, perhaps earlier, on the question of the war with Austria. Danton was abhorrent to the Rolands, to Madame Roland in particular, who professed to shudder at the sight of his leonine head and pockmarked face. Marat had the distinction of being disliked almost as fervently by his supporters among the Montagnard deputies as by his detractors among the Girondins. In all three of these Montagnard deputies the Girondins thought they detected aspirants to a dictatorship over France. Then there was the Girondin complex against Paris. Most of these deputies came from the provinces and resented the excessive influence that the Paris Commune and the Parisian populace had assumed over the national assemblies. They felt themselves insecure in the capital, insisting that "Paris must be reduced to its one-eighty-third degree of influence like every department," and that the national govern-

ment must function legally, unhampered by the threats of insurrectionary mobs of workers. But more than anything else, at first,
it was the memory of August 10 and the September massacres that
united the Girondin deputies against their rivals in the assembly.
At the time of the massacres they had maintained a neutral aloofness, afraid to condemn and loath to participate in the odious
butchery; but later they cast the charge of "Septemberers" at all
those who had ordered or taken part in the massacre.

The personal rivalries might have been assuaged, the fear of
Paris lessened, and the memory of September weakened, but there
were more fundamental differences between them which in the
poisoned atmosphere of the revolutionary turmoil could not be
composed. Essentially it was a difference in social outlook that
separated them. Politically, there was little to choose between
them. All were loyal revolutionists. All were converts to the
religion of national patriotism without being apostates to catholicism. There were no royalists or counter-revolutionists among
them. Not a single deputy whom one would today call a socialist
or a communist sat in the new assembly. In the beginning almost
all of them belonged to and attended the sessions of the powerful
middle-class Jacobin club of Paris.[3] The extremists with a socialistic
program, those who later imposed some of their views upon the
Montagnards, were isolated and scattered, without an organization
or even a large following. The majority of the Girondin deputies
were lawyers, cultivated, idealistic disciples of the *philosophes* and,
in their social philosophy, of Turgot and the Physiocrats. They
were unblessed either with sympathy or with understanding of
the inarticulate needs of the peasants and the city artisans. They
unconsciously sponsored the claims and interests of landowners
and men of affairs. Socially—this point is important—as well as
intellectually, they were linked by a strong bond of sympathy to
men of wealth and property. Their political and social ideal was
a state where trade and industry would be free and unregulated,
where foodstuffs would be imported and exported without the
supervision or the interfering regulation of a central administration, where private property would be inviolable and well-nigh as
sacred as life itself. They had consented to the establishment of a

[3] After August 19, 1792, the official title of the Club was changed from "The
Society of Friends of the Constitution" to "The Society of Friends of Liberty and
Equality."

republic, but they could not resign themselves to the rule of the lower classes without which a republican government could not then exist. For them the Revolution had gone far enough; further progress spelled anarchy and the end of their economic security.

Yet the Montagnards whom they accused, in the electoral campaign, of fostering an attack upon private property, of favoring the violent expropriation and forcible redistribution of landed property, were in most respects as socially respectable as they themselves. The nucleus of their party was the deputation from Paris, around which there were many decided republicans from the departments. They were dominant at the Jacobin club, indorsed by the Commune, and enthusiastically supported by the *sans-culottes* of the sections. The Montagnards also believed in the institution of private property and in the maintenance of a competitive economic order. But some of them from their reading and study and others from association and experience had acquired a sympathetic attitude toward the world of the lowly, the petty tradesmen and the artisans. They believed in that which the more legal-minded and individualistic Girondins could not accept, in the constitutional or unconstitutional intervention of the government in private affairs, provided that that direct action served the interests of all citizens, poor ones included. This was their famous *loi de salut public* ("law of public safety"), a point of view borrowed from Rousseau's famous doctrine of the "general will" and developed by the Jacobins to excess in 1793–1794. Without desiring a social revolution, they were more inclined to appeal to the lower middle classes and to the proletariat of the country and the city for support. No doubt their leaders were less eloquent and less cultivated than the Girondins, but they were more daring, more realistic, and certainly less scrupulous as to means.

In order to gain and hold political power they had to satisfy the demands of the masses; and they felt that they, infinitely better than the Girondins, could wield political power to crush the various enemies of the Revolution. Thus gradually they took over some of the more radical social demands of the popular leaders, less out of political conversion than out of political expediency. At first locally and later on a national scale they insisted upon governmental regulation of prices and wages, a policy which roused the apprehensions of the producers and their Girondin adherents. They also tempered their acceptance of private property with vigorous attacks against certain types of private wealth, the estates of émigrés and priests. This policy exposed them to the charge of being "anarchists," but the property that they expropriated was, in their opinion, the property of enemies of the state, not that of real Frenchmen. They regulated prices and wages not merely to serve the consumers at the expense of the producers, as the Girondins claimed, but because they saw the imperative need in time of war of guaranteeing the food supply and defeating the real or imagined machinations of profiteers and speculators.

Under ordinary circumstances the solution of their difficulties would have been a peaceful one, and a *modus vivendi* might have been established. But under the extraordinary circumstances in which they lived, revolution, war, civil strife, plots, food shortages, and recurrent crises, passions ran high, and each side saw only the justice of its views. Disagreement was not a mere difference of opinion; it was treason, and presumption passed readily for proof. Thus they never achieved unity, that unity which circumstances seemed to favor in the autumn of 1792, which was so sorely needed to solve the problems of the new government. Efforts were made, most notably by Danton, to heal the breach, but the bitter personal rivalries, the political incompetence of the Girondin chieftains, and the tactics of the Montagnard extremists defeated all attempts at reconciliation. So long as the possibility existed that August 10 and the September massacres might be repudiated, the Girondins, who were not contaminated with those proceedings, played safe. Therefore, every consideration of political strategy impelled the Jacobin deputies to force the Convention along the radical road to the point where all, Girondins as well as Jacobins, would be too deeply committed to turn back. From the end of September, 1792, to the beginning of June, 1793, the rivalry steadily grew more intense, and quarrel followed quarrel until a veritable coup d'état cleared the political atmosphere.

TRIAL OF THE KING

The times were indeed propitious for united action in the Convention. The Commune of August 10, existing only on sufferance, for the Legislative Assembly had ordered the immediate election of a new municipal government, was not inclined to challenge the national assembly. The foreign war was taking a favorable turn, and Paris was quiet. Danton extended the olive branch of peace to the Girondins, but it was spurned, largely because of the personal animosity of the Rolands toward Danton. Instead of unity, the Girondin leaders desired victory. For weeks they attacked the triumvirate of Montagnard leaders, Danton, Marat, and Robespierre. They accused Danton of being an instigator of the September massacres, they charged him with the misuse of secret funds which he had received as minister of justice, and they upbraided him for aspiring to a dictatorship. The immediate effect of their tactics was to push Danton all the more solidly into the ranks of their opponents.

So too with Marat. Despite his keen intelligence, his sterling honesty, and his sympathetic advocacy of the poor and the disinherited of the earth, he was hated and feared. His violent words, calling for a dictatorship and mass extermination, his theatrical gestures, his repulsive physical appearance, made him one of the most thoroughly loathed of all the deputies. But by attacking him and linking him with Danton and Robespierre, indeed with all the deputies implicated in the September massacres, the Girondins forced him upon the Montagnards, who with some reluctance undertook his defense.

Roland, that personification of domestic virtues and political ·ineptitude, fanned the flames by abusing his ministerial powers in the Girondins' behalf. He interfered with the mail service of the Jacobins. At his instigation many pamphlets, vehement in their denunciation of Paris, were printed and distributed all over France. Worse still, he made the ill advised suggestion that the Convention have a paid guard composed of fédérés from the departments in order to protect the deputies against the Parisian populace. The motion was not carried, but the fédérés came trooping into Paris anyhow, and by the middle of October there were some sixteen thousand of them in the capital. The Jacobins were not undone; they paid court to the volunteers, wooed their favor, and finally won them over. Before the conversion of the fédérés was completed, however, their presence gave the Girondins sufficient courage to make a bitter personal attack upon Robespierre. As in the case of Danton and Marat, the Girondin charges against Robespierre fell flat, save no doubt to strengthen Robespierre's bid for leadership in his party.

Then the Girondins tried a new tack. They attempted to detach the local Jacobin clubs throughout France from their affiliation with the *société mère* in Paris; but the effort, like the preceding attacks upon individuals, was a failure. Baffled in their plan to make the Convention independent by surrounding it with a paid guard, they fell back upon a more dangerous expedient of convoking the primary assemblies in order to have the election of various Montagnard deputies nullified. Had this maneuver succeeded, the purged assembly would not have long existed, and wild anarchy would have ensued. Thus the Girondins failed in all their attacks and succeeded only in arraying the Montagnards, the Commune, the Jacobins, and the sections solidly against them.

The Mountain did not remain on the defensive. In the Assembly itself the deputies of the Plain, discouraged by the rash tactics of the Girondins, slowly assumed a more friendly attitude toward the latter's opponents. By the middle of November the first non-Girondin president (for a fortnight) was elected, the honor falling to Grégoire of the Plain. In the election of a new minister to succeed Servan as the minister of war, a creature of the Jacobins, the notoriously incompetent Pache, was named. In the new Commune the two most important posts, those of procurator and assistant procurator, were filled by extremists, Chaumette and Hébert, the latter being the popular editor of the widely read *Père Duchêne*. While the Girondins attacked Paris, the Montagnards circulated the charge that their rivals were federalists, that is, supporters of a loose federation of little states. This accusation was all the more effective in that many political liberals, who thought that a republic was an ideal form of government for a small state, feared that if a large country (such as France) adopted the republican form of government, it would break up into a loose federation. The experience of the Swiss and Dutch federations seemed to confirm that fear. The Girondins, by stressing the equality of the departments, laid themselves open to the charge of federalism, and consequently of violating the intent of the decree of September 25 which proclaimed the French Republic "one and indivisible." Meanwhile, the Mountain waited for an opportunity to take the offensive in its turn, and this opportunity to involve the Girondins it found in the discussions concerning the fate of Louis XVI.

By the end of the autumn of 1792, this issue overshadowed all others. The deposed monarch and his family were under close watch in their narrow quarters in the Tower of the Temple, but his power was still greatly feared. The public mind, influenced by the popular clubs, agreed that he should be punished, but the deputies were far from agreed on the procedure to adopt in his case. There was substantial agreement that Louis Capet, as he was now known, could not be liberated to become the nucleus of fresh intrigues and counter-revolutionary plots. His followers had been punished. Why not he, himself? But what was to be done with him? Was he to be imprisoned for the duration of the war, or banished from France, or was he to suffer the fate of the hapless Charles I, victim of an earlier revolution?

The Girondins played for time. They placed obstacles in the path of a speedy trial, sought and found various diversions without daring openly to flaunt the popular sentiment for Louis's punishment. On the other hand the Montagnards expressed their views with brutal simplicity. They wanted a trial, they desired the royal prisoner's death. They intended to make impossible any return to the monarchy, and they hoped, by the condemnation of the king, to rally the support of the violent parties as well as to tar the Girondins with the same brush that had already tarred them in September. The youthful Saint-Just in his first appearance in the tribune maintained that Louis XVI was a captured enemy, who was to be tried by the rules of war. Robespierre was equally direct: "Louis is no prisoner before the bar; you are not judges; you are, and you can only be, statesmen and deputies of the nation. Yours is not to sit in judgment for or against a man; yours is to take a step for the public welfare." [4]

During all of November the Convention discussed the report of the committee on legislation, which had decided that the former king was not inviolable and could be tried as a private citizen. The Girondins did not dare to flaunt popular animosities by declaring Louis inviolable, but they protested strongly against the Montagnard proposal that he be condemned without a trial. Accordingly they swung the assembly in favor of a trial. Louis was formally arraigned on December 3, and his trial dragged on for more than a month. At the last moment it might have been averted or at least postponed, had it not been for the timely discovery of fresh evidence of Louis's counter-revolutionary activities. A secret cup-

[4] Danton was averse to a trial, again in the interests of peace with the powers; but he let it be understood that if a trial were held, he would vote for the death penalty.

board, closed by an iron door, which Louis, who was a skilled locksmith, had helped make in the wall of his royal apartments, was revealed to Roland. The minister brought its contents to the assembly. They disclosed Mirabeau's relations with the crown, the monarch's correspondence with a secret agent who had been entrusted with the delicate operation of bribing popular agitators and fomenting counter-revolutionary disturbances, and Louis's relations with the émigrés across the frontiers. This theatrical coup made a trial inevitable and silenced the opposition, for now to oppose a trial or plead the inviolability of the king seemed *ipso facto* a profession of faith against the republic.

Louis XVI appeared twice before the Convention, the first time on December 11 to hear the indictment read, and the second and last time on December 26 to hear Desèze, one of his three counsel, read an eloquent defense. His dignity and poise impressed the deputies most favorably, but he spoiled that impression by making a denial of every article of the indictment, even those which were thoroughly substantiated. After an interminable series of passionate debates in which the Girondins' attempt to save Louis by having a popular referendum was defeated, the deputies finally came to the vote on January 15, 1793. It had been decided, on Barère's proposal, that the vote should be by roll call, which gave the gallery, packed with fierce viragoes from the Central Markets and vociferous agitators, an opportunity to distinguish between the "pure" deputies and the "corrupt."

Four questions were put to the deputies: first, "Is Louis guilty of conspiracy against public liberty and of plotting against the general security of the State?" To this all the deputies present, 707, answered in the affirmative. To the second question, "Will the verdict of the National Convention against Louis Capet be referred to the people for ratification?" 424 deputies voted in the negative and 287 in the affirmative. The Girondins wished to save Louis, but they feared the imputation of royalism. By referring the sentence of the Convention to the popular assemblies they hoped to accomplish their aim without exposing themselves to the charges of the Mountain. On the third question, "What penalty will be imposed on Louis?" the voting was intensely dramatic. Each deputy in turn mounted the tribune and recorded his vote aloud. For twenty-four long hours they voted, and at the end the former king was condemned to death by 387 votes against 334.

Though twenty-six of the 387 were in favor of postponing the execution, which seemed to reduce the absolute majority of the advocates of the death penalty to one vote, the fact remains that they voted for death. The correct majority for death was thus fifty-three. Among those who voted for the death penalty were several of the Girondin leaders. On the 19th, they made a final desperate effort to postpone the execution, which, according to revolutionary practice, was to be carried out within twenty-four hours of the sentence; but a respite was rejected by 70 votes, 380 against 310.

The voting had lasted for more than 100 continuous hours, from the evening of January 15 to the early hours of January 20. The execution took place on the morrow, Sunday, January 21, 1793. Up to the last moment the royalists hoped to save the monarch; but their bribery and threats were unavailing against popular animosity and intimidation. Louis took leave of his heartbroken family on the evening before. A nonjuring priest accompanied him to the scaffold. Paris was feverish, for attempts at rescue were feared and a double line of troops hedged the road from the Temple to the Place de la Révolution, where the scaffold had been erected; but outwardly, the city maintained its calm. Louis, whose courage had never been higher, mounted the steps, the abbé by his side. He tried to speak. The drums drowned his words, and a dripping head fell heavily into the basket. The knife had done its work. A loud shout, "Vive la nation!" split the air. His body was buried in quicklime in the cemetery of the Madeleine Church, and his blood cut a chasm behind the regicides. "Now it can truly be said," wrote one of them, "we must live free or die."

Louis XVI was the victim of his errors and his weaknesses and those of his royal predecessors. His tragic death redeemed his memory, indeed placed a halo around him. His long martyrdom in prison, which he bore with marked patience and resignation, his kindliness and manly courage, his simple composure in the face of death, have served to palliate a personal mediocrity, a revolutionary policy that was tortuous and obstructing. But the conscience of the Montagnards was clear. On the night before the execution, Le Peletier de Saint-Fargeau, a distinguished deputy, guiltless of violence or fanaticism, had been stabbed to death by a rabid royalist because he had voted for the king's death. He was the first deputy to suffer a violent fate in the performance of his duties. His colleagues exalted him as a "Martyr of Liberty" and gave him the honors of a great public funeral. And every Montagnard must have trembled at the dread thought that perhaps his turn might come next. In a very literal sense the death of Louis XVI was the signal for a life-and-death struggle between the revolutionaries and their enemies.

Republican Victories and Propaganda

In spite of their sorry rôle in the trial of the king, the Girondins still enjoyed great prestige. The foreign war had placed them in a position of power. By the success of their generals they held their position. After the repulse of the Prussians at Valmy, the enemy had retreated slowly through the plains of Champagne, unharried by any pursuing troops though ravaged by dysentery. Inspired by Danton, the ministry gave Dumouriez full powers to negotiate with the Prussians, trusting that the discussions would eventuate in the rupture of the Austro-Prussian alliance and perhaps in the cementing of a Franco-Prussian alliance against Austria. The exact nature of the *pourparlers* remains a mystery; but the Prussian troops withdrew slowly and unmolested from French territory. Dumouriez prepared to invade the Netherlands, while General Custine marched against the Austrians in the Rhineland and Generals Montesquiou and Anselme received orders to advance into Savoy.

The first triumphs came in the southeast. In September, General Montesquiou entered the territory of Savoy, whose king was bound by treaty to Austria, and General Anselme occupied Nice at the end of the month. In both regions the French troops were enthusiastically acclaimed by the civil population, which met them singing the "Marseillaise" and waving the French tricolor. A "national sovereign assembly" of Savoy assembled a few weeks later and formally declared the union of its country to France, sending a deputation to Paris in order to obtain the ratification of the Convention. If possible, the enthusiasm of the somnolent, placid Rhine provinces was even greater. Valmy gave them the chance to express their cordial sympathy with the principles of the French Revolution, and the nearness of the French troops gave them hope that soon those principles would be triumphantly proclaimed in their own states. General Custine was equally inspired by the enthusiasm of the new converts and the negligence of the allies, who had withdrawn their troops from the Rhineland. He made a sudden and highly successful raid, captured Speyer and Worms without a struggle, advanced upon the Rhine fortress of Mainz and, after the surrender of Mainz, crossed the Rhine and occupied Frankfort. The local princes and the privileged subjects fled at his approach, and to the enthusiastic inhabitants who remained Custine promised all the blessings of freedom *à la française*. After a short time, however, the Rhinelanders found these blessings decidedly too taxing.

In the north Dumouriez utilized the opportunity afforded both by the retreat of the Prussians and by the advance of Custine to turn his attention to the Austrians who were before Lille. He raised the siege of Lille, pursued the Austrians under the duke of Saxe-Teschen across the French frontier into the Austrian Netherlands, and, at the heights of Jemappes on November 6, carried the day in the first great victory of the French troops. Brussels, Antwerp, and Liége fell soon after, and within three weeks all of the Netherlands was in the possession of the French. Dumouriez had not been mistaken in believing that the bourgeoisie and the peasantry would rally to his support. Before advancing he had issued appeals to the civil population, promising the leaders the aid of the French in renouncing the rule of the Hapsburgs and in organizing their own government.

These rapid triumphs of the revolutionary armies greatly increased the prestige of the new republic, but they also increased the problems of the deputies of the Convention, who now had to fix the government's policy toward the provisional administrations in Savoy, Nice, and the Rhineland. Could France abandon the revolutionists of those regions who had seized power with the aid of the French troops? If it did so, never could France expect aid from them against its enemies. Furthermore these victories could be made profitable to the republic, for at least one of the conquering generals, Custine, levied military contributions upon the civil population in order to defray the costs of operations. On the other hand, the French government had renounced wars of conquest and had pledged itself not to interfere in the internal affairs of its neighbors. Among the generals there was no unanimity of procedure; instructions from the Convention were lacking. The propagandist spirit, so strong in the Girondin deputies, swept the Montagnards and the Plain. On November 19 the Convention voted the first of the "propaganda decrees" which allied the French nation with its revolutionary supporters outside of France: "The National Convention declares in the name of the French nation that it will bring fraternity and aid to all peoples that wish to recover their liberty and charges the executive power to give the generals all necessary orders to bring aid to those people and to defend the citizens who have been or may be molested in the cause of liberty."

More and more the enthusiastic supporters of the Revolution were coming to regard it as a universal crusade of *peoples* against *aristocrats* and *kings*. The internationalism of the decree of November 19 is identical with the internationalism of contemporary socialism and communism, which summon the proletarians of all countries to unite against their bourgeois exploiters. One has only to change the nomenclature: for peoples read proletarians, for aristocrats read bourgeoisie, and for kings read capitalist governments. Yet the debates preceding this decree reveal clearly that in the minds of many deputies there was, underneath their revolutionary idealism, a firm desire to extend the boundaries of France to its "natural frontier" of the Alps and the Rhine. Consequently, when the delegation from Savoy presented its petition, the Convention voted to accept it on two grounds: first, that the people of Savoy shared the sentiments of France, and secondly, that the territory of Savoy was enclosed within "the limits set by the hand of nature to the French Republic." By that decision Savoy became a part of France.

The second, complementary, "propaganda decree" of December 15, which was voted in consequence of the situation in the Netherlands, modified whatever undue idealism may have manifested itself in the first decree. In the political agitation of the Belgians, Dumouriez's rôle was that of a more or less peaceful bystander, for his purpose was to use the Netherlands as a base for further operations against the Austrians. But the incompetent Pache, the new minister of war, mistrusted the general and demoralized the army services, making Dumouriez's further advance extremely difficult as well as dangerous. An increasing number of deputies, too, shared the conviction that the costs of war should be defrayed by the "liberated peoples." To investigate the situation in the Netherlands the Convention sent several deputies there, and these summoned a number of Jacobin stalwarts from near-by

French towns to assist them in the "investigation." In close co-operation they extended their aid to the small minority of Belgians who wished a French régime and intimidated the more reluctant natives into demanding French institutions and, in some instances, annexation to France. Upon the return of the deputies the Convention voted the decree which formulated the intention of France to stir up rebellion in every neighboring country.

The decree stipulated that in all occupied states the system of taxation, the tithe, titles of nobility, all special privileges, and all feudal dues were to be abolished. The property belonging to the local ruler and to the various religious communities was to be entrusted to the French Republic. This meant the sequestration of the property as security for a new issue of assignats. The existing authorities were to be replaced by an administration chosen by the "friends of liberty," so that members of the old government and members of the privileged classes were excluded. The assignat was to be accepted at its face value and the enfranchised peoples were to defray the costs of their liberation. All peoples rejecting this proffered assistance of the French were to be regarded as enemies. Within a few months' time this decree was applied in all its provisions to the Netherlands and to the territory between the Moselle and the Rhine.

This new French policy of territorial aggrandizement and financial exaction accomplished by force and coercion, turned the liberated peoples against their benefactors. Even before the decree of December 15 was passed, many of the Belgians had outraged their French liberators by manifesting great reluctance to accept the depreciated French assignats. To avoid counter-revolution in the occupied territory the Convention decided upon a policy of annexation. Nice was annexed at the end of January, 1793, on the very day that Danton proclaimed that the boundaries of the French Republic were those "marked by nature." City by city, province by province, the local patriots of the Netherlands and the Rhineland, supported by French bayonets, voted for annexation, and in March the Convention ratified their votes and decreed the annexation of these lands to the French Republic.

This new policy gained a new and a most formidable enemy for France. Formal diplomatic relations with England had been broken after August 10, and the situation became tense after the September massacres. The recognition of the new republic by the

English government was a forlorn hope even before the French invasion of the Netherlands in November. But strained relations were not necessarily a prelude to a declaration of war. The French invasion of the Netherlands made war a possibility, even a strong probability, for it threatened the security of the United Provinces, which Great Britain had guaranteed by an earlier treaty. Before the first of the "propaganda decrees" could be utilized by the Dutch malcontents against their government, the Convention had already menaced the interests of the Dutch and English merchants by opening the Scheldt River to commercial navigation.[5] The French occupation of Antwerp (later characterized by Napoleon as "a loaded pistol aimed at the heart of England") undoubtedly threatened the English sense of military security. Accordingly the English government, under the direct inspiration of the younger Pitt, took the precautionary measures of opening negotiations with the Germanic allies and speeding military preparations. To the English ministry the second of the "propaganda decrees" seemed full justification for its actions.

The decision reached by the Tory government in England in the period between November, 1792, and January, 1793, to wage war upon France was typical of the attitude of other European governments. In that period three important developments had finally convinced Europe that the French Revolution was a devastating menace to established governments and society. First, the Revolution was pursuing an aggressive policy of conquest (Belgium, the left bank of the Rhine, and Savoy). Secondly, these acts of military aggression were being rationalized in terms of a universal crusade to liberate all oppressed peoples (the propaganda decrees). Thirdly the revolutionists had executed the king. It was now clear that the French Revolution was more than a revolution in France. It was taking on the aspect of an international movement which, if successful in France, would overflow the frontiers and undermine governments and society in Europe. To crush the menace of the armed doctrine of the French Revolution became a matter of life and death to all legitimate governments.

If England took the lead in organizing the European opposition, it is because England's position was most seriously threatened. The opening of the Scheldt was a serious blow to her commercial classes. The French occupation of the Austrian Netherlands was a

---

[5] The control of the Scheldt was secured to the Dutch by treaties.

direct military menace to England herself, while the French conquests in general destroyed the delicate political equilibrium in Europe. Lastly, the radical movement at home was assuming alarming proportions. Pitt's solution of this complex of domestic and foreign problems was to direct public opinion in favor of a *patriotic* war to protect England's legitimate rights, her glorious traditions, and her king against what Burke had already called "this wild, nameless thing . . . in the heart of Europe." War became inevitable early in January, 1793, and the execution of Louis XVI furnished the pretext. The French diplomatic agent at London received his passport on January 24, 1793, and on his return to France on February 1, the Convention declared war upon England and her Dutch ally, the United Provinces. On the day preceding the declaration of war, Dumouriez received instructions to invade the Dutch provinces, Amsterdam, the financial center of Europe, being his objective.

Military Reverses and Civil Strife

Within a month's time the ranks of France's enemies were swelled by new recruits. The execution of Louis XVI was the direct cause of the break with Bourbon Spain, against which the Convention declared war on March 7 as the culmination of a long series of provocative acts. Spain's entry gave England access to the Mediterranean and encouraged the lesser Italian states, Sardinia and Naples, to come out openly against the French republic. Early in 1793 Europe, excepting Russia, Switzerland, Denmark, Sweden, and Turkey, was at war with France.[6] By the end of the year England had made separate treaties of alliance and subsidies with all these powers, thus constituting the first coalition against France. On all sides the republic was threatened by the armies of its enemies, by Austro-Sardinians in the Alps, Spaniards in the Pyrenees, Austrians, English, and Dutch in the Netherlands, more Austrians between the Meuse and the Moselle, and Prussians and Austrians on the middle and upper Rhine. All told, nearly 350,000 men were soon in the field against the republicans. Nominally the allies were in the lists, each to safeguard its particular interests against the unjust aggressions of France. Their

[6] The Holy Roman Empire declared war on France in 1794, which brought the smaller German states into the coalition.

official pronouncements displayed their high concern over the preservation of the political balance on the Continent and the defense of European civilization against French barbarians. But under these sonorous pronouncements lay the vital consideration of keeping intact those principles of government and society which the Revolution had destroyed in France and was threatening to destroy everywhere in Europe. Their defense against the revolutionary doctrine of an armed crusade for liberty was a monarchical crusade against the government which embodied the doctrine. To destroy the doctrine, to crush the strength of the idea, they agreed to despoil France of her rich provinces, which would make her weak, and restore the Bourbons, which would make her docile.

On February 20, the Convention passed a decree for a new levy of 300,000 men to fight the enemy. Every able-bodied and unmarried man from eighteen to forty was liable to service, but enlistment was compulsory only if volunteers did not fill the local quota. To supervise the enrollment, deputies of the assembly were sent into different departments as commissioners with extraordinary powers.[7] No precedent for this course of action existed, and some serious blunders and vexatious decisions were made in the enrollment of troops. On the whole, the levy was moderately successful save in the Vendée.[8] The attempt to muster men there provoked open rebellion in March among the fanatical Catholic peasants, whose opposition to the government's religious policy had been carefully nursed by various noble conspirators. "It was inevitable," says Mignet, "that the two fanaticisms of monarchy and of popular sovereignty, of the priesthood and human reason, should raise their banners against each other, and bring about the triumph of the old or of the new civilization." But the insurrection of the peasantry was not spontaneous. The levy provided the occasion; it was not the cause. The immediate cause was the discovery of the plans of a conspiracy organized by noblemen, which gave the counter-revolutionaries implicated no other course than to flee the country or rebel openly. The peasants seized towns, formed small bands under local leaders, and by the end of March had a self-

[7] The majority were Montagnards, for the Girondins kept their party at full strength in the Convention.

[8] Vendée was the name of the department in the west which comprised part of the old provinces of Poitou and Anjou, but the entire region of the war became known as "la Vendée."

styled Grand Army. There were similar uprisings in Brittany. In May the rebels established the *Grande Armée Catholique Royale* and issued a proclamation in the name of Louis XVII. For many months these rebel troops caused the government the gravest apprehensions.

In February too began the series of military reverses abroad and economic crises at home which gradually weakened the prestige of the Girondins and undermined their position. Their best general, Dumouriez, had staked all on a surprise invasion of Holland, but during his absence from the Netherlands Coburg led his Austrians in a fresh offensive against Dumouriez's generals. These fell back from Aix-la-Chapelle and Liége and retreated farther into the country whose long-suffering inhabitants threatened to rise against the French and cut Dumouriez off. Upon the receipt of this discouraging news the Convention promptly recalled Dumouriez from Holland, and he returned, grumbling, into the Austrian Netherlands, disgusted over the incompetence of the war bureau and the Jacobins' ill treatment of the Belgians. His views were known to some of the deputies, for he expressed them vigorously enough in a letter to the Convention, but his letter was purposely kept secret. One could tolerate such independence from the foremost military commander of the country. But treason was another matter, and treason the adventurous Dumouriez intended after he suffered two successive defeats at the hands of the Austrians (March 18 and 21). Even earlier he had entertained a fantastic notion of uniting the Netherlands and Holland into a single state under his protection. Now, beaten by the Austrians and assailed by the Jacobins, he saw no other recourse than desertion to carry out his plans. He negotiated with the Austrians and agreed in return for their inactivity to evacuate Holland and Belgium; after which he would march upon Paris with the aim of restoring the monarchy and reëstablishing the Constitution of 1791. But his plans went wrong, for the rank and file of his troops refused to follow him to Paris. From his headquarters in France, where he had delivered four of the Convention's investigators to the Austrians, he fled across the frontier to the Austrians, accompanied only by a few of his officers and two squadrons (April 5). The Convention promptly outlawed him and put a price on his head. In the meantime General Custine had lost the Rhineland to the strongly reënforced Prussians under Brunswick and was slowly retreating before them (March 27). The outburst of fear and frenzy that swept over the citizens at the news of Dumouriez's defeats and subsequent desertion, Custine's reverses on the Rhine, and the outbreak of civil war in the Vendée was accentuated by an acute shortage of food and supplies. Unemployment was increasing, food was scarce, and prices rapidly mounting. Grain speculators and war contractors were reaping an ill-gotten harvest. The flood of new assignats, real and bogus, added to the distress of the consumers. Such extraordinary misfortunes, reasoned the people, must assuredly be the work of "false patriots," and with the normal instinct of simple folk the people demanded a scapegoat. In the large cities of Lyons, Orléans, and above all Paris, in many districts of central France, the peasants and the city proletariat rioted against the government and clamored for radical measures. These the Girondins, true to their convictions and their prejudices as well, could not grant, which only added to their unpopularity.

Paris saw bread riots at the end of February, and hostile crowds sacked and plundered the shops for foodstuffs. Step by step the Montagnards in the Convention and loyal republicans in the departments came to the realization that no solution of the internal difficulties and the problem of waging war was possible save by acceding to the program of the Enragés ("Madmen"). Enragés was the name applied to the small groups of radicals who were led by a certain Varlet and the constitutional priest Jacques Roux in Paris, Chalier and Leclerc in Lyons, and a lawyer, Taboureau, in Orléans. Their political program called for unity in the Convention, which meant the expulsion of the suspected Girondin leaders and the concentration of power in the hands of the Montagnards. Their social program called for a heavy graduated tax upon the wealthy citizens in order to pay for the costs of war and the support of the needy. They demanded governmental regulation of food prices, requisitions for the troops, subsidies for the poorer citizens, and the creation of a revolutionary army in which the unemployed might serve with pay.

An attempted insurrectionary movement in Paris against the Convention on March 9–10, coming on the heels of Dumouriez's retreat from Holland, convinced the deputies that the strengthening of the national government could no longer be delayed. In the emergency measures which were passed during March and April, Danton and the Montagnards took the lead; Danton possibly to lessen the suspicion that he had been implicated in Dumouriez's intrigues, and the Montagnards in order to win over the support of the National Guard and the troops of the sections which were under the domination of the Enragés. The arrangement might be called a political "deal." The Enragés turned over their troops to the Montagnards who, in return, adopted their program of reforms.

The following were the emergency measures which the Convention decreed in March and April, 1793: the conferring of almost unlimited power with the title of representative on mission upon the deputies whom it sent out into the departments and cities and to the armies; the organization of a new revolutionary tribunal for the trial and punishment of counter-revolutionary agitators; the institution in each commune and in each section of the larger cities of a surveillance committee to watch over the movements of foreigners; [9] harsher, even vindictive, penalties against refractory priests; a censorship law against seditious writing; the banishment of all émigrés and the infliction of the death penalty on all rebels and returned émigrés, including a provision for the confiscation of their property; a special tax on the rich and the creation of a revolutionary army. But the most important of all was the establishment of the famous Committee of Public Safety (*comité de salut public*).[10] This executive committee was given supervisory control over the ministry and irresponsible disposal of one hundred thousand livres for its expenses. No outstanding Girondins were named to the first committee, of which Danton was the guiding spirit. The Convention timorously limited the tenure of office to one month, but successive reëlections of the members kept this "Danton Committee" intact until well into July.

Jacobin Triumphs

The machinery for the suppression of disorder at home and the repulse of the enemy was now created, but a harmonious per-

[9] These committees were later known as revolutionary committees, and kept a watchful eye on Frenchmen as well as on foreigners.

[10] Somewhat earlier the Convention had established a Committee of General Defense, which might be regarded as a precursor of this famous group.

sonnel to control the machinery was lacking. These measures enacted, the party struggle broke out anew and in more virulent form. Dumouriez's treason provoked the first of the new clashes. Each faction accused the other of complicity with the arch traitor. The Mountain accused the Girondins of being the accomplices of Dumouriez in a royalist plot; while the Girondins, somewhat earlier, accused the Mountain of being Dumouriez's accomplices in a plot to make the former duke of Orléans king. As the prominent leaders of both sides had been friendly with Dumouriez, there was as much or as little truth in one set of accusations as in the other. Then it was that the Convention, in Danton's vivid phrase, became "an arena of gladiators." Almost at every session there were disgraceful scenes, taunts and jeers, insolence and disorder, provocative petitions and addresses. Such were the commonplaces of parliamentary procedure which constituted one long Roman holiday for the galleries. Finally, to counter the Girondin attack upon Danton, the Mountain called upon their supporters among the members of the Jacobin clubs. On April 5, the Jacobins of Paris issued a circular petition to their local branches assailing the Girondin deputies who had voted to refer the death sentence of Louis XVI to the primary assemblies for ratification. Marat, at the moment the presiding officer of the Jacobins, signed that anti-Girondin petition, an act which drew their full fire upon him. Using their numerical superiority in the Convention, they had the "Friend of the People" arrested and impeached.[11] Marat went into hiding until his case came before the revolutionary tribunal (April 24), which acquitted him of the charges of seditious and libelous writing against the Convention. From the court he was brought back into the assembly in triumph, a triumph which his admirers repeated several days later at the Commune.

From that moment on, there was no respite in the concerted attack of the Mountain and the Parisian sections against the Girondins. Even before Marat's case came to court, delegates from a majority of the sections, headed by the mayor of the city, signed a petition for the expulsion of twenty-two of the leading Girondin deputies. This was the first of an unbroken series of petitions, for the Convention's weakness made loose talk astonishingly safe.

[11] Marat himself had been instrumental in having the parliamentary immunity of the deputies removed, though it was no part of his scheme to enable the Girondins to begin impeachment proceedings against him.

Rumors circulated that the Commune was making ready to dissolve the Convention in order to force the expulsion of the obnoxious Girondins. The sections afforded themselves the luxury of several illegal acts, such as the appointment of one of their men to the command of the National Guard, and a meeting of their representatives to form an insurrectionary committee. At the same time the Montagnards renewed their support of the economic demands of the Enragés. During the month of April various local administrators had of their own authority fixed a maximum price for grain and taken several other measures to avoid a food shortage in urban centers. On May 4 the Convention voted a decree which incorporated most of these measures and extended their application to the entire country.[12]

The Girondins were not idle. In what appears to be a concerted plan elaborated at Paris, they stirred up the departments against the capital. There were insurrectionary movements of the moderates against the local Jacobins in Lyons, Bordeaux, Marseilles and Nantes, where the Girondins hoped to raise a military force great enough to march against Paris. In Paris they planned to dissolve the Commune, summon the supernumerary deputies of the Convention and reconvene the national assembly away from Paris at Bourges. This thoughtless motion to remove the assembly to Bourges was tabled in the Convention (May 18), but a substitute measure was decreed on Barère's proposal—that a commission of twelve be appointed to investigate whether the Commune and the sections had acted illegally. The commission was created, a Girondin commission, whose members followed the mobile promptings of their hearts more easily than the sober dictates of reason. The twelve ordered the sections to turn over their registers, forbade nocturnal meetings, and placed three of the most prominent popular leaders of Paris, among whom were Hébert and Varlet, under arrest.

Hébert's arrest in particular kindled the insurrectionary populace, for his outspoken newspaper had many devoted readers. Moreover, was he not assistant procurator of the Commune! The Commune, astounded and outraged, sent a delegation to lodge a protest before the Convention (May 25). To the threatening

[12] This first "maximum law" remained virtually a dead letter, for many local administrations failed to enforce it.

words of the delegation Isnard, the Girondin president of the Convention, answered in words more threatening still:

> Give heed to the truths that I am going to tell you. . . . If ever . . . as a result of one of these constantly recurring insurrections, the national assembly should be molested, I declare to you in the name of all France, Paris will be destroyed. . . . Soon people will be searching the banks of the Seine to see whether Paris had ever existed.

The stupidity of his threat was matched only by its vain presumption. It sounded like a new Brunswick manifesto, and the incensed Parisians answered it as they had answered Brunswick's declaration. They prepared a coup against the national assembly and the Girondin leaders. Insurrection was now the order of the day.

The events of the next week were a crowded panorama of illegal violence and parliamentary vacillation with a catastrophic end looming ominously. On the 27th, the Mountain employed its temporary majority in the Convention to order the dissolution of the commission and the release of its various prisoners. The next day the Girondin deputies and their sympathizers regained the majority and reinstated the commission though recognizing the release of Hébert and the other prisoners. On the 29th Danton made a supreme effort toward reconciliation. In a report read by Barère, for the Committee of Public Safety, he inserted a paragraph pleading with the deputies to lay aside their differences lest they all be buried in a common fate. But his appeal to reason came too late. Paris had already taken the direction of events out of the powerless hands of the deputies.

That very day delegates from the more radical sections formed a general revolutionary assembly which forthwith declared that Paris was in a state of insurrection and ordered the barriers closed. On the 30th, the Parisian authorities carried out these measures. In the early hours of May 31, the insurrectionary assembly selected a small Central Revolutionary Committee of nine men, of whom Varlet and Dobsen were the best known. Varlet and his colleagues worked fast, profiting from the precedent of the insurrectionary Commune of August 10. Late in the afternoon they withdrew the powers of the legal Commune, then reinstated the members and joined forces with them, thus creating a new municipal administration. In several instances, however, the central revolutionary committee functioned independently of the Commune. They ordered the tocsin rung, and the alarm cannon fired to arouse the populace. To gain the support of the National Guard of the capital they had Hanriot, one of their stalwarts, appointed as commanding officer. In addition, 30,000 *sectionnaires* took up arms in their various districts, prepared to march in support of the revolutionary committee. To each of these volunteers forty sous a day had been allotted, to make sure that they would be loyal. While troops surrounded the hall of the Convention, delegation after delegation presented petitions within for the arrest of the Girondin leaders and the enactment of various measures of economic relief. The deputies held their ground. They referred the various demands to the Committee of Public Safety and voted only the definitive dissolution of the commission of twelve. This was a check for the rebels, but the day ended peacefully in unexpected fraternizing between the deputies and the sectionnaires outside of the assembly.

The latter renewed their efforts on the morrow (June 1), but another petition for the arrest of the twenty-two Girondins was again referred to the Committee of Public Safety, the latter body being requested to report within three days. With this second check the revolutionary committee determined to stop sending petitions and to use its troops. The night was spent in making preparations. Early in the morning of Sunday, June 2, came the final effort of the insurrectionists. Hanriot surrounded the Tuileries, where the Convention had been holding its meetings since early May, with 80,000 men and sixty cannons, announcing that no deputy was to be allowed to leave the hall until the Girondins were given over. Many of the attacked Girondins were absent, but some courageous deputies, such as the bold Lanjuinais and the fiery Barbaroux, were there to brave their enemies. A few deputies defied Hanriot's order and filed toward the door, but they were pushed back into the hall. A compromise solution involving the voluntary suspension of the proscribed deputies was defeated. A feeble attempt to have the deputies leave their hall *en masse* ended in inglorious failure and the Convention returned from the Tuileries Gardens, defeated. In the dismal silence that ensued the semiparalytic Couthon proposed the arrest of the Girondin leaders, and the session ended with the arrest of twenty-nine Girondin deputies, including two Girondin ministers, and the twelve members of the commission. The arrested deputies were not imprisoned, but placed under surveillance at their own homes. From this moment the Convention was no longer free.

Among the illustrious victims of the insurrection there were Vergniaud, Brissot, Gensonné, Buzot, Guadet, Isnard, Barbaroux, and the two ministers, Lebrun and Clavière. Roland succeeded in escaping; but Madame Roland was less fortunate and was imprisoned. The Girondin control was now a thing of the past. From now on the Montagnards were masters of the Convention, and the Commune the master of the Montagnards. But unity did not follow this political insurrection; nor did the masses get immediate satisfaction of their demands. Vergniaud's dire prophecy that the Revolution like Saturn would devour its own children seemed to be approaching fulfillment. First the nobles and the priests, then the constitutionalists, and now the moderates were proscribed by the revolutionists in power.

Jacobin Defeats

It remained to be seen whether the rest of France would acquiesce in this coup against the Girondins. Paris once again was tranquil, the debates in the Convention became orderly, since only the Mountain and its sympathizers dared speak up, and the purged assembly ostentatiously proclaimed that the Parisians had helped save Liberty and the Republic. The Committee of Public Safety was still inclined to temporize and pursue its former conciliatory policy, but the arrested Girondins threw conciliation to the wind. Of the detained deputies the more venturesome eluded their guards and escaped from Paris, twenty of them fleeing the capital before the month had ended. At Caen in Normandy, where Buzot, Barbaroux, and Salle took refuge, they organized an insurrection, formed an army, appointed a royalist general commander, and prepared to march on Paris. Brittany, ardently royalist, joined this so-called federalist revolt against the national assembly. Lyons also took arms, and Marseilles and Bordeaux arose. By the end of June more than sixty departments, including the great provincial cities, were in arms against Paris and the Convention, while only the departments around Paris, in central France, and on the eastern frontier remained loyal.

This revolt was begun by the Girondins, but other parties, particularly the royalists, sought to take advantage of it. The situation in Lyons was all the more fraught with danger to the government in that Lyons was the center of a movement which was supported by arms in the south and in the west. From an early date in the Revolution there had been disturbances at Lyons, whose industries and trade had been heavily hit by the defection of the privileged classes. Even before the Parisian insurrection on May 31 the moderate and royalist sections of Lyons had succeeded in overthrowing the municipal administration and in terrorizing the local Jacobins. After the news of the revolt in Normandy, the Lyonnais openly rebelled against the Convention, welcomed the émigrés, and raised a large army which was entrusted to a royalist leader. At Marseilles the royalists also gained control of the rebel troops, as they did at Toulon and in the principal towns of the Midi.

The royalists in the Vendée meanwhile extended their operations until all of Poitou, Anjou, and Brittany was under their control. From their own country they tried to cut their way to Paris in one direction and to establish communications with England in another. At its greatest strength the "Royal Catholic Army" could muster 80,000 men; but, fortunately for the republic, which could spare only a handful of troops against them, the rebels usually dispersed after each skirmish. The guerrilla warfare in the Vendée was savage and ferocious, no mercy being shown on either side. Sickening tales of torture, mutilation, and the burial of soldiers still alive besmirch the account of the struggle. In June and July the Vendeans advanced steadily. After their capture of Saumur and Angers the road to Paris lay open before them, but their leaders hesitated and ultimately went down the Loire to effect a junction on the coast with the English and with the rebels in Brittany (the Chouans). Repulsed at Nantes, where their leader Cathelineau met his death, they recrossed the Loire into the Vendée, and beat off the republican troops that tried to rescue Angers. For the present the southwest from Nantes to Bordeaux was lost to the republic; Lyons and Marseilles had thrown up fortifications, and the English fleet was blockading Toulon.

The situation on the eastern frontier was equally desperate. After the reverses of the early spring Danton had tried secretly to negotiate with the enemy and to gain allies for France. To reassure the powers the Convention renounced its propaganda decrees and voted a decree (April 13) promising that France would not "interfere in any way with the government of other states." But so long as the victory lay with Europe, so long as Danton's position in the government was insecure, the hostile states turned down his proposals. Besides, they had their own plans for the future peace of Europe.

Almost on the very day that France renounced its propaganda policy, the allies, assembled in secret conference in Antwerp, discussed plans for a Bourbon restoration and a dismemberment of France (April 17). The representative of Russia at this conference put the matter tersely: "Let us work in concert to give to what remains of France a stable and permanent monarchical government; it will become a second-rate power, which will no longer frighten any one, and thus we shall extinguish the flames of democracy which bid fair to enkindle all Europe." Ultimately these high aims were defeated, for not only did the allies fall out on the division of the spoils and on the conduct of the war, but while they fought they had no unity of command, no coördinated plan for the disposal of the troops and their available material resources; and not one of them dared to change its method of warfare to meet the challenge of the new revolutionary strategy and tactics. These shortcomings were only gradually revealed; up to the autumn of 1793, their troops carried all before them, though aided, to be sure, by internal circumstances in France.

After Dumouriez's retreat from the Netherlands, Coburg's Austrians crossed the French frontier and laid siege to the border fortresses of Condé and Valenciennes.[13] The siege was conducted in leisurely fashion, and not until July did the garrisons surrender, Condé on the 10th and Valenciennes on the 28th. Custine worked marvels in restoring the morale of his troops and in enforcing discipline, but he received no coöperation from Bouchotte, the minister of war, who vetoed Custine's excellent plan of stripping the Rhine and the Moselle armies in order to force the Austrians to raise the siege of the frontier fortresses. After their surrender Custine fell back along the Scarpe, covering Lille but leaving the road to Paris open. Farther south on the Rhine the Prussians also advanced, crossing the river after Custine's retreat, isolating the great fortress of Mainz and forcing the French back

---

[13] Dampierre, the successor of Dumouriez, was killed in battle early in May, and Custine was called from the Rhine Army to take command and restore discipline.

upon Landau. For four months the garrison at Mainz held out heroically against its besiegers, but on July 23 the city opened its gates to the Prussians. In the south the Spaniards had cleared the Pyrenees and were advancing on French soil. To the southeast the Sardinians were advancing from the Alps. And the English government declared all the ports of France in a state of blockade, thus forbidding neutral ships to bring in supplies.

All these evils were still further aggravated by the growing acuteness of the economic crisis and the financial disorder. The maximum for prices (fixed by law on May 4) was a virtual dead letter when the Convention formally suspended its application in July. At the front the troops were short of clothing, food, and munitions; at home the distress of the poor people was equally dire. Grain markets were half empty, for few of the peasants were willing to market their grain in the prevailing financial uncertainty. Other necessities were not less scarce and sold at constantly soaring prices. The assignats kept steadily depreciating, being worth less than thirty per cent of their nominal value. For this depreciation the financiers of the Convention who augmented the number of assignats in circulation were largely to blame; but the English government which shipped counterfeit assignats into France, the speculators of the stock exchange, and the unpatriotic bankers who exported their capital from France must also share part of the blame. Holders of government securities and *rentiers* with modest incomes suffered only slightly less than the poorer citizens.

Such were the staggering catastrophic burdens of the republic. What solution could unite the nation, bring peace between the factions, and expel the enemy from the land? Manifestly only by the most heroic measures would France be saved from her desperate situation. There was no lack of individuals to aspire to leadership, no dearth of suggestions for relief; and ultimately in the course of the summer months the Montagnard deputies established their dictatorship over the country. We shall now examine the methods they pursued and the results they accomplished from the summer of 1793 to the summer of 1794.

XI. THE CONVENTION: THE JACOBIN COMMON-
WEALTH (1793-1794)

AT first the Committee of Public Safety was loath to use force against the federalist revolt and sent out deputies to the centers of the rebellion with instructions to negotiate. On June 6 it proposed to send an equal number of Montagnard hostages to the departments whose deputies had been arrested, but Robespierre succeeded in having the motion tabled. An immediate consequence of the Committee's conciliatory proposal was the draft of a petition, signed by seventy-five Girondin sympathizers, condemning the events of May 31 and June 2. Not until the end of June did the Committee act to raise an armed force to quell the insurrection. Finally on July 8, in response to popular agitation, the Committee, through the voice of Saint-Just, presented a bill outlawing the active leaders of the rebellion. This bill the Convention promptly decreed. Of the various pacific measures that the Convention took against the rebels none was more effective than the constitution which the Montagnard deputies voted hastily between June 10 and June 24.

The original object of the Convention, it will be recalled, was to draft a constitution to replace the obsolete monarchical Constitution of 1791. A document, drawn up largely by Condorcet under the inspiration of the Girondins and bitterly contested by the Montagnards, was available; but since it was the work of Girondins, it was manifestly impossible for the Jacobins to accept it. Yet a constitution was imperative to unite the disaffected provinces to Paris and reassure property owners that the rule of the Montagnards did not spell anarchy. Accordingly the latter bestirred themselves, and in a few days presented a document which, after the downfall of Robespierre, was regarded as a magic text and the gospel of pure political democracy.

This Montagnard constitution, the famous stillborn Constitution of 1793, did effectively guarantee political democracy as it was then organized. It provided for universal manhood suffrage without property qualifications either for voters or for candidates. The election of representatives was to be direct and exercised by the voters in their primary assemblies. The legislative body was to consist of one chamber, to which the executive council would be responsible. To overcome the fears held in the departments that Paris would become the dictator of the government, the executive authority was entrusted to a board of 24 officials chosen by the departments from a larger panel. But the Jacobin constitution did little to organize a social democracy. It recognized the social right of insurrection against an unjust government, but nowhere did it adequately recognize any fundamental obligation on the part of the government to insure the social rights of the poor citizens. It contained provisions for public relief, and it recorded the workers' right to subsistence, but otherwise it strongly emphasized the rights of property owners. It omitted the four famous articles that Robespierre had submitted in an earlier Declaration of Rights, whereby poor citizens received tax exemptions and monetary support from the fortunes of the rich. It is possible that the Montagnards deliberately falsified their social program in their effort to win the wealthy bourgeoisie away from the Girondin leaders, though it seems more likely that the great majority of Montagnards had no other social policy than that expressed in the constitution.

Yet undeniably this document was a potent factor in the defeat of federalism. Quite the shrewdest move in the Montagnard game of removing suspicion against Paris was the decision to have the constitution ratified by popular referendum before it could become valid. The voting took place in July and coincided with the debacle of the federalist insurrection. Only a small proportion of voters turned out to the polls, but the recorded vote of 2,000,000 was practically unanimous in favor of the new constitution. At the same time the Convention took other steps to win popular support. It decreed the immediate sale of the confiscated estates of the emigrants, dividing the property into small plots and allowing the purchasers ten years for full payment. Another decree divided the common lands for the benefit of the villagers and, on July 17, the last legal vestiges of feudalism disappeared with the abolition of all existing feudal rights without indemnification to their owners.

These measures were insufficient to stifle hostile criticisms of the Committee of Public Safety. It was assailed for its failure to arrest the course of the federalist revolt, for its failure to end the civil war in the Vendée, and for the failure of the French troops on the frontiers. Not even the great prestige of its unofficial leader, Danton, saved it against the attacks of Hébert and the active Jacobins. On July 10, it fell, and a new Committee of nine members, to which Danton was not reëlected, was named by the Convention. The majority was resolutely Montagnard, actively pro-war and against Danton's policy of negotiation. During the course of the summer the Committee became relatively homogeneous and functioned in that dictatorial fashion which saved France from her foes. But even in July the personnel of the new Committee was such as to constitute a strong central government. The events of July 10 were thus in a very real sense the complement of the political revolution of June 2.

Before the new Committee settled down to its tasks, on July 13, the knife of the assassin ended the career of one of the ablest, yet one of the most grossly vilified of the Montagnard deputies. Charlotte Corday, a reserved, mannerly young woman from Caen, was inspired by the discourses of the refugee Girondins to seek and find martyrdom, quite in the spirit of those heroes and heroines of her beloved Plutarch, by ridding France of Jean Paul Marat, the sickly and persecuted "Friend of the People." Marat she held responsible for all the woes of her country; Marat removed, peace would once more prevail. Her deed, for which she bravely accepted the penalty, only accentuated the morbid suspicions of the patriots who saw in it the hand of the proscribed Girondins. It also hastened the entry of Robespierre into the new Committee (July 27), for with Marat dead and Danton under a cloud, the "Incorruptible" was popularly regarded as the leader of the Montagnards.[1]

For the next three months the Committee bent all its efforts to organizing France for simultaneous military operations against its many enemies. In July the only heartening development was the collapse of the federalist insurrection. The strength of the rebels was more apparent than real. Despite the great number of departments which opposed the government, there was no unity of command, no community of purpose. After the first shock of

---

[1] Robespierre succeeded Gasparin, who resigned because of ill health.

revolt was over, the local Jacobins appealed to public sentiment in the threatened regions to remain loyal to the government. The city workers and many of the peasantry refused to enlist in a movement which was captured by royalists and converted into a counter-revolutionary attack upon the Convention. In some regions the pro-Girondin authorities voluntarily renewed their allegiance to the government, after a brief experience with the insurrectionists. The voting on the new constitution contributed in no small measure to the breakdown of the revolt. A small skirmish at Vernon in Normandy sufficed to crush the insurrection in the northwest. The southwest likewise submitted, save for Bordeaux, which held out until September. In the southeast the advance of the republican troops quickly subdued the rebels, though Marseilles did not open its gates until the end of August. Only two cities still resisted—Toulon, the great naval base on the Mediterranean, and Lyons on the Rhone. In the former city the royalists called upon the aid of Admiral Hood and his fleet, and by the end of August the English were in control of the local government. Against Lyons, where class war raged between the royalists and the Jacobins, the republicans began a systematic siege early in August.

THE MIDSUMMER CRISIS OF 1793

On the other fronts the results were less happy. The stalemate in the Vendée continued. The rebels were still formidable and an equal match for the loyal troops. The republican reverses on the northern and eastern fronts have already been recorded—the capitulation of Condé and Valenciennes and the surrender of the Mainz garrison to the Prussians.

In France and particularly in Paris the financial crisis and the food shortage were still acute. The spokesmen of the Enragés continued their violent attack upon the Convention. Robespierre saw, or professed to see, the hand of Pitt in the radical proposals of Roux and Varlet, whom he vigorously denounced as secret counter-revolutionaries. But the militant left-wing republicans, those later known as the Hébertists or the ultra-revolutionaries, took over the social program of the Enragés. The strength of these radicals was not to be ignored. They were intrenched in the Commune, in the Cordelier Club, in the war ministry, and they had behind them the nameless thousands in the poor sections of Paris. Unless the Convention followed their lead, a new Parisian insurrection against the government was inevitable. Through the energetic efforts of its commissioners in near-by departments the Committee of Public Safety gathered sufficient grain to provision Paris for several weeks. But the deputies still refused to institute governmental regulation of prices of all commodities of prime necessity. Instead, they decreed the closing of the Bourse, which was the stronghold of the speculators and stockjobbers, and they made profiteering a capital crime.[2]

The month of August began with a series of energetic decrees. These were the adoption of new tactics in the Vendée, the arrest of all the nationals of enemy countries, the closing of the barrier gates of the capital, the transfer of the queen to the Conciergerie (whence she was to be sent before the revolutionary tribunal), and the destruction of all the tombs of the kings of France at Saint-Denis. The last was an act of patriotic vandalism, understandable if not excusable under the circumstances. It was occasioned by the finding of the papers of an English spy which revealed a plan of firing arsenals and fortresses and of assassinating prominent revolutionary leaders.

In the first week of August the delegates of the primary assemblies began to arrive in Paris, bringing to the Convention the official results of the referendum on the constitution. The national assembly planned a hearty welcome for them on August 10, so that the promulgation of the constitution would coincide with the first anniversary of the overthrow of the monarchy. The fête was brilliantly successful, and a happy symbol of the reunion of France after the unfortunate events of June 2; but the constitution, a copy of which was solemnly placed on the altar of the country in the Champ-de-Mars, was not applied. Little argument was needed to convince the enthusiastic delegates that the dissolution of the Convention and new elections at this tragic moment of war and economic crisis would only court disaster. So the application

[2] Profiteering meant the failure of the retail merchant to declare his stock to the authorities and post his list at the door of his shop. Since the sale was to be at the "current prices," the merchant could readily get around the intention of the law. In many cases the retailer was more sinned against than sinning, for he had to buy at the unregulated prices made by wholesalers and middlemen and sell at the low patriotic prices demanded by the consumers. Hence his eagerness to conceal his goods and make private sales at a profit.

of the constitution was indefinitely postponed, and the permanency of the Convention until the end of the war was accepted.

The delegates brought with them to the capital various summary demands of the masses who were weary of halfway measures. Let all suspects be arrested! Let the nation rise in its might and move on to the front, driving the suspects before them! To the first demand no objections were made, but to a levy in mass, stated in that crude form, the deputies took objection, fearful of the consequences of a profound dislocation of the nation's normal activities. Under the pressure of the Jacobins and the delegates from the departments the Committee slowly yielded, first adopting the principle of the levy in mass, and on August 23, presenting a systematic scheme for the war-time organization of the entire nation. The accents of the most exalted nationalism rang through the celebrated decree, which Barère proposed to the Convention at the instance of the Committee. "All citizens must discharge their debt to liberty. Some will give their labor, others their wealth, some their counsel, others their strength; all will give it the blood that flows in their veins. Thus all Frenchmen, all sexes, all ages are called by the patrie to defend liberty." For the present all unmarried men from eighteen to twenty-five were called to the front, but all other citizens were liable for work in the munitions factories and in the service of supplies. To requisition supplies and munitions, to raise and drill the new conscripts, deputies were dispatched into all the departments. France was to become an armed camp, a nation in arms under the command of the Convention. The decree was typical of the prevalent state of mind: nothing was impossible to the enthusiastic zealots of liberty. Without this underlying determination of the people to dare all, "to conquer or die," the Convention and the Committee in particular, for all their energy and resourcefulness, would have failed in their task.

During this same month of August a determined effort was made, under the guiding hand of Cambon, the financial expert of the Convention, to solve the financial tangle and check the inflation of the currency. To end the wild speculations in government securities Cambon proposed and the Convention decreed that all government bonds, irrespective of the date of their origin or of their maturity, should be inscribed in a national register. The old securities would be burnt and a certificate bearing a statement of the debt and its amount would be given to each creditor. In that way no one would be able to distinguish between the bonds of the Old Régime and bonds of the Revolution. Moreover, this decree funded the national debt by converting the capital of each bond into a perpetual annuity paying five per cent interest. Thus the treasury would be freed of the embarrassing necessity of paying the principal, so long as it met the interest. The problem of the assignats was met by decreeing that after January 1, 1794, the royal assignats, i.e., those issued before the republic, were to lose all legal value. And to raise immediate funds, the Convention decided to enforce the compulsory loan (which had been decreed in principle in May) upon all citizens. The amount levied was proportionate to the income of the individual, but such citizens as had incomes above ten thousand livres were expected to lend the government all of the surplus—with interest if given voluntarily, otherwise without. In passing, it may be noted that these decrees did not solve the financial difficulties of the government, for the attempts to enforce them were not successful.

INAUGURATION OF TERRORISM

September opened under grim auspices. The food supply of Paris again was low; and a long drought which blighted the new crop hampered efforts at relief. Once more the exasperated populace threatened violence upon lukewarm deputies who refused to vote governmental regulation of food prices. Hot-headed patriots angrily attacked the revolutionary tribunal for its slowness in condemning prisoners and criticized the Committee of Public Safety for its retention of noble generals at the front. From the departments came discouraging news concerning the obstacles raised against the levy in mass. Billaud-Varenne returned from the Army of the North with vehement criticisms of the disorganization of the staff. On September 4 the news of the surrender of Toulon to the English was officially confirmed. At the news of that treason the excitement reached its height; and the extremists in Paris organized their new offensive against the Convention. Hébert and Billaud joined with them, the Jacobins followed suit, and the Commune gave its blessing. On the 5th a mob of petitioners, with Chaumette, the procurator of the Commune, at their head, invaded the assembly hall and presented their demands for bread and a revolutionary army of the interior. Before the tumultuous day was over, the Committee had yielded, adopting their slogan that Terror should be the order of the day. Thus it kept itself in power. On the following day Billaud-Varenne and Collot d'Herbois, both sincere republicans and fanatical terrorists, were elected to the Committee of Public Safety, thereby establishing a direct contact between the government and the world of the popular societies and the sections of Paris.

The meetings of the sections were limited to two per week in order to give the "true," i.e., the poor, patriots an opportunity to attend, while a subsidy of forty sous was allotted to those who attended in compensation for the loss in wages thus incurred. To provide for the food supply of Paris and to coerce the secret counter-revolutionaries around the capital, the revolutionary army of the interior was finally organized under the command of Ronsin, a staunch Hébertist and a power in the war ministry. Moreover, the revolutionary tribunal was reorganized and divided up into four sections, two groups of two working alternatively. The number of judges was increased from ten to sixteen, the jury to sixty, and the public prosecutor, the methodical Fouquier-Tinville, was provided with five assistants to aid him in his work. The entire personnel was to be designated by and subject to the close supervision of the Committee of Public Safety and the committee of general security. Up to now the tribunal had functioned too slowly to please the warm patriots. By this new arrangement it was prepared to handle many more cases, and it became an integral part of the revolutionary machinery. Up to now the Terror had been spasmodic; henceforth it would become permanent. Suspects had been arrested and released for want of evidence; now the revolutionary tribunal would have work to do. On September 17, the famous jurist Merlin de Douai presented the first comprehensive law of suspects, which the Convention voted:

Immediately after the publication of the present decree all suspects who are in the territory of the Republic and who are still at liberty shall be placed under arrest. These are accounted suspects: first, those who by their conduct, their connections, their remarks, or their writings show themselves the partisans of tyranny or federalism and the enemies of liberty; 2nd, those who cannot, in the manner prescribed by the decree of March 21 last, justify their means of existence and the performance of their civic duties; 3rd, those who have been refused certificates of civism; 4th, public functionaries suspected or removed from their functions by the National Convention or its commissioners and not reinstated, especially those who have been or shall be removed in virtue of the decree of August 14 last; 5th, those of the former nobles, all of the husbands, wives, fathers, mothers, sons or daughters, brothers or sisters, and agents of the *émigrés* who have not constantly manifested their attachment to the revolution; 6th, those who have emigrated from France in the interval from July 1, 1789, to the publication of the decree of March 30–April 8, 1792, although they may have returned to France within the period fixed by that decree or earlier.

The surveillance committees established according to the decree of March 21, last . . . are charged to prepare, each in its district, the list of suspects, to issue warrants of arrest against them, and to cause seals to be put upon their papers.

The police reports in Paris alone make it evident that the incarceration of many persons was required for the safety of the state. The weakness of this law of suspects lay not in its severity, but in its vagueness, which made abuses inevitable.

The committee of general security, however, which had supervision over the surveillance committees, was precisely the nest of the deputies whose financial operations and relations with various foreigners in Paris were most suspicious. Danton notwithstanding, the Committee of Public Safety won the right to nominate the members of the above committee as well as those of all the other governmental committees. Exercising its rights, the Committee of Public Safety forthwith eliminated Basire, Chabot, Julien de Toulouse, and Osselin, all of them implicated in contracting scandals and financial intrigues. By that one stroke the *grand comité* acquired full executive control of the government. In the reformed police committee, the committee of general security, the majority were fierce terrorists, men who suffered no qualms in making arrests and dispatching prisoners before the revolutionary tribunal. That very day, September 13, when the domination of the Committee of Public Safety became a reality, another decree incorporated the Jacobin clubs into the governmental system. Those clubs, of which there was one practically without exception in the principal town of every department and district, were charged, officially at least, with denouncing all suspects and unworthy officials and making articulate the voice of the sovereign people whom they represented.

A new attack upon the dominant Committee came at the end of the month, this time from various disaffected Montagnards acting in concert within the assembly. Ever since the decree of the

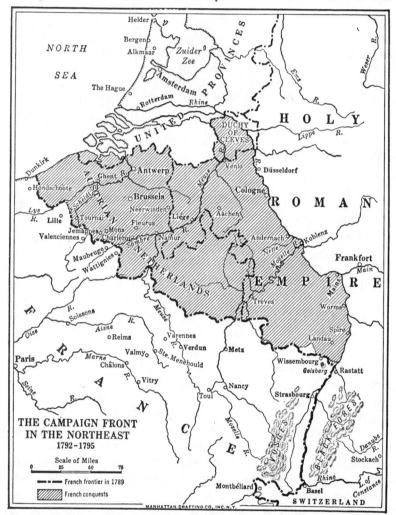

THE CAMPAIGN FRONT
IN THE NORTHEAST
1792–1795

Scale of Miles
0   25   50   75

▬ ▬ ▬ French frontier in 1789
▨ French conquests

MANHATTAN DRAFTING CO. INC. N.Y.

levy in mass the Committee had directed its efforts to improvising equipment and supplies for the troops, to efface among them all signs of the military system of the Old Régime, and to "republicanize" the major staffs of the different armies. This "purification" of the staffs and the arrest of General Houchard of the Army of the North provoked a furious attack upon the Committee in the assembly on September 24 and 25 which coincided with the agitation in the streets of Paris, where the masses still clamored for the trial of Marie Antoinette and the imprisoned Girondins as well as for the definite beginning of governmental regulation of prices. For a moment, the Committee seemed swamped by the criticisms of its erstwhile member, Thuriot, who had just resigned, and of the various deputies on mission who had been recalled from the front. At first, Billaud-Varenne alone was present at the assembly to defend the Committee against its critics, but Barère, Jeanbon, and Robespierre hastily rushed to the rescue and won a vote of confidence from the Convention.

The opposition scattered and Danton withdrew—to recover his health—to his country home at Arcis-sur-Aube, near Paris. But the Committee paid for its strengthened position by granting the demand of the Parisians. The law of the maximum, fixing maximum prices on commodities of prime necessity, was finally decreed on September 29. That decree was the entering wedge of the economic Terror, as the decrees of September 5 had introduced the political Terror. By its provisions it regulated not only prices, but also the wages of workers throughout the country. On October 3, the Convention adopted the report of the lesser committee which recommended that forty-one of the imprisoned Girondins should be brought before the revolutionary tribunal. That report placed the seventy-five deputies who had protested against the events of June 2 under arrest, and only Robespierre's intercession prevented them from being added to the list of the forty-one. That same day the trial of Marie Antoinette was voted by the deputies. In the armies the Committee pursued its "republicanizing" of the major staffs and appointed three young generals, who had just risen from the ranks, Jourdan, Pichegru, and Hoche, to the supreme command of the armies of the North, the Rhine, and the Moselle, respectively. And on October 10 Saint-Just summed up the events and the policies of the past three months and outlined the policy for the future by proclaiming that "the provisory government of France is revolutionary until the peace."

TURNING OF THE TIDE

In the meantime the tide of battle slowly began turning in favor of the revolutionists. Until the end of September no success of any significance was attained, but a feeling of confidence gradually replaced the tragic spirit of despair which had prevailed earlier in the summer. In August two important additions were made to the great committee in the person of Lazare Carnot and Prieur (de la Côte d'Or), both experienced engineers and men of courage and ability. Prieur assumed charge of munitions and equipment for the troops, while Carnot supplied unity of purpose and efficient central control over the armies and military operations. The representatives on mission resolutely and in the face of many obstacles enforced the provisions of the levy in mass. They called out the conscripts, equipped them, drilled them, requisitioned for them supplies and munitions, and prepared them for the great rôle that was to be theirs in the spring of 1794. Preparations for the future were not enough; the dangers of the present had to be met. By August 650,000 men were available for service on the different fronts.[3] Their leaders were, for the most part, the new republican generals whom the Committee substituted for the older generals inherited from the Old Régime. The Committee's ruthless policy of punishing generals who, through incompetence or lack of resolution, failed to take chances, brought to the front new leaders of daring and initiative, men who pounced upon every mistake committed by the generals of the coalition.

The most serious of these mistakes and the one most salutary for the republic was the decision of the British government to separate the British forces under the duke of York from the Austrians along the Scarpe and to send them against Dunkirk on the coast. York divided his army into two sections and disposed his men in exposed positions which could have been strengthened only by his immediate capture of Dunkirk. But the republicans did not give him a chance. Houchard's Army of the North was hastily reënforced and concentrated against York. Spurred on by an energetic representative on mission, Houchard attacked at Hondschoote (September 6 and 8), using the mass attack for the first time, and forced York to raise the siege. But he failed to follow up his victory and allowed the English to escape. Subsequently, after a minor defeat, he was removed from his com-

[3] The levy of 300,000 men decreed on February 20 was completed in the course of the summer. In addition to these new troops the French troops consisted of the old regular troops and the volunteers of 1792.

mand and paid for his negligence by being condemned to death on the charge of treason. However, his success at Hondschoote gave the patriots good cause for rejoicing. Coburg meanwhile continued his advance and moved on to besiege Maubeuge, which he needed as a base for the campaign of the following spring. Again the republicans concentrated for a mass attack, profiting this time by the inactivity of the Prussians along the Rhine and Moselle fronts. Carnot himself joined the new general Jourdan and led the attack. A frontal charge failed on October 15, but on the 16th the sans-culottes turned Coburg's flank at Wattignies and forced him to raise his siege. This was the first major victory of the republicans, a tribute to the organizing skill of Carnot and Jourdan and to the daring mass tactics followed by the men. On the eastern front, along the Moselle and the Rhine, the Prussians advanced until Carnot was able to strengthen the armies of the East with the victorious troops of the Army of the North. In November and December Hoche and Pichegru attacked again and again, and on December 26 their combined forces carried the heights of Wissembourg and forced the Prussians to raise the siege of Landau. At last on all fronts the invaders were expelled or held in check. In the south the Spaniards had retreated to the frontier stream of the Bidassoa, and Savoy was cleared of the enemy in October.

While the French passed from the defensive to the offensive on the northern, eastern, and southern fronts, the situation in the royalist centers also became less critical. Lyons resisted until October 8, when the mass attacks of the peasants under Couthon forced its surrender. After the fall of Lyons the siege of Toulon was vigorously pressed and brought to a successful issue in December. In the recapture of Toulon from the English a young captain of artillery named Napoleon Bonaparte first drew attention to himself as a strategist of rare ability. In the Vendée fortune finally smiled on the "Blues," i.e., the republican troops, after the collapse of their offensive in September. On October 17 the joint republican troops inflicted a crushing defeat upon the "Whites" at Cholet. But the Vendée was not secure until the end of the year, for from Brittany, where the fugitive Vendeans had taken refuge, they advanced anew southward into the Vendée. The bulk of their forces were massacred in the terrible carnage of Le Mans, and the remainder scattered or crushed in a horrible slaughter at Savenay

(December 23). Desultory fighting continued in the almost impenetrable marshes and thickets of Brittany and the Vendée, while the republican troops and the military commissions exacted fearful vengeance against the unfortunate inhabitants.

THE CAMPAIGN FRONT
IN
WESTERN FRANCE

Despite these victories the authority of the Committee was still ill established throughout the whole of France. The direct link between the local elected administrations and the national assembly was the deputies sent out by the Convention on civil or military missions. Their power was practically unlimited, and the Committee's check upon them slight. Their principal objects in the summer and fall of 1793 were to carry out the levy in mass, to detect, check, and punish counter-revolutionaries, and to aid the poorer citizens. These deputies on mission were the real rulers of France up to the end of 1793. The Committee tried but failed to regulate their actions, for they were far from Paris, communication was slow, and the time too short to wait for instructions. Consequently, their procedure varied amazingly, for each acted according to his own inspiration. The extremists among them were in a minority, strong-arm tactics and terrorism being less common than energetic coöperation with local Jacobins and the surveillance committees. It must not be forgotten that circumstances also varied greatly throughout France, perhaps as greatly as the personal character and the views of these "proconsuls." Moreover, they were compelled to delegate some of their powers to local republicans, with whom their coöperation often took the form of personal rivalries and conflicts of authority. When all due credit is given them for their great work of raising troops, stimulating the revolutionary sentiments of the country, and succoring the poor, the fact remains that by their arbitrary actions, their freedom from discipline, and their lack of a common policy they constituted a potential threat to the central government. Accordingly in November the Convention decreed the recall of many of them. But the Committee was determined to extend its authority in a more orderly and systematic fashion. The recall of the deputies on mission was not an abandonment of governmental centralization; it was a step in the perfection of the system.

The economic situation also called for the extension of the central administration. The earlier decree against food speculators and hoarders and the decree establishing granaries in each district for the collection of taxes in grain had been only paper solutions of the difficulties. The execution of those measures was left to the local elected authorities, and the latter, we have seen, were frequently far from trustworthy. On September 29 all commodities of prime necessity were subjected to the application of the law of the maximum. By that law a uniform price throughout the country was fixed for cereals, flour, tobacco, salt, and soap; while for other commodities the new price was to be one-third higher than the local price prevailing in 1790. Farmers had to declare their harvest, and merchants the inventory of their stock, to the district administrations which were empowered to inflict severe penalties on all violators of the law. But no allowance was made for the cost of transportation, and the rate of profit was not legally fixed. And a provision regulating wages had already been incorporated into the law, its application being entrusted to the administrators of the commune. The new wage was to be the local wage of 1790 plus an increase of fifty per cent.

The difficulties which the Committee anticipated were not imaginary, and the measures of enforcement that it decreed proved unavailing. Buyers sped to acquire their necessities at the new price, which was measurably lower than the current one demanded by the shopkeepers. In no time the shops were emptied, and disappointed purchasers congregated in noisy groups on the streets. In Paris and in the larger cities the municipal authorities averted famine by a strict rationing system and the use of food cards. But reprovisioning was even more of a problem than distribution of the existing supplies, for the merchants derived no profit by renewing their stocks. On October 22 the Committee appointed three deputies to form a food commission which was given the right to make seizures of food supplies with full control over transportation, agricultural and industrial production. While this commission began its slow task of gathering data throughout all of France for a revision of the maximum which would revive trade and allow a graduated and uniform profit to wholesaler, transporter, and retailer, the country had to live on expedients. Since the projected revision of the maximum would not be effected until the spring of 1794, the sequel to the formation of the food commission was still further strengthening of administrative centralization. To this development the Committee was inevitably forced lest the entire economic foundation of France collapse. In November the food commission was given the monopoly of import trade, and in December the right to authorize exports. On December 4 all the various emergency measures were coördinated in a comprehensive decree which is rightly called the "Constitution of the Terror," for it defined the purpose and the forms of the revolutionary government. From piecemeal beginnings and haphazard additions, starting in April, 1793, and continuing with each new danger that rose against the government, administrative unity was finally achieved.

The Terror Government

In essence, it was a war government, not constitutional but "revolutionary until the peace"; centralized and dictatorial, with the right of invoking terror against the foreign enemy and all internal enemies of the republic. Its constitution was the law of December 4, and its architects were the members of the Committee. "We wish an order of events," declared Robespierre, "where all base and degrading passions are chained . . . where distinctions are born out of equality itself." To good citizens the revolutionary government owed protection; to unworthy ones it owed nothing but death. To quote from Robespierre once more: "The mainspring of popular government in a revolution is at once virtue and terror; virtue without which terror is baleful, terror without which virtue is powerless." "What constitutes the Republic," stated Saint-Just, "is the complete destruction of everything that is opposed to it." Virtue did not mean individual morality; virtue meant love of the patrie, the sacrifice of personal interests to the interests of the state, the quasi-mystic absorption of the individual will into the general will, as defined by Rousseau, the prophet of the revolutionists.

The decree of December 4 named the Convention as the motive force of the government, the sole center of all revolutionary activities. This provision guaranteed that the government would remain democratic—at least in form. But the assembly tacitly accepted the dictatorship of the great Committee of Public Safety which had seen the country through the grave crisis from July to December. The formation of the first Committee of Public Safety in the spring of 1793, as well as its career under the guidance of Danton up to July 10 and under Robespierre from July on have already been recorded. Each phase of the republic's struggle strengthened the personnel and the powers of the Committee. The disorders in the Vendée and the federalist movement gave it a more forceful membership, the crisis of July and August added Robespierre, Carnot, and Prieur de la Côte d'Or, and the combination of food shortage and danger on the frontiers added Collot d'Herbois and Billaud-Varenne in September. From September, 1793, its personnel was kept intact and reëlected every month.[4] Saint-Just, Couthon, Collot, and Billaud had charge of the general administrative policy; Carnot and Prieur de la Côte d'Or directed the armies and provided munitions and equipment; Jeanbon de Saint-André and Prieur de la Marne managed the navy; the indefatigable Barère was entrusted with the diplomacy and

---

[4] Hérault de Séchelles was found guilty of counter-revolutionary actions and eliminated from the Committee. Later he was guillotined with the Dantonists.

the drafting and reading of reports to the Convention; Robert Lindet assumed control over food supplies; and Robespierre, with probably the least specific duties of all the members, intervened in almost all affairs and gave his moral leadership to the entire committee. The "decemvirs" came from all parts of France. All were well educated, all were experienced and capable. Their sincerity and devotion to their cause were uncontested. All were scrupulously honest and, with unlimited opportunities for corrupt practices, remained poor and above considerations of personal profit. Innumerable subordinate officials and a swarm of clerks and assistants aided them in their work. All were equal in authority; there was no responsible head to formulate a general policy. Several signatures sufficed to validate a decree or an executive order, which made rapid decisions possible. But the absence of a responsible head was bound to create dissension if serious differences arose among the members, as they later did. Many of the excesses of revolutionary justice, as well as the failure of the Revolution to develop in a scientific fashion, are due to this single fault.

The Committee of Public Safety shared its vast powers with the committee of general security, whose members it appointed from the deputies of the assembly. On several points there was no strict delimitation of the frontier between the two committees, but the specific jurisdiction of the less famous body extended over everything pertaining to the general police and the activities of individuals. It had to ferret out suspects, indorse arrest warrants, and send prisoners before the revolutionary tribunal. By virtue of those sweeping and terrifying powers, this group of men, even more than the Committee of Public Safety, held a controlling hand over the Terror both in Paris and in the provinces. Vadier, a gaunt, mocking old man, and Amar, who drew up the indictment of the Girondins, were its two outstanding members.

The Convention and the two committees were the propelling force of the revolutionary mechanism which functioned through various agencies. Of the latter, the revolutionary tribunal must be mentioned first. It was an extraordinary criminal court, reorganized on March 10, 1793, to take cognizance of every counterrevolutionary enterprise and every plot against the security of the state. Like the other revolutionary courts which sat in the departments, it was provided with judges, a prosecuting attorney, and a jury. But the personnel was nominated by the Convention, its judgments were final, and its sentences were carried out immediately. The property of the condemned was confiscated and placed on sale by the state. Dilatory and ineffective for six months after its establishment, it really entered on the activity which gave it its evil reputation after the Hébertist movement of September, 1793, when its personnel was increased and its judges and jury appointed by the two committees. The most prominent member of the revolutionary tribunal was Fouquier-Tinville, a methodical, systematic individual who applied himself to his duties with amazing stolidity and nerveless precision.

Then there were the deputies on mission, whose actions we have already noted. By the decree of December 4 their number was reduced, the Convention's surveillance over them tightened, and the field of their activity was limited. One still found them in 1794, but their great days were over.

Of the local administrations the least important was that of the department, while the district authorities and the municipal administration were considerably more influential and corresponded directly with Paris. But the executive power (after December 4) was exercised by the national agents, of whom there was one in each district or commune. The function of these national agents was similar to that of the deputies on mission, but their responsibility to the Committee was much greater. Where they still existed, the surveillance committees (or more popularly "revolutionary committees") performed a useful service as a sort of political police. But the deputies on mission purified their personnel with perhaps overscrupulous zeal; their numbers dwindled, and few traces of their activity remained. The popular societies (Jacobin clubs) were at the base of the administrative pyramid of the Terror government and no large center was without one. Despite deeply rooted opinion to the contrary, these clubs did not play a decisive part in fashioning the new government. On the whole they were dominated by the deputies on mission, who purified their personnel with little interference and consulted only with local leaders, not with the club as a whole, in the execution of the revolutionary laws. With regard to political activities, the popular societies fulfilled the functions of auxiliary administrative bodies, attending to the innumerable concerns which overwhelm even long-established governments in time of war. Examples are not lacking of Jacobin self-assertiveness against the central administration, but after 1793 these are exceptions rather than the rule. The popular societies, whose total membership assuredly was not less than 500,000 during the Terror, were absorbed into the governmental system, because no other rôle was left them, save being eliminated entirely. This alternative was out of the question, because the revolutionary government was the government of Jacobins, who had gained control of the state by defeating the Girondins in June and July.

In October began the ill famed activities of the revolutionary tribunal, for then the desire for vengeance against royalist and federalist traitors and morbid fear of traitors had reached their height. The first of the prominent victims was Marie Antoinette, "the widow Capet," as she was then called, whose trial was brief, for the result was a foregone conclusion. After the queen came the turn of the arrested Girondins, twenty-one of whom were led from the Conciergerie in creaking tumbrils to the Place de la Révolution, where the guillotine stood (October 31). They were sincere republicans, upright and courageous, but they had stirred up civil war, and no responsible government in time of war would have treated them more leniently. Next came the duke of Orléans, who was guillotined because of his royal birth; Bailly, the former mayor of Paris, hated by the populace for his part in the massacre of the Champ-de-Mars in July, 1791; Madame Roland, the soul of the Girondins, who died calmly, with an apostrophe to liberty on her lips; Barnave, once a leader of the National Constituent Assembly, several former generals, and a number of more obscure individuals who were sacrified to the prevailing wrath and fear of the patriots. Most of the condemned Girondins who escaped the guillotine in Paris met tragic deaths elsewhere; Roland and Condorcet committed suicide, Barbaroux was guillotined in Bordeaux, and Buzot and Pétion died of starvation after being pursued relentlessly from point to point.

The Terror was more sanguinary in the provinces, where the number of those who received the semblance of a trial before execution reached the total of 12,000. Summary punishment without even the semblance of a trial brought the figures to the high total of 20,000 for all of France. Aside from all exaggerated accounts, the butcheries, as they actually were, were horrible enough. In Lyons, now renamed Ville Affranchie (Liberated City), Fouché and Collot commandeered a detachment of the revolutionary army and embarked upon a senseless and odious butchery of the popu-lace that nothing can justify, that shocked every principle of justice and humanity. Fréron and Barras exacted vengeance against the two rebellious cities of the southeast, Marseilles and Toulon, in similar spirit though in slightly less murderous fashion. In the Vendée, where the most atrocious reprisals were practiced by both sets of combatants, where the worst of human passions were aroused, military columns systematically ravaged the country, making it a veritable desert. At Nantes, the deputy on mission, Carrier, yielded to the hysterical fears of the local Jacobins and organized frightful massacres whose ferocious cruelty surpassed even the horrors at Lyons. Yet the situation in Nantes was scarcely worse than elsewhere in the Vendée, where the record of man's inhumanity to man is unparalleled.

The question that arises, whether or not the Terror was justi-fied, is essentially irrelevant. Under the circumstances sanguinary and arbitrary violence was unavoidable. Life proceeded under tremendous tension. Patriotism was at white heat in the embattled country, which was beleaguered by the foe without and honey-combed with enemies within. The spirit of intolerant suppression of opposition was firmly embedded in Jacobin practices long be-fore the Revolution entered upon the Terror proper, and the use of violence, of eliminating voluntary consent, was implicit in the fundamental faith of the revolutionists. When the tragic occasion arose, when the patriots fought for the existence of their republic against federalists, royalists, and the coalition without and, as they fervently believed, myriads of suspects within the country, their impulse toward violence became a sort of collective psychosis. Those upon whom responsibility rested did not dare to manifest softness or sentiment. The sans-culottes and their wretched victims were alike prisoners of a nation-wide hysteria which expressed it-self in the most odious forms of butchery. Where the danger was greatest, the repression was most sanguinary. However, if the recourse to arbitrary, blind violence was spontaneous on the part of the avengers, it was organized at the initiative of the various deputies on mission, who acted without instructions or serious re-strictions from Paris. Some of them, like Tallien at Bordeaux, were bribed into moderation. Others, more notorious, gratified the worst impulses of human nature, fear, vengeance, personal rivalry and hatred, and unbridled abuse of authority. Not all of France suffered. Many regions, indeed most of France, knew the Terror in its mildest form of repression of constitutional liberties and patriotic intimidation of nonconformists. Terror in this guise is a phenomenon not unknown to our generation.

PARLIAMENTARY OPPOSITION

For all its successes the Committee of Public Safety was constantly attacked by its critics in Paris. Not until the spring of 1794 did it succeed in destroying the two factions which made its security so precarious. The members of the government administration were firmly convinced that these attacks were not legitimate criticisms of an opposition, but the dastardly consequences of a complex, highly ramified conspiracy organized by the coalition. Absurd as this seems on the face of it, the rulers of France had no doubt whatever (if they entertained any doubt at first, constant reiteration of this thesis finally dispelled it) that the group of extremists called the Hébertists, or the *ultras*, as well as the group of moderate deputies known as the Dantonists, or the *citras*, were false patriots plotting to overthrow the republic and reëstablish the monarchy. In some ways the attitude of the Russian revolutionists, who live in constant fear of a coalition of bourgeois states and of the sabotage of professing revolutionists within their state, helps us to grasp the psychology of Robespierre and Saint-Just and their colleagues. To be sure there was reason for this dread of conspiracy. There were active agents of the allies and of the royalists in France, intrenched in strong places, living on intimate terms with many patriots, using their funds and their guile to embarrass and hamper the government. But all they could do was to assist those in the opposition. The opposition can be explained in very simple ordinary terms as the division of the revolutionaries into one group, left-wing republicans who wanted more vigorous support of the sans-culottes, and another group, right-wing republicans who wanted to check the social policy of the committee and institute a government of the solid middle class.

The nucleus of the Hébertists was the little group of men in control of the Paris Commune, of the Cordeliers, and of the war ministry. There were Hébert, Momoro, Vincent, Ronsin, and Bouchotte. The officers of the revolutionary army of the interior were with them and several of the notorious deputies on mission, like Fouché and Carrier. Certain foreign refugees and adventurers, such as Anacharsis Clootz, who was an apostate Prussian baron, the Belgian Proly, and the bankers Koch, Dutch refugees and republicans, were also closely associated with this group. They had no particular political program save that of war to the bitter end and the severest repression of all suspects. Their social program was exceedingly vague and ill defined, more sympathetic on the whole to the city workers than that of the Committee and louder in its denunciation of speculators and monopolists, but fundamentally inclined in favor of the same petty bourgeoisie from which the Committee drew its support. They were rabidly anti-Catholic and took the lead in the famous dechristianization movement of the fall of 1793.

The citra-revolutionists, the Dantonists so called, were venal politicians each with personal grievances against the Committee and united only by a common desire to retard or turn back the Revolution. Among them were discontented deputies on mission who bitterly criticized the incompetence of the committees and of the war office, corrupt deputies implicated in stock-jobbing and contracting scandals, others whose private life and connections with financiers or émigrés or royalists made them anxious to end the unconstitutional régime of the committees and the revolutionary tribunal. In a way they were a permanent parliamentary opposition, representing the opinions of the majority of the deputies who secretly hated the policy pursued by the Committee. By their pin-pricks against the guiding committees they succeeded in impairing the efficiency of the administration, but not until the return of Danton to political life did they become a serious menace to the Committee.

Danton's opposition was neither entirely disinterested nor yet entirely treacherous. He was by no means a conspirator against the Revolution, as Robespierre alleged at the time of his trial. He was sick at heart of the cruelty and abuses of the Terror, for his was an ardent nature, expansive and generous. He regretted his inability to save the queen from the scaffold; he had wept at the execution of the Girondins. A great sorrow had come into his life with the death of his first wife, and his second marriage only intensified his yearning for peace and rest. He was a bluff, hand-shaking, back-slapping politician, loud and coarse in his speech, intensely courageous, and thoroughly unprincipled. He detested single-minded, fanatical natures, men who were wedded to principles, particularly to principles which threatened his security. Proof, at the time only suspicion, now exists that his humanity was tinctured with studied calculation. He amassed a fairly large fortune during the Revolution and owned considerable property at his home near Paris. His new interests as a property owner were injured by the social policy that the sans-culottes impressed upon the government. Of late he had appealed more and more to the men of means in the Convention. He was a close friend of the corrupt deputies of the Convention, to whom he was in loyalty bound. He desired peace with the foe because he was an opportunist, an optimistic improviser, who had given more proofs than one of his genius in secret negotiations. Peace would bring him prestige and power, and his friends security against that revolutionary justice which threatened them. He was sincerely conciliatory by nature, but conciliation toward the factions, as the Committee rather vaguely perceived, would end the revolutionary régime and inaugurate a middle-class republic of those very financiers and speculators, of venal representatives whom Robespierre and his associates opposed. And Robespierre, acutely suspicious of all differences of opinion, saw at last the golden opportunity to usher in the Republic of Virtue and Equality, which his intellectual master, Rousseau, had envisioned.

In struggling against these groups the Committee fought for the stability of the government and for the perpetuation of the power of its members. In the course of the struggle the latter gained a clearer conception of their ideal state, and two of them, Robespierre and Saint-Just, eloquently defined the object of the Revolution and its goal. The exceedingly complex and dramatic details of this bitter struggle are much too full to reproduce here. They are replete with personal rancors, denunciations, retractions, intrigues, attempted insurrection, trickery, and bad faith. The first threat which came from the ultras was definitely checked in December, 1793, when they were forced to cease their attacks against the churches and several of their adherents found themselves compromised in the "foreign plot." [5] Ronsin and Vincent were im-

---

[5] In October and November two of the corrupt deputies, Fabre d'Eglantine and Chabot, both of them deeply involved in the falsification of the decree which liquidated the French East India Company and in the ensuing stock-jobbery, made secret revelations to the Committee. Among the individuals that they named, several were prominent Hébertists. Accusers and accused were arrested and imprisoned by the Committee.

prisoned, and, with Robespierre's approval, Camille Desmoulins attacked the extremists in the first two numbers of his new newspaper *Le Vieux Cordelier*. Precisely at this moment Danton left his retreat and returned to the political stage to encourage the moderates, who were busily pushing their campaign directly against the extremists and indirectly against the government. The subsequent numbers of *Le Vieux Cordelier* were brilliant arraignments of the entire revolutionary régime, its draconic law of suspects, the mistakes and haughtiness of the committees, the unbridled excesses of the deputies on mission. When Camille pleaded for a committee of clemency a crowd of weeping women came to the Convention to beg for the release of prisoners. But brusquely the tide turned against the moderates. Robespierre, aware now that Desmoulins's campaign had gone too far, assumed the defense of the Committee's policy and roundly denounced the two sets of internal enemies, both inspired by foreign gold, who were marching toward the same goal of disorganizing the government.[6] Vincent and Ronsin were released, and the Dantonists were temporarily silenced.

For two more months the factions fought each other, but the climax was reached in February, when the Hébertists tried to take advantage of an acute food shortage in Paris to incite the populace to a new insurrection. They denounced Robespierre and his associates, whom they called the "*Endormeurs*" (the "Pacifiers"), and veiled the Declaration of Rights at the Cordelier Club, as if to signify by that gesture that justice was dead. "Insurrection, a sacred insurrection, that is what we must give the scoundrels," counseled Carrier at the Cordelier Club. The movement fizzled, for the Parisian sans-culottes and the Commune refused to follow the would-be insurrectionists. At first the Committee of Public Safety was inclined toward a conciliatory policy, but strengthened by the return of Robespierre, who had been away because of illness, it struck sharply not merely at the Hébertists but at the Dantonists

---

[6] The proof of Fabre's guilt in falsifying the decree came to light in January, 1794, and convinced the committees that the dishonest deputies concerned, whom Chabot had denounced, were also parties to the dread "foreign plot." In Robespierre's own words: "Two kinds of factions are directed by the Foreign Conspirators . . . those who have an ardent nature and a violent character propose ultrarevolutionary means; those who are milder and more moderate propose citrarevolutionary means. They combat each other; but whether the one or the other is victorious is immaterial; . . . either system is intended to ruin the Republic. . . ."

as well. "Let conspirators of all kinds tremble," exclaimed Barère, "we must watch over the faction of the Indulgents and the Pacifics as much as that of the so-called Insurgents," thus maintaining the government's favorite thesis that the two factions were secretly working together despite appearances to the contrary. During the night of March 13–14 the leading Hébertists, Hébert, Momoro, Ronsin, and Vincent, were placed under arrest. With them were associated several others seized by the government, the most notable being the foreigners Clootz and Proly. Their trial was brief. The revolutionary tribunal found them guilty, and on March 24, they were guillotined for having plotted to starve Paris, dissolve the Convention, and reëstablish tyranny.

The moderates and all their sympathizers who saw in the arrest of the extremists the sign of a speedy overthrow of the rule of the sans-culottes were hopeful, but the turn of the Dantonists soon followed. While the Hébertists were on trial before the revolutionary tribunal, the committees arraigned the "corrupt deputies." [7] Hérault, the former member of the great Committee, was also under arrest, accused of relations with the enemy. Only Robespierre's scruples remained to save Danton, for it was illogical to have the supposed ringleader escape while his followers were apprehended. Robespierre had cherished his fallen opponent; they had been associated throughout the entire course of the Revolution; only recently he had defended Danton at the Jacobins. Billaud narrates how at length he overcame Robespierre's objections, how Robespierre "consented to give up Danton." During the last week in March the committees prepared their accusation, Saint-Just working from Robespierre's notes against Danton, "the rotten idol." On March 30, six days after the end of the Hébertists, the Dantonists were placed under arrest,[8] charged with conspiracy to reëstablish monarchy and destroy the republic. Danton did nothing to avert his inglorious end. "Better a hundred times to be guillotined," he cried, "than to guillotine." Before the revolutionary tribunal he regained his boldness, and his vibrant eloquence stirred the jury and resounded in the street outside. But his defense, like that of the Girondins, was stifled. The debates were cut short, and the jury deliberated, soon returning with a verdict of guilty. The death sentence was executed that very day (April 5).

[7] Fabre, Delaunay, Chabot, and Basire.
[8] Danton, Camille Desmoulins, Philippeaux, Delacroix.

Danton was the last to mount the steps of the scaffold. "You will show my head to the people," he told the executioner; "it is well worth while."

The execution of the extremists and the judicial assassination of Danton and his supporters introduced a new era in the Revolution. In all previous crises the existing government had followed the lead of the Parisian patriots; this time it crushed and guillotined their leaders and proceeded with rare energy to make its power supreme in Paris. It dissolved the revolutionary army, placed men on whom it could rely in control of the Commune, closed the Cordelier Club and the popular societies that were meeting in the sections, and made the food commission responsible for the food supply in the capital. Would the revolutionary masses still give their support to the government? Manifestly, the terrified deputies could not be counted on to oppose it. They had surrendered Danton to the committees, but almost entirely from fear of Robespierre, for whom as an individual they held no affection, and for whose views they entertained distrust.

THE REPUBLIC OF VIRTUE

The most varied judgments have been passed on "the Incorruptible," the scrupulously neat, elegantly attired deputy who was the living symbol of the revolutionary government. The masses admired him without measure, most of his colleagues respected him highly, and some detested and feared him with deep passion. Historians are equally divided. For some he is a great humanitarian, an apostle of social justice, the most lofty figure of the entire Revolution. Others see in him an owlish and scheming intriguer, ambitious and unscrupulous, or yet a mediocrity elevated by circumstances and schemers cleverer than himself to the summit of revolutionary power.[9] Ambitious he undoubtedly was; perhaps without realizing it consciously, for he sincerely believed that all his actions were for the benefit of humanity. He was sincere, fanatically sincere, with the type of narrow dogmatic sincerity which marks single-minded reformers and religious crusaders. In his private life he was austere and simple to the point of asceticism. He was aloof in his personal contacts, incapable of arousing the

---

[9] Lord Acton calls him "the most hateful character in the forefront of history since Machiavelli reduced to a code the wickedness of public men."

emotions of others or even of expressing his own. Moreover, he was morbidly suspicious, describing himself somewhat unctuously as "one of the most suspicious and melancholy of patriots." His gifts had developed remarkably since the opening of the Revolution. Finicky and diffident at the outset, prone to making pedantic and declamatory speeches, he learned how to talk extempore with eloquence and appeal. He had gained his ascendancy in the Committee partly because the other members were too deeply occupied with their own tasks, largely because he more than all the others (with the exception of Saint-Just and Couthon) had the ultimate goal of the Revolution in mind. For these three men the Terror was more than an instrument of national defense; it was to be the instrument of social justice. From Rousseau they had caught the vision of an ideal republic, founded on virtue, where there would be neither rich nor poor, where excessive wealth would be a social crime, where the highest goal of the citizen would be to serve the general will, where jealousy would give place to trust, hatred to love, cruelty to justice and reason. However, when we examine their efforts to usher in this Utopia, to realize heaven on earth, we can perceive the inadequacy of their program and distinguish those misguided attempts which awakened the fiercest of opposition and brought about their downfall.

Their social-economic policy ultimately proved a dismal failure, for they had no comprehensive plan and were forced to sacrifice one large section of their followers in order to retain the rest. War needs had forced the government to nationalize a large part of the country's economic activities. It established munitions plants, drafted the great technical specialists, controlled export and the import of raw material, requisitioned supplies and equipment, regulated production, and fixed prices and wages. This unprecedented concentration of economic activities was sufficient to insure the defense and to start the armies on their imperialistic conquests. But this partial success was achieved despite woeful inefficiency, wasted efforts and duplication, haphazard development and corrupt practices on the part of the administrators, and indifference, secret resistance, and open sabotage by a large part of the population. Without the drastic application of the Terror to stimulate the patriots and restrain all others, not even this partial success would have been gained.

The millions of landless peasants and city workers who favored governmental regulation for its supposed social value to them were grievously disappointed in the failure of the triumphant committee to introduce a thorough sans-culotte policy. There are several reasons for its failure. The majority of the deputies in the committees were concerned exclusively with safeguarding the stability of the government. The Robespierrists sympathized strongly with the sans-culottes but could do little. They too were politicians, anxious to remain in power. To remain in power they required the support of the strategically important patriots, and the latter were not landless peasants and city workers. Moreover, their policy was not socialistic; their ideal state was a state of small traders and dealers and cultivators of moderate means. With the poorer citizens they sympathized; but they did nothing in their behalf, except at the expense of enemies of the republic such as émigrés and convicted suspects. Their social and economic policy was doubly mischievous, for it was radical enough to antagonize the propertied classes without being sufficiently radical to satisfy the demands of those without property.

They removed many of the restrictions upon foreign trade, Robespierre himself appealing directly to the mercantile interests and defending the patriotic services of merchants and traders. Furthermore, in the spring of 1794 the Committee weakened the application of the maximum on prices while it endeavored to maintain it stringently on wages paid to the workers, which were considerably less than the unofficial scale. At the same time that the Committee refused its intervention to guarantee the grain supply of the civilian population and forbade the local authorities to requisition other prime commodities, the Robespierre group voted the famous Ventôse [10] decrees in behalf of the landless cultivators. Much has been written recently in praise of these decrees, which proposed to transfer the lands of convicted suspects and émigrés to indigent peasants. The intention back of them was highly commendable, but their social significance seems greatly exaggerated. On the one hand, many of these enemies of the Revolution had little or no land; moreover, no systematic classification of "indigent peasants" was ever made. On the other hand, the indigent peasants clamored for the abolition of the share-cropping system and the division of large estates into small plots, but were not heeded by

[10] Ventôse was the month in the new revolutionary calendar which corresponded to thirty days between the end of February and the end of March.

the Robespierrists. In short, neither the city proletariat nor the poor peasants gained much satisfaction from the government. The economic situation was grim in the summer of 1794; and the threatened failure of crops, together with the unabated inflation, foreboded disaster. The Committee fell back upon another expedient, the systematic inculcation of orthodox republicanism in the new generation; but it did not survive long enough to make that effort successful.

Robespierre understood very clearly that he could not inaugurate his ideal state based upon civic virtue without the unifying moral force of religion. But that religion could not be Catholicism, nor could its official spokesmen be Catholic priests. The latter had been discredited by their actions during the Revolution, the nonjuring priests by their early opposition and the juring clergy by their part in the federalist revolt. The very dogma of Catholicism was giving ground rapidly to the new revolutionary faith, the worship of national patriotism. We have called attention to the steady growth of this new faith, which substituted revolutionary principles and la patrie for God, developed its sacred traditions and its martyrs, its ritual and its civic fêtes. In the fall of 1793 the revolutionary opponents of Catholicism made their most determined effort to extirpate the old faith and establish the new state religion. Between October and November the Convention voted the measures making up the new revolutionary calendar, which did away with the Sabbath and the saints' days of the old calendar.[11]

One object of the revisionists was to commemorate the triumphs

[11] The new era and the new year were designated as beginning on September 22, 1792, the day following the abolition of the monarchy and by a happy coincidence the day of the autumnal equinox. The year was divided into twelve months of thirty days each, and each month into three ten-day periods called *décades*. To maintain the coincidence of the new revolutionary year with the solar year there were to be five additional days (six in leap years) at the end of the year known as *sans-culottides*. In place of the old names of the months the Convention adopted an entirely new nomenclature which substituted "the truth of nature and the realities of reason for sacerdotal prestige and visions of ignorance." The autumn months were named Vendémiaire, Brumaire, Frimaire; the winter months Nivôse, Pluviôse, Ventôse; the spring months Germinal, Floréal, Prairial; the summer months Messidor, Thermidor, Fructidor. To supplant the Sabbath and the saints' days an elaborate scheme was devised whereby the days of the year were to be named for "the true treasures of rural life," while the sans-culottides were to be dedicated to festivals of Virtue, Genius, Labor, Opinion, Rewards. The new calendar was in official use until January 1, 1806.

of the Republic; another, and the more important, to destroy the influence of Christianity and the Catholic Church. At about the same time a formidable dechristianization movement was launched by several deputies on mission and Chaumette, procurator of the Paris Commune. Churches were closed and converted into temples of reason, priests forced to unfrock themselves, and anti-Catholic demonstrations held. The movement culminated in the Festival of Reason at the cathedral of Notre Dame in Paris (November 10). Robespierre and the Committee decried these excesses, for fear that they would turn millions of believing citizens against the republic. The Convention halted the dechristianization movement and forbade all violence and measures hostile to the freedom of religious worship. But most of the churches remained closed, and the religion of patriotism flourished vigorously.

After the fall of the factions Robespierre became actively engaged in preparing the bases of the official religion. From Rousseau he had learned that it was the duty of the state to assume charge of souls; the reports of the deputies on mission and his own shrewdness as a politician confirmed that conviction. On the 18th of Floréal, year II (May 7, 1794), he read his famous report on the relationship of moral ideas and revolutionary principles, in which he outlined the national religion. It was to be free from degrading superstition and the corrupt influence of a priesthood; it was to have only two positive articles of faith—belief in a Supreme Being and in the immortality of the soul. To impress the moral ideas of Virtue upon the nation and to mold the spiritual character of the citizens, regular ceremonies were to be held on each *décadi* [12] in honor of various generous abstractions, such as "liberty and equality," "filial piety," "the benefactors of humanity," "paternal devotion," and "modesty." Each year the republican authorities would celebrate the four great events of the Revolution, which were the capture of the Bastille, July 14, 1789; the deposition of the monarchy, August 10, 1792; the execution of the king, January 21, 1793; the Parisian insurrection that led to the overthrow of the Girondins, May 31, 1793.

A month later, on the 20th of Prairial (June 8) Robespierre formally inaugurated the new religion in a solemn ceremony in honor of the Supreme Being. The scene of the celebration was the

---

[12] This was the tenth day of the *décade*, of which there were three in each month of the revolutionary calendar.

Tuileries gardens and the greatest artists of the time had been pressed into service to make the ceremony as impressive as possible. All public officials were assembled, the deputies of the Convention, and many thousand Parisians. Robespierre welcomed the assemblage, delivered a lengthy oration, and then proceeded, allegorically, to show triumphant Wisdom destroying Atheism, Vice, and Folly. He set fire to the statues representing those undesirable abstractions, from whose ruins emerged the lofty wooden figure of Wisdom.[13]

Then, at the head of a long procession, holding a bouquet of flowers in his hands, Robespierre marched to the Champ-de-Mars, where on the symbolical Mountain that had been constructed all the participants took an oath of allegiance to the Republic. A few skeptical freethinkers among the deputies grumbled over the ceremonies, but the Catholics and the sans-culottes were pleased—the former because the new religion seemed to be the old Catholicism in another form, and the latter because the ceremonies organized the new civic faith. The foreign press hailed the ascendancy of Robespierre, confidently expecting him "to fill in the abyss of the Revolution." But shortly after the Fête of the Supreme Being the Terror in Paris reached its height.

To understand the significance of the law of the 22nd of Prairial (June 10, 1794) which completed the process of concentrating the administration of revolutionary justice in Paris, the events preceding it must be noted. After the execution of the Hébertists and the Dantonists the local revolutionary tribunals were abolished, and a decree created six popular commissions to select only the most culpable of the imprisoned suspects for trial in Paris and release the others. There was need of such centralization, for the spring of 1794 was marked by a revival of local Terror which turned only too frequently against the innocent sans-culottes. But only two of these popular commissions were established, and these too late and too imperfectly to be effective. Moreover, the dominant Committee of Public Safety was under suspicion of attempting to wrest control of revolutionary justice from the lesser committee of general security. It has recently been proved that the Robespierrists did

---

[13] Some mechanical defect in the arrangements prevented the statues from burning cleanly, so that the Wisdom which finally emerged came out blackened by smoke, much to Robespierre's annoyance. The gay Parisians laughed heartily over this unexpected and irreverent diversion.

not use the separate police bureau which they established as an instrument to supplant the committee of general security, but the suspicion existed at the time. The last and the least successful step the Committee of Public Safety took to gain control was its decision to reorganize the revolutionary tribunal and its procedure, without consulting in advance the members of the committee of general security. The law that Couthon proposed in its name, the law which the Convention voted after fierce protest on the part of certain deputies, speeded up the working of the revolutionary tribunal, deprived the accused of all legal defense, eliminated all other verdicts than acquittal or the death penalty, and defined "the enemies of the people" in so vague and sweeping a fashion that the infliction of the death penalty became virtually mandatory upon the four sections of the revolutionary tribunal. In brief, all opposition to, even disagreement with, the régime of virtue was to be punished by death, a social consequence which would hasten the execution of the recently passed Ventôse decrees.

Applied conscientiously and concurrently with the preliminary investigation of the popular commissions, the 22nd of Prairial law would scarcely have altered the existing procedure, for under the prevalent system the guilt of the accused was already taken for granted when he came before the revolutionary tribunal and none of the judges or jurors dared brave the anger of the mob by relaxing their severity. But applied dishonestly, without a preliminary sifting of local prisoners being made, the law enormously swelled the number of prisoners sent before the revolutionary tribunal. Its application, moreover, was falsified by the terrorists in the committee of general security, who grouped the prisoners sent into Paris in "batches," invented conspiracies and conspirators, and thus instituted the "Great Terror" when "heads fell like slates from the roofs." More than thirteen hundred persons were guillotined in the six weeks that elapsed between June 10 and July 27, almost two hundred more than in all the fourteen preceding months of the tribunal's existence.

FALL OF THE ROBESPIERRISTS

If Robespierre was not personally responsible for these legal butcheries, he had done little to prevent them, and the entire nation regarded him as the personification of the Great Terror,[14] which was precisely the result expected by his opponents in the committee of general security. He had defended the law before the infuriated deputies, when it deprived them of their parliamentary immunity. But the need for revolutionary excesses no longer seemed apparent. The country was out of danger. The reorganized armies were sweeping on to victory and by their brilliant triumph at Fleurus on June 24, 1794, had opened the way to a second conquest of the Austrian Netherlands. The middle-class patriots, now safely installed for the most part in the local administration, were averse to further revolutionary exertions. The sans-culottes were bitterly disappointed in the failure of the social and economic experiment of the government. Robespierre was the official defender of the government's policies, and upon Robespierre all his critics now turned, skillfully exploiting the popular sentiment to overthrow "the Incorruptible."

In substance the final attack against Robespierre was a new version of the earlier frustrated plan of extremists and moderates to overthrow the government. The earlier attacks had been upon the Committee as a whole; this one was against Robespierre in person, for such was his ascendancy that his enemies could denounce him as a dictator. In the second place, the moderates and the extremists had failed on the earlier occasion to unite their forces; this time they joined hands. Of his colleagues in the great committee the terrorists Collot and Billaud were his implacable enemies. Only Saint-Just and Couthon were loyal to the end. Barère was for no man unless it were himself. The others, like Carnot and Lindet, were troubled with many misgivings over Robespierre's ultimate intentions. They were all alike worn out by their herculean labors of the past twelve months, overworked, testy and irritable from lack of sleep and the overpowering summer heat, their nerves frazzled and out of their control. Carnot and Saint-Just almost came to blows. Robespierre himself was suspicious and intractable, a constant source of irritation to his colleagues. In addition to his critics in the Committee, there were the many deputies who were hostile to his general policies and fearful of his vengeance. The committee of general security, inspired by the cynical Vadier who

[14] With his customary legal and ethical scrupulousness he had tried to distinguish between the guilty and the innocent whenever he had occasion to ratify arrest warrants, but such palliative efforts meant very little.

despised Robespierre as a religious hypocrite, resented his moderation and his part in the reorganization of revolutionary justice.
Lastly, there were the former deputies on mission whom he had
recalled for their excesses and their dilapidations, Carrier, Fouché,
Tallien, Fréron, Barras, all of whom feared him for his severity.

Robespierre knew that a plot was being formed against him, and
he welcomed a show of strength, for he was confident of the support of the Convention. Skillfully conducted, his defense might
have succeeded, but he misjudged the situation and played directly into the hands of his political opponents. He had stopped
attending the sessions of the Committee at the end of June.
Couthon and Saint-Just favored a working arrangement with the
schemers (to eliminate them at some later date), but Robespierre
pressed the issue in a defiant speech before the Convention on the
8th of Thermidor (July 26, 1794). This speech sealed his doom,
but it vindicated his sincerity and his disinterestedness. To remain
in power all that he had to do was to extend the olive branch to
the corrupt deputies. His final address did just the reverse. It was
vigorous in its denunciatory qualities and in its appeal for complete
reorganization of the two committees; but he strangely refused to
name all his enemies outright. His inexplicable reticence gave the
plotters a respite. Overnight they evolved their plans for the
morrow and rounded up all his enemies in the Convention. To
some they imparted the information that Robespierre was preparing a long proscription list; to others, that he was a moderate,
unworthy of revolutionary confidence. That night Robespierre enjoyed his final triumph at the Jacobin Club, where he repeated his
Convention speech.

The dénouement came on the following day, the 9th of Thermidor. The opposition was in full control of the Convention, and its
program was followed to the letter. Saint-Just's indictment against
the leaders of the plot, which he had prepared during the night,
could not be read; Robespierre was denied the floor, and his enemies reveled in the luxury of denouncing him who had always
denounced others. Late in the afternoon, the Robespierrists, Robespierre and his brother, Couthon, Saint-Just, and Le Bas, were arrested and conducted to different municipal prisons. The friendly
Commune delivered them from prison and rebelled against the
authority of the Convention. But the insurrection was unprepared
and proved abortive. Robespierre would have taken his chances

with the revolutionary tribunal, but when he learned that the Convention had outlawed him and his followers, he joined the insurrectionists at the Hôtel de Ville and addressed an appeal for arms to the sections. It came too late. Early in the morning of the 10th of Thermidor (July 28) the hastily recruited troops of the Convention penetrated into the Hôtel de Ville. To judge from the evidence, Robespierre tried to shoot himself, but he succeeded only in shattering his lower jaw with the bullet. Saint-Just gave himself up. Couthon and the younger Robespierre failed to escape. At seven that evening the "Triumvirate" and the nineteen adherents were guillotined; and in the following week a hundred more. The joy of the populace was unbounded, though not for long. Thus ended the homicidal venture to establish the republic of virtue and equality, and the future of the Revolution now lay with the solid middle class and its sorry leaders of terrorists, trimmers, and grafters.

XII. THE CONVENTION: THE REËSTABLISHMENT OF A CONSTITUTIONAL RÉGIME (1794-1795)

THE THERMIDORIAN REACTION

THE Terrorists who overthrew Robespierre had no intention of relaxing the severity of the revolutionary régime. Their first intention had been to save themselves. But the pressure of events and public opinion forced the new leaders to pursue a systematic policy of undoing the work of the Terror. To that transformation of the revolutionary régime and its accompanying tactics of prosecuting the leaders of the Terror and compensating those who had been persecuted, the term "Thermidorian Reaction" has been given. The leaders of the reaction are known as the Thermidorians. With Robespierre out of the way, Paris and all France breathed more freely. The chained press threw off its shackles and came to life. Opinion once again became free, at least to condemn all those who actually or seemingly had been sympathetic to the program of the dead "tyrant." This was the period in which the legend of Robespierre's cruelty, Robespierre's rapacity, Robespierre's duplicity began to flourish, in which all the crimes of the Terror were unloaded on the shoulders of that one man. The dread accusation of being a "Robespierrist" hung like a pall over the deputies, over the deputies on mission, over the old committee members, and over the very Thermidorians who had destroyed Robespierre. To escape that accusation, to make manifest by their attitude and their actions that they had nothing in common with Robespierre, to attack the institutions that Robespierre treasured most dearly, became the first preoccupation of the Terrorists who had overthrown him. Tallien, Fréron, and Barras discovered to their great surprise that they were popular heroes, the unwitting champions of a strong reaction against the government of the revolutionary dictatorship. They quickly realized the situation and assumed the rôle that was created for them. At first the deputies of the Plain, such as Sieyès, Thibaudeau, and Boissy d'Anglas, who had been silent during the Terror, held a balance between the

293

Thermidorians and the revolutionary democrats. But the increasing bitterness of the political strife in and out of the Convention made them join the repentant Terrorists against the remaining Montagnards.

Centralization of powers and stability of administration had been characteristic of the revolutionary régime. For these the Thermidorians substituted decentralization and frequent renewal of the administrative personnel. Within a few months' time the personnel of the Committee of Public Safety was altered. The leading Terrorists were eliminated and replaced by Thermidorians. In order to end the centralization of the administration the work was distributed between sixteen committees, while the powers of the Committee of Public Safety were limited to diplomacy and the prosecution of the war. It also lost all of its former dictatorial powers of arrest and surveillance. The revolutionary tribunal, before its ultimate dissolution in the spring of 1795, was reorganized and its membership changed. With the repeal of the law of the 22nd of Prairial the accused were given adequate means of defense, and the new revolutionary tribunal subsequently acquitted about eighteen times as many as those that it convicted. The Terror was coming to a close. The Paris Commune automatically ceased to exist by the outlawry of all its members on the 9th of Thermidor, and the administration of Paris was placed under the control of several executive commissions of the Convention. The local revolutionary committees were greatly reduced in number and disappeared entirely somewhat later. The Jacobin clubs in the departments were forbidden to affiliate and correspond with the mother society. On November 12, 1794, the doors of the mother society in Paris were closed by the Convention after its hall had been invaded by the young hooligans who called themselves "The Gilded Youth." The great Jacobin Club thus passed into history. The Ventôse decrees, like the law of the 22nd of Prairial, were repealed in August, 1794.[1] In December, 1794, the law of suspects and the law of the maximum were also repealed, to the great joy of traders.

As the reaction gathered force, individual deputies came in for their share of vengeful attention. Between the closing of the Jacobin Club in November and the readmission of the outlawed Girondins in March, 1795, there was a regular succession of acts

[1] For the Ventôse decrees and the law of the 22 Prairial, see above pp. 285–289.

of clemency for the victims of the Terror and vengeance against the Terrorists. Carrier, the notorious deputy on mission to Nantes, was condemned to the guillotine for his crimes. Fouquier-Tinville, the public prosecutor, met his death unflinchingly, protesting his innocence of any personal acts of terrorism and proclaiming his loyalty to the instructions that he had received. Then the members of the old committees were again attacked for their real and alleged misdeeds. In December, 1794, a commission was appointed to investigate the charges against Barère, Billaud-Varenne, Collot d'Herbois, and Vadier (who took refuge in flight). Marat's remains were formally removed from the Pantheon and bands of foppish young men manifested their patriotism and amused themselves by breaking his bust in its places of honor in the cafés and theaters.

In the meantime the suspects were being released from prison, and many thousands rejoined their families. Their presence gave an added impetus to the movement of repudiating the Terror government. Despite strong opposition, the Convention decreed the return of the imprisoned seventy-three Girondins who had been among the first victims of the Terror. In December, 1794, these deputies took their seats in the Convention. Three months later those Girondins who had escaped from Paris after June 2, 1793, and had been in hiding ever since, were also readmitted with the restoration of their full rights. Some of them had learned generosity in the course of their sufferings, but most of them were rancorous and intent only on full and speedy reparation for their past sufferings. The dominant group in the Convention was now the Girondin deputies, who joined with the Plain and the Thermidorians in effecting a republican counter-revolution, their ideal being a constitutional republic that would be safe against royalism. The victors of the 9th of Thermidor were all freethinkers and had not dreamed that their overthrow of Robespierre would eventually lead to a revival of Catholicism. At first, the Convention held firm to its policy of a religion of patriotism. As the decree of September 18, 1794, made clear, the Convention did not favor a separation of church and state, but the ruthless elimination of every cult, philosophical and civic, that competed with the official worship of the Supreme Being. The pensions that the republic had been paying to the constitutional clergy were withdrawn. No effort was made to protect either the constitutional or the nonjuring priests, and in the departments many deputies on mission continued to enforce their anti-Catholic measures. The revolutionary calendar was kept intact, and the civic fêtes of the décadi were strictly observed, even if only sparsely attended. The Convention even attempted to complete the organization of the national religion on the basis of the outline that Robespierre had drawn up; but its efforts were doubly defeated. It failed to make the worship of la patrie uniform and exclusive, and it failed to suppress Catholicism.

There were many reasons for that failure. The revolutionary régime, and the successive decomposition of the constitution of the Terror reacted upon the faith that supported it. The revelation of the crimes that were committed during the Terror further weakened the religion. The high idealism that marked the apogee of the Terror was gone, and its disappearance was reflected in the disillusionment of the former devotees of the new faith. The closing of the clubs and the release of many juring priests from prison further weakened the new religion and at the same time strengthened the revival of the old. Besides, the religion of patriotism was highly artificial, a compound of popular philosophy and classical mythology which never appealed to the real religious emotions of the masses. Consequently, the renaissance of Catholicism was rapid.

In January, Bishop Grégoire reopened the churches of his diocese, an example which was widely followed elsewhere. Shortly after, a decree of the Convention recognized religious liberty; but the priests were obliged to take an oath to observe the laws of the republic, the acts of worship were narrowly restricted, and the use of public funds for the support of services forbidden. Still, this decree created great enthusiasm all over France, and religious services were attended by great throngs of faithful Catholics. On May 30, 1795, the Convention reluctantly permitted the use of unsold confiscated church buildings upon the petition of the citizens, provided the officiating clergy made a declaration of submission to the laws of the republic. Many more churches were thus reopened, but the principal beneficiaries of the Convention's new policy were the nonjuring priests, who returned illegally into the country in droves. An acute observer, Mallet du Pan, at once realized that the Convention had inadvertently aided its enemies: "By reviving Catholics, it revives royalists. Whoever will attend mass is an enemy of the Republic."

Indeed, the political situation of the republic was still extremely precarious. On the one hand were the gilded youth of Paris, young men of varying degrees of affluence and elegance, dressed in the height of a new fashion and armed with clubs, who had pursued and fought with the Jacobins on the streets of the capital. Many of these *muscadins*, as they were also called, had been war slackers during the great critical period of the republic, others deserters, and most of them were deeply royalist at heart. Behind them were the unnumbered legions of malcontents—released political prisoners, widows and children of the victims of the guillotine, war profiteers, repentant terrorists, and many partisans of a royalist restoration. Their journals goaded the gilded youth on; the fashionable salons, which were reopened after Thermidor, encouraged and praised them, and they went on their way with good will, chasing Jacobins, destroying the presses of Montagnard journals, breaking the busts of Marat.and bawling out the strains of the newly composed royalist song, "Le Réveil du peuple." The stage also reflected the reaction against the terrorists, and anti-Jacobin plays were given to packed houses. On the other hand, there were the remaining Jacobins and their supporters among the poor masses, who criticized the Convention as sharply for its conservative measures as the muscadins did for the insufficiency of such measures. They organized counter-manifestations and defended each other in the Convention against the accusations of the Thermidorians. They paraded their past services to the state and tried to stem the tide of the reaction which threatened to sweep them along to the fate of all outworn revolutionists.

THE JACOBIN INSURRECTIONS

The general want as well as fear of proscription soon disposed the Jacobin survivors to revolt. The winter of 1794–1795 was unusually severe. More than forty consecutive days of freezing weather exhausted the supplies of combustibles and rendered the transportation of food difficult, where food was available at all. The pinch was felt not only in Paris but in all of France, for the crisis was general and the catastrophe unprecedented even for the revolutionary period. The repeal of the maximum law and the resumption of private trading were fundamentally to blame for this violent crisis, which traders and farmers turned to account by shameless and heartless monopoly and jobbing. The paper assignat of 100 francs, worth 34 gold francs in Thermidor, fell to 8 in March, and the end was not yet in sight. The government's frantic emission of additional assignats made the distress worse. Farmers and dealers and the propertied class refused to accept paper money in payment, and economic activities all but discontinued. The municipalities were forced to ration supplies and fuel, and in the summer of 1795 the regulation of the grain trade was again employed. In the meantime the crisis was acute. The price of flour was a hundred times higher than it was in 1790, and that of sugar, seventy times. Butter sold at a prohibitive price, and bread became so scarce in March, 1795, that not even the official ration of one pound per day to each head of the family could be distributed. Many died of starvation and many others of the cold. Suicides became alarmingly frequent. The government was helpless, because it had almost reached bankruptcy. The economic crisis assumed a political complexion, for the poor people blamed their distress upon the moneyed class and the government, recalling with bitter pleasure that in the days of the Montagnards they had had both food and power.

The revolutionary populace lost all confidence in the Convention. They wanted bread and work, a new regular election and the democratic Constitution of 1793. It was in this atmosphere that the trial of the four former members of the great Committee began in March, 1795. In spite of the rumblings of their protests the Thermidorians held fast to their goal of vengeance and refused to suspend the trial of the four members, Barère, Billaud, Collot, and Vadier. For nine days the trial continued, the accused defending themselves with vigor and courage. Outside, excitement grew higher, and the aggrieved, famished populace moved to suspend the trial. On the 12th of Germinal (April 1, 1795), a mob, mostly of women and children, invaded the Convention, bearing banners and shouting for "Bread," "the Constitution of 1793" and "Liberty for the Patriots." Several Montagnard deputies had connived with the popular leaders to stage that demonstration in the hope of intimidating the Thermidorians. That complicity cost them dear. The crowd was easily and quickly dispersed by the citizens of the more prosperous sections of Paris. There was no violence on either part, but this demonstration gave the Thermidorians an excellent pretext to finish with the arrested committee members. These were immediately ordered deported on the ground that their continued presence in the Convention was an incitement to disorders. The hapless Montagnards who protested against that summary action were placed under arrest, on the supposition that they had shared in the hostile move against the assembly. Pichegru, who was appointed general-in-chief of the Paris National Guard, restored the semblance of order in the city, but the ferment was not ended.

Paris continued to live a hand-to-mouth existence, and the bread ration of the municipality dwindled to half a pound or less *per diem*. The paper franc [2] continued to depreciate. More than ever the workingmen regretted the fall of "the good Robespierre." A decree of the Convention, restoring the property of the victims of all the revolutionary tribunals to their families, increased the temper of the poor workers. For more than a month a commission of deputies labored on a revision of the Constitution of 1793, finally making it clear that this document of terror could no longer be maintained or revised. Its partisans promptly organized a new insurrection in order to maintain it. On the 1st of Prairial (May 20) the plans of the new insurrection were completed, and a mob of workingmen and women marched on the Convention. For several hours, after an initial repulse, they turned the hall into a field of battle, stormed, murdered one of the deputies, and shouted out their demands for a new assembly, for the "Constitution of 1793," for the release of the imprisoned patriots, and, principally, for bread. Toward evening only a handful of Montagnard deputies remained in the hall. These voted all the demands of the mob and formed a provisional government. But their victory was momentary, for the insurgents had no military support. The Convention called out the National Guard and volunteers from the more prosperous sections, which toward midnight cleared out the mob and gained control of the assembly hall. The intervention of the troops proved decisive.

The absent deputies returned, closed the doors on the Montagnards, and began their work of retaliation. Fourteen of the latter were arrested, and subsequently six of them, honored as the "Last of the Montagnards," were condemned to death. All the measures voted in the interim were of course canceled. On the following day (May 21) the insurrection broke out again in the Faubourg Saint-Antoine, and the National Guard was called to

[2] The Convention decreed on April 7, 1795, that the "franc" should replace the "livre" as the monetary unit. Its value was substantially the same.

suppress this last effort of despair. Within three days the entire
movement was quelled by the soldiery. The Convention's punishment was swift and harsh. A military commission condemned
hundreds of insurgents to death, including the six Montagnard
deputies. The populace was disarmed. Only three of the old committee members were spared; the rest were dead, under arrest,
or in hiding. Carnot, too, would have been arrested, had not an
indignant deputy protested that he had "organized victory." The
triumphant Convention suppressed the revolutionary tribunal entirely, officially abolished the use of the term "revolutionary," and,
as we have noted, voted the reopening of the churches. With this
repulse the rule of the revolutionary multitude was finally terminated. It no longer had leaders, nor clubs, nor arms, nor constitution—for the Constitution of 1793 was abolished also.

The reaction which spread to the provinces was attended by
unspeakable atrocities. A "White Terror" now swept the south
and the west. It was directed against all who had not opposed the
fanatics of the "Red Terror." Returned émigrés and royalists were
the allies and associates of the government agents and of the
escaped victims of the Jacobins who directed the acts of reprisal.
In the southeast royalist bands, calling themselves "Companies of
the Sun," or "Companies of Jesus," which had been organized
somewhat earlier, fell upon isolated individuals and murdered
Jacobin prisoners who were awaiting trial. In the west the rebels
and the royalists also attacked the purchasers of national property.[3]
The Convention could not or would not moderate the savage
reaction, for several of the deputies were secret partisans of the
royalist faction which controlled the press and salons of the capital.
Despite the death of the young dauphin in June and the alarmingly reactionary proclamation issued by the new pretender, the
count of Provence, the royalist intrigues continued. The plotters
in Paris were in close communication with each other and with
Wickham, the agent of the English government, who from Basel
in Switzerland directed their movements and distributed their
funds. But two series of reverses dispelled the fear of a speedy
royalist restoration in 1795. A combined English and émigré expedition to Quiberon Bay in Brittany ended disastrously with the
defeat of their little force and the merciless massacre of the

[3] The Thermidorians had voted an amnesty to the Vendean rebels, but this
attempt at conciliation was ill advised and premature.

prisoners. More important still, the Convention carried through its peace negotiations with Prussia, Holland, and Spain and broke up the first great coalition of powers against revolutionary France.

THE END OF THE FIRST COALITION

France and several states of the coalition were anxious for peace. The French armies had begun their second conquest of the Austrian Netherlands with the battle of Fleurus on June 25, 1794. Their advance to the Rhine was steady, and by the end of October the coalition troops held only Luxemburg, Mainz, and Mannheim. Mannheim fell into French hands in December, and Mainz early in January, 1795. In the dead of winter Pichegru led his tattered troops into Holland, on to the capital, Amsterdam, where they were eagerly expected. A committee was formed there to prepare for the organization of a provisional government. The Dutch cities opened their gates to the invaders. The stadholder, the prince of Orange, withdrew to England, and the old Estates General dissolved itself, making way for a new body composed of sympathizers with the French revolutionists. The Dutch fleet, blocked by the ice at Zeeland, surrendered. From the North Sea to Basel, almost the entire left bank of the Rhine was held by French troops. These conquests not only opened great avenues of wealth to the manufacturers and traders of France, but greatly weakened the military position of several of the states of the coalition. England was deprived of a powerful support along the North Sea, while Prussia, threatened both on the Rhine and from Holland, sued for peace in the autumn of 1794.

Negotiations dragged, because the aims of the negotiators were modified in the course of the discussions and neither the French nor the Prussian diplomats were free to take the final steps until the spring of 1795. The Thermidorians in France who desired the annexation of the Austrian Netherlands and the left bank of the Rhine had to overcome the objections of Carnot, who rejected the annexation of Belgium (the Austrian Netherlands) and the Rhine frontier in favor of such partial annexations as would strategically strengthen the French boundaries. Carnot's expulsion from the Committee of Public Safety in March, 1795, effectively disposed of his objections. Public opinion, educated by the military traditions of the Old Régime and by the revolutionary propaganda of the Convention, also supported the policy of extending France to her "natural frontier" of the Rhine. A still more important consideration was the necessity of satisfying the republican soldiers and their leaders. The troops could not be disbanded, for the Thermidorians needed the support of the soldiery; and since the army was to be maintained, only the conquests of war could pay for its maintenance. The occupied territory paid dearly for its deliverance from the armies of the coalition. The agents of the French Republic extorted sixty million livres from the people of the Netherlands and twenty-five million from the region held between the Meuse and the Rhine. Pictures were removed and art galleries looted of their treasures. The acceptance of assignats was made compulsory in Holland. Only the annexation of the occupied territory could prevent the outbreak of a bitter reaction against the French.

Events outside of France aided the designs of the annexationists. Despite the opposition of the Prussian statesmen who stood firmly for a general pacification of Europe and the guarantee of the territorial integrity of Germany, the contrary view of the minister Haugwitz gradually prevailed. His group sponsored a separate peace treaty between Prussia and France with the surrender of Prussia's territory on the left bank in return for compensation elsewhere in Germany. For them the defense of Prussia's interests in Poland was fully as important as the settlement with France; and any delay in negotiations with France would keep Prussia from using her forces to prevent Austria from gaining an advantage in the third partition of Poland.[4] To release his troops from the Rhine for service in Poland was the motive which forced Frederick William of Prussia to direct his envoys to conclude peace with France.

The treaty was signed on April 5, 1795, at Basel. The French troops evacuated the territory on the right bank but were to hold the Prussian possessions on the west bank of the Rhine until the conclusion of peace between France and the empire. In a secret

---

[4] Austria had been excluded from the second partition, but her statesmen were busily preparing to defend her interests in the third carving. They arranged a secret agreement between Austria and Russia in January, 1795, in which they agreed to limit Prussia's share, while Austria was to receive additional territorial compensation for her exclusion from the second partition in 1793 as well as for her probable loss of the Netherlands. While the terms were temporarily kept secret, rumors of the agreement reached Prussian ears.

THE CONSTITUTIONAL RÉGIME 303

article, however, it was agreed that should France gain the Prussian left bank at the general peace, suitable territorial compensation for the dispossessed German princes would be found within the empire. The German states north of a line of demarcation along the Rhine and the Main rivers were to be considered neutrals and closed to the movement of troops. In appearance, then, Prussia became the defender of the territorial integrity of the empire, but in secret she was committed to its eventual dismemberment. Doubly to secure immunity from the war Prussia also signed an agreement with Russia and Austria which guaranteed her neutrality on the Rhine. Thus in return for furthering the French in their acquisition of the "natural boundaries," Prussia obtained peace on the western front and freedom of action against Poland. This cautious double-edged policy ultimately led to disaster, but for ten years it preserved northern Germany from the ravages of war and allowed Prussia all the advantages of a neutral state.

Peace with Holland followed. Negotiations dragged for several months, but as soon as the news of the treaty of Basel reached Paris, the Committee of Public Safety sent two of its members, Reubell and Sieyès, both of them strong annexationists, to The Hague with a threat to use force. The country was occupied by French troops and could offer no resistance. The treaty of The Hague was signed on May 16, 1795. Holland ceded Dutch Flanders, Maestricht, and Venloo to France and promised to pay a war indemnity of one hundred million florins to her well-nigh bankrupt conqueror. The Dutch government was to be reorganized and bound by an offensive and defensive alliance with France against England. The navigation of the Rhine, the Scheldt, and the Meuse was to be free to both nations. Bound thus to France, Holland was drawn into the war against England and within a year's time lost most of her colonial possessions, including Ceylon, the Cape of Good Hope, and nearly all her colonies in the West Indies.

A secret convention, duly accepted by the French assembly in March, 1795, ended hostilities with Tuscany, to the great satisfaction of the bankers and traders of Florence and Leghorn. On July 22, 1795, peace was made with Spain. The Spanish monarch recognized the French republic, thus abandoning the cause of the Bourbons, and ceded only the Spanish part of the island of Santo Domingo, which made the island entirely French. In return,

France abandoned her recent conquests in Spain, forbore to impose an indemnity, and made no interference in the customs tariff of her neighbor.

The peace treaties added vastly to the prestige of the republic, but Austria and England, the two most formidable enemies, were still in the field against France. Catherine of Russia gave half-hearted and ineffectual aid to the coalition in the west, reserving her forces for the important business in Poland. Peace with Austria was possible, provided that France renounced her annexation policy along the Rhine and in the Netherlands. The royalists' threat, however, and the renewal of the Anglo-Russian-Austrian pact against France strengthened the Convention in its determination to pursue the policy of the "natural frontiers." In October, 1795, it took the decisive step and voted to annex the Austrian Netherlands to France as an integral part of the republic. At the same time the deputies decided to carry the war against Austria by a simultaneous attack in southern Germany and Italy.[5]

Victories were not won during the remaining days of the Convention. The campaign in southern Germany turned disastrously against the French. For a time the flanking operations of Jourdan, who advanced along the Main, and Moreau, who went down the Danube, were successful, and several states of southern Germany sued for peace. But the Archduke Charles, who commanded the Austrian forces in Germany, profited by the inactivity or the treason of General Pichegru, who failed to support Jourdan's troops. He crushed Jourdan's army and forced it to flee in disorder across the Rhine. Moreau's troops retreated more stubbornly, but by the close of October, the Austrians had crossed the Rhine and recovered part of the left bank from the French. The fighting then ceased until the following spring. The campaign in northern Italy was also ended by an armistice after the failure of the French to invade Piedmont.

England, meanwhile, hoped for peace and waited for definite overtures from France. The summer and autumn of 1795 were

[5] The Convention offered the Austrian emperor compensation in Bavaria for the loss of the Belgian provinces, but he rejected the proposal. Had he accepted the offer, he would have become involved with Prussia, for the latter country would not have permitted Austrian aggrandizement in Germany without compensation for herself. The responsibility for the renewal of the war rests largely with the French annexationists, who had committed the republic to a policy of intervention in the internal affairs of the empire.

difficult for Pitt's government. The finances were exhausted, business conditions bad, food scarce, and political ferment high. The future relations of the two countries lay in the hands of the new government in France.

THE CONSTITUTION OF THE YEAR III

The second phase of the Thermidorian reaction began after that series of events which curtailed the menace of the surviving Jacobins, dashed the hopes of the royalists, and concluded peace between France and four of its enemy states. This phase was marked by an attempt to return to a system of legal order, by the organization of the power of that substantial middle class which wanted neither democratic radicalism nor a Bourbon restoration. The distinctive event of this second period was the drafting, in August, 1795, of the essentially sane and conservative republican Constitution of the Year III, which replaced the stillborn democratic Constitution of 1793.[6]

It had as a preface a declaration of the rights of the citizen which carefully omitted all references to the legitimacy of rebellion as well as all stipulations concerning state assistance to the poor. A corollary declaration of duties more fully revealed the temper of the new document, for it stressed the necessity of safeguarding the rights of private property and respecting law and the established order. However, the confiscation of the estates of the emigrants was declared irrevocable. In respect to the rights of sovereignty the new document bore a marked resemblance to the bourgeois constitution of 1791. Property qualification for the voters and the intermediary electors and indirect elections in two degrees were reaffirmed in the express determination of insuring the supremacy of the middle class and moderating hasty popular action. While these suffrage provisions were certainly not democratic and perhaps not even liberal, they in no sense prevented a slow and gradual democratization of political life.

The legislative power was entrusted to the *Corps législatif*, which was composed of two councils, the Council of Ancients and the Council of Five Hundred. The obvious reason for two legis-

---

[6] The original intention of the constitutional committee had been to revise and modify the Constitution of 1793, but the popular insurrections of Germinal and Prairial induced the committee to drop entirely the "constitution of anarchy" and present a new document instead.

lative bodies instead of one was the desire both to avert the unchecked despotism and the abject servility that at different periods had characterized the Convention. For election to the Five Hundred one had to be thirty years of age or over, and for election to the Ancients (made up of 250 councilors), forty years or more. Under ordinary circumstances the two councils were to sit separately, the Five Hundred initiating and discussing bills and the Ancients adopting or rejecting them. Under exceptional conditions the two councils combined and sat as the Corps législatif. Also, for the first time in the Revolution, the reëlections were to be partial, so that no sudden innovations might be made in policy. No elections were to be held until the spring of 1797; after that they were to be held annually.

The organization of the executive power was entirely different from that prescribed in the Constitution of 1791. There was to be a board chosen by the Ancients from a list of nominees made by the Five Hundred. No one was eligible to the Directory unless he were forty years of age or over, and either a former administrator or a former deputy. After 1797, one of the board, determined by lot, was to retire annually, and his successor was to be chosen by the due process of law. For three months one of the five was to serve as presiding officer, the others following in rotation. This was the closest concession to a real president, who was not wanted because of his disturbing resemblance to a monarch. The directors had no control over legislation nor over financial matters; nor could they be dismissed by the councils. They appointed ambassadors, ministers, commanders of the armed forces, tax officials, and certain minor functionaries and, with the approval of the councils, they could declare war and sign treaties of peace.

The existing administrative divisions of local government were all retained with the exception of the district, which was abolished. The smallest communal administrations were combined into cantonal municipalities of almost uniform size, while the prerogatives of the largest municipalities, like Paris, Lyons, Bordeaux, and Marseilles, were curtailed. Though each local division had its elected councils and executive officers, the Directory at Paris established close surveillance over local affairs by appointing a resident commissioner to each canton and department. The judicial administration prescribed in the Constitution of 1791 was also retained in its essentials, the number of tribunals being somewhat reduced.

On the whole the new constitutional charter established a system of checks and balances, designed to prevent the unrestrained control of the people and the concentration of power in the hands of an individual. The powers of government were strictly divided into the several branches in order to prevent the dictatorship of a single assembly and make possible a legal order. But the different parties in the country did not want legal order; each wanted control of the government. By failing to provide for a peaceful, legal solution of disputes between the executive and the legislative branches of government, the drafters of the new constitution committed their gravest error. When the disputes arose, as they did almost at once, the only solution available was an appeal to force. Thus in spite of all the elaborate precautions the country was foredoomed to further coups, and the reign of law was indefinitely postponed.

Before holding the first elections the deputies voted several supplementary decrees which, like the constitutional document itself, were to be ratified by popular vote. Fearing a royalist victory at the polls—and the fear was not exaggerated, for the Vendeans were up in arms again and the Quiberon expedition had just taken place—the deputies decreed that five hundred members of the Convention, roughly two-thirds (hence the name, the "two-thirds decree") should be selected to serve in the new councils. To keep up the pretense of free election, these old deputies were to be re-elected by the electoral assemblies; but if those precautions failed and the requisite number of deputies was not elected, the Convention itself was to name the rest from its own ranks. The country received these decrees with high disapproval. Just as it was preparing to rid itself of its unpopular representatives, these "perpetuals" (as the deputies were promptly dubbed) made ready to stay indefinitely in power. The plebiscite on the constitution and the supplementary decrees was most illuminating: the constitution was accepted by a large majority, but the opposition to the two-thirds decree was very pronounced, particularly in Paris, where it was overwhelmingly rejected. Thanks to the vote of the army and navy, however, it received sufficient votes to be carried, and late in September, 1795, the Convention declared that both the constitution and supplementary decrees were the law of the land. The elections were set for the 20th of Vendémiaire, year IV (October 12, 1795).

THE INSURGENTS OF VENDÉMIAIRE

All but one section in Paris had rejected the supplementary decrees. The dissatisfied sections were not entirely royalist in sympathy. They were inhabited by men who were thoroughly sick of the Revolution and its worthless currency, its hardships upon legitimate trade, its food shortage and disorders. Their sentiments were exploited by various schemers and royalist journals. These aroused public opinion against the illegal acts of the Convention, smuggled emigrants into the disaffected sections, and organized an insurrectionary committee. In the name of the sovereign people the committee, directed by royalists, brusquely challenged the authority of the national assembly. On the 13th of Vendémiaire (October 5) the insurrectionists marched against the Tuileries, where the Convention was assembled. To meet the 20,000 or 25,000 men that the insurgent sections mustered against it, the Convention had barely 4000 soldiers of the regular army and a small detachment of volunteer patriots. By a strange irony of fate, most of the volunteers were revolutionists who had been imprisoned after the events of Prairial by the very assembly that now released them to defend its existence. Despite the numerical inferiority of the government forces these had two advantages which brought them victory. They had artillery, and they had a commander who knew how to use it. This was the young Corsican, Napoleon Bonaparte, who had been appointed second in command to the titular commander Barras. Bonaparte posted his men and his guns at strategic points about the assembly hall and easily broke the attack of the royalist insurgents. By this famous "whiff of grapeshot" Bonaparte made a name for himself and opened the way to fame and power. His "star" had risen. Several hundred men were killed on either side in the mêlée, but no violent reprisals marred the victory of the Convention.

With the restoration of order the Assembly proceeded with the election of the new councilors and the organization of the new government. The new third was rapidly chosen by free election and showed itself favorable to the reaction. But the nation elected only 379 of the requisite 500 deputies from the Convention, and this body constituted itself into a national electoral assembly in order to nominate the remainder. The councils were then constituted and selected the five executive directors. Before adjourning for the final time the deputies renewed the revolutionary legislation against the emigrants and refractory priests and extended an amnesty to all save these and the plotters of Vendémiaire. It ordered the name of the Place de la Révolution to be changed into Place de la Concorde and then declared its sessions ended, on October 26, 1795. To the government of the Directory its final legacies were vigorous anticlericalism and a financial bankruptcy at home and war with Europe abroad.

THE SALE OF NATIONAL LAND

The history of the three most stirring years of France's existence is incomplete without a brief survey of the more positive achievements of the National Convention. It had saved the republic from the hostile powers of Europe, but it did more. Its various committees made profound changes in the social, educational, legal, and cultural life of the nation. The efforts of Cambon and the finance committee to unravel the financial tangle have been noted. For a brief period during the Terror the value of the assignats was artificially "pegged up" by voluntary loans and capital levies and by the obligatory acceptance of assignats in payment of all transactions. But from January, 1794, the assignats dropped again, at first slowly, and after Thermidor rapidly. Inflation was primarily a consequence of the depreciation of the paper money and only secondarily a cause of that depreciation. The more fundamental causes of the depreciation were loss of popular confidence in the paper money (as evidenced by the decree compelling the acceptance of the assignats), financial errors on the part of the finance committee of the government, disorders within France, the monumental expenses of foreign war, and, lastly, inflation. When the Convention came to an end, the assignat had lost ninety-seven per cent of its face value. The government continued to accept the paper money at its nominal value in collecting taxes, but bankers and financial agents discounted it at its real or market value. This monetary catastrophe ruined many families of the old bourgeoisie and enriched many speculators and adventurers, who gave their support to the government which had made their wealth possible.

The destruction of the feudal régime, which was begun in the Constituent Assembly, by the August 4 decrees and continued under the Legislative Assembly, was consummated under the Convention. After the fall of the Girondins the Mountain, anxious to give its victory more than a political significance, tried to win the support of the peasants by voting the absolute abolition of all feudal rights without indemnification to the owners (July 17, 1793). The decree stipulated that within a period of three months all feudal titles were to be burned publicly in all the municipalities of France. It is likely that the difficulties of redeeming the feudal titles have been exaggerated and that the feudal régime would have disappeared more slowly even without this decree; but on the other hand this radical measure was of undeniable profit to the mass of peasants. It gave them gratis what elsewhere in Europe the peasantry received much later and at a higher price, free and absolute title to their land.[7]

The consequences of the sale of public land were also very significant. During the Convention the estates of the emigrants and of convicted counter-revolutionaries were acquired by the state and placed on sale along with the domains of the clergy. To encourage peasant buyers the Convention (in June and July, 1793) voted to sell the land in small plots and on easy terms payable over a period of ten years. The sales were widespread and continuous, though motives of purest patriotism were not always predominant in the minds of the purchasers. In measure as the real value of the assignat depreciated and particularly after the full collapse of the paper money, the shrewd investor actually paid less and less for the land he purchased. At all times he had the advantage of making deferred payments in constantly depreciating assignats. According to the official statistics for the years of the Convention and the Directory the bourgeoisie profited most by the sales, even though the peasantry bought more rural land. If one considers, however, that much of the land acquired by the bourgeoisie was bought for speculation or on account, occasionally for émigrés and more frequently for the peasantry, it

[7] The division of the common lands, decreed in June, 1793, among the rural population gave small plots to many landless peasants.

seems evident that the permanent purchases of the peasantry were actually greater.

Not all peasants profited alike. In general—and the variations in the different regions are enormous—the revolutionary land settlement did not break with the traditional development of the eighteenth century. It merely accelerated that development. The Revolution did not divide; it freed the land. It is true that it brought into the market the church property and many of the estates of the nobility, but the bulk of these lands passed into the hands of those who already held land. Consequently, no great increase in the number of proprietors took place. Wealthy peasants greatly increased their holdings. A few peasants of moderate-sized farms also made vast additions to their holdings, but the great majority of small landowners only added slightly to their land possessions. Of the former pre-revolutionary landless peasantry many graduated into the ranks of small proprietors, but many more were no richer in land after the Revolution than they had been before. It is true that the class of small peasant proprietors in France was more numerous and more influential than in any other European state, but they and the rural proletariat beneath them in the social scale still had many grievances. They still lacked enough land to support them and their families, and they still were forced to engage in rural industry. What they desired was the legal abolition of share cropping (*métayage*) and the break-up of large estates; but these boons the Revolution did not grant them. In short, the agricultural crisis of France was alleviated but not solved between 1789 and 1795.

LEGAL AND EDUCATIONAL REFORMS

From the very beginning of the Revolution the deputies endeavored to meet one of the most frequently repeated demands of the cahiers, to substitute a single code for the many existing local codes. The various assemblies proceeded slowly. The legislation based upon the principles of canon law and feudal law were abolished by 1793. From 1789 to 1793 the deputies passed new organic laws concerning inheritance, marriage and divorce, rural property, the civil register, and mortgages. The first systematic attempt to draft a complete civil code, based upon the customary law of the country, was made by the legislative committee of the Convention at the very height of the invasion and civil war. This first draft, for which Cambacérès was largely responsible, met the fate of those that succeeded it between 1793 and 1796: it was discussed but not promulgated. However, the systematic and methodical work of the eminent jurisconsults of the legislative committees was not wasted, for it made possible the ultimate successful codification of the civil laws under Napoleon. It is no exaggeration to state that in practice France already had a uniform civil code when the Convention ended its sessions.

The cahiers had also desired the substitution of a uniform system of weights and measures for the confusing and infinite variety that plagued society before 1789. The first two revolutionary assemblies enlisted the services of the Academy of Science, and in 1793 the Convention made ready to introduce the compulsory use of "the new system of weights and measures, based upon the measure of the meridian of the earth and the decimal division" throughout the entire republic. The people were still rooted in their old habits and both unable and unwilling to use the new terms and units of the meter, the gram, the liter, and the franc. With time, however, their objections vanished, and the Convention's introduction of the metric system and the decimal system has since been recognized as one of its greatest positive achievements.

The nationalization of the language, like the nationalization of the civil law and weights and measures, was another essential step in the unification of France. The deputies of the Constituent Assembly hoped that their projected system of primary education in French would gradually eliminate the use of the local dialects and non-French languages, such as Italian, German, and Spanish, that were spoken throughout the land. Otherwise, they reasoned, the new laws and principles of the Revolution would remain closed books to the great majority of the citizens. Yet primary schools were not established, and many peasants were still speaking their local dialects when France was plunged into the Terror and war against the coalition. The solution for the anomaly seemed clear: "The unity of the republic dictates unity of speech," said Bishop Grégoire. Accordingly the Convention decided to use strong methods to extirpate the dialects and the foreign languages. An instructor of French was to be sent to the necessary regions to teach the French language and to expound the Declaration of Rights to the children. On the décadi days he was to read aloud for adult citizens "the laws of the republic, preferably those concerning agriculture and the rights of the people." At the same time the Convention decreed that all public deeds should be written in French and private deeds should not be registered unless in French.

This régime of intellectual coercion was modified later. French did not displace the local patois among the peasantry and in the primary schools. Still, this effort of the Convention to employ educational forms and methods in order to stir up the patriotic sentiments of the people was partly successful in its immediate consequences in 1794. In conjunction with other measures it helped suppress local dissension by utilizing the martial and patriotic ardor of thousands of young Frenchmen. It was unquestionably the first application of a doctrine which all governments subsequently employed in the nineteenth and twentieth centuries, the inculcation of national patriotism through a system of universal elementary education. A second doctrine, extensively utilized and abused by modern governments, the dissemination of nationalistic propaganda, was also effectively applied by the Convention. To combat a return to the older ideals and institutions which the Revolution was destroying, the Convention counted not only upon its armies, but upon the younger generation. It intended to make the young Frenchmen loyal, public-spirited citizens who would defend the patrie and the republic against all internal and foreign foes. Since the citizen was born for the republic, the republic itself would mold him in his formative years to love and cherish his patrie. Hence its organization of public games and national festivals which would generate sentiments of fraternity and patriotism by allowing the citizens to share in national activities. During the Directory these public ceremonies, organized by the foremost artists and musicians of the state, played an important part in the revolutionary and republican education of the people.

The Convention's definitive decree on the organization of a public-school system was not passed until October 25, 1795, the day before that assembly was dissolved; but it had long struggled with the problems of primary and secondary education which were a legacy from the Old Régime. During the Constituent Assembly, Talleyrand prepared a comprehensive plan, and the principle of free elementary education was inserted in the Constitution of 1791. Condorcet, the leading member of the committee of public instruction of the Legislative Assembly, presented another, more famous report, on April 20, 1792, which, though tabled, served later as the actual basis of reform. In the words of his latest biographer, J. Salwyn Schapiro, "Condorcet . . . clearly realized the importance of popular education as an instrument of national power and as a means of safeguarding progress and of advancing social equality. His report is a landmark in the history of education." In the meantime the existing system was thoroughly disorganized in consequence of the Constituent Assembly's ecclesiastical measures and its destruction of corporate teaching bodies. During the period of the Mountain's control, the Convention decided that primary education should be free and attendance compulsory. The final law abandoned this principle of free instruction and obligatory attendance. It provided for a limited number of primary schools, but also made provision for home and private instruction. Competent teachers, however, were few, the salaries provided by the state pathetically small, and the opposition in royalist and Catholic regions to the republican "godless" schools pronounced. Consequently the public primary schools did not prosper, whereas private schools were more flourishing.

The same law of October 25, 1795, established secondary schools, the "central schools" which were to teach languages, drawing, and natural history in the first and second year, sciences in the third and fourth, and literature, grammar, history, and law in the fifth and sixth years. There was one "central school" in each department but five at Paris. These schools encountered many difficulties at first, but the teachers were of exceptional ability, and the establishments made great progress during the Directory and the Consulate up to 1802, when they were summarily suppressed by Napoleon. On the other hand, the private secondary schools, dominated by the church, were also very prosperous.

The Convention was most successful in its organization of higher education. Only two war-time establishments, the École de Mars, which was a revolutionary military academy, and the École Normale, a training school, ended with the Revolution. Other scientific schools were permanent. The School of Public Works (later called the Polytechnic School) was established in 1794 to train civil and military engineers. To keep intact France's close contacts with the East, a school of oriental languages was founded. In 1793 the Jardin du roi was reorganized and enlarged into the Museum of Natural History. Its collection was enriched, and France's most distinguished scientists were given subsidies to carry on their researches in its laboratories. Subsequently public lectures were given gratis by these savants. A National Conservatory of Arts and Industries was organized as "a museum and a school for industry." Three schools of medicine, giving theoretical and practical instruction to students who were chosen on a competitive basis, were founded in 1794. These special schools as well as the service of the state absorbed the energy of the country's scientists and artists. To replace permanently the abolished universities and the academies of the Old Régime, the Convention created the National Institute (also on October 25, 1795), which was to attest the unity and the solidarity of human knowledge. It was divided into three classes: physical and mathematical sciences, moral and political sciences, literature and the fine arts. More than one hundred members resident at Paris, France's most distinguished savants, were summoned by the government to make the Institute "the representative body of the republic of letters."

It is unfortunately true that many irresponsible individuals and revolutionary mobs indulged in wild and wanton destruction. Private residences, churches, and rich abbeys were sacked, and their artistic treasures stolen or destroyed. All the assemblies warred upon vandalism. Both the Constituent Assembly and the Convention appointed commissions to protect the artistic treasures of the country. Severe laws were passed and executed against pillagers. The deputies, who represented the cultural élite of France, frequently recognized their obligations to safeguard the artistic treasures of the past as well as to minister to the cultural needs of the new France. The Royal Library was reorganized as the National Library, and its rich collection still further enriched by books from private and monastic collections. The National Archives were established with a precious collection of books, manuscripts, and documents from France's past. The Louvre Museum, today one of the world's greatest collections of art treasures, was established to house the royal collection of paintings and thrown open to the public. A central museum of sculpture, also open to the public, was founded on the site of a former convent.

To elaborate upon individual achievements in the arts, literature, philosophy, and science during the period of the Convention lies outside the scope of this volume. The mere mention of such names as Lavoisier, Laplace, Lamarck, Cabanis, Madame de Staël, André Chénier, Condorcet, David, Grétry, and Gossec is an indication sufficiently eloquent that France's cultural life was far from stagnant even during the Terror. It is impossible even to evaluate the release of new intellectual energy and the liberation of men's thoughts from the thralldom of past customs and beliefs. When one considers that France was continuously at war from 1792 to 1795, that there was civil war, dictatorship, food shortage, and an economic and political crisis, the Convention's achievements appear stupendous. Not the least of its services, it saved France from its enemies.

These accomplishments are seen in retrospect, in the perspective of time. The immediate gifts of the Convention to the government of the Directory were war and bankruptcy.

XIII. THE EXECUTIVE DIRECTORY AND THE RISE OF NAPOLEON BONAPARTE

THE PROGRAM OF THE DIRECTORS

THE new constitutional government of the executive Directory and the two legislative councils took office on October 27, 1795. No elections were to be held, no replacement of directors to be made until the spring of 1797. Thus the government had eighteen months to liquidate the Revolution and the war, eighteen months in which to return to normality after six years of turmoil and profound agitation, immense labor and ruthless demolition.

The France of 1795 was far removed in spirit from the France of July 14, 1789, when generous enthusiasms ran high, convictions were deep, and public morality exercised a firm sway over private individuals. It was equally remote in spirit from the France of the Terror, when a fanatical sect imposed its faith and its rule upon the population, binding the people by their hopes and their fears to the government of equality and virtue. France in 1795 was tired and worn out. The revolutionary fever had exhausted it. People wanted rest and order after the hurly-burly and the privations of revolution and war. Their enthusiasm had given place to disillusion. Their long and painful sacrifices for the common good, for liberty, equality, and fraternity, made them all the more anxious to reap, if not advantages, at least security for their personal interests. To the play of party passions and the call of political doctrines they were now indifferent, when aware of them at all. Many were anxious to rear their children in the ancient faith of Catholicism which was vigorously regaining its hold over the country. They demanded the protection of the government against the "brigands," that is, the motley bands of deserters, unemployed, dismissed officials, vagrants, and criminals who, under the leadership of men hostile to the government, were terrorizing the country. They wanted an end of emergency political and economic measures. The city workers wanted steady employment, a living wage, and above all food and shelter. The business interests wanted peace, some only with the Continent in order to market their manufactured products, others with England as well as with Europe in order to share in foreign trade and financial transactions.

The five directors and the deputies worked with zeal and courage, if not always with great wisdom, to satisfy the demands of the country. The majority in the councils (the five hundred former deputies of the Convention who had been elected in consequence of the two-thirds decree) were on the whole tried revolutionists of moderate views, though there were many radicals and some secret royalists among them. Many of them were "regicides" who had voted the death of Louis XVI. They had served the Revolution for many years and were anxious to remain in public life, which sheltered them against the rancor of individual vengeance and the menace of a Bourbon restoration. They were haunted, however, by the strong conviction that they would not be reëlected. Consequently they succeeded through a political artifice in having selected as directors five men of opinions similar to their own, on whose protection they thought they could count.

Of these five directors (Barras, Reubell, La Révellière, Le Tourneur, and Carnot), only the first did not come from the revolutionary bourgeoisie. All with the exception of the Alsatian lawyer Reubell had voted for the death of the king. Excepting Barras, the only ex-noble among them, they were hard-working and honest and sincere in their revolutionary convictions. Barras was indolent and fond of pleasure, surrounding himself with all that was disreputable of the Old Régime and the Revolution. He was a clever schemer, constantly involved in political and financial intrigue, and thoroughly dishonest. Carnot, who took over the war office, was high-minded and courageous, though too inflexible for a position which required much political versatility. Le Tourneur and La Révellière were eclipsed by the imperious Reubell, whose energy and forcefulness made him the leading member of the board. In the beginning the executive heads collaborated with the "two-thirds" in the councils, but within a year they fell out over the solution of the many national problems.

A manifesto issued by the directors shortly after they assumed office outlined their domestic program. Their first concern was with the restoration of political stability, "to wage active war upon royalism, stimulate patriotism, vigorously to crush all factions, extinguish partisan feelings and all desires for vengeance, to make concord reign." This was an opportunist and conservative program, a policy of republican concentration. Profiting by the temporary cessation of the war in Italy and along the Rhine the Directory turned its first efforts against the royalists. The greatest menace came from the Vendée, where defeats had not extinguished the hopes of the rebels. General Hoche, whom the government sent to end the disturbances, did his work speedily and well. Having pacified the Vendée, in the spring of 1796 Hoche led his troops against the Chouans in Brittany; and within a few months he gained full control of the situation. While Hoche was bringing the civil war in the west to a close, a new peril was rising in the capital, the conspiracy of the radical malcontents of Paris to overthrow the government.

THE INTERNAL POLICY OF THE DIRECTORY

The malcontents had been meeting in a former convent near the Pantheon at a club which the government had founded for its own purposes, and among whose members were many secret government agents. Two other groups soon swelled the membership of the Pantheon Club. One of these groups consisted of former radical Jacobin deputies of the Convention who had personal grievances against the members of the administration. The second group consisted of "Gracchus" Babeuf and his handful of nondescript followers who for reasons peculiar to themselves gave him their support. Babeuf, a petty official before 1789 and a revolutionary journalist since, had gradually evolved a crude communistic philosophy in the course of a checkered career in prison and out. In his journal, *Le Tribun du peuple,* he began to preach his ill digested, makeshift creed of the community of goods and the abolition of private ownership. Tracked by the government's agents and deserted by his confreres in the radical press, Babeuf and his associates of the "Society of Equals" also drifted into the Pantheon Club. By the beginning of the year 1796 the number of club members and adherents outside of the club ran well into the thousands.

The government closed this "den of anarchists," but since it did not remove their grievances the Pantheonists continued their opposition, secretly and underground. In the spring of 1796 they completed their plans for an insurrection, concentrating their propaganda in the small cafés of the workingmen and among the garrison troops. Babeuf, almost single-handed, planned a communist régime; the others of the secret insurrectionary committee looked forward to a democratic dictatorship and back to the Constitution of 1793. A traitor revealed their plot to Carnot, and the directors swooped down upon their leaders. The conspirators were arrested in May and held for a year before coming to trial. In the interval between their arrest and their trial there occurred what seems suspiciously like a police "frame-up" against the Parisian radicals, which gave the government the necessary pretext to break up the solidarity of the radical opposition. In this atmosphere of official terrorism the first elections under the new government were held in the spring of 1797 and the arrested conspirators (the Babouvists) were brought to trial. Babeuf and one accomplice were guillotined, and several others deported. These proceedings temporarily brought the Directory a measure of security against the radicals, but they only increased the danger from the side of the conservative opposition.

Another of the problems which the Directory was called upon to solve was that of reorganizing the religious and moral foundations of society. The libertinage of social life during this period has often been portrayed and frequently exaggerated. That in the reaction to the Spartan simplicity and the involuntary sacrifices of the Terror there should have been a sharp revival of the forbidden joys of private life is a phenomenon understandable by the student of human nature. The return of salon life, of theatricals, dancing, and gambling, and fastidiousness in food, speech, and costume was not unnatural to those who had money for such pleasures. What was unnatural was the coarseness of taste, the vulgarity of tone, and the flagrant immorality which the parvenus contrived to give to their amusements. They revived the salon life of the Old Régime, but they revived only its worst features and almost none of the ineffable charm and distinction which made eighteenth century salon life a rare moment in the history of refined society. Most of the revelers were war profiteers and their sycophants, who were unaccustomed to the refined pleasures which wealth could procure, who surpassed themselves in cheap and ostentatious display of their fortunes. A neurotic spirit was abroad, a post-war madness driving these people to all sorts of excesses which denied the humdrum virtues of morality, sobriety, economy, and plain living. But their number was slight if their deeds were loud and malodorous. The mass of people had neither the money, nor the leisure, nor the desire to emulate the exploits of worldly society.

For the benefit of the masses the government sought to give new vigor to the fêtes and rites of the civic religion, to infuse the philosophic and abstract patriotic cult with an emotional vitality which could check the alarming revival of Catholicism. But the government was miserably poor and lacked the resources necessary to give an artificial prop to a decaying faith. An independent venture sponsored by intellectuals who had much in common with present-day ethical culturists, a deistic religion named theophilanthropy, also failed to take root among the masses. Catholicism continued its rapid recovery.

The last of the great problems which the Directory had to meet was that of restoring financial and economic stability. When the government entered upon its functions, the treasury was empty, and money was lacking for the barest needs of the administration and the troops. National property was still being sold, but for assignats. The returns from taxation were far from sufficient for the needs. A compulsory loan was decreed, a relic of revolutionary procedures, but it was adopted half-heartedly, executed still more feebly, and in the end it failed utterly. Between thirty-five and forty billion francs in assignats were in circulation, which had to be retired in part or in whole before relief could be found. Early in 1796, the printing plates of the assignats were destroyed, and in March the first partial repudiation of the paper currency was effected. The assignat was stabilized at slightly more than three per cent and replaced by a new paper currency, *mandats territoriaux*, which were to be accepted in payment for public land. This operation retired less than half of the assignats, while the new paper currency also steadily depreciated until it fell to one per cent of its face value. In February, 1797, the régime of paper money came to an end when the Directory suppressed the enforced acceptance both of assignats and of mandats in private transactions and made obligatory the payment of taxes in specie. Nearly forty billions of francs in paper were thus repudiated, but the greatest benefit of this repudiation fell to the speculators who had hastily bought national land at grotesquely small prices.

In the fall of the same year the Directory extended its venture in national bankruptcy. In a desperate effort to stabilize the budget it sharply curtailed expenditures and reorganized the service of the internal debt. Two-thirds of the debt, amounting to 177,000,-000 francs, was reimbursed to security holders in territorial bonds, and the remaining one-third, amounting to 83,000,000, was inscribed on the government register as three per cent bonds on which the government was to pay the interest annually. Officially this operation was called the "consolidated third," actually, it was the expunging of two-thirds of the internal debt, for the territorial bonds speedily lost their credit and fell to one-half per cent of their face value.[1] The obligations of the state were decreased, but the measure cost it the support of the holders of government bonds and inflicted a severe shock upon public credit.

Public revenues were low, for the economic situation of the country was still chaotic after the vicissitudes of government regulations during the Terror. The Directory failed to adopt a clear-cut policy which would satisfy either the merchants and financiers who clamored for a return to free trade and *laissez faire* or the manufacturers who wanted high tariffs, government subventions, and tax exemptions. Moreover, the economic policy of the government was dependent upon as well as a determinant of its foreign relations, at least until the genius of Napoleon Bonaparte willed it otherwise.

The Foreign Policy and Napoleon Bonaparte

The object of the Directory was to end the war and guarantee the security of France. Prussia, Spain, Holland, and Tuscany had already signed peace treaties with the republic. The north German states had been neutral, and the south German states were ready to desert the coalition at the first advance of the French beyond the Rhine. In Italy, Venice, and Genoa had been neutral from the commencement of hostilities, and the lesser states were only of doubtful assistance to the allies of the coalition. England had just arranged a new alliance among the enemies of France, but her own situation was such that Pitt did not hesitate to listen to offers of peace. Of the other two states of the coalition Austria relied upon the assistance of Russian troops for the fighting in the west, but Russia saved her forces for her affairs in Poland.

---

[1] In 1801 the consulate government called them in at a fraction of their value.

The military situation of France was not brilliant in this autumn of 1795. The Rhine frontier was open, the Army of Italy was on the defensive, and the French and Dutch coasts were exposed to the English Atlantic fleet. Two things the French government was determined not to do—to make a peace which would restrict France to the old royal boundaries, and to conduct a war of revolutionary propaganda. The positive alternatives were not clear, but the recent annexation of Belgium greatly strengthened the position of those who favored a peace upon the basis of France's "natural frontier" of the Rhine.

This policy would necessitate compensation for Prussia within the empire with a consequent diminution of Austrian prestige. Hence Austria continued the war, confident that the expected assistance of the Russians would bring her victory in the spring of 1796. Had the English bid for peace with France succeeded in March, 1796, hostilities would not have been resumed; but the British foreign office could not make a peace which would leave Belgium and Antwerp in French hands. Though for a long time the war had been profitable to the English oligarchy, the peace treaties of 1795 which broke up the coalition against France had also brought distress to England. Her war manufactures fell off sharply, many of her continental markets were closed, and the financial investments of English bankers brought dwindling returns. A partial failure of the grain crop added to the difficulties which brought on the familiar and disheartening symptoms of economic depression—falling prices, unemployment, privations, and bitter criticism of the government. Meanwhile, in 1794, England negotiated the Jay Treaty with the United States, which closed the Atlantic to French trade and released the British patrol fleet for active duty.[2] Under these circumstances the French plan of action was clear. Naval operations were restricted to retaliatory commercial decrees against British and American shipping, and a concerted effort would be made, with the assistance of the Spanish fleet, to defeat the English in the Mediterranean. The major operations were to be on the Continent: (1) against Austria in Germany and Italy, and (2) against English shipping on the North Sea. Such was the French plan of campaign for 1796, a plan which

[2] The Senate did not ratify the Jay Treaty until 1795, and the House did not vote appropriations until 1796, so that the execution of its terms was delayed for two years.

Bonaparte's military genius and political ambition were to alter. Napoleon Bonaparte was then only approaching his twenty-seventh birthday. He was born at Ajaccio in Corsica in 1769, a year after France acquired the island from Genoa. His family belonged to the impoverished patriotic Corsican nobility, and the youthful Bonaparte dreamed romantically of leading his people to a reconquest of their independence. Thanks to his father's belated conversion to a pro-French attitude, the slenderness of the family purse was overcome and a friend was found to have the boy educated at state expense at various military schools in France. There the influences of his Corsican heredity and the dominant characteristics of his own personality manifested themselves. An alien in a foreign and a hated land, he was driven inwards on himself. He became taciturn and meditative, an omnivorous reader and a diligent student particularly of history and geography. In 1785, when he was only sixteen years of age, he was appointed second lieutenant of artillery; but his prospects of advancement were slight, and his sentiments toward France were still far from the friendliest. He plunged all the deeper into study and meditation, thus compensating himself unconsciously for the dreary future before him, but preparing himself also, somewhat more consciously, for the great military career which ambition outlined for him.

The Revolution dramatically changed his prospects. Although he became a first lieutenant in 1789, he still remained a Corsican patriot at heart. For several years he divided his activities between his duties as an officer in the French army and his career as a Corsican agitator. On August 10, 1792, at Paris, he had his first experience with a revolutionary mob, an experience which left him with an unconquerable aversion for demagogues and their radical followers. In 1793 a final dispute with Paoli, the venerable patriotic leader of the Corsicans, forced Bonaparte and his entire family to flee their native island. He renounced his earlier projects, identified himself with his adopted country, and became an ardent patriot and Jacobin. At the height of the civil war between the Girondins and the Montagnards, he took sides with the latter and the government and wrote a dialogue, *Le Souper de Beaucaire*, that was intended to bare the folly of the Girondin position. A grateful government saw to it that his pamphlet was reprinted and widely distributed at public expense. Toward the end of 1793 he took a distinguished part in recapturing Toulon from the royalists and the English. As a reward the government promoted the young officer, then a captain of artillery, to brigadier general. At Toulon he gained the friendship of the younger Robespierre, who was serving as a deputy on mission from the Convention, and the attention of Barras. He was sent to Genoa, ostensibly on an official mission, but in reality to acquaint himself with the terrain of that region, for even then he was harboring his grandiose vision of conquering northern Italy.

For the next two years his fortunes varied. The fall of Robespierre compromised his position, but after his temporary arrest on the suspicion of being a Robespierrist, he was released and later assigned to command an infantry brigade in the Army of the West, which was under the supreme command of Hoche. He refused to go, disgruntled that he, an artillery leader, should be asked to command an infantry brigade under Hoche; besides, his heart was set on the Italian command. During the better part of 1795 he tasted the bitterness of virtual oblivion, working in the topographical division of the Committee of Public Safety and frequenting the salons of the Thermidorians. His name was struck off the army list, and his request to be sent to Turkey to reorganize the sultan's artillery was denied. But a fortunate accident, the Vendémiaire uprising in Paris, recouped his fortunes and he was at once appointed commander-in-chief of the Army of the Interior. In March, 1796, he obtained his heart's dream, the command of the Army of Italy.

THE FIRST ITALIAN CAMPAIGN (1796-1797)

The plan of operations assigned only a lesser rôle to the Army of Italy. The major part of the military movements devolved upon the two French armies along the Rhine commanded by Jourdan and Moreau, which were to converge upon Vienna by different routes, the former along the Main River and the latter along the Danube. The military campaign in Italy, according to Carnot's original intentions, was only to supplement the main operations in Germany. The goal of all the military efforts was the capture of Vienna, which would induce Austria to withdraw, and the conclusion of a final peace with Prussia that would give France the Rhine frontier. Such conquests as would be made in northern Italy would be utilized to compensate Austria for the loss of her Belgian provinces that France would retain in the final peace with the empire. But Austria did not break off the armistice on the Rhine until well in the spring and by that time Bonaparte had, by his victories, completely altered the nature and scope of the campaign in Italy.

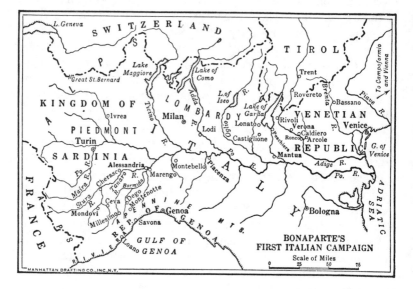

BONAPARTE'S FIRST ITALIAN CAMPAIGN
Scale of Miles

The short, emaciated young general assumed command of his troops at his headquarters near Genoa in April. The veteran commanders, such as Augereau and Masséna, who were to serve as his subordinates, were at first inclined to challenge his authority, but their first encounter with "General Vendémiaire" changed their grumbling into respect. To the miserably clad, unpaid, inactive, and half-famished soldiers Bonaparte addressed the first of his stirring proclamations, as we have it in a later version:

Soldiers! You are naked and hungry. The government owes you much, but can give you nothing. Your patience and your courage are admirable; but they can win you neither glory nor prestige. I will lead you to the most fertile plains in the world. Rich provinces and great cities will be in your power; there you will find honor, glory, and riches! Soldiers of Italy! Will you lack courage or constancy?

The soldiers responded enthusiastically, dazzled by his promises and electrified by his vibrant power.

In less than three weeks he accomplished the first part of his campaign plans and fulfilled his promises to his men. From the Riviera they struck north into the passes of the Apennines, cut the connections of the Austrian and the Sardinian troops and defeated each in turn. The Austrians were driven toward Alessandria down the valley of the Bormida toward Mantua and the fortresses of the Quadrilateral, and the Sardinians beyond the Po River toward Turin. An armistice, granted to the king of Sardinia, gave Bonaparte control of the military roads from Piedmont to the neighboring plains of Lombardy across which the Austrians were driven by his lightninglike thrusts. In the middle of May he made a triumphal entry into Milan, the Lombard capital, and the retreating Austrians shut themselves up in the great fortress of Mantua, which blocked his further advance to the Tirol in the north and Trieste in the east.

Peace with Sardinia was made shortly after the armistice. Sardinia formally recognized France's earlier annexation of Nice and Savoy, agreed to pay a heavy war indemnity, demolished three and turned over eight other fortresses to the French. The lesser Italian princes also hastened to make peace with the conqueror, who levied heavy war indemnities upon them all—the dukes of Parma and of Modena, the king of Naples, and the pope. More than sixty million francs in currency, the treasures of libraries, museums, and galleries, and the English goods in the harbors of Naples and of Leghorn in neutral Tuscany were the official price that northern Italy paid for its liberation from the Austrians. Unofficially, though not less effectively, subordinate generals extorted and soldiers pillaged and plundered.

In this conduct Bonaparte was not exceeding his instruction from the bankrupt Directory. But his ultimate plans for Italy were by far loftier than the Directory's prosaic scheme of exchanging Lombardy for Belgium. In the intervals between the fighting he addressed appeals to the national sentiments of the Italians, summoning them to revolutionary independence and national unity. His appeals were disingenuous, but his policy demanded a state closely allied with France and guaranteeing France's control of the Mediterranean, and affording him a point of departure for certain eastern ventures that troubled his repose.[3] Assuredly this "Italian system" of Bonaparte upset the calculations of the Directory, but could it dare oppose so useful a general! He protected local uprisings, raised legions of Italian volunteers and, in December, 1796, without official instructions, granted recognition to the union of Reggio, Modena, Bologna, and Ferrara in the Cispadane Republic of Lombardy.

The second phase of the Italian campaign opened with the siege of the Austrians in the citadel of Mantua, which held out longer than seven months and blocked Bonaparte's advance toward Vienna. Twice the Austrians under Würmser advanced from the river valleys of the eastern Lombard plain to aid their besieged countrymen, and twice they failed in the course of the summer. In the fall 50,000 victorious Austrian troops came down the Adige from Germany, where they had pushed back the French generals to the Rhine, but at Arcola Bonaparte stopped their advance. Their final repulse by Bonaparte and Masséna at Rivoli on January 14, 1797, sealed the fate of Mantua. On February 2 the French flags were flying over the city. The immediate aftermath was the signing of a definitive peace treaty with the pope. By the treaty of Tolentino, February 19, 1797, Pius VI paid dearly for his rupture of an earlier armistice. He recognized the French annexations of Avignon and the Comtat-Venaissin, agreed to an additional indemnity of fifteen million francs, and ceded Ancona and the legations of Bologna, Ferrara, and the Romagna. Rome was saved for the papacy, but France gained control of the Adriatic and an opportunity to take part in questions relating to the Balkan states of the Turkish Empire.

In the meantime the course of events had forced the English government during the autumn to renew peace negotiations; but like the earlier negotiations, these broke down. Before they came to a close, a French expeditionary force under Hoche attempted to carry the war directly to the British Isles by setting sail for Ireland. The venture miscarried for want of good weather and expert seamanship, and the French troops never made a landing, to the deep disappointment of the expectant Irish insurgents. Hoche,

---

[3] In the summer of 1796 France negotiated a naval and commercial pact with Spain. The menace of the combined French, Spanish, and Dutch fleets was sufficient to force the English fleet to raise the siege of Cadiz, abandon Corsica, and put in at Gibraltar.

however, made good his return to France and was appointed
Jourdan's successor as commander-in-chief of one of the armies
operating along the Rhine. The failure of the Irish expedition
confirmed the decision of the Directory to wage its war against
England on the Continent with armies and with commercial decrees against British merchandise.

In the spring of 1797 the simultaneous advance of the French
in Italy and in Germany was resumed. Bonaparte pushed his way
from Mantua through Carinthia and Styria and was less than a
hundred miles from Vienna when he offered an armistice to the
enemy. Hoche and Moreau were advancing too rapidly into Germany, and Bonaparte was anxious to conclude peace with Austria
single-handed, without sharing his honors with rival generals. On
April 18, 1797, acting alone and against the deepest wishes of
the Directory, he signed the preliminaries of Leoben with the
Austrian plenipotentiaries. The open provisions of this preliminary
peace gave to France Lombardy and Belgium, which were hers
already by conquest, and to Austria, Istria and Dalmatia, which
she did not have. In the secret provisions Austria was promised
compensations at the expense of Venice. In order to maintain his
"Italian system" and save Lombardy from Austria, Bonaparte was
silent concerning the left bank of the Rhine, generous with Venetian territory upon which he had neither claim nor hold, and
respectful of Austrian supremacy within the empire. Though faced
with the repudiation of its entire policy of the Rhine boundary
for France, the directors ratified the terms, being unable for reasons of internal politics in France to do otherwise.

THE COUP OF FRUCTIDOR

The conservative opposition to the Directory slowly gathered
force after the Babouvist plot was suppressed, for there was wide
dissatisfaction throughout the country and in the councils with
the Directory's domestic policies and its measures concerning the
war. Various interests sought to take advantage of the discontent.
Several influential deputies of the minority group in the two councils formed a habit of meeting more or less regularly at a private
home in the rue de Clichy, where they elaborated plans for winning the coming elections and strengthening the prerogative of
the councils against the executive Directory. Most of them were

sincere in their professed adherence to the constitution and at first had no intention of acting otherwise than through legal means. They wanted to abrogate the existing laws against émigrés and deported priests, a program which they pressed very vigorously and with marked success. A small minority of these *Clichiens*, however, collaborated with royalist plotters who also sought to win the election of 1797. These formed local election committees throughout the country, "Friends of Order," in which the émigrés and deported priests who were coming back in thousands gained control. This electoral campaign, backed by an active royalist press and English subsidies, scored a clean triumph at the polls in the spring of 1797 over the Conventionals in the councils. Out of 216 former members of the Convention who stood for reëlection only 13 were reëlected, and their successors were all either partisans of a monarchy or lukewarm revolutionists totally out of sympathy with the course of events since 1791. Thus the members of the new two-thirds majority in the councils were solidly antiradical and antidemocrat, though divided in their views on the restoration of a monarchy.

With General Pichegru as the presiding officer of the Council of Five Hundred and Barthélemy, another secret royalist, in the Directory (in place of Le Tourneur, who retired according to law), the royalist campaign made rapid headway. But the plotters, encouraged by the illegal reëntry into the country of many thousand émigrés, overreached themselves and lost the support of their more moderate followers. Opposed to these schemers were three directors (Reubell, La Révellière, and Barras) who had the support of the loyal revolutionists in the Constitutional Club as well as of the government troops. Carnot, the fifth of the directors, supported by several conciliatory deputies, attempted to heal the breach, but his effort failed. Under the circumstances an appeal to force was in order.

The three directors appealed to Bonaparte, who needed no urging, for a royalist restoration would disavow and end his Italian diplomacy. He threatened to march his men over the Alps, and he sent hot notes to the government protesting against the personal attacks that were being made upon him. When the directors appointed his emissary, the blustering General Augereau, to command the National Guard of Paris, and these 30,000 men fixed their camp on the outskirts of Paris, standing ready to act at an order from their commander, the explosive atmosphere needed only a spark. This was supplied by the secret decision of the councilors to arrest and impeach the three directors and proclaim martial law.

The latter acted first. They ordered the barriers of the city closed, called in the troops; and at dawn on the 18th of Fructidor (September 4, 1797) Augereau and his men invested the assembly hall in the Tuileries. When the populace awoke, it found the city placarded with the news of the discovery of a royalist conspiracy. The rump of the councils was convoked and proceeded to make the government safe for democracy. The election of almost 200 councilors was nullified, and more than fifty individuals, including Barthélemy and Carnot, were condemned to deportation. In their place in the Directory the councils named two staunch revolutionists, Merlin de Douai and François de Neufchâteau. The legislation against émigrés and the refractory clergy was renewed, and the liberty of the press was suspended for one year. Arrest warrants were issued against citizens who had returned illegally, and many of them were condemned to the guillotine by local military boards.

Royalist hopes were annihilated by the coup of Fructidor. The royalist party was broken up not only in Paris but throughout the country wherever it had established itself. The Directory had triumphed, but with the aid of the troops. It had destroyed the legal government and reëstablished a revolutionary dictatorship, but its power rested upon the support of the armies. Would it now succeed in holding the ambitious generals in check? Could it oppose the will of Bonaparte?

THE TREATY OF CAMPO FORMIO

Bonaparte had established himself at Montebello, near Milan, where all summer long he carried on the final negotiations with the Austrians and continued his reorganization of Italy. Out of the heart of Lombardy he created the Cisalpine Republic, whose constitution he dictated, and whose first officials he named. He had no illusions on the score of Italian capacity for self-government; but he consciously appealed to the most progressive Lombards and kindled their hopes of Italian unity, because he needed their manpower, their material resources, and their strategic location for the furtherance of his own plans. The short-lived Cispadane Republic disappeared, its territory and seaport south of Genoa being incorporated into the Cisalpine Republic. The ancient republic of Genoa was abolished, and the new Ligurian Republic, protected by a French garrison, took its place. The mainland of the Venetian Republic had been promised to Austria at Leoben, and Bonaparte found a pretext to treat the Venetian government as an enemy. Threatened with invasion, the government abdicated, and with the new administration Bonaparte signed a treaty which placed his men in control of the city of Venice and netted the Directory additional spoils.

Negotiations with the Austrians dragged, for the latter expected much from the new conservative majority in the councils. Fructidor dashed their hopes and greatly strengthened Bonaparte's hand. He was desperately anxious for peace, for he needed peace on the Continent in order to complete his reorganization of Italy and to embark upon that venture to the east with which his correspondence to Talleyrand was full. Venetia on the mainland he would concede to Austria, but not the Venetian islands of the Levant, for his eyes were fastened upon the sea. From the pope he had obtained Ancona on the Adriatic, and he now occupied the Ionian Islands and planned to seize Malta. But he knew that unless he obtained the left bank of the Rhine for France the Directory would never ratify his peace. This the Austrian envoy Cobenzl also knew. So he drove as hard a bargain with Bonaparte as was possible under the circumstances. The final terms were incorporated in the treaty of Campo Formio (October 27, 1797).

Austria recognized the French annexation of the Belgian provinces. She agreed (in secret articles) to cede approximately two-thirds of the imperial territory on the left bank of the Rhine to France, from the Swiss frontier down the river to the confluence of the Main with the Rhine, provided that this cession were ratified at an imperial congress to be held at Rastatt. The German princes thus dispossessed from their territory were to receive compensation elsewhere within the empire. Moreover, it was agreed that, if France should obtain any additional territory in Germany at the final peace with the empire, Austria was to obtain an equivalent amount. Prussia, however (this too in a secret article), was not to share in the dismemberment of the Holy Roman Empire, as had been stipulated in the treaty of Basel in 1795, for Prussian territory on the left bank was to be restored to her by France. In

Italy, for her loss of Lombardy, Austria received Istria and Dalmatia and the Venetian mainland, including Venice itself, as far as the Adige River (instead of the Oglio, as provided at Leoben). The rest of Lombardy was added to the Cisalpine Republic, whose existence Austria formally recognized. The Ionian Islands including Corfu, Zante, and Cephalonia, which Bonaparte was so anxious to gain, went to France. The duchy of Modena also went to round out the Cisalpine Republic, and the duke obtained the Austrian territory of Breisgau in exchange. Austria's compensation for the loss of Breisgau was to be the rich bishopric of Salzburg and some Bavarian territory between the city of Salzburg and the mountains of the Tirol.

Such were the main provisions of the treaty of Campo Formio which the French government was asked to ratify. The most serious objections to it from the French side were: (1) the affront to nationalist sentiments in the concessions concerning the Rhine frontier; (2) the possibility that the violation of the treaty of Basel might embroil France with Prussia; (3) the probability that France would become involved in a new war with Austria over Napoleon's Italian policy. The advantages to France, however, more than outweighed the disadvantages. In the first place, the treaty broke the hold of Austria over northern Italy, the arrangements concerning Venetia notwithstanding, for Venetia was at the mercy of the French. Secondly, this treaty, together with the treaty of Basel, made Austria's position in Germany precarious, for it laid the foundation for the secularization of ecclesiastical territory and the absorption of the small states in southern and western Germany; and it was precisely upon the ecclesiastical rulers and the princes of the small states that Austria's position in the Holy Roman Empire rested. Thirdly, the treaty was the decisive step in a policy which, within a few years, gave France not only the Rhine boundary, but the dominant position in Germany and Italy. Sieyès spoke wisely when he said, "This treaty is not peace; it is a call to a new war." It was an imperialistic peace, and a sorry end to the revolutionary crusade begun in 1792 to bring the blessings of liberty and equality to France's neighbors.

The Directory and the councils were forced to ratify the treaty, for the entire nation enthusiastically welcomed the news of peace. The secret terms were not known, and the momentous significance of the treaty was not generally realized. Bonaparte had conquered in peace as he had in war, and the government appointed him commander-in-chief of the Army of England to carry on the war against the islanders. For a short time during that summer of 1797 peace between England and France seemed possible, but the negotiations finally collapsed. Now only the two great rivals, England and France, still remained in the field.

THE EGYPTIAN EXPEDITION

The conqueror of Italy returned to Paris by way of Rastatt, where the imperial congress of German states was assembled.[4] He stayed long enough to arrange the exchange of Mainz for Venice and proceeded to Paris in December, 1797. There the wild applause of the populace, the obsequious flattery of the press, and the constrained congratulations of the Directory welcomed him. Honors were accorded him such as no general ever before had received from the republic. Though he bore himself with studied simplicity, his independence and ambition revealed themselves, as on that public occasion when he permitted himself to criticize the existing constitution. His popularity was too disquieting and his very presence in the capital overshadowed the existence of the government. Bonaparte himself was no more anxious to remain, inactive, in Paris than the directors were to have him stay. At the formal reception of the Directory, Barras exhorted him to crown his achievements by a conquest of England. With England unconquered and the colonial empire which made possible her prosperity intact, France lived in constant uncertainty of the future. It was wholly natural that the war against the proud islanders should be entrusted to the conqueror of the Continent. Accordingly Bonaparte was appointed general of the Army of England with instructions for an invasion of England.

Preparations were begun for this invasion, though not seriously, and largely to satisfy public opinion. Bonaparte and the wily Talleyrand, recently returned from America to become minister of foreign affairs, had a more dazzling scheme in mind, a scheme to which the latter was a new convert, but which Bonaparte had dimly entertained for a long time. Bonaparte was fully aware of the difficulties of the English venture and personally loath to

---

[4] The congress was dissolved in the spring of 1799 without accomplishing the object for which it was convoked.

undertake it. A brief tour of inspection along the coast had convinced him that the French fleet was incapable of conducting operations successfully. The recent naval defeats of the Spanish and Dutch allies of France rendered them doubtful aids against the English sailors. In his mind the English expedition was manifestly out of the question. During his absence on the Channel coast Talleyrand elaborated their scheme and officially laid before the government the project of an Egyptian expedition. To his secretary Bourrienne, Bonaparte confided his secret hopes early in 1798: "I know that if I remain here, I shall soon be discarded. Everything wears out here. My glory is already threadbare. This little Europe gives scant opportunity for more. I must go to the East. It is there that great glory can be won."

The responsibility for the Egyptian expedition rests squarely upon Talleyrand. Bonaparte's soaring imagination had long been fired by the romantic and mysterious lure of the East, by the grandiose vision of a new Alexander winning fame eternal by a conquest of the Orient. But not until Talleyrand read his *Essay on the Advantages to Be Gained from New Colonies Under the Present Circumstances* (at an open meeting of the Institute on July 3, 1797) did Bonaparte's hopes germinate. During that entire summer he thought and spoke constantly of this old pre-revolutionary project, now revived by Talleyrand, of wresting Egypt from the rule of the Turkish Empire. He mentioned it to the directors in a brief dispatch, and in his correspondence with the minister he returned to it constantly, bidding Talleyrand to sound the Sublime Porte on its reaction to a French expedition to Egypt. Early in 1798 Talleyrand addressed an outspoken report to the Directory in which he prognosticated the speedy dissolution of the Turkish Empire and urged that France seize the choicest parts either independently or in conjunction with Austria and Russia.

Shortly after, he submitted a long and optimistic report solely on the question of Egypt, discussing the manner in which an expedition should be conducted and the advantages that a seizure of Egypt would bring to France. Once Egypt was conquered and fortified, the isthmus of Suez would be cut through again, as it had been in antiquity, and French trade with India would follow this shorter Mediterranean route while England would be compelled to follow the longer and commercially ruinous route around the Cape of Good Hope. Not only would England's commercial prosperity be ruined by this blow, but her very political empire would quiver under the shock. From Suez a force of 15,000 men would leave for India. There it would meet the troops of Tippoo Sahib, the sultan of Mysore, and the joint forces would end English rule in India.[5]

Once determined, the expedition was organized with the utmost rapidity and comparative secrecy. The war fleet and the convoy ships set sail from Toulon on May 19, 1798, carrying 16,000 sailors and more than twice as many soldiers. A distinguished staff of scientists, artists, and men of letters accompanied the fighting forces. On the way to Alexandria Bonaparte risked a surprise attack upon the island of Malta, which he had been given secret orders to seize, and captured the formidable fortress. Four weeks later, on July 1, the French forces landed at Aboukir in Egypt and captured Alexandria without firing a shot. Admiral Nelson, who had been scouring the Mediterranean in quest of the French, left Egypt barely three days before the arrival of the French. These two fortunate events presaged a happy conclusion to the venture, and the brilliant French victory against the Mamelukes three weeks later at the foot of the Pyramids gave Bonaparte control of Cairo and confirmed the optimism of the invaders.

A single naval defeat, however, ruined his enterprise. Nelson had finally learned the true destination of the French fleet. From Sicily he sailed toward Egypt, and on August 1 he surprised the anchored French fleet in Aboukir Bay and destroyed it almost to the last ship. By this one stroke England became mistress of the Mediterranean. The communications of the French forces with France were cut, and Bonaparte became a prisoner in the land that he had conquered. He put a bold front on a situation which undid all his plans of using Egypt as a base of operations against India. Covering his discouragement, he summoned his officers to greater determination and higher courage. "Here is an occurrence which forces us to do greater things than we expected. We are perhaps destined to change the face of the East, and to place our names by

---

[5] Tippoo Sahib, one of the most powerful of the native princes who opposed the English rule in India, had been defeated in 1791, but since his defeat he had allied himself with the remaining French. Upon the advice of his Jacobin allies he appealed for aid to the Directory and to the governor of the French colony in the Île de France. The latter raised volunteers and proclaimed a revolt against the English. Tippoo Sahib offered an alliance to the Directory, but the two French envoys who were sent to India failed to arrive at their destination.

the side of those whose brilliant achievements are recorded in history." For weeks the scientists and savants of his expedition pursued their investigations into the nature of the country and its resources, while Bonaparte waited for news from Europe and nourished his hopes.

Again the news was evil, for in September the sultan declared war upon France, allied himself with Russia and England, and summoned the faithful everywhere in Egypt to expel the impious French. A rebellion broke out in Cairo, but it was ended by the French artillery. Then, in the following January, Bonaparte learned that the vizier and governor of Syria, Achmed Pasha, had gathered an army for the invasion of Egypt, and that one of the frontier fortresses had fallen into the hands of his advance guard. The British fleet and a convoy were to coöperate with him in his advance. Bonaparte welcomed the opportunity to march into Syria and stir its population to revolt.

At first his small expeditionary force won one victory after another as he proceeded toward Acre, where Achmed Pasha had taken refuge. For two months he besieged Acre, but without a fleet his efforts were fruitless. Plague attacked his troops; his ammunition ran low, and his food supply was almost spent. Then came the report that the English fleet was transporting a Turkish army of 20,000 men to the Nile. Bonaparte raised the siege and hastened to Egypt before the enemy could arrive. His sick and wounded were abandoned in his precipitate march, but he made good his entry into Cairo; and then from Cairo he marched to the sea, arriving just as the Turks were landing at Aboukir. On July 25, 1799, almost exactly a year after his great victory before the pyramids, he annihilated the Turkish army, shooting down those who held their position and driving the others into the sea. The reverse of Acre was avenged, but the victory was a hollow one, for he was none the less a prisoner in the conquered land.

His hopes of expelling the English from India were also frustrated. When the English governor-general learned of the possibility of a French invasion he tightened his lines of defense. After he learned of the news of Aboukir, he advanced against Tippoo Sahib and isolated him. The latter's native ally deserted, leaving Tippoo to face the English alone. The subjugation of the luckless rebel was completed by the brother of the governor-general, Arthur Wellesley, who was later to gain lasting fame as

Lord Wellington. Wellesley invaded the state of Mysore and captured the last stronghold of Tippoo, the native prince meeting his death in the siege. Just as the reverse at Acre ended Bonaparte's dream of conquering the Ottoman Empire, so this English victory against Tippoo Sahib closed the road to India to the French.

THE SECOND COALITION AGAINST FRANCE

The first intimation of military reverses and domestic strife in France reached Bonaparte when he was conducting the siege of Acre. The news was abundantly confirmed several months later when a packet of newspapers fell into his hands. From these journals he learned of the formation of the second coalition against France and its successful offensive against the republican troops.

Even before he had embarked for the East, the Directory had taken steps against Holland, the cantons of the Swiss federation, and the states of the pope. Anxious to strengthen Holland's defenses against England, the Directory used the political disorder in that country as a pretext and ordered the French troops there to move against the provisional government. After its downfall the government of the Batavian Republic was organized on the model of the directorial government of France, and an alliance with France was imposed upon it. Thanks to this arrangement France obtained valuable military subsidies, even though the Dutch were brought to the verge of financial and commercial ruin. A pretext was also found to extend the republican system to the Swiss cantons, whose government was changed into the centralized Helvetic Republic. While thus promoting the democratic cause, the agents of the Directory imposed a heavy indemnity upon the Swiss burghers, part of which also helped finance the Egyptian venture, and seized control of Simplon Pass for the benefit of French troops. Ostensibly to end smuggling activities in Geneva, France annexed that republic outright, together with the small republican state of Mulhouse and the principality of Montbéliard. Switzerland thus became a French highway into Italy. The procedure was very similar in the case of the states of the pope, where a popular insurrection afforded the necessary pretext for French intervention. The city of Rome was occupied by the republican troops, whose general transformed its government into the Roman Republic (February, 1798). The customary war indemnities were also employed in part for the financing of the Egyptian venture.

French aggression in Italy continued after Bonaparte's departure. In the Cisalpine Republic the systematic plundering by French agents who interfered in the administration of the government continued, provoking bitter animosity against the erstwhile "liberators." In December, 1798, the French troops were in possession of Piedmont, whose king had abdicated and fled to his island possession of Sardinia, protected by the English ships. The king of Naples opened the ports of his country to the English fleet and marched his troops to the relief of Rome; but the effort turned against him, and in January the French occupied Naples. There the fourth of the "sister republics" of Italy was established under the name of the Parthenopean Republic. With the four vassal republics in Italy and the two in Switzerland and Holland, the Directory had set up six new governments since the conclusion of the peace of Campo Formio. This was reason enough for the great states of Europe to take fright; and in addition there was the Egyptian venture.

Under the careful ministrations of the British diplomatic agents the powers of Europe once more drew together to oppose the armed doctrine of the French revolutionists. On the Continent the principal rôle devolved upon Paul I, the czar of Russia. He found cause for hostility in the French expedition to Egypt and in Bonaparte's seizure of Malta, of which he considered himself the protector by virtue of his title grand master of the Order of Malta. Besides, he had recently been converted to the belief that one of the secret aims of French policy in Europe was to place a French candidate upon the throne of a revived Polish nation. The grievances of Austria were multiple—the unsatisfactory terms of the treaty of Campo Formio, the extension of French influence in Italy, and the protracted and indecisive course of negotiations at Rastatt. In September, Turkey allied herself with England and Russia against France. In December, Naples and England reached an accord; and at the end of the month the Anglo-Russian and the Russo-Neapolitan treaties of alliance and subsidy were signed at Saint Petersburg. Without signing a treaty until later Austria made satisfactory arrangements with England on their respective aims in the approaching war with France. Of all the great states

Prussia alone maintained her neutrality; and again England had become the paymaster of Europe against France.

Before actual hostilities broke out, the Directory passed the first general conscription law in September, 1798, in a desperate effort to raise the number of French troops against the superior forces of the coalition. But against the 320,000 men whom the allies put in the field the Directory could oppose fewer than 200,000 on the long front which extended from the North Sea to the Ionian Sea. The campaign opened in earnest in the spring of 1799 with fighting in northern Italy. There a strong Austrian army, later reënforced by the Russians under Suvarov, inflicted successive defeats upon the French. By the end of the summer all Italy was lost to the republican forces save Genoa, where Moreau shut himself in to guard the mountain passes of the Apennines. The newly founded Italian republics disappeared as if by magic, and the old aristocratic governments were restored. The combined Austro-Russian forces then directed their strength upon Switzerland, where the position of Masséna near Zurich was highly precarious. In the fighting along the Rhine the Archduke Charles had already forced Jourdan to fall back upon Strasbourg. At this moment his troops received reënforcement from the Russians, and he prepared to cross into Alsace. At the same time the Anglo-Russian army under the duke of York effected a landing in Holland. Everywhere the prestige of the French armies was shaken, and the French frontier was once more exposed to invasion.

INTRIGUES AGAINST THE DIRECTORY

The domestic situation was no less troubled. The former Jacobins who had profited most by the coup d'état of Fructidor were successful in the elections of 1798 and returned a great many of their candidates to the councils. But the directors were no more eager to have a majority of republican extremists in the councils than they were to have the constitutionalists and royalists in control. Exercising their power of "judging" the operations of the electoral assemblies, they forced the Corps législatif to annul many elections and fill a sufficient number of vacant seats with governmental candidates to have a majority in the councils. This action was designated as the coup of the 22nd of Floréal, year VI (May

11, 1798). For a year the discontent of the political parties was stifled within the country; meantime outside of France the course of events was one of unbroken military defeats.

The elections of 1799 were also republican, like those of the preceding year. The distraught Directory, already weakened by military defeats, did not dare arouse fresh political passions by attempting to repeat its tactics of the preceding Floréal. The new republican majority in the councils opened a political fire upon their opponents in the Directory, one of whom they forced out on technical electoral grounds, replacing him with Gohier, the former minister of justice. Unable to find constitutional grounds to oust Merlin de Douai and La Révellière, they put sufficient political pressure upon these two directors to force their resignation. For their successors the councils chose General Moulin, a militarist though an innocuous one, and Roger Ducos. Reubell, meantime, had retired from the Directory, his successor being the inveterate constitution maker Sieyès. These comprehensive changes in the personnel of the Directory constituted the so-called coup of the 30th of Prairial, year VII (June 18, 1799), which was the retaliation of the councils against the directors for the illegal acts of the latter during the past two years.

Both branches of the government had now violated the constitution; and Sieyès was confident of success in striving to give the republic a more effective charter of government. On his side were Roger Ducos in the Directory, a majority of the Council of Ancients, and many republicans of moderate and conservative views. The opposition to his plan of strengthening the executive power came from his two colleagues, Gohier and General Moulin, from the Council of Five Hundred, and from the influential Jacobin Club, which had been reëstablished at the Manège under the name of "Society of Friends of Liberty and Equality." That club with its 3000 members, including several hundred deputies of the councils, had a powerful organ of expression in its newspaper, the *Journal des hommes libres,* through which it defended the Terror and the Constitution of 1793. The fifth member of the board of directors, Barras, was also opposed to Sieyès without, however, being a partisan of the more extreme republicans. He judged that the events of Prairial were merely a prelude to a sweeping royalist reaction and restoration and deemed it good politics to anticipate the march of events and guarantee his own safety by treating secretly with the pretender, the count of Provence.

In truth, the danger from the royalists was temporarily as pronounced as the threat of a revived Jacobin rule. The victories of the second coalition raised the hopes of the royalists in the south and the west; while the enactment of the laws which levied a compulsory loan upon the rich parvenus and abolished their exemption from military service, together with the law of hostages, which compelled the families of emigrants to give guarantees to the government, terrified the moderates and the conservatives. Fortunately for the republic and for the plans of Sieyès, the menace both from royalists and from Jacobins subsided in the course of the summer.

The expectations of the royalists, who counted upon the military aid of the victorious Russians, were dashed at the resumption of republican victories. After wresting Italy from the French the Austrian and Russian troops had separated, the Austrians remaining in that Italy which was so dear to their emperor and the Russians under Suvarov moving toward Switzerland to join Archduke Charles and their own countrymen under Korsakov. But then the order was given to the archduke to advance upon Mainz, which left the defense of Switzerland to the two Russian armies, still widely separated from each other. Masséna did not waste this golden opportunity to attack each commander in turn. For two weeks he attacked the advancing Russians, defeating both Korsakov and Suvarov in successive battles and culminating his campaign in a decisive victory at Zurich. A month later, in the middle of October, General Brune drove back the forces of the duke of York in Holland and forced him to sign a convention whereby the Anglo-Russian troops agreed to evacuate the territory of the Batavian republic. After the reverses in Switzerland the Russian troops forsook the coalition and returned home. Thus the Austrians held Italy, but the allies had fallen out, and the French frontier was secure against attack.

In the meantime Sieyès pursued his campaign against the extreme republicans. Through Lucien Bonaparte, the younger brother of the absent general, he played upon the fears of the moderate deputies in the Council of Five Hundred. Through Fouché (the ex-terrorist of 1794 and the future minister of police under Napoleon), the minister of police, he struck at the Jacobins by closing their club and suppressing their influential journal.[6] Their final threat came in September, when the leaders of the radicals appealed to General Bernadotte, the minister of war, to head a democratic movement against the government, while General Jourdan pleaded with his colleagues in the Council of Five Hundred to decree that the patrie was in danger. Had the latter motion passed, terrorist tactics would have ensued. With the aid of Barras and Lucien Bonaparte, Sieyès parried the thrust, forcing Bernadotte from office and prevailing upon the Five Hundred to reject Jourdan's motion.

Sieyès was now secure against a popular insurrection, and he resumed his quest of a general who could serve his purpose of protecting the republic without placing it in under his heel. Joubert, his first choice, had been killed in action in the fighting in Italy. Hoche had died of tuberculosis. Moreau's conduct was equivocal, Masséna was unsuited for the delicate task, and both Bernadotte and Jourdan were too radical. Thus only Bonaparte remained, but Sieyès was sorely troubled by doubts as to whether Bonaparte would consent to play a secondary rôle.

THE COUP D'ÉTAT OF BRUMAIRE

When the news of the events that had occurred in France and in Europe reached Bonaparte,[7] his patriotic convictions and his personal ambition happily united to convince him that his place was in France and his duty to save his country. The difficulties of the Directory had created the opportunity he sought to enhance his own glory. Accompanied by several of his most trusted officers, he secretly stole away from Alexandria in August, informing Kléber by letter that the command of the Egyptian expeditionary forces had devolved upon him. Six weeks later, on October 9, he effected a safe landing at Fréjus in southern France, and proceeded directly but slowly toward Paris. Although he was unaware of the fact at the time of his departure, the Directory had already ordered his return to France. His ill fated army held out until 1801, when it was forced to surrender, thus bringing the Egyptian ven-

[6] Talleyrand resigned from the ministry the very day that Fouché entered it. He sensed the wind and abandoned the sinking ship of the directory.

[7] The packet of newspapers which he received in August, 1799, disclosed the news up to June 6. Consequently he was ignorant of the coup of Prairial and the victory of the republican troops.

ture to an inglorious close. Unsuccessful as the campaign was in its military aspects, its incidental results were significant. The economic life of Egypt was rescued from its deadly languor. The Institut d'Égypte was founded, and the fortunate discovery of the trilingual inscription on the Rosetta Stone, which Champollion later deciphered, laid the foundations for the reading of the Egyptian hieroglyphs and for the new science of Egyptology. Bonaparte himself gained new glamour from his exploits in the land of classical antiquity, for his military bulletins had concealed or minimized his defeats and lavishly extolled his triumphs. The entire venture had dazzled the imagination of the French and, by contrast, revealed all the more clearly the nullity of the existing government.

His long trip from Fréjus to Paris was a splendid triumph. The news of the victory at Aboukir Bay had reached France only a short time before Bonaparte's return, and the public gazed with awe at the new Caesar who had conquered in the East as brilliantly as he had in Italy. The crowds were so thick that his carriage could barely advance. All the roads were lighted to welcome and to speed the hope of France. To save France against her enemies he no longer had the opportunity, for the victories of Masséna and Brune had already accomplished that much; but there was still time to pacify the Continent, even as he had done at Campo Formio.

The glory that he had sought in the East was his. What would he make of it? He would, most assuredly, not use it to strengthen the Directory; for even at the time of his triumphs in Italy he had revealed his secret thoughts on that subject. "Do you believe that it is to increase the grandeur of the lawyers in the Directory . . . that I win triumphs in Italy? They [i.e., the French] need glory, the satisfaction of their vanity; but as for liberty, they know nothing about it. . . . The nation needs a leader, a leader made illustrious by glory." He knew that his moment had come. He listened without committing himself to the solicitations of the different factions, sounded out popular opinion, and carefully studied the political situation. Through Talleyrand, who was promised a suitable reward for his services, Bonaparte established contact with Sieyès. Contact established, agreement followed.

Their plans were rapidly laid. Roger Ducos, Talleyrand, Lucien

Bonaparte, Fouché, and Cambacérès, the minister of justice, were active in the service of the plotters. The moneyed interests favored, and probably financed, those operations which promised them relief from the revolutionary expedients of forced loans and worthless paper currency. The plans had the merit of simplicity. Under the persuasive arguments of Lucien and Sieyès the Council of Ancients would be induced to remove the sessions of the legislative bodies to Saint-Cloud, just outside of Paris, where their deliberations would be undisturbed by the workingmen of Paris. General Bonaparte was to be appointed to the command of the armed force in Paris, which would force the resignation of the obdurate directors and the dissolution of the councils. This accomplished, an executive commission of three provisional consuls was to be created for the purpose of drafting a new constitution, which would then be submitted to the electoral assemblies of the country for ratification. The date fixed for the execution of the coup was the 18th of Brumaire (November 9, 1799).

On the eve of the dénouement such deputies of the Council of Ancients as were aware of the plot were notified to assemble early the following morning. This notification was not extended to the republican deputies, whose presence was not desired. At that morning session the alarming announcement was made that a formidable Jacobin conspiracy against the government had been unearthed, and that this conspiracy could be surmounted only by taking two decisive steps. The first of these was to appoint General Bonaparte commander-in-chief of the armed forces in Paris; and the second was to transfer the meetings of the two councils to Saint-Cloud, where the Jacobins could not disturb the solemnity and the freedom of legislative procedure. These steps were taken at once, in the early morning. In the course of the day Sieyès and Roger Ducos presented their resignations; and Talleyrand used his gift of subtle intimidation so effectively that Barras also resigned and accepted a safe-conduct for his departure. The other two directors, Gohier and General Moulin, refused to resign, but Bonaparte placed a guard over them at the Luxembourg. Thus the executive branch of the administration automatically came to an end. While the republican generals, Augereau, Jourdan, and Bernadotte, were kept under surveillance, Bonaparte himself rode down the Tuileries, surrounded by his subordinates, entered the hall of the Council of Ancients and swore an oath of loyalty. He did not take the oath to the constitution as required by law, but an oath to maintain a republic based upon freedom and equality.

On the following afternoon (the 19th of Brumaire) the plot almost miscarried at Saint-Cloud. The deputies of the Council of Five Hundred and the republican minority of the Ancients had at last sensed the trend of developments. They realized that the troops which surrounded the assembly halls were not there to protect them against a conspiracy. In the Five Hundred a motion to renew the oath of loyalty to the Constitution of the year III was carried unanimously and with such enthusiasm that Bonaparte could well entertain misgivings over the successful issue of the plot. Learning what had occurred in the Five Hundred, he determined to crush the opposition before it made further progress. He went first to the Council of Ancients, his officers following him. There he spoke in ominous terms of the dangers surrounding the government, attested his patriotic loyalty, and exhorted the deputies to adopt measures which he could execute. When interrupted by a deputy who reproached him with forgetting the constitution, he broke into a torrent of passionate language: "The constitution? You violated it on the 18th of Fructidor, on the 22nd of Floréal, on the 30th of Prairial. . . . The constitution is invoked by all factions, and violated by all; . . . the constitution being violated, we must have another compact, new guarantees." This outburst and a veiled threat to use his troops overcame the resistance of the Ancients, and the council rose in approval of his remarks. Only the Five Hundred now opposed him.

There his reception was more stormy. He had left his bodyguard at the door, but the mere sight of their gleaming bayonets roused the fury of the councilors. Cries of "Down with the dictator," "Outlaw him," rang through the hall, and several of the deputies tried to reach him. He was jostled and pushed about, but his grenadiers protected him with their bodies from the blows and dragged him, fainting, into the open. All seemed lost, but Lucien retrieved the situation. While the deputies demanded a decree of outlawry against Bonaparte, Lucien as the presiding officer held up the vote and tried to calm the storm. The uproar was so great that he could not make himself heard above the noise. Assuming that his brother had in fact been outlawed, Lucien resigned his presidency of the council, but sent word to Bonaparte to act in haste, whereupon the latter sent a squad of grenadiers to rescue Lucien from the hall.

Sieyès and Roger Ducos were ready to take flight, and Bonaparte had not yet recovered his full composure and initiative. Lucien took in the situation at a glance and saved the day for the schemers. On horseback, sword in hand, he improvised a mendacious harangue to the soldiers and summoned the troops to rally behind him and expel the "brigands" who were in control of the hall. Then, turning toward Bonaparte, he swore to plunge his sword into his brother's heart if ever the latter plotted against the liberty of the French people. That act of cheap theatricality swayed the befuddled and impatient soldiers. Bonaparte now addressed his men, his composure regained. Assured of their loyalty, he gave the order to his officers to clear the hall of the Five Hundred. Led by Murat and Leclerc, the grenadiers invaded the Orangerie, where the session was being held, and in a few moments all was over. The deputies fled before the troops, pouring helter-skelter through the windows into the sheltering woods. The plot was consummated, not peacefully and constitutionally as the plotters had wished, but by the force of arms.

That same evening, the rumps of the two councils assembled to cloak the late proceedings with constitutional legality. They named Bonaparte, Sieyès, and Roger Ducos provisional consuls and appointed two commissions, one from each of the councils, to aid the consuls in drafting a new constitution. The republic still existed in name; actually the rule of the man on horseback had begun. Ten years of revolution had culminated in the rule of a military adventurer.

XIV. THE PACIFICATION OF FRANCE AND EUROPE (1799-1802)

THE PACIFICATION OF FRANCE: THE CONSTITUTION OF THE YEAR VIII

On the whole France tamely accepted the warrior who had made himself master of the republic. In the first place, the real events of Brumaire were not fully known; if the country did not actually believe in the existence of the Jacobin plot which Bonaparte had supposedly suppressed, at least it accepted his official version. Moreover, ten years of revolutionary turmoil had dimmed the fire of political idealism and made the citizens indifferent to plots both "Red" and "White," predisposing them to accept the accomplished fact, whether it was legal or illegal. Despite the right of universal suffrage which the Revolution had given them, very few people had taken any active part in the government. Their political education had been restricted to the lessons given at the revolutionary clubs; and fundamentally, they were in 1799 what they had been a decade earlier, monarchists at heart. They were ready to support any leader who would maintain the advantages that they had gained and restore tranquillity. The rise of stocks after Brumaire indicated the confidence of the business interests in Bonaparte, but most of France remained indifferent to the change.

Bonaparte himself, ever a superb realist even when he dissembled most, struck the correct pose. He was not overthrowing the republic; on the contrary, he was consolidating it. In one of his earliest statements after the coup he sagely remarked: "My policy is to govern in accordance with the wishes of the great majority. That, I believe, is the way to recognize the sovereignty of the people." What the great majority desired in 1799 was the preservation of the civil conquests of the Revolution; above all others, social equality. Bonaparte's task, then, was at once to dispel the fear of a reaction which would undo the vast social and economic transformation of the past ten years and to rid the country of the anarchy which prevented the resumption of normal activities. Brumaire had given him not power, but an opportunity. His government was only a provisional one. His future actions alone could determine whether lasting mastery of France would also be his; and the events of the next few years were dictated by that necessity. In the words of a contemporary: "On the 18th of Brumaire, year VIII, Bonaparte contracted an immense debt whose extent he alone realized and he alone could pay."

To pay that debt he had to suppress the cumulative disorder of a decade. Police reports and information gathered on the spot by agents of the provisional consuls graphically described the situation. In the west there were forty thousand Chouans overrunning the country, cutting communications between Paris and the Atlantic and defying the representatives of the government. The entire south and the valley of the Rhone were prey to robber bands who attacked the coaches, robbed the mail, sacked the homes of the well-to-do, and perpetrated all sorts of outrages upon "the patriots." Taxes were unpaid, the currency worthless, and the credit of the government was ruined. The clergy were in rebellion against the state, and the very servants of the government exacted tribute from the governed. The workers in the large cities suffered from unemployment, and merchants and manufacturers from the suspension or abandonment of economic activities. With great energy and unsurpassed tact Bonaparte began the work of pacification and reconstruction which he was so brilliantly to complete within a few years.

In the meantime the two commissions that had been formed on the 19th of Brumaire to revise the directorial constitution were hard at work upon their project. The guiding spirit of their labors was Sieyès, the oracle of constitutional wisdom, who, boasting that he had mastered the "science of politics," at last had an opportunity to elaborate his revision of the much-criticized constitution of 1795. But the commission and Sieyès worked too slowly to satisfy Bonaparte. On December 2, he first summoned the commission to the Luxembourg, where the three provisional consuls were living, and virtually dictated a text, blended in part of Sieyès' ideas and in part of his own, which was promulgated December 15. The nation accepted it enthusiastically by 3,011,107 votes against 1562, and ever afterward the Bonapartists contended that Bonaparte owed his power to the sovereignty which the nation had solemnly conferred upon him. It is worthy of note, however, that the plebiscite, distinctive as it was of the Napoleonic régime, was not a referendum or a free popular consultation, but the ratification of an accomplished fact. The plebiscite was not completed until February, 1800, but Bonaparte had the Constitution of the Year VIII (1799–1800) put into effect by December 25, 1799. On that day the provisional government gave place to the Consulate.

The constitutional document itself partook of the same disingenuous characteristics that marked its acceptance. Externally, it retained the liberal forms of the Revolution; in reality it organized a strongly autocratic and paternalistic régime. Universal suffrage was reëstablished: every male citizen, twenty-one years of age or over, with a fixed legal residence for one year had the right to vote, but this right was rendered useless by the method of election. The voters met in the principal town of the district (the arrondissement) to choose one-tenth of their number, this tenth constituting the communal list. These communal groups then met in their several departments and selected one-tenth of their number, the new groups being designated as the departmental list. By the same procedure the latter selected one-tenth of their members, who were eligible "to the national public functions." From the list of five or six thousand candidates whom the voters had nominated by this ingenious winnowing process of indirect election, the Senate was to select the officials of the administration and the deputies of the legislative bodies. In truth, Sieyès' principle that "confidence comes from below, power from above" was vindicated by this arrangement; however, this arrangement was reserved for the future. For the immediate present, before the various lists were formed, the selections were made from lists drawn up by Sieyès and his friends.

The legislative power was divided among several bodies whose effectiveness was carefully restricted by an elaborate system of checks and balances. The initiation of the legislation belonged to the Council of State, whose members Bonaparte nominated. The Tribunate, composed of one hundred members twenty-five years of age or over, could discuss and criticize proposals brought before it, but could not vote upon them. The Legislative Body (the Corps législatif), of three hundred members, listened in silence to the proposals of law which were brought before it and voted for their acceptance or rejection without discussing them. Thus the one assembly could discuss without voting, and the other voted without discussing and without the power to amend the bills. A third assembly, the Conservative Senate, was also provided for in the constitution. To it was assigned a double rôle: to annul or confirm the measures which either the government or the Tribunate deemed unconstitutional, and to select the consuls and the members of the Tribunate and the Legislative Body from the national list. By virtue of its veto over legislation the Senate had in its power to make the effectiveness of the two other legislative assemblies still more illusory. As for its constitutional right to name the three consuls, the Senate never had an opportunity to exercise it, for the constitution had already designated the original consuls. Nor did the Senate name the tribunes and the legislators, for the first choices, as we have already noted, were made from lists drawn up before the groups of Notables were formed. The majority of the sixty original senators was named by the junior consuls—the two junior consuls of the provisional government and the two junior consuls of the regular government. This majority subsequently chose the other senators.

The electoral system and the division of the legislature were Sieyès' contribution to the new constitution, to which Bonaparte gave his whole-hearted approval. But he entirely disapproved of Sieyès' organization of the executive power, in which he had a rather markedly personal interest. Sieyès had contrived a balanced bureaucracy composed of two consuls, one for foreign affairs and the other for domestic affairs, above whom he had placed a grand elector of no real authority but with a large salary and high decorative honors. Bonaparte, for whom the part of the last-named was intended, disrupted the entire scheme. In reality a person of his energy, ambition, and prestige could not be reduced to the empty ridiculous rôle of "a disembodied shadow of a do-nothing king," as Bonaparte vigorously characterized Sieyès' conception of the grand elector. He altered the original project, making provision for three consuls and casting himself for the office of the first consul. "How can you imagine," he exclaimed, "that a man of any talent or activity would consent to settle down like a pig fattening on so many millions?"

There was no question of equal powers for the three consuls, even though they were all chosen for ten years and were eligible for reëlection. On the first consul the constitution, as Bonaparte rewrote it, virtually bestowed dictatorial power. Through the

Council of State he proposed legislation. He appointed (and dismissed) his councilors, the ministers, the ambassadors, the officers of the army and the navy, and the government commissioners assigned to the tribunals. Though the Senate could nominate certain lesser officials, a special act allowed Bonaparte to name the prefects of the departments. This act largely nullified the constitution so far as local administration was concerned. Further, the first consul appointed all the magistrates of civil and criminal courts, other than the lowly justices of the peace and the magistrates of the court of cassation. He also signed treaties, subject to the ratification of the legislative assemblies. Thus he controlled the military and diplomatic service and the general administration without being responsible for his actions to the legislative assemblies. The second and third consuls were allowed a consultative voice in "the other acts of the government," signing the register of these acts in order to attest their presence. If they wished, they could record their opinions; "after that, the decision of the first consul suffices." In other words, the two colleagues of the first consul were supernumeraries. The consuls received for their residence the Tuileries palace, which was the home of the former kings of France. The first consul was to receive 500,000 francs a year, the other two 166,666 francs each for their services.

A special decree, conceived in the same spirit as the constitution, organized the new Council of State, which was little else than the royal council of the Old Régime under a new name. It was divided into five sections—civil and criminal legislation, domestic affairs, finance, war, and the admiralty. Composed originally of thirty, and later of forty-five members, who were appointed and dismissed at will by the first consul, it was at once the screen for his dictatorship and the instrument of his power. The duty of the councilors was to prepare the laws, issue administrative regulations, and modify or elaborate such statutes as the first consul desired by issuing "opinions." The Council of State served also as the supreme court of administrative justice. The activity of the councilors, considerable at the very outset, increased steadily, and their control became all-embracing; but, influential as they were, these hand-picked servitors were not likely to thwart Bonaparte's wishes. The ministers were in many ways less influential. Like the councilors, they were nominated by the first consul and selected as much for their amenability as for their professional worth. Of all officials they alone were made responsible to the legislative assemblies. Still further to weaken their solidarity, Bonaparte divided the functions of the leading ministers between two holders, and founded a general board within each ministry, whose head was not the minister but Bonaparte's direct agent, a councilor of state.

The Constitution of the Year VIII had a liberal façade, but it built up the autocratic régime of one man, Bonaparte. The republic still existed in name, but the constitution made Bonaparte the real ruler of France. It organized the rule of the drillmaster and disciplinarian who had no other conception of government than that of a nation yielding prompt obedience to his commands. By what it stated and by what it omitted to state—the absence of a general declaration of rights or principles, failure to define the limits of the arrondissements, incomplete organization of the department, lack of provisions for the filling of vacancies in the legislative assemblies, only the barest sort of outline of the system of judicial administration—the hastily drawn-up document sounded the knell of republican government. Nevertheless, it was, as we have seen, enthusiastically accepted by the French; and for the first six years of his régime at least Napoleon was right enough in saying that he ruled by the will of the people, that his system was a "democratic empire."

The Pacification of France: The Restoration of Order and Prosperity

The gaps in the constitution and the insistent needs of the moment led Bonaparte to the first of his enduring reforms—the reorganization of the local administrative system, which was effected by the law of February 17, 1800. It is a tribute to his genius that this reform still serves as the basis of the French administrative system. What the Revolution did in this respect, Bonaparte undid. He repudiated the two cardinal principles of revolutionary legislation concerning local administration, popular election and local self-administration of national laws. He retained the geographical divisions established by the first of the Revolutionary assemblies, but he ended the autonomy which the elective departmental councils had enjoyed—in theory, if not always in practice. Each department was put under the direct responsibility of a prefect, each district under a subprefect, and each municipality under a mayor. To assist the prefect (although almost entirely in matters connected with the allocation of the direct tax), a council of prefecture and a general council were established; and, in similar fashion, the subprefect had the aid of a district council and the mayor of a municipal council. The first consul appointed all the executive officials and the members of the councils. In this way the centralization of the Old Régime was reëstablished, a change that was perhaps necessary at the time, though it was not without its manifest limitations upon liberty.

In fact, the centralization effected by the law of February 17, 1800, was more pronounced than that which had been so abused in the Old Régime. In the Old Régime various powerful local and regional bodies, such as the parlements and the provincial estates, had rather effectively obstructed the power of the royal intendants. But in 1800 all obstacles to the omnipotence of the state were gone. As one of the councilors saw it, the law "singularly facilitated despotism," and it is certain that Bonaparte intended to substitute an orderly uniformity, inspired by himself, for disturbing local initiative. To respectable citizens of the time, orderly uniformity was unquestionably a real blessing in comparison with the insecurity of pillage and brigandage which local initiative had been incapable of suppressing during the past decade. Particularly grateful were they for those blessings when in later years Bonaparte protected national industry, built his great roads and harbors, cut through canals, and spanned turbulent rivers with durable bridges. These material reforms may have been the work of a despot, but of a benevolent despot who was keenly alive to the need of firing the imagination of the well-to-do citizens.

The reorganization of the judiciary followed shortly after, being effected by the law of March 18, 1800. Again centralization was the goal. The law established a civil court of the first instance in each district, a court of appeal for every two or three departments (twenty-nine for the whole country), a criminal court in each department, and a supreme court of cassation. With the exception of the local justices of the peace at the bottom of the judicial hierarchy and the magistrates of the court of cassation at the summit, all the judges were named by the first consul. A governmental commissioner was attached to each court, partly to represent the administration, and partly to supervise the procedure. In addition, Bonaparte revived a system of administrative justice for his officials, the administration of which was entrusted to the councils of prefecture and the Council of State. Thus, directly and indirectly, the judicial reforms extended and consolidated the power of the central government.

These vast powers which the constitution and the first reforms placed in Bonaparte's hands, powers which in his mind were only the beginnings of the authority that he intended to win, were used to secure peace and order. Soldier and disciplinarian that he was, he "imported a cold and wholesome dose of inhumanity into the conduct of affairs." "When my service is in question," he observed, "all passions must be laid aside." To build for the future, he had to disregard the past. He meant to recruit his new officials from all classes, from the old revolutionaries, from royalists, from experienced officials of the Old Régime, and from promising new men who were coming to the front. For him the revolutionary past was over; and he had no intention of rekindling the fires of ancient passions.

When the constitution became effective, two of the provisional consuls, Sieyès and Roger Ducos, retired from office and entered the Senate. The new second consul was the former regicide Cambacérès, an able jurist and a wise and prudent adviser. The new third consul was Lebrun, a man thirty years older than Bonaparte, who had served the king in the Old Régime and was strongly suspected of royalist sympathies. His political career had been without distinction, and his name was not even well known. But in selecting him Bonaparte made it manifest that royalist views were no more of a bar to service in the Consulate than the revolutionary antecedents of the Montagnard Cambacérès. The same broad tolerance was exercised in the nomination of the members of the Corps législatif, the Tribunate, and the Senate. More than two-thirds of the new parlementarians came from the councils of the Directory. The most signal illustration of the catholicity of Bonaparte's nominations was seen in the new administrative personnel of councilors, ministers, and local officials. Among the ministers were Fouché, now minister of police, and Talleyrand, now minister of foreign affairs. "What revolutionist," exclaimed Bonaparte, "can fail to have confidence in the social system when Fouché, the Jacobin, is minister of police? What nobleman would be unwilling to live under Talleyrand as minister of foreign affairs?" In the Council of State Bonaparte had placed the specialists, experts in law, finances, administration, military affairs, with whom he consulted regularly and informally, and with whose aid he elaborated all his great projects. The prefects of the departments were recruited from the members of the old revolutionary assemblies, from military leaders, from wealthy landowners, and from the most experienced and capable of the returned émigrés. It was indeed fortunate for Bonaparte that he had it in his power to dispose of so many important positions. No systematic opposition to his government was likely to be established, when almost every man in public life of merit and docility could find service in the new administration. Without exaggeration one may speak of this bureaucracy as Bonaparte's party. To them as well as to him goes the credit for what the new government accomplished.

As provisional consul Bonaparte took active steps to end disorder and pacify the country. He reassured the vested interests by suppressing the forced loan. He recalled the citizens who had been proscribed without trial by earlier assemblies. He rescinded the law on the seizure of hostages. Toward the Chouans in the west he first practiced a policy of conciliation, which resulted in an armistice and the beginnings of peaceful negotiations. After December 25, when the new constitution came into effect, and the provisional consul became the all-powerful first consul, Bonaparte's methods changed. As circumstances and inclination decreed, he employed alternately repression and indulgence. A proclamation, offering an amnesty to the Chouans who laid down their arms and extermination to those who refused to surrender, failed of its effect. Sterner measures were promptly determined, and preparations for vigorous war against the rebels were made. At the same time the first consul pursued the method of indulgence toward the former nobles, the relatives of émigrés, and the priests. One immediate consequence of this attitude was the return of many erstwhile "suspects" to political life. The leaders of the rebels were induced, by Bonaparte's tactics, to submit, and by February, 1800, organized Chouannerie was a thing of the past. Bonaparte's strong methods had prevailed, and he was free to use the troops in the west against the forces of the coalition in the campaign which soon opened.

While continuing his overtures to the emigrants and the Catholics, Bonaparte gave the republicans an inkling of the course that he would take against their criticism. Several members of the

Tribunate having indulged in their constitutional right of discussion first by criticizing the autocratic tendencies of the first consul and then by supplementing oral criticism with written commentaries in the newspapers, Bonaparte cut the matter short. Within two months' time the rash liberal critics were silenced and the press muzzled. The number of political newspapers in Paris was cut down from seventy-three to thirteen, and a theatrical censorship was soon established to coöperate with the already existing official press bureau. The security of the country in times of war—such was Bonaparte's euphemistic explanation of his high-handed attack upon free speech and press. In the manufacture of friendly public opinion Bonaparte needed no instruction, though the Jacobin rule abounded in excellent examples.

There was only slight protest from business men against the shackling of opinion because the new government persisted steadily in its great work of restoring law and order. The measures taken to ward off and end the disturbance were supplemented by the winning of financial stability. The business world and financial circles welcomed the coup d'état of Brumaire which they had helped to finance. Their confidence in the accession of Bonaparte was not misplaced. Before Brumaire the state bonds, the Consolidated Third, had fallen to seven francs on the Bourse; within several weeks they had risen to twenty. By suppressing the capital levy and instituting a direct twenty-five per cent war tax in its stead Bonaparte's new minister of finance further impressed capitalists and bankers, from whom he secured sufficient advances to meet current expenditures. Immediately after the coup d'état a sinking fund was instituted in order to raise the national credit. It had at its disposal part of the vast unsold national land which could be employed to redeem state bonds in circulation. In order to relieve the money market, which was flooded with more than sixty different paper securities, all of them greatly depreciated, Gaudin, the new minister, called these in and gave consols or other forms of governmental obligations whose value was slightly in excess of the current market value of the old securities. This operation was not strictly equitable and may even be considered a partial repudiation, but it was absolutely necessary and decidedly more justifiable than the open jobbery that had prevailed under the Directory. In February, 1800, the Bank of France was established in order to stabilize the public debt and to promote commerce and industry. The first great function of the Bank of France was to pay the holders of annuities, which it did in coin, and to issue bank notes up to a certain amount. It prospered from the very beginning, and its shares, to which several Parisian bankers and Bonaparte and his family had subscribed, soon doubled in value. In 1803 it gained the exclusive right of issuing bank notes for Paris.

A large part of the resources that enabled the government to discharge its existing obligations came from various extraordinary sources, both internal and external. The external income came from the conquered countries in the form of contributions, subsidies, and confiscations. The extraordinary internal receipts came largely from the administration of the unsold national land, which brought in an appreciable sum annually. The ordinary receipts were also thoroughly reorganized by Bonaparte's financial experts, who, in this respect, followed the lines laid down by the ministers of the Directory. An office for the collection of the direct taxes, which had been the principal resource of the revolutionary governments, was established in Paris under the direct control of the minister of finance, with a smaller board in each department. Instead of allowing the municipalities to continue to draw up the tax rolls, which had varied considerably from year to year, the personnel of the new central office took over the work in vigorous fashion. The assessment rate was definitely regulated. The tax lists in arrears were prepared, and those of the current and the coming fiscal year made, so that collections could begin promptly. An exact survey of all real estate and the thorough reorganization of the customs bureau and the bureau of landed property greatly increased the revenues from public property. The budget was pared down to the lowest possible point. The new tax collectors collaborated with the central office, and the collection of taxes henceforth went on efficiently. In later years Bonaparte was also to revive the system of national indirect taxation, but up to 1800 he limited indirect taxation to local purposes. Thus for the first time in many years the credit of the government was restored and the finances stabilized. During the Consulate too began the industrial regeneration of France. While French commerce suffered continuously from the prolongation of the maritime struggle between France and England, industry began a slow recovery. Bonaparte was particularly interested in industry and took especial pains to protect French products against English competition. Under the active leadership of Chaptal, his minister of the interior, serious efforts were made to stimulate industrial production. A Society for the Encouragement of National Industry was founded, local investigations carried out, and important data compiled. French textile manufacturers copied the models of English machines and vigorously extended the use of such mechanical appliances as had been introduced in France before 1789. Progress in the application of new machinery was, on the whole, very slow. The steam engine, for instance, was not used in French mills until 1810, though its use had been successfully demonstrated in England long before. Nevertheless industrial progress was continuous in a small way, as the success of the various expositions held during the Consulate and the empire showed.

Bonaparte's interest in industrial production was as well received by the workers as it was by the manufacturers. This seems all the more surprising because in many respects his attitude toward the workmen was unfavorable. Fear of food shortage, especially in Paris and the larger cities, prompted him to reëstablish the old guild system in the meat and bread trades, but he refused to allow a complete reëstablishment of guilds. Once more the workers in these trades were subjected to the rigorous surveillance of the police. The legislation against striking workmen and even against unions of workmen was strengthened. Workers were required by law to provide themselves with a *livret*. This industrial passport was kept by the employer so long as the worker was in his service. Upon the termination of the service the employer surrendered it to his former employee, with his signature affixed to it to show that the previous contract had been fulfilled. Without a livret duly signed, the worker's quest for a new job was bound to be difficult if not impossible. Wages were perhaps higher than they had been earlier, though living costs had also increased. The working population were among Bonaparte's most enthusiastic supporters. They overlooked the discriminatory legislation for several reasons. In the first place they were not class-conscious. Secondly, they had good wages and steady employment. Lastly, they were intensely patriotic, chauvinistic, to use a more modern term, and enthusiastic over Bonaparte's vigorous policy of conquest.

The Pacification of Europe: The Treaties of Lunéville and Amiens

The campaign of 1800 interrupted Bonaparte's pacification of France, which was to culminate in the reconciliation of the Revolution and the Catholic Church. The majority of Frenchmen desired peace, being weary of the long years of continuous war and satisfied that the conquest of the natural frontiers guaranteed the independence of their country. But peace was impossible in 1800. The disorder of the finances was not yet remedied; only the foundation of reform had been laid. The very existence of the government depended upon contributions from the dependent republics and levies from the occupied territory. A peace which gave up the system of dependent states would also deprive the French treasury of the funds which the conquered territory provided, and on no other terms was peace then possible. The demobilization of the returned soldiers might precipitate grave social disorders. Most important of all, Bonaparte needed victorious war to consolidate his power in Europe, even as his domestic policy was consolidating his authority within France. "Our task," he proclaimed to his soldiers, "is not to defend our own frontiers, but to invade the territory of our foes."

Nevertheless, to George III of England and to Francis II of Austria he publicly expressed his desire for peace. These peace offers, if offers they were, deceived no one, and they even failed of the only effect that Bonaparte hoped to achieve through them, which was the division of the allies. The English ministry refused to treat on terms of equality with a man whom they considered an adventurer. Underestimating the vitality of French resources and overconfident in the ultimate success of the coalition—for the English were blockading Malta and Egypt at the time of Bonaparte's offer—Pitt refused to entertain any proposal for peace. Austria, fresh from her recent military successes in northern Italy, also rejected his advances, but left the door open for future negotiations. Satisfied, nevertheless, that he had thrown the responsibility of war upon the enemy, Bonaparte made energetic plans for the resumption of hostilities.

From the Army of the West, which the final pacification of the Vendée had released, and from new contingents he was able to muster between 40,000 and 50,000 soldiers. These he at first intended to send to the Rhine to effect a union with Moreau's troops, but the latter's reluctance to serve under Bonaparte forced the first consul to give up his first plan. Skillfully concealing the full extent of his revised plan, he decided to lead his troops into northern Italy and cut the Austrian communications with Vienna. Meantime Masséna was to hold the Austrians under Melas in check as long as possible and then retreat slowly to Genoa.

In Germany, Moreau swept all before him. Early in May he crossed the Rhine and by a surprise flanking movement drove the Austrians beyond the Danube to the city of Ulm. Masséna fulfilled his requirements in northern Italy with sufficient dispatch and vigor to create the opportunity for Bonaparte's great offensive. Into the immense hole which Moreau's operations in Germany and Masséna's in Italy had created between the Austrian armies, he poured his fresh recruits. With the lightning stroke of the military genius that he was—and with the eye for theatricality that rarely failed him—he led his men (May 15–31) over the Alps through the Great Saint Bernard Pass and took possession of the Po valley before the enemy realized that an invasion of Italy was even contemplated. On June 2 Bonaparte entered Milan, having encountered only the slightest opposition from the scattered Austrian detachments to his triumphal march.

While he rested his troops, strengthening them with the fresh contingents which Moreau had now sent, the Austrians were deciding to concentrate all their troops on Alessandria and join battle there with the invader. While Bonaparte was dividing his forces to cut off any possible retreat by the enemy the Austrians fell upon him suddenly on June 14 in the plain of Marengo to the east of Alessandria. After six hours of fighting Melas' troops had won the day, and the Austrian commander dispatched a courier to Vienna to announce the glad tidings to his government. Melas' rejoicing was premature, for General Desaix, receiving word from his chief, halted his troops and hastened back to succor Bonaparte. With Desaix's fresh troops Bonaparte resumed the battle and turned defeat into victory, driving the Austrians under the walls of Alessandria. The latter lost more than 9000 men killed and wounded and the French 7000, including Desaix himself who was killed almost at the resumption of the battle. On the following day Melas sued for an armistice, which Bonaparte granted on the condition that the French occupy Lombardy as far as the Mincio River.

The results of the victory of Marengo were not exclusively military. Had Bonaparte suffered a reverse on the battle field, there is no doubt that the secret combination of his political enemies, including several members of the government, would have cast him from power. Marengo, in the words of one of the royalist conspirators, "was the consecration of Napoleon's personal power." To the count of Provence, who had sought to enlist his aid in the restoration of the Bourbons, the first consul now wrote: "You should not desire to return to France; you would have to march over 100,000 dead bodies." Shortly after, the czar expelled the count from his territory, and the latter was forced to seek temporary refuge in Warsaw. The royalist agencies in France were broken up, and only bands of brigands masquerading under the banner of the cross remained in the south of France to remind the government of the royalist threat that had once existed. An expected insurrection in Brittany failed to materialize, degenerating into pure brigandage which was handled by the gendarmerie and military commissions. Bonaparte then played his trump card. Sanguine that the royalist party in France was broken up, he issued a decree which at one stroke removed more than 50,000 names from the list of so called émigrés, many of whom were royalist sympathizers who had not actually left France! The measure was a daring one and a clever move, not to mention the fact that it was also illegal, for it deprived the pretender of almost half of his faithful adherents. The only condition imposed upon the amnestied émigrés was that they take an oath of loyalty to the constitution.

While Moreau continued his campaign in Germany, steadily driving Kray's troops to the east until a new armistice suspended hostilities and left the French in control of Bavaria, negotiations toward peace with Austria were carried on first at Lunéville and later at Paris. It was not long before Bonaparte discovered that the Austrians had no real intention of concluding peace at that time without the concurrence of their English allies, or on the terms that the French offered. Both sides prepared for the resumption of the campaign, which opened with the formal termination of the armistice at the end of November, 1800. Meantime Bona-

parte had attained the financial object of the war, for the governments of the conquered territory in northern Italy and southern
Germany were forced to contribute generously to their French
conquerors. The winter campaign was brief and decisive. Again it
was upon Moreau that the honor of victory fell. On December 2,
he won the most decisive and the bloodiest battle of the entire war
against the second coalition of Hohenlinden, which is not far from
Munich. Continuing his advance, he was within fifty miles of
Vienna when he yielded to the Austrian demand for an armistice.
In the meantime Brune and Murat were completing the French
reconquest of Italy, the former driving the Austrians out of the
Po valley and the latter expelling the English and Neapolitans
from Tuscany. These military triumphs and France's improved
foreign relations, particularly with Russia, forced the hand of
the Austrians, who on February 9, 1801, signed the treaty of
Lunéville.

The treaty confirmed the arrangements made by the treaty of
Campo Formio concerning the cession of territory in Belgium,
along the Rhine, and in Italy. The emperor, who signed as the
head of the Holy Roman Empire, recognized the Batavian, Helvetic, and Ligurian Republics, and agreed to the incorporation of
Modena and the Papal Legations into the Cisalpine Republic. He
also agreed to the formation of the kingdom of Etruria (Tuscany),
which was given to the duke of Parma, the husband of the Spanish
Infanta (as part of Bonaparte's bargain with Spain over Louisiana). The expelled duke of Tuscany was to be compensated for
the loss of his state by land in Germany. The provision in the
treaty of Campo Formio which promised Austria territorial compensation in Bavaria was not renewed, while on the other hand,
France gained the right to supervise the arrangements concerning
indemnifications for the dispossessed princes of the left bank of
the Rhine. All that Austria now retained of her former possessions
in Italy was Venetia, for the peace deprived her of her last territorial foothold in central Italy. A treaty with Naples on March
18, 1801, gave the French the right to maintain an expeditionary
force at the important eastern port of Taranto, while at the same
time the king of the Two Sicilies promised to close the harbors
of his state to the English.

England held out alone against the conquering French; but the
sentiment for peace was strong in England, and Bonaparte himself

was anxious for a truce. He had failed to make headway on the seas against the British. In September, 1800, the French garrison in Malta was forced to surrender, and in the summer of 1801, the British regained Egypt. Secure in their control over the Mediterranean, the British emphatically asserted their supremacy in northern waters by breaking up the League of Armed Neutrality which the principal Baltic states had formed against England. These victories not only strengthened the determination of Bonaparte to sue for peace, but made it possible for the English to conclude peace with honor. Pitt's government had fallen in the spring of 1801, and the new ministry of Addington gave a friendly reception to peace overtures from Paris. The English desired peace largely to regain the European markets that the French had closed to them. Bonaparte desired a truce mainly to complete his pacification within France and to consolidate his position in Europe.

Negotiations began in the spring of 1801; and in October, 1801, the preliminaries of peace were signed at London. Great Britain restored to France and her allies, Spain and Holland, all her naval conquests except Ceylon, which had been taken from the Dutch, and Trinidad, which had been won from Spain. The Cape was returned to Holland with the understanding that it would be open both to British and to French commerce. Malta was to be restored to the Knights of Saint John, one of the conditions being the guarantee of its integrity by the great powers. The British also withdrew from the island of Elba. In return the French agreed to evacuate the kingdom of Naples, to guarantee the integrity of Portugal (which Bonaparte had violated in June, 1801, by forcing that kingdom to close its ports against the English), to restore Egypt to Turkey (the news of the surrender of Alexandria was not known until after the signing of the preliminary terms of peace), and to recognize the independence of the Ionian Islands. A fortnight later France and Russia came to terms. In secret articles these two countries agreed to regulate in common the question of territorial compensation for the dispossessed German princes. They also agreed to settle the Italian question in so far as it was not regulated through France's existing treaty arrangements with the papacy, Naples, and Austria.

The burst of joy which greeted the news that the preliminaries of peace had been signed lasted only a short time in England. Statesmen were dumfounded when they scanned the document and found no mention of the Rhine, Italian states, and Switzerland, which Bonaparte refused to discuss on the ground that he had already made arrangements in the treaty of Lunéville. Militant patriots bristled indignantly over the surrender of most of England's maritime conquests. The business world was aghast over the failure of the negotiators to conclude a favorable treaty concerning British commerce with the Continent. Hopes of revived prosperity were bitterly dashed to the ground. A chorus of criticism and recrimination fell upon the government, but it was too late for major changes in the treaty. Six months later, on March 25, 1802, the treaty of Amiens was signed by representatives of the two nations. The most important modifications concerned Malta and the Cape. The latter was returned to the Dutch in "full sovereignty" and the arrangements in respect to the English evacuation of Malta were altered and amplified.

Unquestionably France profited most by the treaty. It left her in control of Holland, Belgium, the left bank of the Rhine, and Italy, without obliging her to guarantee the independence of the new republics. By this singular lack of precaution the English negotiators gave Bonaparte a free hand on the Continent. The return of the Cape of Good Hope to the Dutch in "full sovereignty" and the surrender of Malta to weak authorities whom he could intimidate made it possible for him to renew his eastern projects. The failure to include the renewal of a treaty of commerce with France placed a check upon the economic life of England and excluded her products not alone from France, but from the French colonies which the treaty restored and from the new republics in Europe which France controlled. After ten years of war England had obtained only two islands, while France emerged the most powerful state in Europe. "One may state without the slightest exaggeration," wrote Talleyrand, "that at the time of the peace of Amiens France enjoyed abroad, thanks to its military supremacy, such power, glory, and influence that the most ambitious person could desire nothing more for his country. And what made this state of affairs still more marvelous, was the rapidity with which it was accomplished. In less than two and a half years, . . . France had climbed from the depths of degradation, into which the Directory had cast it, to the highest position in Europe." France was indeed victorious, and Europe enjoyed the blessings of peace amidst the rumblings of a coming war. The questions that Amiens left unsolved and the questions that Bonaparte's aggressive acts aroused after the peace, once more brought France and Europe to grips.

THE PACIFICATION OF FRANCE: THE CONCORDAT

Within a month after the signing of the treaty of Amiens the dignified cathedral of Notre Dame in Paris echoed to the sound of a great celebration which marked the final reconciliation of the Revolution with the church. Indeed, the first acts of the provisional consuls had given reason to hope that the persecution of Catholicism would be ended. Subject to certain restrictions, churches were opened for services on the Sabbath, the clergy were liberated from the hostile surveillance of the government, and the vexatious oath of fidelity to the republic was replaced by a simple oath of fidelity to the constitution. The official revolutionary religion was, if not abandoned to its fate by the government, at least left to its own resources to survive or fail. The religion of patriotism was decaying, but the religious spirit of the masses was strong. In addition to the variant forms of Catholicism, there were at least five minor cults that had adherents in greater or lesser number. It has been argued with great cogency that the benevolent neutrality which the state observed at the beginning of the Consulate would, if continued, have ultimately solved the problems of religious dissent in France; but for a variety of reasons which we shall examine, Bonaparte chose to intervene and regulate the religious life of the nation.

Bonaparte himself had no pronounced religious beliefs. If not an agnostic, he was at the most a vague deist. "Let them call me a papist," he said. "I am nothing. I was a Mohammedan in Egypt; I shall be a Catholic here for the good of the people. I do not believe in religions. . . . It was by becoming a Catholic that I terminated the Vendean war; by becoming a Mussulman that I obtained a footing in Egypt, by becoming an Ultramontane that I won the Italian priests, and had I to govern a nation of Jews I would rebuild Solomon's temple." Personally indifferent to religious dogma, he felt very strongly that France was fundamentally Catholic. Reconciliation with the church would be as beneficial to the people as it would be advantageous for his own policy. Mankind in general, he firmly believed, required the authority of revealed religion to be happy or resigned to its lot. If he was sincere in thinking that the promise of eternal felicity reconciled men to their misfortunes on earth—and there is no reason to doubt his sincerity—it is also true that he counted upon the people's submission to the laws of the church, upon their obedience of the traditional rules of morality, to facilitate his task of ending the revolutionary ferment and restoring law and order. The bishops and priests he later referred to as "my sacred gendarmerie." In this he once more revealed his military training; the prospect of policing the mind appealed to the drillmaster. But he also expected to derive great and immediate political advantages from a settlement of the religious question.

He knew that the purchasers of ecclesiastical property would never be easy until the church formally validated their titles or made some other definitive and friendly arrangement. The unsold ecclesiastical property which the state held was decidedly less salable than other national land because of the insecurity of the title rights. The question of the legitimacy of children born of civil wedlock and of their inheritance rights was equally perplexing. The fear of a royalist restoration could never be allayed unless the Catholics in France were detached from the emigrant ecclesiastics who continually denounced the existing régime. "I must detach the Catholics of France from those bishops in Vienna, London, or Madrid whose opposition to the republican government penetrates into the family hearth. . . . The pope could not do me a greater service; he alone, without the shedding of blood, without any commotion, can bring the Catholics of France to obey the republican government." An equally important consideration in his mind was that of effacing the Jacobin taint that clung to his name. By solving the religious question he would destroy the notion that prevailed in Europe that the Revolution connoted anarchy in government and atheism in religion. He would make himself acceptable to the old monarchies of Europe.

Negotiations with the newly chosen pontiff, Pope Pius VII, began shortly after the battle of Marengo, when Bonaparte first felt strong enough to mature his plans; and they were conducted both at Rome and at Paris. When the pretender learned that the papal envoys had gone to Paris, he wrote, "Perhaps never has the cause of the French monarchy run greater danger"; and his pessimism was only too well founded. Bonaparte was inclined to bully the papal envoys, whose task was made doubly difficult when French military victories stiffened the tone of the republican negotiators. The negotiations were intricate and prolonged, and twenty-one drafts were made and discarded before the Concordat was signed by the diplomatic representatives of France and Rome and accepted by Bonaparte on July 16, 1801.

The preamble of the Concordat was a compromise between the extreme views of both parties. It stated:

> The Government of the French Republic recognizes that the Roman, Catholic, and Apostolic religion is the religion of the great majority of French citizens. His Holiness likewise recognizes that this same religion has derived, and in this moment again expects, the greatest benefit and grandeur from the establishment of the Catholic worship in France and from the personal profession of it which the Consuls of this Republic make.

By this compromise the papacy was protected against Bonaparte's threat to secularize the state, while Bonaparte succeeded in defeating the pope's desire to have Catholicism declared the state religion. The government agreed to permit the free exercise of the Catholic worship subject to the police power of the state—a most important reservation—and engaged itself to place churches and chapels at the disposal of the bishops. The papacy and the government were jointly to make a new distribution of the French episcopal dioceses, to which new incumbents were to be appointed by the first consul and canonically instituted by the pope. The bishops then were to appoint the curés. The government agreed to pay a suitable salary to bishops and curés, who, before entering upon their functions, were to take an oath of fidelity to the government. In return for the salary list and the use of churches for worship the pope gave up the claim to the confiscated but unsold land of the church. The papacy also recognized the revolutionary land settlement and declared irrevocable the sale of ecclesiastical property. Each bishop was given the right to open a chapter in his cathedral and a seminary in his diocese, and the parishioners were to be permitted to establish church foundations.

Bonaparte thus obtained the main objects for which he had been striving. The Concordat maintained the revolutionary sale of the ecclesiastical land, which satisfied his unalterable determination to perpetuate the civil conquests of the Revolution. It assured the government of the submission of the clergy, who became paid civil servants appointed by the state, bound to it by oath, and regulated in their very acts of worship by its supervisory regulations. During the Old Régime the great wealthy prelates, rich in lands and prebends and linked by blood and loyalty to the nobility, had often tied the hands of the government. All that the Revolution had destroyed, and Bonaparte had no nostalgia for the past. He intended and succeeded in making the Concordat serve his aim of founding a strong autocratic régime. For the present he had detached the church from the Bourbons and taken a great stride toward the perpetuation of the Consulate. Moreover, by this highly realistic act he had gained the church's official indorsement of the Revolution which it once had condemned as "anathema," and this indorsement consequently recognized civil marriage and registration of civil status (births, marriages, etc.).

On the other hand, the papacy had the consolation of masking its real concessions in ambiguous phrases. It gained great prestige by ending the schism and restoring unity of faith. The absence of any specific provisions concerning monastic orders and the reëstablishment of religious congregations was a notable victory for the papal cause. By giving the pope the right to demand the resignation of all the bishops Bonaparte all but rendered illusory his own right to nominate new ones, for never before had the French state or the French clergy attributed such sweeping powers to Rome. By this provision as well as by his virtual incorporation of the bishops and priests into the civil service, Bonaparte almost made it inevitable that all protests on their part would be addressed to Rome. Yet if these consequences be censured, the blame for the concomitant ultramontanism of the clergy and the anticlericalism of the government in the nineteenth century rests with the Revolution and not with Bonaparte.

The Concordat was not altogether popular in France. It had the enthusiastic support of fully half of the nation, upon which Bonaparte had counted; but the small minority represented by the intellectuals, the administrative and political personnel, and army circles were bitterly opposed to the agreement. The rest of the country was more or less indifferent. To surmount the expected opposition of the critics Bonaparte had reserved for himself the right of "providing by regulation against the more serious inconveniences that might arise from a literal execution of the Concordat." By this right, phrased so euphemistically as to constitute a masterpiece in ironic understatement, Bonaparte made effective the police regulations given to him by article one of the Concordat; viz., that the worship of the Catholic religion should be "in conformity with the police regulations which the government shall deem necessary for the public tranquillity." These "regulations," which not only filled in the omissions of the Concordat, but also provided for the state regulation of Protestantism, were known as the Organic Articles. The Concordat and the Organic Articles were combined in one text, so as to give the impression that the "regulations" were an integral part of the arrangement that had been made with the papacy, and issued as a single law on April 8, 1802. The pope, however, knew nothing of the Organic Articles until they were passed, and he never accepted them as provisions of the Concordat. These articles, in so far as they dealt with the Roman Church, fully elaborated the "rights and prerogatives" of the state in its relations with the Catholic Church in France. But they did so in a spirit which violated the terms of the Concordat. They reasserted the militant claims of the Gallican clergy, but a Gallican clergy thoroughly subordinated to the state. The Organic Articles were an error and Bonaparte lived to regret them.

After the Tribunate and the Legislative Corps had accepted the Concordat and adopted the Organic Articles, there was another delay caused by the refusal of several of the constitutional (or juring) clergy to confess penitence for their sin of schism. Until they agreed to do so the papal representative refused to institute them into office. They finally retracted, so at least the pope was led to believe, and most of them were received again into the fold of the church. The solemn Te Deum at Notre Dame on Easter Sunday, April 18, 1802, publicly celebrated the return of peace. Delayed until after the peace of Amiens, this solemn religious ceremony really celebrated a double pacification—the restoration of order within France and the restoration of peace in Europe. The genius of Bonaparte had accomplished within three short years that to which all Frenchmen had looked forward—vainly for many long years—the end of the revolutionary upheaval and war. Thus reasoned the majority of Frenchmen, who now were confident that France would enter upon a new era of peace and prosperity.

XV. BEGINNINGS OF THE EMPIRE IN FRANCE AND EUROPE

THE LIFE CONSULATE

FROM the very first, as his summary revision of Sieyès' constitutional project clearly indicated, Bonaparte aimed at personal rule.
Great as his power was under the Constitution of the Year VIII,
the first consul chafed at the restrictions imposed upon his authority. As early as November, 1800, his brother Lucien sounded
public opinion on the question of making Bonaparte's rule hereditary, but the occasion was not yet ripe for change. The royalists in
France, who were not slow in realizing that Bonaparte stood between them and the realization of their hopes, made a desperate
effort to remove him from their path. On a little side street in
Paris which they knew he would traverse on his way to the Opera
on Christmas Eve, 1800, they set a mechanical device so arranged
as to explode when his carriage passed. The machine exploded,
killing more than a score of people, but the first consul miraculously escaped injury. The police readily ascertained that the plot
was the work of royalists, but it suited Bonaparte's political purposes to place the responsibility upon the Jacobins. From the old
revolutionaries he had more to fear for the moment than he had
from the opposition of the Right.

Aware that the legislative assemblies would strongly dispute
the voting of repressive measures against the Jacobins, he put
pressure upon the more subservient Senate to issue a Senatus Consultum ordering the deportation of more than a hundred outspoken Jacobins. This procedure, which he justified as necessary
for the preservation of the constitution, set a precedent, for in
the future Bonaparte largely ignored the assemblies and acted
through Senatus Consulta which had the force of law. During the
remainder of the year 1801, the first consul intensified his campaign against liberals and radicals throughout the country, procur-
ing through special tribunals the arrest and imprisonment of more
than seven hundred Jacobin sympathizers.

For all his efforts the liberals in the Tribunate and the Corps législatif continued their bitter opposition to his internal policy. Bonaparte had little patience with their attitude and spoke ominously of drowning the "vermin" that opposed his will in the assemblies. In the spring of 1802, when the first election of one-fifth of the members of the assemblies was to take place, Bonaparte showed his hand. Instead of following the constitutional provision of determining by lot the deputies who were to resign their seats, he had the Senate select the four-fifths that were to keep theirs. By that simple maneuver he excluded the liberals, while at the same time the Senate named new deputies whose compliance with Bonaparte's policy could be taken for granted. Thus, by 1802, the first consul had effectively silenced liberals and radicals outside of the assemblies and nullified all parliamentary restrictions upon his authority.

After the ratification of peace on the Continent and the celebration of the signing of the Concordat in a solemn Te Deum of Easter Day, April 18, 1802, he felt strong enough to make a sweeping bid for the support of the emigrant royalists and all other nobles who, without actually emigrating, had their names on the official list of émigrés. After Marengo he had stricken 50,000 names from the list of emigrants, but an equal number were still proscribed. By a Senatus Consultum dated April 26, 1802, he now extended full amnesty to all but about one thousand die-hard emigrants on the condition that they return to France before September, 1802, and take the oath of loyalty to the constitution. To those whose property had been seized but was still unsold, full restoration of their estates was promised. This measure completed his systematic destruction of organized opposition. With the republicanism of the armies and the generals hushed, the opposition of the legislative bodies ended, the emigrant royalists no longer dangerous, and his popularity at its height, Bonaparte had good reason to suppose that the moment was ripe to resume his march toward the throne. He knew that he could count upon the compliance of his bureaucracy, which desired nothing better than the permanency of the new régime, as well as upon that of his admirers, who regarded his government as the sole barrier against anarchy.

Upon the instigation of Cambacérès and Lucien, the Tribunate decided on May 6, 1802, to give to General Bonaparte, first consul of the republic, "a signal pledge of the gratitude of the nation" for his great work of pacification and reorganization. The occasion was well chosen, for this was the day that the peace of Amiens was formally announced. Two days later, the Senate, to which the decision of the Tribunate had been communicated, resolved to extend Bonaparte's tenure of office for ten additional years. He was bitterly disappointed, for he had expected the senators to propose the consulate for life. But, concealing his feelings, he thanked the Senate (May 9), adding: "You deem that I owe a fresh sacrifice to the nation; I am ready to perform it, if the commands of the people confirm what your vote allows." By this clever move he referred the question from the Senate to the people; and on the following day (May 10) the Council of State, to which the matter was now referred, formulated the question that was to be put to the people in the following words: "Is Napoleon Bonaparte to be made Consul for Life?" Thus by an act of more than dubious legality—for nothing justified the Council of State in its formulation of the question—Bonaparte achieved his end. That same day, a consular decree completed the arrangements for the new referendum or plebiscite. The assemblies bowed before the inevitable, only Carnot lifting his voice in the Tribunate against the consulate for life. The Senate also acquiesced in this violation of the republican constitution. The results of the popular vote, which were announced in August, were overwhelmingly favorable to Bonaparte: 3,568,885 citizens voted in favor of the change, and only 8374 against it. France showed by this overwhelming vote that it gave its full support to Bonaparte, and on that same day the Senate proclaimed Napoleon Bonaparte consul for life. Bonapartism, which like Caesarism depended upon the consent—and the resignation—of the people, became the new political system.

The reorganization of the government was completed two days later on August 4, when Bonaparte's draft of a new constitution was accepted *in toto* by the Senate and issued as the "Organic Senatus Consultum of the Constitution of 16 Thermidor of the Year X." The consuls were to hold office for life, but Bonaparte presented the names of the second and third consuls, who were then appointed by the Senate. He gave himself the right to name his successor with the stipulation that if his candidate were rejected by the Senate the right of nomination would devolve upon the other consuls. He created a Privy Council, whose members he named from the ministers and councilors, to which treaties were henceforth referred for ratification. This Privy Council was also given the right to lay projects concerning the constitution and matters not provided for in its text before the Senate; if accepted, those projects were to have the force of Senatus Consulta. The number of senators was to be increased, the arrangements for the nominations of the new senators giving Bonaparte additional power. In measure as his control over the Senate became greater, its powers were correspondingly increased. Beginning in the year XIII (1804–1805), the Tribunate was to be reduced to fifty members. The local and national lists of eligible candidates were abolished in favor of district and departmental electoral colleges which were composed of the most prosperous citizens. These colleges were granted certain rights of nomination to vacancies in local and national assemblies, but the actual appointive power was vested in the first consul. The civil list of the first consul was increased from 500,000 to 6,000,000 francs. This Senatus Consultum is generally known as the Constitution of the Year X, even though the Constitution of the Year VIII was not formally discarded. Despite the retention of the three consuls, the government that it established was a monarchy in fact if not in name. The proclamation of the empire two years later should have surprised no one. The preliminary steps were already taken in 1802.

As it became more and more evident, in particular after the establishment of the consulate for life, that Bonaparte was aiming at personal rule, social life in Paris took on a new character. Bonaparte early realized that manners and customs, as well as institutions, would have to be revised in order to consolidate his government. Under the able and discreet influence of Talleyrand the society of the Old Régime made its peace with the France of Bonaparte. A new court gradually reappeared at the Tuileries and royal usages and etiquette slowly replaced the informality of republican customs. Busts of Brutus and other Republican heroes were no longer to be seen. Madame de Campan, who had once been a lady-in-waiting to Marie Antoinette, impressed the ways of good society upon the young ladies of the day, and the beautiful Madame Récamier set the tone of refined salon life in Paris. Slowly Paris reasserted its pristine supremacy in politeness, in elegance of dress, and in the culinary arts. The loutish *nouveaux riches* of the Directory were carefully ostracized by the court and the refined salons. The Opera balls were held again, for the first time since the Revolution. Sumptuous fêtes were celebrated in the fashionable salons and châteaux which the great ladies of the aristocratic Faubourg Saint-Germain deigned to grace with their presence. Provincials and foreigners once more flocked to the capital, and Paris regained that charming and elegant gayety which was hers by tradition.

The Founding of the Empire

The life consulate was only a stop-gap of two years' duration, an interval which Bonaparte employed to good advantage in furthering his personal interests. The success of his sweeping reforms in internal affairs [1] swelled the popularity that he gained by his restoration of order in France and his termination of the war. With the exception of the few uncompromising Jacobins, who were quiet, and the royalists, who were soon to be discredited, all classes sang his praise. He seemed a bulwark against disorder. Yet his life was still endangered by secret conspiracies, although, since the explosion of the "infernal machine" in 1800, he had taken the most careful precautions and never showed himself in public without a large escort of police. The most famous of the plots against him, which was disclosed in 1804, bears examination, for it was the suppression of the conspiracy which gave Bonaparte the opportunity to make his rule hereditary.

Toward the end of 1803, various royalist emigrants living in London drew up an elaborate plan involving uprisings in the west and south of France, the abduction or assassination of the first consul, and the return of a Bourbon pretender to France. From supposedly royalist sources in France the émigré conspirators received funds, and from the mouth of a presumed French royalist they obtained firm assurances that the republican opposition in France would join them against Bonaparte. As we now know, Bonaparte himself supplied the funds, while the French royalist who gave them assurances was a secret agent of Fouché, Bonaparte's former minister. In short, the first consul manufactured a plot which at all times he controlled and which he could disclose when disclosure served his ends.

The occasion came early in 1804, when the Breton, Georges

[1] These great reforms are discussed in detail in Chapter XVIII.

Cadoudal, and General Pichegru, the leaders of the conspiracy, secretly met General Moreau in Paris and tried to win his support. All three were arrested and imprisoned, Moreau unjustly, for he had refused to join the conspirators. While the press bared the horrible details of what seemed a dastardly plot, the government's secret police hunted high and low for the Bourbon prince who was expected in France. They knew that it could not be the count of Artois, who had not budged from England, so they sought to pick up the scent elsewhere. The trail led to Baden, where the young prince of Enghien, the grandson of the duke of Condé, was living. It was reported that he came secretly into Strasbourg, received secret English agents, and was in communication with the traitor Dumouriez. Upon the receipt of these reports, even before the arrest of Cadoudal, Bonaparte jumped to the conclusion that Dumouriez and Enghien were the active leaders (or dupes) of the plot. Inspired by Talleyrand and Fouché, who were anxious to compromise him by a crime which would make him their accomplice and end his reproaches against their revolutionary past, Bonaparte made a grievous decision. He ordered his soldiers to invade the territory of Baden, seize Enghien, and speed him to Paris for trial. When he gave those orders he had already decided to condemn the young Bourbon to death. The arrest took place in the night of March 14. On the 20th, the last of the Condés was brought to the castle of Vincennes and a scant six hours after his arrival, at eleven o'clock at night, he was subjected to the indignity of a hollow military trial. Before the break of dawn he was shot, and his body thrown into an open grave that had been dug before his arrival at Vincennes.

In the meantime, long before Enghien had reached Paris, the first consul had learned that the prince was entirely innocent. Why then did Bonaparte persevere in that act of extraordinary violence and crime which sullied his entire career? He never dodged the responsibility for this act. In his will he wrote:

I caused the duke of Enghien to be arrested and judged, because it was necessary for the safety, the interest, and the honor of the French people when the count of Artois, by his own confession was supporting sixty assassins at Paris. Under similar circumstances I would again act in the same way.

In other words, the murder of the duke was at once an act of reprisal and a warning to the Bourbons, a terrible declaration that reconciliation between them and Bonaparte was impossible.

The punishment of the royalist conspirators soon followed. A fortnight after the execution of Enghien the hapless Pichegru was found strangled in his cell. Cadoudal and several other conspirators were condemned to death and executed. Moreau, whose quiet self-possession and dignity during the trial won the sympathy of the court and audience, was first condemned to a brief imprisonment and later pardoned on condition that he accept exile to America. Thus the first consul removed one of his dangerous military rivals and the leader of the moderate republican opposition.

The horror that filled Paris at the news of the execution of the duke of Enghien found its echo in a temporary depression of the stock market and in a momentary decline of Bonaparte's great popularity. On the whole, the stirring events of the conspiracy, the trial, and the punishments rebounded in favor of that ambitious project which he had unceasingly nursed, the establishment of his hereditary rule. A current of opinion, in part genuine and in part sedulously inspired by the government, swept the country in favor of Bonaparte. His political henchmen guardedly advanced a project for the consolidation of his régime. They stressed the main argument that he and he alone stood between France and the renewal of the revolutionary upheaval. The peasantry, the military, and the middle class for whom Bonaparte's rule meant prosperity and peace were quite indifferent to the secret intrigues which prepared the way for the establishment of the hereditary empire. Even those who had distaste for his methods and ambition felt that the moment had come for France to put an end to foreign intrigue and to make such changes as would place the stability of their government beyond the question of Bonaparte's continued existence or his sudden death at the hands of an assassin. The contemplated change was inevitable. It completed the dictatorship begun in Brumaire.

Within a week after the execution of Enghien, the Senate petitioned Bonaparte "to complete his work by rendering it, like his glory, immortal." While the first consul bided his time, allowing public opinion to seize the full implications of the Senate's petition, one of his admirers presented a motion in the Tribunate to have Napoleon Bonaparte proclaimed emperor and the imperial dignity declared hereditary in his family. Only Carnot, "the Organizer of Victóry" of 1793, dared risk Bonaparte's wrath and speak against it. The Corps législatif meekly voted in favor of the project. On May 4 the Senate, to which the vote of the assembly had been communicated, declared: "Glory, gratitude, devotion, reason, the interests of the state, all unite to proclaim Napoleon hereditary emperor." Napoleon then busied himself, as the head of the government committee, with drawing up a new constitutional document. After a short debate in the Council of State the document was transmitted to the Senate which adopted it as the "Organic Senatus Consultum of 28 Floréal, Year XII" (May 18, 1804).

The first title of the new constitution (the Constitution of the Year XII) reads as follows: "The government of the French republic is entrusted to an emperor . . . Napoleon Bonaparte, present first consul of the republic, is emperor of the French." The second title provided for the inheritance, which was to be in the direct, natural, and legitimate and adoptive lineage of Napoleon. No radical innovations in the machinery of government were made. The changes in detail that the new constitution demanded completed the subjection of the legislative bodies. The Tribunate was divided into three sections and lost the right publicly to criticize the projects of the government. The Corps législatif obtained the right of discussion in secret session, but the discussions were withheld from the public unless authorized by the government. The Council of State, as before, voted decrees which the Senate issued as Consulta. The Senate itself lost whatever independence it had had, though it was given certain illusory rights which could be exercised only with the emperor's consent. A final clause provided for a plebiscite on the following proposition:

The people desire the inheritance of the imperial dignity in the direct, natural, legitimate and adoptive lineage of Napoleon Bonaparte, and in the direct, natural, and legitimate lineage of Joseph Bonaparte and of Louis Bonaparte, as is regulated in the organic Senatus Consultum of this day.

This referendum, like the preceding ones of the year VIII and the year X, implied that Napoleon would not proceed without the consent of the people, but in reality it was the seal of their resignation. It assumed their *acceptance* of the establishment of the imperial dignity and all that it submitted for their ratification was the *manner of inheritance* of the crown. As the popular vote for the empire was slightly less than that for the life consulate, Napoleon delayed publishing the figures until he had "corrected" the vote so as to show a higher total than that of 1802.

Napoleon's choice of the title "emperor" was not haphazard. He could not assume the title "king," for the Bourbon princes had not renounced their claims. Even as a legitimate king of revolutionary France, he would have placed himself in a ridiculous position. His idea was to go back to an earlier French line, to the dynasty of Charlemagne, and represent himself as the legitimate successor of the great warrior who had been emperor as well as king of the Franks. The empire was to serve as the instrument of his policy, a policy which only gradually became clear in his mind, but which even then was dimly fashioned in his thoughts. Thus the first sentence of the new constitution was highly significant, for it intimated that the empire was to be European even though the emperor ruled over the French Republic.

Having become emperor, Napoleon had to establish an imperial court and assume the ceremonies and the habits of monarchy. Invested with the imperial title, Napoleon still retained many of his old habits, but to maintain his new dignity he surrounded himself with great dignitaries, grand officers, grand marshals, and many other minor holders of titles. The second and third ex-consuls, Cambacérès and Lebrun, became arch-chancellor of the empire and arch-treasurer. His brother Joseph became grand elector, his brother Louis, constable, his brother-in-law Murat, grand admiral, and his uncle Fesch, grand almoner. Fouché received his reward in his reappointment as minister of police, a position which brought him close to the ear of the emperor. To reward Talleyrand, Napoleon was to revive the office of the old court, grand chamberlain; and his companion generals, all without exception men of the people, became grand marshals.

Haunted as he was by the name and the image of Charlemagne and anxious to impress himself upon France as the successor of the mighty Teuton, Napoleon now visited Aix-la-Chapelle, where Charlemagne's relics were buried, and he returned to Paris bearing the insignia and the sword of that ruler. Like Charlemagne, he needed the consecration of the Catholic Church; and shortly after the founding of the empire he entered into negotiations to induce Pope Pius VII to come to Paris and bestow his religious blessing at the ceremony of coronation. In the eyes of both men the matter had a political as well as a religious significance. The pope allowed himself to be convinced that the prestige of the church would be enhanced by the spectacle of the mighty emperor of the French bowing before the head of the church, and he made the arduous trip to the French capital to anoint the Corsican upstart. The coronation took place on December 2, 1804, at the cathedral of Notre Dame. No pains had been spared to make the proceedings resplendent, though a modern historian has aptly remarked, after attesting the great pomp that prevailed, that "the occasion was remarkable rather for splendor than for popular enthusiasm." It was remarkable also for its dramatic climax. As the pope was on the point of crowning the emperor, Napoleon took the crown from the hands of Pius VII and, turning his back on the venerable pontiff, faced the people and crowned himself, as if to show by that gesture that he owed it to none other than himself. After crowning himself, Napoleon crowned Josephine. He was now doubly consecrated; by the *vox populi* in the plebiscite and by the *vox Dei* in the religious ceremony. Of all the expectations of Pius VII, only one, and a minor one, was realized. Napoleon agreed to reëstablish the Gregorian calendar, beginning with January 1, 1806.

It remained to be seen whether the monarchs of Europe would recognize Napoleon's title. No perspicacious statesman in Europe could fail to realize the implication of Napoleon's new dignity. "It was not only the consecration, almost the sanctification of the Revolution, not only a thrust to legitimacy and an offense to every established right, but a frightful threat against old monarchic Europe. . . . It was the Revolution projected forward by its own triumphant strength." [2] From England, then at war with France, no greetings came to the new emperor. Gustavus IV, king of Sweden, scornfully referred to him as "Mister Napoleon Bonaparte." In Russia there was no question of recognizing Napoleon's new title, so strained had relations become between Alexander and

[2] E. Driault, *Napoléon et l'Europe: Austerlitz, la fin du Saint Empire* (*1804–1806*), p. 69.

Napoleon; and the sultan of Constantinople was too closely dominated by Russian influence to dare extend official recognition. On
the other hand, formal letters of felicitation came promptly from
the Batavian and the Italian Republics, the Helvetic Confederation, Spain, and the petty German princes. The Prussian court followed suit, as did Austria, ungraciously and after several months
of diplomatic bargaining.

The Corsican adventurer was now emperor of the French. In
four brief years he had ended "the romance of the Revolution"
and established his authority over the country. He had imposed
his will on France because of his practical intelligence and his soaring imagination, his boundless confidence and his tireless energy,
and his genius for combining a meticulous attention to details with
an undimmed vision of the ultimate object that he desired. The
reorganization of France was his work. He closed the chapter of
republican violence and royalist reprisal. To people sick of the
Revolution he brought peace and stability without restoring the
Bourbons or sacrificing the benefits of the Revolution. He would
not undo the work of the Revolution; but he could not continue
it, for he was hostile to the idea of liberty which had inspired
the revolutionists. For the idea of liberty he substituted the idea
of authority. He retained the essentially democratic society that
the Revolution had created, but he restored and perfected the
centralized administration of the Old Régime. He might con-
ceivably have ended his days as emperor of the French and perpetuated his dynasty, for the people at first welcomed his autocratic
rule. But he could not pursue the safe course of peace. On more
than one occasion he declared that war was essential to his political purposes; and the war which he renewed in 1803 mapped the
road to his ultimate failure.

The Rupture of the Peace of Amiens

The responsibility for the rupture of the peace of Amiens rests
squarely with Napoleon. He had never considered Amiens as more
than a truce in his struggle to humble England and destroy her
colonial empire and commercial position. He provoked the war
that was renewed in May, 1803, by a deliberate policy which made
it apparent to all that he was bent on an enormous expansion of

French power in Europe and a revival of that French naval and colonial supremacy which England had destroyed in the eighteenth century.

To maintain that Napoleon fought wars solely because he was under the irresistible sway of blind ambition is scarcely adequate as an explanation of the actions of the profound statesman that he was. On the other hand, it is inexact to suppose that the war which he provoked in 1803, like the wars in which he engaged subsequently, was a studied move toward a clearly determined goal. He himself gives a clue to his actions, for he once declared to an intimate that "he will not go far who knows from the first whither he is going." From the first he did not know whither he was going. Ambition, of course, played a great part in his actions, romantic ambition, love of glory and power, thirst of fame that would make his name immortal.

Ambition alone does not explain his actions. In the first place, he understood that he was a military upstart in the society of ancient European royalty. His position was insecure, dependent upon military triumphs and the adulation of the French nation. He was completely convinced that the great powers would not passively accept the new government in France as a permanent part of the European system of states. And in this surmise he was entirely correct. France, he concluded, must be first or fail entirely. Secondly, his attitude toward France's weaker neighbors was radically different from that of the great European powers. Napoleon regarded these smaller states as so many props to his military projects and as so many different regions in which he could settle the beneficial revolutionary institutions. In his relations with them he was moved by "the genuine desire of the born administrator to rid the world of the accumulated débris of worn-out institutions." Perhaps one could say that he considered himself the knight paladin of the Revolution, as Charlemagne had regarded himself as the champion of Christianity. England, however, dependent for her prosperity and her very political existence upon a European balance of power and allies on the Continent, could interpret his aggressions in only one way, as a new version of the ancient French ambition for military domination in Europe. Thirdly, he was the prisoner of a fixed idea, of the overpowering conviction that until he had broken England's colonial and commercial supremacy and forced her to modify her maritime code, his own rule in France rested on fragile foundations. In his economic thinking, he was essentially a Physiocrat, and was convinced that England's prosperity was artificial, resting upon her commerce, which, in turn, rested upon her colonies. In the last analysis he provoked the war of 1803 in order to close the Continent to British products and thus destroy the prosperity which had made England the irreducible foe of France and the Revolution and of his larger designs.

The Napoleonic aggressions which awakened British fears of French military hegemony on the Continent took place in Italy, Switzerland, and Holland. Between 1801 and 1802 Napoleon revised the provisional administration of the Cisalpine Republic, forced his own draft of a constitution upon the inhabitants and had himself named president. To gain the military support of the Lombards he changed the name of the republic from "Cisalpine" to "Italian," a gesture flattering to the national aspirations of the population. The adjacent state of Piedmont suffered the rule of a military administration before it was annexed outright to France some months after the Peace of Amiens (September, 1802). The Ligurian republic also received a new constitution à la française and its great port, Genoa, which was also the principal outlet of Piedmont, fell into French hands (June, 1802). Farther south, the kingdom of Etruria (established by the peace of Lunéville), also felt the Napoleonic heel, while its principal port, Leghorn, like Genoa of strategic importance in the event hostilities were resumed with England, fell under French control. With the annexation of the small island of Elba and the strengthening of French control over the tiny republic of Lucca, all of northern Italy with the exception of Venetia was now directly or indirectly under French control.

To cover his approach to northern Italy Napoleon acquired full control of the Simplon road through the Alps by the simple expedient of separating the canton Valais, through which it ran, from Switzerland. Switzerland, too, was essential for Napoleon's purposes, for he needed there a firm government, friendly to France, which would cover the approach to the southeast frontier of France. Lunéville had guaranteed the independence of the Helvetic Republic, but nothing in the treaty prevented Napoleon from intervening to settle political strife. Intervene he did and successfully, both for himself and for the discordant Swiss factions, the aristocratic Federalists and the more democratic Centralists or Unitarians. By the compromise Act of Mediation, which was thrust upon selected Swiss delegates at Paris (1803), he ended the internal strife (which, in passing, his agents had stirred up) and transformed the Helvetic Republic into the Swiss Confederation, which became a military ally and satellite of France. The strengthening of French control over Holland had been part of Napoleon's earlier preparations on the Continent for the defense of France's frontiers. Military occupation in 1800 was followed by an enforced revision of the constitution and the payment of heavy indemnities by the Dutch burghers (October, 1801).

A second set of developments which aroused English apprehensions was Napoleon's steadfast refusal to arrange a commercial treaty and his rigorous enforcement of the existing French laws against products of British origin. If the situation before Amiens was grievous from the English standpoint, it was doubly serious after. British products were now excluded not only from France, but from the European states that Napoleon controlled and the colonies which England had returned to France and its allies. The new tariff law of April 28, 1803, was a clear indication of the policy of the French government to make the home market secure for the native manufacturers. The English concluded bitterly that Napoleon was intent on killing their industrial prosperity, and English merchants found that the peace cost them more dearly than the war.

Fears no less lively than those provoked by Napoleon's continental and commercial policies were raised by his project of winning a great colonial empire in the West as a balance to the loss of Egypt and Syria. The island of Haiti in the West Indies was to be the nucleus of the new France overseas, but in the West Napoleon's plans encountered two obstacles. The first of these was the talented, pathetic figure of the negro, Toussaint L'Ouverture, in whom the natives of the island had found a leader of genius. Over a period of almost a decade he had established his personal ascendancy in the island, from the western French part to Santo Domingo, which Spain had ceded to France in 1795. He had assured a plentiful supply of negro laborers for the white planters, established the necessary commercial relations with England and the United States, reformed the administration, and reëstablished order and prosperity. Napoleon had his own reasons for refusing to accept the *status quo* and the virtual autonomy of the island under the rule of Toussaint. It was no part of his plans to allow autonomy to a French colony, nor to allow it to trade freely in British products, nor yet to perpetuate the abolition of slavery and the slave trade, which the negro administrator had effected. Moreover, Toussaint was an obstacle to the realization of his colonial project. To undo Toussaint's able work was not difficult by decree, but the French expeditionary forces sent to the island in February, 1802, found the execution of the decree another matter, though Toussaint himself fell into the hands of the French, who sent him, the unhappy victim of their broken faith, to a French prison, where he died within a year. The second obstacle to Napoleon's plans was the outbreak of a terrific epidemic of yellow fever. General Leclerc, Napoleon's brother-in-law and the leader of the expeditionary force that was sent to Santo Domingo, fell victim to the fever and his successor surrendered to the negroes (1803). Of the 33,000 men sent in February, 1802, to reassert French supremacy, 24,000 were dead and an additional 7000 lay suffering in military hospitals a year later.

This grim fiasco ended the colonial project in the West. The collapse of the venture in Santo Domingo and the imminence of war with England determined him to sell Louisiana to the United States rather than run the risk of losing it completely to the English. The sale was consummated in 1803 for $15,000,000—a sales price that must be considered extraordinarily cheap in view of President Jefferson's strong desire for the territory.[3]

The fourth source of English misgivings lay in Napoleon's Mediterranean and eastern policy. By his aggressions in Holland he made the English route to India precarious, for the Cape had been returned, by the treaty of Amiens, to the Dutch, and now Napoleon controlled the Batavian Republic. To offset the danger from that source, England had to safeguard the overland routes to India from the Mediterranean, but there too Napoleon was threatening. He had strengthened his hold over Italy, and he gave intimations to the czar that the partition of the Turkish Empire was imminent. While English fears and resentment were at their height and English newspapers published biting attacks upon him, he suddenly raised the question of Egypt by publishing in the

[3] It is more than likely that Napoleon's colonial project in the West was an incident in his European schemes and concerned him much less than students of American history have thought.

official *Moniteur* the sensational account of Colonel Sébastiani, a military observer whom he had sent to that country. The account described the military weakness of Egypt and the unpopularity of the British forces there. It concluded that a small French expeditionary force could easily reconquer the country.[4] Meanwhile French agents fomented disturbances against Turkey in southern Greece, and the governor of the French East India colonies received instructions to prepare for active developments in India.

Against all these acts of aggression, indeed these incitations to war, England made sharp protest, relations becoming so bitter that in 1803 peace hung by a thread. In a long and acrimonious diplomatic controversy, during which the entire range of Napoleon's activities was discussed, neither country yielded its claims. So long as England refused to evacuate Malta, that small Mediterranean island south of Sicily whose broad harbor and strong fortress were the last English defense against his eastern project, Napoleon refused to evacuate Holland and restore Genoa and Piedmont. But his very refusal to make concessions in Holland and Italy made it impossible for England to yield on Malta. From a strictly legal point of view England stood condemned as the violator of treaty rights; from the larger point of view which considered England's prosperity, security, and historic tradition, no one can doubt that Napoleon's intolerable acts amply justified her stand. War became a reality in May, 1803, a war of which all shades of political opinion in England heartily approved.

The humbling of England and the destruction of its preponderant influence in Europe soon became a pretext for a vaster scheme which brought not only Europe but the Near East into its range. This scheme was at first ill defined, but during the early days of the empire its essential details became fixed in Napoleon's mind. He then spoke of it in the following vein: "Europe cannot be at rest except under the rule of a single head who will have kings for his officers, who will distribute his kingdoms to his lieutenants." But in 1811 he remarked to a confidant: "I have not yet fulfilled my mission and I mean to end what I have begun. We need a European code of law, a European court of appeal, a uniform coinage, a common system of weights and measures. The same law must run throughout Europe. I shall fuse all the nations into one."

[4] It is likely that Napoleon published this account in order to divert public attention from the reverses that the French had just suffered in Santo Domingo.

A decade earlier he thought more directly of preparations against England. It was in the course of these preparations, which eventually drew England, Russia, and Austria together in the third coalition, that there came the thought of substituting the Napoleonic empire for the Holy Roman Empire in Germany and Italy.

NAPOLEON AND THE REORGANIZATION OF GERMANY

At the opening of the nineteenth century Germany was only a vast mosaic of states, large and small, which formed part of the Holy Roman Empire. The two largest states were formed of the territorial possessions of Austria and Prussia, the foremost rivals for mastery within the empire. There were also a number of secondary states, such as the electorate of Saxony, the electorate of Hanover, the landgraviate of Hesse-Cassel, the principality of Nassau, the duchy of Berg, the duchy of Westphalia, and the bishopric of Münster in northern and central Germany; and the electorate of Bavaria, the margraviate of Baden, the duchy of Württemberg, the landgraviate of Hesse-Darmstadt, and the archbishopric of Salzburg in southern Germany. These were not so large as Austria or Prussia, but still large enough to take rank with the secondary states of Europe. Then there were many hundreds of small states, so small, so numerous, and so diverse that in the course of a single day's journey the traveler of those days might have traversed the territories of half a dozen or more. Some were free cities, such as Hamburg, Bremen, Lübeck, Frankfort, Nuremberg; some were ecclesiastical states, and the most numerous and insignificant were the territorial possessions of counts, barons, and knights of the empire.

Over this bizarre aggregation of principalities the emperor (who, for the past three hundred years had been chosen from the Hapsburg family) had only nominal authority; while the imperial diet, composed of representatives of the various states, was both cumbersome and ineffectual. No common feeling of nationality existed to overbalance the disadvantages of political diversity and disunion. Religious differences and an ancient tradition of territorial aggrandizement helped, on the contrary, to make Germany politically negligible. The rivalry of the leading states, their incessant machinations to round out their territorial possessions at the expense of the smaller states within their boundaries, and the imperial administrative inefficiency made Germany a prey to the greedy ambition of covetous princes within and outside of its boundaries.

The reconstruction of Germany had been determined by the left-bank policy of the Directory and confirmed by the treaties at Campo Formio and Lunéville. By the treaty of Basel in 1795 Prussia was promised compensation east of the Rhine for the cession to France of her territory west of the Rhine; in 1797 and again in 1801 Austria also agreed to the sacrifice of the left bank to France on the condition that the princes dispossessed of their territory there should take over certain smaller German states east of the Rhine. That such a procedure was agreeable to Napoleon is uncontested, for it afforded him an opportunity that Richelieu and Mazarin had earlier sought for France. This was the opportunity to intervene in Germany and build up a federation of states, bound by territorial interests to France and strong enough collectively to hold Austria in check in southern Germany. The procedure contemplated was agreeable to the rulers of the larger secondary states, especially to the rulers of Bavaria, Württemberg, and Baden. who saw in it their long awaited opportunity to despoil the smaller ecclesiastical states within their boundaries. The tentative plan, already adopted at the abortive Congress of Rastatt, provided for the secularization of much of the ecclesiastical territory. Territorial appetites were sharpened, and greedy eyes looked toward Paris, for the various treaties since 1795 had given France the right to intervene in the settlement.

There was good reason to look toward Paris, for the imperial government in Germany proved incapable of devising a basis of territorial indemnification suitable to the conflicting interests of the various larger states. Prussia, Austria, and the group of large secondary states were hopelessly divided in their schemes. While the emperor sought to maintain the existing constitution of the empire and the influence of the Catholic Church in the administration by opposing secularizations on a large scale, Prussia and many of the secondary states favored a policy of the widest secularization of ecclesiastical territories. Besides, the entire problem had become European in scope, for the grand duke of Tuscany, the duke of Modena, and the stadholder of Holland were also concerned in the redistribution of territory. To end the deadlock the imperial diet agreed to turn over the problem to an imperial deputation (*Reichsdeputation*) of eight members; but before the deputation was constituted Napoleon began to make his own arrangements.

Russia was associated with France in the regulation of German affairs, being bound by a treaty for that purpose. Once before, in 1779, the ruler of Russia had intervened as a mediator in Germany, and this precedent together with the fact that Alexander I had relatives on the thrones of Baden and Württemberg gave him a special interest in the settlement. Napoleon was all the freer to intervene, not only because he had admitted Russia into the negotiations, but because the preliminaries of London had ended the war with England. Acting through Talleyrand, his minister of foreign relations, who reaped a golden harvest in bribes and gifts from the petty German rulers gathered in Paris, Napoleon concluded separate treaties with Prussia, Bavaria, Baden, Württemberg, Hesse-Cassel, and the towns. These treaties formed the basis of a comprehensive plan of secularization. By the spring of 1802 the French plan had been accepted by Russia and half of the members of the imperial deputation and eventually it was accepted by the diet and Francis II.

This settlement, which is known as the Imperial Recess of 1803, did far more than settle the question of indemnifying the dispossessed princes. It effected a veritable territorial revolution, recasting and simplifying the entire map of Germany. A sixth part of all the land and some 4,000,000 Germans were involved in the new distribution of power. One hundred and twelve states of the Holy Roman Empire were destroyed. Of the fifty-two free-city states, only six remained—Hamburg, Lübeck, Bremen, Frankfort, Augsburg, and Nuremberg. Of the many ecclesiastical states, especially in the south and the west, only one was left. The largest of the destroyed ecclesiastical states were Salzburg, Würzburg, and Münster. The archbishop-elector of Mainz lost most of his land, but received the title of prince-primate of Germany. Thus, two types of states virtually disappeared: the free cities and the ecclesiastical states. The imperial knights (counts, barons, knights) also suffered, but their total spoliation was to come somewhat later. All these states lost their independence, and their territory was incorporated with the larger states which had profited by the changes. Prussia and Bavaria each gained about five times as much territory within the empire as they lost on the left bank of the Rhine. The most important of the Prussian acquisitions was its share of the progressive bishopric of Münster. Württemberg and Baden were the chief beneficiaries in Germany, gaining much territory and rounding out their possessions. Austria too profited by the exchange to strengthen her military frontier toward Italy (receiving the bishoprics of Brixen and Trent), at the cost of its western possessions.

The Recess completely altered the distinctive features of the governmental system of the empire. By secularizing the ecclesiastical states it severed the close association between the church and the old empire, and it deprived the Hapsburgs of their staunchest adherents. It raised four lay rulers of secondary states (Baden, Württemberg, Hesse-Cassel, and Salzburg) to the dignity of electors, strengthened Prussia, and dealt a heavy blow to Austrian ascendancy. It sounded the knell of the empire that was the keystone of the political structure of old Europe. In many other ways the Catholic Church suffered a loss as severe as that incurred during the Protestant Reformation.

The greatest benefit came to France, for Napoleon was on the verge of realizing Mazarin's dream. He had gained the Rhine frontier for France and laid the foundations of a "Third Germany" of secondary states in southern Germany which could check the ambitions both of Prussia and of Austria. He had isolated Austria, attached Prussia to France without permitting her to extend her possessions too closely to France or over the center of Germany, and he had built up in the south those secondary states that naturally looked to France for further favors. Within a few years he was to intervene once more, to build up the Rheinbund (the confederation of states along the Rhine frontier), and to substitute the Napoleonic empire for the Holy Roman Empire in Germany and Italy. The first German revolution was accomplished for the benefit of France and a handful of German princes.

For the present Napoleon was too concerned with his preparations against England to exert his extraordinary influence in the renewal of German territorial disputes. One of the problems left unsolved by the Recess was the status of the many hundred tiny principalities ruled by the imperial knights. Immediately after the settlement of 1803 the south German states had pounced upon the petty states, occupying many of them and taking over their governments. But the Emperor Francis II supported the protests of the latter and annulled the annexations (1804), particularly those made by Bavaria, in whose territory the knightly states were extensive. Bavaria backed down before the determined attitude of Austria, but this surrender only increased her dependence upon France, which took full advantage of the situation in the following year.

Formation of the Third Coalition

In the meantime Napoleon was using the pretext of his war with England to continue his coercion of France's neighbors. The war began with a fresh revelation of France's naval inferiority. Her remaining colonies were seized by the enemy and her naval squadrons blockaded in their harbors at Brest, Rochefort, and Toulon. Pending the construction of enough new ships, at which the Dutch and French shipwrights were actively engaged, and the invasion of England by the large army that he had assembled on the coast, Napoleon proceeded vigorously on his program of closing the continental ports to English shipping. He tightened the restrictions against British shipping by ordering the exclusion of all colonial wares and products, irrespective of origin, coming from British ports. He ordered that the Neapolitan ports of Brindisi, Otranto, and Taranto be occupied by French troops, using the pretext that the English were still in possession of Malta. His troops occupied Hanover in northern Germany, where he hoped to get timber for his ships, horses for his cavalry, and the control of the Weser and the Elbe against British commerce. He put pressure upon the Spanish government and exacted heavy financial subsidies from the king. In Italy he raised contingents of Italian republicans. He posted a strong French force along the Simplon Road and coerced the Swiss confederation into signing a treaty which promised him additional military support. The government of the Batavian Republic was browbeaten into fulfilling its military agreement, which meant auxiliary troops, the support of a French army of occupation, and the closing of its ports to the English. Portugal purchased neutrality by agreeing to make heavy monthly payments to the French.

With Russia, Napoleon's relations grew more and more chilly. As joint mediator of the Recess of 1803, Czar Alexander I was offended by Napoleon's violation of the German settlement, and he protested sharply against the seizure of Hanover and the free Hanseatic cities. He waxed indignant over the French occupation of the Neapolitan ports, not only because he had a treaty of alliance with the king of Naples, but also because Napoleon's control of the Adriatic menaced Russia's interests in the Turkish Empire. The Russians, meanwhile, occupied the island of Corfu, at the invitation of the queen of Naples. The presence of new Anglophile counselors at Alexander's court had already begun to influence his attitude toward Napoleon when he received the news of the execution of the duke of Enghien. He demanded explanations of this act, and his court went into mourning. Lastly, his efforts to act as mediator between England and France failed, leaving in his mind a firm conviction that Napoleon's coercive policy was a grave menace to his own plans concerning the Balkans. In measure as Alexander became estranged with Napoleon, Russia's relations with England grew more cordial, and in 1804-1805 negotiations for a comprehensive treaty of alliance against France were earnestly conducted.

Unsuccessful in retaining his Russian alliance, Napoleon played for the support of neutral Prussia, which Alexander also tried to win. The French occupation of the electorate of Hanover could easily have given the Prussian king a pretext for war. Frederick William III continued, however, to follow his cautious policy of neutrality, cleverly, perhaps cravenly, avoiding the compromising alliance that Napoleon offered. A year elapsed after the invasion of Hanover before Prussia signed a purely defensive alliance with Russia.[5] It is interesting to note that in these negotiations of 1804 with Prussia Napoleon employed the same tactics that he was to use in the negotiations of 1806. He wished to embroil Prussia with Austria over the Recess of 1803, with England over Hanover, and with Russia over the Italian states by having the Prussian government guarantee the changes that he had made there.

Austria had the most to fear from Napoleon's policy of coercion, but Francis II warily bided his time until his financial and military positions were strengthened. He had already suffered greatly from the events in Germany and Italy and he was extremely reluctant, as may well be understood, to lose Venetia to Napoleon or sacrifice his imperial title. At the proclamation of the

---

[5] For a moment there was tension, when Napoleon's soldiers kidnaped Sir George Rumbold, the British consul at Hamburg and the accredited agent to a district under Prussian control. Napoleon released Sir George at the energetic protests of the Prussian ruler.

Napoleonic empire he took his precautions by conferring upon himself the new title of Francis I, Hereditary Emperor of Austria. That Napoleon sanctioned the new empire of Austria only indicated that he too was biding his time, in expectation of its speedy break-up. Austrian neutrality, however, came to an end when the court at Vienna learned that Napoleon was taking steps to obtain firmer control over northern Italy. Aroused by this menace, which presaged still more threatening French acts, Francis signed a defensive treaty with Alexander I, which bound Austria and Russia to resist further French aggressions in Italy or in Germany (November, 1804).

The creation of the Napoleonic empire was generally regarded as a forboding of changes in the constitution of the Italian Republic, for Napoleon could hardly reconcile his position as emperor of the French with that of president of the Italian Republic. Without informing Austria of his intentions, he planned to transform that state into a kingdom, offering or pretending to offer the throne first to his brother Joseph and then to the son of his brother Louis. Their refusals, which were probably inspired by Napoleon's hints or orders, then placed him in a position where he had to take the throne for himself. Accordingly, in March, 1805, he announced the projected changes. The Italian Republic became the kingdom of Italy, of which Napoleon became king. But as soon as the foreign troops evacuated Malta and Corfu, ran the official proclamation, Napoleon was to give up the throne to his heir or adopted heir with the stipulation that his successor waive his rights in the French empire. Shortly after his coronation at Milan he gave a further challenge to the empire of Austria. He created the first of the imperial fiefs, bestowing the tiny principalities of Piombino and Lucca upon his sisters, with the binding stipulation, however, that they were to remain loyal to the emperor of the French.

Meantime the protracted diplomatic pourparlers between England and Russia reached a successful issue, helped by the return of Pitt to the ministry. In April, 1805, the two governments signed the convention of Saint Petersburg, which was ratified three months later. This Anglo-Russian accord of 1805, which was the foundation of the third coalition, has been characterized by a modern student as "the first official attempt at reëstablishing the European system on firm and just foundations." For the historian this treaty is of interest largely because of its anticipation of the final settlement of 1815—an independent Holland, enlarged by the Belgian provinces, to form a barrier against France on the north, and an independent kingdom of Sardinia, enlarged by Genoa and Savoy, to guard France on the south. Moreover, at the end of the successful war a congress of states was to assemble to discuss the basis of a new European system "founded upon the sacred rights of humanity." Ratification was delayed, for the idealistic young czar was at the same time pursuing a highly realistic policy under his sonorous phrases about "the sacred rights of humanity." He proposed that the Anglo-Russian negotiations be communicated to Napoleon, to whom he would offer compensations in Germany, while Russia kept Corfu and England gave up Malta and established a maritime code protecting the rights of neutrals. On these last points Pitt's refusal was adamant, for he keenly suspected that Russia's designs upon the decadent Turkish Empire were as great a menace to British interests as the French plans, and that the Russian indignation over the situation in Italy was a screen for Alexander's real concern with the Balkans.

Ratification became possible at the news of the turn that events took in Italy. At the end of May, Napoleon placed the iron crown of Lombardy on his head, and a fortnight later he adopted his stepson Eugène de Beauharnais and made him viceroy of the kingdom of Italy. At the same time he formally annexed Genoa to the French empire. This act proved decisive in the formation of the third coalition. England and Russia exchanged ratifications of their convention in July; Austria, dismayed by the turn of events in Italy, hastened her military preparations and worked out a plan of campaign in collaboration with the Russians. Another month was to elapse before Francis II gave his adherence to the Anglo-Russian pact, for he was none too assured about the wisdom of allying himself with his eastern rival, Russia. Even after he made his arrangements with the other two powers, which entitled him to British subsidies, he still continued his negotiations with the French. Napoleon was not outwitted in this diplomatic game, for the Austrian mobilization gave him a pretext to carry the war to the Continent. As we shall see presently, he had ostentatiously elaborated and advertised the "immense project" of invading England from Boulogne on the French side of the Channel. Now he could allege that the Austrian mobilization and the Austrian aggressions in southern Germany made it necessary for France, in self-defense, to suspend the "immense project" against England and use the Army of England at Boulogne, henceforth called the Grand Army, against the continental enemies of France. Without losing any more time he ordered his troops to advance from northern France and Belgium to the line of the upper Rhine, where they guarded the eastern frontier. Simultaneously he renewed his bid to Prussia (which had refused to join the continental allies), and concluded offensive and defensive alliances with Baden, Bavaria, and Württemberg. Again the bait for the support of these German states was increased territory, for the treaties promised that their territories should be conveniently rounded out.

The Project of Invading England (1803–1805)

Napoleon's contemporaries and most historians ever since have interpreted his descent project as a ruse whereby he could find a pretext for raising and drilling troops without alarming the continental powers. This interpretation, consecrated as it is, is highly questionable, for it seems more likely that he was in deadly earnest in his varied projects for the invasion of England. His first plan contemplated a descent upon English shores late in the fall or winter of 1803. He assembled a large body of troops, 150,000 men, at Boulogne on the coast, had 1200 flat boats built, and his men trained to disembark rapidly from the unprotected flotilla. The preparations were extensive and well advertised, and English apprehensions were keen. Early in 1804 his dispatches gave the first hint of a revised plan, for actual experimentation and sound technical advice convinced him that his first plan was unfeasible. The revised plan proposed the movement of the transport flotilla in conjunction with two or more French fleets, which were to slip out from their blockaded ports at Toulon, Rochefort, El Ferrol, and Brest, lure the English squadrons to the high seas, escape their pursuers and effect a rapid concentration in the Channel. Like his original plan, this second scheme depended for its success upon several favorable contingencies, the most vital of which were the division of the English fleets and weather favorable for the French naval concentration in the Channel.

It depended also upon the success of Napoleon's diplomacy with respect to Austria. During almost the entire year of 1804 the project was not pressed, but in the fall of that year the French emperor renewed it with increased vigor. His sincerity may be gauged from the fact that he followed a conciliatory diplomatic policy toward Austria, even though he realized fully that Austria was slowly drifting toward a war psychology, and that the aim of the Austrian diplomacy was to gain time to complete her arrangements against the French. Had he so desired, Napoleon could have struck then at Austria, without giving her time to strengthen her diplomatic relations with Russia or complete her military preparations. Feeling certain, however, that he had the military situation on the Continent well in hand, he was all the more determined to carry out his projected English invasion because the French fleet could count upon the active support of Spain, which had become involved in war with England.

Following his instructions, the French fleet stationed at Toulon and the Spanish squadron made good their escape from the English patrol and sailed for the West Indies (March 30, 1805). A full month elapsed before Nelson learned the true destination of Admiral Villeneuve's squadron which sailed from Toulon. He followed the French admiral to the West Indies, arriving there before Villeneuve could do much damage to the British colonies. When Villeneuve learned that Nelson was in the West Indies, he turned about and set sail for Europe, Nelson in pursuit. A fast brig that Nelson had sent ahead overhauled Villeneuve's fleet and, noting its direction, informed the British admiralty. The British promptly concentrated their ships off the northwestern coast of Spain to check Villeneuve. The French admiral escaped defeat, but failed to shake off his pursuers and reach the Channel.

The project now entered upon its final phase, in respect both to the actual invasion and to the reënforcement of French defenses on the Continent against Austria. To Villeneuve, Napoleon's final instructions were to sail directly from Spain, join with the Brest squadron, and gain control of the Channel. Villeneuve entertained no enthusiasm for the venture, whose success he regarded as more than dubious. In this attitude he was corroborated by the French minister of the navy, who also feared a general naval engagement with the British. Villeneuve made a faint effort to follow instructions, but almost immediately after setting out for the Channel, he veered about and made for Cadiz (August 15), as his discretionary power permitted him to do, in case of difficulty or great misfortune. Napoleon meantime was at Boulogne, burning with impatience and sending telegraph instructions by semaphore to hasten Villeneuve's approach. But even before he came to the realization that the admiral's caution had prevailed over his valor, Napoleon raised the entire descent project and gave orders for the Army of England (the Grand Army) to advance to the line of the upper Rhine (August 24). His pretext was the Austrian mobilization; his real reason was unquestionably the news that Nelson had returned, and that the British now had naval superiority over the combined French and Spanish fleet. It is certain, moreover, that Napoleon's difficulties would only have begun if he had succeeded in reaching England. Even if he had captured London, which is extremely doubtful, he would have remained a prisoner, cut off from the sea, in a country systematically denuded of all supplies that could sustain him.

His wrath against Villeneuve, whom he wished to make the scapegoat for the failure of his plans, helped precipitate the disastrous ending of the "immense project." To that admiral, blockaded in Cadiz by a large British fleet which Nelson now commanded in person, Napoleon sent fresh instructions, couched in withering terms of contempt, to reach the Mediterranean. These orders fitted in perfectly with Nelson's own plans, which were to give battle to the French and Spanish squadron whenever he contrived to draw them out of Cadiz. Since his guard ships had picked up the signal communications of the enemy, he had the advantage of employing his own tactics. The decisive engagement took place on October 21, 1805, off Cape Trafalgar, and the result was the crushing victory of the British. After six hours of ship-to-ship action more than half of the combined French-Spanish fleet of thirty-three ships was destroyed or captured. Of those that escaped four were subsequently captured by their pursuers. The British fleet was intact, without the loss of a single ship, but Nelson himself lay dead, a sacrifice to his own victory.

The victory at Trafalgar was decisive in determining the continuation of England's mastery on the seas, but Napoleon's future unwillingness to challenge that mastery anew helped make it so. In so far as the actual invasion of England was concerned, Trafalgar hardly affected the situation, for the invasion had been abandoned definitely two months before the naval engagement at Trafalgar. Indeed, Napoleon had already reached the Austrian capital before he received the news of the disaster.

XVI. THE GRAND EMPIRE

THE WAR OF THE THIRD COALITION

THE fighting on the Continent against Austria and Russia was brief and decisive, and Napoleon's victories resulted in significant modifications of the political balance in Europe. A fortnight before Vienna formally declared war (September 3, 1805), the Grand Army was on the march from northern France to the line of upper Rhine. Napoleon had more than the advantage of a highly trained, mobile army of more than 200,000 men and experienced generals. He had a strategy that confounded the enemy by its brilliant daring. According to the original Austrian plan of campaign the Austrian army in Italy was to begin operations, while the Austrian forces in southern Germany were to effect a junction with the Russians and advance through Bavaria and beyond the Iller River into France. The Russian vanguard was expected to reach the Inn River by the middle of October. General Mack, who commanded the Austrian forces in Germany, was misled by his overconfidence into ruining the cause of his country. His first error, based upon the assumption that Napoleon would not be able to appear in Germany with any considerable force, nor before the arrival of the Russians, made him advance, prematurely, deep into Bavaria. But his hope of winning Bavarian support for a rapid invasion of France was crushed, for the Bavarians retired before him and, according to the new treaty, joined forces with the French. Mack then committed the graver error of continuing his advance to the Iller, thus isolating himself still farther from the Russians, who were slowly coming toward the Inn. He now planned to hold the line of the Iller at the fortified city of Ulm, while waiting for the Russians to reënforce him.

Napoleon's plan was a brilliant improvisation dictated by the information that he received from spies when he reached the Rhine with the bulk of his army, which lay stretched from Strasbourg to Würzburg. Essentially, his operations resolved themselves into a major flanking movement against Mack at Ulm. Swinging his troops in a wide arc from the valley of the Main and the Neckar, he brought them down south on the Danube in the rear of Mack's troops and cut the Austrian line of retreat. Murat, meantime, with the cavalry reserve continued his demonstrations in the Black Forest so as to conceal the advance of the infantry corps that were moving against Ulm along the Danube. The French corps methodically closed the net around the Austrians and in several minor engagements cut off all avenues of escape. It is difficult to explain Mack's inactivity save on the charitable grounds that he was completely misinformed by false reports concerning the movement of the French troops. On October 20 he surrendered with all his remaining forces to Napoleon. More than twenty thousand Austrians fell prisoner to the overjoyed French commander, while the unfortunate Austrian general was released to languish for several years in an Austrian prison, pondering on the fatuity of his miscalculations.

From Ulm, Napoleon hastened on to Vienna, for the destruction of Mack's forces removed from his path the last obstacle to the Austrian capital. It was there, in the middle of November, that he received the discouraging news of Nelson's victory at Trafalgar. Despite his triumph at Ulm.he had more than one reason for misgivings. In France popular opposition to the war and a major financial crisis disturbed the tranquillity of the state. Though his advance to Vienna had been incredibly rapid, his forces suffered frightfully from shortage of food, being saved largely by an abundant crop of potatoes. A second, even more serious reason for worry was the sudden turn in the Prussian situation. It will be recalled that Napoleon had vainly tempted Prussia with an offer of Hanover "in full sovereignty" as the price of an alliance. Without waiting for an answer he had ordered Bernadotte to march through the Prussian territory of Ansbach, in order to arrive more rapidly on the Danube to the rear of Mack. This inexcusable violation of Prussian neutrality determined Frederick William to listen to the proposals of the czar, who had come to Berlin to win Prussian aid. He opened his frontiers to the passage of the Russian troops and signed an alliance early in November, by the terms of which he agreed to offer his armed mediation to Napoleon. If, by December 15, Napoleon refused to accept the allied terms, which demanded the repudiation of most of Napoleon's achievements in western Europe, Prussia, with an army of 180,000, was to join the war against the French. In return the czar promised to use his influence to secure Hanover for Prussia.

Count Haugwitz, the leading pro-French minister, was commissioned to report this virtual ultimatum to the French. Had the Prussian intervention actually taken place, the French position would have become extremely precarious, but Frederick William was not yet inclined to break with Napoleon. His final oral instructions to Haugwitz were to preserve peace at any cost. Haugwitz made his way slowly to the French headquarters, where Napoleon and Talleyrand, who suspected the nature of the Prussian-Russian agreement, outplayed him in diplomatic maneuvering. While Napoleon held off the Prussian envoy, and made urgent diplomatic bids both to Austria and to Russia, the blunders of the Russian military staff rescued him from his danger and rendered the Prussian mediation innocuous. As a matter of fact Haugwitz followed his instructions so carefully that he kept his demands in his pockets and did not actually present them to Napoleon at either of his two interviews.

After the reverse at Ulm the straggling remains of Mack's army moved north to join the advancing Russians. It was Napoleon's hope to defeat the latter before they could make a junction with the Austrians or receive reënforcements from a second Russian army; but they retreated into Moravia, pursued by the French. Napoleon was now exposed to the Russian attack on the north, confronted on the south by the troops of Archduke Charles, who was hurrying up from Italy to join the Russians, and menaced by Prussian intervention. Fortune came to his aid. Before the general concentration was completed, the Russians had resolved to attack the French single-handed. The responsibility for this tactical error must rest upon Alexander and his younger military advisers, who were confident of the Russian ability to cut Napoleon off from Vienna and defeat the great French general. As soon as the latter perceived their intentions, he saw his opportunity and planned his moves accordingly.

The great battle which ended the third coalition was fought near the little Moravian village of Austerlitz on December 2, 1805, the first anniversary of Napoleon's coronation. He had so maneuvered his troops as to choose the terrain himself, a terrain with which he was thoroughly familiar. Unknown to the Russians, his generals had rushed all available reënforcements to the front, and Napoleon's troops now exceeded seventy thousand men. On the eve of the battle they were deployed along the muddy stream, the Goldbach, with Davout commanding the right in the ice-covered swamps between Telnitz and Sokolnitz, Soult in the center, and the cavalry of Murat and the troops of Lannes guarding his left. Napoleon's plan was audacious, yet extremely simple. Realizing that the Russians planned to cut him off from Vienna he purposely encouraged their expectations by weakening his right wing and inviting a Russian attack there. His tactics succeeded almost as well as though he himself had been giving orders to the enemy. To concentrate their troops against the French right the Russians were obliged to weaken their own center on the plateau of Pratzen, directly across the Goldbach. As soon as they attacked his right wing, Napoleon planned to hurl the infantry regiments of Soult and Lannes and the cavalry of Murat against the weakened center, then, having thrust it back, to turn rapidly against the advanced Russian left and cut it off.

The battle began in the early morning with the first beams of the radiant "sun of Austerlitz" lighting up the thick wintry mist, and it lasted until dusk, when the triumphant emperor of the French rode over the field viewing the grandeur and the misery of victory. Murat's cavalry cut down the Russian infantry on their left; Soult and Lannes scaled the heights of the Pratzen and drove the Russian center in retreat, and the Russian right, caught between the forces of Davout and the combined troops of the other French generals behind them were cut down or crushed in the icy marches. This terrible defeat cost the allies almost thirty thousand casualties. Napoleon had lost nine thousand men, including the dead and wounded. This "model battle" filled Napoleon with pride. "The battle of Austerlitz," he wrote home, "is the most splendid of all I have fought."

The Break-Up of the Third Coalition

The consequences of the overwhelming victory that Napoleon had just gained were of tremendous significance, particularly since he consolidated his success on the battle field by a series of diplomatic thrusts. To the Austrians Napoleon granted an armistice, according to the preliminary terms of which the Russian army was to be removed and the Prussian forces denied entry into Austrian territory. Moreover, he would refrain from despoiling Austria provided that Russia made peace concurrently with Austria. Though the czar informed the Austrian emperor not to count on the Russian troops any longer, he refused to conclude a peace on the terms offered by Napoleon. He also informed the king of Prussia to make what arrangements he could with Napoleon. With her erstwhile Russian ally retreating through Poland and the Prussian envoy cringing before the victorious Napoleon, Austria was helpless before the ever more stringent demands that the latter put upon her. "Every hour witnesses the birth of new exactions," complained the Austrian envoy. On December 26, 1805, she was forced to sign the disastrous treaty of Pressburg, which stripped her of all her outlying territory. She recognized all the changes that had been made in Italy and ceded Venetia, including Istria and Dalmatia (though not the port of Trieste), and Cattaro as well, to the king of Italy, on the old condition that the two crowns of Italy and France would be separated at the general peace. In Germany, Austria gave up the Tirol and Trent to Bavaria, while her possessions in Swabia were divided up between Württemberg and Baden. Francis II renounced his imperial rights over Bavaria, Württemberg, and Baden and recognized the electors of the first two as kings. In this fashion Napoleon redeemed the promises in his new alliances with the south German allies. He also struck the death blow at the Holy Roman Empire. Austria was completely excluded from Italy and southern Germany. The formation of a new German confederation was expressly recognized in this treaty. Now the Empire which was "neither Roman, nor Holy, nor an Empire," was also virtually without an emperor. The substitution of the French empire for the defunct Holy Roman Empire was near at hand.

There was another tottering empire that engaged Napoleon's attention. This was the Turkish Empire. Talleyrand, among other counselors, had advised Machiavellian leniency in dealing with Austria, but Napoleon rejected his minister's proposal to give Austria compensations in the Balkans for her losses in Germany and Italy. His own eastern projects prevented him from following Talleyrand's counsels. With Venetia annexed to the kingdom of Italy and the Dalmatian coast as far as Ragusa under his control, the French sphere of influence now reached as far as the Balkan Peninsula. Napoleon could now promote his old plan of playing a determining part in the affairs of the Turkish Empire. His designs were temporarily thwarted, a few months after the treaty of Pressburg, by the Russians' occupation of Cattaro in Montenegro, which Austria surrendered to them in violation of the treaty.

Napoleon also used his victory to impress upon the Prussians the futility and the danger of their policy of armed mediation. He was now unwilling to allow Prussia to remain neutral. By a judicious mixture of reproaches, threats, and flattery, he induced the Prussian envoy, Haugwitz, to sign the preliminaries of Schönbrunn on December 15. By its terms Prussia gained Hanover, which her troops already occupied, but pledged herself to recognize the important changes in Italy and to cede Cleves on the right bank of the Rhine to a prince of the French empire, Neuchâtel to France, and Ansbach to Bavaria. Moreover, Prussia agreed to form a defensive and offensive alliance with France and to recognize an enlarged "kingdom of Bavaria."

When the Prussian State Council met to consider the ratification of the preliminaries of Schönbrunn, it was already in possession of an alternative proposal from Great Britain. In lieu of Hanover the English envoy had offered Prussia a stretch of territory west of the Rhine and subsidies for an army of two hundred and fifty thousand men. But Frederick William was not disposed, after Austerlitz, to run the risk of war with Napoleon. Disregarding the indignant manifestations of the irate Berliners he persevered in his policy of playing off the French against the English. Accordingly, he adopted Haugwitz's counsel to revise the preliminaries of Schönbrunn, so that Prussia was not to annex Hanover outright, but to occupy it provisionally until the general peace as a guarantee of the neutrality of northern Germany. Again, Haugwitz was selected to announce the Prussian decision to Napoleon. Frederick William ruined all his chances, however, by demobilizing the Prussian army before Haugwitz presented the demands to Napoleon. He had consented to the demobilization because he was misled into believing that Napoleon would accept the revised terms. This false economy worked havoc with his political opportunities. The French forces of 200,000 men were still in southern Germany, and in southern Germany they remained despite the peace with Austria. For their presence Napoleon had a plausible pretext; namely, the Austrian surrender of Cattaro to the Russians.

The Prussian decision rejecting the British proposals was the direct cause of the death of Pitt. All his last efforts had been directed to win the alliance of Prussia without losing Hanover, but all were fruitless. First, the czar had reached an agreement with Prussia, pledging his aid in the legal acquisition of Hanover for Frederick William III. Then, in rapid succession came the terrible news of Austerlitz, the shipwreck of an expeditionary force that England sent to recover Hanover, the withdrawal of Russia from the third coalition, the humiliation of Austria, and, worst of all, the tidings that Prussia had assented to Napoleon's terms and had agreed to retain Hanover. Pitt's health was poor, nor had it been improved by the fierce opposition raised in Parliament to his continental policy. When the news trickled through that his efforts at Berlin had failed, he abandoned the struggle. He died on January 23, 1806, convinced that all his efforts had been wasted.

The Pitt ministry was succeeded by the so-called ministry of all the talents, in which the peace-inclined Fox, the champion of the American revolutionists and the open admirer of Napoleon, was the minister of foreign affairs. In the field of foreign affairs the program called for the withdrawal of England from the costly coalition and the negotiation of peace with Napoleon. The latter was pleased with the nomination of Fox; and he wrote to Talleyrand that now he would not give up Hanover to Prussia unless the cession were part of a general arrangement to end hostilities. He had already made up his mind to make Cleves the nucleus of a buffer state between France and an enlarged Prussia. As no immediate overture came from Fox, Napoleon decided upon a firm course with Prussia.

When Haugwitz presented himself at Paris he met with a harsh reception. Napoleon may have simulated his anger, as occasionally he did to achieve his purpose in diplomatic negotiations, or his anger may have been real. In any case Haugwitz was overwhelmed with accusations of Prussian faithlessness. Since Napoleon threatened to employ his troops in Germany against Prussia, the unfortunate envoy had no choice but to accept, and his monarch to ratify, the new terms that Napoleon imposed as a substitute for the preliminaries of Schönbrunn. By the terms of the treaty of Paris (February 15, 1806) Prussia was not only to annex and occupy Hanover at once but also to close the coast of Germany to English commerce. Further, in addition to the earlier provisions of

Schönbrunn, Prussia agreed to guarantee Napoleon's forthcoming changes in Naples and, as before, to guarantee the integrity of the Turkish Empire. Thus Napoleon schemed to embroil Prussia with Russia over Turkey and Naples and with England over Hanover. The popular opposition in Berlin to this treaty, which was even more onerous and humiliating than the preliminaries of Schönbrunn, was intense, but the monarch could not repudiate it. Hanover was occupied and formally annexed by the end of March, an act which Fox denounced as "a compound of everything that is detestable in servility with everything that is odious in rapacity." The scorn of the English minister was well founded; Prussia's conduct struck the very depths of national degradation. England promptly recalled her ambassador from Berlin, blockaded the Prussian ports, and captured several hundred small vessels lying in British ports. Late in April, England declared war upon Prussia.

THE GRAND EMPIRE

The immediate consequences of Austerlitz, which were the break-up of the third coalition, the humiliation of Austria, and the studied coercion of Prussia, have been recorded. A consequence not less significant than these mentioned was the evolution of Napoleon's views on the organization of western Europe. From that time on he referred openly to the "Grand Empire," an enlarged Napoleonic empire which was to replace the dying Holy Roman Empire in Germany and Italy. In studying the modifications that he made there after his victory at Austerlitz, we must always be guided by the conception Napoleon himself entertained of his historic mission. In setting up kingdoms for members of his family and in carving out dependent duchies and fiefs for his great civil and military officers Napoleon was carefully tracing the outline of the hierarchic empire of which he was the head. In prescribing with minute exactness the relations between himself, the emperor, and his imperial subordinates he was carefully emphasizing the personal and paternalistic character of the Grand Empire.

The first of the great changes took place in Italy. In Italy there were still two large stretches of territory which blocked his efforts to exclude the English from the Continent. These were the kingdom of Naples and the states of the church. He had an old score to settle with the Bourbon rulers of the kingdom of Naples. Contrary to their promise of neutrality, they had invited the British and Russians to occupy the ports of Naples at a moment when Napoleon was busily engaged in southern Germany. Even more, Queen Marie Caroline, who was the sister of Marie Antoinette and the aunt of Francis II, had "thrown off the mask" and actively sided with the coalition against the French. With this enemy then Napoleon dealt in summary fashion. A military order declared the Bourbon rulers deposed, and a detachment of troops under his brother Joseph was sent to occupy the capital, which both the Russians and English evacuated. A month after Joseph had taken Naples, Napoleon announced in a decree to the French Senate that he had made Joseph king of Naples and Sicily (March, 1806). While the crowns of Naples and France would remain separate, Joseph was to retain his status as a grand dignitary of the French Empire and as a member of Napoleon's family. In other words, he became subject to the imperial authority of the French emperor, and his kingdom took its place as a dependent member of the Napoleonic empire. But Napoleon was still effectively checked in his designs upon the Turkish Empire. The deposed Neapolitan rulers had taken refuge in Sicily, where they had the active support of the British troops from Malta, and the Russians were firmly lodged in the island of Corfu and in the Montenegrin city of Cattaro.

The elevation of Joseph to the throne of Naples was an indication of Napoleon's future course in organizing the Grand Empire. The existing territorial divisions in Italy made that peninsula peculiarly appropriate for his policy of establishing a landed aristocracy. He had already created thrones for his sisters Elise and Pauline. Bernadotte, now a member of the Napoleonic family through his marriage with the sister of Joseph's wife, became the prince of Ponte Corvo; and Talleyrand fell heir to another papal enclave in the territory of Naples, becoming the prince of Benevento. From the income of domain lands in the dependent kingdoms in Italy, Napoleon endowed a score of duchies, which he later assigned as fiefs of the empire to his military subordinates. To provide for future benefits and a reserve fund he diverted more than two million francs from the incomes of the kingdoms of Italy and Naples to a special fund, first known as the war treasury.

His relations with Pope Pius VII had become more and more strained from the time of the signing of the Concordat; and with the pope too Napoleon took the position of a new Charlemagne.

In substance, his major interest in the papal states lay in having the pope renounce his neutrality, expel the Anglo-Russian forces from his territory, and close his harbors to the English. This the pope refused to do, opposing a quiet but unalterable firmness to all the Napoleonic blustering. When his threats to degrade the pope to the status of bishop of Rome proved unavailing, Napoleon had recourse to deeds. He now occupied Civita Vecchia on the west coast, even as he had seized Ancona on the east coast late in 1805. For both of these acts Napoleon could plead the military necessity of protecting himself against the English and Russians in the Mediterranean and the Adriatic.

The new dynasties that he established in Italy were the forerunners of others elsewhere. For his younger brother Louis he reserved the crown of Holland, ironically overriding the weak protests of the half-blind old grand pensionary of the Batavian Republic (June, 1806). For his brother-in-law Murat, the husband of Caroline Bonaparte, Napoleon created the Rhine duchy of Berg, the nucleus of which was that territory of Cleves which Prussia had recently ceded. This new duchy provided Napoleon with a small state, later enlarged, which could serve as a military buffer against Prussia. Like their princely relatives in Italy, Louis and Murat were bound by personal ties of allegiance to the French emperor. As a step toward the realization of his full control of Germany the latter ordered the following dynastic marriages: the marriage of his stepson Eugene to a Bavarian princess of the house of Wittelsbach, and the marriage of Josephine's niece to the hereditary prince of Baden.[1] These marriage alliances gave a certain stamp of respectability to Napoleon's intriguing adventure in statecraft.

The most momentous change took place in the constitution of the Holy Roman Empire. Austerlitz and Pressburg had already shattered the old empire, and none of Napoleon's client princes in southern Germany had any reason to oppose a further simplification of the map of Germany. As in 1803, Talleyrand was the official agent of Napoleon's policy, and again he amassed a royal fortune from the envoys of the anxious German rulers. In private conversations with each of them he frightened them with threats of France's military power and impressed upon them the necessity

---

[1] He also contemplated the marriage of Jerome to a princess of Württemberg, though it was first necessary to dissolve Jerome's morganatic marriage with a young American from Baltimore. The marriage took place in 1807.

of having protection against a rancorous Austria. When he concluded the series of separate treaties, Talleyrand called in the German representatives on July 13, 1806, and presented to them a collective text which established the Confederation of the Rhine. The fifteen states admitted to it had no other course than to sign, for the alternative was either complete absorption or else the risk of not gaining any additional territory.

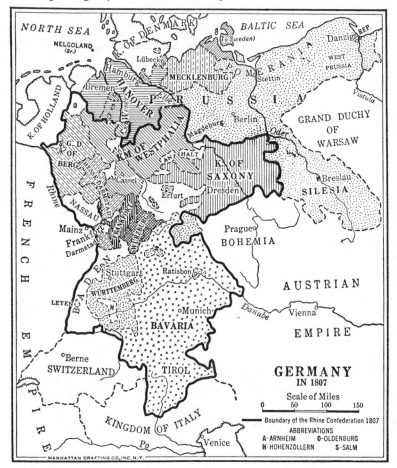

GERMANY
IN 1807

Scale of Miles

0   50   100   150

━━━ Boundary of the Rhine Confederation 1807

ABBREVIATIONS

A - ARNHEIM   O - OLDENBURG

H - HOHENZOLLERN   S - SALM

Prussia and Austria were, of course, excluded from this "Third Germany" of Rhine states. The kingdoms of Bavaria and Württemberg, the grand-duchies of Baden, Hesse-Darmstadt, and Berg, and the archbishopric of Mainz were the most important and the largest of the states that entered the confederation. Almost seventy smaller states were absorbed in the territories of the Napoleonic clients, including three of the six remaining free cities, all the countships, and many other tiny principalities. Moreover, all the imperial knights, who had escaped annexation in 1803, now lost their sovereign rights in the old empire. By this one stroke Napoleon once again hastened the final unification of Germany, ruthlessly sweeping out the cobwebs of waste, inefficiency, and disorder in the Germanic constitution. For the present he had created a united confederation which recognized him as protector, agreed to support him in his wars and to furnish him with a military contingent of 63,000 soldiers.[2]

The final act in remaking the map of Germany was the formal dissolution of the Holy Roman Empire. The states belonging to the Confederation declared that they no longer recognized its existence, nor any claims that it might put upon them. On August 6, Francis II was forced to recognize the accomplished fact. He humbly renounced his titles and prerogatives as its head and definitely assumed his new title of Francis I, Hereditary Emperor of Austria. The thousand-year-old Holy Roman Empire thus passed into history, and Napoleon had taken a long step forward in the realization of the ideal he had voiced on his ceremonial trip to Aix-la-Chapelle in 1804. For it was there that he had said: "Europe cannot be at rest except under a single head who will have kings for his officers, who will distribute his kingdom to his lieutenants."

The War of the Fourth Coalition (1806–1807)

One explanation of Napoleon's haste in rushing through his reorganization of southern Germany was his expectation of coming to terms with Russia and England. Another, more likely, explanation was that these negotiations were never serious on his part and were purposely extended in order to give him time to arrange affairs in southern Germany, after which he would deal with Prussia. It is probable that the diplomats of Russia and England also played for time during the summer of 1806, pretending to negotiate with Napoleon but actually trying to arrange treaties with each other and with Prussia. To be sure, Napoleon was not

[2] In 1808 the number of states in the confederation had increased to thirty-eight.

at all averse to the idea of separating Russia from England and concluding a separate treaty with each. If he seriously thought of concluding peace, his hopes were disappointed, for before the year was over his armies were again on the march.

The negotiations with Russia turned entirely on the question of the Russian occupation of Cattaro and the island of Corfu. Napoleon inveigled the Russian representative to agree to the Russian evacuation of Cattaro, but the czar refused to ratify the terms. Instead, he proposed alternative terms which he knew Napoleon would not accept and immediately gave orders for the mobilization of the Russian armies (August, 1806). The negotiations with Fox must be treated in conjunction with Napleon's secret plans for the future position of Prussia in German affairs. Had Napoleon desired, he might have perpetuated the old French tradition of friendly alliance with Prussia; but a united and enlarged Prussian state did not suit his purposes. He finally made it clear to the English envoy that in order to obtain the island of Sicily for Joseph's unstable kingdom of Naples he was prepared, on certain conditions, to restore Hanover to England, even though it was already occupied by the Prussians. As compensation for Prussia he had in mind some territory in Germany, probably Hesse-Cassel. The news of his intentions came to Prussia during a studied after-dinner indiscretion of the English ambassador at Paris. Napoleon's cool duplicity was too much for the Prussians. To acquire Hanover they had suffered humiliation and material loss; in the most positive manner Napoleon had reassured them that Hanover would not be returned to the English. Now he was blandly offering it to the English, provided that he could satisfy Prussia with some other territory instead. In any case the negotiations with England broke down with her refusal to give up Sicily. The major consequence of the Anglo-French negotiations was the revelation to Prussia of Napoleon's double-edged policy concerning Hanover.

Another cause for Prussian bitterness was Napoleon's secret opposition to a confederation of the north German states under Prussian control. He himself, to sweeten the pill of the Confederation of the Rhine, had made the suggestion that the Prussian king assume the imperial rank in this confederation. The project of a north German Confederation, as Napoleon well knew, was difficult to accomplish at best; but he rendered it impossible by encouraging the existing objections of Saxony, Hesse-Cassel, the Mecklenburgs, and the Hanseatic towns. At this moment Murat, the new grand duke of Berg, was already testing the Prussian spirit by a provocative policy of enlarging his state at the expense of adjoining Prussian territory. The long-suffering Frederick William appealed to the czar, "He [Napoleon] intends to destroy me; will you see this, Sire, with indifference?" Through Hardenberg, Frederick William reached a secret agreement with Alexander (July, 1806), binding Prussia not to take part in any attack upon Russia and binding the latter country to aid Prussia in the event of an attack by France. Prussia's position had become ridiculous, for she was bound to France by one treaty (the treaty of Paris) and by this treaty against France. Before the Russian ratification of the new treaty reached him, the Prussian ruler mobilized his army against France (August 9, 1806). The coincidence of Prussian preparations for an attack with the Russian rejection of the peace negotiations led Napoleon to believe that a new coalition was being formed against him. During the same week that he received the Russian rejection of the terms concerning Cattaro, a Prussian envoy arrived with the demand that the French remove their troops from southern Germany.

While the war temper in Prussia was steadily rising, southern Germany was not silent. Pamphlets, vigorously couched, denounced the exactions and the gross outrages of the French troops quartered in the land and demanded an end of German subservience. This movement was the first sign of an awakening German nationalism, a sentiment that Napoleon neither understood nor tolerated. He ordered the arrest of the authors and booksellers, and some six of these were brought before a French military court in a small Austrian town. Among them was a certain peace-abiding Palm, a bookseller in Nuremberg, who had helped circulate a pamphlet entitled *Germany in Her Deepest Humiliation*. The booklet appealed to Saxony and Prussia to save Germany from destruction at the hands of the French emperor. For his offense Palm was condemned to death and executed, to the horror and indignation of all Germany (August 25, 1806).

Napoleon's act of primitive morality was the spark that kindled the flame. The enemies of France, those publicists and administrators who were denouncing Napoleon's encroachments and preaching the cause of German nationality, overcame the timidity of Frederick William. Prussia plunged into war under the stimulus of the national sentiment of hatred for France. To Napoleon's de mand that the Prussian troops be demobilized Frederick William replied with a renewed demand that the French withdraw from Germany, and that Napoleon accept the principle of the confederation of the north German states. Napoleon did not wait for the ultimatum to expire on October 8. Without sending a reply, and weeks before the time limit expired, he began moving new levies in the direction of the Rhine. His answer to the Prussian threat was his troops. Thus, after ten years of equivocal neutrality Prussia plunged rashly and prematurely into war. England was still at war with her; Austria was neutral and not at all loath to witness the humbling of her old rival; and Russia a distant and suspicious ally. The fourth coalition against France was never formidable. Prussia's own army was no match for Napoleon's veteran fighting machine, her forces were scattered, the commanders were old and without resourcefulness, and the ministerial board both irresolute and timorous in its policy. Baron vom Stein, the most resolute of the ministers who opposed Frederick William's unprogressive rule, was without power in the government. Under the circumstances the military future held nothing bright in store for Prussia.

The first blow of the military campaign fell with devastating rapidity. The bulk of the French forces were in southern Germany resting from the last campaign and preparing for the one that was coming. Their advance began in the first week of October, 1806, Napoleon's first plan being to force the concentration of the Prussians and have them attempt to block his march upon Berlin. Learning that the Prussians were marching into Thuringia, without waiting for the Russians to come up, and attempting to cut him off from the Rhine, he changed his strategy. From the upper Main valley where his men had been concentrated, he marched them rapidly in three great columns, each column separated from the next by not more than a day's march, across the watershed of the Franconian Wood. By October 9, a day after the expiration of the Prussian ultimatum, his columns had streamed out into the open plains of Saxony. He then rested his troops in order to give Murat's cavalry a chance to catch up, and then the whole army pivoted toward the left and advanced directly upon the Prussian lines.

There all was confusion. Jealousies divided the two Prussian commanders, Prince Hohenlohe and the duke of Brunswick. Staggered by the unexpected advance of the French, the Prussian war council futilely debated the plan of campaign, neither concentrating for battle nor deciding upon a retreat. When finally they determined to fall back upon the Elbe, Napoleon was upon them. While Napoleon with the main body of the French fell upon Prince Hohenlohe and the Prussian rear guard at Jena on October 14 and crushed the foe by sheer weight of numbers, a fiercer engagement took place at Auerstädt, twelve miles to the north. There Marshal Davout, commanding the advance guard of the French,

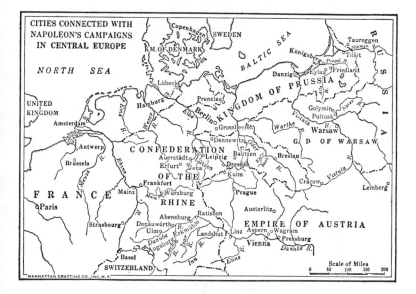

attacked the bulk of the retreating Prussians under the duke of Brunswick. After stubborn fighting, in the course of which Brunswick was fatally wounded, the Prussians yielded before the French offensive. As they fell back, they were joined by the stragglers from Jena, and the whole Prussian retreat became a rout.

The French pursued the demoralized enemy relentlessly through their own country. Marshal Ney occupied the garrison fortress of Magdeburg. Other fortresses, Küstrin, Spandau, and Stettin, without adequate means of defense, surrendered to the invader. By October 25 the French were in Berlin, while Frederick William and the court retired from fortress to fortress, finally taking refuge in Memel, deep in East Prussia. Within a month after the opening of the campaign the kingdom of Prussia had collapsed; only a detachment of 15,000 troops in Silesia and the garrison troops in the Baltic fortresses of East Prussia still defended the Prussian eagle. Prussia was a conquered country and in its capital flew the standards of the victorous French.

As the primary object of the war upon Prussia was to establish French domination in northern Germany, Napoleon proceeded forthwith to utilize his victories. He detached the elector of Saxony from his unwilling alliance with Prussia. He increased the elector's territory, which was transformed into a kingdom, and drew it into the Confederation of the Rhine, binding it to France by a rigid military alliance. The other clients of the Prussian state fared worse. Like Prussia they all paid heavy war contributions. In addition the elector of Hesse-Cassel, the duke of Brunswick, and the prince of Orange were deposed, and their states occupied by the French. The emperor's demands upon Frederick William were even more rigorous, and the latter could prevent the full destruction of his kingdom only by casting himself humbly upon Russian support. Napoleon was now the master of northern Germany, but Russia still opposed the execution of his grandiose conception of a European union against England.

THE DEFEAT OF THE RUSSIANS

Russia was a more formidable opponent than Prussia. In the first place, the fighting was shifted to the vast swampy Polish plains of East Prussia, where the great desolate stretches, the bitter cold of the approaching winter, and the scarcity of food and fodder placed heavy obstacles in the path of the invaders. Secondly, the diplomatic situation was fraught with perils for Napoleon. The Austrian troops were mobilized, prepared at the signal to fall upon the right flank of the French. As Napoleon neared the old Polish capital of Warsaw, the Polish patriots lashed themselves into a frenzy of enthusiasm in their mistaken belief that the new dawn of Polish independence was at hand. But Napoleon understood that a restoration of the Polish kingdom was the most effective way of reuniting Austria and Russia, for both countries had shared in the partitions and would lose their Polish provinces by such a move. "By conceding then to the full measure of Polish aspirations Napoleon would have committed the supreme folly of making peace with Russia impossible and war with Austria certain." [3] This folly he did not commit. He carefully encouraged the Poles in their hopes with vague and ambiguous phrases which gained him the food resources of the country and the support of the Polish cavalry, but he made no definite statements which could compromise the diplomatic situation. Meantime Austria pursued her policy of watchful waiting. Her forces, mobilized to guarantee her neutrality, were a fearful menace to Napoleon's long line of communications. To cut his communications with Berlin was also the first objective of the Russians.

Napoleon's first attempts to end the military campaign with a decisive victory over the Russians ended with a serious check. He attempted a wide circling movement against them in December, but the heavy snows, the sudden thaws and the thick mud made rapid maneuvering impossible, and the Russians escaped him. In February, 1807, while hurrying north to parry a Russian thrust against Danzig, which Marshal Bernadotte was successfully besieging, Napoleon met the Russians at Eylau, near Königsberg. There in a blinding snowstorm Marshals Murat and Soult fought against the rear guard of the Russians in the bloodiest battle of the campaign. The Russians finally gave way, but the appalling carnage had also taken heavy toll of the French who were too exhausted to pursue. After this setback the dispirited Grand Army fell back into East Prussia, while Napoleon's enemies grew more sanguine, confident that the French colossus was tottering at last. But they reckoned without heeding the marvelous abundance of Napoleon's diplomatic resources and the tantalizing slowness of their own efforts at union against him.

In the early spring Prussia and Russia signed a military convention in accordance with which they pledged themselves to deliver Germany and Italy from Napoleonic control. Austria and England and the Baltic states were asked to give their adherence to this arrangement concluded by the treaty of Bartenstein. Austria found plausible pretexts for delaying military action, for under the pressure of Napoleonic diplomacy, her government had consented to offer her services as mediator to the combatants. England promised subsidies without formally joining this fourth coalition, but her subsidies came too late. Meantime French diplomacy

[3] H. A. L. Fisher, *Studies in Napoleonic Statesmanship, Germany.*

was netting tangible results in the Near East. At Constantinople, General Sébastiani aided the sultan to repulse an English squadron in the Dardanelles. He tried also to persuade the Turks to attack the Russians, who had invaded Moldavia and Wallachia, the two Danubian provinces of the Turkish Empire, but all the vigor of the Turks, so far as that territory was concerned, was expended in words. French diplomacy was more successful in the Middle East. Persuaded by Sébastiani, the sultan sent a force to defeat a British expeditionary force to Egypt. A diplomatic mission to Teheran, the Persian capital, flattered the shah into sending plenipotentiaries to Napoleon. With them the emperor signed an offensive treaty which obligated Persia to attack the Russians from the south and to break off relations with England and incite the Afghans into an attack upon India.

With each passing day Napoleon's position was strengthened. Spring was on the way, the roads were drying, and the grass for his horses was sprouting. From France and Italy he summoned 80,000 raw recruits, the conscripts of 1808, with whom he reconstructed his reserve army in Germany for a defense against the Austrians and increased his main army for the offensive against the Russians. In May he occupied the port of Danzig, where he found fresh supplies for his men. A month later the decisive battle was fought at Friedland in East Prussia, where the inept strategy of the Russians and the numerical superiority of the French gave Napoleon a crushing victory.

THE TREATIES OF TILSIT

Despite his huge losses at Friedland, Alexander could have continued the military struggle against Napoleon, had other considerations not become uppermost in his thoughts. A growing consciousness that the prolongation of the fighting might encourage a national Polish uprising, angry resentment over the lukewarm attitude of England and Austria, and a strong desire to seek his own profit in the liquidation of the troubled affairs of Europe made him resolve to seek peace with Napoleon. The latter encouraged him in his new attitude, for he too desired peace to rest his tired troops and utilize his victory for the fulfillment of his vast continental designs. An armistice ended the hostilities on June 21, and four days later the two rulers held the first of their formal conferences on a raft moored in the Niemen River near Tilsit. For three hours Napoleon and Alexander I discussed the terms of their rapprochement while the scorned and unhappy Frederick William, the erstwhile ally of the czar, rode helplessly up and down the shore, a prey to the darkest conjectures. His fears were not imaginary, as Napoleon made clear to him when he was presented to the French emperor. Prussia did indeed pay the costs of the war.

The treaties of Tilsit (July 7–9) consisted of an open and secret treaty between Russia and France and an open treaty between France and Prussia. In the diplomatic duel which the two monarchs fought under the friendly setting of long intimate discussions and sumptuous entertainments, it was not Napoleon who fared second best. The vanquished Alexander paid a heavy price for the integrity of his state and his alliance with Napoleon "to assure the happiness and tranquillity of the globe." He recognized the great changes that Napoleon had already effected in Holland, Germany, and Italy, and declared himself ready to accept all additional changes that Napoleon should make there. He gave his assent to the dismemberment of Prussia, who lost some of her most precious possessions and half her population. From the Prussian territory west of the Elbe (to which were added lands from Hesse-Cassel and the duchy of Brunswick), Napoleon created the kingdom of Westphalia, which he assigned to his brother Jerome. Prussia's Polish provinces in the east, with the exception of the district of Bialystok, went to form the grand duchy of Warsaw under the rule of the king of Saxony. To connect this new territory with his old possessions the king of Saxony was given the right to use a military road running through Silesia. The unfortunate Frederick William retained only his provinces of East Prussia (together with West Prussia and Ermeland), Brandenburg, Silesia, and a portion of the duchy of Magdeburg.[4] By a separate military convention, however, the French troops were to occupy various fortresses in these provinces until the payment of war contributions, the exact amount of which was not fixed until September, 1808. Pending the conclusion of a general peace with England, French garrisons

---

[4] Frederick William saved as much as he did through the "friendly intercession" of Alexander; but it is likely that Alexander's intercession in his behalf was as calculated as it was generous. By preserving Prussia from total extinction he won a claim to Prussian gratitude and also a possible barrier against the extension of French influence.

also occupied the port of Danzig, now a free city, and the ports of the duchy of Oldenburg and Mecklenburg. Frederick William also recognized the Confederation of the Rhine, Louis as king of Holland, and Joseph as king of Naples. Lastly, in secret articles, Prussia was required to close her harbors to the English and take common action with France and Russia against "the Mistress of the Seas."

In the secret treaty of alliance between France and Russia the terms of their future joint action were elaborated. Here Napoleon's diplomatic genius reached the heights, for he beguiled the czar into believing that the French emperor threw open to him the East, whereas in reality Napoleon never for a moment contemplated so generous a settlement. The czar offered his mediation in the struggle between France and England. England would be summoned by November 1, 1807, to return all the conquests she had made since 1805 and to grant complete independence upon the seas. In the event of her refusal, Alexander was to declare war, close the ports of his country to British products, and summon the Baltic states, Austria, and Portugal to follow suit. Similarly, Napoleon offered his mediation to end the war between Russia and Turkey. Were Turkey to refuse, at the end of three months Napoleon would make common cause with Russia against the Porte in liberating the European provinces, Roumelia and Constantinople excepted, from the Turkish yoke. Alexander was convinced that Napoleon had committed himself to the eventual partition of the Turkish Empire, and that his own share would be Moldavia and Wallachia; and Napoleon's ambiguous language was not designed to disillusion him. Meanwhile Napoleon prevailed upon the czar to remove his naval forces from the Mediterranean, surrender Cattaro to the French and recognize the French sovereignty over the Ionian Islands.

Such was Tilsit, which left each monarch with the comforting feeling that he had outwitted the other. Alexander lost no territory and gained an alliance. He was content with the arrangements concerning the grand duchy of Warsaw, for they ended the danger of Polish independence and placed the sycophantic Saxon king, whom Alexander expected to dominate, in control. Yet the king of Saxony was a prince of the Confederation of the Rhine and a military dependent of Napoleon. Confident that Sweden would refuse to join in a war against England, Alexander saw himself free to seize her province of Finland, which lay within Russia's "natural frontiers." Best of all, he and his soldiers saw in him the emperor of the East, even as they saw in Napoleon the emperor of the West. Napoleon, too, had no cause for regret. He had broken Prussia and gained full military control over Germany from one end to the other. In the kingdom of Westphalia he had a French outpost in Germany, and in the grand duchy of Warsaw a military march against Russia. He lost no time in reducing the sovereignty of the Saxon monarch to a minimum and in reserving the essentials of power for himself. He had misled Alexander, in exchange for vague phrases about the Balkan provinces, into recognizing a Grand Empire that protruded dangerously into Poland and the eastern Adriatic. He had played his cards well; indeed too well. By refusing to reconstruct an independent Poland under the guarantee of Russia, he willfully neglected and endangered the final consolidation of his domination in Italy and Germany and turned his interests too far into eastern Europe. By scheming to thwart Russia's secular ambitions in the Turkish Empire, he was to gain the bitter and determined hostility of Alexander I. At a crucial moment in his career he had committed a gigantic blunder. He sacrificed the reality of domination in Europe for the shadow of a universal empire. But the blunder had fashioned itself in his mind long before he executed it on the paper of the treaties. To gauge its extent we must turn our attention to that vast continental conception which he called the Continental System.

XVII. THE CONTINENTAL SYSTEM

THE MEANING OF THE CONTINENTAL SYSTEM

THE Continental System is the term that Napoleon himself applied to that set of measures by means of which he confidently expected to ruin English economic prosperity as a preliminary to the destruction of England's political influence. The Continental System introduced only one novel factor into the century-old commercial war between England and France. This was the association of the entire Continent with France proper in the execution of the various acts of policy which France had hitherto employed single-handed against England. At the moment that Napoleon formally established the continental blockade, he was in sufficient control of Europe to resist England by forming a military alliance with Prussia and a maritime alliance with Holland and Spain. His aim, however, was not exclusively the ruin of the English, as the famous English historian Seeley maintained; rather it was a European confederation of states under his personal domination. By establishing a continental blockade against English products and vehemently condemning English maritime practices, Napoleon could pose as the defender of continental interests against an unprincipled England and still inflict as crushing a blow upon the English economic system as he could have done by following any other tactics. If England agreed to modify her maritime code and restore the colonies of France and her allies, Napoleon's grand design in Europe and in the East would progress rapidly. If England refused to come to terms, Napoleon would confront the English —as for a brief moment he was able to do—with an armed Continent. Though his ultimate goal of a European confederation was clearly premature and the ruthless violence of his methods doomed his venture to failure, it is only by correlating the continental blockade with his general policy of imperial conquest that we can understand why he was inevitably led to renew his war against Austria, Prussia, and Russia.

The idea of compulsory regulation of commercial policy and

maritime intercourse was not new, and the theory underlying it was considerably older than the Revolution. Up to the time of the commercial treaty of 1786, the normal state of relations between France and England was that of commercial war and mutual embargo. Following the mercantile theory that a country was strong in so far as its exports exceeded its imports, and that the mother country should have the monopoly of trade with its own colonies, the two states professed a policy of general prohibition of each other's goods. In practice, smuggling on a very extensive scale and the use of the license system made the actual intercourse between the two countries far different from what it was supposed to be in theory. This divergence between reality and professed policy became all the more pronounced in the latter half of the eighteenth century, when the forces of the industrial revolution and the doctrines of economic liberalism (*laissez faire*) helped to weaken the old mercantile ideal. The commercial treaty of 1786 openly recognized the great change in the commercial relations of the two countries and allowed the entry of British manufactured goods into France. So unpopular, however, was this treaty with the French textile manufacturers, who were crippled by English competition, that they endeavored to end it at the first opportunity. This opportunity came in 1793, with the outbreak of war between France and England; and from 1793 till the close of the Napoleonic era the commercial relations between the two states consistently followed the older traditions of blockade and restrictive commercial policy.

From 1793 to 1799 the revolutionary assemblies passed severe if not draconic decrees for the exclusion from French markets of various classes of British manufactured products, such as cotton and woolen fabrics, iron and steel products, and refined sugar. They also pursued a strongly protectionist policy against all foreign goods, levying heavy customs taxes on such products when conveyed on foreign ships. This policy of French self-blockade was in practice modified by regulations and seriously weakened by extensive smuggling operations.

The English government during the same interval professed a policy of blockade, but it made no effort to starve out France or to stop French imports. It was always the desire of the English to regulate French trade for their own benefit and never to encourage the French self-blockade of British products. The English policy actually was an effective method of strengthening the commercial prosperity of Great Britain. It helped to hinder the trade of the French colonies of the West Indies with France and her European allies to the advantage of the British colonies, and it enabled England to convey the products of the enemy colonies to her own ports. It served also to increase in extraordinary fashion the total foreign trade of the United States, whose merchants and shipowners gained enormous profits in transporting the produce of French, Dutch, and Spanish colonies to Europe. Though this carrying trade of the American vessels had been declared legal by an eminent British authority, the position of the American and European neutral was fraught with some danger. The legal status of the neutral shipper was protected, but this legal protection scarcely checked the damaging activities of British ships of war and privateers. In fact, Great Britain used its uncontested naval superiority to indulge in extralegal and injurious practices which often eventuated in the confiscation of the neutral's cargo. Nevertheless, despite the interference of British warships and French privateers and prize-court condemnation the years up to 1807 were prosperous for American merchants, farmers, and shippers. "The whole situation was remarkably similar to the first years of the World War, 1914–1917, when the United States, as the great neutral, profited from supplying foodstuffs and other products to the warring nations."

With Napoleon's seizure of power in 1799 the commercial war between France and England grew more severe and gradually involved the whole Continent. Like many of his contemporaries in France, Napoleon was convinced of the hollowness of the English economic system. As he firmly believed that a country's trade was of slight value in comparison with its industry and agriculture, he was certain that England's apparent prosperity was fictitious. He could therefore bring about the economic strangulation of England by closing her continental markets. "Deprived of these immense markets," he wrote, "harassed by revolts and internal disturbances which will be the consequence, England will have great embarrassment with her colonial and Asiatic goods. These goods, being unsalable, will fall to low prices, and the English will find themselves vanquished by excess. . . ." Furthermore, he thought he saw the signs of economic decay in England in the extraordinary increase of the funded debt, in the suspension, on the part of the Bank of England, of the redemption of its notes, and in the gradual inflation of the currency. Hence, by closing the Continent to the English and forcing them to buy their foodstuffs from France, paying for them in metallic currency, he would deplete the gold reserves of the Bank of England. The English credit system would then collapse, English subsidies to the Continent would cease, and France would emerge victorious.

Such was the Napoleonic conception of the commercial war. To make good his aim of closing the Continent to the English, he extended the practices of the revolutionary assemblies to the North Coast, to Italy and Switzerland. Although he had offered, in 1800, to revise the revolutionary decrees against British merchandise, pressure from French manufacturers induced him to maintain the restrictions. Consequently nothing was stipulated in the treaty of Amiens. In April, 1803, the Corps législatif voted a new tariff law which made no concessions to English commerce, thus making inevitable the renewal of the war in the following month. After the outbreak of the implacable war, Napoleon tightened the restrictions upon colonial wares from British sources, also against neutrals that lent themselves to smuggling activities. On the British side, the most important measures taken were the extension of the paper blockade to the coast between the mouth of the Elbe and the port of Brest and the reversal of the policy concerning the broken voyage of American vessels (1806).[1]

After his victory at Austerlitz (December 2, 1805), Napoleon was free to promote systematically his great plan of conquering the sea by the land; that is, of using his military domination on the Continent to close European markets to the English and, at the same time, to win those markets for French manufacturers. The new tariff of April 10, 1806, which he later characterized as "a real coup d'état," was a clear indication of his policy. All colonial products were subjected to heavy customs duties. Raw cotton became dutiable, subject however to a drawback if the goods manufactured were subsequently exported. Cotton manufactures, with certain exceptions for such as could not be produced in France, were excluded *in toto*. He foresaw the difficulties that the measure

---

[1] The earlier decision peculiarly favored the American neutral, whose long coast line, remote from the European belligerents, allowed him to break his journey from the colonies to Europe. But the legitimate scope of the neutral American trade no less than the evasion of the regulations on the part of her enemies, determined England to protect her own "neutralization." Henceforth, ran the ruling, the intention of the shippers must be examined to determine whether or not the "Rule of War of 1756" had been infringed.

would bring to French manufacturers, but was sanguine that after a year or two of hardship French manufacturers would be grateful to him for removing foreign competition.

The Decrees

The immediate occasion for the establishment of the Continental System was the issue of the English order in council of May 16, 1806, which declared the entire coast beween Brest and the Elbe, that is, the ports of the North Sea and the English Channel, in a state of blockade. This first order in council was in itself an answer to Napoleon's earlier order for the closing of the neutral north German coast to British goods. Napoleon's next move was delayed until after his defeat of the Prussians at Jena and Auerstädt (October, 1806). He then gave orders to his commander in northern Germany to occupy Hamburg, Bremen, and Lübeck, close the Elbe "hermetically," and seize all English goods in that territory. It was through these Hanseatic towns that Great Britain landed most of her colonial goods and manufactured products on the Continent, for from there the goods went to Germany and the rest of Europe. Much of the trade of the American shipper with Europe was also carried on via the Hanseatic towns.

The consequence of this brusque order was the confiscation of vast quantities of British merchandise stored in the warehouses of the Hanseatic cities and the enrichment of Napoleon's war treasury. On November 21 the emperor of the French issued the famous Berlin Decree, in which he posed as the champion of European economic interests and as the defender of the liberty of the seas. The preamble denounced the British blockade as a violation of the accepted principles of international law. The decree itself declared the British Isles in a state of blockade, forbade all trade in British goods, ordered the arrest of British subjects in territory occupied by the French, made British products liable to seizure, and refused to every vessel coming directly from ports of Great Britain or her colonies, or calling at them after the proclamation of the decree, access to any port on the Continent. As this decree was binding upon all of France's allies and dependencies, it virtually established, at least theoretically, a cordon against British commerce from northern Germany to southern Italy. Without a fleet Napoleon could not actually enforce, nor did he intend to enforce, his blockade of the British Isles, so that the principal consequences of that declaration were felt by neutrals like the American shipper, who ran the risk of capture at the hands of French privateers. The prohibition of trade with England was also felt by the neutrals in Europe, who were exposed to Napoleon's armies. For thus needlessly antagonizing the neutral carrier and cutting off neutral trade from France, Napoleon has been severely criticized by many students of his policy. But Napoleon aimed precisely at conquering the British economically by a self-blockade of all the Continent; this object he never could have attained by allowing neutral trade to continue. He realized that the ensuing privations would be great in France and among her allies; but he judged that the injury to Great Britain would be even greater, if not fatal.[2]

Great Britain's defense against the Berlin Decree and its execution was to break through the continental blockade and maintain its connection with Europe. The first attempt at reprisals took the form of another order in council (January 7, 1807), which forbade neutrals to trade between the ports of France and her allies (i.e., the coasting trade) under pain of seizure and confiscation of ship and cargo. Because of British supremacy on the seas, the neutrals, particularly the American and Danish ships plying in the Mediterranean, suffered more keenly from the British order than they did from the more sweeping Berlin Decree. Napoleon had already taken pains to have the American minister in Paris reassured that the Berlin Decree did not apply to ships owned by his fellow citizens, though this exception was later canceled. As this measure of reprisal was only of slight importance, steady pressure was put upon the British government for a more forcible policy.

Napoleon was not free to execute his various regulations against English commerce until after the successful termination of the war of the fourth coalition. The treaty of Tilsit contained careful provisions with regard to the Continental System, which Prussia and Russia observed by closing their ports after the failure of Russian mediation between France and England. Denmark, Sweden, Austria, and Portugal remained to test the common action of Russia and France in winning their adherence to the continental block-

---

[2] In a message to the Senate Napoleon explained his action. "It has cost us dearly to expose the interests of the private individual to the quarrels of kings . . . ; but we have been forced for the good of our peoples and our allies, to employ against the common enemy the same weapons that he used against us."

ade. The first trial of strength came in Denmark. The strategic location of Denmark gave her control of the Baltic, a factor which could be used against England's efforts to land an expeditionary force on the Swedish shore. In addition, her fleet held the balance between the combatants, for should Napoleon win the reënforcement of Danish naval forces, the fleet of France and her allies would almost equal that of England. Before the Napoleonic powers could complete their plans for the coercion of Denmark, England acted with unceremonious rapidity. It offered Denmark a secret defensive alliance, in return for which the Danes were to turn over their fleet to the English for safe-keeping until the peace. On the firm refusal of the Danish government an English fleet bombarded Copenhagen for three days, compelled its surrender (September 5, 1807), and took possession of the coveted fleet. While this outrageous proceeding gave especial point to Napoleon's charges against English practices toward neutrals, it nevertheless turned the naval balance against the French. Denmark immediately concluded a military alliance with Napoleon and entered into the Continental System, but her fleet was lost to the French. In the interim, while Napoleon was elaborating his plans for the subjection and partition of Portugal, Alexander carried out his treaty obligations. On November 7, 1807, Alexander declared war against England. Sweden remained to be coerced. Upon the refusal of the Swedish to give up their alliance with the English, Alexander invaded Finland, expelled the Swedes, and procaimed himself ruler of that country.

With Russia, Prussia, and Denmark actively on the side of France, and the Iberian and Italian peninsulas almost entirely under Napoleonic control, it behooved the English to devise immediate ways of preventing the strangulation of their economic system. The regulations that were issued in the very important orders in council of November–December, 1807, were largely expedients for turning the measures of France against herself, that is, to injure the trade of France and her allies in the same way that Napoleon had endeavored to injure that of Great Britain. These orders in council reaffirmed the principle of a paper blockade by maintaining that all ports from which British ships and goods were excluded should henceforth be subject to the same restrictions in regard to trade and navigation as though they were actually blockaded by a British fleet. All trade in the articles of the states that adhered to Napoleon's system or of their colonies was held unlawful, and all such merchandise and the ships that carried it were to be considered lawful prize goods. Any neutral vessel that carried "certificates of origin," that is, papers which declared the cargo to be of non-British origin, was to be considered lawful prize of war. By these provisions Great Britain penalized neutrals that complied with the decrees of the Continental System. But in order to win neutrals over to its cause, the British government held out certain inducements to them. It permitted direct neutral trade between British ports and the enemy ports in the colonies, and between neutral ports and any enemy colonial port not actually blockaded by British ships. Furthermore, the neutral trade with blockaded continental ports was also permitted, but only on the condition that the neutral first put in at a British port, unload his cargo and pay charges virtually equivalent to an import duty before he could obtain the right to proceed to a European port. Since British wares required no reëxport certificate, this provision materially favored the carriage of British goods, especially sugar, coffee, and cotton, to the Continent on British bottoms. Meantime, the immense importations made by British merchants were bonded and kept in warehouses at different British ports in England and the colonies.

In short, despite the formal renewal of the blockade, the English government was primarily concerned with forcing goods, whether colonial or manufactured, British or enemy, upon the Continent via a British port. These orders in council of the autumn of 1807 were wholly consistent with the traditional English policy of commercial warfare. The trade of American shippers was particularly molested by the new English regulations. It exposed them anew to the British right of search and cut off their lucrative trade between the enemy colonies in the West Indies and the European mainland unless they agreed to put in at a British port and pay the dues. And if they did comply with this regulation, so heavy a charge was put upon their profits that the honest neutral shipper was threatened with ruin.

The next move in the commercial struggle lay with Napoleon, who retorted to the new orders in council with the Milan Decree of December 17, 1807. Alleging that all ships that submitted to the search of the British on the high seas lost their national character (were "denationalized"), he decreed that they should be considered lawful prize of war if captured by French or allied vessels. His decree stated, furthermore, that every vessel that put in at any port in Great Britain or in its colonies and possessions and paid duty would also be held lawful prize if captured by a French warship or privateer. The Milan Decree was the logical conclusion of Napoleon's policy of forbidding the export of British goods on neutral vessels. For him there were henceforth no more neutrals, inasmuch as neutrals either were English in disguise or had become the accomplices of the English by obeying the orders in council. Since the year 1807 had witnessed such a great increase in his power, from his standpoint England was now cut off from the Continent and isolated from all save its colonies.

In fact, the Continental System on the one hand and the various British orders on the other wrought such hardships upon neutral shipping as to threaten the neutrals, particularly the American traders, with ruin. The first significant act of retaliation by the United States was the Embargo Act of 1807; but the damage it caused to American interests was so great that in March, 1809, it was repealed. It was replaced by a Non-Intercourse Act, which prohibited trade only with Great Britain and France and their possessions.[3]

The commercial warfare in Europe continued under the formal rules laid down by the various decrees throughout the years 1808 and 1809, neither England nor France altering the conditions of the struggle save to extend them and introduce secret and important modifications. These extensions and modifications, particularly those effected by licenses, will be taken up in the final estimate of the consequences on each set of antagonists. Beginning with 1810 Napoleon followed a new policy which led him far from his original intentions. In the meantime, the Continent was nominally closed to England except for the considerable operations of smugglers and the leaks in the Spanish and Italian and Balkan peninsulas. In Spain and Portugal the situation was particularly unsatisfactory.

The Political Consequences in Spain and Portugal

In 1806 Napoleon had already made plans with Spain for the

[3] In 1810, the Non-Intercourse Act was also repealed, and new legislation provided that as soon as either England or France revoked its decrees against American shipping, the Non-Intercourse Act would be renewed against the other country. When Napoleon repealed the Berlin and Milan decrees against the United States, in 1810, President Madison immediately revived the Non-Intercourse Act against Great Britain.

partition of the territory of England's loyal ally, and now, fresh from his triumph at Tilsit, he returned to his project of crushing Portugal in order to strike at England. It had been agreed at Tilsit that Portugal would be treated as an enemy if it refused to make a declaration of war against England. On October 27, 1807, the secret treaty of Fontainebleau between France and Spain determined the partition of Portugal. The northern part of the country was to be made into a kingdom and given to the queen of Etruria in exchange for her kingdom, which, with its important port of Leghorn, was to be surrendered to Napoleon. Godoy, the "Prince of Peace," as he styled himself, and the paramour of the Spanish queen, was to gain the southern section, while the central and the largest portion, including Lisbon, the most active and flourishing port of all Portugal, was to be held by Napoleon until the conclusion of the general peace. In a secret military agreement, the Spanish government promised to occupy northern and southern Portugal with 16,000 troops. Even before the treaty was signed, Marshal Junot was given orders to invade Portugal from his headquarters at Bayonne in southwest France, reach Lisbon and seize the Portuguese fleet. Struggling along under great hardships that decimated his troops, Junot raced through Spain and reached Portugal just too late, for the Portuguese royal family had escaped and was en route to Brazil, conveyed to the New World by the Portuguese fleet under the protection of a British squadron (November 27, 1807). Napoleon had other objectives in mind in the Iberian peninsula than the subjugation of Portugal. He had particular interests at stake in Spain, where the misrule of the Spanish Bourbons threatened the success of his full efforts in Europe.

To find a pretext for intervention in Spanish affairs was comparatively easy for the emperor, as the Spanish government itself provided him with an opportunity. For years the French alliance had been cordially detested in Spain. It had cost Spain the naval disaster at Trafalgar, English attacks upon her South American colonies, and grievous tribute, both in men and in money. Moreover, it suspended a sword of Damocles over the heads of the Bourbon rulers. With Bourbon rule ended in France and in Naples, the senile Charles IV and his intriguing and superstitious spouse lived uneasily under the menace of deposition. Spain, under their weak rule and the guidance of the queen's lover, the grasping, unscrupulous Godoy, had sunk to the depths of national degradation. In

1806 while Napoleon was waging the campaign of Jena, Godoy thought he had an opportunity to cast off the Napoleonic hold. He had issued a proclamation to the army, which he hurriedly retracted upon the news of Napoleon's victory. Godoy did not proceed from any motive of national consideration; his action was prompted by nothing loftier than thwarted greed and disappointment over the abandonment of the first project to partition Portugal. After Tilsit, Napoleon returned to his projected partition, beguiled Godoy into believing that his explanation of the abortive proclamation to the Spanish troops was accepted, and renewed the offer to the minister of a share in the Portuguese partition.

Meanwhile, happily for Napoleon's schemes, Marshal Junot's invasion of Portugal took place just at the moment that Godoy and Prince Ferdinand were both engaged in a palace intrigue against the bloated and degenerate Charles IV. The bitterness of the family quarrel, which was reflected in the growing hostility of the Spanish masses toward Godoy, afforded Napoleon the súpreme pretext that he sought to intervene in Spanish affairs. From Bayonne, Marshal Dupont invaded Spain with 40,000 men, and other French corps followed in December, 1807, and January, 1808. By February the strongholds of northern and western Spain were in the hands of the French armies. The natives welcomed them, thinking they had come to overthrow Godoy and set Ferdinand upon the throne. As Marshal Murat, commander-in-chief of the invaders, advanced upon Madrid, the Spanish capital, its inhabitants, suspicious of Godoy, broke out in revolt. In the ensuing disorder Charles IV was cowed into abdicating in favor of his son Ferdinand, the darling of the Spanish patriots. Murat, however, refused to recognize Ferdinand, seeing an opportunity to deliver the Spanish throne into the hands of Napoleon—and ultimately into his own.

With Madrid occupied by Murat, Napoleon prevailed upon the royal family to cross the border to Bayonne, where presumably the reconciliation of quarreling Spanish royalty would be effected by the emperor. With consummate skill in trickery and deception Napoleon played off one member of the family against the other and cowed them both by threatening reprisals for the bloody insurrection that had taken place in Madrid on May 2 (the famous Dos de Mayo) against Murat's troops. He terrified the supine Ferdinand into abdicating in favor of the former ruler, Charles IV, but not until he had taken the precaution of extracting a signed abdication in his own favor from the latter. Both father and son signed away their rights, the former becoming a pensioner of the emperor in Italy, while the son was virtually imprisoned at Talleyrand's castle in Valençay. The rule of the Spanish Bourbons was now ended, and the throne vacant. Napoleon saw himself free to add an epilogue to the agreeable Spanish interlude. Since his rôle presumably was that of arbitrator, he played his part to the end by giving the Spaniards a monarch of their own choice. The enterprising Murat fell in with this game and summoned responsible officials and notables to petition the emperor to grant them Joseph Bonaparte as king. Napoleon graciously complied with their request and ceded his rights in Spain to Joseph, while the latter's now vacant throne in Naples was given to Napoleon's brother-in-law Murat (June, 1808). This transaction ended the first act of the Spanish tragedy.

THE RIFT WITH ALEXANDER I

The same year of 1808 saw fresh advances for Napoleon's broad plan of a confederated Europe under his control. He forced Austria to break with England and to join in the Continental System. The kingdom of Etruria (Tuscany) was annexed to the empire, its territory divided into French departments, and its dowager queen forced to flee. At the same time Corsica and Elba were formally annexed to France. Only the papal states still lay outside Napoleonic Italy, and in the following year this defect was remedied. It was essential to Napoleon's purposes to absorb Rome into the Italian confederation of Bonapartist states, but he could not accomplish his ends because of his failure to intimidate Pius VII into entering the Continental System against England. Ancona on the Adriatic and Civita Vecchia, the seaport of the papal city, were already in French possession. Early in 1808 a French army of occupation took possession of Rome, while three provinces (the legations) on the Adriatic were incorporated with the kingdom of Italy. Now all Italy, Portugal and Spain, Prussia, the Hanseatic cities, Austria, Russia, and Denmark were partners with Napoleon in his commercial war with England.

The year 1808 was marked also by a significant readjustment of the French and Russian alliance. Despite the unpopularity of Tilsit with the Russian court Alexander I had proceeded to fulfill his treaty obligations. He broke off relations with England after his mediation had been rejected and gave his support to the continental blockade. Upon Sweden's rejection of his proposal for Swedish participation in the continental war against England, Alexander had occupied Finland (February, 1808) and proclaimed himself grand duke of that country. But his move engaged Russia in a perilous adventure in the north, for Sweden assumed a vigorous offensive against the Russian invaders. Corfu had already been surrendered to the French. Finally Russia began, then abruptly discontinued, her evacuation of Moldavia and Wallachia in the Danubian region, for the preliminaries of peace with Turkey contained nothing concerning the cession of the two principalities to Russia. Alexander still waited for the realization of the hopes that Napoleon had kindled at Tilsit, but the emperor made no move to partition Turkey. Alexander's slow realization that he had been duped lent a sharp tone to his subsequent diplomatic negotiations with Napoleon. His minister at Paris demanded France's recognition of the Russian conquest of the Danubian principalities and the evacuation of Prussia by the French troops. The French reply, dictated by Napoleon, added to Alexander's anxiety. Prussia, the emperor would not evacuate, since the French occupation was based upon a separate treaty with Frederick William, which the latter had not yet fulfilled. The Danubian provinces he would allow Russia to keep, provided he received compensation in Silesia—at Prussia's expense. The implication to Alexander was clear; if he agreed, Napoleon would bolster up his power in central Europe preparatory to the revival of an independent Polish state. But Alexander could not agree to any spoliation of the territory of Prussia. He rejected the proposal and kept his troops on the Danube—an act which enabled Napoleon to pose in Constantinople as a friend of the Turkish Empire.

These diplomatic discussions outlined the policies of the two rulers. Like Alexander, Napoleon was vitally interested in the East, but he could not run the risk of falling out with the czar on that score until after the termination of his Spanish venture. Not until the ports of Spain were under his control and all Italy subjected to his power would Napoleon hold the whip hand over the Russian czar. He would then be ready to renew the discussions concerning the Turkish Empire, secure in his control of the Mediterranean from Spain to the Dalmatian coast. In the meantime he needed the support of Russia against England in order to maintain his domination in Europe. He sought a personal interview with Alexander, hoping once again to dazzle the young czar with fantastic plans of conquests in the Near East and India. To gain time he made a proposal in a letter to Caulaincourt, the French ambassador at Saint Petersburg, that the two monarchs take joint action against Constantinople. After the partition of Turkey they would cross into Asia Minor and march victoriously against India. Enticed by these prospects the czar agreed, in the spring of 1808, to the interview, the date being left for future agreement; and then Napoleon left for Bayonne, as we have noted, to exercise his wiles upon the Spanish royal family. Thus far he had moved with remarkable dexterity, but in the summer of 1808 came such disquieting news from Spain that Napoleon was compelled to modify his plans and contend with a new perplexing and dangerous situation.

Spain had risen against her conqueror. Love of the young Ferdinand, who was idolized by the populace for his opposition to the detested Godoy, hatred of the old king who had sold his birthright for a castle and a pension, fanatical loyalty to the Catholic religion whose spiritual head Napoleon had oppressed, the reactionaries' bitterness against the revolutionary French, and the progressives' shame at their country's degradation—all these factors united the proud and sensitive Spaniards into a national resistance. Before the French troops had escorted Joseph to his capital at Madrid in July, 1808, the various provinces had broken out in bloody rebellion. While Joseph was still on the road toward Madrid, a column of 20,000 French soldiers under General Dupont, which was fighting its way from Madrid to Seville, was forced to surrender to a superior Spanish army at Baylen.

The reverse at Baylen was the beginning of a long succession of popular attacks upon the invaders. Shortly after, the inhabitants of Saragossa in northeastern Spain drove the French army from their city. The warfare in Spain was to continue until 1814—a guerrilla warfare to which the geography of the country particularly lent itself, a quasi-religious warfare in which the Spaniards fought as crusaders against the heretical French, and above all a national war in which a whole people fought in defense of its country against a foreign oppressor. The Spanish venture was a blunder of the first order. Napoleon had counted on 20,000 men to conquer Spain, but for

the following six years, when their presence was absolutely necessary in central Europe, hundreds of thousands of tried veterans
were rushed to Spain.

THE INTERVIEW AT ERFURT

The English government, realizing its unique opportunity to
open the Continent to British goods and to harass Napoleon, eagerly
gave promises of help to the Spanish rebels. To Portugal it dispatched a small expeditionary force under Sir Arthur Wellesley,
which late in the summer inflicted a decisive defeat upon Junot.
Meantime the Spaniards whom Napoleon had summoned to
northern Germany escaped on British ships to their own country,
an incident which produced an effect as electrifying as the news
of Baylen.

These events were a terrible blow to Napoleon's prestige and
power. Spain and Portugal, with their money subsidies, were lost
to him. The surrender of French troops that had long been regarded as invincible gave new hope to the patriots of the conquered
states. Austria pushed its military reorganization. Prussia lifted its
head. Thus Napoleon had to turn his attention to central Europe
before he could continue his subjugation of the Iberian Peninsula.
He postponed his eastern schemes, and withdrew many of the
veterans of the Grand Army from Prussia for the fighting in
Spain. Disturbed by the tokens of national resistance in the Prussia
that he had humbled so thoroughly, he imposed a treaty upon her
king (September, 1808) definitely fixing the amount of her war
indemnity, but at an impossible figure, insisting upon the surrender
of several garrisons on the Oder and limiting her active army to
42,000 men. In the event of war with Austria in 1809 Prussia was
to furnish him with 12,000 men. But in order to secure Russia's
good will, he agreed to remove his troops from Prussian territory.
Then, before leaving for Spain to direct operations in person, he
held his long projected interview with the czar at the small
Thuringian city of Erfurt, between September 27 and October 14,
1808.

More than ever he needed friendship of the czar and the renewal of the alliance that had been struck at Tilsit. The situation
at Erfurt was different from that at Tilsit, where he had held the
whip hand. Now it was the czar who was the stronger. Fascinated

as he undoubtedly was by the Napoleonic blandishments, the young ruler of "All the Russias" had between Tilsit and Erfurt made up his mind to end the French alliance. He came to the realization that Russia's real policy lay in an alliance with Austria, rather than in the strengthening of Napoleon's control over Austria and Germany. Between the two interviews, he employed all the artifices of his complex and cunning temperament to conceal his true intentions from Napoleon. To his sister he confided that "Bonaparte" considered him a fool but he would have the last laugh. On the eve of Erfurt in a letter to the Russian ambassador at Vienna he made the following revelation of his diplomatic game: "The wisest course for Austria would be to remain a spectator of the Napoleonic struggle in Spain. There will always be time later to adopt the policy that circumstances will suggest. By following this course Austria will free me of the painful obligation of taking up arms against her, for I am not obliged to do so unless she attacks first." This letter reveals a full understanding of his position: if Austria made war upon Napoleon, the defeat of Austria would be the preliminary to the subjection of Russia. He saw that, inasmuch as Russia was now essential to Napoleon, he would be allowed to have his own way on the Danube. Now to come to the aid of Prussia and Austria would defeat his own purpose—the acquisition of Moldavia and Wallachia. Hence his keen desire to dissuade the German states from forcing war upon Napoleon in central Europe. With Napoleon occupied in Spain, Alexander foresaw the realization of his own dreams on the Danube, and perhaps in Constantinople.

The dazzling setting at Erfurt that furnished the background of his discussions with Napoleon, the military reviews and the imposing spectacles at the theater and the opera, even the apparent intimacy and cordiality that prevailed between rulers, only concealed the real divergences between them. Alexander, timid and irresolute in manner, was obdurate to all of Napoleon's guiles and manifestations of anger. With the utmost skill he avoided accepting all proposals which would involve him in war with Prussia and Austria and remove his troops from the Danube. The interview ended with a superficial and secret renewal of the Tilsit alliance. Russia and France were to continue their common efforts against England until the latter state agreed to a peace on the basis of present possession. But in the end Napoleon agreed to withdraw his mediation in Turkey and to come to the aid of Russia in case the Austrians sided with Turkey. Conversely, the czar agreed to make common cause with France in the event that Austria took the initiative in declaring war upon France. At the successful termination of the war with England the czar was to retain the Danubian provinces, while Napoleon would keep his conquests in Spain. Napoleon refused to discuss the terms of the partition of Turkey, but he made slight concessions to the czar in the Prussian question by agreeing to scale down the total of the Prussian war contributions. The Tilsit alliance was indeed renewed, but the interview was a diplomatic reverse for Napoleon and a success for the czar. Russia did renew her alliance against Austria, but Alexander never intended to (and actually never did) live up to his treaty obligations.

Half reassured that there was nothing to fear in the immediate present in central Europe from either Austria or Prussia, Napoleon led more than 200,000 of his veterans into Spain. A brief and brilliant winter campaign in northern Spain ended the feeble, unorganized Spanish resistance and resulted in the restoration of Joseph early in December. To win the sympathy of the Spaniards the French emperor decreed the abolition of feudal rights, the suppression of the Inquisition, and the reduction by two-thirds of the number of monasteries. His attempt was fruitless. The intellectual climate of Spain was centuries behind that of France, and those liberal eighteenth century ideas which had fired the French revolutionaries met a chilly reception south of the Pyrenees. From Madrid, Napoleon had intended to march against southern Spain and against Lisbon in Portugal, but learning that a British force under Sir John Moore was near, he set out in pursuit. He pursued the English through Leon to Corunna in the foothills of Galicia, where he turned over the command to Marshal Soult, who received the surrender of the enemy, though not their fleet, which escaped (February 15, 1809). Napoleon had meanwhile hastily returned to Paris, for he had received both the news of a ministerial intrigue against him in the French capital and the news of Austria's warlike preparations.

The unpopularity of the Spanish war had indeed provoked political intrigues in Paris against the emperor. During his absence, Fouché and Talleyrand, who detested each other cordially, were brought together by a plot for Napoleon's deposition. A telltale letter to Murat was intercepted en route and sent to Napoleon along with the reports of Talleyrand's indiscreet remarks on the subject. Napoleon's precipitate return to Paris ended their conspiracy. He spared Fouché for the moment, but upon Talleyrand fell a stream of unprintable invective unparalleled in the political relations of a monarch and his adviser. When Napoleon finally drew breath, his disgraced official retired unabashed, remarking softly, "What a pity, what a pity that so great a man has been brought up so badly!"

The War of the Fifth Coalition

An additional reason for Napoleon's hasty departure from Spain was the disquieting news that the war party in Austria had won control over the Emperor Francis and was forcing his hand. Indeed, in the years following the humiliating peace of Pressburg (1805) the sentiment of German nationalism developed rapidly among the five million German-speaking inhabitants of the Austrian duchies. Many circumstances contributed to this development of a national consciousness, of what the most recent historian of the movement has called "a feeling of cultural unity and identity with a common group of people, a desire for political union . . . in a distinct national state." [4] The French troops spread with them in their march the concept of nationalism, and the humiliation and the material distress into which their defeats had cast Austria prepared for the application of that concept among the subjects of Francis I. More immediate factors in its extension were the simultaneous retirement of the older leaders and the entry upon the scene of younger, more forceful men, the news of the patriotic uprising of the Spaniards, and the organization of national propaganda on an extensive scale.

The new chancellor was the highly intelligent, energetic, and resolute Count Philip Stadion, the champion of a national war against the French invaders. The new commander-in-chief of the Austrian forces was Archduke Charles, the younger brother of the emperor and the military hero of the people. These men and the new empress, Maria Ludovica, played the leading part in the preparations for a national uprising. Archduke Charles introduced

[4] Langsam, W. C., *The Napoleonic Wars and German Nationalism in Austria*, p. 16.

urgent military reforms and utilized the services of men of letters to stimulate the ardor of the men by appeals to Austria's glorious past. The number of troops in active service was increased to 300,000, and an additional force of 200,000 was drilled and enrolled in the reserve army (the *Landwehr*, created in 1808). Stadion fully appreciated the value of nationalist propaganda in creating public opinion and summoned to his side such vigorous publicists as Friedrich von Gentz and Pozzo di Borgo to direct the campaign against Napoleon. From Prussia came the dismissed Baron Stein and the Hanoverian novelist Friedrich von Schlegel. A press war was instituted, and the campaign of the newspapers was supplemented by the distribution of many pamphlets and fly sheets, the publication of popular songs, poems, and dramatic works that all took for their themes the revival of Austrian sentiments against Napoleon. Early in 1809 the French chargé reported to Paris that "the newspapers contain nothing but tirades against France, and advertisements of patriotic works and accounts of the prowess of Austrian heroes." [5]

The Austrian statesmen were eager to profit by Napoleon's difficulties in the Spanish peninsula, and they were hopeful of military aid from Prussia and Russia and subsidies from England. Even after the king of Prussia and the czar indicated that their governments would not break with Napoleon, popular enthusiasm in Germany was so strong for a war against France that the Austrian emperor at last yielded to the contagion. Early in 1809 the Austrian government decided upon war, a war which Napoleon had hoped to avert in his present difficulties. Austria's purpose was clearly stated. It was a war of liberation, not against France, but against the system of constant expansion, against a state that was crushing the independence of European nations, obliterating their boundaries, and imposing upon the different peoples the revolutionary system of France. To his army Archduke Charles addressed an appeal: "The liberty of Europe has taken refuge under your banners; your victories will loosen its fetters, and your German brothers, now arrayed in the ranks of the enemy, await liberation at your hands."

The Prussian monarch refrained from coming to the aid of the Austrians, partly from fear that the time was not yet come when he could formally throw down the gauntlet to Napoleon, and

[5] Langsam, *op. cit.*, p. 95.

partly from unsettled differences with Austria over the German situation. Russia was formally bound by the agreement reached at Erfurt to come to France's assistance, though the czar gave the Austrian emperor assurances that he would do all that was diplomatically possible not to injure the chances of the Austrians or further the interests of Napoleon. In this campaign of 1809, the war of the fifth coalition against Napoleon, Austria had only her own resources to count on, an informal alliance with the insurrectionary force in Belgium as well as the promise of customary British financial subsidies.

Napoleon was in difficult straits. He soon learned that the alliance with Russia was dead, for while Alexander I overwhelmed him with promises of aid, he forbore to send troops. To overcome the numerical superiority of the Austrians, Napoleon was forced to summon young conscripts to the colors before their time and to fill in the gaps in the ranks by recalling older classes to the front. From Spain he hastily recalled two divisions and the Guard. By these heroic exertions he succeeded in gathering in Germany some 200,000 troops. His tactics in the first part of the campaign clearly showed that he had lost none of his military genius. In a masterly campaign of less than a week's duration (battles of Abensberg, Landshut, and Eckmühl) he drove Archduke Charles out of Bavaria (April 19-23); and within three weeks he was in the Austrian capital. Instead of waging an offensive campaign, the Austrians were forced back upon the defensive. In five days they had lost more than 50,000 men.

The second part of the campaign proved more difficult for the French. It is no disparagement of the valor of the Austrians nor the prowess of their commander, the Archduke Charles, to note that Napoleon's army of young and raw recruits in 1809 was vastly inferior to the disciplined and tried veterans of the Grand Army of 1805 that had shattered the Austrians at Austerlitz. Napoleon's first attempt to cross the Danube from the wooded island of Lobau that divided the river near Vienna failed in the desperate fighting at Aspern and Essling on May 21-22, which cost both antagonists 50,000 casualties. His bridge of boats to the capital broken, he fell back upon Lobau, awaited fresh troops from Italy and the Tirol, improvised a boat service of supplies from Vienna, and with great secrecy perfected his plans for a surprise crossing of the river. His chance came during the violent storm of the night of July 5, when he established himself on the northern bank. The following day witnessed the fighting of the decisive battle of Wagram where the Archduke Charles, vastly outnumbered by the French, suffered defeat and was forced to retreat. But he retreated in good order; Wagram was no repetition of the rout of Austerlitz. Luckily for Napoleon, the Austrian emperor was disheartened by the reverses of his troops and sued for an armistice, which served as a prelude to the peace that was signed three months later at Vienna.

Napoleon was fearful of the effect of the Austrian resistance upon Prussia and his nominal and unwilling ally, Russia. His anxiety on that score was allayed in the summer of 1809 by the failure of either country to attack him while he was recovering from his losses against Austria. Another source of anxiety to him was the expected British diversion in the Baltic and northern Germany. The projected British expedition was first delayed and then sadly bungled. Instead of landing at the mouth of the Elbe, the British force landed in July on an island off Holland, hoping, from there, to capture Antwerp. Several months later the expeditionary force, decimated by typhus, returned in disgrace to England. The Prussian temper was sharply impressed upon Napoleon in the sporadic insurrectional movements that broke out in northern Germany during the course of the campaign. But these attempts were premature and unsupported, and the rash enthusiasts who embarked upon them were crushed and dispersed. Frederick William did indeed yield to the warlike sentiments of his people so far as to stop the payment of his indemnity and to consent to secret preparations for war, but beyond that he dared not go. An uprising in the Bavarian, formerly the Austrian Tirol, which, if successful, would have cut Napoleon's communications with Italy and the Rhine, was also subdued. After Wagram the heroic leader of the Tirolese, the innkeeper Andreas Hofer, was betrayed to the French and executed. Even more symptomatic of the rising national spirit in Germany than the scattered uprisings was the attempted assassination of Napoleon by a young Saxon student, who averred that he considered it his duty to rid the world of Napoleon.

Her own reverses and the failure of attempts at relief rendered Austria powerless to oppose the rigorous peace terms that Napoleon dictated, and that Francis I signed in the treaty of Vienna on October 14, 1809. Austria lost three and one-half million of her population and a great stretch of territory. To Bavaria, Napoleon's ally, fell Austria's western provinces, the duchy of Salzburg and the Engadine. The important harbor of Trieste and the strategic coastal territory around the head of the Adriatic were also ceded, and then joined to Dalmatia to form the Illyrian provinces of the French empire. Austria also gave up the Polish province of Galicia, the western part of which was ceded to the grand duchy of Warsaw, while Russia received the eastern portion. By creating the Illyrian provinces he insured communication between Italy and the eastern Adriatic. Austria again agreed to break with England and join the Continental System. Francis I was also required to pay additional war indemnities and to reduce his active army to 150,000 men. In return for Napoleon's guarantee to respect the integrity of what remained of Austria, Francis I gave his sanction to all changes made, or to be made, by Napoleon in Spain, Portugal, and Italy.

The transfer of Galicia to Warsaw was in flagrant violation of the assurance that Napoleon had given earlier to Alexander. Russia's acquisition of the eastern portion in no way lessened Alexander's fears that Napoleon was secretly planning to reëstablish the kingdom of Poland. From this date began the czar's determined diplomatic negotiations to force Napoleon to sign an agreement never to restore Poland. Here was the beginning of the final estrangement between Napoleon and Alexander, an estrangement brought about fundamentally by the fact that a restored Poland was vital to Napoleon's scheme of conquest. It is certain that he planned to break with Russia after he had used her aid to subdue England. The war of 1809 forced him to disclose his Polish policy before he was really in a position to carry it through.

In the meantime, in that same summer which saw the defeat of the Austrian armies and the revival of French strength after the setbacks of 1808, all that remained of an independent Italy fell under Napoleon's sway. The papal legations east of the Apennines had already been annexed to the kingdom of Italy in April, 1808. Between the kingdom of Italy in the north and the kingdom of Naples in the south lay the territory of the papal states west of the Apennines. The territory, occupied and administered by the French since 1808, was formally annexed to the French empire in May, 1809, or "reannexed," as Napoleon, the successor of Charlemagne, styled the act. To his logical administrative mind the continued existence of the papacy as an independent power was harmful and an anachronism. That attitude of mind helps explain the decree that he proposed to the pope after Tilsit, whereby the college of cardinals was no longer to be recruited predominantly from Italy but reconstituted so that a third of the cardinals would be selected within the French empire. This Pius VII had refused, retaliating by ceasing to give canonical institution to the new bishops named by Napoleon to vacant dioceses. Anticipating Napoleon's formal annexation of the papal territory the pope had prepared a formal bull of excommunication of the emperor. On receiving this news Napoleon ordered the arrest and imprisonment of the head of the church. "The pope is a raging maniac whom we must incarcerate," he wrote to his representative in the kingdom of Naples. Pius was arrested in the Quirinal and imprisoned at Savona on the Riviera. By that summary act, which still did not complete the long series of aggressive moves against the church, Napoleon gained the eternal hostility of every devout Catholic in Europe and created an extremely embarrassing situation concerning the institution of clergy for vacant bishoprics in France.

The Working of the Continental System

At the close of 1809 Napoleon's political position on the Continent was safe against immediate attack, but meantime his economic position had been weakened by the failure of the commercial war. The decrees, culminating in the Milan Decree of December, 1807, had not accomplished their avowed objective of shutting the Continent to English products. Attention has already been called to the fact that neither country actually intended to maintain a blockade of the other, the formal declarations to that effect notwithstanding. Insuperable difficulties soon arose to militate against the success of the continental self-blockade during the early years from 1806 to 1810. The major obstacles were three: the deficiency of the administrative personnel, the extensive ramifications of smuggling activities, and the wide use of English licenses to trade with the Continent. The Napoleonic conception of a Continent hermetically sealed to the English was so heroic in its vastness that its effectiveness depended upon agents similarly inspired. Instead, the entire staff of civil and military authorities employed in the execution of the Continental System suffered both from unwillingness and from incapacity to carry out instructions. Graft and corruption, laxity, indifference, or hostility characterized the great majority of the emperor's servants. The military corps, the naval port officials, the customs staff, the border police, and the local administrators, with few exceptions, could not be relied upon. They found it profitable to encourage the commercial traffic which they were employed to suppress.

The operations of smugglers were a notable instrument of this commercial intercourse. Smuggling, which had played an extremely important part in the commercial relations of France and England during the entire eighteenth century, not only acquired greater scope, but also became an ordinary, quasi-respectable method of trade. It was based upon definite business practices, with fixed commissions proportionate to the risks involved. A large part of the smuggling trade was carried on through northwest Germany and Holland, whose affable monarch, Louis Napoleon, entertained slight hope for the success of his brother's scheme. The emperor threatened, as early as 1807, to annex Holland to the French empire, but in the meantime he contented himself with closing the French frontier to all colonial goods coming from Holland. The Channel Islands, Sardinia, Sicily, and Malta were also favorite points from which smugglers carried on their trade with European ports, while from Saloniki goods were carried overland into Hungary and then sent up the Danube into central Europe. In the early years of the Continental System, the small island of Helgoland in the North Sea, not far from the mouths of the Weser and Elbe, and the Hanseatic cities Bremen and Hamburg assumed a vital importance in smuggling operations. Occupied by the English late in 1807, it soon became a veritable "Little London," its volume of business for 1808 being reported as eight million pounds sterling or a sixth of the total exports of Great Britain. The homely expedients of the small army of smugglers included such devices as the mixing of sand with raw sugar, false declarations, concealing of colonial products on one's person, organization of mock funerals in which hearses rolled solemnly along laden with colonial goods or bales of merchandise, and many others too numerous to mention. These devices of human ingenuity coupled with the corruption and the almost open connivance of customs officials, reduced the efficiency of the self-blockade to the vanishing point.

The expenses and risks of the smuggling trade swelled the price of the forbidden goods for the petty consumer, but the latter's desire for them was sufficiently strong to insure a large turnover for the smugglers. Even with the higher prices and the risks the smuggler's profit ran up to forty or fifty per cent. Despite the risks the contraband trade was profitable because the British machine-made goods were in competition with the vastly more expensive goods produced in France. In other words, the profits of the smugglers were so many francs subtracted from the customs receipts of the French treasury, which decreased by eighty per cent between 1806 and 1810.

The tightening of French military control over the north German coast and the welcome adherence of Denmark to the Continental System tended to diminish the volume of traffic in the North Sea after 1808, but the smuggling activities were then transferred to Sweden and the ports of the southern Baltic, whence the goods were carried as before into Germany. Königsberg, Riga, Stralsund, and Memel replaced the Hanseatic towns and the Dutch ports as centers of the contraband trade. England's breach with the United States (following the enactment of the Embargo Act) temporarily diminished her exportation to the Continent, but the decline was more than balanced by England's gain in Central and South America. After the flight of the Portuguese royal family to Brazil the ports of the latter country were reopened to British shippers. The deposition of the Bourbons in the Spanish peninsula had its political consequences oversea in the revolt of the Spanish colonies, with which England had long enjoyed a profitable contraband trade, and in the formal opening of the Spanish colonial ports to British and neutral commerce. This move enabled England to gain control of the colonial trade, most markedly that of Cuba and Porto Rico, and to open new markets for the immense accumulations of manufactured products (cotton cloth in particular) that were stored in the warehouses. As a result there was a boom in sales and industrial activity and frantic speculation in the South American trade, which lasted for two profitable years, from 1808 to 1810.

The situation, from Napoleon's point of view, grew worse during 1809. The war against Austria was in full swing, and Napoleon's preoccupation with the military situation in central Europe resulted in diminished vigilance in the northern ports. The volume of English and American commercial relations, despite the Ameri-

can legal prohibition of trade, and the enhanced activity of smugglers in the Baltic ports still further lessened the emperor's
prospects of success. Finally, the third of the factors militating
against Napoleon made itself most sharply felt. The sale of licenses
to trade had increased enormously, from some 2000 in 1806 to
18,000 in 1810. A license saved the shipper, whether English or,
as was more likely, Prussian, Russian, or Swedish, from capture at
sea by British war vessels and privateers, netted the English
treasury a handsome income from fees, and kept the Continent
open to British goods. On arrival at an enemy continental port
the master of the ship produced his easily procured false paper,
which proved the non-English character of his cargo and his departure from a non-British port. Not without reason has this supple
system of commercial intercourse been characterized as a parallel
to open smuggling.

The failure of the self-blockade prompted Napoleon in 1810
to adopt a policy which led him far from the original purposes of
the Continental System. Publicly and formally Napoleon never
admitted that his original aims had in any way been modified.
The underlying cause of the new system was his inability to interrupt the carriage of colonial and manufactured goods to the Continent. The hope which inspired it was that of a substantial increase
in the French customs revenue, and the consequences were the
ruthless promotion of French interests at the expense of the Napoleonic allies and dependencies. "I have found a combination,"
he exclaimed, "for turning the tables on the English and the smugglers." In January, 1810, he authorized the sale at auction of
prize cargoes, prohibited goods included, provided that the purchaser paid a duty of forty per cent. To make sure that the revenue
from these sales would be sufficient to offset the steady losses in
the ordinary French customs dues, he let customs officials understand that prohibited goods might be admitted into the ports, on
the condition that they were falsely labeled as "prize goods." Cotton, however, was not included in these operations, being destroyed
in return for an indemnity to the captors. In August he established
the fundamental law of his new system, the Trianon tariff. By this
measure he legalized the importation of such colonial products as
coffee, cocoa, and sugar on the payment of a duty amounting to
fifty per cent. The duty on raw cotton, however, was more severe
and, in the case of American cotton, prohibitive. In this way he

became his own smuggler, adding to the revenues of the state in customs duties approximately the same percentage of profit that private smugglers had derived from their illegal operations. The revenue of the treasury immediately showed a prodigious increase, but the difficulties that these measures caused to dealers in colonial products and to cotton manufacturers speedily contributed to a fatal depression. Thus he hoped to make the profits of the treasury pay for the costs of the war against England.

By the Trianon tariff Napoleon had endeavored to regulate colonial trade so as to make his government rather than smugglers the beneficiary of this trade. At the same time, further to increase his fiscal revenues, he encouraged on a large scale and at a high price the sale of temporary trading licenses to favored French merchants, who could now evade in secret those laws which he rigorously defended in public. The importation of British colonial goods and most of the prohibited manufactured products was permitted on condition that French products of equivalent value were exported by the merchant. So far as the importation of these French silks and cloths into England was concerned, the situation was hardly affected, for these products were excluded from England and not many of the favored French merchants complied honestly with the regulation concerning the export of French products of an equivalent value. Instead they shipped empty chests or chests full of sand, which were cast into the sea as soon as the vessel left the shore. On the other hand, Napoleon hoped, by means of the license system, to promote the exportation of French manufactured products to the continental states in which British goods were still forbidden.

Napoleon's more pressing concern at that moment was in suppressing what remained of illicit colonial trade and in rendering impossible sales of British industrial products not permitted by his licenses. This he endeavored to effect by the Fontainebleau Decree of October, 1810, which ordered the destruction everywhere in the empire of all British manufactured products except the comparatively few articles that had been admitted under licenses. To enforce the decree he spurred on the confiscatory activities of his military corps in Germany and established customs courts for the trial and punishment of all violators. This decree was rigorously executed. The seizures of presumed British goods, particularly in the north German states, excited popular feeling to a pitch of fury against the French military agents. Some of the goods were sold at auction, but cottons and silks were publicly burned. Napoleon firmly believed that these holocausts of British merchandise insured the success of his mighty efforts. But the loss incurred was not felt by the British, for the greater part of the goods destroyed had already been paid for by French or German merchants. He had by now completely denatured the great aim of his Continental System. His later system stood fully revealed as a pernicious and imperialistic fiscal expedient which, under the pretext of combating the English, contrived to squeeze money out of his continental allies and to promote the growth of French industries at their expense. Economic retribution was soon to come.

THE CONSEQUENCES OF THE CONTINENTAL SYSTEM

The consequences of this economic struggle must now be noted. From 1807 to 1810, thanks to the license system and smuggling activities, English exports were not adversely affected by the Continental System, though the British shippers suffered a severe loss by having neutrals monopolize most of their reëxport of foreign goods to the Continent. In compensation they found new markets, especially for calicoes and prints in South America and the West Indies. During that same period France made strenuous efforts to find native substitutes for the colonial products of which the country was deprived. Chicory was cultivated to replace coffee. The increased use of potatoes and of French-grown tobacco was encouraged. In 1811 a satisfactory substitute for imported cane sugar was found in the domestic sugar extracted from beetroot. French indigo took the place of the indigo formerly imported from English colonies. French industries also profited temporarily from Napoleon's policy of economic imperialism. The silk industry of Lyons expanded so rapidly by the particular protection that Napoleon gave the manufacturers of that city that the number of looms almost doubled that under the Old Régime. Other industries to gain were the cotton and woolen manufactures. These gains were made primarily at the expense of the British competitors, but not exclusively so, as the situation in the kingdom of Italy clearly showed. In that country the effects of his policy were to create a virtual monopoly for the French and to increase fourfold the volume of French exports. Those were the beneficial results of Napoleon's vast effort to make commerce "maneuver like a regiment."

After 1810, both sets of combatants felt the struggle much more keenly. The English speculative boom collapsed suddenly in the summer of 1810, resulting in heavy unemployment and a marked depreciation of the British currency. The pound sterling was quoted more than twenty per cent off on the Continent. The depression was the inevitable reaction to the wild speculative activities of merchants and manufacturers in the markets of South America and the West Indies, a speculative outburst that had been aggravated by rapid inflation and the excessive granting of private credits. The immediate occasion for it was the parallel phenomenon of an enormous importation of raw materials and colonial goods and a sudden sharp decline in exports both to the Continent and to the United States. The decline in trade with the United States followed President Madison's revival of the Non-Intercourse Act against England late in 1810. Trade with the Continent fell off in consequence of Napoleon's fiscal measures in 1810. To that extent the Trianon tariff and the Fontainebleau Decree, together with Napoleon's annexations in northern Europe, contributed directly to the British crisis.

With the self-destruction of Napoleon's system after 1812, the situation in Great Britain improved. During the crucial year of 1810, in order to increase the revenue of the French treasury Napoleon permitted the export of huge shipments of grain from Europe to England. It is probable, as he himself realized, that even if he had used his control of the great wheat port of Danzig to prevent exports of grain to England, the islanders would still have found relief in imports from Prussia and Poland on the Continent and from the United States. In any case it is extremely doubtful that he could have starved Great Britain into submission. Napoleon's system inflicted temporary hardships upon Great Britain, but it failed of any permanent effects. It did not in any way retard the rapid rate of British industrial development, nor did the bitter suffering of the workers from 1810 to 1812 turn public opinion against the government. The British public credit system was scarcely affected, and Britain's subsidies to her continental allies did not diminish.

In France and the allied and subject states the crisis was no less pronounced. To bolster up the execution of the new tariff war of

1810, Napoleon adopted the policy of annexing the territory where smuggling was most active. In that year Holland, part of the kingdom of Westphalia, the northwest coast of Germany including the Hanseatic cities, and the republic of Valais in Switzerland, which controlled the Simplon Pass into Italy, were all annexed to the French empire. Within the newly annexed territory as within the earlier annexations, French trade was unrestricted. Up to 1810 French prosperity was real. But the emperor's ruinous fiscal policy had so thoroughly disrupted the normal economic activities of the mainland of Europe that this last territorial extension of the French empire did not stave off disaster. The dislocation of normal economic relations, brought on by the license systems, the decrees, the confiscation of British goods, the government sale of these goods, and the sudden fluctuation in prices, had produced an orgy of speculation.

In France itself the new economic policy of 1810 increased the price of colonial products to such an extent that the shock to this exceedingly speculative trade engulfed many Parisian dealers in ruin. The loss of the Spanish market brought many to bankruptcy. The manufacturers fared no better, since the period of speculative expansion terminated with the tariff of 1810, which greatly increased the price of raw materials. The havoc that Napoleon's new policy created among the continental allies of France closed their markets to French goods that were produced especially for them. The artificial prosperity of the new agricultural cultivations and, more particularly, of the new manufacturing industries disappeared. The banks curtailed their loans, and credits were strained. The discounts of the Bank of France fell from 715 million francs in 1810 to 319 million in 1811. Without the support of the banks the manufacturer could not carry the burden imposed by falling markets and rising costs. Business failures in Germany and Holland, involving French manufacturers, precipitated the debacle. Two successive years of inadequate harvests in 1810 and 1811 and the steadily increasing demands of the armies created an appalling food shortage, and prevented a liquidation of the industrial and financial crisis. Soaring prices, unemployment, and a general economic paralysis, which lasted to the end of the empire, was the state of affairs in France which Napoleon vainly sought to improve by secret advances and loans to manufacturers. Foreign trade which in 1806 had reached 933 million francs fell to 605 million in 1813.

In the allied and vassal states the suffering and the exasperation caused by the economic war stiffened the opposition of the patriots to Napoleon's control. By putting pressure upon the czar to end the neutral and the smuggling trade in the southern Baltic, Napoleon only increased the tension between himself and his nominal ally. On the last day of 1810 the czar defied Napoleon by permitting the virtual import of colonial goods into Russia, and in the following years military events completed the breakdown of Napoleon's grandiose experiment of the Continental System.

XVIII. IMPERIAL FRANCE

THE MARRIAGE WITH MARIE LOUISE

THE course of continental affairs during 1809 and 1810 had run favorably for Napoleon. Central Europe was under control, the situation in Spain hopeful, and the bludgeon blows at England had borne telling effect. By the end of 1810 the emperor's power appeared greater than ever, and the territory of his empire reached its widest extent. But there was one element of insecurity, for Napoleon had no son to inherit his crown and possessions. The question of succession troubled the beneficiaries of Napoleon's favors almost as greatly as it did the emperor, for until it was satisfactorily settled they had no security for the enjoyment of their privileges and prerogatives. For a long time he had considered the advisability of putting away his wife, the Empress Josephine, who had not borne him any children, but it was not until after the last Austrian campaign that he decided definitely upon a divorce. The decision was a painful one, for even if he no longer loved Josephine, he was bound to her by innumerable ties of affection. Josephine had lived in fear and trembling of that decision, but after the first hysterical outbreaks she resigned herself with great dignity to the sacrifice. A Senatus Consultum proclaimed the civil divorce, and the metropolitan of Paris annulled the religious marriage which had been performed in 1804. The unhappy Josephine then retired to her château at Malmaison.

Napoleon's second wife and the new empress was Marie Louise, the eighteen-year-old daughter of the Austrian emperor, whom he married on April 1, 1810. When he had decided upon a dynastic marriage, Napoleon opened negotiations both with Russia and with Austria. He knew that his request for the hand of the czar's younger sister would be denied; but it was good diplomacy to frighten the Austrians with the possibility of a Franco-Russian family alliance. By the time that Alexander gave the anticipated reply, that his sister was too young for marriage, Napoleon had completed the arrangements for his marriage with Marie Louise.

In formally polite terms he informed the czar that he now gave up his thought of marriage with the latter's sister. If Napoleon were anxious to have Austria as an ally against Russia, with whom he would sooner or later come into conflict, Austria was no less eager to enjoy peace and security through an alliance with France. Marie Louise was a pawn in the skillful hands of Metternich, who was now—and for many years to come—the head of the government. His policy was to pretend to be friendly with France. In reality he was preparing to utilize all diplomatic means to undermine Napoleon's European power and hold a balance between France and Russia. "We must confine our system to tacking, and turning, and flattering. There remains but one expedient, to increase our strength for better days and to work out our preservation by gentle means."

By contracting this marriage Napoleon supplemented his military victories of the preceding year and gained the great advantage of claiming relationship with the oldest reigning house and the proudest royal family in Europe. Furthermore, it promised to usher in an era of peace in Europe; and when the promise was redeemed by the birth of a son a year later, Napoleon was sanguine that the last obstacle to the stability and security of his empire was removed. Indeed, between 1810 and the opening of the Russian campaign in 1812 the empire was more nearly at peace than it had ever been for a similar period of time. Before entering upon a discussion of the extent and character of the Napoleonic empire of that date, we may turn our attention to events in imperial France from the time of the establishment of the empire to the zenith of its glory in 1810.

The founding of the empire in 1804 had brought about no profound modification in the system of government. Napoleon's powers as consul for life were already so sweeping that the change from a consular form of government to an empire hardly added to them. At first the old political bodies continued to function; but as time went on all semblance of their legislative powers disappeared, and Napoleon's government became a personal dictatorship. In 1807 the Tribunate was completely suppressed. The Legislative Corps did little more than register the bills that were proposed and, in one instance, was not even convoked for an entire year. Legislative procedure in the Senate was an empty formality, for despite its theoretical rights the Senate did not oppose Napoleon in any of his measures. Out of one hundred and forty members of the imperial Senate, almost ninety were Napoleon's appointees, men who had every inducement and reason to give their full support to the emperor. The deliberations of the Council of State still remained exceedingly important, and the number of plenary sessions that were held increased appreciably. Promising young men, selected from different parts of the French empire, were encouraged to attend the debates of the council and gain first-hand experience in the problems of government. Frequently, however, the emperor dealt directly with the individual ministers rather than with the plenary session of the Council of State. When he had made up his mind, he communicated his decision to the Council of State, which enacted it into law by a decree. With the entire administrative system under his surveillance and the legislative system virtually nonexistent, Napoleon ruled through imperial decrees and Senatus Consulta. Dictatorial centralization could go no further; even more than Louis XIV, Napoleon could say, "I am the State." If after the revolutionary turmoil France needed a strong government, Napoleon gave more than was needed—a despotism.

The passage of years and the long series of unbroken successes had left their mark upon the emperor. The pale and cadaverous young general of 1796 whose long hair fell in poetic disorder had become the thickset emperor of 1807. He had grown stout and somewhat bald. His pallor had given place to a dull, unhealthy leaden color, and his features were rounded and full, with the hardness of expression that marked the man of resolute and untrammeled will. But the piercing blue-gray eyes had not lost any of their fire; the full features could be mobile; and the sharp Corsican accent still grated harshly on sensitive French ears. In the early years of the empire, Napoleon retained his irregular habits of life. He bolted his food, slept a few hours when he was tired, whether the time was day or night, and worked with that terrific activity which made his career the greatest explosion of human energy that history has ever recorded. During those years he lived almost in the saddle, spending much of his time in his campaigns, first against one enemy then another. But toward 1809 and particularly after his second marriage he began to conserve his strength. He lingered over his meals, would indulge in an occasional afternoon siesta, and slept regularly like any good burgher, from ten to seven.

The greatest change, however, was in his moral character. His most marked characteristic was the nervous tension under which he worked, a tension which he displayed at all moments and which drove him occasionally to commit acts of great violence. It was betrayed in his quick, jerky conversation which he did not allow any one to interrupt, in his handwriting which was so scratchy as to be illegible, in the speed and frenzy of his dictation at which he exhausted his secretaries, in the impatient way in which he tore off and scattered his clothing. On important occasions he seemed incapable of controlling his soaring imagination by reason. Though in the organization of his work he was a model of orderliness, he scorned advice, reducing his former collaborators to the rôle of subordinates or replacing them with more complaisant successors.

For mankind in general and idealists in particular he entertained a deep feeling of contempt, a feeling which his own miraculous rise to power and the habit of command encouraged. In the end it was his violence that ruined him. He was spoiled by continuous success. His keen intelligence and his power of analysis remained sharp to the last; his attention remained riveted for hours if necessary to a single object, and his memory was still as keen; he displayed exceptional, superhuman energy as late as 1814, and his personal magnetism still fascinated all those who came in contact with him. But the realization of his superiority, his pride in his accomplishments, his uncontrolled egoism and ambition, and his *idée fixe* to stabilize and perpetuate his rule, all these characteristics turned his own country against him. The immense popularity that he enjoyed in 1804 had disappeared in the later empire, and France did indeed give a sigh of relief at his downfall.

The Codes

During the Consulate, Napoleon began to lay the bases of his system in France. He pacified the factions, brought Jacobins and royalists under his control, ended disorders, stabilized finances, reformed the administration, and terminated the bitter struggle between the Revolution and the church. The wars of the empire distracted him from his program of reform, but in the intervals of peace the reorganization of French life and institutions continued. The measures which were begun during the Consulate were completed, and several new projects taken up. One may profitably examine these reforms to ascertain what Napoleon did with his unrivaled opportunities, to determine the validity of his proud boast that he was a child of the Revolution.

In his last years at Saint Helena, Napoleon maintained that his glory rested in great part upon the draft of the famous Civil Code, which bears his name in well deserved tribute to the important rôle that he played in its completion. But if the glory of its completion rightly belongs to him, the idea of legal unity and the inspiration of the articles that composed the Code belong to the past history of France. The traditional obstacles that prevented the achievement of legal unity under the old monarchy were swept away in the revolutionary maelstrom of idealism, optimism, and violence. All the old social barriers of France's past—feudalism, regionalism, privileged classes and intrenched corporations, the church, and the crown—disappeared between 1789 and 1795. A mighty current of liberal legislation completely remodeled the spirit and form of the existing law of persons and property. But the revolutionary era was too troubled to allow its legislators to terminate their great work in a single code of all the laws. Several times they attempted to reach this goal, but all that survived in 1800 of their efforts was three incomplete drafts of a code of civil laws. Napoleon's opportunity to complete the work came after his victory at Marengo. On August 12, 1800, he appointed a committee of several of France's most eminent lawyers to draw up a project of a Civil Code. Within six months the rough draft was prepared and printed. After receiving the benefit of specialized criticism and revision the draft was discussed, article by article, in the plenary sittings of the Council of State.

Concerning Napoleon's rôle at these general deliberations, Roederer, one of his intimates, has the following praise: "In these sittings the First Consul manifested those remarkable powers of attention and precise analysis which enabled him for ten hours at a stretch to devote himself to one object, or several, without ever allowing himself to be distracted by errant thought." There is no doubt whatever of the passionate interest that he displayed in the discussions, of the intelligence and imagination that he manifested in the larger social and political aspects of the legal questions, nor, unfortunately, of the incisive imperiousness of his intervention. The Tribunate and the Legislative Corps retarded the speedy completion of the work by criticizing and rejecting the first articles, and the Code was not completed until the very end of the life consulate. On March 21, 1804, the same day that saw the judicial murder of the duke of Enghien, the various articles were promulgated as a single law under the title of the Civil Code.

The Code was profoundly national. It maintained the social conquests of the Revolution, but it reverted in part to the juristic traditions of France and the authoritarian instincts of human nature to correct the philosophical abstractions that gave so extravagant a note to revolutionary legislation. It was at once "a summary and a correction of the Revolution." It gave the unity of legislation that France had so long desired. It maintained the emancipation of civil law from religious influence, for the state remained secular. It defended the revolutionary principle of equality by guaranteeing civil liberty and civil equality. Hereditary nobility was not reëstablished. It followed the general principles of revolutionary legislation concerning the land and the equality of inheritance.

It also bore the impress of Bonaparte's authoritarian views, particularly in those provisions that were incorporated to restore the unity of family life. The authority of the father in the home was restored, "and the despotism of the State repeated in the structure of the family." The status of women was systematically depressed. The Code contained a number of reactionary provisions subjecting the wife to the power of the husband, debarring her from the administration of their common property, and requiring the husband's written consent for her acquisition of property. The right of divorce was recognized when the divorce was requested both by husband and by wife, but it was strictly regulated in the interests of family unity. Though the right of testamentary bequest was widened, the law of inheritance in general followed the revolutionary principle that there should be an equal division of property among the heirs.

Compared to the legislation of the Revolution, the Code was reactionary; in comparison with the legislation of the Old Régime, it was revolutionary. Its great virtue lay in its admirable brevity and clarity, in its remarkable application of deep-rooted human impulses and juristic traditions to regulate and systematize the revolutionary enactments. Everybody could appeal to its general principles, and everybody could understand its specific provisions. With all its defects, it was immeasurably more progressive than any other civil code that Europe then had. Wherever Napoleon's armies introduced it in the course of their conquest of Europe, and in all the other countries that it reached, Egypt, Canada, Central and South America, Japan, it brought the social and political ideals of the French Revolution. In that sense, it became as universal as Roman law and a permanent factor in promoting the democratic ideals of 1789. In France itself, it served to illustrate once again that the first consul was systematically bent upon reconciling the old France with the new.

The codes which were promulgated during the empire all bore the impress of the harsh paternalism and despotism which characterized Napoleon's imperial conceptions. A Code of Civil Procedure, upon which work was also begun during the Consulate, was completed in 1806. In the main its provisions restored the procedure of the Old Régime. The Code of Criminal Procedure and the Penal Code were also begun during the Consulate, but not completed until 1810. They perpetuated many of the changes that were introduced during the Revolution but weakened the application of these revolutionary principles. Equality before the law was recognized by having the same penalties for all citizens. The penalties stipulated were harsher than those invoked during the Revolution, and included life imprisonment and the death penalty. In the main the use of torture was proscribed. The citizen was legally protected—at least in theory—against arbitrary arrest and imprisonment. Though the procedure was a vast improvement over that of the Old Régime, a public trial with witnesses and a jury was not invariably given to all criminals. Nevertheless, after due allowance has been made for the reactionary elements that Napoleon introduced into the criminal procedure, the Criminal Code still remains a consolidation of revolutionary accomplishments. The Commercial Code (1807) also served as a model for many countries in Europe, being in force at the present day in Belgium and Italy.

In their totality these codes represent the most comprehensive effort ever made in France to achieve legal unity. If in France the later codes reflected the imperial despotism of the emperor, elsewhere, in Italy, Switzerland, Germany, and the Netherlands, the codes stood for the principles of equality. Everywhere they were a civilizing and refining influence and the instrument of the triumph of revolutionary principles over conservatism and reaction.

THE NEW NOBILITY

The one great social change that the empire introduced was the creation of a new nobility. The transformation of republican habits which had begun late in the Consulate was brought to full completion after 1804. An imperial court was organized. The emperor's family constituted a new dynasty of French princes. Surrounding the person of the emperor were the six great dignitaries: the grand elector, who was Joseph Bonaparte; the arch-chancellor of the empire, Cambacérès; the arch-chancellor of state, Eugene de Beauharnais, who was Josephine's son by her first marriage; the arch-treasurer, Lebrun; the constable, Louis Bonaparte; and the grand admiral, Murat. There were also two hierarchies of grand military officers and grand civil officers. Another hierarchy of prefects of the palace, chamberlains, equerries, and pages made up the imperial household. There was the empress's household, similar ones for the princes and princesses, and the military household of the emperor, that boasted the famous Imperial Guard. Each of these courtly charges brought in high salaries to the titulary, which were still further increased by the enormous bequests and donations of fiefs in Germany and Italy that the emperor showered upon the generals in order to retain their allegiance.

Napoleon established military fiefs in the Venetian and Dalmatian provinces and elsewhere "so that at the most perilous angle of the Empire there might be a cluster of military families pledged, like the frontier feudatories of the fifth century, by urgent considerations of the pocket, to defend it." The dignitaries in their embroidered uniforms of silk and velours, in their gold and precious stones, followed a code of etiquette as stiff as that which had prevailed under the Bourbons. But the charm and the ease of the Old Régime could not be recaptured. All of Napoleon's efforts to lend dignity and prestige to his dynasty resulted in little more than the building of a wall between him and the masses. Like his Bourbon predecessors he had isolated himself from his subjects.

Apart from the great court nobles, there was the lesser imperial nobility which was created with the establishment of the Legion of Honor and widely extended in 1808 with the creation of titles of hereditary nobility. To reward service to the state, both of a military and of a civil character, Napoleon had in 1802 conceived an "intermediary corps," the Legion of Honor. Public opinion gave a harsh welcome to his scheme, and the legislative assemblies criticized it severely. Their orators pointed out the political implications of the Legion of Honor: the affront to democratic equality by the elevation of a small number of individuals to a special status and the menace of reviving a hereditary nobility by the creation of a bourgeois aristocracy. Napoleon defended his project by insisting that it was no real violation of the democratic conceptions of the Revolution, for nomination to the Legion was open to all men of eminence, irrespective of blood or wealth. In short, he was throwing open careers to talent. Distinctions, he maintained, were essential even in republics. To confidants he pointed out that while one could call the distinction of belonging to the Legion of Honor an empty bauble, it was precisely by baubles that men were led. Nevertheless, he took heed of the popular dissatisfaction and did not venture to confer the first formal decorations until after the establishment of the empire. By the end of the reign, excluding the members of the Bonaparte family and a few favored individuals who held the title of prince, there were thirty-one dukes, some four hundred counts, more than one thousand barons, and about fifteen hundred knights, many of whom had hereditary estates. The old nobility remained suppressed, but the establishment of the new imperial nobility was a markedly reactionary measure and must be regarded as a profound modification of the social order created by the Revolution. Though Napoleon took great pride in the creation of the new nobility, it failed to achieve the objects that he had in view. Those were to reconcile Napoleonic France with Europe and imperial France with Bourbon France and to extinguish the old feudal nobility.

THE FINANCIAL ADMINISTRATION

In another important respect Napoleon undid the work of the Revolution and reintroduced the characteristics of the Bourbon régime. In order to raise money for the expenditures of the state, which rose rapidly from 1804 to the end of the empire, Napoleon fell back upon the system of indirect taxation which the Revolution abolished. "My financial system consists," he said, "in creating a great number of indirect taxes, whose lowly level could be raised in proportion to my needs." His needs became so pressing that the indirect taxes, *les droits réunis*, on the use of tobacco, salt, and liquors furnished, along with the customs duties, forty per cent of the state's income in 1813. On the other hand, he never increased the direct taxes nor issued paper money. All state expenditures were carefully audited, and France enjoyed monetary stability throughout the entire empire. In reality, he was able to balance his budget during most of the imperial period by having recourse to extraordinary financial expedients, such as the sale of national property and the imposition of indemnities upon the enemy and subject states.

To a special fund, ultimately known as the "Extraordinary Domain," went a large part of the war indemnities, revenues from dependent countries and the proceeds from the sale of confiscated British goods and the customs duties on colonial goods. Just as he constantly sought to popularize his empire with the generals, so he endeavored in his fiscal policy to win the support of the merchants and the manufacturers. Partly for their benefit he had revised the aims of his Continental System. Almost entirely to retain the good will of his French subjects he made it a point of his policy to throw the financial burden of his wars upon the non-French states of his empire. From the latter he extorted what he needed in specie as well as in man power and requisitions. So long as he was victorious on the field, the enemy paid the cost of his operations and contributed to the maintenance of his troops. But once he was defeated, as was the case in Spain and in the disastrous Russian campaign of 1812, the weaknesses of his financial system were revealed. At the end of his reign his financial difficulties were almost as pronounced as those that overwhelmed the government of the Old Régime.

It is true that France's credit remained unimpaired, and her currency sound. A great part of the public indebtedness stemmed from the obligations which the empire inherited from the revolutionary assemblies. In 1805 there was a severe financial crisis which extended to trade and brought on several disastrous bankruptcies. The crisis arose when the Bank of France issued notes to save an association of bankers that had undertaken to advance money to the state. Its notes fell in value, making the situation still more serious. Napoleon averted financial disaster for the time being by replenishing the reserves of the bank with war indemnities from Austria and by taking over all the assets of the company of bankers. The bank was then reorganized and brought more closely under government control in the form of a limited liability company. He established a treasury board for the administration of finances. To the financial debacle of the later empire, the partial paralysis of economic life during the Continental System contributed in no small measure. The greater part of receipts from abroad consisted of war indemnities and requisitions from defeated states. A lesser, though still considerable, portion was in the form of landed property and other wealth that Napoleon reserved for himself.

Nevertheless, up to the collapse of economic activities that the later Continental System brought about, France was prosperous, and her people enjoyed many material comforts. Population figures for France proper show a steady increase up to 1810, but even in 1814, when the population had decreased, there were still twenty-nine million inhabitants as compared with the twenty-seven at the beginning of the empire in 1804. On first thought it seems amazing that the peasants who had most cause to hate Napoleon because of the great demands that he laid upon them with his wars and the hated conscription remained, almost to the end, his warmest partisans. But the contradiction is explained if one considers, first, that the conscription system did not become intolerable until after his return from Russia, and second, that he was always extremely careful to maintain the revolutionary changes concerning the land. For this the peasants were eternally grateful, and their prosperity was due in no small measure to that fact that Napoleon recognized the titles to the land that they had purchased and prevented a return to the odious tithes and feudal rights of the Old Régime. If the Revolution struck off the shackles from agriculture, Napoleon saw to it that they were never put on again. Agricultural prosperity, based upon improved technique and more extensive and varied production, marked the lot of many French peasants during the empire. In 1811, however, a partial failure of the grain crops once more brought harsh suffering to the farmer.

Industrial production also entered upon a transitional state in which the technique and the distribution of the old guild system was gradually abandoned without, however, being entirely replaced by the methods of modern industrial society. Financial stability, the opening of new continental markets, and protective tariffs greatly accelerated the rate of industrial progress until the pause of 1810. From the time of the crash to the end of the empire, industry languished, for the artificial prop formerly afforded by the later Continental System no longer sustained the manufacturers. Socialists and Laborites of the nineteenth and twentieth centuries have bitterly criticized Napoleon's attitude toward industrial workers, which subjected the latter anew to the rigorous supervision and control of their employers and the police.

On the whole, the most permanent of Napoleon's industrial achievements were what he called "his treasures." Between 1804 and 1813 more than a billion francs was spent in public works. These were the great canals that he had dug, the swamps that were dredged, the harbors that were enlarged, the broad system of highways that linked France to the countries beyond her old frontiers, to Belgium, to the Rhine, and through the passes of the Alps to Switzerland and Italy, and the imposing monuments that his architects built in order to beautify Paris and its environs. The most famous of these monuments were the Austerlitz and Jena bridges across the Seine, the triumphal arches and columns, the Stock Exchange (Bourse), and the classic church of La Madeleine.

INTELLECTUAL REPRESSION

Just as Napoleon's autocratic state destroyed the political liberty that the Revolution had gained for the French, so his growing despotism made short shrift of their personal liberty. In theory the Civil Code maintained civil liberty, but it was the fate of the Civil Code to be used mainly for export. Napoleon displayed a tireless zeal in waging war upon all individuals and all agencies that advocated the untrammeled liberty of thought and expression. Liberty was not for the common people, he maintained. The eighteenth century rationalists—the "Ideologists," as he scornfully referred to them—had corrupted public opinion by inspiring thought in people "who had never taken it into their heads to think before or who had forgotten how." A highly ramified and complex system of police surveillance interfered constantly in the private life of the citizens. There was a plague of domiciliary visits in the case of political suspects for whom habeas corpus was suspended, and very little justice. Merely an indication from the emperor or his administration sufficed to lodge suspects in the reconstituted state prisons. Hundreds of police agents and spies were in his employ. One estimate of the number of political prisoners in France in 1814 gives the high figure of twenty-five hundred.

The revolutionary ideal of liberty yielded to the paternalism that inspired Napoleon's discipline of the mind and conscience. In order to keep printing under control the number of printers in Paris was limited to sixty, each being required to take an oath of obedience to the government. Liberty of the press completely disappeared. Paris, which had more than seventy newspapers in 1800, had only four after 1810 and these were scarcely more than mouthpieces of the government. More than a hundred important provincial journals were suppressed; in their stead each department was granted an official bulletin, which was edited at the prefecture. The French press thus became a branch of the political administration, printing little more than government-inspired articles that were intended to keep the French ignorant or misinformed of all real news, particularly of military reverses. Napoleon's attitude toward the theater and men of letters was of a piece with his views on the press. The number of theaters was fixed by governmental regulation; the plays, both old and new, rigidly censored, and the administration of the theaters given over to government agents. No writer could publish his work until it had obtained the approval of the censor. Consequently, at the very moment when the French empire reached its widest extent and French was spoken all over the Continent, the quantity of French literary production fell to a shamefully low total. Meantime, thousands of unhappy French émigrés still scattered over the face of Europe sowed fresh seeds of interest in the older forms of French literature and thought.

It was not the quantity alone that suffered from Napoleon's effort to force men to think along patriotic imperial lines. The quality suffered marked deterioration. In the history of French literature the two outstanding writers of the Napoleonic age were Madame de Staël, the last of the eighteenth century ideologues, and Chateaubriand, the first of the romanticists of the nineteenth century. Napoleon has to his discredit the sorry distinction of persecuting both of them and driving them into exile. No Jacobin fanatic of 1793–1794 could more effectively have organized the domination of the state over the individual than did Napoleon. His system reduced the individual to helplessness; and no criticism was tolerated, lest protest swell into disloyalty toward the supreme ruler.

Nowhere was Napoleon's paternal solicitude over the mental speculation and the spiritual growth of his subjects more vividly displayed than in his views on education. His reform of the national educational system was begun during the Consulate. It has long been a popular misconception that the revolutionary reformers did little more than maintain the abolition of monastic and clerical education and make generous but futile plans for a system of national education in primary, secondary, and advanced schools. This view is approximately correct in so far as it applies to the organization of primary education, which, at the beginning of the Consulate, was shamefully inadequate. But the central schools, of which there were five in Paris and one in each department, made brilliant progress after a slow start, and at the opening of the nineteenth century had reached their full development. They were financially prosperous, with funds for libraries, laboratories, botanical gardens, and scientific collections. Attendance was heavy and the professors were men of merit—"perhaps the most remarkable teaching personnel that France ever had." In each department they were the centers of the intellectual activity of the younger generation.

Napoleon's educational policy did not encourage the free development of man's moral and mental faculties. He desired a system which would teach men to think loyally and uniformly on the problems of religion, politics, and social organization. The educational system that he had in mind would be a division of the political administration. In defending his educational project before the Tribunate he frankly stated his views: "The system that we propose is not only moral; it is also a political system. Its purpose is to rally behind the government both the new and the old generation, the old through their children, and the children through their parents, to establish a sort of public fatherhood."

His project, reorganizing the revolutionary system, became law on May 1, 1802. It made the scantiest provision for elementary education, the establishment and supervision of elementary schools being turned over to the voluntary action of the communes. It did away with the flourishing écoles centrales, which were replaced by a limited number of local and private secondary schools and lycées under direct government control. The organization of the lycées made them effective nurseries of patriotism. The central administration appointed the teaching staff, provided for its salaries, and presented detailed regulations of conduct, which extended even to the wearing apparel of the professors. The administration also determined the curriculum and the teaching schedule of each lycée and dispatched inspectors to enforce regulations. The training was extremely military; lessons began and ended with the rolling of the drums, students in residence wore prescribed military uniforms and received military instruction from a retired officer. Napoleon devised a liberal scheme of free scholarships, particularly for the sons of men in military service, but even with that artificial stimulus the lycées languished during the greater part of the empire.

His educational reforms were completed during the empire in 1808, by the establishment of the Imperial University, which acquired a monopoly over public instruction in France. The Imperial University was not a university in our sense. It included the entire system of education, from the elementary schools to the institutions of higher learning. His own words best reveal the purpose of this monopolistic régime:

There will never be a fixed political state of things in this country, until we have a body of teachers instructed on established principles. So long as the people are not taught from their earliest years whether they ought to be republicans or royalists, Christians or infidels, the State cannot properly be called a nation.

The exact provisions of this decree in respect to the different stages of instruction need not concern us here. Private and church schools were not entirely subjected to the full control established by the Imperial University. Vastly more important is an appreciation of the guiding spirit of the University. All the schools were required to take for the basis of their instruction the precepts of the Catholic religion, fidelity to the emperor, and "obedience to the rules of the teaching body, which have for their object the uniformity of instruction, and which tend to train for the state citizens attached to their religion, to their prince, to their fatherland, and to their family." In that way Napoleon hoped to fashion the new generation into a body of obedient subjects, profoundly Catholic and conservative in their views and inoculated against the subversive germs of revolutionary discontent. If we ignore the specifically imperial aims of Napoleon's educational policy, it is at once apparent that he was simply elaborating upon the revolutionary educational policy. Like the revolutionists themselves, he created a public school system which kept the church out of education, or at least, permitted the church to establish private schools, subjected to the authority of the state. His own state schools never achieved a high measure of success, but his system succeeded in that it perpetuated the principle of lay education, controlled and supported by the state, and available to all citizens of the country.

Napoleon also elaborated upon his conception of priests as a "sacred gendarmerie" of the state. In an imperial catechism, which school children were expected to learn, a catechism approved by the papal legate, there was a remarkable passage that illustrates Napoleon's use of religion to insure social stability. The duties that Christians owed "to the princes that govern them . . . and in particular to Napoleon I," were enumerated as "love, respect, obedience, fidelity, military service, and the tributes laid for the preservation and defense of the empire or of his throne." Further, pursued this catechism, all those lacking in their duty toward the emperor "would be resisting the order established by God Himself and would render themselves worthy of eternal damnation."

The amicable relations between Napoleon and the church had already broken down when the catechism became law in 1806. We have already noted that, while in the early days of the empire the régime of the Concordat functioned smoothly and Napoleon surpassed any pious mediaeval ruler in multiplying the marks of the imperial favor toward the church, after 1805 the relations became strained. The Concordat was disregarded, the papal states were annexed to the empire, the pope was a prisoner of the emperor, first at Savona and later at Fontainebleau. Napoleon was excommunicated by Pius VII; and the majority of Catholics in France were bitter in their denunciation of the ruler whom they had earlier regarded as the restorer of religion. In the end Napoleon's high-handed persecution of the clergy and his attempt to dispense with papal authority led to failure. His coercion of the pope and the clergy only stiffened their opposition, and in 1814 he was forced to consent to the liberation of the pope, who returned in triumph to Rome.

On the other hand the state regulation of the Protestant cults, which was prescribed in the regulations of the Organic Articles of

1802, functioned satisfactorily. The Jews, who made up the only other organized religious group in France, also fell under the regulations of the state. Limitation of space forbids a discussion of the fortunes of the different communities of Jews in France to whom the Revolution gave a political and civil status, and forbids an analysis of all the motives that Napoleon had in mind when he organized the relations of the Jews and the state between 1806 and 1808. In some respects the problem was more complex than that of regulating the relations of either the Catholics or Protestants, for many of the Jews in the eastern departments of France had recently emigrated to France, and the great majority even of those who were natives was wholly un-French in its outlook and customs. Consequently the decrees that established a scheme of local government for Jewish communities by consistories under the surveillance of the regular administrative authorities and made provision for the assimilation of the Jews as well as for the settlement of their financial difficulties with their peasant debtors must be regarded as exceptional emergency legislation. By some critics they have been assailed as "oppressive in character"; but most students of the question are of the opinion that Napoleon's solution benefited both the Jews and the state. In any case, it laid the basis of the free economic activity of the Jews in the nineteenth century as well as of their active participation in the cultural and political life of France. In its essentials Napoleon's policy toward the Jewish religion was similar to the policy of civil control of religious opinion that he followed in the case of Catholics and Protestants.

XIX. THE GRAND EMPIRE AT ITS HEIGHT

By 1807, Napoleon's conception of the character of his imperial authority in Europe was fairly clearly defined in his own mind. It was not until 1810, however, that this imperial authority reached its fullest extent. The French empire stretched from the Hanse city of Lübeck on the Elbe to the Pyrenees and from the English Channel to Rome. More than one-third of the 131 departments into which it was divided were non-French in language and in inhabitants. To the France of the revolutionary period, which already included the Belgian provinces, the German territory west of the Rhine, Savoy, and Piedmont, Napoleon had annexed territory which carried the French boundary far beyond the "natural frontiers." In the south, between 1805 and 1810, he had annexed Genoa, Tuscany, Parma, Piacenza, the states of the church, and the Illyrian provinces on the eastern shores of the Adriatic. All this territory was incorporated directly with the French empire and divided into departments, administered by prefects. In 1810, in a final effort to enforce the Continental System, he also annexed the northern portion of the electorate of Hanover, the Hanseatic towns of Bremen, Lübeck, and Hamburg, part of the Prussian provinces that had originally been set aside for the kingdom of Westphalia, all of Holland (from which his brother Louis had fled), the republic of Valais, and the duchy of Oldenburg (1811).

Such was the French empire. But Napoleon's European empire, his Grand Empire, comprised enlarged France, the territories ruled under the protection and supervision of the emperor, and the states allied with and dependent upon him. Napoleon was king of Italy (ruled in his name by the viceroy Eugene), which in 1810 included all northern and central Italy that lay outside of the borders of enlarged France. Through members of the imperial family, he controlled Spain, the kingdom of Naples, and the kingdom of Westphalia. On the Spanish throne sat his older brother Joseph, uncertain of the future and ready for flight; in Düsseldorf, the capital of Westphalia, ruled his younger brother Jerome; in Naples, his brother-in-law, the swashbuckling cavalry leader Joachim Murat, was king. Napoleon was mediator of the Swiss Confederation and protector of the Confederation of the Rhine, which then included all the large secondary states of Germany with the exception of Prussia. Through his resident he had effective control over the grand duchy of Warsaw, even though the titular head was the king of Saxony. Out of German territory he carved two additional states, the grand duchy of Berg and the grand duchy of Frankfort, both of which were ruled almost directly from Paris. The diminished kingdom of Prussia and the landlocked empire of Austria were dependent vassal states. Denmark was an ally, earnestly fulfilling her obligations to enforce the Continental System. In 1810, Russia was still a nominal ally, though the quality of the czar's friendship was more than dubious. In addition to Russia the list of states that lay beyond Napoleon's control included only England and Portugal, Sweden, and the Ottoman Empire.

To what use did Napoleon put the enormous power that his military victories had given him? If one accepts at its face value his apologia composed during the exile at Saint Helena, or his statements of 1811, his great design was to make France the center of a federal empire, radiating the light of its splendid civilization over Europe. He loved peace and respected the principle of nationality. From France he would spread the principles of enlightenment to vanquish the stubborn forces of feudalism, clericalism, and deep-rooted traditions that defied reason and equality. He would establish a constitutional régime in Spain, restore the kingdom of Poland, and create an independent and united Italian state. In England and in Ireland he would found free republics; in Germany, a group of states under French control. He would lure the Russians, "the barbarians of the North," toward the East and remove the menace of Slavic influence from central Europe. True that his government had been a dictatorship, but he had only adjourned the era of constitutional government until he had gained security for France from her enemies in Europe. Such, he averred, was his plan, which only the incompetence of his subordinates, the bludgeoning of fate, and the implacable hostility of England prevented him from carrying out.

More than one critical historian has expended time and effort to

prove that Napoleon's real actions and his avowed intentions in
many respects totally contradicted the intentions that he later attributed to himself during the period of his captivity. His rule was
neither that of a thwarted Prometheus, nor the scourge of an
Attila nor the violence of an unchecked Jacobin. His rule was one
of mixed blessings. The long period of French ascendancy in the
arts and sciences, the universality of the French language, and the
force of French arms prepared many regions for Napoleon's domination. The intrinsic strength of revolutionary principles had been
tested for more than a decade of years; and the excellence of the
alert, intelligent, and enterprising bureaucracy that Napoleon built
up helped not a little to popularize those principles in the annexed
and occupied territories. Then there was the incalculable force of
Napoleon's genius, directed toward selecting and driving his assistants, supervising their activity, correcting their shortcomings,
elaborating suggestions, gathering into a mighty whole the many
divisions of administrative policy.

The weaknesses of his rule were the weaknesses of men and the
errors of policy. Along with administrators of highest integrity
and of admirable, disinterested zeal, there were all too many
Frenchmen who entered the imperial service largely for the opportunities that it offered for rapid promotion, power, and fortune.
Such officials made themselves personally detestable; even worse,
they discredited the emperor and the country that they served. Napoleon himself discredited the Napoleonic rule and gave it a taint
of odium that can hardly be effaced. By his vulgar ambition for
universal power and his despotic coercion of intellectual and spiritual expression he imposed upon his non-French subjects burdens
of tribute, conscription, increased taxes, and commercial and industrial hardships that amounted, in many cases, to ruin.

It is clear that Napoleon was building up a European federation of states. His writings at Saint Helena notwithstanding, he
never fully elaborated a single principle of political organization
for his federation of miscellaneous territories and heterogeneous
populations. The European states under his control had no firm
structural foundation, because his federation was basically unsound.
Napoleon acquired new territory in order to have each new de-
pendency contribute its own peculiar share to the defense of enlarged France. Yet it is true that everywhere, in varying degrees of

scope and permanence, his administrators introduced rights and institutions that had slowly been elaborated in France. The administration of the governments was simplified and unified. The franchise was extended, political assemblies were created, and municipal institutions were strengthened. The administration of finances was placed on a scientific basis, the liquidation of the public debt was begun, and tax equality was introduced. The Codes were applied bodily, and new principles and new procedures, in most instances much more enlightened and humane than the old, came into common practice. Serfdom was done away with, feudal dues abolished, the inheritance of large estates prohibited. The new officials suppressed public violence, discouraged vagrancy, and instituted systems of poor relief. Guild corporations were dissolved and the principles of scientific agriculture were introduced. Uniform weights and measures and standard coinage replaced ancient forms. A system of elementary public instruction was laid down; monastic establishments were abolished, and their wealth taken over; and the supremacy of the secular government over the church was everywhere enforced. Public works and material improvements swelled the prosperity of the native population. In the administration, in commerce and industry, and in the army, careers were opened to the talents of all social classes.

The other side of the French rule shows the crushing force of Napoleon's despotism—secret police agents, spies, a muzzled press, a rigid censorship, and the stifling of all hostile criticism. It shows the suppression of political liberty and the introduction of the same "model despotism" that the Constitution of the Year XII gave to France. It shows the exigencies of Napoleon's imperial policy in conflict with the real needs of the various subordinate states. The continental blockade forced hordes of French customs agents and inspectors into prosperous, thriving communities. Goods were confiscated, the avenues of trade were choked up by a ruinous tariff, prosperity was destroyed. Brutal administrators, civil and military favorites living on fiefs created out of the domain land, armies of occupation, heavy war indemnities, staggering taxes, and the weight of conscription awakened national sentiments against the French emperor. Religious feeling also turned against him when he revived the worst error of the revolutionary assemblies and became the oppressor of the Catholic Church.

French Rule in Italy and Spain

"Nowhere outside of France had the French revolutionary principles of equality been so completely put into effect as in the Italian states," writes a profound student of our own generation. Yet an analysis of the steps which led up to the various territorial changes in the peninsula shows that Napoleon's interest was always calculated, always inspired primarily by the motive of making Italy serve his own ends. At the height of Napoleon's powers the peninsula was divided into three large states—the kingdom of Italy, the kingdom of Naples, and "French Italy"; and in each of these divisions a single plan, inspired by Napoleon, guided the ruler. Established in 1805, the kingdom of Italy was subsequently enlarged by the additional territory of Venetia (1806), the march of Ancona and the papal legations (1808), and the Italian Tirol (1810). To Napoleon's stepson Eugene de Beauharnais, who was viceroy for him at the capital city of Milan, as well as to the emperor, must go the credit for the magnificent success of French rule. Eugene, who was amiable, upright, and industrious, surrounded himself with a splendid staff of administrators, combined severity with tact, and rigid honesty in financial affairs with sensitive moderation in cultural activities. He simplified the administration, introduced the Civil Code, and prepared for the establishment of an enlightened judicial procedure. Criticism of the administration was, as one may expect, severely forbidden, but in other respects, the rule was one of benevolent despotism. The budget was carefully balanced, and the assessment of taxes, while higher than during the earlier days of Austrian rule, was more evenly distributed. Crime and brigandage were diminished, vagrancy largely eliminated, and a system of public instruction uniform throughout the entire kingdom was introduced. Through the equalization of taxation and the completion of lasting public improvements the material prosperity of the Italians was promoted. Most significant of all, the army service, in which Italians from Lombardy, Venetia, Modena, and Ancona served with equal readiness, provided them with a school for patriotism. One may safely state that this military service contributed greatly to the eradication of provincial and social distinctions and impressed upon thousands of these veterans of the Napoleonic wars the ideal of an independent and united Italy.

The most important districts of "French Italy," that is, Italian territories annexed to the French empire, were Piedmont, Tuscany, and the papal states. The administration of this territory illustrated the flexibility as well as the advantage of French rule. The Codes were introduced, the simplified French financial system adopted, and the forms of political representation established. In Piedmont, which was divided like the other regions into departments, French became the official language, but Italian was not proscribed. In Rome and Tuscany, the use of the Italian dialects was maintained. The least opposition to French rule came from Piedmont, which was longest in the hands of the conqueror (1802–1814). There, feudal dues and the tithes of the church were abolished, a system of poor relief instituted, brigandage suppressed, and a comprehensive program of public works laid down. The French government took over the public debt. The innovations of French rule in Tuscany were in the main not superior to the existing institutions in that state, where the Hapsburg rule had been both mild and enlightened.

The most pronounced opposition came from the inhabitants of the papal city. The pretexts for occupying and annexing Rome were specious, and the arrest and imprisonment of the pope a humiliation to the Romans' pride. The French administration proved itself sound and beneficial, though the disadvantages of French rule figured more highly with the Romans than the benefits of the Codes, the equalization of taxes, the confiscation of monastic wealth, the encouragement to industry and agriculture, and the suppression of disorder. Though Rome was given a municipal senate and proclaimed the second city of the empire, its inhabitants, like the Tuscans and, to a lesser extent the Piedmontese, resented the burdens of Napoleon's imperial policy of conquest. In Rome the staunch resistance of the priests constituted a serious problem for the new administration.

The first French ruler of the kingdom of Naples was Napoleon's older brother Joseph, and he was succeeded after a short reign of two years (1806–1808) by Joachim Murat, the husband of Napoleon's sister Caroline. Several years elapsed before French rule was secured by the subjugation of the rebellious Calabrians in the southeast and the repulse of English invaders from Sicily. The government of the kingdom presented staggering difficulties; in no other region of western Europe were the vices of the Old Régime so deeply rooted. The indomitable energy of the new officials slowly but steadily brought gratifying results in the regeneration of the backward state. Yet Murat, like his fellow administrator Marshal Marmont, the governor-general of the Illyrian provinces, complained bitterly that Napoleon's policy destroyed the effectiveness of reforms. After the restoration of the Bourbons in Naples in 1815 little of the French reforms in fiscal administration, sequestration of the domain lands, feudal legislation, legal procedure, remained. The Civil Code survived, as did the new judicial procedure. Of Marmont's notable accomplishments, the greatest were the construction of a great highway from Zara to Spalato and the reduction of the robber bands that infested his territory.

French ideas did not take root in Spain, for Joseph's reign was largely the history of the unsuccessful effort of the invaders to maintain themselves in the country. In 1808 Napoleon had begun what he expected to be the transformation of Spain's institutions by issuing four decrees. These abolished the Inquisition, destroyed feudal rights, did away with provincial tariffs, and reduced the number of monastic establishments. But the enforcement of these decrees was a more difficult matter than their promulgation. Coming from a foreign invader, from the persecutor of the pope, these measures excited the hostility rather than the approval of the Spaniards. In the course of the national uprising against Napoleon, an extraordinary Cortes or assembly was elected in 1810 in which the dominant influence was held by delegates from the coastal and more democratic provinces. These delegates used their influence in elaborating, after two years of discussion, the liberal constitution of 1812.

From 1813 to 1815, or from the evacuation of Madrid by the French up to the restoration of the Bourbon ruler Ferdinand VII, the constitution was applied, though not with great effectiveness. In many respects this charter, which proclaimed the principles of liberty and equality, derived from the French Constitution of 1791, from the defects of that document as well as from its strong points. The return of Ferdinand VII sounded the knell of the constitutional régime. But the Constitution of 1812 lived in the memories of Latin reformers, for in 1820–1821 it was readopted in Spain, proclaimed in the kingdoms of the Two Sicilies and Sardinia, and used as a model in Portugal. Again the epilogue was disappointing, for within a few years the revolutionary movements of 1820–1821 were effectively suppressed.

REFORMS IN BELGIUM, HOLLAND, AND GERMANY

The possibilities of settling French institutions were greater in the former Austrian Netherlands than they were in the kingdom of Holland. The former territory had been incorporated with France during the Revolution and remained in French hands for two decades; the latter was annexed to France in 1810, and three short years proved insufficient to remold Dutchmen into Frenchmen or Dutch institutions into French. The history of the nine Belgian departments of France presents a series of contrasts, beginning with the exactions and privations during the Revolution and the Directory, which gave place to the beneficent rule during the Consulate and the early empire, only to revert to the hardships during the later empire. The fate of the seven Dutch departments under French control was almost unrelieved misery for the native population. The advantages that resulted from the wise reforms of the excellent French prefects in Belgium were in the long run outweighed by the injury to commerce by the blockade, the domiciliary visits of the police, the strain of finances, the conscription, and the later Napoleonic persecution of the church. These hardships were also felt, and more keenly, in Holland, where Napoleon exerted himself to leave almost nothing Dutch in the country. While the use of the Dutch language was not forbidden, the French administration made strenuous efforts to rear the younger generation in a French spirit. The administration of the two most prosperous and important provinces, of which Amsterdam and Rotterdam were the capitals, was entrusted not to natives, but to Belgians. All books were rigidly censored. One-third of all the officers of the Dutch army were required by law to be Frenchmen. The permanent legacies of French rule were the perpetuation of the Codes and the judicial procedure—and marked distaste for the invaders themselves.

French influence in Germany varied according to the different localities, both in intensity and in beneficial results. Napoleon's simplification of the political geography of Germany, his destruction of Austrian influence in southern Germany, and his creation of the

Confederation of the Rhine represent his claim as the founder of a united Germany. From the point of view of results ultimately accomplished, his claim is valid. It is worthy of note, however, that it was never part of Napoleon's program to encourage the national aspirations of the Germans. His ultimate plan was to establish a federation of states under the domination of France. Directly and indirectly French influence affected the fortunes of several separate regions in Germany. These were the territory annexed to France, the independent and temporary states created by Napoleon, the states of the Confederation of the Rhine, and Prussia.

The territory on the left bank of the Rhine was occupied by the French as early as 1794 and organized into four departments in 1802. The native population, having only the thinnest cultural ties with the interior of Germany, was at first enthusiastic over the prospects of French rule. But five unbroken years of misgovernment and misfortune at the hands of the French commissioners turned the enthusiasm into loathing. With the establishment of the Consulate the situation changed almost miraculously for the better, and nowhere was the work of reorganization along French lines more successfully accomplished. In his final summary of Napoleonic statesmanship in the Rhenish provinces, H. A. L. Fisher states that there "the system of the Empire was at its best, repairing material waste, obliterating senseless divisions, driving into a torpid populace its keen and vital energies, and in the ordered structure of French law bequeathing one of the most splendid legacies which a conqueror has ever left to a vanquished province." [1]

The work of reorganization began much later in the German territories that were annexed late in 1810 and early in 1811. These were the Hanseatic cities, the northern part of the electorate of Hanover, and the duchy of Oldenburg. It began later and still remained unfinished at the collapse of the empire. The confusion and the hardships incidental to the task were at their worst in the two departments that were created out of the territory of the Hanseatic cities of Hamburg, Bremen, and Lübeck. The cities were long under the control of French troops before their formal annexation in 1810. Napoleon required them to prop up his imperial system and spared neither their pride nor their purse. With their commerce ruined by the Continental System, their finances shat-

[1] H. A. L. Fisher, *Studies in Napoleonic Statesmanship, Germany*, p. 384.

tered by the costs of the emperor's wars, their streets filled with troops of the army of occupation, the stout burghers of northwest Germany had slight cause to feel beholden toward their conqueror.

The evils were less marked, but not different in kind, in the grand duchy of Berg and the grand duchy of Frankfort. The first of these artificial creations came into being in March, 1806, out of the Prussian territory of Cleves and the Bavarian district of Berg. Subsequently enlarged in 1808, it remained what it had been from its inception, a military "march" against Prussia, a sort of French outpost on the Rhine. Though the French imperial commissioner, Beugnot, was an excellent administrator and effected many sound reforms from his residence at Düsseldorf, the military and financial exigencies of Napoleon's policy provoked dissatisfaction not less lively than in many other vassal states. The benefits of his administration were the familiar fruits of French rule—a simplified administration, judicial reforms, stimulation of a public works program, abolition of castes, increased commercial and agricultural activity. The once free imperial city of Frankfort acquired the status of a grand duchy in 1810 after being for four years part of a principality created for Dalberg, the prince-primate of the Confederation of the Rhine. Dalberg meant well, but was checked in his efforts by the French resident at his capital, who received his instructions from Paris. After the overthrow of Napoleon only the new judicial system survived, and memories of taxation, conscription, and injury to commercial ventures.

The first two years of the kingdom of Westphalia were productive of many useful and necessary innovations in the life of its inhabitants. The monarch of this new realm which was created in 1807 out of the duchy of Brunswick, Hesse-Cassel, the Westphalian provinces of Prussia, and the southern portion of Hanover, was Napoleon's amiable younger brother, Jerome. The population was mixed, as were the historic traditions of this unnatural state of some two million inhabitants, but the possibilities were great. Napoleon intended to make the kingdom an inspiration to Germany, and he instructed Jerome in most explicit terms: "It is necessary that your people should enjoy a liberty, an equality, and a degree of well-being unknown to the people of Germany." For so lofty a goal Jerome was hardly the man, as Napoleon should have realized. Apart from Jerome's facile morals, his wasteful expenditures, and his administrative incompetence, much of the blame for the failure of the presented program rests with Napoleon himself. Knowing what should be done, he interfered constantly in the administration and exploited the kingdom for his own financial and military ends. From 1807 to 1809 the new constitution, which was adapted from the French constitution of the empire, was slowly put into force, and the most active elements of the state rallied to the support of the monarch. Careers in the administration, the courts, and the army were open to them, abuses were slowly eradicated, differences were reconciled, and high hopes were excited. But the policy of the later empire intensified the existing opposition to the reforms. Beginning with 1809, no fewer than seven uprisings against the French broke out. Napoleon stripped the country of its wealth and saddled it with his troops. At the same time he increased the burden of armament and raised the levy of Westphalian troops from 125,000 men to 375,000. The costs of enforcing the Continental System and the passage of French troops through the country completed the ruin of the hopeful experiment that was to bring the Westphalians "a degree of well-being unknown to the people of Germany."

The states of Berg, Frankfort, and Westphalia were members of the Confederation of the Rhine, which, formed in 1806 with fifteen members, grew steadily in membership until it included virtually all the secondary states of Germany. In 1813 the defection of Bavaria sounded the knell of this "Third Germany" that Napoleon had created. French influence over the member states (other than the three states already mentioned) was exercised indirectly through the sovereigns allied with Napoleon. Attention has frequently been called to the peculiarity of Napoleon's relations with the princes of the Confederation. Since he needed them primarily for such military assistance as they could give, he found it expedient to have them strengthen their autocratic authority at the expense of their subjects. In doing so, he ran counter to the basic spirit of the Revolution, which stood for constitutional rule and the safeguard of civil and political rights. What he would have done at the conclusion of a successful war against Russia and England is problematical, his statements at Saint Helena notwithstanding. At any rate the opportunity never came. He himself destroyed the opportunity by provoking into a defensive and victorious war the only power in Germany that challenged his domination—the regenerated kingdom of Prussia. Of the south German states within the Confederation the kingdom of Bavaria distinguished itself most in reorganizing its institutions in the spirit of French principles. Equality of taxation was introduced; the control of education given to the state; the enormous power of the church was broken and its wealth expropriated; and the existing system of feudal rights was substantially modified. Opposition to Napoleon came at first from the secularized clergy and the humbled aristocracy, but in the end Napoleon's policy of using the states as powers on his continental chessboard aroused the animosity of all elements of society.

The king of Saxony, which belonged to the Confederation of the Rhine, was also nominal head of the grand duchy of Warsaw. Since he was not even permitted to have a viceroy represent him at Warsaw, the real power was exercised by the French resident. He, in turn, followed instructions sent from Paris. The grand duchy was formed in 1807 from the Polish territory that Prussia had gained in the three partitions, and it was subsequently enlarged in 1809 with a portion of Galicia that was torn from Austria. The province of Bialystok, however, was given to Russia, and the city of Danzig was made free under the protection of Prussia and Saxony. Napoleon never intended to have the grand duchy develop other functions than that of protecting his creations in central Europe against the menace of Russian penetration. With England subdued, Napoleon planned to attack Russia and push this essentially Asiatic power east of the Dnieper. He has been reproached for his faithlessness toward the Polish patriots, for encouraging their hopes of a restored Polish kingdom without ever seriously intending to have these hopes realized. The criticism is unwarranted. Napoleon's whole Polish policy is inexplicable apart from the supposition that the restoration of Poland was of vital importance to his later schemes of bringing all Europe, including Constantinople, under his imperial control. What ruined his plans was not his bad faith with the Poles, but the war of 1809, which forced him to advance his program and take Galicia before he was ready to break with Russia. And in fact the rupture with Russia really came over Poland.

As Napoleon's chief concern in Poland was to make it a strong bulwark against Russia, the matter of reforms never received more than perfunctory attention. A constitution that was reminiscent of the French Constitution of 1791 was granted, but its theoretical provisions were largely ignored in practice. Similarly, the abolition of serfdom was not enforced save on paper. On the other hand the inhabitants felt the weight of the heavier taxation that Napoleon's needs imposed. To Napoleon's marshals and generals fell domains and revenues within the duchy amounting to more than twenty-six million francs. The strict enforcement of the Continental System cut off the export of their timber and grain to England, while the war between Russia and Turkey prevented them from trading with the Turkish Empire. The number of men required for military service increased steadily until it reached 85,000 in 1812—this out of a total of fewer than 3,000,000 inhabitants. Yet despite the disappointments of the new régime Polish patriots still cherished the hope that the existing arrangements were only temporary, and that in time the reëstablished national kingdom of Poland would take its place in the society of European states.

The Spiritual Regeneration of Prussia

In 1807, some twenty years after the death of Frederick the Great, Prussia had lost all the military prestige that her kings had won in the preceding century, and suffered a complete inner collapse. The treaty of Tilsit forced the king to give up one-half of his territory to Napoleon's dependents. The key fortresses to the defense of the remaining territory were garrisoned by French troops. The obligations to enforce the Continental System played havoc with the fortune of the Prussian merchants, while the strain of maintaining the enormous body of the French army of occupation exhausted the financial resources of the population. In contravention of the treaty of Tilsit, Napoleon had forced a military convention upon the defeated state (July 12, 1807), whereby the conquered land was not to be rid of the victorious enemy until all contributions and indemnities should have been discharged. But the maximum amount of the contributions was not specified, and it was Napoleon's intention to "make the provinces pay all they can."

Napoleon's plans for Prussia were dependent upon other political combinations. By keeping his troops in the kingdom he had a telling and characteristic argument against any other attempt on the part of Alexander I to retain the provinces of Moldavia and Wallachia. Should Russia make that attempt, Napoleon would demand the cession of Silesia to France. On the other hand, he could repay any concessions that Alexander I would make by lessening the amount of the Prussian indemnity or by withdrawing his troops. Meantime, French troops, totaling 150,000 men, lived off the Prussian land. Pending a definite financial settlement vast sums of money were exacted for the benefit of French officials and the emperor's special war fund. Such was the financial background of the movement for reform and for throwing off the yoke of the conqueror.

This movement was well under way before the final financial arrangements were concluded for the evacuation of the army of occupation. Men of the pen and practical men of affairs came to the realization that the bases of the Prussian state would have to be widened if Prussia were to regain her place among the great states of Europe. Under their leadership an admirable program was launched "to regenerate the state as a better instrument for national defense under dynastic leadership." [2] Their purpose was to draw the entire population into the active service of the state, and not merely the nobility and the bureaucracy; to give the towns and the middle class a more vigorous rôle than that of mere taxpayers. Under the impact of the Napoleonic armies they saw the necessity of introducing into their still essentially mediaeval state a large part of the new social order that had been established in France. But their program was none the less Prussian and not French, "because it embodied a new realization of the necessity to that state [Prussia] of free citizens, who would be ready to serve in the ranks of the national army which Scharnhorst was planning against the day of national uprising." [3]

The intellectual preparation for this regeneration had been begun in the days preceding the military catastrophe at Jena. The shock of the French revolutionary armies carrying their new gospel of equality shattered the old indifference of German intellectuals to public life and the concerns of the ordinary individual. In remote, sleepy Königsberg the imperturbable Immanuel Kant defended the principles of the Revolution against the hostility of his auditors. A colleague, Professor Kraus, indoctrinated a generation of students and future Prussian administrators with Adam Smith's teachings of economic liberalism. The voices of the Romantic move-

[2] G. S. Ford, *Stein and the Era of Reform in Prussia 1807–1815*, p. 222.
[3] Ford, *op. cit.*, p. 212.

ment sang the love of the German land and sounded the glory of the simple, honest German folk. By their interest in the Germany of the Middle Ages, in its history and its ancient lore, they strengthened the feeling of patriotism to a German fatherland. Public-minded Germans from the various states of the Holy Roman Empire accepted service in Prussia and bent themselves to the task of reform. Among these civil servants were Baron Stein, who was born at Nassau in the Rhineland, Hardenberg and Scharnhorst, who came originally from Hanover, and Gneisenau and Fichte, who were Saxons. Now in Prussia's moment of deepest despair the undismayed guides of her future greatness pointed the way to a new and higher conception of civic duties and awakened the sentiments of national patriotism.

The major prophet of this movement of regeneration was the philosopher Fichte. His resounding series of lectures called Addresses to the German Nation (*Reden an die deutsche Nation*), that were given in Berlin in the fall of 1807, sounded a new note in Prussian history. Inspired directly by the Kantian ideal of moral obligation, he delved into the treasury of Prussia's historic past and appealed to the highest conceptions of ethics and religion in his effort to lay the foundations of a new politics. He denounced the jealous sectionalism and the devotion to petty interests that held in check the growth of national German unity. He called for a new and broader system of education that would inculcate in the younger generation a lofty zeal for German welfare. Like the French patriots of the Revolution he glorified the ideal of national patriotism and summoned all Germans to dedicate themselves, even unto death, to the security and greatness of their nation. Veiling his allusions, so as to defeat the vigilance of the French censor, he exhorted his listeners to rise, like their ancestors in the days of Roman rule, against the foreigners that oppressed their land.

The fierce national insurgence of the Spaniards gave point to Fichte's appeal. The changed spirit in the schools of primary instruction and in the *Gymnasien* (secondary schools) showed that his words had taken effect. The most important development was the establishment of new universities in Berlin and Breslau.[4] Several months after the presentation of a report by the famous sci-

[4] The immediate occasion for the establishment of the University of Berlin was the loss to Prussia of the University of Halle, which lay in territory that Prussia ceded by the treaty of Tilsit.

entist, Wilhelm von Humboldt, the king gave his consent to the establishment of a new university at Berlin (1809). The university was opened in 1810 with a faculty comprising the most illustrious scholars of the realm—Fichte for philosophy, Savigny for law, Schleiermacher for theology, Niebuhr for history, and Humboldt for science. Despite the appalling poverty of his state, Frederick William assigned a generous sum to the young institution, which became one of the influential centers of the new national movement. There, as at the newly founded University of Breslau in Silesia, distinguished scholars taught and enthusiastic students absorbed their teachings of civic duty and devotion to the national welfare. It was through no accident that professors and students alike rushed to arms in 1813 in the War of Liberation.

Another factor in the movement to infuse into public life the new moral idealism of the reformers was the famous *Tugenbund.* This Moral and Scientific Union was founded in 1808 by a group of somewhat impractical enthusiasts, who hoped to make it a nucleus for "the revival of morality, religion, serious taste, and public spirit." The influence of the Tugenbund was not profound, nor yet were its aims Jacobin and revolutionary, as many of its critics maintained. Despite the fact that the leading practical reformers refused to become enrolled as members, their efforts were undoubtedly aided by the members of the association. A year after its founding it was declared illegal, but the work continued through secret channels.

STEIN AND THE ERA OF REFORMS

The man called to the helm of the government after the treaty of Tilsit was the masterful Baron Stein. All the progressives in the kingdom appealed to this experienced administrator and man of resolute determination to save the situation. Only recently Stein had been dismissed by Frederick William and characterized as "a refractory, insolent, obstinate, and disobedient official," but after Tilsit the reluctant monarch was forced to turn to him. Stein assumed office as minister on October 1, 1807, and at once ended the rule of the king's private advisers, of the "kitchen cabinet," that had hampered the work of the official ministers. For fourteen months he enjoyed virtual dictatorial powers, both in domestic and in foreign affairs; and in those fourteen months he instituted and associated himself with a program of reforms that revitalized Prussian life. Yet at no moment was he free from the almost intolerable financial burdens that the French occupation imposed upon the land. The best of his efforts were directed to obtaining relief in that direction, yet for all his endeavors the relief obtained was slight.

One expedient that he employed was to dispatch the king's brother, Prince William, to Paris, there to bargain for more favorable terms from Napoleon, even at the cost of binding Prussia to a French alliance and sanctioning her entry into the Confederation of the Rhine. He himself left the court at Königsberg and went in person to Berlin to seek concessions from the French military governor. Meantime, he made drastic economies, slashing pensions, whittling down court expenditures, reducing the salaries of officials and soldiers and officers in the army. By using the royal domain as collateral he succeeded in floating debentures or mortgage bonds and raising more than 70,000,000 francs toward payment of the indemnity and costs of occupation. But the unfortunate interception of a letter that he had written determined both the fall of his ministry and the imposition of despairingly severe financial terms. In that letter this responsible head of the government indiscreetly wrote that war between Austria and France seemed a certainty, that Germany's interests would best be served by fanning the growing resentment against the French, and that the national uprising in Spain was an example for German patriots. The final settlement of September 8, 1808, marked Napoleon's wrath at Stein's activities. The indemnity was fixed at 140,000,000 francs, and the Prussian army was limited to 42,000 men. The French army of occupation was bound to evacuate Prussia shortly after the ratification of the arrangement, but the fortresses of the Oder were to remain in French hands until the full settlement had been paid.

Napoleon now outlawed Stein and set a price upon his head, insisting vigorously, meantime, upon his resignation from office. Stein accordingly resigned in November, 1808, and fled for safety to Austria, but not before the reforms associated with his name were thoroughly begun. In point of time, if not of importance, the first of these reforms was the one dealing with the peasantry and the land. On October 9, 1807, the king gave his signature to the Edict of Emancipation, which abolished serfdom, with its many personal obligations, throughout his kingdom. This momentous change was to take effect at the expiration of three years, on October 8, 1810.[5] The first two articles of the edict were no less important than those articles which abolished serfdom, for they removed the existing mediaeval restrictions on the holding of land and the choice of occupation. The transfer of land from one class to another was now legalized by royal permission, the only safeguard being measures to protect the diminution of peasant property. The classification of labor was also ended. The noble was now legally permitted to take up occupations hitherto restricted to the middle class, and the burgher could legally pursue the callings previously limited to the peasantry. This edict was a tremendous step in the direction of free economic enterprise. It favored the development of agriculture by attaching capital to the land, particularly to the unproductive land of impoverished noblemen. It removed all social stigma from occupations formerly classified as ignoble and enabled enterprising men, irrespective of their class origin, to develop their economic abilities without fear of reproach.

This edict did not free the peasants from their feudal obligations, whether paid in labor, in kind, or in money; nor did it end the manorial jurisdiction of the noble over the peasantry. But if feudalism were not yet abolished and manorial justice still existed, nevertheless this reform was fundamental in transforming the Prussian peasant into a citizen of the state. The fuller realization of this program was essayed by Hardenberg after the fall of Stein. By the vigorous decree of September 14, 1811, the peasants on private estates were divided into two classes, both of which were "to be freed from dues and labor duties to the landowner in return for their relinquishment to him of all claims to a certain fraction of the holdings in which they had by custom or law possessory rights." The hereditary peasant proprietors gave up one-third of their holdings; the peasants without hereditary rights and renters of noble land on a lease basis were to give up one-half of their tenure. These were by far the larger class. The measure was hedged in by many reservations and was strenuously opposed by the privileged landowners. Moreover, the provisions were not observed in the troubled years of the War of Liberation, and the

[5] Two royal edicts, the one of October, 1807, and the other of July, 1808, completed a reform already under way, that of liberating the serfs on the royal domain and commuting their dues into property rights. It has been estimated that many thousand free peasant proprietors were created in consequence of these edicts in East and West Prussia and Lithuania.

edict of 1816 superseded them and limited their application to the larger holdings. Nevertheless, the change from feudal tenure to freehold was begun, and the peasants now had their first opportunity to become an economically independent landowning class. On the other hand the privileged land barons gained greatly from the conservative elaborations of the original measure and built up still larger estates at the expense of free, but landless, peasants.

Stein had a greater share in the reform of municipal government than in the agrarian measures, but in both instances the preparation of the project antedated his assumption of office. On November 19, 1808, the great edict which laid the foundation of local government in Prussia during the entire nineteenth century was signed. In contradistinction to the French municipal code of December 14, 1789—by which the framers of the Prussian law were clearly inspired—this law was not primarily an effort to guarantee the rights of man and the citizen. It was an attempt to revitalize the state in the interest of national defense. This was accomplished not by increasing the state's authority over the towns, which was already enormous, but by entrusting large powers to the local citizens, without entirely depriving the state of its general supervision. On the other hand the law did away entirely with the rights of lords of manors over towns and villages with more than 800 inhabitants. The framers of this law were not unmindful of the fact that in some towns the memories of civic rights dating back to the Middle Ages still survived; nor did they neglect the worth of the new patriotism taught by the great intellectual leaders of their time. Lastly, they were well warned by the sad example of the first French experiment of 1789–1790 in local government, and they placed their faith in a slow and controlled training of citizens for public life. This faith, as subsequent events showed, was entirely justified.

Stein also projected a thorough reform of the central administration as well as of its agents in the local administrative divisions. There was much to do, for the well regulated state of Frederick the Great had degenerated, once his controlling hand was removed, into a cumbersome bureaucracy. Stein's ministry was too brief to permit the full realization of his plan of reform, but he made a start in the right direction. His later successors carried some of his ideas through to completion. He increased the importance of the ministers and gained a degree of real responsibility for them. He also planned the creation of a true royal council, but after his re-tirement his successors succeeded only in establishing a smaller ministerial council that convened under the presidency of the mon-arch. The administration of justice was separated from the admin-istration of government, and the various special treasuries were consolidated into one central treasury.

During his ministry, too, a new military system was established, with profound consequences for the fate of Prussia. Shortly after the signing of the treaty of Tilsit, Frederick William appointed a military commission, of which the reformers Scharnhorst and Gneisenau were the most prominent and influential members. To these two men Frederick William gave a large measure of sup-port in their efforts to create a truly national army. Many old officers were cashiered; others responsible for the military degrada-tion of their country in the campaign of 1806 were severely pun-ished. The king assented to Scharnhorst's demand that the use of mercenary troops be abandoned, which was in itself a step forward toward enlisting every citizen in the work of national defense. But he withheld his support from Scharnhorst's proposal of a national militia, preferring to reorganize the existing cantonal system of recruiting.

Nevertheless, Scharnhorst's ideas actually prevailed when Na-poleon limited the effectives of the active Prussian army to 42,000 men and forbade the organization of a militia. In order to defeat this provision the reformers devised their famous "shrinkage sys-tem" (*Krümpersystem*), whereby the ranks of the regiments were periodically filled with recruits who, after a brief period of train-ing, passed into the reserves. Carried out with a very high degree of secrecy, this system enabled Prussia by the year 1812 to have a well trained force of 150,000 men in addition to the nominal total of 42,000 soldiers in the active army. Despite the king's reluc-tance to go the full length of reforms, the whole male population actually received a longer or shorter training in military service. The reforms also did away with the degrading punishments for-merly imposed upon the soldiers. Though the highest positions in the service were still reserved for the nobility, it now became pos-sible for commoners to rise rapidly from the ranks and become of-ficers. Great improvements modernizing the entire system of the eighteenth century army were introduced in weapons, uniforms, drill, and tactics. Heavy baggage trains were to be given up, as well as supply stations, and in times of war the army was to live by requisitions. Ultimately, in 1814, universal military service was made legal throughout the entire system; but in practice universal service was already in existence.

Military disaster had brought Prussia under the yoke of the conqueror. At the same time it made possible an amazingly rapid regeneration of the country which no policy of neutrality and time-serving could possibly have effected. In her hour of deepest darkness her thinkers and statesmen saw clearly that new light and new life could come only by introducing in their dynastic kingdom the leading principles of that Revolution which made the French armies at once a blessing and a scourge in Europe.

XX. THE COLLAPSE OF THE EMPIRE

The Weakness of the Empire

Until about 1807 one has the feeling that Napoleon is riding the storm easily and successfully. He appears to control events. But from the intervention in Spain, and especially in connection with the war of 1809, which he did not want, one has the feeling that the situation is getting out of hand. Henceforth he is struggling more and more in vain to master situations which he has not foreseen and which he can never solve to his satisfaction. With his usual political acumen Talleyrand sensed this trend of events and began, as early as 1808, to weave the intricate plot which was to make him indispensable to the conquerors of Napoleon. In 1809 one of Napoleon's ministers spoke prophetically of "a frightful catastrophe" that would destroy the foundations of the emperor's power. From 1809 on, great as the empire was, its stability was more apparent than real.

Within France itself, a mounting tide of discontent and war-weariness undermined the stability of the government. Napoleon's repression of political liberty, his despotic organization of educational and intellectual activities, and his unfailing recourse to the police alienated the intellectuals and the old partisans of free parliamentary government. Another cause of grievance, which has been described elsewhere, was the economic stagnation and the financial disorder that ensued from the strict enforcement of the Continental System. This discontent cost him the support of the solid middle class of merchants, manufacturers, and bankers. Then there was the increasingly onerous burden of conscription. While rumors of the appalling losses in Spain were in wide circulation, the peasants learned that their emperor contemplated a new war in distant Russia. Their consternation was universal. Thousands of young men who were eligible for service sought to escape, whether through purchasing exemption or through flight. The government used its power to enforce the conscription law, but neither prison penalties, nor heavy fines, nor flying squadrons of troops, nor garrisons stationed at strategic villages prevented the flight from the colors. To illiterate peasant women, who were too backward to appreciate the cosmic vastness of the emperor's projects, Napoleon had now become "the Corsican monster." Lastly, the clergy and the faithful Catholics opposed his rule.

Conditions outside France were equally disturbing. The burdens of conscription and the hardships of the Continental System aroused fiercer discontent in the allied and vassal states, because that discontent was fanned by the spirit of national patriotism. Patriots everywhere in Napoleonic Europe bitterly resented the presence of arrogant French officials, army officers, and soldiers in their land. Common people were thoroughly disillusioned by Napoleon's failure to give them the blessings of political liberty. The privileged aristocracy of the conquered states scorned and hated the "child of the Revolution." Since events in Spain had shown that Napoleon's armies were no longer invincible, his enemies took heart and envisaged his overthrow. Even France's nominal allies could not be counted upon, for both in Austria and in Prussia resolute men were planning to end the rule of Napoleon. But the emperor was confident that the Continental System would prevail against England; and with England subdued, only Russia remained to block his path to universal dominion. To conquer England was difficult, even with the aid of Russia; to break with Russia before England was settled was to invite disaster, and toward this disaster Napoleon was now heading.

The Break with Russia

The Franco-Russian alliance of Tilsit had been the personal work of Napoleon and Alexander, and had always been opposed in Russia. It had been renewed at Erfurt; but the formal renewal was vitiated by the events of 1809. Officially it still subsisted in 1810, but circumstances steadily estranged the two rulers and impelled them toward the final rupture and war. As soon as it became clear to both authors of the alliance that neither was to derive as much benefit from it as he had expected, all justification for its continuation disappeared.

In 1807 and 1808 Napoleon had given definite assurances to the czar that Russia would not be compelled to restore the Polish territory that she had gained in the partitions of the eighteenth century. The sincerity of those assurances was highly questionable, for reëstablishment of an enlarged and independent Polish state was essential to the success of Napoleon's great plan to bring all Europe under his imperial control. Sooner or later he intended to break with Russia, push it beyond the Dnieper, create the kingdom of Poland, and take over the Balkans, including Constantinople. In 1807 and 1808 he knew that the occasion when he might with impunity alienate Alexander had not yet risen, but in 1809, in spite of himself, he was forced to move more rapidly than he had intended. The war against Austria forced him to transfer most of Galicia, with some 1,500,000 Polish-speaking inhabitants, to the grand duchy of Warsaw. This move aroused the deepest suspicions of the czar, for it pointed directly toward an independent Poland, and a restored kingdom of Poland would not be complete unless it included the broad plains of Lithuania which Russia had taken in the partitions of the preceding century. Once Napoleon came to the conclusion that he could deal with Russia on the Continent even before the issue with England was settled, he made slight effort to allay Alexander's suspicions or make concessions to his nominal ally. Feeling that war with Russia was now a certainty, he played hard for the support of the Poles. This consideration explains his provocative act in 1810 when he refused to ratify an agreement drawn up by Caulaincourt, the French ambassador in Russia, to the effect that he would never restore the kingdom of Poland, or even use the term Poland in public documents.

Napoleon's policy in European Turkey was a second great factor in embittering his relations with the czar. At Tilsit he had dangled before Alexander the spectacle of a Turkish Empire partitioned between Russia and France; and at Erfurt he had consented to Russia's retention of the two Danubian principalities at the conclusion of the war between Russia and the Turkish Empire. Now, directly contrary to those promises, agents of the emperor were stiffening the resistance of the Turks to the Russian armies and preventing the speedy end of hostilities. Napoleon's ultimate intentions concerning the Balkans are not entirely clear, but there are memorandums, prepared for him by a Turkish renegade, outlining various plans, some of which suggest the union of the Balkan states, like the Confederation of the Rhine. It is certain that his

earlier declarations at Tilsit and at Erfurt were gestures to beguile
Alexander into false security. Napoleon never contemplated
abandoning Constantinople to the Russians.

The third source of irritation lay in the question of Russia's
adherence to the Continental System. Without Russian coöperation the system could not succeed, but the coöperation of Russia
was impossible on Napoleon's terms. From 1807 to 1810 Russian
merchants had protested more and more vigorously over the
rupture of direct commercial relations with England, their best cus-
tomer for wheat, timber, hemp, and tallow. Without some alleviation of the conditions governing Russia's support of the blockade,
the country was headed for economic and financial ruin. Instead of
modification, however, Napoleon proposed still greater stringency
of enforcement, summoning Alexander, in 1810, to confiscate
neutral vessels in Russian ports on the ground that they carried
only British goods. The czar refused, alleging that Russia's prosperity depended on the trade of neutrals. Had Napoleon been
willing to make the necessary concessions concerning Poland and
the Balkans, or concerning Poland alone, it is likely that Alexander
would not have made an open issue of the Continental System. As
his refusal legally opened the Continent to British exports conveyed on neutral bottoms, it could be construed as a definite indication that he had broken with his French ally. Even before
Alexander learned that Napoleon had annexed to France the northwest coast of Germany, including the duchy of Oldenburg, whose
ruler was the uncle of the czar, he made the rupture with Napoleon
definite. On December 31, 1810, he issued a decree which at the
same time favored the entry of neutral ships into Russian ports
and virtually excluded, through high protective duties, the importation of silks, wines, and brandies, which were the chief exports of
France to his country.

For the following year and a half both rulers engaged in extensive military and diplomatic preparations for the impending
struggle. Alexander's first intention was to carry the war into
northern Germany, but without assurances of the military support
of the Poles in the grand duchy of Warsaw, the plan was impossible of realization. In an effort to trump Napoleon's bid to the
Polish patriots the czar revived his old plan of establishing an
autonomous Polish kingdom within the Russian empire. The idea
was dropped when the Poles gave clear signs that they would sup-

port their great French patron, and Alexander reconciled himself to waging a defensive campaign within his own country. Napoleon had good cause for satisfaction in the failure of Alexander's efforts. The czar's Polish project weakened the possibility that he would gain the support of Austria and Prussia, while his final decision not to invade Germany ended the danger of a Prussian uprising against French rule.

Patriotic statesmen in Prussia saw in the rift between France and Russia an opportunity to liberate their country from Napoleon's control—provided that Alexander came to their aid and the emperor of Austria joined them in an alliance against Napoleon. Neither condition was fulfilled. The Prussian monarch, hemmed in on all sides by French troops or the troops of France's allies in southern Germany, was obliged to accept the terms of a military alliance that Napoleon thrust upon him. On February 24, 1812, the onerous treaty of alliance was signed. Prussia agreed to furnish 20,000 troops subject to the orders of Napoleon, and to garrison the Silesian forts, the Prussian commandants receiving their orders from the French general staff. The Prussian contingent was to take service anywhere in Europe except Spain, Italy, and Turkey. The French armies had the right to march through Prussian territory, and their generals could requisition supplies, the value of which was to be taken as part payment of Prussia's still unpaid war contributions. Metternich also signed a treaty of alliance with Napoleon. Russia's policy in Poland and along the lower Danube only endangered Austria's interests in the same regions, whereas Napoleon's offers promised to strengthen her position in Germany and Illyria. On March 14, 1812, the military alliance between France and Austria was signed. Austria agreed to furnish 30,000 men, who were to serve under the general direction of Napoleon, but directly under Austrian officers. In return, it was understood that Austria would recover part of the Illyrian provinces, gain territory in Bavaria up to the Inn River, and recover the lost province of Silesia at "the first mistake that Prussia makes."

Successful in winning the support of Prussia and Austria, Napoleon failed to get that of Sweden or the Turkish Empire. In the former country he had to cope with his former marshal Bernadotte, now crown prince and heir apparent to the Swedish throne. Bernadotte guarded his popularity too closely to risk an alliance which would bind Sweden to enforce the Continental System and expose her to the attacks of a Russian army and the British fleet. In April, 1812, Sweden concluded an alliance with Russia, by the terms of which Bernadotte pledged the support of a Swedish corps in northern Germany and received from Russia the promise of Norway at the conclusion of a successful war. A month later the French emperor suffered another diplomatic reverse when the Turkish Empire made peace with Russia. By the provisions of the peace of Bucharest (May 12, 1812) Russia gave up her claims to the two Danubian provinces of Moldavia and Wallachia and accepted instead the province of Bessarabia. The sultan won a lenient peace for his country, and the czar regained, for active use in the north against Napoleon, the use of those Russian armies which had been campaigning against the Turks in the south.

THE OPENING OF THE CAMPAIGN

The campaign opened without any official declaration of war. To Alexander's ultimatum that he would negotiate with France only on the condition that the French evacuate Prussia, Napoleon responded by ordering his troops to advance to the line of the Vistula. He himself repaired in the interim to Dresden, where he received the homage of the rulers of the Confederation of the Rhine. From Dresden he proceeded eastward to Königsberg in East Prussia (May 31), where he gave directions for the advance of the Grand Army into Lithuania. The movement of troops continued steadily from the last days of May until June 23, when the Niemen was reached. For three days the main army, which Napoleon commanded in person, filed over the bridges of the river immediately south of the city of Kovno without meeting any opposition in its course.

The troops that began this great invasion constituted by all odds the largest army that Napoleon or any other general had ever assembled or was to assemble again up to 1914. More than 400,-000 men stood ready to march into Lithuania and, with the reserves in Germany, the total forces operating in this mighty expedition came to the amazing figure of 600,000. The Grand Army of "twenty nations," which included Frenchmen, Germans from Prussia, Austria, and the states of the Confederation of the Rhine, Spaniards, Italians, Dutchmen, Croatians, and Poles, was divided into three large parts. The main army under Napoleon counted

250,000 men and included the guard and the corps under Marshals Davout, Oudinot, Ney, Macdonald, and Murat. All these were French except two Württemberg divisions under Ney and the Prussians under Macdonald. Eugene, the viceroy of Italy, commanded the second army of 80,000 men, which included the Italian and Bavarian corps and a French corps of cavalry. King Jerome of Westphalia was at the head of the third army, also of 80,000 men, which included Poles, Saxons, Westphalians, and a corps of cavalry, partly French and partly Polish. South of the Grand Army were the Austrians at Lemberg, whom Prince Schwarzenberg commanded. Fewer than 200,000 of these soldiers were French, for the best French troops were still in Spain under Masséna and Soult.

If the raising of these great armies was a "supreme example of military tyranny"—for the cause in which they were to lay down their lives was not their own—it was also a masterpiece of organization. Once Napoleon overcame his fleeting misgivings and decided to carry out his plans, he bestirred himself to take all human precautions to provide for the needs of the men. Nothing was left to chance. Siege trains and horses were in readiness to carry the heavy pieces and ammunition trains for the corps. Enormous depots storing both ammunition and food supplies were established in the French garrisons in Germany, along the Oder and the Vistula. Oxen pulled innumerable wagons carrying provisions of rice and wheat, and transports were prepared to ship flour and biscuit by water to Vilna. Not even pontoon bridges were neglected. To avoid carrying fodder for the 150,000 horses, the campaign was delayed until the early summer when the fresh grass grew high in the fields and meadows.

Since the Russians were in ignorance of the exact course that the Napoleonic troops would pursue, they divided their forces to avoid being surprised. One Russian army of 130,000 men under General Barclay de Tolly was stationed to the north of Vilna, while the second Russian army of 43,000 men under Bagration lay south of the Pripet marshes. Still farther south in Volhynia a third Russian army under Tormassov was in the process of formation, though auxiliary forces in Moldavia and in Finland were not yet free to share in the campaign. Napoleon's numerical superiority was considerably greater than he himself realized, and so great indeed that it defeated the plan of campaign that he had worked out. In substance this plan was to drive an ever deepening wedge between the two Russian armies, surround them with superior numbers, and defeat each in detail. The wedge was to be made at Kovno and deepened by the entry of the second and third armies into Lithuania at Grodno. The emperor would then pass the winter at his headquarters in Smolensk, take over Lithuania and unite it with Warsaw, and come to terms with the defeated czar. If the czar, however, failed to come to terms, the campaign would be resumed in the spring of 1813 with Moscow as the final objective of the drive.

It is at once apparent that this plan was predicated upon two assumptions: first, that Napoleon would defeat the Russian armies in Lithuania in 1812, and second, that the Poles of Lithuania would rally to his cause against their Russian masters. But his very numerical superiority allowed the Russians to stumble upon Fabian tactics of defensive warfare which nullified all his expectations. At the same time the Polish patriots failed to greet him with the martial enthusiasm upon which he had counted. Indeed, far from aiding him and flocking to his troops, the benighted peasantry of the endless Lithuanian plains placed totally unexpected difficulties in the path of his advance. Expecting liberators, the peasantry found marauders and pillagers in the army of invasion. In truth the disorder ensuing upon the breakdown of the service of supplies and the laborious advance of the expeditionary forces became marked in the first week of the march into Lithuania. Recruits who were left behind formed pillaging bands, while those who faced starvation when food trains stuck in the mud and flour transports ran aground in the shallow waters of the Niemen fell like a plague of locusts upon the land. While these events embittered the peasantry against the invaders, Napoleon chilled the ardor of the patriotic leaders by giving evasive answers to their request for a proclamation of Polish independence. Such a proclamation, he reasoned, not only would be premature, but would surely cost him the military support of Austria which had its own reasons for objecting to the restoration of the kingdom of Poland.

THE ADVANCE TO MOSCOW AND THE RETREAT

By the time Napoleon reached Vilna, Barclay was on his way to a great fortified camp at Drissa on the Dvina, where he awaited the coming of Bagration. When Barclay learned that Bagration had retreated in a wide detour southward without daring to fight his way through, he too fell back eastward along the Dvina. Had he stayed on at Drissa to face Napoleon the entire course of the campaign would have been different, but he gave way, leaving there only his right wing under Wittgenstein to hold back Marshal Oudinot. Napoleon followed in relentless pursuit, driving his men along the blackened plains under a merciless July sun. Every day the heat, disease, desertion, and hunger took their toll of his men—and of the horses of the cavalry that dropped under their riders. For a few days in the last week of July the emperor's hopes ran high, for he thought that he would at least have the pitched battle that he sought. Again he was doomed to disappoint-

ment. Barclay had made a stand at Vitebsk, counting, as earlier at Drissa, on being supported by Bagration. Once more, however, the French [1] numerical superiority forced the latter to retreat eastward, now by a long detour toward Smolensk. The effect of this maneuver was to dissuade Barclay from offering battle. In the dead of night, July 27, his troops abandoned their line of battle and on the morrow no foe opposed the French advance.

The demoralization of his troops forced Napoleon to order a two weeks' rest at Vitebsk. It was high time. The muster was now reduced by almost a third. Moreover, the Prussians had been dispatched northward to Riga, while the Saxons were ordered south to reënforce the Austrians against the third Russian army, which meantime had advanced from Volhynia. Oudinot had failed to

[1] The third French army was now commanded by Davout. Jerome had been sent back for his failure to coöperate energetically with Davout in the first attempt to cut Bagration off.

budge Wittgenstein at Drissa, even after receiving reënforcements under Marshal Saint-Cyr. And the fourth Russian army in Moldavia was now free to take part in the campaign against Napoleon. Still Napoleon pressed on, confident that the retreating foe would make a stand at Smolensk, the city of the Holy Virgin and the gateway to old Russia. Popular sentiment did compel the czar to give orders to Barclay to defend Smolensk, but sound military sense compelled Barclay to fight only a rear-guard action when he saw the possibility of being outflanked by the superior French troops. On the 17th of August Napoleon's advance guard entered the city, but the enemy had escaped him and the half-burned city was smoldering in its ruins.

At this crisis Napoleon made a disastrous blunder. He was urged by his subordinates to adhere to his first plan of establishing winter quarters at Smolensk. He might have retreated to East Prussia. But victory had thus far eluded him and the prospect of humiliating inactivity held no appeal for him. Retreat he would not, for retreat was a confession of failure. There were several months of good campaigning weather left: why not press on to Moscow? Under the sway of this obsession for a decisive victory he threw caution to the winds. He defied the force of patriotic resistance that welled up in the hearts of the Russians, and he defied the forces of nature, of distance, and weather. On September 7 his rapid advance brought him face to face with the Russians at Borodino on the Moskwa. Kutusov, a popular Russian hero, had replaced Barclay as commander of the Russian troops with instructions to block the road to Moscow. He occupied a long, extended position on the hills back of Borodino. There was a small valley to his right and sloping ground before him, where he had thrown up earthworks. Napoleon attacked him directly, in his left and center, eschewing his favorite flanking tactics for fear the enemy would retreat. There, at Borodino, in a horrible carnage that yielded 70,-000 victims in dead and wounded he forced Kutusov to give up his redoubt. Borodino was no victory, but the way to Moscow was clear. On the 14th the advance guard of the French entered the western gates of the holy city.

At Moscow, the goal of his efforts, Napoleon's cup of misery was filled to the brim. The city was virtually deserted by its inhabitants. No deputation waited upon him to conclude terms. Even before the French made their way into the city, they had discerned from afar the clouds of smoke that rose to greet them. Two days after their entry the entire city was aflame, fired one knows not for a certainty by whom; and within a week three-quarters of Moscow lay in ashes. Kutusov's men, who lay south of the city, pounced upon French stragglers in quest of food. Communications with Smolensk, where Napoleon had left a garrison were difficult and precarious. Alexander refused to treat with Napoleon. Did not his subjects thirst to exterminate the unhappy foe? Did not Baron Stein at his side counsel firmness against the invaders? Had he not received assurances of the support of Bernadotte's Swedish corps, of Wittgenstein's numerical superiority over the French at Drissa, and of the junction of the army from Moldavia with Tormassov's troops that engaged the Austrians? For five long weeks of suspense Napoleon tarried in the doomed city, and on October 18 he finally gave the order for the retreat.

The retreat began on the 19th, the most famous and the most terrible retreat of history. The first check came when Kutusov blocked Napoleon's retreat along the southern and the shorter route to Smolensk and forced him to fall back along the line of his advance. On the heels of the French, as they made their way past the charnel house at Borodino, were Kutusov and the Cossacks; before them the oncoming winter; in their midst, hunger, cold, and despair. When they reached Smolensk, half of the army of 100,000 men had disappeared; and still Napoleon could not rest for long. At Smolensk, Napoleon learned that Victor, whom he had left there with a garrison, had suffered defeat at the hands of Wittgenstein when he fell back to give help to Saint-Cyr. With the line of the Dvina and the Dnieper now untenable, for the Russian armies of the north and south would try to effect a junction, Napoleon could only continue his retreat lest he be encircled.

The retreat then became a ghastly rout, with only 25,000 men left to answer the roll call. The real Russian winter was setting in, though the occasional thaws that turned the roads into wildernesses of mud were perhaps only slightly less deadly than the cold. To gain greater mobility the French burned their pontoon bridges, confident that they would at least gain safety beyond the bridge at Borissov on the Beresina. Then the Russian armies from the south wrested the town of Borissov from its defenders and, before losing it again to Marshal Oudinot, burned its only bridge. Through the junction with Victor and Oudinot the strength of the

French main army had again risen to 40,000. In the last week of November came the murderous crossing of the Beresina, when Oudinot's ruse and the heroism of his engineers enabled the French to build two wooden bridges across the river. There the Russian armies pursuing the French and the Russian forces in front of the French turned a shattering fire against the retreating foe. One bridge broke down under the weight of numbers and the French rear guard fired the remaining one in time to escape, but too soon to allow the thousands of stragglers to cross. The French losses at the Beresina were stupendous: half of the army was gone. By the 16th of December, of the 100,000 men who had left Moscow and the thousands who had joined them from garrisons on the route, some 20,000 human skeletons staggered back to Kovno on the Niemen. Of these not more than 1000 of the Guard remained in orderly formation. These 20,000, the two wings under Schwarzenberg and Macdonald, the Poles (who crossed the Niemen elsewhere), and stragglers, amounting altogether to about 100,000 men, were all that were left of the Grand Army. In all, 500,000 were lost: 250,000 lay dead in Russia; 100,000 were prisoners; the remainder were wounded or had deserted. Napoleon was not at Kovno to witness the end of his venture. On December 5 he had left the army, turning the command over to Murat, and sped back to Paris, which he reached on the 18th.

NAPOLEON'S NEW PREPARATIONS

The last bulletin of the Grand Army, dated December 3, barely preceded the emperor to his capital. It is significant as much for what it concealed of the disaster and Napoleon's own blame for it as for the hints it threw out of the true magnitude of the horrible retreat. Despite the official censorship during the course of the campaign inklings of the French reverses had appeared in Paris, and it was partly to counteract in person the disquieting rumors that Napoleon had entrusted his army to Murat and sped back to Paris. Not only rumors, moreover, but the ferment caused by an abortive republican plot that had broken out during his absence (October 23). The plot had miscarried, and the conspirators had been executed, as he well knew while he was still in Lithuania; but the significance of the situation had not been lost to him. During the momentary flurry of the plot no one had thought of his son, the infant king of Rome, as his successor. On the contrary the idea of a provisional government seemed acceptable. Nothing could have illustrated more graphically the fundamental lack of attachment to the Napoleonic dynasty and the fragile bases of the imperial régime. Napoleon's provision against his absence or his possible death was to force through a Senatus Consultum (February 15, 1813), which designated, in that eventuality, the Empress Marie Louise as regent for her minor son.

Talleyrand's comment upon the Russian disaster reveals his keen understanding of the European situation. He remarked, with apparent casualness, "Now is the moment to overthrow him [Napoleon]," meaning that, if the European powers could present a united front against the emperor, his downfall was certain. Their inability at that moment to reach a basic understanding with one another only postponed the final outcome, but it gave Napoleon a respite and an opportunity to display anew his remarkable genius as administrator and military organizer. No one may presume to deny that his spirits were dampened, but they were not crushed. He had no sympathy with the desire of many of his subjects for a peace that would end his sway in Europe. He would consider a peace that preserved his conquests for France, a peace that in his eyes at least would not weaken his country. In short, he planned to renew his campaign against his two enemies, Russia and England, which had come to terms in the summer of 1812. All his actions subsequent to his return to Paris not only indicate his intention of maintaining intact his European domination, but illustrate the almost awe-inspiring efficacy of his preparations for a new campaign.

His first hope had been to keep the army under Murat beyond the line of the Niemen at Vilna; but that was an empty hope, for the stragglers retreated across the Niemen to Königsberg. Nor did they have the support of the Prussians under Macdonald or of the Austrians and Saxons under Schwarzenberg. Undismayed, Napoleon appealed first for the support of the government in his attempt to raise a fresh army. The appeal to the administrators and the legislators, couched as it was in a heroic vein, with careful allusions to the fact that he alone had once saved the state from anarchy, carried weight. The assurances of loyalty and devotion that he received quieted whatever misgivings he may have had. Even more, when Murat had to give up the line of the Vistula and fall back to Posen, a complaisant Senate voted the necessary decree to strengthen his retreating forces. By calling upon the conscripts of 1813 and having at his disposal for the spring the class of 1814, by recalling 100,000 men who for various reasons had been exempted from the draft, and by gaining the right to use the National Guard for service outside France, Napoleon counted on raising a new army of 600,000 men for the spring campaign. Decrees, however, were not enough; the support of the people was essential to the realization of his plans.

Hence he took special pains to bolster up his waning prestige. He explained anew how the cold had destroyed his army, and that, after he had turned the command over to Murat. That he might weaken the ill will of many million conscientious Catholics, particularly in the west and in the south, he made an agreement with the imprisoned pope and signed a new concordat in January, 1813. The settlement scarcely outlived the tolling of the church bells that chimed the glad news, yet the proclamation of peace between Napoleon and the papacy appreciably aided the emperor's military preparations. Simultaneously, he gave assurances—wholly specious assurances, in passing—to the taxpayers that their financial obligations would not be increased by his military activities, so that they might support him in his preparations. Then in a speech to the Corps législatif in February, which was in the nature of a public communication to the entire nation, he summed up his efforts and spoke optimistically of the renewed support that his allies would give him. For the most part his faith in the allies was not belied, but in the attitude of the Prussian people and of the Austrian government he was to discover overwhelming evidence that heroic exertions, surpassing everything that he had ever done, would be required to maintain his domination in Europe.

Preparations for the War of Liberation

The amazing rapidity with which Napoleon pursued his military preparations after the destruction of the Grand Army made it extremely difficult for the princes of the Confederation of the Rhine to disregard their obligations to him. Only in Prussia and in Austria were the consequences of that great disaster quickly utilized against the French. Metternich at all times maintained full control of Austria's foreign policy, but Frederick William III, timorous and hesitant as ever, followed the lead given by others—by

Russia, by the Prussian commander of the forces that had operated
with Napoleon, and by the national uprising in northern Germany
against Napoleon.

Alexander himself was at first undecided as to his future policy,
but ultimately, encouraged by his two intimate advisers, Baron
Stein and the young Russian diplomat Nesselrode, he decided not
to conclude peace single-handed with the French, but to ally himself with Prussia for the purpose of liberating Germany and restoring the balance of power on the Continent. The first step toward
the rapprochement of Prussia and Russia came shortly after the
close of the Russian campaign. On December 30, 1812, General
Yorck, the commander of the Prussian contingent of 18,000 men
who had fought under Marshal Macdonald, made a momentous
decision. Acting "according to circumstances," as he had been instructed, he signed the military convention of Tauroggen, by which
hostilities between the Prussians and the Russians were suspended
until March 1, 1813, pending further orders from Frederick William, and the territory immediately surrounding the Prussian corps
was neutralized. Out of fear of the French garrisons in his country, Frederick William disavowed the action, but it was too late.
A subordinate Prussian officer, acting on his own initiative, had
forced the French to retreat to the line of the Vistula and made
possible the occupation of East Prussia by the Russians. Early in
January the latter occupied the city of Königsberg, and a fortnight
later Baron Stein, armed with a commission from the czar, arrived
to begin the organization of the military resources of East and
West Prussia.

Heartened by Stein's energetic efforts, in particular his measure calling for the levy of a volunteer army (*Landwehr*) of 20,000
men, Frederick William began to act. Quitting his capital at Berlin—with Hardenberg offering explanations to Napoleon that his
monarch had left to raise the Prussian quota to assist Napoleon in
the coming campaign—he rode off to Breslau in Silesia, where he
issued a call for volunteers. A few days later the troops of the line
in Silesia and Pomerania were mobilized for active service. And
before the month of February had run its course he reached a
definite military agreement with the Russians. On March 1, 1813,
the treaty of Kalisch, the cornerstone of the final alliance against
Napoleon, was ratified. It provided for the restoration of Prussia
to a territorial position as strong as that of 1806, but only part of

the provinces incorporated in the grand duchy of Warsaw was to be returned. This part was a strip large enough to connect Silesia with West Prussia. The armies of the two countries were to co-operate in the coming campaign, and no peace was to be made without common accord. The territorial dispositions left Russia free to reconstruct an independent Poland, but they indicated also that Prussia would find compensation in Saxony, an arrangement which was mutually satisfactory.

The terms of the treaty were communicated to Austria, Sweden, and England, along with an invitation to join the allies, and then published. On March 17, 1813, Prussia declared war upon France, and the long-desired War of Liberation began. On that day Stein made his appearance at Breslau. Frederick William addressed a moving appeal to his people, to which there came a vibrantly enthusiastic response. Patriotic feeling had been running high ever since the news of Tauroggen, which was like "a flash of lightning that transfigured the entire horizon," and the first appeal for volunteers required no repetition. Especially high-spirited were the students and the professors at the newly founded universities of Berlin and Breslau, but everywhere in Prussia the soldiers of the regular army and volunteers hastened to take their places in the ranks. This was one of the greatest moments in Prussia's history, a moment comparable to the stirring days in France in 1792, when patriotic resentment against the rule of the foreigner raised ordinary mortals above their normal stature and inspired them with the courage of heroes.

The two allies also issued a proclamation to the princes and the peoples of the Confederation of the Rhine, appealing for their aid in the liberation of northern Germany from the French. A central administrative commission of four members, with Stein at the head, was formed and endowed with full powers to govern the states of the Confederation, to raise troops and make military requisitions.

The signing of a subsidy treaty between England and Bernadotte, crown prince of Sweden (March 3), strengthened the arrangements of the allies. In return for English subsidies Bernadotte promised to put 30,000 Swedish troops in the field for the German campaign. England also maintained an earlier arrangement not of her making, promising Norway to Sweden, an agreement which had the not unforeseen consequence of strengthening Denmark's alliance with Napoleon.

Meantime Metternich utilized the French disaster in Russia to weaken the bond of the Franco-Austrian military alliance of 1812. In October, 1812, during the invasion of Russia, Metternich's fears of French success led him to conclude a secret arrangement with Russia; but now the fear of Russian preponderance had supplanted Metternich's fears of a French victory. By removing the theater of war from Austria, he could husband his country's resources until that day when her strength could be employed against the greater peril, whether Russian or French. Consequently in acknowledging Napoleon's request for additional troops he proposed Austria's mediation toward a general pacification. Some time later, acting under instructions from Vienna, Schwarzenberg, safe in Warsaw with the Austrian contingent that had fought in the Russian campaign, signed an armistice with the Russians. His pretext was the necessity of saving his troops from the advancing Russians. The consequences were the retreat of the French from the line of the Vistula and their withdrawal to the line of the Oder. From a diplomatic point of view the Austrian armistice with the Russians effectively, if not legally, terminated the Franco-Austrian alliance of 1812.

Two months later, on March 29, Metternich advanced his program. By a secret military convention with the Russians the Austrian troops in Warsaw were permitted to retire from the duchy, first to Cracow and then to Bohemia. In Bohemia they could join with an Austrian reserve army, and the combined forces could be employed to enforce the policy that Metternich had now adopted, the policy of *armed* mediation. While the Austrian troops were retiring into Bohemia, Metternich conducted masterly diplomatic campaigns on two fronts, with France and with England, masking his ultimate intentions so completely as to bewilder his compatriots at Vienna.

Yet the main lines of his diplomacy are clearly visible—a diminished, but not too greatly weakened France, and a restoration of the old Germanic system sufficient to give Austria her former influence. Though the position of Austria was uppermost in his mind, he believed that a confederation of German states was necessary both as a part of the European state system and as a barrier to external aggression. Hence his steadfast insistence upon a strengthened Prussia, large enough to hold Russia in check on the east. Under this separatist arrangement of a German confederation—as opposed both to Stein's conception of a united Germany and to the idea of an Austrian empire in Germany—Austria would have many advantages and few responsibilities.[2] In order to reach his goal he needed first to cut himself loose entirely from his bond to France. And this he accomplished in April, when he formally announced Austria's position as an "armed mediator" in the coming struggle between France and her enemies.

THE SPRING CAMPAIGN AND AUSTRIAN MEDIATION

The spring campaign opened in Saxony with Austria observing an armed neutrality. The French troops, numbering 250,000 men, were concentrated in the angle formed by the Saale and the Elbe, threatening both Dresden and Berlin. Napoleon planned to carry the war to the Oder and relieve his garrisons there, but the enemy invaded Saxony. On May 2 his untried troops defeated the Russo-Prussian forces at Lützen, but his lack of cavalry prevented him from turning the enemy's flank and making the victory decisive. Metternich, however, prepared to reap the fruits of Lützen, for with the Austrian army in Bohemia threatening Napoleon's right and the new levies of the allies coming up, his policy of armed mediation was greatly strengthened. On May 21, at Bautzen on the Silesian frontier, Napoleon again defeated the allies, but once more the victory was indecisive for want of cavalry. After Bautzen, on June 4, Napoleon agreed to the terms of an armistice which was to last until July 20.

The armistice was a gigantic military blunder, as Napoleon later recognized. It afforded him an opportunity to rally his raw troops, maintain his hold upon Saxony, and draw up reënforcements, especially cavalry from Spain. Nevertheless it strengthened the position of his adversaries more than it did his own. It enabled Russia and Prussia to make use of their reserves, and it gave Metternich the time required for the completion of Austrian military preparations and of his own diplomatic arrangements with Prussia and

[2] The Austrian-Saxon treaty of the spring of 1813—which Saxony later repudiated because of Napoleon's military threats—illustrates Metternich's effort to assure the secondary German states that freedom from French tyranny would not mean subjection to Austrian domination.

Russia. In brief, Metternich, who had first proposed an armistice after Lützen, so that he might offer his mediation for peace, now reached an understanding with Napoleon's enemies on the basis of a common and united offensive against him.

As a mediator acceptable to Russia and Prussia, Metternich submitted to the two allies the conditions that he was prepared to lay before Napoleon. The four indispensable points were the dissolution of the grand duchy of Warsaw,[3] the enlargement of Prussia through this dissolution and by the cession of Danzig, the restitution of the Illyrian provinces to Austria, and the independence of the Hanseatic cities in northwestern Germany. In addition, Austria was prepared to support two other points "with all the weight of her mediation"; namely, the dissolution of the Confederation of the Rhine and the reconstruction of Prussia to the position she had held in 1806. However, under the pressure of the allies—with whom the conditions of a triple alliance had been discussed for more than a month—Metternich had to concede that these points sufficed merely as a preliminary program. On June 27 at Reichenbach in Silesia a secret treaty was signed by the representatives of Austria, Russia, and Prussia binding Austria to declare war upon France if the minimum proposals were not accepted by Napoleon by July 20; but Austria agreed also to support the additional conditions put forward by her allies. These were the separation of Holland from France, the restoration of the Bourbons in Spain, and the exclusion of French influence from Italy.

The shadow of England's financial and naval power was thus thrown upon the diplomatic screen of Europe. Some two weeks earlier than this treaty of Reichenbach, though in the same city, England had signed treaties with Prussia and Russia, by which she promised them financial subsidies in return for their engagement not to conclude a separate peace with France. There was nothing in these arrangements between England and the two continental powers that referred openly to Holland, Spain, or Italy. But the instructions forwarded by Castlereagh, the English secretary of state for foreign affairs, to the English diplomats on the Continent, which they duly communicated to Prussia and Russia, were explicit enough. English subsidies would not be given for the achievement of such a peace as Metternich had in mind. Castlereagh worked for

---

[3] Austria's demands relating to Poland were directed also against the czar's plan for taking a larger part than he had formerly had.

a peace that would maintain the colonial and maritime supremacy of Great Britain, fulfill England's obligation to her European allies (i.e., Spain, Portugal, Sicily, and Sweden), establish a military barrier on the eastern frontiers of France, and create a European alliance that would guarantee the continuance of that peace. It was the need of British subsidies and the realization of Castlereagh's policy that compelled Russia and Prussia to insist upon those additional demands which Austria accepted in the treaty of Reichenbach of June 27.

Still concealing his ultimate intentions as well as Austria's commitments to the allies, Metternich held his famous and stormy interview with Napoleon at the latter's headquarters at Dresden. There it was agreed verbally that the armistice should be extended until August 10, that the Franco-Austrian alliance of 1812 should be considered defunct, that Austrian mediation would be accepted, and that the specific proposals of Austria would be stated and discussed at a peace congress to be held at Prague.

The news of the latest military developments in the Iberian Peninsula reached Napoleon and the allies shortly after he had accepted Metternich's mediation. From 1809, when Sir Arthur Wellesley, the future duke of Wellington, assumed full control of the British expeditionary forces, the fortune of the French declined. Against that dogged commander Napoleon was to send his best marshals—Victor, Jourdan, Soult, Masséna, Marmont—and 300,000 of his grizzled veterans, but nothing availed him. Methodically Wellington intrenched himself in Portugal, and from Portugal he pursued his grim advance into Spain. In the spring of 1813 Joseph Bonaparte, the titular ruler of Spain, fled from his capital at Madrid, but Wellington caught up with him and his treasure vans and store trains at Vittoria, near the French frontier, and overwhelmed the fleeing foe (June 21, 1813). The disaster at Vittoria, which sealed the fate of Spain and exposed southern France to Wellington, was the news that Napoleon and the allies received on the eve of the peace congress at Prague. Metternich could now safely drop the mask of armed neutrality and come out openly into the opposition against Napoleon.

The Congress of Prague could not be other than a hollow formality. Napoleon's hope of making a separate peace with Russia failed of realization, for in July, at the castle of Trachenberg, Alexander, Frederick William, and Bernadotte drew up the allies' plan of campaign. Napoleon delayed sending Caulaincourt to Prague until the end of July, and it was not until August 8 that Metternich presented his terms. These included the four points of his minimum program and in addition the supplementary two points, couched in the form of an ultimatum. If by midnight of August 10 Napoleon failed to accept them, Austria would join the allies. Caulaincourt's letter, pleading with the emperor to accede to the ultimatum, reached Napoleon on the 9th. He drafted a reply, accepting part of the terms, meantime bidding the Austrian envoy to send a courier to Prague with the news that a reply was on the way, and that Napoleon was ready to conclude peace. Napoleon's reply was at hand on the 11th, but at the stroke of midnight of the 10th, Metternich announced that the congress had ended, and on August 12, Emperor Francis declared war upon the French.

The Fall Campaign and the Liberation of Germany

The diplomatic die was cast, and the military struggle began. Napoleon had employed the armistice to draw up his reënforcements, and he now put 440,000 men into the field. The main army, which he commanded in person from his headquarters at the strongly fortified city of Dresden, guarded the line of the Elbe; Ney and Macdonald commanded the troops in Silesia; Oudinot was north of him at Wittenberg, and Davout had his base at Hamburg. The Bavarian corps under Wrede was at Munich, while Eugene was dispatched to gather an army in northern Italy. West of the Elbe, guarding the emperor's communications were Jerome in Westphalia, Augereau at Frankfort, and Kellermann at Mainz.

The allies had also completed their concentration. The main army of Austrians, Prussians, and Russians was in Bohemia, south of the Erzgebirge, 250,000 men under the supreme command of Schwarzenberg. With this army were the allied rulers—Alexander, Francis, and Frederick William. Blücher commanded the Silesian army of 100,000 Prussians and Russians, while Bernadotte in northern Germany commanded an army of 150,000 Swedes, Germans, and Russians. There were also 25,000 Austrians on the Bavarian front to hold Wrede and 50,000 more in Styria to head off Eugene. Napoleon's plan of campaign was conceived on his boldest lines. With his forces in Saxony and Silesia he would fall upon the forces of Schwarzenberg and Blücher, while from the north Oudinot and Davout would sweep on to Berlin and the fortresses on the Oder, which were still defended by their compatriots. Wrede was to advance into Bohemia and Eugene through Styria to Vienna. The plan bore all the Napoleonic marks of clarity and imagination; but its execution was miserable, partly out of Napoleon's own indecisive fumbling and partly because the allied plan of campaign circumvented his project.

The campaign opened with a resounding victory for the French. Napoleon drove Blücher deep into Silesia, left Macdonald there to hold him, and then marched west with 100,000 men to cut off Schwarzenberg, who had crossed the mountain passes and was moving down the valley of the Elbe. Informed that Dresden was endangered, Napoleon left a corps under Vandamme to wait for Schwarzenberg and made one of his most extraordinary marches, returning to Dresden, ninety miles away, in seventy-two hours, in time to hurl Schwarzenberg back (August 26–27). This was his last great triumph, for then the French reverses began. Oudinot, striking northeast from Wittenberg, was checked by Bülow at Grossbeeren and driven back to the Elbe. Blücher defeated Macdonald in Silesia, scattered his army, and advanced upon Bautzen. Vandamme, in pursuit of the retreating forces of Schwarzenberg, was surrounded by superior forces in the mountains and forced to surrender his entire corps. A week later Ney, who had replaced Oudinot, was defeated at Dennewitz by Bernadotte. In a few days Napoleon had lost the offensive. The brilliant plan of campaign that he had drawn up was now useless.

He stayed on at Dresden, sallying forth against Blücher and Schwarzenberg but incapable for some reason of giving up his old plan and formulating a new one. While desertion and illness cut heavily into his ranks, the allies converged slowly upon Leipzig in order to force him out of the angle of the Elbe and the Saale. The army of Bohemia moved northward; the army from the north advanced southward, while Blücher, by a daring flank march, crossed the Elbe to join with it at Wittenberg (October 3). Napoleon then hoped to cut the communications of the enemy both with Berlin and Bohemia, but as the iron ring drew closer around Leipzig he realized that the decisive engagement would take place there. He was anxious for battle, for only a clean-cut victory could restore the fading morale of his men. The allies outnumbered him, but he was Napoleon, and he had unity of command against their divided control. His hopes lay in defeating the army of Bohemia south of Leipzig before Blücher and Bernadotte could arrive to engage the French north of the city.

The struggle began on October 16 in the villages south of Leipzig. In the desperate fighting against the army of Bohemia the French held back Schwarzenberg's troops, but their triumph was not decisive. Napoleon had already summoned Marmont and Ney from the north to lead the final charge when his trained ear heard the rumble of artillery fire, and he knew that Blücher had arrived. The most savage fighting of the day was at Möckern, north of Leipzig, where for hours Marmont held Blücher at bay, only to yield before the final onslaught and fall back in disorder upon Leipzig. The murderous fighting of the day had cost the combatants more than 60,000 lives. On the 17th the allies were ready to renew the battle, but Napoleon did not attack, and they took advantage of the respite to rest the men and await the coming of Bernadotte and Bennigsen. The delay was a blunder of the first order. Napoleon should have retreated at once or renewed the battle immediately against the weakened army of Bohemia in the south. He did neither, but remained inactive at Leipzig, waiting —so it seemed—for the blow to strike. It fell on the 18th when Bernadotte and Bennigsen had arrived to fill in the gap between Schwarzenberg and Blücher. Again the carnage was murderous, 50,-000 men falling in the struggle which ended with Blücher driving the French back into the city. That night, after the Saxon contingent had gone over to the enemy, Napoleon ordered a general retreat. All night and during the following day his men streamed through the three eastern gates of the city, fighting stubbornly against their pursuers in the narrow streets of Leipzig. There was only one gate at the western end of the city by which they might escape, and to make the confusion and order still greater the narrow bridge over the Pleisse River was blown up.

Such was Leipzig, "the battle of the nations." In the four days' fighting more than 120,000 men had fallen. Napoleon's position was critical, almost desperate. Had the allies been capable of energetic action they might have cut off his retreat through a hostile country and kept him from reaching the Rhine. Only the Bavarians offered serious opposition at Hanau near the Rhine, but the French cut their way through to safety. The Bavarians were no longer the allies of Napoleon. Even before the battle of Leipzig was fought their ruler had signed a treaty with Austria, severing his bonds with the Confederation of the Rhine and promising a force of 30,000 men in return for the recognition of his political independence and territorial integrity (October 8, 1813). It was in conformity with this treaty that the Bavarians had blocked the retreat of the French toward the Rhine. A few days after the engagement at Hanau the latter reached the Rhine and safety. Fewer than 100,000 soldiers and stragglers had escaped. In slightly more than a year two Imperial armies, amounting altogether to almost one million men, had been destroyed.

The overwhelming victory at Leipzig was the military seal of Metternich's diplomacy, for at Töplitz in Bohemia, on September 9, the three allies signed treaties which confirmed their earlier agreement concerning the prosecution of the war. On October 9, Austria and England signed a similar treaty, based upon the conditions submitted at Prague. In addition, these treaties recognized the full and unconditional independence of the states lying between the frontiers of the reconstituted Prussia and Austria. This provision marked the defeat of Stein's patriotic dream of German unification and guaranteed a leading position for Austria in southern Germany. Before the year was over, Austria had given assurances of territorial integrity and autonomy to Bavaria and Württemberg. To avoid discord no arrangement was made in these treaties for the future settlement of liberated Europe. This was to be the work of Castlereagh in the following spring. Meantime the risks of dissension had to be avoided.

The battle of Leipzig and the retreat of the French to the Rhine had liberated Germany. The Confederation of the Rhine was ended. After Bavaria other states made their peace with the allies. The kingdom of Westphalia came to an end with Jerome's flight to the Rhine. The grand duchy of Berg and the grand duchy of Frankfort were dissolved. From Frankfort, the seat of the central administrative commission, Stein ruled over the territory of the former Confederation. The extent of his authority and the vigor with which he employed it explains why some of his supporters wished to have him elected emperor of Germany. Yet the crafty Metternich, who hated Stein and regarded him as a revolutionary firebrand, had already rendered Stein's program of unity impossible of execution.

Napoleon not only lost Germany, but suffered reverses elsewhere which, for the first time since 1799, exposed France to invasion. Bülow invaded Holland, and the prince of Orange made his entry into Amsterdam. The Austrians defeated Eugene in northern Italy and regained the territory at the head of the Adriatic. Wellington pushed aside the last French barriers in northern Spain and led 80,000 men across the muddy Bidassoa into France.

THE INVASION OF FRANCE

The allied armies occupied the line of the Rhine, and the sovereigns and their ministers were at Frankfort early in November. The invasion of France was in order, but the allies were uncertain as to how the French would take an invasion. They knew that the French people cared little for the Grand Empire, but France itself was a different matter. The allies could remember 1793. Besides there was discord among them. The czar was for pressing on to Paris, despite the advice of his military staff, but the other sovereigns hesitated to continue the campaign in France. Francis I was reluctant to make fresh sacrifices of men and money. Frederick William also drew back, while Bernadotte, with his eye to the possibility of succeeding Napoleon on the French throne, had no strong desire to alienate his former countrymen. Largely from those considerations and also to win Napoleon's assent to terms which Metternich knew would not be kept, the Austrian diplomat offered to make peace if Napoleon would accept the natural frontiers for France. As Metternich himself avows in his Memoirs, the offer was disingenuous, for all the allies would not have adhered to it. But he counted upon Napoleon's refusal, knowing well that the French emperor was no tyro at such double-edged diplomacy. Napoleon realized at once that Metternich was setting a trap for him. If he accepted the offer in good faith and were subsequently forced to take less than the natural frontiers, his prestige in France would be ruined; if he refused it outright, he would shoulder the onus of refusing a good peace and needlessly prolonging the war.

Napoleon countered Metternich's move by proposing a peace congress. Then, after a delay of a fortnight, through Caulaincourt he declared his willingness to accept the offer as the basis of negotiations. The delay and Napoleon's first evasive reply served

Metternich almost as well as a blunt refusal, for now he could withdraw the offer, feeling assured that it had accomplished the purpose for which it was intended. It had become known to men in influential circles at Paris, such men as Talleyrand, Pasquier, and Baron Louis, who grasped the import of Metternich's move. Napoleon's cautious reply convinced them that he meant to fight on for his universal empire. The only safe course for them to pursue was therefore to cut themselves off from the emperor and negotiate behind the scenes for the restoration of the Bourbons. Such a policy had the advantage of being patriotic and profitable: patriotic because a Bourbon restoration undoubtedly would insure lenient terms for France from the conquerors and profitable be-cause it would keep them in power.

Metternich was now in a position to appeal to the French over the head of Napoleon, for he could represent the emperor's evasive answer as the equivalent of a refusal of his own generous offer. Accordingly, on December 1, the allies issued a manifesto subsequently known as the Declaration of Frankfort in which they announced to the French people that they were not at war with France, "but with that haughtily announced preponderance . . . which Napoleon has for too long a time exercised outside of the boundaries of his empire." In other words, they distinguished clearly between the French people and Napoleon. Then, unable to state explicitly that Napoleon had refused their offer, for he had not actually done so, they used an ambiguous phrase to convey the impression *to the French people* that Napoleon had refused: "An attitude reënforced by the assent of all the sovereigns and princes of Germany has not had any influence upon the conditions of peace." Such being the case, the blame for their invasion of France lay not with them, who were anxious to avoid it, but with Napoleon himself. Since Napoleon had refused peace on terms which offered France "an extent of territory which France never knew under her kings," the allies meant to press on. The phrase, "an extent of territory which France never knew under her kings," was no doubt an intimation that if and when the kings were restored, France would be restricted to her boundaries of 1789.

Metternich's adroitness and Napoleon's manifest intention to continue the struggle contributed alike to turning public opinion against the emperor. Still bent on victory before concluding peace, he alienated many of his supporters by his tardy acceptance of negotiations as well as by his demand for a new levy of 300,000 men. The deputies of the Corps législatif protested vehemently in a report which drew loud applause in the assembly, but the publication of which was forbidden by Napoleon. The shortage of funds was an additional handicap to Napoleon, as the day had passed when the emperor could levy tribute upon dependent states. The French imperial government bonds were quoted fifty per cent off. A domestic crisis was approaching, while the party of peace worked furiously behind the political scenes to end Napoleon's rule.

The spring campaign (1814) postponed the solution of the internal difficulties in France, but the intrigues of Talleyrand and his group continued while the guns were being fired. The events of the first three months of 1814 cannot be followed without taking into account the close interdependence of intrigue, warfare, and diplomacy. Three allied armies invaded France, from Switzerland, the middle Rhine, and Belgium, and by the end of January had pushed the French generals into the basin between the Marne and the Seine. Napoleon had gone to extremes to raise a new army, but never was the total of his troops greater than 90,000, and in most of the engagements it was considerably less. The position of the allied armies made it impossible for him to attempt to organize an army of the interior. His small army was woefully short of guns and ammunition, and his marshals were grumpy and discouraged. Yet he fought one of the greatest campaigns of his long military career, a model illustration of what a general of genius with a small army operating on interior lines could do against vastly superior forces under a divided command.

His victories only postponed the day of reckoning. True, they spread panic in the headquarters of the allies, where dissensions—over Saxony and Warsaw and over the question of a new government in France—more than once threatened to destroy their coalition. Napoleon's victories ultimately strengthened the efforts of Castlereagh, who had come in person to the Continent and was at that moment working desperately to compose the differences of the allied leaders and bind them together in a comprehensive alliance. It was Castlereagh who prevailed upon the Austrians to drop the idea of an armistice and continue fighting, and upon the Russian monarch to continue negotiations while fighting. These parleys were conducted during February and March at Châtillon, where twice Caulaincourt was bidden by Napoleon to reject the allied terms. Those terms were no longer "the bases of Frankfort," but the conditions of France limited to her old frontiers (as of 1792) and excluded from all discussions relative to the new organization of Europe. Meantime Napoleon was winning his electrifying victories over Blücher on the Marne and holding Schwarzenberg in check on the Seine.

At last, on March 9, Castlereagh gained his great objective. By the comprehensive treaty of Chaumont (signed on March 9, but antedated to March 1), the four allies reached an understanding without which their dissensions would have forced them to make a peace "which, sooner or later, would have left Europe again at the mercy of Napoleon." They agreed to use all their resources in the vigorous prosecution of the war, if Napoleon refused the terms now proposed. No separate negotiations would be begun or treaties signed with the enemy. Great Britain promised a subsidy of £5,000,000 for the remainder of 1814. The allies reserved to themselves the right to work together, after the conclusion of peace, to guarantee its continuance, agreeing that if one of them were then attacked by France, each of the others would intervene with 60,000 troops. Lastly, the treaty was to be binding for twenty years, with the option of renewal three years before its expiration. This treaty was Castlereagh's greatest achievement; it united Europe against Napoleon. And its secret articles concerning the settlement in Europe were substantially those incorporated three weeks later in the first treaty of Paris between the allies and France.

Negotiations ended on March 19, when the congress at Châtillon was dissolved. Napoleon's minor victories were without profit to him now, for he received no reënforcements to make good his losses. He formed the desperate resolution to fight his way through to Lorraine, raise fresh troops and force the allies to retreat by cutting their supply lines. But his rule had already crumbled. Talleyrand's group had sent one of their number, an old royalist officer, to the allied headquarters with the advice to march directly upon Paris. On the 30th of March, 200,000 troops under Blücher and Schwarzenberg carried the heights of Montmartre and on the following day Alexander and Frederick William made a triumphal entry into Paris. Napoleon sped back to his capital in the mad hope that if Paris held out only for a few days he would succeed in crushing the enemy at its very gates. He was within fifteen miles of Paris when he learned the news of the capitulation; and he retired to Fontainebleau to await his army and recapture his capital. His hope was an empty one. His rule was over.

XXI. THE RESTORATION IN FRANCE AND EUROPE

The Fate of France

THE first question before the conquerors was the determination of the fate of Napoleon and the selection of his successor. Serious differences of opinion had divided the allied sovereigns and diplomats. Alexander favored the candidacy of Bernadotte, crown prince of Sweden; Metternich was not averse to a regency for Napoleon's son, while Castlereagh firmly supported the cause of the emigrant Bourbon prince, the count of Provence. But these differences were almost entirely composed by the time that Alexander entered Paris at the head of the victorious army. Metternich's fears of what Alexander might do if he obtained a free hand in Paris prompted him to join with Castlereagh in advocating a Bourbon restoration. Bernadotte helped ruin his own chances by engaging in secret intrigues of which Alexander soon got wind. Meantime the coterie of royalists in France, of which Talleyrand was the spokesman, won the czar over to the Bourbon cause by demonstrating that the interests both of Europe and of France were best served by recalling the brother of Louis XVI. Alexander gave his consent when Talleyrand assured him that the procedure for the deposition of Napoleon would be scrupulously correct, but he gained his point that Bourbon France should be granted a liberal constitution. In a proclamation to the French nation (March 31), signed by Alexander, the allies declared that they would no longer treat with Napoleon, and they invited the Senate to form a provisional government to revise the administration and draft a new constitution for France.

The transition from the Napoleonic empire to the Bourbon monarchy was smoothly and speedily effected in the first days of April. Events moved smoothly because the civilian population of France had already abandoned Napoleon, while his marshals refused their support to his plan for the continuation of the unequal military struggle. Talleyrand as vice grand elector convoked the Senate, which established a provisional government, of which he became the dominant spirit. Two days later (April 3) the Senate formally deposed Napoleon and released the army from its oath of loyalty to the emperor. On the 4th Napoleon abdicated in favor of his infant son, and at the same time made a final desperate but unavailing appeal to Alexander I to renounce his support of the Bourbons. On the 6th the Senate issued its hastily formulated constitution and summoned the count of Provence to the throne, making his acceptance of the constitution the prerequisite to his restoration. On the 11th Napoleon announced his unconditional abdication, resigning both for himself and for his family the thrones of France and Italy. That very day his future was settled by the terms of the treaty of Fontainebleau. The allies—with the exception of England—allowed him to retain the title of emperor, but confined his rule to the tiny island of Elba, which he was to have in full sovereignty, but which he was never to leave. His annual revenue was to be 2,000,000 francs, payable by the French government from the income of his domain in France. The duchies of Parma, Piacenza, and Guastalla were granted in full ownership and sovereignty to the Empress Marie Louise, and were to pass to her son and his line. Liberal financial provisions were made for other members of his family.

On the 20th Napoleon took leave of his Old Guard at Fontainebleau and set out on the dismal journey to his future home. With Napoleon out of the way the allies turned to the question of making peace with France. The secret provisions of the Chaumont treaty had already outlined the nature of the forthcoming peace treaty between France and the conquerors of Napoleon. What delay there was in ratifying the terms was due largely to Talleyrand's efforts to get more favorable boundaries for his country. Still one of the outstanding characteristics of the first treaty of Paris (May 30, 1814) was the moderation displayed to the conquered country. The French boundaries were fixed as of January 1, 1792, and in addition she was allowed to retain Avignon and the Comtat-Venaissin and received concessions in Savoy and at Landau and Saarlouis. She paid no indemnity and was not forced to support an army of occupation.

On the other hand British interests were carefully safeguarded. Holland was returned to the House of Orange and was promised (in a secret article) an increase of territory in the former Austrian Netherlands. In return for a money compensation for the loss of the Cape, Holland was to erect frontier fortresses against France. Thus England established a barrier state on the northeastern frontier of France and placed the mouth of the Scheldt River in the hands of a country that could defend Antwerp. The rest of the territory on the left bank of the Rhine that France gave up was to compensate Prussia and other German states for their losses. The English position in the Mediterranean was secured by the retention of Malta, while her long route to India was protected by the Cape, Mauritius, Saint Lucia, and Tobago. The menace of French penetration toward the Mediterranean was met by extending Austrian control in northern Italy up to the Mincio River. The king of Sardinia was to regain Piedmont, Nice, and the greater part of Savoy, and gain an extension of territory from the state of Genoa.

The greatest shortcoming of the treaty was its failure to determine the reconstruction of Europe. Excepting the provisions concerning Holland and the Netherlands, Austrian control of northern Italy, and the establishment of a federation of German states, the continental settlement was not attempted. This was left for a congress, to be held shortly at Vienna. But a secret clause of the treaty gave the allies the right to determine among themselves the settlement of the conquered territory and bound France to their decisions. "No one at this time," says C. K. Webster, "regarded the coming Congress as anything more than an opportunity for communicating the decisions of the Great Powers to the rest of Europe and for adjusting minor points."

While the treaty of Paris was being negotiated, the count of Provence was making his way from England to assume the throne of the country from which he had fled almost a quarter of a century earlier. There was no overwhelming enthusiasm in France for the Bourbons. The royalist demonstrations in Paris were the work of Talleyrand and the agents of the royal princes. The greatest single factor that promoted the chances of the "legitimate" ruler of France was the general aversion to Napoleon's insensate policy of war. Certainly the French nation would not permit the beneficial accomplishments of the revolutionary era to be undone, and of this profound sentiment the count of Provence was entirely aware. Speaking in his name, his brother, the count of Artois, who had returned to Paris in April, accepted the basis of the liberal senatorial constitution but found it unacceptable in detail. As the future Louis XVIII approached Paris he issued a proclamation from Saint-Ouen which reassured public opinion that he would not attempt to turn back the hands of the clock. He declared that he would disturb no one for his earlier opinions, and promised, with the aid of the constituted authorities, to grant France a liberal constitution that would retain the essential conquests of the Revolution. The new king fully understood the imperative necessity of making a compromise between the old France and the new. Besides he was getting old and feeble, and the memory of his many tribulations in exile made him determine never again to "set out on his travels."

Shortly after he took up his residence at the Tuileries, he appointed a committee of men, all of whom had served Napoleon, to draw up the new constitution. The document which they prepared in redemption of Louis XVIII's promise at Saint-Ouen was the famous Charter of 1814. Despite a number of vague statements and contradictions it contained the possibilities of a liberal constitutional régime. Best to appreciate the measure in which Louis XVIII accepted the permanent gains of the Revolution, one should compare it either with typical cahiers of 1789 or the Constitution of 1791. In the main it accepted the provisions of the Declaration of the Rights of Man, established a parliamentary form of government, maintained an independent judiciary, guaranteed the public debt, and declared that the sale of national property was irrevocable. To be sure, the Roman Catholic religion was declared the religion of the state at the same time that freedom of worship was guaranteed; and the preamble of the Charter announced that the document was the king's gift to France, which he had "granted" in the "nineteenth year" of his reign. Louis XVIII's "voluntary grant" of a constitution to his people indicated very clearly that the Bourbons still did not recognize the fundamental doctrine of popular sovereignty. Yet the Charter was acceptable, and Louis XVIII began the "nineteenth year" of his reign with a fair assurance of success. Time alone would show whether or not the new monarchy and its émigré supporters could regulate their actions by the terms of the Charter of 1814.

THE CONGRESS OF VIENNA

The deliberations at Vienna began on September 15, 1814, with the preliminary discussions of Castlereagh, Metternich, Nesselrode, and Hardenberg, and continued until June 9, 1815, when the Final Act summarizing the many decisions was issued. Strictly speaking, the congress never formally opened. Talleyrand, as the representative of France, found slight difficulty in preventing the adoption of the proposed plan of deliberation by which the diplomats of "the Big Four" intended to arrange all matters among themselves before communicating their decisions to the lesser powers. There was no exchange of credentials and no plenary sessions of all the diplomatic representatives. The decisions at Vienna were arranged in special committees and in the informal conferences of sovereigns and diplomats. In many of these committee meetings and conferences Talleyrand found himself included, despite the secret clause of the treaty of Paris which had bound France to accept in advance the decisions of the four great powers. His much vaunted diplomatic finesse may account for his presence at the deliberations of the conquerors, but one should not overlook the fact that Castlereagh was anxious, on certain occasions, to have him attend the conferences and throw his support to the English plans.

The brilliance of the congress is almost proverbial. Emperors, kings, princes, victorious generals and famous statesmen, proud noblemen and great prelates, and a swarm of lesser notables assembled at the Austrian capital to forget the tribulations of the past in a round of gayety—and to lay the ghost of Jacobinism and Bonapartism. The care-free dancing, the lavish entertainment, the gay theatricals, the charming masquerades, and the merry hunting parties were at once a foil for and an instrument of the intensely serious business that had brought these grandees of Europe to Vienna. Theirs was indeed a sober task, the task of settling the fate of territories and peoples liberated at last from Napoleon's control, the heavy task of bringing peace and security to a Continent that for a quarter of a century had been convulsed by a gigantic revolutionary upheaval.

Their method of procedure has been noted. In what spirit did the sovereigns and diplomats shoulder their enormous responsibility to millions of people, to their contemporaries of the upheaval, and to the generations yet unborn that would be bound by their decisions? Would they satisfy the hopes of enlightened men who had looked forward for years to just such a congress, men "who had promised themselves an all-embracing reform of the political system of Europe, guarantees for universal peace, in one word, the return of the golden age"?

We know that the congress failed utterly to satisfy such liberal aspirations. Friedrich von Gentz, who was secretary of the congress, confessed his disappointment in the following words:

> The Congress has resulted in nothing but restorations which had already been effected by arms, agreements between the Great Powers of little value for the future balance and preservation of the peace of Europe, quite arbitrary alterations in the possessions of the smaller states; but no act of a higher nature, no great measure for public order or the general good which might compensate humanity for its long sufferings or pacify it for the future.[1]

The victors over Napoleon could not break through the hard shell of their fears, fears of Napoleon's military prowess and fears of the revolutionary ideas which he had translated into new institutions and new relationships between peoples and their governments. They regarded themselves as the saviors of European civilization, and their mission as to undo the work of the Revolution, dissolve Napoleon's military empire, and, so far as possible, restore the political system of Europe to the condition in which it had found itself in 1789. Their duty therefore was, where practicable, to restore legitimate rulers to the thrones from which Napoleon had driven them, to compensate them for their losses, and to establish guarantees against all future menaces to what they sonorously called "a durable peace based upon a just division of power."

Alexander I was the closest in spirit to the liberals who hoped that a finer Europe would be created at Vienna. He was generous by nature, he had his moments of humanitarian sympathies, and he believed—at times—in liberal, constitutional government. But he could not forget—nor did he try to forget—that Russia's historic mission was in his hands; and Russia's mission, when expressed in terms of territorial expansion beyond the Vistula, awakened the apprehensions of her three allies, England, Prussia, and Austria. Hardenberg, the facile and gallant courtier who represented Prussia, knew the meaning and the need of liberal reform. Had he not been associated with Stein in the great movement of Prussian reconstruction after the collapse at Jena? But in the diplomatic bargaining at Vienna he put the interests of Prussia above those of Germany and sacrificed the greater purpose for a

[1] W. A. Phillips, *The Confederation of Europe* (London, 1914), p. 118.

selfish one. Viscount Castlereagh, the most influential mediator of the congress, was thoroughly honest in his thinking and wholly consistent in his actions. But neither in his thinking nor in his actions could he find place for those principles of national independence and popular institutions which had become potent during the generation of upheaval from 1789 to 1815. He came to Vienna to negotiate the sort of peace that William Pitt would have made —the safeguarding of England's maritime and colonial supremacy, the erection of barriers to French extension on the eastern frontier, and the establishment of a "just equilibrium" in central Europe.

And Metternich? His hostility to the ideals of political liberty and nationalism is a matter of record, and the consecrated phrases, the "Era of Metternich" or the "Metternich Reaction," eloquently bespeak his conservatism. Yet his opposition was not the hostility of an unintelligent reactionary blind to the new forces of the century. On the contrary, every consideration of intelligent, realistic politics urged him to fight the extension of those ideals in the empire of Austria. The empire was a hodgepodge of nationalities, races, and creeds. Once the movement for political liberty and nationalist unification gained a foothold in Austria, the empire was doomed as the history of Austria from 1875 to 1919 subsequently proved. Unless he were anxious to hasten the dissolution of the empire, the statesman had no other course than to try to suppress those persistent revolutionary ideals. And such was precisely the endeavor of Metternich at the Congress of Vienna. In his eyes nationalism was a phase of the democratic movement for constitutional government, leading straight to revolution and anarchy. He would establish a "moral pentarchy" in Europe, a union of the five great states of Austria, Prussia, Russia, France, and England to combat the spirit of nationalism and preserve peace and order. He opposed all efforts to unite the German states, believing that such a union would create an abortive monstrosity. His ideal form of the state system in Germany was a loose confederation, which would end the agitation for a united monarchy, combat the leveling of the different German cultures, and keep Austria dominant in Germany and secure against military threats from France and Russia. All his efforts since 1813 had been to defeat Stein's farsighted plans for a united German Fatherland, and the Congress of Vienna unfortunately crowned his efforts with success.

Of all the questions that divided the negotiators the thorniest was the settlement of the rival claims to the grand duchy of Warsaw and the kingdom of Saxony. By arrangements concluded in 1813 Prussia agreed to Alexander's plan of joining the territory of Warsaw to the Polish territory acquired by Russia in the partitions in order to restore the kingdom of Poland. The czar's intentions were to grant a liberal constitution to the new kingdom and bind it by a personal union with Russia. In return, Russia promised her support to the Prussian claim upon the territory of Saxony, whose king had been loyal to Napoleon in the final struggle. In the bitter dispute that broke out over this territorial "deal," Castlereagh played his not unfamiliar rôle of mediator with great courage and flexibility. Uppermost in his mind was one consideration, to establish a strong central Europe that would be as much a bulwark against Russian aggression from the east as against French threats from the west. To establish this central bulwark between the Rhine and the Vistula a federation of German states was necessary, and to create the federation he had to bring Austria and Prussia together against Russia, end their rivalry and establish good relations between them.

Such was the goal toward which Castlereagh moved. His path was difficult, for with the Austrian diplomats objecting strenuously to the Russo-Prussian agreement and the Prussians and the Russians adopting a menacing tone, the possibility of war as a solution was great. The climax of the dispute was reached in January, 1815, when Castlereagh admitted Talleyrand in the armed mediation and arranged a secret treaty which bound Austria, England, and France each to contribute 150,000 men if attacked by Prussia. This precautionary measure insured the success of Castlereagh's compromise solution. All the powers involved saw the need of abandoning their extreme positions, and the main issues of the Saxon and Polish question were soon settled.

Less difficulty was experienced in settling other disputed points, and Napoleon's return to France helped not a little in speeding up the deliberations. The congress broke up in June, 1815, with the issue of the Final Act. Russia retained Finland which she had wrested from Sweden, and Bessarabia which she had acquired from Turkey. The solution of the dispute over the grand duchy of Warsaw gave her the lion's share of that territory, which Alexander incorporated with his Polish provinces in forming the separate kingdom of Poland. Austria recovered the province of Galicia which she had sacrificed in 1809; and Prussia obtained the province of Posen and the fortress of Thorn. Cracow was established as a free city. The king of Saxony was restored to his throne. To compensate her for the loss of her Polish provinces Prussia received from him about two-fifths of Saxony, Pomerania from Sweden, and territory on both sides of the Rhine, in which the important cities of Cologne and Koblenz were included. She received back her other territories in northern Germany. Austria, which had suffered so severely at the hands of Napoleon, profited greatly by the arrangements at Vienna. In addition to recovering Galicia, Austria regained Lombardy, the Tirol, and other lands that she had possessed on her western frontiers. In compensation for her loss of the Netherlands, she received Venetia, the Illyrian provinces, and Salzburg. England gained no territory on the Continent, but added to her colonial possessions and safeguarded her commercial route by acquiring Malta and the Ionian Islands (as Protector) in the Mediterranean; the Cape of Good Hope in South Africa; Trinidad off the coast of South America; Ceylon, Île de France, Saint Lucia, and Tobago. Sweden was given Norway to compensate for the loss of Finland and Pomerania.

The Bourbon kings were restored in France, Spain, and Naples. The House of Braganza was restored in Portugal. The king of Sardinia was restored to his throne, the pope in his territorial possessions, and Austrian princes were restored in Modena and Tuscany. Austrian influence again became dominant in Italy, a settlement which answered English fears of French penetration toward the Mediterranean. Italy became, as Metternich wished, "a geographical expression." The many hundred petty rulers of Germany whose states Napoleon had abolished between 1803 and 1806 were not restored, but the thirty-nine German states were united in a loose German Confederation in which Austria enjoyed a commanding position. The arrangements in Italy and Germany effectively killed all hopes of unity and liberal government.

In their effort to establish guarantees against future French military aggressions the Rhine barrier was created. On the lower Rhine was the enlarged kingdom of Holland, which now included the Austrian Netherlands. That was Holland's compensation for the loss of the Cape and Ceylon to England. South of Holland were the Prussian possessions on the Rhine. Farther south was the Swiss Confederation, augmented in territory by three new cantons and guaranteed in its neutrality by the great powers. Below Switzerland was the enlarged Sardinia, strengthened by the inclusion of Genoa.

No provisions were made to revise or modify any of the terms of the settlement. Consequently the settlement at Vienna was the point of departure for the history of the century, 1815–1914, in which the aspirations of the nationalists and the liberals were largely realized. For the present the settlement along the lines of restoration, compensations, and guarantees gave the measure of the fears of the conservative sovereigns and diplomats. It attempted to elevate the natural desire for repose and tranquillity into a principle of statesmanship, and it failed because it ignored or disregarded the new forces which the Revolution had released.

The First Restoration and the Hundred Days

The Charter of 1814, as we have seen, was rich in possibilities. It was markedly antidemocratic, for the king had the exclusive initiative of legislation, and the high property qualifications disbarred the great majority of his subjects from active political life; but it entrusted the government jointly to the monarch and to such political representatives as the country had. It retained the administrative system of the empire, and with the system many of its experienced officials; and it had accepted many of the fundamental changes of the Revolution. But the Bourbon government failed signally to rally public opinion behind it. The country could not forget that its new ruler and his émigré supporters had come back to France in the "baggage of the allies." The nation was not permitted to forget that the Charter was Louis XVIII's gift to France, because various groups of emigrants who were more royalist than the king himself gained control of the situation and destroyed the liberal possibilities of the Charter. These men of violent royalist and reactionary views, who soon were known as the Ultraroyalists or the Ultras, found their leader in the bigoted and embittered count of Artois, the brother of the king. While his agents unquestionably had much to do with turning liberal opinion solidly against the Bourbons, the new government itself was guilty of certain blunders which arrayed the different social classes against it.

One mistake concerned its policy of financial retrenchment.

Economies were imperative, for the deficit was mounting and the floating debt enormous. While Napoleon was still emperor, royalists had promised the people that his deposition and the conclusion of peace with Europe would result in the reduction of taxes. But the Bourbon government found it impossible to reduce taxes, which it continued to collect despite many violent protests. In the interest of economy the war machine of the empire was put on a peace footing, but this measure reduced the pay of thousands of officers by fifty per cent and condemned many more veteran soldiers to leave for their homes clothed in the tattered uniforms of the last campaign. And once at home they found themselves under police surveillance. At the same time, as though to add political insult to the financial injury of these Napoleonic veterans, the government appointed many emigrant officers to high posts in the army and reëstablished the military household of the Old Régime—at a cost, approximately, of 20,000,000 francs.

The Bourbons also alienated many manufacturers by attempting to remove the high prohibitive duties of the Continental System. The attempt was almost mandatory, as all the frontiers of France were open to her foreign enemies and competitors; but the attempt was none the less resented by those to whom it meant ruinous competition. Liberals grew fearful over the efforts of an extreme group of returned ecclesiastics who unleashed a systematic attack upon the Concordat of 1801, upon Napoleon's educational system, and upon the liberty of the press. This movement seemed a war of revenge against the Revolution. The purchasers of national land, in particular the peasantry, became apprehensive as they saw the government restoring great stretches of unsold national land and heard of proposals in the upper house for the indemnification of noblemen whose property had been confiscated during the past generation. How different were the good old days of Napoleon, who had scrupulously respected the property rights of these now frightened purchasers of national land!

"From his exile in Elba Napoleon had taken note of the new features on the horizon, of the recrudescence of the revolutionary hatred of priest and noble among the peasantry, of the chagrin of the old soldiers, of the power of the liberal opposition in Paris; and recognizing the altered mood of France, he determined to accommodate himself to it."[2] He had taken note also of the dissen-

[2] H. A. L. Fisher, *Bonapartism* (Oxford, 1914), p. 108.

sions among the allies at Vienna and determined to take advantage of so favorable an opportunity to recover his control. As pretexts for violating the treaty which confined him to Elba he could allege the failure of the Bourbons to abide by its terms; for not one sou had Louis XVIII paid of the money due him. Rumors were afoot, moreover, of a plot to kidnap him from Elba and remove him to the Azores; and Napoleon hastened preparations to escape and return to France.

The escape was not difficult, as no adequate provisions could be made, under the treaty, to prevent it. Profiting by the temporary absence of the English commissioner from the island, Napoleon embarked the small army of his faithful adherents on several frigates, and on March 1, 1815, after a trip of several days, he landed on the coast of southern France. The record of his triumphant march to Paris is more stirring than fiction. To avoid passing through Provence, where royalist sentiment ran high, he led his men over mountain passes into Dauphiné, whose inhabitants gave him a rapturous welcome. Near Grenoble a company of soldiers blocked his advance; but Napoleon dramatically bared his breast to their fire, and they threw down their arms, shouting, "*Vive l'Empereur!*"

Never did Napoleon's remarkable political intuition serve him so well as at this juncture of his career. As peasants and his old soldiers, the "grumblers" of his many campaigns, rallied to his standard, he voiced such sentiments as would hold their allegiance forever. He proclaimed himself the champion of the people, the savior of the masses from the slavery which engulfed them during the rule of priests and emigrants, the child of the Revolution, and the apostle of peace. In these utterances en route to Paris and in all his deeds during the crowded moments of the Hundred Days, Napoleon began the creation of that Napoleonic Legend which he so carefully elaborated in the dreary days of captivity at Saint Helena. On the 20th of March he was at Fontainebleau; and in Paris, Louis XVIII was entering his carriage and starting out on his travels again, journeying until he reached the protection of the allied troops in Ghent.

There was no difficulty in reorganizing the administration, for many of Napoleon's former officials accepted service under him. Reluctantly, for his profession of liberal faith was insincere, Napoleon bowed to the force of public opinion which wanted neither the arbitrary rule of the Bourbons nor a return to the despotism of the empire. He was summoned to make good his boast that he was sprung from the Revolution. He won over to his side the most influential publicist in Paris, Benjamin Constant, an implacable foe of the Bourbons and a former critic of the empire, and he commissioned Constant to draw up a constitution for his new liberal régime. The document which was mainly the work of Constant was entitled the Additional Act and published in the *Moniteur*. It was designed as a supplement and a corrective of the earlier constitutions of the empire, as a new pledge of those liberal projects which Napoleon would have carried out earlier had he not been forced to fight in self-defense against the kings and the aristocrats of Europe. Aside from the speciousness of the explanatory preamble the Additional Act was indeed a liberal document. It broadened the basis of the suffrage, restored the freedom of religious worship, established a responsible ministry, and removed the censorship of the press. Napoleon made strenuous efforts to overcome the skepticism of middle-class liberals, who remained not unnaturally suspicious at the miraculous spectacle of the lion's transformation into a lamb, but he might have saved his energy. Time was too short to put the new constitution into operation; and Napoleon had to leave for the war front in Belgium.

The news of his return to France had thrown the plenipotentiaries at Vienna into consternation, but they speedily recovered from the shock. On March 13 the powers publicly outlawed him "as an Enemy and Disturber of the tranquillity of the World." On the 25th they put teeth in their public declaration by renewing the appropriate provision of the treaty of Chaumont. England, Russia, Austria, and Prussia each agreed to keep in the field 150,000 men and not lay down arms "until Buonaparte shall have been put absolutely beyond the possibility of exciting disturbances and of renewing his attempts to seize upon the supreme power in France." Once more the stability of Europe rested precariously upon the test of arms.

THE SECOND RESTORATION

The action of the allies closed all diplomatic channels to Napoleon. In vain he protested that he would respect the provisions of the treaty of Paris, that his empire would be a force for peace in Europe. Their response was to speed the mobilization of their armies. Napoleon's last resource rested with his troops. Among the hundreds of thousands of veterans who had returned to their fatherland from garrisons or prisons in Europe he hoped to find many loyal supporters. But their hatred of the reactionary Bourbon rule was not synonymous with an active desire to share in Napoleon's new military ventures; and not more than 60,000 answered his appeals. To avoid appearing the aggressor Napoleon had postponed his military preparations, putting off the conscription of 1815 until the last moment. In June his total forces were well over 200,000, but at the most only 125,000 followed him into Belgium, the remainder serving in the interior against the royalists or defending the eastern frontier.

He planned an offensive campaign outside of France, partly to spare France the burden of a new invasion, partly to sow political discord among the allies by winning a decisive military victory over the Prussians and the English in Belgium before the Austrians and the Russians could complete their mobilization. The former were already assembled in Belgium near the French frontier, the 120,000 Prussians under Blücher having converged from the Rhine and the 95,000 Belgians, Dutchmen, Germans, and English under Wellington from the Channel ports. Napoleon struck before either of the allied commanders had any definite information of his movements. On June 15 he crossed the Belgian frontier and occupied Charleroi, believing that he had cut the two armies at their point of junction, and that he could now defeat each army in detail. This was the first, though a minor, miscalculation; other errors more grievous were to come within the next few days. Only Blücher's outposts had been engaged at Charleroi; with the bulk of his troops he resisted the French when Napoleon attacked him at Ligny on the 16th. Aware of his error Napoleon sent couriers to recall Marshal Ney, whom he had dispatched earlier with 50,000 men in the direction of Brussels. Ney, however, could not fall upon the right flank of the Prussians as his superior ordered him to do, for he himself was engaged at Quatre Bras, where Wellington's divisions stayed his advance. Ligny was a victory for Napoleon, for the Prussians yielded before his attacks. But in their retreat their commander made a courageous de-

cision to retire northwards to Wavre, from which point they could
give support to Wellington in the battle which they knew to be
imminent. Again Napoleon miscalculated. So certain was he that
the Prussians had fallen back to the east, in the direction of Namur,
in order to rally their forces, that he sent off Grouchy with 30,000

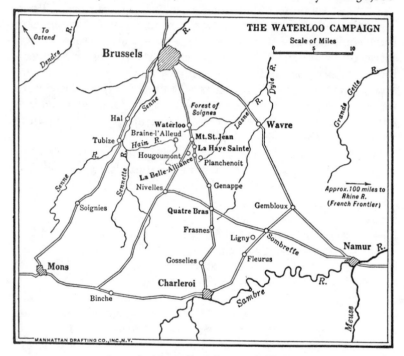

men to pursue them in that direction and block them if they attempted to advance again toward the west. Meantime, on the 17th,
the main force of the French under Napoleon marched toward
Quatre Bras to reënforce Ney.

Wellington had taken his position several miles south of Waterloo, stationing the bulk of his forces behind a ridge which concealed their number and their movements from the enemy. A
group of farmhouses in the valley before the ridge, at Hougomont
on his right and at La Haye Sainte in the center, which he had
hastily fortified, constituted his first line of defense. Napoleon
rested his men on the 17th after their fighting at Ligny and their
heavy march toward Wellington's line, and he did not begin the
fighting until noon on the 18th in order to allow the ground to dry

after the heavy rain of the preceding night. He saw no cause for haste. Was not Blücher far from the field! His greatest fear was lest Wellington endeavor to escape. But unknown to him, from Wavre, Blücher had sent assurances of his support to the English commander; this at a moment when Grouchy with 30,000 Frenchmen was miles away from the battle field.

Napoleon held Wellington in scant respect, but Wellington was not to be taken lightly; not even by Napoleon. He had arranged his troops in the position that had brought him victory after victory in the Peninsular campaign, in a combination that had never failed to hurl back the magnificent charges of his French opponents. Without the aid of Blücher and the absence of Grouchy the outcome of the epic struggle might have been different; but Grouchy was not there, and Blücher's hardened veterans came in time to turn the scales against Napoleon. The "hollow squares" of the English held their ground against the furious assaults of the French cavalry and the Prussian divisions thrust back Napoleon's right. When the fierce combat ended in the darkness of that memorable June night, the French forces were in panicky flight toward Quatre Bras and the French frontier; and the exultant Blücher, much the worse for the blood of the fray and the smoke of the guns and many copious libations, clasped hands with a saddened English duke.

Napoleon still hoped. "Courage, constancy," he wrote to his brother in Paris, but his hopes were empty. Again he abdicated in favor of his son, and for a second time Louis XVIII regained his throne, this time never to lose it. Napoleon fled to the coast to escape the Prussians, whose grizzled commander had given orders for his capture alive or dead. Failing to escape the vigilance of the British ships that prevented him from embarking for America, he threw himself upon the generosity of that perfidious Albion which had defeated him and took refuge with Captain Maitland of the *Bellerophon*. To the British was left the thankless task of serving as his jailers. They hurried him off to his captivity, and in October he landed at Saint Helena, a distant island in the Atlantic, whose "salubrious climate" he enjoyed until his death on May 5, 1821.

Had he been left to the tender mercies of Blücher or the stern justice of other conquerors, his fate would have been grimmer, if not sadder. And had his country been left to the rancor of Austria and Prussia, there is no doubt that it would have been bled white.

But the sterling common sense of Castlereagh, which was ably seconded throughout by the humanity of Wellington and the generosity of Alexander I, prevailed over the bitter passions of the other victors. Castlereagh saw that, other than reducing France to a third- or fourth-rate power, there was no alternative to leaving her substantially intact in territory:

> The more I reflect upon it the more I deprecate this system of scratching such a Power. We may hold her down and pare her nails so that many years shall pass away before she can again wound us . . . but this system of being pledged to a continental war for objects that France may any day reclaim from the particular states that hold them, without pushing her demands beyond what she would contend was due to her own honour, is, I am sure, a bad British policy.[3]

In the end he defeated the proposals to take from France a large slice of her territory and bind her to a peace that could lead only to revenge. By the second treaty of Paris (November 20, 1815) France suffered a heavy punishment, but not a cruel one. The few square miles of territory that she lost reduced her boundaries substantially to those of 1789. She was required to pay an indemnity of 700,000,000 francs within five years, part of which the allies used to erect barrier fortresses on her northeastern frontier. An allied army of occupation of 150,000 men occupied her northeastern departments—at French expense. The ambassadors of the Big Four were permitted to proffer advice and suggestions to her government, even in matters of domestic policy. But her position in Europe was secure.

The epic of Napoleon was ended, but the glory of the Napoleonic Legend was yet to be. From his lonely rock in the Atlantic, the new Prometheus—so Napoleon chose to consider himself—did not tear at the chains that bound him. He prepared a subtler revenge upon the forces of conservatism that had chained him to his rock. He occupied his dismal leisure in rearranging the acts of his life so as to insure the triumph of his dynasty at some later date when Europe, tired of repression, would examine anew the record of his miraculous career; and examining, would find fresh courage and new hope in the profession of his liberal faith.

[3] From a dispatch of Castlereagh to Lord Liverpool, August 17, 1815. Quoted in *The Cambridge History of British Foreign Policy*, edited by A. W. Ward and G. P. Gooch, Vol. I, p. 511.

BIBLIOGRAPHY

I. The Old Regime

Notes on Historiography

Little now remains of a conventional approach which would make the weaknesses and imbalances of the Old Regime both the necessary and sufficient conditions for the revolution of 1789. There is ample recognition of the strength, the cultural ascendancy of France, and the fluidity of its social structure. Fresh regional studies succeed each other on social mobility and on the differences within as well as between the various social groups. The so-called "feudal reaction" is seen as part of the broader phenomenon of an aristocratic resurgence directed against the state, which took place concurrently with what may be called a "democratic" movement both against the aristocracy and the absolute state. There is increasing agreement, too, about the considerable effort made by the crown and its ministers to modernize the administration and the institutions of government, and on the degree of success effected by that effort.

Thanks to C. E. Labrousse and French scholars of his school, we possess far greater information and understanding than ever before on the long term and shorter cyclical movements of French economy in the eighteenth century, and of the relationship of those movements to political and ideological changes.

The study of the Enlightenment has also been renewed and on an appreciably less polemical basis than was long the case when historians gave themselves ardently to proving either that the major *philosophes* exercised an all-beneficent influence upon men's thinking or conversely produced a baleful effect upon historical developments. Our views of Voltaire, Diderot, Montesquieu, and particularly Rousseau have been significantly modified. Not only the differences between the intellectual spokesmen but the unifying strand which bound them together in a common desire to make the betterment of man's social and personal condition the effective gauge of governmental action have been made clear. That none of them advocated revolution is also clear.

The place of America in the causal pattern of the French Revolution has received long overdue attention; and the pre-revolutionary program in France has been situated in the larger frame of the democratic, revolutionary ferment of the Atlantic community. Much of the old historiographical dispute as to whether ideas or material circumstances "caused" the Revolution has become irrelevant. Finally, the coming of the Revolution between 1787 and 1789 is being carefully reviewed in the light of the new knowledge and the new angle of vision which these studies have given.

The following works provide a useful introduction to the revisionist studies of the Old Regime: A. Cobban, *The Myth of the French Revolution* (London,

1955), and his *Historians and the Causes of the French Revolution*, rev. ed. (London, 1958); C. Brinton, *The Anatomy of Revolution*, rev. ed. (1952), also in Vintage paperback; R. R. Palmer, *The Age of the Democratic Revolution:* Vol. I, *The Challenge* (Princeton, 1959), a pioneering study of the larger democratic agitation in the Western world. For Palmer's own digest of his thesis, see L. Gottschalk, ed., *Generalization in the Writing of History* (Chicago, 1963), pp. 66–76. L. Gottschalk's two interesting studies, *The Place of the American Revolution in the Causal Pattern of the French Revolution* (Easton, Pa., 1948), and "Philippe Sagnac and the Causes of the French Revolution," *Journal of Modern History*, Vol. XX (1948), pp. 137–148, discuss both the place of the American Revolution and the role of the *philosophes*. The latter topic is trenchantly treated in H. Peyre, "The Influence of Eighteenth-Century Ideas on the French Revolution," *Journal of the History of Ideas*, Vol. X (1949), pp. 63–87. J. L. Talmon, *The Origins of Totalitarian Democracy* (Boston, 1952), is suggestive but unduly severe on Rousseau as a founding father of illiberalism. S. J. Idzerda's booklet, *The Background of the French Revolution* (Washington, D.C., 1959), briefly presents and evaluates the newer approach and contains a good selected bibliography. The best single work is J. Godechot, *Les Révolutions, 1770–1799* (1963), with a remarkably full bibliography.

BIBLIOGRAPHICAL AIDS AND BIBLIOGRAPHIES

The most useful general bibliographical guides are: *A Guide to Historical Literature*, G. M. Dutcher, H. R. Shipman, S. B. Fay, and others, eds. (Washington, D.C., 1931), and *The American Historical Association's Guide to Historical Literature*, G. F. Howe and others, eds. (Washington, D.C., 1961). Current publications, listed annually, are in *International Bibliography of Historical Sciences*, 27 volumes to date (1926–   ). The national historical bibliographies for particular states or regions, e.g., H. Pirenne, *Bibliographie de l'histoire de Belgique*, 3rd ed. (Brussels, 1931), are in both Dutcher and Howe. For bibliographical guidance to the Old Regime in France, see C. du Peloux, *Répertoire général des ouvrages relatifs au XVIIIe siècle français, 1715–1789* (1926). E. Saulnier and A. Martin, *Bibliographie des travaux publiés de 1886 à 1897 sur l'histoire de France de 1500 à 1789*, 2 vols. (1932–1938); G. Lanson, *Manuel bibliographique de la littérature française moderne*, Vols. II and III (1909–1914), which should be complemented by *A Critical Bibliography of French Literature:* Vol. IV, *The Eighteenth Century*, G. R. Havens and D. F. Bond, eds. (Syracuse, 1951). The valuable bibliographies in many of the longer general works, such as E. Lavisse, ed., *Histoire de France*, Vols. VIII, Part Two, and IX, Part One (1909–1910), will be noted at the appropriate place.

SOURCES AND REFERENCE WORKS

For the seventeenth century there is an exhaustive systematic guide to the sources in L. André and others, eds., *Sources de l'histoire de France, XVIIe siècle*, 8 vols. (1913–1935), but there is nothing comparable for the eighteenth century. Obviously, there is a great wealth of material in the literary masterpieces, the critical works of the *philosophes*, memoirs, and letters, most of which have been translated and are readily available. Of the many travel accounts for the last years of the Old Regime one could begin with A. Young, *Travels in France during the Years 1787, 1788, 1789* (in the Cambridge University Press edition of 1929), and Dr. E. Rigby, *Letters from France*, new ed. (London, 1880). There are also the *Almanac royal*, published annually during the Old Regime, a source book of statistical information; A. de Clercq and J. de Clercq, *Recueil des traités de la France*, new ed., Vols. I and II (1880), a standard collection of treaties; J. B. Duvergier, *Collection complète des lois, décrets, règlements*, Vols. XIII–XIX (1824–1828); J. Flammermont and M. Tourneux, *Remontrances du parlement de Paris au XVIIIe siècle*, 3 vols. (1888–1889). For the cahiers of 1789, the scholarly researches of Beatrice F. Hyslop are indispensable: *A Guide to the General Cahiers of 1789, with the texts of unedited cahiers* (1936); *Répertoire critique des cahiers* (1932); *Supplément au répertoire critique des cahiers* (1953); and "Les cahiers de doléances de 1789," *Annales historiques de la Révolution française*, Vol. XXVII (1955), pp. 115–123. Many of the secondary cahiers are reprinted in Vols. I–VI of the *Archives parlementaires*, first series, J. Mavidal and E. Laurent, eds., (1862–1896). The publication of this series, which stopped with Vol. LXXXII, was resumed in 1961. The memoirs, which are legion, cannot possibly be listed in full. The most important will be given at the appropriate places.

Among works of reference see M. Marion, *Dictionnaire des institutions de la France aux XVIIe et XVIIIe siècles* (1923); such standard biographical dictionaries as the older *Biographie universelle*, the *Nouvelle Biographie universelle*, the *Larousse*, the *Grande Encyclopédie*, and the more recent *Dictionnaire biographique français*, T. Balteau, A. Rastoul, and M. Prévost, eds. (1933), a cooperative work of French scholars with letters A–D thus far. See also, L. Mirot, *Manuel de géographie historique de la France* (1929), many maps which cover the Old Regime, and A. Brette, *Atlas de bailliages* (1906), invaluable for administrative France in 1789.

GENERAL ACCOUNTS

1. *Background studies*

C. Seignobos, *The Evolution of the French People*, Eng. trans. (1932), remains an excellent introductory survey; the second volume of the broadly conceived manual of G. Duby and R. Mandrou, *Histoire de la civilisation française*, 2 vols. (1958), covers the eighteenth century and the first sets forth the historical origins; R. Mandrou, *Introduction à la France moderne, 1500–1640* (1961) is a fascinating study in social and cultural anthropology; the five volumes of A. Adam, *Histoire de la littérature française au XVIIe siècle* (1949–1956) is a detailed panorama correlating belles lettres with intellectual and social movements; A. L. Guérard, *The Life and Death of an Ideal: France in the Classical Age* (1928) presents a brilliant but outmoded cultural history, to be corrected by the relevant chapters of P. Barrière, *La Vie intel-*

lectuelle en France du XVIe siècle à l'époque contemporaine (1961); E. B. D. Borgerhoff's luminous *The Freedom of French Classicism* (Princeton, 1950), and P. Bénichou, *Morales du grand siècle* (1948), the last two pointing up the intellectual probing of the great seventeenth century authors. G. N. Clark, *The Seventeenth Century*, 2nd. ed. (1947 and in paperback), is a thoughtful topical survey drawing heavily on French examples; J. Lough, *An Introduction to Seventeenth Century France* (1954), sets forth a balanced, reliable treatment abreast of recent research. The following selected studies illuminate various problems and issues in the formation and deformation of absolutism: the two popular accounts of G. Pagès, *Naissance du grand siècle: la France de Henri IV à Louis XIV, 1598–1661* (1948), and *La Monarchie d'ancien régime en France de Henri IV à Louis XIV*, 4th ed. (1946); V. L. Tapié's authoritative *La France de Louis XIII et de Richelieu* (1952); the still useful J. B. Perkins, *France under Richelieu and Mazarin*, 2 vols. (1886), and the more recent popular A. Bailly, *Mazarin* (1936); P. Gaxotte, *La France de Louis XIV* (1946), extols the "Grand Monarch," while the convincing monograph of E. L. Asher, *The Resistance to the Maritime Classes* (Berkeley, 1960), uses local archives for the opposition to Colbert's policy of naval recruitment; W. C. Scoville, *Persecution of Huguenots and French Economic Development, 1680–1720* (Berkeley, 1960); W. J. Stankiewicz, *Politics and Religion in Seventeenth Century France* (Berkeley, 1960); W. H. Lewis, *The Scandalous Regent: a life of Philippe, duc d'Orléans, 1674–1723, and of his Family* (1961), interesting for its treatment of early reactions against the Louis XIV pattern, which Lewis examines sympathetically in *The Splendid Century* (1954) and in *Louis XIV: An Informal Portrait* (London, 1959).

2. The eighteenth century

Recent brief accounts are in J. Lough, *An Introduction to Eighteenth Century France* (1960), a valuable handbook in English; the scholarly and brilliantly written A. Cobban, *A History of Modern France*, 2 vols. (1957–1961), of which Vol. I covers the Old Regime and the Revolution; the section on the eighteenth century by R. Mousnier in M. Reinhard, ed., *Histoire de France*, Vol. II (1954); A. de Tocqueville, *Oeuvres complètes*, J. P. Meyer, ed., 2 vols. (1952–1953), best French edition of Tocqueville's famous *L'Ancien Régime* with his preparatory notes and drafts on the revolution and the empire (also in English translation); G. P. Gooch, *Louis XV, The Monarchy in Decline* (London, 1956); F. Funck-Brentano, *The Old Regime in France*, Eng. trans. (1929), a learned apologia, as is P. Gaxotte, *Le Siècle de Louis XV*, rev. ed. (1958). On foreign relations, there is G. Zeller, *Les Temps modernes de Louis XIV à 1789*, Vol. III in the Histoire des relations internationales series, P. Renouvin, ed. (1955); and for church-state relations, E. Préclin and E. Jarry, *Les Luttes politiques et doctrinales aux XVIIe et XVIIIe siècles*, 2 vols. (1955–1956). Of the longer studies, there are P. Sagnac, *La Formation de la société française moderne*, 2 vols. (1946), covering the two centuries before 1789; Vols. VIII, Part Two, and IX, Part One, in the *Histoire de France*, E. Lavisse, ed. (1909–1910); and the still brilliant, but hostile, unreliable H. Taine, *L'Ancien Régime*, Eng. trans.,

The Ancient Regime (1875), the first volume of his comprehensive series, *Les Origines de la France contemporaine.*

SPECIAL STUDIES

1. *Administrative and political*

F. L. Ford, *Robe and Sword: The Regrouping of the French Aristocracy after Louis XIV* (Cambridge, Mass., 1953), a penetrating study of the aristocratic resurgence; P. N. Ardascheff, *Les Intendants de province sous Louis XVI*, 3 vols. (1909), valuable for regional administration and reforms; both A. Cobban, "The Parlements of France in the Eighteenth Century," *History,* Vol. XXXV (1950), pp. 64–80, and L. Gottschalk, "The French Parlements and Judicial Review," *Journal of the History of Ideas,* Vol. V (1944), pp. 105–112, examine the strategic position of the high magistrates; G. T. Matthews, *The Royal General Farms in Eighteenth Century France* (1958), on the collection of indirect taxes.

2. *Social and economic*

In addition to the second volume of Sagnac's *La Formation,* there is a brief but admirable account in H. Sée, *Economic and Social Conditions in France during the Eighteenth Century,* Eng. trans. (1927); L. Ducros, *French Society in the Eighteenth Century,* Eng. trans. (1929), is good particularly for descriptions of social life; while the interpretations and conclusions in the monographs of Albert Babeau may be challenged, the studies themselves retain their value as works of reference: *Les Artisans et les domestiques d'autrefois* (1886), *Les Bourgeois d'autrefois* (1886), *La Ville sous l'ancien régime* (1884), *La Province sous l'ancien régime,* 2 vols. (1894), *Le Village sous l'ancien régime* (1879), and *Paris en 1789* (1891). P. Ariès, *Centuries of Childhood,* trans. from the French by R. Baldick (1962) throws great light on social evolution through the study of changing attitudes toward children; C. Kunstler's two vols., *La Vie quotidienne sous Louis XV* (1953) and *La Vie quotidienne sous Louis XVI* (1950), are facile descriptive accounts which make interesting reading; G. Lefebvre, *Études orléanaises:* Vol. I, *Contribution à l'étude des structures sociales à la fin du XVIIIe siècle* (1962), its title notwithstanding, this posthumously published work is a major contribution to the study of social structures in France as a whole. There is a mine of information in the old classic work of E. Levasseur, *Histoire des classes ouvrières avant 1789,* Vol. II (1901); C. E. Labrousse, *Esquisse du mouvement des prix et des revenus en France au XVIIIe siècle,* 2 vols. (1933), the first of the author's great inquiries into economic developments; M. Marion, *Histoire financière de la France depuis 1715,* Vol. I (1914), a standard account; on the peasantry, there are also M. Bloch, *Les Caractères originaux de l'histoire rurale française,* rev. ed. (1952), and G. Lefebvre, "Les Recherches relatives à la repartition de la propriété et de l'exploitation foncière à la fin de l'ancien régime," in *Revue d'histoire moderne,* March–April, 1928, pp. 103–130. Various special topics are taken up by J. Bourgeois-Pichat, "Evolution de la population en France depuis le 18e siècle," *Population*, Vol. VI (1951), pp. 635–660; G. Martin, *La Grande Industrie en France sous le règne de Louis XV* (1920); H. Cavaillès, *La Route française, son histoire et sa fonction* (1946); C. A. Julien, *Les Français en Amérique de 1713 à 1784*, 2 vols. (1955); H. Blet, *Histoire de la colonisation française*, 3 vols. (1946–1950), see Vol. I.

3. *The three legal classes*

On the clergy there are Abbé A. Sicard, *L'Ancien Clergé de France*, 5 vols. (1894–1912); C. L. Chassin, *Les Cahiers des curés* (1888); F. D. Mathieu, *L'Ancien Régime en Lorraine* (1907). The conclusions of H. Carré, *La Noblesse de France et l'opinion publique au XVIIIe siècle* (1920), and P. de Vaissière, *Gentilshommes compagnards de l'ancienne France* (1904), concerning the position of the nobility are modified by R. Forster, *The Nobility of Toulouse in the Eighteenth Century* (Baltimore, 1960). *The Memoirs of Madame Campan*, Eng. trans. (1887), and *Recollections of Baron Frénilly 1768–1828* (1909), deal with the court nobility on whom there is also rich material in A. Castelot, *Queen of France*, Eng. trans. (1957); L. and C. de Loménie, *Beaumarchais and His Times*, Vols. I and II, in trans. (1861); and G. Lacour-Gayet, *Talleyrand, 1754–1838*, 3 vols., trans. from French (1928–1931), of which the first volume deals with the Old Regime. E. Barber, *The Bourgeoisie in Eighteenth Century France* (Princeton, 1955) is an admirable monograph on the progressive alienation of the upper middle classes. Under the impress of G. Lefebvre's *Les Paysans du Nord pendant la Révolution française*, 2 vols. (1924), recent researches have critically re-examined the position of the peasantry in several regions: P. de Saint-Jacob, *Les Paysans de la Bourgogne du Nord au dernier siècle de l'ancien régime* (1960); P. Bois, *Les Paysans de l'Ouest* (1960); P. Goubert, *Beauvais et le Beauvaisis de 1600 à 1730* (1961); A. Soboul, "The French Rural Community in the Eighteenth and Nineteenth Centuries," in *Past and Present*, no. 10 (1956), pp. 78–95, a useful approach.

"THE CLIMATE OF OPINION"

1. *European thought and culture*

E. Cassirer, *The Philosophy of the Enlightenment*, trans. from German (Princeton, 1951); A. Cobban, *In Search of Humanity* (London, 1960), a stimulating revaluation of the intellectual and moral temper of the European Enlightenment; P. Hazard, *The European Mind, 1680–1715*, Eng. trans. (New Haven, 1953), a probing presentation of the "crisis of the European conscience"; P. Smith, *A History of Modern Culture*: Vol. II, *The Enlightenment, 1687–1776* (1934), sympathetic and learned, covering all aspects of the period; the old classic of L. Stephen, *History of English Thought in the Eighteenth Century*, 2 vols. (1896); F. C. Green, *Minuet* (London, 1935), a sprightly and learned survey of French and English literary relations; A. Reichwein, *China and Europe: Intellectual and Artistic Contacts in the*

Eighteenth Century (1925); A. Wolf, *A History of Science, Technology, and Philosophy in the 18th Century*, 2nd ed., 2 vols. (Torchbook paperback, 1961) is useful for reference; J. U. Nef, *War and Human Progress* (Chicago, 1950), a stimulating refutation of the thesis that militarism was a barometer of cultural and scientific progress; F. E. Manuel, *The Eighteenth Century Confronts the Gods* (Cambridge, Mass., 1959), a brilliant and original study; V. L. Tapié, *Baroque and Classicism: The Age of Grandeur*, trans. from Fr. (1960), and L. Réau, *Histoire de l'expansion de l'art français*, 4 vols. (1924–1934) do full justice certainly to French artistic domination.

2. The French Enlightenment

K. Martin, *The Rise of French Liberal Thought*, rev. ed. (1956); D. Mornet, *French Thought in the Eighteenth Century* (1929); and G. R. Havens, *The Age of Ideas* (1955), present the main currents of liberal thought in brief compass, while Mornet's *Les Origines intellectuelles de la Révolution française*, rev. ed. (1954), minimizes the social background but is otherwise authoritative. A. Lichtenberger, *Le Socialisme au XVIIIe siècle* (1895), takes up the more radical aspects of French speculation. The following works bear directly on the key concept of liberal rationalism: J. B. Bury, *The Idea of Progress* (1920) and in paperback; the controversial classic of C. Becker, *The Heavenly City of the Eighteenth Century Philosophers* (1932), which is critically re-examined a quarter of a century later in R. O. Rockwood, ed., *Carl Becker's Heavenly City Revisited* (Ithaca, 1958), C. Frankel, *The Faith of Reason: The Idea of Progress in the French Enlightenment* (1948), and R. V. Sampson, *Progress in the Age of Reason, The Seventeenth Century to the Present Day* (Cambridge, Mass., 1956), defend the essential validity of the concept; and F. E. Manuel, *The Prophets of Paris* (Cambridge, Mass., 1962) brilliantly situates Turgot and Condorcet in the mainstream of utopian thought; see too the work of J. S. Schapiro, *Condorcet and the Rise of Liberalism* (1934). The brief monograph of H. Vyverberg, *Historical Pessimism in the French Enlightenment* (Cambridge, Mass., 1958), shows, so to speak, the other side of the coin. J. S. Spink, *French Free Thought from Gassendi to Voltaire* (London, 1960), and L. G. Crocker, *Man and World in Eighteenth Century French Thought* (Baltimore, 1959), both emphasize the moral aspects of French philosophical speculation. R. R. Palmer, *Catholics and Unbelievers in Eighteenth Century France* (Princeton, 1939), brings out the scope of religious controversy, and P. Trahard, *Les Maîtres de la sensibilité française au XVIIIe siècle*, 4 vols. (1931–1933), gives an exhaustive account of the humanitarian-philanthropic mood among the men of letters. In E. G. Léonard, *L'Armée et ses problèmes au XVIIIe siècle* (1958), and E. Carrias, *La Pensée militaire française* (1960), military developments are linked to movements of thought.

3. The philosophes

The literature on the *philosophes* is vast, and the following titles represent only a very small sampling of the more recent works. For Rousseau there are his own writings, such as C. E. Vaughan, *Political Writings of J. J. Rousseau*, 2 vols. (1915); T. Dufour and P. Plon, eds., *Correspondance de J. J. Rousseau*, 20 vols. (1924–1934); and C. W. Hendel, ed., *The Citizen of Geneva: Selections from the Letters of Jean-Jacques Rousseau* (1937). E. H. Wright, *The Meaning of Rousseau* (1929), treats Jean-Jacques with greater sympathy than does the vivid biography of F. C. Green, *Jean-Jacques Rousseau* (London, 1955). A. Cobban, *Rousseau and the Modern State* (London, 1934) along with A. Derathé, *Jean-Jacques Rousseau et la science politique de son temps* (1950), are good for the basic unity of Rousseau's political views. The Protean character of Diderot's speculation receives its due in L. Crocker, *The Embattled Philosopher, A Life of Denis Diderot* (East Lansing, 1954); A. M. Wilson, *Diderot, The Testing Years, 1713–1759* (1957); and in the more technical study of A. Vartanian, *Diderot and Descartes* (Princeton, 1953). Peter Gay, *Voltaire's Politics: The Poet as Realist* (Princeton, 1959), is an able study which emphasizes the extent to which Voltaire was courageously committed to reform, as does the Introduction to the same author's translation of the *Philosophical Dictionary*, 2 vols. (1962). G. Lanson, *Voltaire* (1906), is the best of the older biographies; and G. Desnoiresterres, *Voltaire et la société au XVIIIe siècle*, 8 vols. (1871–1876), remains a matchless source. R. Shackleton, *Montesquieu: A Critical Biography* (1961), incorporates the results of recent research. For the vogue of Franklin, see A. O. Aldridge, *Franklin and his French Contemporaries* (1957).

THE REFORM MOVEMENT IN EUROPE

1. *General works*

M. S. Anderson, *Europe in the Eighteenth Century, 1713–1783* (London, 1961), an excellent manual, topically arranged, covering Europe as a whole rather than particular states; E. Préclin and V. L. Tapié, *Le XVIIIe Siècle*, 2 vols. (1952), in the Clio series, sober on the facts, but useful for discussion of interpretations; the older studies cited in the original bibliography are superseded by R. Mousnier, C. E. Labrousse, and M. Bouloiseau, *Le 18e Siècle; révolution intellectuelle, technique et politique, 1715–1815* (1953), Vol. V in the Histoire générale series. G. Lefebvre, *La Révolution française*, Vol. XIII in the Peuples et civilisations series, rev. ed. (1957), Book One is a symphonic treatment of Europe in the eighteenth century and contains an admirable bibliography. P. Sagnac, *La Fin de l'ancien régime et la Révolution américaine*, Vol. XII of the same series (1941), also up to date and good for the extra-European world. Three consecutive volumes in the Rise of Modern Europe series (bibliographies) deal in detail with pre-revolutionary Europe: P. Roberts, *The Quest for Security, 1715–1740* (1947); W. L. Dorn, *Competition for Empire, 1740–1763* (1940); and L. Gershoy, *From Despotism to Revolution, 1763–1789* (1944), all with revised bibliographies in Harper Torchbooks paperbacks.

2. *Enlightened despotism*

The volumes of Dorn and Gershoy, cited above, give detailed bibliographies. G. Bruun, *The Enlightened Despots* (1929), is a crisp, suggestive introduction to the subject. Among noteworthy works on Prussia, see W. Oncken, *Das Zeitalter Friedrichs des Grossen*, 2 vols. (1881–1882); W. H. Bruford, *Germany in the Eighteenth Century* (1952), a reliable survey, stressing literary developments; R. Koser, *Geschichte Friedrichs des Grossen*, 5th ed., 4 vols. (1912–1914); P. Gaxotte, *Frederick the Great*, trans. from Fr. (New Haven, 1942); G. P. Gooch, *Frederick the Great: The Ruler, the Writer, the Man* (1947); H. Brunschwig, *La Crise de l'état prussien à la fin du XVIIIe siècle* (1947), on the costs of Frederick's enlightened despotism. For the Hapsburgs, there is F. Valsecchi, *L'assolutismo illuminato in Europa; l'opera riformatrice di Maria Teresa e di Giuseppe II* (Milan, 1952); in English, the brief biographies of J. F. Bright, *Maria Theresa* (1897) and *Joseph II* (1897), readable but sketchy; S. K. Padover, *The Revolutionary Emperor: Joseph II* (1934), very eulogistic; E. M. Link, *The Emancipation of the Austrian Peasant, 1740–1798* (1949), a useful monograph; H. Marczali, *Hungary in the Eighteenth Century*, trans. from Hungarian (1910), and R. J. Kerner, *Bohemia in the Eighteenth Century* (1932), the last two lighting up the resistance to the Austrian centralizing authoritarianism. On Catherine, apart from the general histories, one has K. Anthony, *Catherine the Great* (1925), sketchy; two still useful studies of K. Waliszewski, both in translation, *Romance of an Empress* (1894), and *Story of a Throne*, 2 vols. (London, 1895); and E. A. B. Hodgetts, *The Life of Catherine the Great of Russia* (London, 1914). J. Fabre, *Stanislas-Auguste Poniatowski et l'Europe des lumières* (1952), is a fresh account of the ill-fated Polish reformer. R. N. Bain, *Gustave III and his Contemporaries*, 2 vols. (1894), is sharply critical of enlightened despotism in Sweden, while Beth Hennings, *Gustav III. En Biografi*, 2nd ed. (Stockholm, 1957), is a major rehabilitation. G. Natali, ed., *Il Settecento*, 3rd ed., 2 vols. (Milan, 1930), is basic for the Italian Enlightenment; for reforms in Hapsburg Italy, the earlier work of F. Valsecchi, *L'assolutismo illuminato in Austria e in Lombardia*, 2 vols. (Bologna, 1931–1934), is useful. The two standard histories of Spain are R. Altamira y Crevea, *Historia de la civilización española*, 4 vols., rev. ed. (Barcelona, 1913–1914); and Vols IV and V of A. Ballesteros y Beretta, *Historia de España y su influencia en la historia universal*, 9 vols. (Barcelona, 1918–1941). Though G. Desdevises du Dezert, *L'Espagne de l'ancien régime*, 3 vols. (1897–1904), is the once classic study, both J. Sarrailh, *L'Espagne éclairée de la seconde moitié du XVIIIe siècle* (1954), and R. Herr, *The Eighteenth-Century Revolution in Spain* (Princeton, 1958), throw fresh light on the scope and the uniqueness of the Spanish Enlightenment. For the Spanish colonies, there is A. P. Whitaker, *Latin America and the Enlightenment* (1942). M. Cheke, *Dictator of Portugal: Life of Marquis de Pombal, 1699–1782* (London, 1938), is hostile and uncritical, and a good biography in English still remains to be written.

THE REFORM MOVEMENT IN FRANCE, 1763–1789

1. *From 1763 to 1787*

The extraordinary impact of the Physiocrats on the reform movement is exhaustively treated in G. Weulersse, *Le Mouvement physiocratique depuis 1756 à 1770*, 2 vols. (1910), *La Physiocratie à la fin du règne de Louis XV, 1770–1774* (1959), and *La Physiocratie sous les ministéres de Turgot et de Necker* (1950); and in brief compass there is H. Higgs, *The Physiocrats* (1897). For light on Turgot, G. Schelle, *Oeuvres de Turgot et documents le concernant*, 5 vols. (1913–1923), is the primary work of reference; D. Dakin, *Turgot and the Ancien Régime in France* (London, 1939), is broader and generally more revealing than the more recent E. Faure, *La Disgrâce de Turgot, 12 mai, 1776* (1961). L. Gottschalk's articles on America in the causal pattern of the French Revolution, cited under "Notes on Historiography," are elaborated on in D. Echeverria, *Mirage in the West: A History of the French Image of American Society to 1815* (Princeton, 1957), and L. Villard, *La France et les Etats-Unis: échanges et rencontres, 1524–1800* (1952), which are more balanced than B. Faÿ, *The Revolutionary Spirit in France and America*, Eng. trans. (1927). The waning of the prestige of England is ably discussed in F. Acomb, *Anglophobia in France, 1763–1789* (Durham, 1950), and G. Bonno, *La Constitution britannique devant l'opinion française de Montesquieu à Bonaparte* (1932). The false antithesis between "ideas" and "circumstances," is well handled with references to the literature in Palmer's *The Age of the Democratic Revolution*, given under "Notes on Historiography." R. Priouret, *La Franc-maçonnerie sous les lys* (1953), which maintains that freemasonry was less influential than generally supposed, is the most recent of the works on that subject which include the balanced G. Martin, *La Franc-maçonnerie française et la préparation de la Révolution*, 2nd ed. (1926); G. Huard, *L'Art royal: Essai sur l'histoire de la franc-maçonnerie* (1930); and A. Lantone, *Histoire de la franc-maçonnerie française; la franc-maçonnerie dans l'état* (1935). Various aspects of reform under state aegis are treated in the great work of C. Bloch, *L'Aissistance et l'état en France à la veille de la Révolution* (1909); S. McCloy, *Government Assistance in Eighteenth Century France* (Durham, N.C., 1946), a useful study, and the same author's *The Humanitarian Movement in Eighteenth-Century France* (Lexington, Ky., 1957). The reforms and discussion of military reforms are examined in R. S. Quimby, *The Background of Napoleonic Warfare* (1956). For the stirring of French conscience, in addition to the works given under "The Climate of Opinion," see also E. D. Seeber, *Anti-Slavery Opinion in France during the Second Half of the Eighteenth Century* (Baltimore, 1937); C. L. Lokke, *France and the Colonial Question, 1763–1801* (1932); E. V. Souleyman, *The Vision of World Peace in Seventeenth and Eighteenth Century France* (1941); M. T. Maestro, *Voltaire and Beccaria as Reformers of Criminal Law* (1942); R. Anchel, *Crimes et châtiments au 18e siècle*, 2nd ed. (1933); and D. Bien, *The Calas Affair* (Princeton, 1960), a careful monograph on Calas in particular and on the spread of religious tolerance in general.

2. The coming of the Revolution, 1787–1789

The best brief introduction to this subject is G. Lefebvre's *The Coming of the French Revolution*, trans. by R. R. Palmer (Princeton, 1947), the work of a master. E. Labrousse, *La Crise de l'économie française à la fin de l'ancien régime et au début de la Révolution* (1943), is a pioneering work of the highest importance; R. W. Greenlaw, ed., *The Economic Origins of the French Revolution: Poverty or Prosperity?* (Boston, 1958), excerpts from the historians with critical commentary, which puts the popular old E. Champion, *La France d'après les cahiers* (1897), in better perspective. J. Egret, *La Prérévolution française* (1787–1788) .(1962), is a valuable work which sums up his earlier studies and discloses the vitality of the monarchy in its last years. The calculated maneuvers of all concerned on the eve of 1789 are painstakingly traced in M. B. Garrett, *The Estates General of 1789* (1935); B. C. Shafer, "Bourgeois Nationalism in the Pamphlets on the Eve of the French Revolution," *Journal of Modern History*, Vol. X (1938), pp. 31–50; B. F. Hyslop, "French Gild Opinion in 1789," *American Historical Review*, Vol. XLIV (1939), pp. 252–271; A. Goodwin, "Calonne, the Assembly of French Notables of 1787 and the Origins of the 'Révolte nobiliaire'," *English Historical Review*, Vol. LXI (1946), pp. 329–377; L. Gottschalk, *Lafayette between the American and the French Revolution* (Chicago, 1950); A. Cobban, "Historical Revisions, No. CVII: The Beginning of the French Revolution," *History*, Vol. XXX (1945), pp. 90–98; and G. Rudé, "The Outbreak of the French Revolution," *Past and Present*, no. 8 (1955), pp. 28–42. The memoirs of Mollien, Talleyrand, Madame de Staël, Ferrières, Malouet, Frénilly, Hardy, Barère, and Saint-Priest are rich in descriptive material. For biographies of the early leaders of 1789, see the section below on the Revolution.

II. THE REVOLUTION

NOTES ON HISTORIOGRAPHY

Perhaps the first observation concerning the historiography of the French Revolution should be recognition of revived interest and research in an old field at the very time that fresh issues and new problems are understandably enlisting the intellectual energies of professional historians. Much of this vitality manifests itself in study of aspects and facets which had either been entirely neglected or had not received due attention. Though it would be hopelessly naive to state that political and religious passions have disappeared in the newer works, it is correct to say that they have appreciably abated. More and more, the revolutionary decade is being set in a broader frame, as a sociological and anthropological phenomenon not unrelated to revolutionary movements elsewhere, before and after.

If the Revolution was a watershed in the history of the modern world, it also maintained continuity with the past. The revolutionists destroyed much, it is true; they also preserved and honored many of the cultural and scientific achievements of their ancestors, particularly those of the age of enlightenment.

Politically radical from the outset, the Revolution was traditionalist with respect to the great legacy. From the outset, too, conservatism jostled radicalism, but it was a conservatism that was inherent in French thinking. The Revolution gave it fresh direction and new depth. The permanent counter-Revolution had many faces.

So too did the Revolution. Many careful monographs have taken up the aspirations and actions of the peasantry, particularly the poorer ranks, as well as the autonomous strivings of the urban masses. The groups that conservative historians uniformly and the liberal historians intermittently once characterized as "the mob" have been rebaptized under the neutral appelation of "the crowd," and their social composition and behavior have been examined with sympathetic new understanding.

We now know much more than ever before how far—and how little—the social idealism of the Robespierrists carried them toward meeting the needs of the proletariat and satisfying the hopes of the anonymous underprivileged. The domestic and foreign policies of the post-Terror governments have been realistically reassessed, presenting a revaluation which puts Bonaparte's seizure of power in Brumaire in a new light. A virtually new body of literature has come into being on the related topics of foreign war and revolutionary ideological expansion. The decisive impact of war on the national economy as well as on political radicalism and governmental coercion has been closely studied. The reception of the Revolution outside France, and its rejection too, has been traced in studies of individual and group Francophiles in neighboring states and in the United States as well. The study of the French Revolution has not been exhausted.

The standard historiographies of G. P. Gooch, E. Fueter, and J. M. Thompson (given in Howe) discuss earlier interpretations. Useful brief accounts stressing the researches of Aulard, Mathiez, and Lefebvre will be found in the revised Torchbook (1963) paperback edition of Crane Brinton, *A Decade of Revolution, 1789–1799*, and in R. R. Palmer's Introduction to his translation of G. Lefebvre's *1789* under the title of *The Coming of the Revolution* (Princeton, 1947); other brief accounts are in L. Villat, *La Révolution et l'Empire, 1789–1815*, new ed., 2 vols. (1940–1942): Vol. I, *Les Assemblées révolutionnaires, 1789–1799*, and G. P. Gooch, "The Study of the French Revolution" in his *Maria Theresa and Other Studies* (1951); and a longer, interesting discussion in P. Farmer, *France Reviews Its Revolutionary Origins* (1944). Both P. Beik, *The French Revolution Seen from the Right* (Philadelphia, 1956), and S. Mellon, *Political Uses of History: A Study of Historians in the French Restoration* (Stanford, 1958), analyze the writings of the conservative-minded historians. The view that the Revolution was radical from the start is vigorously presented in Palmer's *The Age of the Democratic Revolution*, given under "Notes on Historiography" in the Old Regime bibliography; also his interesting article, "Recent Interpretations of the Influence of the French Revolution," *Cahiers d'histoire mondiale*, Vol. II (1954), pp. 173–195. Both J. H. Stewart, "The Era of the French Revolution: Opportunities for Research and Writing," *Journal of Modern History*, Vol. XXIX (1957), pp. 85–98, and R. Cobb, "The Era of the French Revolution; Some Comments on Opportunities for Research and Writing," *Journal of Modern*

History, Vol. XXX (1958), pp. 118–131, make interesting suggestions. The new approach and the controversy over it are in Godechot, *Les Révolutions, 1770–1799*, already cited.

BIBLIOGRAPHICAL AIDS AND BIBLIOGRAPHIES

Besides the relevant references given under the Old Regime, see particularly P. Caron, *Manuel pratique pour l'étude de la Révolution française*, rev. ed. (1947); the exhaustive titles in M. Tourneux, *Bibliographie de l'histoire de Paris pendant la Révolution française*, 5 vols. (1890–1913); G. Walter, *Bibliothèque nationale: Répertoire de l'histoire de la Révolution française, travaux publiés de 1800 à 1940*, Vol. I: *Personnes* (1941), Vol. II: *Lieux* (1951), Vol. III: *Matières* (1953); A. Martin and G. Walter, *Catalogue de l'histoire de la Révolution*, 5 vols. (1936–1955); A. Monglond, *La France révolutionnaire et impériale; Annales de bibliographie méthodique et descriptive des livres illustrés*, 7 vols. (Grenoble, 1930–1953); also A. Soricks, *A Bibliography of the Frank E. Melvin Collection of Pamphlets of the French Revolution in the University of Kansas Libraries*, 2 vols. (Lawrence, Kan., 1960). Current bibliographical information may be found in the general historical reviews, e.g., *The American Historical Review*; in more specialized periodicals, such as *Annales historiques de la Révolution française*, and in the periodical retrospective articles in *Revue historique* and *The Journal of Modern History*.

SOURCES AND WORKS OF REFERENCE

The titles given below refer to the most useful general sources. The invaluable introduction to the manuscript material is A. Tuetey, *Sources de l'histoire de Paris pendant la Révolution*, 11 vols. (1890–1914). For detailed data on manuscript material as well as on the hundreds of critically edited volumes published under official governmental auspices dealing with the laws and decrees of the assemblies, the work of committees, commissions, and municipalities, memoirs, and writings of individuals, the study by Caron is indispensable. Similar information in briefer compass is also to be found in Vol. I of the Villat already cited. For the Estates General, consult the authoritative collection of A. Brette, *Recueil de documents relatifs à la convocation des états généraux de 1789*, 3 vols. (1894–1904); the *Recueil de documents relatifs aux séances des états généraux, mai-juin 1789*, G. Lefebvre and Anne Terroine, eds. (1953), fills the gap between the drafting of the cahiers and the opening sessions of the Constituent Assembly. The official *procès-verbaux* of the debates which each of the revolutionary assemblies published are extremely difficult to find and, in any case, of limited utility. The *Archives parlementaires*, already given, though subject to some caution especially for the earlier volumes, cover the parliamentary proceedings in great detail to January 1794. Beginning with 1793, the annual *Almanac royal* became the *Almanac national*. Of the extraordinarily great number of contemporary newspapers, most of which in one fashion or another gave accounts of the assembly debates (also discussed in Caron), easily the most useful is the reprint, under the title of *Réimpression* of *l'ancien Moniteur*, 31 vols., several editions, of the long-lived *Gazette nationale* ou *Moniteur universel*. The *Histoire parlementaire de la Révolution française*, 40 vols., P. B. Bouchez and P. C. Roux, eds., (1834–1838) is a curiously interesting mélange of data compiled from the sources by two Christian Socialists. The collections of sources edited by F. A. Aulard, long dean of revolutionary studies, are invaluable: *La Société des Jacobins*, 6 vols. (1889–1896), *Recueil des actes du comité de salut public*, 28 vols. (1889–1951), and *Paris pendant la réaction thermidorienne et sous le Directoire*, 5 vols. (1898–1902). Many of the printed minutes of the Jacobin clubs of the provinces are in C. Brinton, *The Jacobins* (1930). Memoirs of contemporaries are given below at appropriate places.

Among the works of reference useful for the entire period from 1789 to 1815 the student should note: J. Godechot, *Les Institutions de la France sous la Révolution et l'Empire* (1951); P. Sagnac, *La Législation civile de la Révolution française, 1789–1804* (1898); E. Faguet, ed., *L'Oeuvre sociale de la Révolution* (1898), interesting articles; M. Deslandres, *Histoire constitutionelle de la France de 1789 à 1815* (1932); M. Marion, *Histoire financiére de la France depuis 1715*, 5 vols. (1914–1932), Vol. I on the Old Regime and Vols. II–IV on the Revolution; G. Six, and others, *Dictionnaire biographique des généraux et amiraux français de la Révolution et de l'Empire, 1792–1814*, 2 vols. (1934), by recognized scholars. Of the documentary collections, there are in English translation the valuable old F. M. Anderson, *Constitutions and Other Documents Illustrative of the History of France* (Minneapolis, 1904); the more recent J. H. Stewart, *A Documentary Survey of the French Revolution* (1951), which gives a running account through the medium of complete and excerpted documents; in the original French text, L. Cahen and R. Guyot, *L'Oeuvre législative de la Révolution française* (1913); J. M. Thompson, *The French Revolution: Documents, 1789–1794* (1933); L. G. W. Legg, *Select Documents Illustrative of the History of the French Revolution: The Constituent Assembly*, 2 vols. (London, 1905); copious debates and excerpts from the parliamentary debates in H. M. Stephens, *The Principal Speeches of the Statesmen and Orators of the French Revolution, 1789–1795*, 2 vols. (London, 1882); also in two works edited by Aulard: *Les Orateurs de la Constituante*, 2nd ed. (1906), and *Les Orateurs de la Législative et de la Convention*, 2 vols. (1885–1886). A. Kuscinski, *Dictionnaire des Conventionnels* (1916–1919), is a convenient and reliable guide.

GENERAL ACCOUNTS

Among the briefer recent treatments there are Brinton and Villat, cited under "Notes on Historiography"; the former, with an excellent bibliography, is brilliantly written, ironic, and thought provoking. J. M. Thompson, *The French Revolution* (1943), based upon the author's long, independent researches in the sources; English translations of the two strongly pro-Revolution and pro-Robespierre accounts by the towering Albert Mathiez, *The French Revolution* (1928), and *After Robespierre, The Thermidorian Reaction* (1931); of the two introductory studies by L. Gershoy, *The French Revolu-*

tion, 1789–1799, in the Berkshire Studies in European History (1932), and *The Era of the French Revolution, 1789–1799: Ten Years that Shook the World* (Princeton, 1957), the latter has accompanying excerpts from the sources; A. Goodwin, *The French Revolution* (1953 and in paperback), especially good on the earlier period; G. Salvemini, *The French Revolution: 1788–1799,* trans. from Italian (1958 and in paperback), reflects the libertarian creed of the great anti-fascist scholar; A. Soboul, *Précis d'histoire de la Révolution française* (1962), succinct synthesis by a leading Marxist scholar; P. Gaxotte, *The French Revolution* (1932), translation of a once immensely popular work sweepingly hostile to the revolutionary movement; N. Webster, *The French Revolution* (London, 1919), a full, almost hysterical elaboration of the "conspiracy" thesis.

Among the earlier brief treatments there are F. Mignet, *History of the French Revolution from 1789 to 1814,* many editions of this thoughtful century-old classic, first published in 1842; Lord Acton, *Lectures on the French Revolution* (1910), excellent, especially for political and constitutional developments; P. Kropotkin, *The Great French Revolution, 1789–1793* (1909), translation of the famous Russian anarchist's study which treats the Revolution in terms of the class struggle between the bourgeoisie and the proletariat; L. Madelin, *The French Revolution,* trans. from Fr. (1916), exciting, learned, and disillusioned. L. Gottschalk's well known college textbook, *The Era of the French Revolution,* first ed. (1929), remains a reliable introduction.

For the longer, detailed treatments, there are, first, two volumes in Lavisse's Histoire de France contemporaine series: P. Sagnac, *La Révolution, 1789–1792* (1920), and G. Pariset, *La Révolution, 1792–1799* (1921); and the modern classic of G. Lefebvre, *La Révolution française* in the Peuples et civilisations series, rev. ed. (1957), of which the first half has been translated as *The French Revolution from its Origins to 1793* (1962), and the second half is forthcoming; also to be used with profit are F. A. Aulard, *The French Revolution, A Political History,* 4 vols. (1910), translation of an earlier work by the then leading French authority, and J. Jaurès, *Histoire socialiste de la Révolution française,* ed. by A. Mathiez, 8 vols. (1922–1924), a remarkable work by the famous socialist leader, stressing economic and social issues. The once classical nineteenth century works include Madame de Staël, *Considérations sur la Révolution française,* 2 vols. (1818), cool and sensible; L. A. Thiers, *History of the French Revolution,* trans. from Fr., 5 vols. (London, 1895), favorable to the early moderate revolution; J. Michelet, *Histoire de la Révolution française,* rev. ed., 9 vols. (1883–1887), dramatic paean to "the people" by a militant nationalist liberal; T. Carlyle, *The French Revolution,* 3 vols., ed. by C. R. L. Fletcher (1912), published originally in 1837, this famous literary extravaganza still maintains its hold on English readers; the still serviceable *Histoire de la Révolution française,* 12 vols. (1847–1862), by Louis Blanc, the first of the many pro-Socialist and pro-Robespierre histories; and the vigorous indictment of H. Taine, *The French Revolution,* 3 vols., in Eng. trans. (1878–1885), the middle part of his *Origines de la France contemporaine.*

SPECIAL STUDIES

The titles which follow should be supplemented by the references given later under specific periods, and also by those under "Revolutionary Expansion." There are many brief articles, largely political, in F. A. Aulard, *Études et leçons sur la Révolution française*, Vols. I–IX (1893–1924), and a convenient collection of Lefebvre's pieces, mainly on social-economic topics, in *Études sur la Révolution française* (1954).

The cultural and scientific achievements in G. Pouchet, *Les Sciences pendant la terreur*, rev. ed. (1896), comprehensive; J. Fayet, *La Révolution française et la science, 1789–1795* (1960), emphasizing the continuity with the work of the Old Regime; H. Guerlac, "Some Aspects of Science during the French Revolution," *The Scientific Monthly*, Vol. 80 (1955), pp. 93–101; L. Pearce Williams, "Science, Education and the French Revolution," *Isis*, Vol. 44 (1953), pp. 311–330, largely on the *écoles centrales* of the Directory; F. Brunot, *Histoire de la langue française*, Vol. IX, Parts One and Two (1927–1937), an admirable study full of fertile suggestions. The continuity with the Old Regime is also brought out in P. Trahard, *La Sensibilité révolutionnaire* (1936), and A. Monglond, *Le préromantisme français* (Grenoble, 1930), while F. Baldensperger, *Le Mouvement des idées dans l'émigration française*, 2 vols. (1924), focuses on the newer currents of thought; H. T. Parker, in *The Cult of Antiquity and the French Revolution* (Chicago, 1937), raises doubts on the phenomenon in question. The volumes by Sagnac and Pariset in the Lavisse series, as well as Godechot's *Les Institutions*, are good on the educational reforms, for which see also B. Bois, *La Vie scolaire et les créations intellectuelles en Anjou pendant la Révolution, 1789–1799* (1929); J. Tiersot, *Les Fêtes et les chants de la Révolution française* (1908), for the utilization of public festivals in revolutionary education; and particularly for cultural propaganda, David L. Dowd, *Pageant-Master of the Republic: J.-L. David and the French Revolution* (Lincoln, Neb., 1948). E. F. Henderson, *Symbol and Satire in the French Revolution* (1912) is an interesting volume of pictorial satires; and two outstanding specialists, P. Sagnac and J. Robiquet, have cooperated on a pictorial history, *La Révolution de 1789*, 2 vols. (1934). For the little facts of everyday life, there is Robiquet's *La Vie quotidienne au temps de la Révolution* (1938).

Three outstanding works on the church are A. Latreille, *L'Église catholique et la Révolution française*, 2 vols. (1946–1950), Vol. I covering the period to 1799; Canon J. Leflon, *La Crise révolutionnaire* (1949) in the Histoire de l'Église series ed. by A. Fliche and Y. Martin; and the superb detailed work of P. de la Gorce, *Histoire religieuse de la Révolution française*, 5 vols. (1909–1923), of which the first 3 vols. go up to Thermidor. In English, C. S. Phillips, *The Church in France, 1789–1848* (1929), largely follows de la Gorce. M. H. Jette, *La France religieuse du XVIIIe siècle, de la Révolution, et de l'Empire* (1956), and C. Ledré, *L'Église de France sous la Révolution* (1949), are intended for the general reader. The now old study by C. Durand, *Histoire du protestantisme français pendant la Révolution et l'Empire* (1902), is supplemented by the useful monograph of B. C. Poland, *French Protestantism and the French Revolution, 1685–1815* (Princeton, 1957); H. Lucien-Bruhl, *La Condition des juifs en France depuis 1789* (1900) is sketchy. Succinct treatments of the economic developments are in S. B. Clough, *France, A History of National Economics, 1789–1939* (1939), Ch. I, and in the introductory chapters of H. Sée, *Histoire économique de la France*, Vol. I (1948). The first volume of E. Levasseur, *Histoire des classes ouvrières et de l'industrie en France depuis 1789*, rev. ed., 2 vols. (1903), like A. Lichtenberger, *Le Socialisme et la Révolution française* (1899), is sympathetic to the working classes. For monetary policy, there are S. Harris, *The Assignats* (Cambridge, Mass., 1930), correcting Marion's hostile treatment, and F. Braesch, *Finances et monnaies révolutionnaires*, 5 vols. (Nancy, 1934–1936); F. L. Nussbaum, *Commercial Policy in the French Revolution. A Study of the Career of G. J. A. Ducher* (Washington, D.C., 1923), deals with nationalist economics. In addition to Lefebvre's *Les Paysans du Nord*, already cited, there are his luminous articles, "La Place de la Révolution dans l'histoire agraire de la France," *Annales d'histoire économique et sociale*, Vol. I (1929), pp. 506–523; "Les Recherches relatives à la vente des biens nationaux," in his *Études;* and the thoughtful essay by R. R. Palmer, "Georges Lefebvre: The Peasants and the French Revolution," *Journal of Modern History*, Vol. XXXI (1959), pp. 329–342. The composition and mentality of the "mobs" are treated with fresh insight in G. Rudé, *The Crowd in the French Revolution*, 2nd ed. (Oxford, 1960); G. Lefebvre, "Foules révolutionnaires," in his *Études;* and R. Cobb, "Quelques Aspects de la mentalité révolutionnaire, avril 1793– Thermidor, an II," *Revue d'histoire moderne et contemporaine*, Vol. VI (1959), pp. 81–120. L. L. T. Gosselin (G. Lenôtre, *pseud.*), *Paris révolutionnaire. Vieilles Maisons, vieux papiers*, roams learnedly and unsympathetically over the field of revolutionary behavior, and P. de Vaissiére, *Lettres d' "Aristocrates"* (1907) gives the course of events as narrated in the private correspondence of the nobility.

THE CONSTITUTIONAL MONARCHY, 1789–1792

1. *The crucial year*

Besides Lefebvre's *The Coming of the French Revolution*, see A. Soboul, *1789, l'an Un de la liberté* (1950), and F. Braesch, *1789: l'année cruciale* (1949), the latter contending that the Revolution could have stopped in that year. The decisive "journées" are examined in J. Flammermont, *La Journée du quatorze juillet, 1789* (1892), and P. Chauvet, *1789: l'insurrection Parisienne et la prise de la Bastille* (1946). For the decrees of August 4 and the peasant and urban uprisings, S. Herbert, *The Fall of Feudalism in France* (1921), and G. Lefebvre, *La Grande Peur de 1789* (1932). The march on Versailles is discussed in detail in A. Mathiez, "Étude critique sur les journées des 5 et 6 octobre," *Revue historique*, Vol. LXVII (1898), pp. 241–281; Vol. LXVIII (1898), pp. 258–294; Vol. LXIX (1899), pp. 41–66. C. B. Rogers, *The Spirit of Revolution in 1789* (1949), and B. F. Hyslop, *French Nationalism in 1789 according to the General Cahiers* (1934) give the mood of exaltation and hopefulness.

2. *Problems and achievements*

The drafting of the Declaration is carefully taken up in S. Kent, "The Declaration of the Rights of Man and Citizen," in R. M. McIver, ed., *Great Expressions of Human Rights* (1950), pp. 145–181. The theory and practice of government are treated in A. Mathiez, "La Révolution française et la théorie de la dictature," *Revue historique* (July–August, 1929), pp. 304–315, G. G. Andrews, *The Constitution in the Early French Revolution* (1927), and R. K. Gooch, *Parliamentary Government in France: Revolutionary Origins, 1789–1791* (Ithaca, 1960). I. Bourdin, *Les Sociétés populaires de Paris pendant la Révolution jusqu'à la chute de la royauté* (1937) is good on the leftist anti-government opposition. The king's flight and its consequences are given in V. Fournel, *L'Événement de Varennes* (1890), an authoritative account; the role of the promoters in O. de Heidenstam, *Marie Antoinette, Fersen, and Barnave* (1913); the political agitation in A. Mathiez, *Le Club des Cordeliers pendant la crise de Varennes et le massacre de Champ-de-Mars* (1910); the opposition to the social legislation, in G. M. Jaffé, *Le Mouvement ouvrier à Paris pendant la Révolution* (1924); and the documents themselves in P. Sagnac and P. Caron, *Les Comités des droits féodaux et de la législation et l'abolition du régime seigneurial* (1907). The growing alienation of the clergy is taken up by A. Mathiez in *Rome et le clergé sous la Constituante* (1910).

3. *The Legislative Assembly*

The sweepingly revisionist monograph of M. J. Sydenham, *The Girondins* (London, 1961), destroys many old legends, including the very existence of a Girondin party; for a Girondin leader, the discriminating biography of E. Ellery, *Brissot de Warville* (1905); on the Girondins' leading lady, the *Mémoires de Madame Roland*, ed. by C. Perroud, 2 vols. (1905), and Vol. II of the *Lettres de Madame Roland, 1780–1793*, also ed. by C. Perroud (1900–1902), which Carl Becker analyzes with his customary incisiveness in "The Memoirs and Letters of Madame Roland," *American Historical Review*, Vol. XXXIII, pp. 784–803; the sensitive biography of M. Clemenceau-Jacquemaire, *Vie de Madame Roland*, 2 vols. (1929). J. H. Clapham's *The Causes of the War of 1792* (London, 1899), distributes responsibilities with an even hand. For the last months of the constitutional monarchy, L. B. Pfeiffer, *The Uprising of June 20, 1792*, (1913); P. Sagnac, *La Chute de la royauté* (1909) stresses the importance of Danton, while A. Mathiez, *Le Dix août* (1931), consistently hostile, attributes a minor role to Danton in the overthrow of the monarchy. The antecedents of the September massacres are given in F. Braesch, *La Commune du dix août, étude sur l'histoire de Paris du 20 juin au 2 décembre 1792* (1911); P. Caron, *La Première Terreur*, 2 vols. (1950–1953) and the definitive study by the same author, *Les Massacres de septembre* (1935), which is well utilized by J. Herissay, *Les Journées de septembre, 1792* (1945), in an excellent study of popular terror and royalist intimidation.

4. *The early leaders*

In addition to the personal accounts in the memoirs of Bailly, Fersen, Malouet, Lally-Tollendal, Bouillé, Lafayette, Talleyrand, and Barère, and the commentaries of foreign observers, such as Gouverneur Morris, *Diary and Letters*, 2 vols. (1888), Vol. II, and B. Mallet, *Mallet du Pan and the French Revolution* (1902), there are many biographies. The following are a cross section of the most useful recent studies: J. H. Clapham, *The Abbé Siéyès* (1912); Ellery's *Brissot de Warville*, already given; J. J. Chevallier, *Barnave . . . deux faces de la Révolution, 1761–1793* (1936), which modifies the more favorable E. D. Bradby, *Life of Barnave*, 2 vols. (1915), Vol. I. J. Egret, *La Révolution des Notables: Mounier et les Monarchiens* (1950), J. J. Chevallier, *Mirabeau* (1947), and O. J. D. Welch, *Mirabeau, A Study of a Democratic Monarchist* (London, 1951), are more realistic than both L. Barthou's laudatory *Mirabeau*, Eng. trans. (1914), and L. and C. de Loménie's study already cited. A. de Bacourt, ed., *Correspondance entre Mirabeau et le comte de la Marck*, 3 vols. (1891), is still excellent for a revelation of Mirabeau's political tactics; for the Anglophiles, there are G. Michon, *Adrien Duport* (1924), and C. Du Bos, *Stanislas de Clermont-Tonnerre* (1931); on Talleyrand's long and fascinating adaptations, the detailed work of G. Lacour-Gayet, *Talleyrand*, 4 vols. (1928–1931), is informed and unfriendly; C. Brinton, *The Lives of Talleyrand* (1936), equally informed and more understanding; D. Cooper, *Talleyrand* (London, 1947), also sympathetic. L. Cahen, *Condorcet et la Révolution française* (1904) is a careful study; D. Walther, *Gouverneur Morris, témoin de deux révolutions* (Lausanne, 1932), is friendly in tone toward the American minister to France. Three collections of vignettes of revolutionary leaders are carefully grounded and interesting: H. Béraud, *Twelve Portraits of the French Revolution*, in Eng. trans. (1928); L. Madelin, *Figures of the Revolution*, in Eng. trans. (1929); J. M. Thompson, *Leaders of the French Revolution* (London, 1929), one of the best of its kind.

REVOLUTIONARY EXPANSION AND COUNTER-REVOLUTION

The most broadly conceived study of ideological and military expansion is J. Godechot, *La Grande Nation; l'expansion révolutionnaire de la France dans le monde de 1789 à 1799*, 2 vols. (1956), with a valuable bibliography; A. Fugier, *La Révolution française et l'Empire napoléonien* (1954), in the Histoire des relations internationales series, links formal diplomacy with social developments and public opinion; Vols. I–V of A. Sorel, *L'Europe et la Révolution française*, 8 vols. (1885–1904), H. von Sybel, *The French Revolution*, trans. from Ger., 4 vols. (1867–1869), and A. Wahl, *Geschichte des europäischen Staatensystems, 1789–1815* (Munich, 1912), all situate the foreign policy of the revolutionists in its European setting; for the British point of view, see Vol. I of A. W. Ward and G. P. Gooch, *Cambridge History of British Foreign Policy*, 3 vols. (1922–1923). The wars are exhaustively treated in A. Chuquet, *Les Guerres de la Révolution*, 11 vols. (1886–1896), going down to 1793, and R. W. Phipps, *The Armies of the First French Republic and the Rise of the Marshals of Napoleon,* 5 vols. (Oxford, 1926–1939). G. Six, *Les Généraux de la Révolution et de l'Empire* (1948) gives brief biographical sketches. The contrary and concurrent counter-revolutionary movement is studied with a fresh eye by J. Godechot, *La Contre-Révolution: doctrine et action, 1789–1804* (1961); and in the solid work of E. Vingtrinier, *Histoire de la contre-Révolution, 1789–1791,* 2 vols. (1924–1925); L. Madelin, *La Contre-Révolution sous la Révolution* (1935), is a more popular work. The cultural counter-revolution among the émigrés, is closely followed in Baldensperger, *Le Mouvement des idées,* already cited under "Special Studies"; A. Challamel, *Les Clubs contre-révolutionnaires* (1895) is informative on the organized opposition; and the reality of the court plot in 1792 is brought out in G. Lefebvre's articles, "Étude sur le ministère de Narbonne," *Annales historiques de la Révolution française* (1947), nos. 105, 107, and 108.

Vols. VI and VII of the great classic, W. E. H. Lecky, *History of England in the Eighteenth Century,* new ed., 7 vols. (1892) offer a comprehensive treatment; the activities of sympathizers and Gallophobes are examined from the sources in A. Cobban, ed., *The Debate on the French Revolution* (London, 1950), which also has valuable data on the controversy provoked by the publication of E. Burke, *Reflections on the Revolution in France,* and T. Paine, *The Rights of Man,* in many editions. P. A. Brown, *The French Revolution in English History* (London, 1918), is an excellent study of public opinion and organized activities; W. T. Laprade, *England and the French Revolution, 1789–1797* (Baltimore, 1909), is good on the government use of the radical scarecrow; W. P. Hall, *British Radicalism, 1791–1797* (1912); H. W. Meikle, *Scotland and the French Revolution* (1912); and R. Hayes, *Ireland and Irishmen in the French Revolution* (London, 1932). For Germany, G. P. Gooch, *Germany and the French Revolution* (1920), and J. Droz, *L'Allemagne et la Révolution française* (1949) are essential works; H. Voight, *Die deutsche jakobinische Literatur und Publizistik, 1789–1800* (Berlin, 1955) on the German radicals. The question of the Rhineland is examined in the following studies: P. Sagnac, *Le Rhin français pendant la Révolution et l'Empire* (1917), H. Oncken, *Die historische Rhein-politik der Franzosen* (Gotha, 1922), and S. S. Biro, *The German Policy of Revolutionary France,* 2 vols. (Cambridge, Mass., 1957) covering the years 1792–1797. On Switzerland see E. Chapuisat, *La Suisse et la Révolution française* (Geneva, 1945). General Belgian developments are in Vols. V and VI of H. Pirenne, *Histoire de la Belgique,* 6 vols. (Brussels, 1900–1926); more specialized studies in two works by S. Tassier, *Les Démocrats belges de 1789* (1930) and *Histoire de la Belgique sous l'occupation française en 1792 et 1793* (Brussels, 1934); also in P. Harsin, *La Révolution liégeoise de 1789* (Brussels, 1954). On Holland, the fifth volume of P. J. Blok, *History of the People of the Netherlands,* Eng. trans., 5 vols. (1898–1912), the best in English. The following general histories of Russia cover this period: V. O. Kliuchevsky, *History of Russia,* Eng. trans., 5 vols. (London, 1911–1931), Vols. IV and V; C. Seignobos, P. Milioukov, and L. Eisenmann, *Histoire de Russie,* Vol. II (1933), which also surveys the period to 1815; and M. T. Florinsky, *Russia, A History and an Interpretation,* 2 vols. (1953), Vol. II.

On the Italian peninsula, A. Franchetti, *Storia d'Italia del 1789 al 1799* (Milan, 1907), is serviceable; see also the suggestions in E. Rota, ed., *Questioni di storia del Risorgimento* (Milan, 1951), with good bibliographies; H. Acton, *The Bourbons of Naples, 1734–1825* (London, 1956), vivid chapters on the anti-revolutionary terror. For the United States, N. Schachner, *The Founding Fathers*, rev. ed. (1954), traces the connection between domestic American politics and the French Revolution; C. D. Hazen, *Contemporary American Opinion of the French Revolution* (Baltimore, 1897), inadequate, but still useful; E. P. Link, *Democratic-Republican Societies, 1790–1800* (1942), a vigorous defense of the American democrats.

Many of the titles given under "The Reform Movement in Europe" are appropriate to the reception of the Revolution outside France.

THE NATIONAL CONVENTION, 1792–1795

P. Mautouchet, *Le Gouvernement révolutionnaire* (1912) is the best single volume for the nature and functions of the Terror government; in much greater detail and with the use of documentary material there are Vols. IV–VIII of L. Mortimer-Ternaux, *Histoire de la terreur*, 8 vols. (1866–1883). R. R. Palmer, "Fifty Years of the Committee of Public Safety," *Journal of Modern History*, Vol. XIII (1941), pp. 375–397, is a critical examination of studies and changing interpretations, while his *Twelve Who Ruled* (Princeton, 1941) has become a modern classic. The activities of two of the most useful of those twelve are closely followed in L. Gershoy, *Bertrand Barère: A Reluctant Terrorist* (Princeton, 1962), and M. Reinhard, *Le Grand Carnot*, 2 vols. (1950–1952), particularly Vol. II on "The Organizer of Victory." M. Bouloiseau, *Le Comité de salut public, 1793–1795*, in the Que Sais-je series (1962), is a brief account incorporating the latest research. For the makings of revolutionary justice (and injustice) in addition to the standard studies of H. Wallon, *Histoire du tribunal révolutionnaire de Paris àvec le journal de ses actes*, 6 vols. (1880–1882), and W. Seligman, *La Justice en France pendant la Révolution*, 2 vols. (1910), only to the execution of Louis XVI, the following monographs are to be consulted: J. D. Godfrey, *Revolutionary Justice. A Study of the Organization, Personnel and Procedure of the Revolutionary Tribunal* (Chapel Hill, N.C., 1951); Arne Ording, *Le Bureau de police du comité de salut public* (1930), exonerating the Robespierrists of seeking to establish a dictatorship; L. Jacob, *Les Suspects pendant la Révolution, 1789–1794* (1952); G. Belloni, *Le Comité de sûreté générale de la Convention* (1924); and the two cool and enlightening studies by Donald Greer, *The Incidence of the Terror* (Cambridge, Mass., 1935) and *The Incidence of the Emigration* (Cambridge, Mass., 1951) which employ statistics to lift the problem above partisan passions. C. Brinton, *The Jacobins. An Essay in the New History* (1930), is a brilliant study of Jacobin faith, ritual, and practice; the systematic and sporadic use of terror in the provinces is covered for the Jacobins in L. de Cardenal, *La Province pendant la Révolution. Histoire des clubs Jacobins, 1789–1795* (1929); for the vigilantes associated with the Jacobins, J. B. Sirich, *The Revolutionary Committees in the Departments of France* (Cambridge, Mass., 1943); and for the new revolutionary soldiery, in R. C. Cobb, *Les Armées révolutionnaires des dé-partements du Midi* (Toulouse, 1956), and his exhaustive study incorporating years of research, *Les Armées révolutionnaires. Instrument de la terreur dans les départements, avril 1793– Floréal, an II*, 2 vols. (1961–1963). A. Soboul, *Les Soldats de l'an II* (1959) is a brief semi-popular account by a leading con-temporary scholar.

For the economic and social policy of the Robespierrists, in addition to the works given under "Special Studies" above, also see A. Mathiez, *Girondins et Montagnards* (1930), and his *La Vie chère et le mouvement social sous la terreur* (1927), a notable introduction to problems of supply of food and other necessities; G. Lefebvre, *Questions agraires au temps de la terreur* (Stras-bourg, 1932), largely a close analysis of the famous decrees of Ventôse for the relief of the indigent peasantry. Though D. Guérin, *La Lutte de classes sous la Ière république: Bourgeois et "bras nus,"* 2 vols. (1946), presents strong arguments for the Terror as a phase of the permanent class struggle, A. Soboul, in *Les Sans-culottes Parisiens en l'an II* (1958), working mainly from manu-script sources, has definitively shown the unique character of *sans-culotterie*. How the Terror government directed war production and sought to control prices and wages is carefully examined in C. Richard, *Le Comité de salut public et les fabrications de guerre* (1921); the suggestive article of G. Rudé, "Prices, Wages, and Popular Movements in Paris during the French Revolu-tion," *Economic History Review*, Vol. VI (1954), pp. 246–267; and in the close, detailed monograph of W. F. Shepherd, *Price Control and the Reign of Terror* (Berkeley, 1953). C. Brinton, *French Revolutionary Legislation on Illegitimacy* (Cambridge, Mass., 1954), on the ideal and reality of the Jacobin social conscience.

Besides the titles on religion listed already under "Special Studies," there are many works bearing more immediately on the years 1792–1795: The earlier work of A. Aulard, *Le Culte de la raison et de l'Etre suprême* (1892), and his *Christianity and the French Revolution*, Eng. trans. (London, 1927), perhaps exaggerate the waning appeal of Catholicism. A medley of studies by A. Mathiez, whose first interest lay in religious problems, tends to stress the strength of the revolutionary cult: *Origines des cultes révolutionnaires* (1904); *La Révolution et l'église* (1910); *La Question religieuse sous la Révolution* (1930); *La Théophilanthropie et le culte décadaire* (1904) on the attempt that failed to introduce a new religious cult in the period following the Ter-ror. The articles by S. J. Idzerda, "Iconoclasm during the French Revolution," *American Historical Review*, Vol. LX (1954), pp. 13–26, and by G. G. Andrews, "Making the Revolutionary Calendar," *American Historical Review*, Vol. XXXVI (1932), pp. 515–532, are revealing brief discussions.

The Girondin death duel with the Montagnards, which was dealt with in the earlier studies of H. Wallon, *La Révolution du 31 mai et le fédéralisme en 1793*, 2 vols. (1886), and C. Perroud, *La Proscription des Girondins* (1917), has been looked at with fresh eyes by R. M. Bruce, *Bordeaux and the Gironde 1789–1794* (Ithaca, 1947); A. Goodwin, "The Federalist Move-ment in Caen during the French Revolution," *Bulletin* of the John Rolands Library [of Manchester, Eng.] (March, 1960); and most searchingly in Sydenham, *The Girondins*, given above under "The Constitutional Monarchy." For the fighting in the Vendee, consult E. Gabory, *La Révolution et la Vendée*, 3 vols. (1925–1928), an exhaustive account rather favorable to rebel leaders; the same author's *L'Angleterre et la Vendée*, 2 vols. (1930–1931); L. Dubreuil, *Histoire des insurrections de l'Ouest*, 2 vols. (1929–1931), a fresh treatment of the subject; and C. Tilly's "Some Problems in the History of the Vendee," *American Historical Review*, Vol. LXVII (1961), pp. 19–33, supplies the social-economic background and shows that the Vendee opposition was far more than religious and political.

The biographies of the later revolutionary leaders are even more numerous than those for the early period. The definitive edition of Robespierre's speeches and writings, *Oeuvres de Maximilien Robespierre*, begun a generation ago, and edited most recently by M. Bouloiseau, G. Lefebvre, and A. Soboul, has reached its ninth volume and is the basic source for the study of "The Incorruptible's" much debated career. Of works which shade from the violently hostile to the relatively unfriendly, R. S. Ward, *Robespierre, a Study in Deterioration* (London, 1934), and G. Walter, *Robespierre*, 2 vols. (1961). The first major creditable biography that saw merit in his life was E. Hamel, *Histoire de Robespierre*, 3 vols. (1865–1867); in our own time, A. Mathiez began the successful rehabilitation of Robespierre's reputation in vigorously partisan studies: *Études Robespierristes*, 2 vols. (1917–1918), *Robespierre terroriste* (1921), and *Autour de Robespierre*, trans. as *The Fall of Robespierre* (1925). Mathiez's scholarship is kept and his polemical defense toned down in J. M. Thompson, *Robespierre*, 2 vols. (Oxford, 1953), and R. Korngold, *Robespierre and the Fourth Estate* (1941). J. Massin, *Robespierre* (1956), and particularly M. Bouloiseau's brief *Robespierre* in the Que Sais-je series (1957), incorporate the most recent research in a sense favorable to Robespierre. On Saint-Just, G. Bruun's *Saint-Just. Apostle of the Terror* (1932), a crisp, brief study that recognizes the zealous idealism of its subject; E. N. Curtis, *Saint-Just, Colleague of Robespierre* (1953), more detailed, more hostile, and less readable; A. Ollivier, *Saint-Just et la force des choses* (1954), the best of the recent accounts; *Saint-Just, Discours et rapports*, Albert Soboul, ed. (1957), gives the definitive text with a sympathetic commentary. Danton, like Robespierre, has ardent champions and passionate detractors. The works of Aulard fall into the first category, those of Mathiez are unremittingly hostile, especially *L'Affaire de la compagnie des Indes* (1921), a detailed study of the "corrupt" deputies; *Danton et la paix* (1917), showing Danton's unpatriotic, "defeatist" policy; and *Autour de Danton* (1926), where he brings his aversion to its peak. It is not surprising that patriotic French conservatives, such as L. Barthou, *Danton*, Eng. trans. (1932), and L. Madelin, *Danton*, Eng. trans. (1914), should find great merit in his "Real-politik" both at home and abroad. A summing up of the latest researches is G. Lefebvre, "Sur Danton," in his *Études*, given above, a model of discernment and discriminating judgment. There are literally hundreds of biographies of other revolutionary figures whose principal activities took place during the years of the Convention. For the Convention deputies themselves, Kuscinski's *Dictionnaire*, already cited under "Reference Works," is a reliable guide. The titles which follow are little more than a sampling of recent works on organization men, extremists, idealists, scoundrels, and deviationists. Recent biographies of Carnot and Barère have been noted above, as has Dowd's study of J.-L. David. L. Madelin, *Fouché*, 2 vols. (1900), Vol. I, is excellent on this supple intriguer; L. Levy-Schneider, *Jeanbon Saint-André*, 2 vols. (1901), an exhaustive, documentary study of a useful worker; L. Jacob, *J. le Bon* (1933), and J. B. Carrier, *Correspondance of Jean-Baptiste Carrier*, Eng. trans. (1920), on two famous deputies-on-mission; General Hérlaut, *Le Général rouge Ronsin (1751–1794)* (1956), M. Dommanget, *Sylvain Maréchal l'égalitaire 1750–1803* (1950), and L. Jacob, *Hébert, le Père Duchesne, chef des sans-culottes* (1960), are serviceable accounts of three extremist spokesmen. L. Gottschalk, *Jean Paul Marat* (1927), is a thoughtful study that gives fertile suggestions on the motive springs of Marat's behavior; also G. Marin, *J.-P. Marat* (1938). G. Avenel, *Anacharsis Cloots*, 2 vols. (1865), an old work which deals sympathetically with this unbalanced, self-styled "Orator of the Human Race"; A. Galante Garrone, *Gilbert Romme, storia di un rivoluzionario* (Turin, 1959), does justice to a warmhearted idealist. L. Jacob, *Fabre d'Eglantine, chef des fripons* (1946), is perhaps more friendly than Fabre merited. C. G. Bowers, *Pierre Vergniaud, Voice of the French Revolution* (1950), is extremely learned but marred by the author's idolatry. There is little else in biographies on the career of the charming Camille Desmoulins than the old eulogistic work by J. Claretie (1876); see also the critical edition of *Le Vieux Cordelier*, based on the notes of Mathiez (1936).

Almost all the works given in this section lead up to the overthrow of the Robespierrists on 9 Thermidor. The brief account of L. Barthou, *Le Neuf Thermidor* (1926) is readable but inadequate; Soboul's *Sans-culottes*, already given, and P. Sainte Claire-Deville, *La Commune de l'an II* (1946), are particularly good on the denouement of the Revolution. For the post-Thermidor period, A. Mathiez, *After Robespierre, the Thermidorian Reaction* in Eng. trans. (1931) is particularly good for the dismantling of the terrorist machinery and for the political retaliations; K. D. Tønnesson, *La Défaite des sans-culottes* (1959), on the vindictiveness of the bourgeois victors; J. B. Sirich, "The Revolutionary Committees after Thermidor," *Journal of Modern History*, Vol. XXVI (1954), pp. 329–339; and best of all, G. Lefebvre, *Les Thermidoriens* (1937), comprehensive and balanced, bringing out the constructive as well as destructive aspects.

THE DIRECTORY AND THE RISE OF BONAPARTE

There are valuable documents in L. Sciout, *Le Directoire*, 4 vols. (1895–1897); good general discussion in M. Reinhard, *La France du Directoire*, 2 vols. (1956); and P. Bessand-Massenet, *La France après la terreur, 1795–1799* (1946). The seamier aspects are given in J. and E. Goncourt, *La Société française pendant le Directoire*, 3rd ed. (1864); A. Mathiez, *Le Directoire* (1934), so far as it goes (to 1797) is vigorously critical of political developments. G. Lefebvre, *Le Directoire* (1946), is marked by his usual masterly, judicious treatment, which emphasizes the long-term achievements of the government. D. Thomson, *The Babeuf Plot* (London, 1947), scholarly and readable, corrects the exaggerated pro-Babeuf version in E. B. Bax, *The*

Last Episode of the French Revolution (1911). M. Dommanget has edited *Pages choisies de Babeuf* (1935), with commentary. M. Buonarroti, *Conspiration de l'égalité, dite de Babeuf*, 2 vols. (1957), with a preface by Lefebvre, is the definitive version of the conspiracy as interpreted by Babeuf's most famous follower.

Foreign policy is carefully traced in R. Guyot, *Le Directoire et la paix de l'Europe* (1911); C. Ballot, *Les Négociatiations de Lille* (1911), why and how peace negotiations with England in 1797–1798 failed; and G. S. Ford, *Hanover and Prussia 1795–1803* (1903), good for Prussian neutrality in 1799. Bonaparte's campaigns and diplomacy in Italy receive admiring treatment in E. Driault, *Napoléon en Italie* (1906); P. Gaffarel, *Bonaparte et les républiques italiennes, 1796–1799* (1895); while G. Ferrero, *The Gamble Bonaparte in Italy, 1796–1797*, trans. from Ital. (London, 1939), places the adventure in its broader European frame. G. B. McClellan, *Venice and Bonaparte* (1931), based largely on the Venetian archives, is thoroughly hostile. F. Charles-Roux, *L'Angleterre et l'expédition française en Egypte*, 2 vols. (1925), is a standard account; J. C. Herold, *Bonaparte in Egypt* (1963), utilizing Arabic as well as European sources, is a study in depth, superseding earlier accounts. The three studies which follow are detailed and reliable on the coups against the Directory and Bonaparte's seizure of power: F. Rocquain, *L'état de la France au 18 Brumaire* (1874); A. Meynier, *Les Coups d'état du Directoire*, 3 vols. (1928–1929); and the classic of A. Vandal, *L'Avènement de Bonaparte*, 2 vols. (1902–1907). Two good popular accounts are B. Morton, *Brumaire, the Rise of Bonaparte* (London, 1948), and J. Thiry, *Le Coup d'état du 18 Brumaire* (1947).

III. The Napoleonic Era

A Note on Historical Interpretations

On Napoleon, too, recent interpretations tend to move away from the long prevailing nationalist bias which so epochal a career understandably generated and also from the "for and against" inclination. Not entirely so; the episodic and the anecdotal still enlist literary efforts which might better be expended on other endeavors. In the main, the cumulative effect of critical archival research has been salutary. The biographies, the specialized studies, and the larger general works on the era set the years of Napoleon's domination in a broader perspective. The decade and a half of his rule is seen less as a disruption, either good or evil, and more as a continuation of both the older development of Europe and of the revolutionary expansion which preceded Brumaire. In those years the rival imperialisms of France and England contended as before; the enlightened despotism of the eighteenth century found new and more effective expression.

The most valuable systematic study is P. Geyl, *Napoleon, For and Against* (New Haven, 1949); A. L. Guérard, *Reflections on the Napoleonic Legend* (1923), an arraignment; J. J. Dechamps, *Sur la Légende de Napoléon* (1931), critical; for the German writers, F. Stahlin, *Napoleons Glanz und Fall im deutschen Urteil* (Berlin, 1952).

BIBLIOGRAPHIES AND BIBLIOGRAPHICAL AIDS

Other than the systematic guides already given above, there are two studies by F. M. Kircheisen, *Bibliographie des napoleonischen Zeitalters* (Berlin, 1902), and *Bibliographie du temps du Napoléon comprenant l'histoire des États-Unis*, 2 vols. (1908–1912); also G. Davois, *Bibliographie napoléonienne française jusqu'en 1908*, 3 vols. (1909–1911).

SOURCES AND DOCUMENTS

Besides the source references already given for the "Old Regime" and "French Revolution," there are *Almanac national* (*impérial* after 1804); *Gazette nationale, ou Moniteur universel* (1799–1815), the official journal; and Vols. I–XII of the 2nd series of *Archives parlementaires*, J. Mavidal and E. Laurent, eds. (1862–1868). F. A. Aulard, *Paris sous le Consulat* (1903), his *Paris sous le premier Empire: recueil de documents pour l'histoire de l'esprit public à Paris*, 3 vols. (1912–1923), excerpts from reports of police and secret government observers. H. Cachard, *The French Civil Code* (1930), presents the text and commentaries. *Correspondance de Napoléon Ier*, 32 vols. (1858–1870), published under the auspices of Napoleon III, this great official collection should be supplemented by other letters of Napoleon, ed. by Du Casse (1887); Lecestre, 2 vols. (1897); and Brotonne (1898 and 1903).

There are several collections of pickings from Napoleon's own writings: F. M. Kircheisen, *Napoleon's Autobiography*, trans. from Ger. (1931); S. de Chair, *Napoleon's Memoirs* (London, 1948); J. M. Thompson, *Napoleon Self-Revealed: Three Hundred Selected Letters* (Boston, 1934), better than most of the compilations; J. C. Herold, *The Mind of Napoleon* (1955, also in paperback, 1961), a selective, critical mosaic; and the first of a projected three-volume work which promises to be most useful of all, *Letters and Documents of Napoleon*, selected by J. E. Howard, Vol. I: *The Rise to Power* (London, 1961).

The memoirs of Napoleon's associates vary greatly in credibility and worth: of his immediate family, those of Joseph, Jerome, Lucien, Eugene and Hortense de Beauharnais; of his subordinates: Bourrienne, Fouché, Méneval, Miot de Mélito, Chaptal, Gaudin, Mollien, Pasquier, Roederer, Talleyrand, Thibaudeau; of his generals: Ségur, Brune, Bertrand, Caulaincourt. L. de Lanzac de Laborie, *Paris sous Napoléon*, 8 vols. (1905–1913), has a little of everything on life in the capital.

GENERAL WORKS

Three works stand up well with the passage of time: A. Fournier, *Napoleon I* (1911), originally published in German in 1886; J. H. Rose, *Life of Napoleon the First*, first published in 1901, mainly political and military; H. A. L. Fisher, *Napoleon* (1912), a brilliant brief sketch, appreciative of Napoleon as a "good European." More works focusing on Napoleon and his family include J. Bainville, *Napoléon* (1931), a dramatic, friendly presentation, popular and accurate; E. Driault, *La Vraie Figure de Napoléon*, 3 vols. (1928–1930), a labor of love by a great sponsor of the Napoleonic legend; W. Greer, *Napoleon and His Family, the Story of a Corsican Clan*, 3 vols. (1927–1929), best of its kind in English, based largely upon Masson's monumental *Napoléon et sa famille*, 13 vols. (1897–1919); E. A. Rheinhardt, *Josephine, Wife of Napoleon*, trans from Ger. (1934); E. M. Oddie, *Marie Louise, Empress of France. Duchess of Parma* (1931). G. G. Andrews, *Napoleon in Review* (1939), has discriminating essays on his personality and achievement. Of the most recent studies on the whole period, G. Lefebvre's *Napoléon*, Vol. IX in the Peuples et civilisation series, 4th ed. (1953), stands at the top of all works for its breadth and profundity; in English, the lucid G. Bruun, *Europe and the French Imperium, 1799–1814*, rev. ed. (1957 and in paperback, 1963), is the best one-volume survey with a fine selected bibliography and notes on historiography; J. M. Thompson, *Napoleon Bonaparte* (1952), good particularly for the Consulate; F. M. Markham, *Napoleon and the Awakening of Europe* (1954), useful introduction; Vol. II of L. Villat, *La Révolution et l'Empire* (1936), a convenient digest. Several famous and once influential works of large compass written during the nineteenth century now appear as almost classical illustrations of special pleading: L. A. Thiers, *History of the Consulate and the Empire of France under Napoleon*, new ed., 12 vols., trans. from Fr. ed. of 1845–1862 (London, 1893–1894), by an ardent French nationalist; P. Lanfrey, *The History of Napoleon the First*, trans. from a study first published in 1867, 4 vols. (1894), reflecting the political discontent during the Second Empire; H. A. Taine, *The Modern Regime*, trans. of the last vols. of his *Origines de la France contemporaine*, 2 vols. (1890–1894), imbued with the conservatism of the Third Republic; and Vols. VI–VIII of A. Sorel, *L'Europe et la Révolution française*, 8 vols. (1885–1904), a sharp study by an historian familiar with the workings of the French foreign office. Vol. IX of the *Cambridge Modern History* cooperative work (London, 1906), G. Pariset's *Le Consulat et l'Empire*, Vol. III of the Histoire de France contemporaine series (1921), and A. Stern, *Die grosse Revolution, Napoleon, und die Restauration, 1789–1848* (Berlin, 1929), Vol. VII of the Propyläen Weltgeschichte series, are standard academic accounts. The studies of the French nationalist historian, Louis Madelin, *Le Consulat et l'Empire*, 2 vols. (1932–1934), and his much more detailed sixteen-volume *Histoire du Consulat et de l'Empire* (1937–1954), are scholarly, lively, and respectful of Napoleon's epic; the veteran German specialist, F. M. Kircheisen, has enriched Napoleonic scholarship with his monumental and eulogistic *Napoleon I, sein Leben und seine Zeit*, 9 vols. (Munich, 1911–1934), and the single volume abridgment, in trans., *Napoleon* (1932).

FRANCE: CONSULATE AND EMPIRE

The institutional foundations of Napoleonic France are covered in Godechot's *Les Institutions*; F. Ponteil, *Napoléon Ier et l'organisation autoritaire de la France* (1956), a brief but systematic presentation of the advance toward governmental dictatorship; more detailed and specialized treatments, mostly in the same critical vein, A. Edmond-Blanc, *Napoléon I, ses institutions civiles* *et administratives* (1880); J. Thiry, *Le Sénat de Napoléon, 1800–1814* (1932); R. Dutruch, *Le Tribunal sous le Consulat et l'Empire* (1921); of C. Durand's several detailed monographs, *L'Exercise de la fonction legislative de 1800 à 1814* (Aix-en-Provence, 1955) is representative; J. Regnier, *Les Préfets du Consulat et de l'Empire* (1913), notes the same trend in the regional administration. The first manifestations of authoritarianism in J. Bourdon, *La Réforme judiciaire*, 2 vols. (Rodez, 1941), and the same author's *La Constitution de l'an VIII* (Rodez, 1941); for a generally friendly appreciation of the Napoleonic Code, H. A. L. Fisher, article in *Cambridge Modern History*, Vol. IX, and an interpretation emphasizing the social inequalities not legally abolished in M. Garaud, *Histoire générale du droit privé français de 1799 à 1804* (1953).

The open and veiled resistance is given in A. Gobert, *L'Opposition des assemblées pendant le Consulat, 1800–1804* (1925); P. Gaffarel's articles, "L'Opposition militaire, républicaine, littéraire sous le Consulat," in *La Révolution française*, Vols. XII–XVI (1887–1889); J. Destrem, *Les Déportations du Consulat et l'Empire* (1885). The military opposition is seen in E. Daudet, *La Police et les chouans sous le Consulat et l'Empire, 1800–1815*, 2nd ed. (1895); L. Dubreuil, *Histoire des insurrections de l'Ouest*, Vol. II (1930); E. Guillon, *Les Conspirations militaires sous le Consulat et l'Empire* (1894); and E. Gabory, *Napoléon et la Vendée*, 3 vols. (1924–1928).

The policing of the mind, exercised more effectively than during the Old Regime, is found in all the longer general histories and R. B. Holtman, *Napoleonic Propaganda* (Baton Rouge, 1950); G. Le Poittevin, *La Liberté de la presse depuis la Révolution, 1789–1815* (1900); W. Welschinger, *La Censure sous le premier Empire* (1882); F. A. Aulard, *Napoléon Ier et le monopole universitaire* (1911), best discussion of Napoleon's educational policy; F. B. Artz, "L'Enseignement technique en France pendant l'époque révolutionnaire, 1789–1815," *Revue historique*, Vol. CXCV (July–Sept., 1946); French intellectual speculation in the larger frame of European thought, in Baldensperger and Brunot, given above, in the concluding section of Lefebvre's *Napoléon*, and in the comprehensive work of T. Merz, *History of European Thought in the Nineteenth Century*, 4th ed., 4 vols. (Edinburgh, 1923–1924).

For the general accounts of religious evolution and church-state relations, see Latreille, Leflon, and Debidour, given under "special studies"; also G. L. M. J. Constant, *L'Église de France sous le Consulat et l'Empire, 1800–1814* (1928), a useful synthesis; the re-establishment of Catholicism as a virtual state religion in A. Boulay de la Meurthe, *Documents sur la négociation du Concordat*, 5 vols. (1891–1897); and his two studies, *Histoire de la négociation du Concordat de 1801* (Tours, 1920), and *Histoire du rétablissement du culte en France, 1802–1805* (Tours, 1925). H. H. Walsh, *The Concordat of 1801* (1933), makes much of the nationalist impress of the agreement. On the Protestants, the study of B. C. Poland already given; on the Jews, R. Anchel, *Napoléon et les juifs* (1928), very detailed and sharply critical of Napoleon's discriminatory policy.

Economic development and social transformations are in the works given in the Revolution bibliography; also R. Stourm, *Les Finances du Consulat*

(1902), the best study of the financial reorganization; E. Levasseur, *Histoire du commerce en France*, Vol. II (1912); C. Ballot, *L'Introduction du mécanisme dans l'industrie française* (Lille, 1923); G. Mauco, *Les Migrations ouvrières en France au début du XIXᵉ siècle* (1932); C. P. Higby and C. B. Willis, "Industry and Labor under Napoleon," *American Historical Review*, Vol. LIII (1948), pp. 465–480. J. Rais, *La Représentation des aristocrates dans les chambres hautes en France, 1789–1815* (1900); P. Brousse and H. Thurot, *Le Consulat et l'Empire* (1905), in the Histoire socialiste series ed. by Jaurès; and G. Hanotaux, "La Transformation sociale à l'époque napoléonienne," *Revue des deux mondes*, Vol. XXIII (1926), pp. 89–123; pp. 562–597, all bring out the social conservatism of the era.

FRANCE AND EUROPE: FOREIGN RELATIONS AND THE WARS

Many of the titles in "Revolutionary Expansion" are relevant for the foreign policy of Napoleon. Both R. B. Mowat, *Diplomacy of Napoleon* (1924), and Vol. II of E. Bourgeois, *Manuel historique de politique étrangère*, new ed., 4 vols. (1945–1949), briefly cover the whole topic. E. Driault, *Napoléon et l'Europe*, 5 vols. (1910–1927); this is an indispensable series for all matters pertaining to Napoleon's foreign policy. Each volume has its own title: I. *La Politique extérieure du Premier Consul (1800–1803)*; II. *Austerlitz. La fin du Saint-Empire (1804–1806)*; III. *Tilsit. France et Russie sous le premier Empire. La question de Pologne (1806–1809)*; IV. *Le Grand Empire (1809–1812)*; V. *La Chute de l'Empire (1812–1815)*; there are two supplementary volumes: *La Politique orientale de Napoléon, 1806–1808* (1904), and *Napoléon en Italie, 1800–1812* (1906). H. C. Deutsch, *The Genesis of Napoleonic Imperialism* (Cambridge, Mass., 1938), a careful study going up to 1805, and H. Butterfield, *Peace Tactics of Napoleon, 1806–1808* (1929), are enlightening monographs.

For the wars, the titles under "The Directory" cover Napoleon's early career, and those below on "The Collapse," his last years. The many studies include: T. A. Dodge, *Napoleon, a History of the Art of War, from the Beginnings of the French Revolution to Waterloo*, 4 vols. (Boston, 1904–1907); Sir Charles Oman, *Studies in Napoleonic Wars* (London, 1929); H. T. Parker, *Three Napoleonic Battles* (Durham, N. C., 1944), which are Friedland, Aspern, and Waterloo; R. J. Burton, *From Boulogne to Austerlitz, Napoleon's Campaign of 1805* (1912); F. L. Petre, *Napoleon's Conquest of Prussia, 1806* (1907), and his *Napoleon's Campaign in Poland, 1806–1807*, 3rd ed. (1906), both for the general reader; and the fighting in Spain and Portugal in Sir Charles Oman's standard, authoritative *History of the Peninsular War*, 7 vols. (Oxford, 1902–1930); also the lively P. Guedalla, *Wellington* (1932); A. T. Mahan, *The Influence of Sea Power upon the French Revolution and Empire, 1793–1812*, 14th ed., 2 vols. (Boston, 1919), has long dominated the field, probably unduly so because of its exaggerations; A. Thomazi, *Napoléon et ses marins* (1950), lights up the inadequacies in the policy of recruitment and naval operations; and E. Desbrière, *Projets et tentatives de débarquement aux îles britanniques, 1793–1805*, 3 vols. (1901), standard. The decisiveness of Trafalgar, is pointed up in A. T. Mahan's *Life of Nelson*,

2 vols. (1897), and R. Maine, *Trafalgar: Napoleon's Naval Waterloo* (1957). E. F. Heckscher, *The Continental System* (1922), and F. E. Melvin, *Napoleon's Navigation System* (1919), deal competently with commercial warfare.

THE GRAND EMPIRE

Europe at the height of Napoleon's power is of course treated in most of the works on diplomacy and war. In addition, there are in German, the sound F. Meinecke, *Das Zeitalter der deutschen Erhebung, 1795–1815*, 2nd ed. (Bielefeld, 1913), which replaces the exaggerated nationalism of earlier German historians like Oncken and Treitschke. Meinecke's *Die Entstehung des Historismus*, 2 vols. (Munich, 1936), along with A. Stern, *Der Einfluss der französischen Revolution auf das deutsche Geistesleben* (Stuttgart, 1928), are valuable on the intellectual ferment, as are F. Valjavic, *Die Entstehung der politischen Strömungen Deutschlands, 1770–1815* (1951); H. Kohn, *The Age of Nationalism* (1962), stimulating essays. H. A. L. Fisher, *Studies in Napoleonic Statesmanship, Germany* (1908); the thoughtful R. R. Ergang, *Herder and the Foundations of German Nationalism* (1931); and the useful but pedestrian R. Aris, *History of Political Thought in Germany from 1789 to 1815* (London, 1936). The studies relating to Prussia are numerous: the still readable and too generous J. R. Seeley, *Life and Times of Stein. Germany and Prussia in the Napoleonic Age*, 3 vols. (London, 1879); a topic which G. Ritter, *Stein, eine politische Biographie*, 2 vols. (Stuttgart, 1931), handles with discrimination, as does G. S. Ford, *Stein and the Era of Reforms in Prussia, 1807–1815* (1922). E. N. Anderson, *Nationalism and the Cultural Crisis in Prussia, 1806–1815* (1939), and W. M. Simon, *The Failure of the Prussian Reform Movement, 1807–1819* (Ithaca, 1955) are good on the resistance to political reform; more effective changes are in W. O. Shanahan, *Prussian Military Reforms, 1786–1813* (1945).

Much of the fresh interpretation of Austrian developments stems from the works of H. von Srbik, *Metternich, der Staatsmann und der Mensch*, 2 vols. (Munich, 1925), and *Das österreichische Kaisertum und das Ende des Heilgen Römischen Reiches, 1804–1806* (Berlin, 1927); his influence is seen in A. Cecil, *Metternich, 1773–1859; a study of his period and personality* (1933). H. Rossler, *Österreichs Kampf um Deutschlands Befreiung, 1805–1815*, 2nd ed., 2 vols. (Vienna, 1947), sums up the recent research; also W. C. Langsam, *The Napoleonic Wars and German Nationalism in Austria* (1930); A. Robert, *L'Idée nationale autrichienne et les guerres de Napoléon* (1933); and P. R. Sweet, *Friedrich von Gentz, Defender of the Old Order* (Madison, Wis., 1941).

General accounts of Italy are in F. Lemmi and V. Fiorni, *Storia d'Italia dal 1799 al 1814* (Milan, 1918); in fuller detail, F. Lemmi, *L'età Napoleonica* (Milan, 1938); and from the French side, A. Fugier, *Napoléon et l'Italie* (1947). For special aspects and particular areas, see E. Tarlé, *Le Blocus continental et le royaume d'Italie* (1928), and M. Pivec-Stelè, *La Vie économique des provinces illyriennes, 1809–1813* (1930), essential for the workings of the Continental System; L. Madelin, *Rome de Napoléon, la domination française à Rome de 1809–1814* (1904), good for relations with the papacy; A. Pingaud, *La Domination française dans l'Italie du nord, 1790–1805*, 2 vols. (1914); E. Rodocanachi, *Bonaparte et les îles ioniennes* (1899); J. Borel, *Gênes sous Napoléon* (1929); R. M. Johnston, *The Napoleonic Empire in Southern Italy*, 2 vols. (1804); and the facile A. H. Atteridge, *Joachim Murat, Marshal of France and King of Naples* (1911). The earlier relations with Spain, in A. Fugier, *Napoléon et l'Espagne, 1799–1808*, 2 vols. (1929–1930), showing how Napoleon's general policy forced him to intervene in Spain; G. de Grandmaison, *L'Espagne et Napoléon*, 3 vols. (1908–1931), best study of the reign of Joseph Bonaparte.

Studies of England during the revolutionary and Napoleonic eras are very numerous. Some representative works suggest their range. General accounts include Volume XI, by B. C. Broderick and J. K. Fotheringham, in the *Political History of England*, ed. W. Hunt and R. L. Poole (London, 1905–1910); P. Coquelle, *Napoléon et l'Angleterre* (1904), from the French side; and the lively trilogy, very patriotic in tone, of Sir Arthur Bryant, *Years of Endurance; Years of Victory;* and *The Age of Elegance* (London, 1942–1950). The mood of the people during the great ordeal is seen in H. F. B. Wheeler and A. M. Broadley, *Napoleon and the Invasion of England: The Story of the Great Terror*, 2 vols. (London, 1908); A. M. Broadley, *Napoleon in Caricature, 1795–1821*, 2 vols. (London, 1910); F. J. MacCunnan, *The Contemporary English View of Napoleon* (London, 1914); O. Darvall, *Popular Disturbances and Public Order in Regency England . . . 1811–1817* (London, 1934). Changes on a higher level of thought and feeling are suggested in A. Cobban, *Edmund Burke and the Revolt against the Eighteenth Century*, new ed. (London, 1961), and with scholarly care in C. Brinton, *Political Ideas of the English Romanticists* (Oxford, 1926). Economic warfare is discussed in the able F. Crouzet, *L'Économie britannique et le blocus continental, 1806–1813*, 2 vols. (1958); W. F. Galpin, *The Grain Supply of England during the Napoleonic Period* (Philadelphia, 1925); the financial stringency in two technical works, N. J. Silberling, "Financial and Monetary Policy of Great Britain during the Napoleonic Wars," *Quarterly Journal of Economics*, Vol. XXXVIII (1924), pp. 214–233, 397–439; and A. Cunningham, *British Credit in the Last Napoleonic War* (1910). For British sea power see C. S. Graham, *Sea Power and British North America, 1783–1820* (London, 1941), and C. N. Parkinson, *Trade in the Eastern Seas, 1793–1813* (Cambridge, Eng., 1937).

Developments in Russia are given in the national histories already listed and also in brief outline in A. A. Lobanov-Rostovsky, *Russia and Europe, 1789–1825* (Durham, N.C., 1947). More detailed treatment is given in K. Waliszewski, *Paul I of Russia* (London, 1913), and *Le Règne d'Alexandre Iᵉʳ*, 3 vols. (1923–1925); A. Vandal, *Napoléon et Alexandre Iᵉʳ*, 3 vols. (1891–1896), less favorable to the tsar. For letters and memoires, there are S. Tatischeff, ed., *Alexandre Iᵉʳ et Napoléon d'après leur correspondance inédite de 1801 à 1812* (1891); C. Mazade, ed., *Alexandre Iᵉʳ et le prince Czartoryski* (1864); and Prince Adam Czartoryski, *Memoirs*, 2 vols. in trans. (1888). Napoleon's Polish policy, in M. Handelsmann, *Napoléon et la Pologne* (1909); and more severely in S. Askenazy, *Napoléon et la Pologne*, (1925).

For the less crucial regions, Pirenne and Blok, already given, on Belgium and Holland; E. Gullion, *Napoléon et les Suisses, 1803–1815* (1910). On the Near East, there are general accounts in W. Miller, *The Ottoman Empire and Its Successors, 1801–1936* (Cambridge, 1936); E. Haumant, *La Formation de la Yougoslavie* (1930); and H. A. R. Gibb and H. Bowen, *Islamic Society and the West* (London, 1950). Special aspects are found in P. Shupp, *The Eastern Powers and the Near Eastern Question, 1806–1807* (1931); G. Lebel, *La France et les principautés Danubiennes* (1955); V. J. Puryear, *Napoleon and the Dardanelles* (Berkeley, 1951).

How Napoleon's foreign policy impinged on the trans-Atlantic world is traced in Vol. IV of H. Adams, *History of the United States of America, 1801–1817* (1890); and W. S. Robertson, *France and the Latin American Independence* (1939). Anna C. Clauders, *American Commerce as Affected by the Wars of the French Revolution and Napoleon* (Philadelphia, 1932) is crowded with details; and both E. W. Lyon, *Louisiana in French Diplomacy* (Norman, Okla., 1933), and A. P. Whitaker, *The Mississippi, 1795–1803, a study in trade, politics, and diplomacy* (1934), treat the Louisiana problem with balanced discernment.

COLLAPSE OF THE EMPIRE AND THE RESTORATIONS

The disastrous Russian venture is in the popular H. B. George, *Napoleon's Invasion of Russia* (1899); P. Ségur, *Napoleon's Russian Campaign*, trans. and abridged by J. D. Townsend (Boston, 1958), the harrowing account of a participant; Vols. I and II of the *Mémoires du Général de Caulaincourt*, ed. by J. Hanoteau (1933), revealing on the campaign and the diplomacy; A. Mansuy, *Jérôme Napoléon et la Pologne en 1812* (1931), graphic account of the chaotic situation. The final military collapse, in E. P. Henderson, *Blücher and the Uprising against Napoleon, 1806–1815* (1911); F. L. Petre, *Napoleon's Last Campaign in Germany, 1813* (1912); O. Browning, *Fall of Napoleon* (1907); H. Houssage, *1814* (1888), excellent on the internal history of France as well as on the fighting; F. L. Petre, *Napoleon at Bay* (1914); and the careful old work, J. C. Ropes, *The Campaign of Waterloo* (1892). The military and political collapse in particular areas, in W. Marin, *La Suisse en Europe, 1813–1814* (Lausanne, 1931); F. D. Scott, *Bernadotte and the Fall of Napoleon* (Cambridge, Mass., 1935); R. J. Rath, *The Fall of the Napoleonic Kingdom of Italy* (1941); P. Vidal de la Blache, *L'Évacuation de l'Espagne* (1914); P. Guedalla, *Wellington* (1930).

The abdication and the restoration, in Vol. III of *Mémoires du Général de Caulaincourt*; Houssaye's *1814* and his three-volume *1815* (1898–1925); E. Le Gallo, *Les Cent Jours* (1924), and J. Thiry, *La Première Abdication de Napoléon Ier*, 2nd ed. (1948), especially good on the political side; while F. Ponteil, *La Chute de Napoléon Ier et la crise française de 1814 à 1815* (1953), the opening chapter of F. B. Artz, *France under the Bourbon Restoration, 1814–1830* (Cambridge, Mass., 1931), G. de Bertier de Sauvigny, *La Restauration* (1955), Part One, and H. Kurtz, *The Trial of Marshal Ney* (1958) all light up the difficulties of establishing the new rule.

The larger European restoration is examined from different angles by H.

Nicolson, *The Congress of Vienna, A Study in Allied Unity, 1812–1822* (1946), almost as a problem in techniques; G. Ferrero, *The Reconstruction of Europe: Talleyrand and the Congress of Vienna, 1814–1815,* (1941), stressing the legitimacy of "legitimacy"; C. K. Webster, in two studies, *The Congress of Vienna* (1919) and *The Foreign Policy of Castlereagh, 1812–1815: Britain and the Reconstruction of Europe* (1931), both focused on the role of Castlereagh.

The epilogue at Saint Helena has had many sympathetic commentators, such as R. Korngold, *The Last Years of Napoleon* (1959); O. Aubry, *St. Helena,* trans. from Fr. (1936); and H. A. L. Fisher, *Bonapartism* (1909). P. Guedalla, *The Second Empire* (1921), has astringent observations on the growth of the Napoleonic Legend, which Napoleon and his companions in exile carefully nurtured; B. E. O'Meara, *Napoleon in Exile,* 2 vols. (1822), the tearful souvenirs of Napoleon's physician; *Mémoires pour servir à l'histoire de France sous Napoléon, écrites à Sainte-Hélène sous la dictée de l'Empereur par les généraux qui ont partagé sa captivité,* 8 vols. (1823); Count E. P. P. Las Cases, *Mémorial de Sainte-Hélène,* 4 vols. (1823), the Old Testament of the accounts; *Mélanges historiques dictés au comte de Montholon* (1822), and C. J. Montholon, *Récits de la captivité de l'Empereur Napoléon à Sainte-Hélène,* 2 vols. (1847); G. Gourgaud, *Sainte-Hélène: journal inédit de 1815–1818,* 2 vols. (1899); and H. G. Bertrand, *Cahiers de Sainte-Hélène,* 3 vols. (1949–1959).

INDEX

Intellectual Repression, under Napoleon, 462-3.
Ionian Islands, 332, 333, 364, 418, 526.
Isnard, 251, 253.
Italy, Bonaparte in, 325-9; and Treaty of Campo Formio, 332-4; French aggressions in, 339-40; campaign of 1800, 361-2; under the Consulate, 383-4; kingdom of, established, 393; and Grand Empire, 405-7; French influence in, 472-4; collapse of French rule in, 513; and Congress of Vienna, 526.

Jacobin Club, 135-7, 177, 183, 191, 211, 226, 229, 231, 235, 265, 275-6, 294, 341-3.
Jacobins, the, 135-7, 175, 177, 191-4, 198-212, 224-6, 230-3, 248-56, 297-301, 305, 319, 371-2.
Jalès, camp at, 177.
Jansenist controversy, 8, 10, 34, 60, 166.
Jay Treaty, 323.
Jemappes, battle at, 240.
Jena, battle of, 413, 424, 523.
Jesuits, 8, 10, 30, 60, 84-5.
Jews, 145, 467.
Joseph II, Emperor of Austria, 84-7.
Josephine, the Empress, 380, 451.
Jourdan, General, 266, 269, 304, 325, 328, 340, 343, 345, 508.
June 20, 1792, events of, 209-11.
June 2, 1793, insurrection of, 251-3.
Junot, Marshal, 429, 430, 434.

Kalisch, Treaty of, 503.
Kant, Immanuel, 481, 482.
Kaunitz, 199.
Kellerman, General, 227, 509.
Kléber, 343.
Klopstock, 182.
Koblentz, 183, 188, 199, 213.
Koch, 279.
Korsakov, General, 342.
Kray, 362.
Kutusov, General, 498-9.

Lafayette, Marquis de, 38-9, 80; and "Patriots," 101; and National Guard, 118; and "October Days," 125, 128, 130-2, 134; and clubs, 137; and

Fête de la Fédération, 138; and king, 172-5; and war policy, 176-9, 193, 194, 200, 204, 209-12; captured by Austrians, 217; and war, 227.
La Haye Sainte, 532.
Laissez-faire, 70, 322, 421.
Lally-Tollendal, 131.
Lamarck, 316.
Lameth, Alexandre de, 38, 135, 175, 194, 195, 200, 202, 204.
Lameth, Charles de, 38, 134, 194, 202, 204.
Lamoignon, 98.
Landau, battle at, 269.
Landshut, battle at, 439.
Landwehr, Austrian, 438; Prussian, 503.
Lanjuinais, 229, 252.
Lannes, General, 401.
Laplace, 316.
La Révellière-Lépeaux, 318, 330, 341.
La Rochefoucauld-Liancourt, 134.
Latour-Maubourg, 191.
Lavoisier, 62, 316.
Law, John, 9.
Law, French, in the Old Régime, 19-20; administration of reorganized, 151-2; see under Codes.
Law of the Maximum, 255, 266, 271, 272, 277, 294.
Law of Suspects, 264-5, 277, 289, 294.
Lebas, 291.
Lebrun, 217, 229, 253, 355, 379, 458.
Leclerc, General, 347, 385.
Legion of Honor, the, 458-9.
Legislative Assembly, 147, 196-202, 205, 209, 211-13, 215-16, 219, 224, 310.
Leipzig, battle of, 510-12.
Leoben, Preliminaries of, 329, 332-3.
Leopold II, Emperor of the Holy Roman Empire, 85, 87, 186, 189, 194, 198-9, 202, 204, 205.
Lepeletier de Saint-Fargeau, 238.
Le Tourneur, 318, 330.
Lettres de cachet, 19.
Levée en masse, 260, 270.
Liége, 182, 240, 246.
Ligny, battle of, 531, 532.
Ligurian Republic, 332, 340, 363, 383, 394.
Lille, 240, 255.
Lindet, Robert, 274, 290.
Lisle, Rouget de, 211.

3 3226 00104 5311